THE BUILDINGS OF IRELAND
FOUNDING EDITOR: NIKOLAUS PEVSNER

NORTH WEST ULSTER
(THE COUNTIES OF LONDONDERRY, DONEGAL,
FERMANAGH, AND TYRONE)

ALISTAIR ROWAN

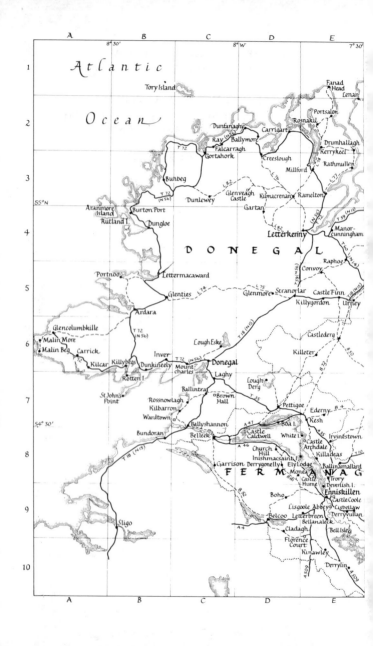

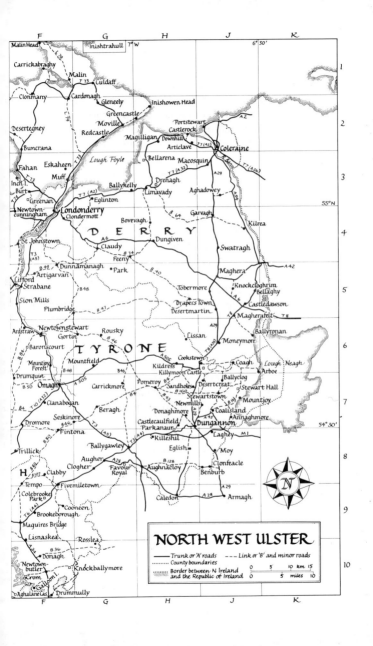

NORTH WEST ULSTER

— Trunk or 'A' roads   --- Link or 'B' and minor roads
‥‥‥ County boundaries
▒▒ Border between N. Ireland   0   5   10 km 15
and the Republic of Ireland   0   5   miles 10

PEVSNER ARCHITECTURAL GUIDES

The Buildings of Ireland series was founded by
Sir Nikolaus Pevsner (1901–1983) as a companion series
to *The Buildings of England*. The continuing
programme of revisions and new volumes has
been supported by research financed through
the Buildings Books Trust since 1994

The preparation of this book has been made possible through
the generosity of the
ESME MITCHELL TRUST
and of
LORD DUNLEATH'S CHARITABLE TRUST
which together made grants to cover the necessary research
work for the Ulster volumes of
The Buildings of Ireland

The continuity of research work for the series
has been supported by
THE LILA ACHESON WALLACE FUND,
THE BANK OF IRELAND,
ARTHUR GUINNESS AND CO.,
and by
MR JOHN HUSTON
and
MR BERNARD P. MCDONOUGH
all of whose assistance is here gratefully acknowledged

North West Ulster

(The counties of Londonderry, Donegal, Fermanagh, and Tyrone)

BY

ALISTAIR ROWAN

★

YALE UNIVERSITY PRESS
NEW HAVEN AND LONDON

YALE UNIVERSITY PRESS
NEW HAVEN AND LONDON
302 Temple Street, New Haven CT 06511
47 Bedford Square, London WC1B 3DP
www.yale.edu/yup
www.yaleup.co.uk
www.pevsner.co.uk
www.lookingatbuildings.org

———

Published by Penguin Books 1979
First published by Yale University Press 2003
2 4 6 8 10 9 7 5 3 1

———

ISBN 0 300 09667 4

———

———

Printed in China
through World Print
Set in Monotype Plantin

———

TO NIKOLAUS

whose lectures in Belfast in 1955
awakened my interest in the history
of buildings and whose encouragement
turned a rash notion into the reality
of which this volume is proof

CONTENTS

Map References

★

The map shows all those places, whether towns, villages, or isolated buildings, which are the subject of separate entries in the text. References to the map square in which each place mentioned will be found are given in the margins of the gazetteer.

FOREWORD

*It is my hope that this book may be the first of a series of volumes
describing the architecture of all the thirty-two counties in Ireland.
That it owes its origin to the example of Sir Nikolaus Pevsner's*
Buildings of England *series, completed in forty-six volumes between
1951 and 1974, will be obvious to anyone familiar with that great
work: the format of* The Buildings of Ireland *is essentially the same,
the publisher is the same, and the text of this volume has been read
by Sir Nikolaus, and prepared for publication by Judy Nairn, joint
editors of* The Buildings of England. *I have benefited greatly from
their support and enthusiasm for this whole project, and by their experience.*

*As Ireland is a very different sort of place from England it may
be as well to explain at the outset the basis on which the following
pages have been planned. The map on pages 2 and 3 indicates the
approximate location of every place for which an entry is to be found
in the gazetteer. Towns, villages, and individual large monuments or
country estates do not pose any problems; but where much of the
countryside is under-populated and without any obvious architectural
focus it is sometimes hard to decide which name to choose for an entry
that may cover a cluster of buildings over a wide area. In the belief
that most readers will use this book as a touring guide I have tended
to prefer those names that appear on signposts – even though the place
so distinguished may be no more than a straggle of houses and a petrol
pump – than to make entries necessarily under the name of the most
interesting building in that area. Thus Banagher church ruin, a noted
example of Irish Romanesque architecture, appears under the modest
village of Feeny. A limited number of cross-references is given in the
main text to indicate where entries for the more notable medieval
buildings and individual houses are to be found. The larger villages
are also cross-referenced in this way. Other place names and outlying buildings are given in the complete Index of Places at the back
of the book. Occasionally entries appear under a parish name. The
spelling of all place names is taken from the Official Irish Post Office
Guide of 1971, and I have followed this in using Derry instead of
Londonderry, except where the prefix London seems appropriate. The
letters* DO, FM, LD, *and* TY *given to the right of each place name*

stand respectively for Donegal, Fermanagh, Londonderry, and
Tyrone, and indicate in which county it is situated.

By European standards churches in Ireland are simple affairs:
very few that date from the Middle Ages are still in use for religious
worship – most are nineteenth-century. Many, indeed the vast
majority, are architecturally undistinguished, though even they may
provide the only characteristic features in a rural Irish landscape.
To provide a selection would not be satisfactory, and as far as
possible every church appears briefly in the gazetteer, either individually or, where several very minor structures exist near at hand, under
a general heading of CHURCHES. The dedication of many Irish
churches, Catholic and Protestant, is often obscure or unknown.
Where it is to a local Irish saint, I have on the whole respected the
spelling used by the church notice boards, though other references to
saints follow the spellings adopted in A. Gwynn and R. N. Hadcock's
Medieval Religious Houses: Ireland. Thus Colmcille appears as
such when referred to as a historical figure, but as St Columb, St
Columba, and St Columbkille in the names of different churches. Catholic churches are entered simply under the name of the saint to whom
they are dedicated or under some other title. For the Church of Ireland, both the dedication and the name of the parish are given, followed by (C of I). Frequently the Catholic and Anglican parishes
have the same name and, though this is far from being always the
case, the Church of Ireland parish name is given in the gazetteer
simply because it is this name, the name of the Established Church
parish until 1869, that is regularly used for entries in the eighteenth-
and nineteenth-century guides to which readers may wish to refer. By
the same token I have made no attempt to keep up to date with the
Church of Ireland parishes. They appear here in their historic state
c. 1850, principally as an aid to further reference.

Distances and dimensions given in this volume may appear to be
inconsistent. I have indicated the approximate distance and direction
of buildings from any centre in kilometres though in Ireland, at the
time of writing, we are still working in miles. The distances are 'as
the crow flies'. The heights of hills or cliffs are similarly given in
metres, but measurements of buildings are kept in feet. In most
cases these measurements apply either to ruined medieval structures, or else to the rooms of country houses. It must be emphasized
that they are given only as a guide to the scale of the buildings and
are not precise. To have translated them into metres or centimetres
would have given a false impression of accuracy and would to my
mind largely defeat the reason for their inclusion. These buildings were
all designed on a foot scale, and I believe a description of a church

ruin as 25 ft by 60 ft with walls 3 ft thick will conjure up a more immediate picture in the minds of most readers than 7.625 m by 18.3 m with
walls 0.915 m thick, which is the metric equivalent.

My hypothetical church ruin may introduce another problem peculiar to the history of Irish architecture. Ireland has never been a rich
country and has had little money for sustained elaborate building.
Perhaps because of the lack of investment in the country Irish buildings tend to be plain constructions with what is often thought of
as a natural life span of two or three hundred years at most. As a
result of this view it is accepted that when they are old they will be
replaced rather than repaired. In the North West of Ulster people
talk of 'tumbling' buildings rather than of demolishing them, but the
effect on the environment is the same. The average Irish town wears
a nineteenth-century expression and the average Irish village – or
at least the average Ulster village – will have a grass-covered mound
with the odd bit of wall as the site of its medieval church, a rectangular
ivy-clad shell left from its seventeenth-century successor, and a trim
hall-and-tower type* Perpendicular church of about 1820, built for
the Church of Ireland, but surpassed in elaboration by a larger, later,
and more authentically detailed Gothic Revival church, built for an
equally larger Catholic congregation and situated perhaps a little way
out of the township itself. There may be a nineteenth-century court
house of modest classical style, an unobtrusive market, and a substantial house or two, but little more. An architectural historian in Ireland
may find much to delight and interest him, but it would be futile to
expect more than a sprinkling of major monuments in any one county.
People who are architecturally curious will however usually prefer
to look at something rather than remain idle, and this is the basic
assumption of the pages that follow. For each town, village, or site,
I have tried to include whatever information has been found – though
it must frequently be inadequate – about the buildings that strike the
eye. Were they elsewhere in Europe they might have been ignored:
in an Irish context they are worth remark.

Buildings for the purpose of this volume begin in the Christian era.
Prehistoric antiquities, earthworks, forts, crannogs, tombs, standing
stones, souterrains, and dolmens are a study in themselves well served
by other authors. With the exception of a very few obvious structures
that even a casual visitor cannot fail to find, they are not included
here. Similarly the vernacular buildings of the countryside cannot
be noted within the limits of the gazetteer, though a guide to the types
and pattern of rural housing in Ulster as a whole is provided in a
separate introduction by Dr Alan Gailey of the Ulster Folk Museum.

* For an explanation of the use of this term here see Introduction, p. 53.

Bridges, railways and roadworks, and rural industrial buildings are noted only where they achieve an architectural character. Church plate is not dealt with, though stained glass and furnishings are included on a selective basis.

As a rule I have personally visited every building described in the text. Where I have not, the fact is recorded in a footnote. As the research for this series has had to proceed on an all-Ireland basis, the visiting has necessarily run ahead of my completion of the text, and in the early years there were often huge gaps in The Buildings of Ireland *files, of which some, but happily not many, still remain unfilled. The visiting for the counties in this volume was carried out in the summer of 1970 in Fermanagh and Tyrone; in the spring of 1971 in Derry; and in the summer of 1971 in Donegal, and a part of north Tyrone and south Derry that had not been completed before. In the spring of 1976 I revisited Derry city and parts of Tyrone and Fermanagh to check entries before the volume went to the printer. On summer visits made in a converted Commer van/caravan I was accompanied by my wife, Ann Martha, who cooked cheerfully in cramped conditions and collated Irish guide books as we lurched along. We were hospitably received by numerous Ulster farmers who let us park on their fields and in their drives and received much kindness from the owners of not a few private estates. For meals, baths, and beds we are extremely grateful to all. In Co. Derry a cold March was offset by the comfort and warmth of Mr Donald Girvan's home at Portstewart, from where Mr Hugh Dixon drove me in loop-like forays of ever-increasing extent in his admirable old Hillman 'Tomato'. For the Derry and Tyrone visiting in 1971 it was Mr Girvan who kept me company in the van.*

Irish buildings are inseparable from their setting, for often it is the setting and not the architecture that claims pride of place. For myself many places are accompanied in the memory by a vivid recollection of other sights and sounds: blustery churchyards full of the sound of cawing rooks, the plastic wreaths round the gravestones hideously pale after years in the sun and rain; the crunch and churn of the Atlantic breaking on a stony beach; the claustrophobic smell of nettles, ivy, and elder thrusting through the ruins of a church or country house; the cold, the bitter cold of Fermanagh when I crouched under an umbrella on Boa Island; or the splendid hedges of Donegal full of fuchsia and roses, ferns and cow-parsley, that gave us such pleasure and Hugh Dixon hay fever. The reader who, like the banished Duke in the Forest of Arden or the Celtic prince Suibhne, is prepared to find good in everything, should enjoy North West Ulster.

The section on sources and further reading at the end of the Intro-

duction gives some of the detail of what has been read to provide the
information for The Buildings of Ireland files to date. Here I must
acknowledge my debt to many research assistants but principally to
Hugh Dixon, whom I lured to Belfast as the first assistant of this project
in 1970. He provided the backbone of research for the next two years
and has accompanied me on much of the visiting. His knowledge of
Irish Victorian architects has saved me many blunders, and his enthusiasm for even the dullest of rural buildings was very sustaining
on poor days. Mr Peter Lamb took on the very considerable task of
noting all the architectural drawings belonging to the Representative
Church Body in Ireland, and in the offices of the major Irish banks.
He also read and noted with exemplary care The Irish Builder from
1859 to 1900, a job that Miss Veronica Aliaga Kelly brought up to
date with the same skill and patience; she also read the Calendars of
State Papers, Official Commission Reports, and material in the Brad-
shaw Collection of Irish books in Cambridge University Library. Miss
Lucy Anne Hunt spent a year extracting information from the major
source books for Irish medieval architecture and Mr Alban Reade
read the Journal of the Royal Society of Antiquaries in Ireland. My
wife and Mrs Anne Simpson have together looked after a great deal
of the Irish interest in the major English building periodicals and have
read various volumes of tours. Others who have helped with the
reading are Mrs Jackie Chadwick, Mr Neil Burton, Mrs A. Bodmer,
Mr James Lawson, and Miss Frances Law. Recent research
assistants who have prepared material for later volumes have also
incidentally contributed to this: they are Mr Christopher Beharrell,
Mr Rory O'Donnell, and Mr Nicholas Sheaff. Finally the job of
filing has been shared by my wife and Mrs Alma Bevan, who
together keep chaos at bay.

  The illustrations for this volume come in the main from my own
collection of photographs taken at the time of our visiting. Ireland
until this year has had no National Monuments Record either in the
Republic or in Northern Ireland nor any full programme for recording
– in a comprehensive way – its rapidly diminishing store of architecture. In such a situation it seemed best that the Buildings of Ireland should provide its own photographic survey, and we have now
a set of some 2,200 pictures of buildings in Derry, Donegal, Fermanagh, and Tyrone. The very considerable job of developing and
printing the films has been undertaken by Mr Douglas Smith of the
photographic department of the Paul Mellon Centre for Studies in
British Art in London, which has given the project invaluable help
through these photographic services. Contact prints of all these Buildings of Ireland Record photographs are deposited with the Institute

of Irish Studies at Queen's University, Belfast, and in the Mellon Centre in London. As the series grows, so will its photographic coverage.

My text has been typed by two kind helpers, Mrs Mary Whitehouse and Mrs Rosemary Gentleman, respectively the secretaries of the Departments of Fine Art and of History in the University of Edinburgh, who have shown more patience with my spelling and scribble than I deserve and have coped with a manuscript that has necessarily come to them in dribs and drabs. Mrs Andrea Stirling helped most kindly and promptly to type additional material at a late stage. The finished text has been read by Mr Dixon and Dr Maurice Craig, the part that deals with Derry City by Mr J. J. Tracey, and some individual entries by a number of different owners and colleagues. My father-in-law, Mr Charles Wrinch, has suggested many improvements and Mr Alan Bell has read, with an eagle eye, a complete set of proofs. I am very grateful to all of them for their help and for the corrections they have made. Any value that this book may have is indeed due largely to those who have helped me. I am nonetheless conscious of its gaps and fearful for its inaccuracies. The responsibility for these, which I hope readers will point out, rests with me alone.

The visiting for this volume ran ahead of the publication by a number of years. Inevitably redevelopment and the effects of continuing trouble in Northern Ireland may make some of the text out of date. This is most likely to apply to sections of the town tours.

Finally I should record my thanks to owners who have let me inspect their property: it should be emphasized here that their kindness to me in no way means that the buildings described in this volume are necessarily accessible to the public.

INTRODUCTION

North West Ulster is not an area of Ireland that is associated primarily with architectural excellence. It is a rugged, rough country, isolated and away from the main traffic routes even within Ireland itself. Its coasts open only to the Atlantic or the North Channel, and it was the sea that provided the main passage for the changes that happened in its history. The sea brought the Norsemen to plunder the monasteries on the coast and around Lough Erne from the eighth to the eleventh centuries; it brought a Scots army under Edward Bruce to the Antrim coast in 1315; and it was by sea that the last of the great native lords, the Earls of Tyrone and Tyrconnell, took their flight, in September 1607. Men from across the water, from Scotland and the north of England, settled their lands in the Plantation of James I that followed. Derry was relieved by sea in 1648 and again in 1689, and a French frigate brought Wolfe Tone into Lough Swilly in October 1798. Finally it was the sea that took thousands of families after the Famine to a new life beyond the Atlantic, leaving the country with less than half the population there had been before 1845. The great port for this emigration was the city of Derry – a boom town throughout the nineteenth century – trafficking not only in the people who drifted steadily from Fermanagh, Tyrone, and Donegal, but also in the flax, linens, and farm produce that the economy of the countryside provided. But Derry stands alone, the only big town in the whole region.

The isolated position of north-western Ireland has meant also that the country has become a stronghold of old ways. Tenacious first of the rites and forms of the early Irish Church, it offered later, under the powerful protection of the O'Donnells and O'Neills, a sanctuary in the sixteenth century to the religious of suppressed monastic establishments, many of whom continued their ministry and community life long after the Tudor conquest of Ireland was complete. The *Annals of the Four Masters*, the most important compilation of Irish history, based on surviving Irish annals, was written here, in a temporary shelter at Bundrowes near the Franciscan friary of Donegal, between 1622 and 1635. The ancient Gaelic tradition made its last stand in Ulster under Hugh O'Neill, the O'Neill, who did not finally submit until 1603, and

Gaelic today is still the first language of the people in the extreme west at Gortahork and Falcarragh. Nor was the native population ever disposed to acquiesce in the imposed English rule. Rebellion became endemic, from the rising of 1641 that wiped out much of the recent Plantation to the '98 and the struggles of Victorian and modern Ireland. The history of this recalcitrant region enriches the literature and lore of Ireland; but while narrative arts flourish on a stormy past and present, the art of architecture does not. Conquest and its resistance brought endless waste, and what had survived the medieval period was paid scant respect in the seventeenth century by administrators with an alien allegiance, religion, and tongue. Sir Henry Docwra, anxious to secure the new anglicized settlement of Londonderry, took down almost all the remains of the Augustinian and Dominican churches there to get materials for his new stone walls, and similar processes have continued throughout the country until recent times. Today it is the turn of the monuments of the Protestant Ascendancy to suffer. As parishes are united, churches are left to decay, while the mansions that provided their congregations are often derelict or roofless, and tenanted only by cows.

The buildings of Ireland that find a place in this volume on North West Ulster are, more often than not, vestiges and fragments rather than complete structures – the history of the area has seen to that; but it should be added here that the area itself – its structure and geography – has also played a part in shaping the architectural scene and in limiting its range. The north west, generally speaking, is a poor area. For the purposes of this volume it has been taken as the four counties of Derry, Donegal, Fermanagh, and Tyrone. (Geographically the western tail of Cavan, which has been kept for the second Ulster volume, might also have been included.) Vast tracts in all these counties are unproductive mountains, moors, or bogs. With the exception of the porcelain factory at Belleek in Co. Fermanagh, and the flax and linen mills of Derry, Sion Mills, Caledon, and elsewhere in the countryside, the economy was essentially agricultural, eked out by fisheries at Killybegs, Greencastle, and on the Foyle and the Bann. Though recently productivity has been raised to a high level – over 80 per cent of the land of Northern Ireland is under active cultivation – the bulk of the population in the past existed in many areas only at subsistence level. Donegal, the largest of the four counties (twice the size of Derry and Fermanagh and half as large again as Tyrone), was and is agriculturally the poorest. Statistics in the *Parliamentary Gazetteer* of 1846, the very year when the

Famine was at its height, illustrate clearly the parlous state of agricultural improvement at that time. By then only 32.9 per cent of Donegal land was under cultivation. Tyrone was better with 55.8 per cent, and Derry and Fermanagh best of all with 61.4 per cent and 63.3 per cent respectively, but even so the average of cultivated land for the region was no more than 48.7 per cent as compared with 83 per cent for the entire province of Leinster or 94 per cent in Meath, one of Ireland's richest agricultural counties. Land as comparatively poor as this could not provide the capital to finance ambitious building projects or to support large towns. Indeed Donegal still has no town of any size. Letterkenny, the largest, had a population of only 4,701 in 1971, and Ballyshannon, the next in size, 2,325.

The area contained by Derry, Donegal, Fermanagh, and Tyrone is 4,650 square miles, just a little over one-eighth of all Ireland. If sparsely populated and not over-endowed with architecture, it is a land that is rich in scenery, often of spectacular beauty and variety. It is, too, a reasonably coherent geographical unit, bounded on the north and west by a dramatic coastline, on the east first by the river Bann and then by Lough Neagh, and on the south by the Leitrim Hills and the Macnean loughs. It is only in the furthest reaches of Upper Lough Erne, at the southeastern tip of Fermanagh between Ballyconnell (Cavan) and Clones (Monaghan), that the border becomes more of an administrative hypothesis than a geographical reality, zigzagging in and out among islets before it runs up the side of Slieve Beagh to join the course of the Blackwater, a not very significant stream that, passing Aughnacloy, Caledon, and Moy, ends back in Lough Neagh. With half the country mountain, it is the lough-sides and river valleys that provide the principal places for settlement and the centres of better building. The lush pasture land around Lough Erne in Fermanagh, with Enniskillen in the middle, is the principal focus in the south. Tyrone has two centres: the wide crescent of farming land east and south of Lough Neagh between Cookstown and Clogher, and the more restricted valleys of the 3 Strule (Omagh), the Derg (Castlederg), and the Mourne – the name the rivers take when they join – which flows north to Lifford, where the Mourne meets the Foyle, the principal river of the district, separating Tyrone from Donegal. Donegal's best land is concentrated around the Foyle and Finn valleys and in the lowlands that border Lough Swilly; in Derry it is the coastal strip between the city itself and Magilligan Point, or the flat land by the Bann and north east of Lough Neagh, that is the richest. The most

1 mountainous regions are around the Sperrins, which rise to 683 m in south Derry and divide east from west Tyrone, and in western Donegal, whose dark blue hills are justifiably famous. It is not that these mountains are high in absolute terms: Errigal, the highest in all Ulster, is 752 m, but it rises to that height from almost nothing in less than a mile, and so too does the great flat-topped bulk of Muckish in the same chain. Other memorable landscapes are provided by Slieve Snaght in Inishowen, a magical and unforgettable peninsula; by the Blue Stack mountains that cluster north-east of Donegal town above the waters of Lough Eske; and in the extreme west of Donegal Bay by Slieve League, a peak of 601 m that drops from its summit to the Atlantic in one continuous bevelled cliff.

The ascent of Slieve League from Teelin Bay to 'One Man's Pass', a giddy track along the edge of the cliff, takes a visitor from a reassuring landscape of small fields and sleepy quays to one of the bleakest prospects in Ireland, where quartzite mountains with bare eroded tops stretch endlessly into the distance. It is the Irish landscape at its most forbidding; yet it is here, on sites like Slieve 2 League, that the buildings of Ireland begin. Just below the peak in the centre of a broad shoulder, a cluster of dry stone walls indicates the location of a primitive church and holy well, the site of an anchorite settlement of the Irish Celtic Church that is typical of a kind of religious life which flourished from the advent of St Patrick in the fifth century until the Synod of Rathbreasail in IIII.

EARLY CHRISTIAN MONUMENTS

The MONUMENTS OF THE CELTIC CHURCH are, for the purposes of this volume, the earliest buildings that need to be described. As the Romans never attempted an Irish conquest there are no classical remains, and the prehistoric and native settlements prior to the Christian period are subjects more appropriate to an archaeological than to an architectural guide. The Ordnance Survey map of Monastic Ireland (2nd ed., 1961) marks no less than ninety-six verified or supposed sites for early Celtic establishments in the four counties. Other anchorite settlements like that 2 at Slieve League abounded in the west, but of all these there are now only a few where clear visual evidence of the communities remains. The simplest monuments of the early Celtic Church are the primitive inscribed crosses put up at holy places. These are often no more than large flattish or shaft-shaped stones from two to five feet high, marked with a Latin or Greek cross or some other device, or roughly shaped with short arms. There is a notable group in the vicinity of Ardara in Donegal and more remain at Glencolumbkille nearby. Others are preserved on the Inishowen peninsula at Clonmany and at Carrowmore; and there are roughly shaped slab crosses near the old churches at Gartan Lough and at Mevagh near Rosapenna, all in Co. Donegal. Fermanagh has at least two, at Teesnaghtan Cross and by Derrynawilt Cross-roads; Co. Derry provides one more on an exposed hilly site at Duncrum and a slab cross at Mullaboy. But the interest of all these is slight: they offer evidence for the existence of early Christian communities at their sites and little more. Much the same is true of the later pillar stones, now used as stations of the Cross, on the celebrated pilgrimage route at Glencolumbkille, and of the reputed anchorite retreats near Malin Head, the Wee House of Malin and the Friar's Cell.

Remains that a non-specialist will find worth going to see occur first among the EARLY SCULPTURED CROSS SLABS. The best of these are in northern Donegal, and the very best all in the Inishowen peninsula, though the fine slab now inside Clogher Cath- 12 edral in Co. Tyrone should also be mentioned. The majority of the slabs are decorated on both faces and are characterized by shallow relief patterns carved all over to a uniform depth. Much use is made of interlaced patterns to define the cross area, and a raised border normally surrounds the slab. The workmanship, with the exception of the Clogher Cross, is generally crude – or now appears so – though the designs themselves can be intricate and of considerable sophistication. The most delicate example, worked with a weave of circles and diagonal crosses, is the broken shaft on the island of Inishkeel near Portnoo, and the most simple at Killaghtee, where the interlace is restricted to a *triquetra* below a plain Greek cross inscribed in a circle. The remaining crosses at Drumhallagh, north of Rathmullen, at Fahan, and at Carndonagh are more closely similar and are best considered as a group. Two remain at Carndonagh: St Patrick's Cross – the first 11 cross in Ireland to break away from the confines of a slab with short but clearly separate arms and head – and the so-called Marigold Cross; at Fahan there is now the splendid St Mura's Cross, 13 finest of the group; and at Drumhallagh a single smallish slab. Various dates from the late sixth to the eighth and even the 'decadent' tenth century have been proposed, but the consensus of critical opinion now places the crosses about the mid seventh century. The key to this dating lies mainly in the use of the broad ribbon interlace derived from Mediterranean – probably Coptic – sources which, though it proved a short-lived fashion, is a distinctive feature of the Book of Durrow written in Northumbria about 670 (now in the library of Trinity College, Dublin).

Equally significant as a feature of the Donegal cross slabs is the use they make of little stumpy figures – like penguins, all head, body, and feet – in the blank areas on the slabs. At Carndonagh they take on a special importance, for St Patrick's Cross is accompanied by two separate *stelae* or pillars that are also carved with small figures and with abstract Celtic patterns on their sides. As with the crosses, the carving is little more than recessed line drawing, but the facial expressions of the figures – full face and profile – and the position of the arms, which are usually crossed, link these tiny figure stones to other developments of PRIMITIVE SCULPTURE existing at various sites around Lower Lough Erne in Co. Fermanagh. The first of these are both earlier and pagan: two figure stones in Caldragh graveyard, Boa Island. One is a small squatting man with folded arms, and with more arms drawn along the sides of the stone. The other is a larger double-headed idol with two identical faces. This double-headed Janus is of a very old type, known widely throughout the Celtic world, and is clearly pagan. A Christian pillar stone is the Bishop's Stone in Killadeas churchyard – a name that records the Culdees, or servants of God, an austere reform group in the Irish church that became established in the late eighth century and that persisted in Armagh and Fermanagh well into the sixteenth century. The Killadeas stone is carved on two faces: the side with the stooped figure of a bishop holding a crozier and bell, and the front with a panel of interlaced ribbon surmounted by a slightly projecting mask-like head. The bishop carving is close in style to the figures on the Carndonagh *stelae*, but the head on the front of the stone is much more fully modelled, a characteristic that it shares with the other Fermanagh figure stones on White Island. These have been found at different times built face-in to a later twelfth-century church. They now number eight figures: two incomplete, and the remaining six modelled on square stone shafts to suggest that they are sitting. Though their exact significance and date – the ninth or tenth century is usually suggested – is still not established, it seems probable that the statuettes, which are of different sizes but in pairs, may have supported the steps of an ambo, that is a pulpit, in a timber church. They were presumably preserved simply because they were useful as stones for the new building.

If the proper architectural context of the White Island figures is now unknown, their original setting may still be described. From the Bronze Age to the end of the Early Christian period and beyond, the standard Irish settlement, either secular or religious, took the form of a large circular enclosure, a rath, cashel, or ring fort, usually of earth or of earth and stone with a surrounding trench or ditch. Within this enclosure a Celtic monastery would consist of a small single-cell church, or a group of small churches, thatched circular huts for the monks, and a number of commemorative pillar stones and crosses. The lack of any formal coordination in planning the layout of the site is best illustrated by the most famous Celtic monastic complex, at Glendalough in Co. Wicklow, though the same may be seen in the north west on Devenish Island, where the small scale and haphazard relationship between St Molaise's House and the early Romanesque church nearby are typical features of a Celtic monastic settlement. 20–3

Irish chiefs, like their clergy, inhabited circular enclosures which survive in hundreds in every county. Frequently they are elaborated by extra defensive ditches or by systems of chambers incorporated within the rath, though the main dwelling was built almost exclusively of timber or of wattle frames. Another type of enclosure that became popular in the Middle Ages was the crannog, an artificial island, circular in form and made with timber staves, sods, and stones, where water provided the main defence instead of an earth bank, though the dwelling house inside was still of timber and wattle. Raths and crannogs still make their impact on the Irish landscape today. The raths of course are often lost behind hedges and later dykes and need to be seen from vantage points, but the crannogs stand out clearly in any lakeland area as neat, round islets – too neat to be natural – usually covered with scrub. Two spectacular raths that must have been seats of considerable power are found at Clogher in the Bishop's Park, and just outside Limavady in Co. Derry. Their sites and scale are both impressive, though being earthworks they cannot rank as buildings for the purposes of this book.

Of buildings in this period little or nothing remains visible except for two remarkable STONE FORTS: the Grianan of Ailech and Doon Fort. Both are splendid monuments, splendid in scale, in situation, and in evocative power, and they lift Ulster architecture to an unaccustomed level of importance. Eminently primitive in appearance, both consist of a great circular cashel built of dry stone walls with a single entrance, with mural passages and stairs within the enclosure that give access to the wall heads. Grianan, the royal seat of the northern branch of the O'Neills, 8–10 is developed inside three defensive rings at the site of an Iron Age hill fort on the isthmus between the city of Derry and Lough Swilly; Doon Fort, an O'Boyle stronghold, rises on a remote island which it occupies completely on Lough Doon near Portnoo. Similar forts exist at other sites in Ireland: Dun Aengus and Dun Oghil on Innishmore in the Aran Islands in Co. Galway, and Staigue Fort near Parknasilla in Co. Kerry, this last the most sophisticated of all; they share the characteristics that they are near the Atlantic coast, open to seaborne attack, and that they are conceived as defensive, not aggressive, structures. In this as in their dry stone construction they bear an obvious similarity to the first-century brochs of northern Scotland, Shetland, and the Western Isles: there is the same pronounced batter of the external wall, the same narrow entrance passage, and the same defensive thickness – up to 15 ft – at the base. But the Scottish brochs are much smaller in plan and far taller in elevation – massive conical towers in contrast to the Irish ring enclosures whose walls seem never to have exceeded 15 to 18 ft and whose diameters are more than twice the width of brochs. Moreover the Irish forts appear to be much more recent. Only Dun Aengus may be dated to the Dark Ages: the others are all of Early Christian origin and are known to have remained in use for several centuries. Grianan was overrun according to the *Annals* in 1101 and destroyed again in 1599, and the O'Boyles of Boylagh held Doon until the sixteenth century.

20   The ROUND TOWER on Devenish Island near Enniskillen is the next building of any importance in these four counties. It is not the only round tower that remains in the North but it is one of the most perfect in all Ireland: complete, finely proportioned,
21 and distinguished by four sculptured heads at its cornice with brilliantly inventive interlace beards. Other towers are the unique example on Tory Island off the Donegal coast, where the tower is built of undressed beach boulders, and the stump at Bruckless, Co. Donegal, now incorporated into a modern belfry beside the nineteenth-century Catholic church.

Round towers were built primarily as places of refuge. Their doors were set high up so that they could be reached only by ladders and (as at Devenish) usually faced the principal church of the monastery of which they formed a part. This position allowed the tower to be stored quickly with the books, relics, and vessels of the church. A window above the door served both to defend the tower and to allow a marksman to shoot at any attackers attempting to break into the church. *Cloicthech*, the Irish word used to denote a tower, means 'bell house', suggesting that in times of peace the towers served an equally useful function as belfries. Their windows at the top would certainly have made them suitable for such a purpose. They served too as lookout towers, and in the thickly wooded landscape of Early Christian and medieval Ireland, when maps were unknown, their function as landmarks was probably of equal importance.

Devenish round tower is usually dated to the twelfth century, two centuries later than the HIGH CROSSES which were the other architectural monuments among the groups of huts and small churches that made up the buildings of a later Irish monastery. The examples in Ulster, of which a good many are in the north-western counties, seem to form a particular group. The finest are the crosses at the old monastic site at Arboe by Lough Neagh [17] and at Donaghmore nearby – both in Co. Tyrone. They are of impressive size: Arboe is 18 ft 6 in. high and Donaghmore (which may not be complete) is 15 ft. Both represent the final development of the Celtic cross in Ireland, far removed from the tentative slab-bound type found at Carndonagh and Fahan. Their form is that of the free-standing 'architectural' cross: stepped base, shaft, and cross, with block-ended arms bound together in a continuous recessed ring or nimbus. The development from the slab to this complete form is not represented in the North of Ireland (crosses at Ahenny, Co. Tipperary, and at Kells, Co. Meath, offer the best examples of the interim stage), but there are instances of the plain form without the sculptural narrative that distinguishes Arboe and Donaghmore. Of these the most impressive is the enormous fallen cross at Ray church in Donegal, 21 ft long, reputedly once destined for Tory Island. At Cooley churchyard, Inishowen, there is another, smaller cross, and stumps or pieces of High Crosses remain at Boho, Lisnaskea, and Galloon Island in Co. Fermanagh and at Camus in Co. Derry. A note must also be added on the curious church-shaped tombs or skull houses that preserve in miniature the forms of early Celtic oratories and occur, here in the north west, in a limited geographical area that was traditionally O'Cahan country. The best example, well preserved, is at Banagher Old Church, another is at Bovevagh, and the remains [19] of a third is at Duncrum, Magilligan, all in Co. Derry. A fourth is at Cooley on the opposite shore of Lough Foyle to Duncrum.

MEDIEVAL ARCHITECTURE

Irish high crosses and round towers, undoubtedly the typical and also the most enduring monuments of the Celtic Christian church, reached their peak in the tenth and eleventh centuries. The twelfth century in Irish history is a century of change: change in the structure of the Irish Church, and in the balance and social hierarchy of Irish society. The events that effected these alterations in a way of life already ancient were the Synod of Rathbreasail of 1111 and the Norman conquest of the country that began in 1169. Taken jointly, the two events may be said to inaugurate the medieval period proper in Ireland; for the Synod was to introduce a new diocesan system based on continental patterns and it followed a thorough reorganization of Irish monasticism – principally the work of St Malachy – while the Norman conquest was to impose a centralized feudal structure in place of the old Celtic pattern of loose family federation that had existed throughout the country. With the religious of the new orders introduced by Malachy and the barons of Henry II's armies came a new architectural style, and indeed a different attitude to the whole purpose of building.

As soon as they had subdued the country, the Normans gave up the earthen mottes that had been their first strongholds and built regular stone castles on a European pattern. The monks of the new orders, where existing Irish monasteries had accepted a different rule, necessarily worked their changes more gradually, though the foundation of new monasteries by the Normans after 1170 tended to accelerate the introduction of new forms in church design as well. The changeover, though by no means immediate, was effected by the early thirteenth century. At the death of St Malachy in 1148 some fifty abbeys of monks and seven houses of nuns still followed an early form of Irish monasticism; by 1171, when Henry II came in person to Ireland, the nunneries had all conformed or disappeared, and the number of male monasteries had fallen to twenty-four; and by the early thirteenth century no Irish forms of monasticism survived beyond the two tenacious Culdees houses at Devenish and Armagh that retained their separate existence until the Elizabethan Dissolution in the later sixteenth century.

How far these changes affected the remote and unruly province of Ulster is not easily told. The Normans under John De Courcy were firmly established in Down and Antrim in 1180, but in the north west they gained only a fleeting hold that culminated in the construction more than a century later of one great castle, North-burg or Greencastle on the Inishowen peninsula, built by Richard 31 de Burgo, the 'Red' Earl of Ulster, from 1305. Within eleven years the castle had been taken by the Scots army of Edward Bruce, and by 1333 it had passed into Irish hands. NORMAN MILITARY ARCHITECTURE is represented solely by Northburg, comparable in its use of polygonal towers and polychrome stonework to the Edwardian castles of Wales, but not a type that naturalized well in an Ulster setting. The scale of the structure with two defensible wards was far in excess of native needs, and significantly large parts were demolished in the later Middle Ages to provide for the O'Donnells a single tower house abutting the north wall of De Burgo's castle. The native Irish lords continued throughout the medieval period to inhabit their raths and stone forts and, with the exception of some Norman towers taken over in the fourteenth century, of which O'Doherty's Castle at Buncrana may be an example, few regular castles were built until the fifteenth century. The one pre-eminent exception to this pattern is Harry Avery's Castle by Newtownstewart, an O'Neill stronghold dating probably from about 1360 of which only the pattern of the layout remains, with two massive drum towers flanking the entrance gateway. Harry Avery marks a stage in the development of the castle from the full strength of a Norman keep-and-bailey design to the forti-fied gate tower types of the later Middle Ages, of which there were at least two examples: on the Donegal coast at Kilbarron Castle, an O'Siggins and O'Clery seat, and Rahan Castle by Dun-kineely built by the McSwineys in the fifteenth century. Very little remains of either today.

LATE IRISH TOWER HOUSES are by far the most common secular remains of the medieval architecture of the north west, though even these are hardly abundant. Tower castles survive in Donegal town, where the tower was altered and extended after the Plantation by Sir Basil Brooke; in Enniskillen, where the core of the Maguire castle was taken over by the incoming Cole family and is now almost unrecognizable in the centre of a nineteenth-century barrack yard; and in Buncrana, where O'Doherty's Castle was adapted by the Vaughans before they built their new house early in the eighteenth century. Two sixteenth-century castles that have remained unaltered since they were ruined are those on Inch Island in Lough Swilly and at Carrickabraghy in In-ishowen. Though both are heavily ruined, Inch retains one com-plete vaulted ground-floor room and a characteristic mural stair-case running in the thickness of the wall round two sides of the

tower. This, besides the usual circular newel stair found in Great
Britain, is a common stair arrangement in Irish sixteenth-century
castles. It occurs again at Carrickabraghy, and at Doe Castle near
33 Creeslough, where the sixteenth-century tower built by the
MacSweeneys and extended in the Elizabethan era has been particularly well preserved, as it was converted into a country house
in the early nineteenth century, when the late medieval parts
were left substantially intact. Doe Castle, which is protected by
a surrounding enclosure with a sixteenth-century casemate, forms
34 an interesting contrast with the near-contemporary Burt Castle
by Newtowncunningham. Burt, though built by the O'Dohertys,
and defended, like Doe, by an outer enclosure and casemate, is
essentially a Scottish type of castle with projecting round towers
at two opposite corners of the main tower, one containing a spiral
stair and both providing protection for the main wall faces.
Though the castle may date from the time of Henry VIII, in many
respects it foreshadows the sort of building that was to be introduced into Ulster in the Jacobean Plantation of the next century.

As with castles, the development of MEDIEVAL RELIGIOUS
ARCHITECTURE in the north west can be traced more usually in
fragments than in complete structures. Indeed, there is no more
compelling proof of the destructive power of the inhabitants of
this part of Ulster than in the paucity of church remains that are
earlier than the seventeenth century. It is possible within these
four counties to trace the development of Romanesque and Gothic
styles through the simple vehicle of the different window shapes
and patterns that survive in the roofless gables of a number of
small rectangular church ruins, but it is hard to do more; and
the habit of robbing ruins of the freestone elements – window
surrounds, tracery, and door frames – has left many an Irish
medieval church in Ulster little better, and of little more interest,
than a deserted barn.

What has been lost may be listed briefly. In 1500 there were
six Augustinian monasteries in the north west, at Clogher, Derry,
Devenish, Dungiven, Lisgoole, and on Saint's Island, Lough
Derg. Of these only the ruins of the churches at Devenish and
Dungiven remain; though modest, they are some of the most
interesting medieval ruins in the area. The Cistercians had two
houses: at Assaroe outside Ballyshannon (of which an ivy-covered
wall still stands) and at Macosquin in Co. Derry, which has left
no appreciable remains. Of collegiate churches at Clogher, Derry,
and Raphoe, only the choir of Raphoe Cathedral remains, and that

is much restored. The nuns' convent at Derry founded about 1218 has left no trace.

Of the four great orders of mendicant friars that brought a renewed religious enthusiasm to Ireland in the thirteenth century, three appeared in the north west. Dominican friars had a house at Coleraine founded in 1244 and another at Derry founded in 1274. Again, neither has left any trace. The Carmelites had one friary at Rathmullen founded in 1403 and refounded in 1516. It remains today as one of the more interesting medieval church ruins, thanks largely to its conversion to a dwelling house and private chapel by the Protestant Bishop of Raphoe early in the seventeenth century. The Franciscans appeared first in 1474 at Donegal Friary, a building whose stormy history and central role during the struggle between Elizabeth and the O'Donnells of Tyrconnell has left little beyond the plan set out in pieces of rubble and two sides of a diminutive cloister. The popularity of the Franciscan system of the Third Order Regular that provided some form of equivalent to the numerous collegiate foundations in England and Scotland in the later Middle Ages is strikingly demonstrated by the quantity of houses founded throughout Donegal and Tyrone, two districts that had hardly been anglicized and where native preferences might prevail. Between 1430 and 1537 seven Tertiary Franciscan houses were founded in Donegal, six in Tyrone, and possibly one in Derry. Significantly, it is the Co. Donegal friaries that have fared best, with substantial if simple structures still to be seen at Magherabeg, Ballysaggart, Killydonnell, and Balleegham. A characteristic of all these foundations is the unusually long and narrow church plan, sometimes more than four squares in proportion. This is most obvious at Magherabeg and Balleegham, where only the church building remains, though the long plan is still evident at Killydonnell, where conventual buildings and a south transept have been added to the church. At Ballysaggart only the east end of the church is standing, with one fine cusped lancet. Of the Tertiary Franciscan friaries in Tyrone, Corickmore alone remains, and it is a simple ruin.

As Ulster chiefs long held out against the armies of the Crown, the suppression of the monasteries under Henry VIII and Elizabeth was completed only in the first years of the seventeenth century: the buildings were then granted to laymen, usually recently settled in the country, to be demolished for their materials. Though their use remained, the parish churches of the Middle Ages have fared hardly better than the abbeys and friaries. The

change to Protestantism and successive periods of rebuilding, first
in the Jacobean Plantation, then in the eighteenth century, and
finally, and more particularly, after the Act of Union, have left
few medieval buildings still in use. Only two, Taughboyne parish
church near St Johnstown and Clonoe parish church by Coalisland, claim to be medieval foundations, and with the exception
of carved late medieval label-stops at Taughboyne neither bears
any visible evidence of its origin. A few later parish churches incorporate medieval fragments: the churches at Carndonagh and
Boho both re-use simple chamfered doors; and one complete traceried window, apparently designed by the master mason *Matthew O'Dubigan* in 1449, has been taken from the Augustinian
abbey at Devenish to be re-erected in the parish church at Monea.
Otherwise the history of Ballywillan parish church near Portstewart may stand as typical of what happened to many medieval
buildings. It is a large rectangular building with high gables.
Originally of the late twelfth or early thirteenth century, with narrow round-headed lancets, the east end was altered later and
given a widely splayed paired lancet window. In the seventeenth
century a third east window was built, much wider and with a
high segmental head. The church survived the eighteenth century
unscathed and in 1837 was described as 'an ancient, spacious and
handsome edifice in the early English style, the only one in the
diocese or county built prior to the Reformation in which divine
service is now performed'. Yet even with this point made in the
first year of Victoria's reign, the Church of Ireland authorities
thought it had better be replaced, and in 1841 built a diminutive
toy church some two miles away, stripping the roof off the last
pre-Reformation church in the diocese. To piece together a
picture of the religious architecture of the Middle Ages in these
four counties, we must pick over the fragments that somehow have
survived the demolition gangs of history. But the gangs have been
at work a very long time, and they are still at work today.

   The oldest churches where interesting details remain to be seen
form a group in Co. Derry at Banagher, Dungiven, and Maghera.
None is straightforward, for the first two have been enlarged and
the last rebuilt. All seem to date from the last years of the Celtic
period and were small single-cell churches built of heavy rubble
masonry. The church at Dungiven preserves, at its east end, corner
18 shafts and horizontal beams in imitation of timber construction
that may be linked with the *antae* or projecting end walls of Early
Christian oratories elsewhere in Ireland, and indeed the same
antae appear at St Molaise's House at Devenish, though only the

sculptured bases, decorated with inverted flower patterns derived from the palmette, survive there. Banagher and Maghera share a type of west door that is found only in one other place in Ireland: at Aghowle in Co. Wicklow. Both doors have inclined jambs of a Vitruvian pattern and are set in a large rectangular ashlar panel which is recessed into the wall and framed by a square stone border. The Banagher door is plain – though the stone border has a complex profile – and may be earlier than the doorway at Maghera, which carries an elaborate Crucifixion scene on the 15 lintel, and billet and scroll patterns on the border at the sides. Pieces of a sculptured lintel preserved at Raphoe Cathedral may 16 once have been part of another doorway of this type which may be dated to the late ninth or early tenth century.

Banagher also provides an example of the Irish style of Romanesque work that followed in the twelfth century, when a chancel was added to the church, decorated with colonnettes on the external corners and multiple roll mouldings framing a window 24 both inside and out. Similar mouldings appear round the aumbry at Ballywillan, on the east window of Killaghtee Old Church at Dunkineely, and at St Molaise's church at Devenish. The only 23 example of an elaborated Romanesque doorway in these four counties is provided by the reconstructed round-headed door with chevron decoration at the church on White Island near Devenish in Lough Erne. A curious east window in the ruined church of Templecrone on Termon Island near Dungloe which has a narrow round-headed lancet, widely splayed inside to a *pointed* and moulded reveal, may date from the late twelfth or early thirteenth century and represents an isolated instance of Romanesque turning to Gothic forms.

The east window of the ruined Temple Douglas Abbey near Gartan is a two-light mullioned type that is probably of the thirteenth century; after this, the next piece of Gothic detail to note is the choir of Raphoe Cathedral which, though it is largely a restoration by *Sir Thomas Drew*, preserves triple sedilia that are also 28 thirteenth-century. These sedilia alone, where the stiff-leaf capitals, colonnettes, and arch mouldings are all original, give some idea of the quality and enrichment that the Gothic churches of the region may generally have possessed.

Two examples of the typically Irish pattern of a tower supported on paired chancel arches are preserved in the Augustinian abbey on Devenish Island and in the Carmelite friary at Rathmullen. The abbey at Devenish, dating from 1449, is the more 30 finely worked, with large ashlar blocks forming the chancel wall,

and an eight-part ribbed vault roofing the crossing. Both sets of
arches considerably constrict the space between the nave and the
chancel, and both are strengthened by extra chamfered arches
within the main arch supported on oddly aggressive inverted
pyramids – the whole style sharp and hard. The cloister at
29 Donegal Abbey, though now only a fragment and on a tiny scale,
bears evidence of the same sharp taste, with oddly chiselled
imposts that die into the reveals of the cloister arcade, and this
firm, crisp style appears fleetingly in a number of fifteenth-century traceried windows in counties Fermanagh and Donegal. The
long, thin window with its cusped head and hood mould at Ballysaggart Friary founded about 1500 is one example close to
Donegal. At Balleegham Friary founded in 1471 a triple light with
complete traceried head survives buried in ivy, and there is of
course the window from Devenish now at Monea of 1449. Two
small Fermanagh churches preserve the cusped frames of their
east windows. One, with a hood mould ending in corbel faces of
25 saints or kings, is at St Naile's church, Kinawley. The other is
in Carrick church ruins by a remote little lough near Derrygonnelly. The frame of a third similar paired light with a curious
moulded hood is at Carnteel crossroads in Co. Tyrone. Of Perpendicular work there is but one example: the east window of Derry-
26 vullan Old Church in Co. Fermanagh, elegantly attenuated, with
four blind panels converting the head to a flat top above two shallow cusped lights.

One monument remains to be mentioned in this bare catalogue
27 of medieval scraps and fragments: the O'Cahan canopied wall
tomb in the choir of Dungiven Priory. The carving of the figure
sculpture suggests a date in the late fifteenth century, and the wide
traceried canopy above the tomb slab, filled with three wheels each
set with three curving daggers, is by far the most eloquent memorial
to the craftsmanship of the late Gothic masons of Ulster, so much
of whose work was to vanish in the aftermath of the Elizabethan
conquest of the province.

The conquest of the north west was complete by 1603. In that
year Hugh O'Neill, who had opened the last sustained rebellion
of Gaelic Ireland in 1595, made his submission at Mellifont in Co.
Louth, as Rory O'Donnell the chief of Tyrconnell had done a
year before at Athlone. The new English king, James I, acted
generously. All who had engaged in the rebellion received a par-
don, and O'Neill and O'Donnell were confirmed in their vast
estates as Earls of Tyrone and Tyrconnell. Yet the days of Gaelic
independence were at an end, and within four years the changed

circumstances of their position forced both men to abandon their
native country.

JACOBEAN AND STUART ARCHITECTURE

The end of the medieval Gothic world is marked quite clearly
in this part of Ireland by the flight of the Earls together with those
heads of the ancient landed families who sailed with them in 1607.
The men who took their place, however much some may have
tried to accommodate themselves to native ways, brought a different language, culture, and religion to the north west, and different traditions too. In a country where the native population
was hostile they also brought over their own artisans, planting
the newly founded towns with Scots or English craftsmen of Protestant stock. And these craftsmen built Scots or English buildings
in Ireland. Perhaps the most enduring element among the
novelties introduced by Plantation settlers was the coordinated
town plan. Docwra's city of Derry, laid out on the regular plan 52
of a Roman camp with four gates, a grid of cross streets, and a
central square – so often in Ulster to be called The Diamond
– is the most celebrated of many early-seventeenth-century
Plantation towns, and its plan remains intact today. Coleraine,
built by the Irish Society, was essentially similar, with a central
Diamond set on an axial street with town gates at either end and
the beginning of a grid plan to the south. Kilrea and Limavady
use simpler cross plans with a central focus, and in Co. Donegal
several settlements, including Donegal town itself, the old town
of Raphoe, and the villages of Castle Finn and Malin, were laid
out round triangular greens. More was imported than plans. At
Coleraine frames for half-timbered houses were brought from
across the water, and indeed the maps of the London Companies'
Estates throughout Co. Derry show that this sort of building was
once widespread. The Ironmongers at Agivey and the Mercers
at Movanagher had built several substantial timber-framed
houses by the mid 1620s, while the Salters' towns at Magherafelt
and Salterstown, had they survived and developed, might have
rivalled Warwick or Chester. But little of this half-timbered work
survived the events of later-seventeenth-century Ireland and none
is left now. The buildings of planters who worked in stone fared
better, and of these there are numerous ruins in various states
of decay throughout the four counties.

The men who settled Ulster were of two races, Scots and
English, and of two types, profiteers and pioneers. The profiteers,

had their intention been other than to make a quick fortune and then sell up – often without meeting the requirements of the original grant of land – might have had the culture to introduce sophisticated architectural styles to the country they had taken; the pioneers had not. These men who came to Ireland and who stayed were generally of tough practical stock. The houses and churches they built were solid and sensible yet, to judge from the evidence of what is left, even if they had had the skilled artisans to employ, which contemporaries complained they lacked, it is doubtful whether their patronage would have produced fine buildings. The London Companies erected plenty of gabled and mullioned manor houses that have all since disappeared, but even these look more like late-sixteenth-century houses than the Jacobean buildings they were. JACOBEAN MANSION HOUSES that 35 deserve the name are few. Best is the gabled wing with mullioned windows built by Sir Basil Brooke at Donegal Castle from 1616 42 with a fine classical doorcase and finer stone chimneypiece in the remodelled keep. A Jacobean delight in fancy plans, reminiscent of Thorpe or Smythson, appears in the use of triple bay windows in a square room that is the tiny remaining fragment of Castle Curlews near Drumquin built by Sir John Davies, the Attorney General for Ireland, whose hope was always that 'this kingdom will grow humane and civil', and whose house must once have been a hostage to that hope. Sir Thomas Ridgeway, the grantee of an extensive estate at Augher in Co. Tyrone, indulged his fancy 38 (and his excellent Devon masons) in the little castle of Spur Royal, a veritable pun in stone, whose plan, an eight-pointed star (four points of which are triangular mullioned bay windows), is based on the reverse of the fifteen-shilling coin of James I's reign which showed a formalized sun with rays resembling a spur-rowel that gave both the coin and the castle its name. Spur Royal is the only Plantation castle still inhabited today. Its cross-mullioned windows appear again at Castlecaulfield, a more extensive three-storey hall house built by Sir Toby Caulfield about 1612, and at Old Castle Archdale built by John Archdale in 1615, of which 39 only a fragment remains. Finally the castle at Newtownstewart built by Sir Robert Newcomen about 1615 should be mentioned. Destroyed by James II in 1689 and now only a gaunt gabled wall, it preserves one fine polygonal chimneystack of cut and moulded brick and a range of typical early-seventeenth-century manorial windows.

All the builders mentioned so far are English and their houses have English details: windows with octagonal mullions and

transoms, label mouldings, and, with the exception of Newtownstewart, smooth gables. PLANTATION CASTLES built by Scots
are more numerous and visually quite different. Perhaps
because Scotland, at least until the late sixteenth century, was as
rough as Ulster, if not rougher, the traditional Scottish vernacular
structure survived better than its English counterpart. There are
many in Fermanagh around Lough Erne where Crichtons,
Balfours, Dundases, Hamiltons, Humes, and Stewarts all settled,
and of these pride of place must go to Malcolm Hamilton's Monea 37
Castle of 1618 whose twin round towers with corbelled square
caphouses strongly recall the celebrated outlines of Claypotts
(1588) near Dundee. Ruins remain of the Balfours' castle at
Lisnaskea, of the Crichtons' at Old Crom, and of the large T-
shaped house at Tully Castle built by Sir John Hume before 1619
on an isolated point between Inishmacsaint and Church Hill. Its
isolation was indeed its downfall, for the family was massacred
there on Christmas Day 1641 and the house has lain abandoned
ever since. All these houses had the traditional barrel-vaulted
ground floors of Scottish seventeenth-century castles, and at
Tully the vault is still complete. Only slightly less defensible is
another group of Scottish-style houses: the L-shaped Derrywoone
Castle of about 1630 at Baronscourt; Old Aughentaine of about
1620, built by Sir William Stewart and though now only a
fragment once also L-shaped with a corbelled spiral stair at the
re-entrant angle; and Mongavlin, another Stewart house built
north of Lifford in 1619 and now little more than a pair of crow-
stepped gables, but preserving an early-seventeenth-century
bread oven at its base. A Scottish house, as opposed to a castle,
is the manor house contrived by Bishop Andrew Knox out of
the Carmelite friary at Rathmullen. Knox remodelled the south 36
transept of the church and added two very Scottish corner bartizans corbelled out from the wall on the end gable of the nave.
    SEVENTEENTH-CENTURY CHURCHES built by Protestant
planters are almost always in a primitive GOTHIC SURVIVAL style
where the differences of Scottish and English patronage are not
so apparent. The largest and today the best preserved, even
though it has been enlarged and restored, is St Columb's Cath- 43
edral in Derry, building from 1628 to 1633. Though its arcades 45
and clerestory were on a scale that was unique in the four counties,
other features are common to the Planters' Gothic church in
general: the big square buttresses, in Derry enhanced with quasi-
classical profiles, and the tendency to place aisle windows as
groups of three or four lights in segmental or even round-headed

reveals inside. In size the Planters' church was usually much the same as its Romanesque or later medieval counterpart, rarely wider than 20 to 25 ft and normally between 40 and 60 ft long. Many were rebuilt on old foundations. Their essential feature is an east window usually of two-centred or semicircular-headed type and filled with simplified Perpendicular tracery with elongated octagonal mullions and round or segmental heads to the individual lights. The east window at Derry is a replica but its pattern is original and suggests that *Parrott*, the mason in charge of the cathedral, worked with more grace than most of the men the planters employed. The old church at Rathmullen has a notable example of an ambitious but botched-up Perpendicular window at its east end, and it has too the big square buttresses already mentioned. The passion for replacement rather than repair that has affected Ulstermen for centuries has meant that few of these Planters' churches are still in use. The most noted exception is 44 Clonfeacle parish church at Benburb, Co. Tyrone, built in 1618 by Sir Richard Wingfield, which despite a west tower added in the late nineteenth century is the most perfect Planters' church to survive, replete with buttresses, curly label moulds, and an unusually elaborate four-light east window. Ruins of the old churches at Cookstown and Fintona in Co. Tyrone, and in Co. Donegal at Fahan and at Raymochy outside Manorcunningham, have all kept their mullioned east windows from the early seventeenth century, and parts of many others – too numerous to list – remain throughout the four counties. One unusually pretty 46 Gothic window of about 1622 survives, with its label-stop heads looking like portraits of Charles I, at Donaghmore parish church, Castlecaulfield, where the structure itself was rebuilt – extended might be a better word – by Lord Charlemont in 1685.

Lord Charlemont's work at Castlecaulfield, though both late and breathtakingly clumsy by comparison with the elegant Gothic window beside it, may introduce a brief account of the few attempts at CLASSICAL CHURCH DESIGN in the seventeenth century. His additions include a south porch with crude Doric columns, broken entablature, and sculpture, and a west tower with a door in a similar style. Much earlier, in 1627, Sir John Dunbar had built the simple rectangular church at Derrygonnelly in Co. Fermanagh with a west door surrounded by the Scottish Renaissance detail of diamond-faceted quoins and voussoirs that would not have disgraced the Old College at Glasgow or Palace Square at Edinburgh Castle. At Castlederg, Sir John Davies, whose Castle Curlews has already been mentioned, built a new church whose tower survived a later rebuilding and still has an elaborate aedicular doorway with a high open pediment and flank- 47 ing Tuscan columns on the rather squat pedestals beloved by Elizabethan and Jacobean designers. Though it must be all of fifty years earlier than Castlecaulfield, this doorway is far more sophisticated than Charlemont's work, and what that ought to have been like is represented by another south porch, added this time to the nave of Raphoe Cathedral, which had itself been adapted by Bishops Leslie and Knox as a Protestant church in the early seventeenth century. The porch was added at a later date, perhaps after 1660, though it looks earlier. It is a rustic attempt at the Baroque, with scrolled volutes to its pediment and a round-headed door inside surmounted by an open segmental pediment supported on inverted console brackets – the vocabulary rich, but the syntax woeful.

A few of the PLANTERS' CHURCH MONUMENTS survive. Of these the finest, though modest by the standards of an English parish church, is the tomb of Sir Richard Hansard and his wife 49 in Lifford parish church, where painted effigies of the knight and his lady dressed in contemporary costume kneel opposite each other across a prayer desk. In Coleraine church are wall tablets with dates of death 1610, 1647, and 1673. The last, to the Mayor, Sir Tristram Beresford, has grotesque *memento mori* 48 and strapwork cartouches which though sophisticated in themselves are old-fashioned for their date. The more modern idea of a mural monument is represented by the Edwards and Elvin memorials of 1675 and 1678 in Derry Cathedral, and with these bizarre concoctions the list of monuments to the early planters, one of whom survived to the age of 102, may end.

Mention has still to be made of the commonest of all the structures erected by the seventeenth-century planters, the PLANTATION BAWNS. From 1618 to 1619 a captain in the English Army, Nicholas Pynnar, was employed to survey the Plantation of Ulster and to prepare a report on the works carried on by the London Companies and individual grantees. The phrase 'a bawn of lime and stone' occurs with monotonous regularity in Pynnar's report, with details of the height of walls, the strength of any house within, and the number of defensive flankers the building had. The bawn was a fortified enclosure that could protect a planter's family and livestock or provide a base for a small garrison. Most of the castles mentioned above were protected by these enclosures, the walls liberally provided with narrow musket loops, splayed inside to allow a maximum field of fire, and reinforced at the angles by circular or salient angled flankers to provide for raking fire along each face. Bawns, or parts of bawns, survive in large quantities in these four counties. Many are no more than rectangular walled enclosures protected by two flankers on diagonally opposite corners. The larger properties however usually included a strong house, and a popular pattern was to build the house across one end of the shorter side of the rectangle approached axially through the bawn, which became the forecourt of the house. The largest of this type was the Skinners' Bawn at Dungiven, now rebuilt as an early-nineteenth-century castle, though the walls of the same company's bawn at Brackfield still stand as an example of the more simple type.

Good examples of the larger plan type, of which substantial parts remain, are Wray Castle by Ballymore in Co. Donegal; Portora Castle near Enniskillen, built by Sir William Cole before Pynnar made his survey; Lough Derg Castle erected as a garrison point by Sir John Davies; and Aghalane Castle, now shrouded in hawthorns and brambles, on the border between Co. Fermanagh and Co. Monaghan, built by Thomas Crichton prior to 1619 and abandoned about 1700. Walworth House at Ballykelly is built on the site of the Fishmongers' Bawn, which was unusual in that the house stood as a detached building within the bawn enclosure. Though the house has gone, three of its flankers and parts of the wall remain among the farm buildings behind the present building. There are similar remains of the Salters' Bawn and Castle on the shore of Lough Neagh near Ballyronan and at Crevenish Castle near Kesh, built by Thomas Blennerhasset about 1615, which came into native Irish hands in the 1630s and was to be the seat from which Captain Rory Maguire planned the Irish rising of 1641. At Benburb, where the Irish were to have one of their most notable successes five years later, the bawn built by Sir Richard Wingfield is now the largest Plantation enclosure extant, preserving four flankers enlarged into gazebo-like towers with an almost complete circuit of wall and many perfect gun loops. Though the smaller bawns are now often no more than a pile of stones, plenty remains of the enclosure of Favour Royal in Tyrone, and at Fort Stewart near Ramelton in Donegal two large flankers survive from the bawn, one by the shore, the other, an acute salient bastion, lying stranded like the bow of a great ship high and dry in the centre of a field.

FORTIFICATION in this period is presented most spectacularly by the city walls of Derry, built first as earthen ramparts but faced in stone from 1618. They survive almost complete. The line of

seventeenth-century earth ramparts may also be traced at
Coleraine, behind the parish church. Captain Legge, reporting
in 1662 on the state of Ulster after the Restoration, recorded a
half-completed square stone fort that had been begun during the
Commonwealth at Coleraine. Here his advice to have it
demolished was followed, but two impressive examples of seventeenth-century fortification survive: at Mountjoy Fort on the
western shore of Lough Neagh, and at Bishop John Leslie's new
palace at Raphoe. Both are rectangular in plan with massive
square flankers, drawn out to a salient at the exposed corners in
the fashion of contemporary treatises on fortification. Mountjoy
dates from 1602; Raphoe Palace, though altered into a classical 41
mansion in the early Georgian period and then romanticized with
battlements in the nineteenth century, still has the essential bulk
and form of the original fortress founded in 1636.

Architecture in the reigns of the later Stuarts, from the Restoration to the death of Queen Anne in 1714, is almost unrepresented
in these four northern counties. Though recent research by Dr
Rolf Loeber has shown considerable activity in the building trade
in this period in Ireland, the confused titles that many landowners
held after the Cromwellian plantation necessarily limited the
scope of such building. Moreover the Williamite war of 1689–
90, which was focused mainly in the North, took its architectural
toll. In the environs of Derry city there are no pre-siege buildings,
nor are there any within the walls. The same is true of the whole
countryside; for though there is evidence of late-seventeenth-century building at a number of sites – Lough Eske Castle, Castle
Coole, or at Thornhill and Ashbrook both outside Derry – all
these places were subsequently rebuilt, leaving nothing but a date-
stone or a reputed tradition of a Stuart foundation. Springhill near 58, 59
Moneymore, an attractive house now of early-eighteenth-century
and Mid-Georgian character, is exceptional in that its seventeenth-century origin can still be discerned in its plan form and
irregular rear elevation.

At Liffock crossroads near Castlerock a cruck-framed single-
storey thatched house has been dated to 1691. Built as the rectory
for Articlave parish church as part of the policy of Bishop King
of Derry to encourage incumbents of the Church of Ireland to
live in their parishes, it is a salutary reminder of the limitations
of architectural endeavour in Ulster at this date. Mount Tilley
barracks, a brick terrace with vaulted ground floors and pedimented Dutch gables that stood until early this century at Buncrana, was more on a par with English provincial building, though

evidently a generation or so behind architectural fashion at the time that it was built. There is indeed only one architectural monument of distinctive character that remains from these years: the great barrack building of 1700 in the centre of Ballyshannon, a severe, plain, brick-built structure, T-plan and of two storeys, with a tall hipped roof and an impressive internal corridor running the entire length of the building. Its architect is presumably *Sir Thomas Burgh*, Surveyor General of H.M. Fortifications and Buildings in Ireland, and the design may bear comparison with Burgh's later work in Dublin or with the contemporary functional designs of the English Office of Works. As the sole substantial structure of late Stuart building remaining in this part of Ireland, it deserves a better fate than to be left to fall down.

EARLY GEORGIAN BUILDINGS

The emergence of 'the Protestant nation' after 1690 and the more settled state of the country in the succeeding century have left their mark on this part of Ireland, as elsewhere, in the quantity of country houses built throughout the Georgian period. Ireland remained a comparatively poor country, and it is not until the 1770s and 1780s that buildings with serious pretensions to architectural style appear in the north west in any quantity. Ascendancy families built houses for themselves, modest public buildings in their market towns, and occasionally simple new churches or meeting houses to replace Plantation structures damaged in the wars. These are the buildings that plot the course of Irish architectural development here and, in an area that was remote, ambitious schemes are not to be expected. Indeed for the first three-quarters of the century a Venetian window, even if the sole decoration of a façade, is very much an architectural event. Adjectives such as 'good' or 'handsome' are the descriptive norm and will often mean no more than that the gentleman's house is on two floors rather than single-storey and that it is slated rather than thatched, this last distinction continuing well into the nineteenth century as a standard of excellence to be applied in gazetteers. Similarly the detailing of these houses is constant from about 1730 even up to 1800. Walls are usually roughcast or whitewashed outside, plain plastered within, and given large, boldly moulded classical cornices of heavy rather than ornate profiles. If there is any stone detail on the exterior it will be limited to a base course, string course, and eaves cornice, with possibly a Provincial-Gibbs surround, a variant of the usual Gibbs surround where every second rustication block is missing, providing a cheaper but weaker architectural effect. There is too a special joinery producing five- or six-panelled doors that depart from standard eighteenth-century practice in their use of one or two long panels across the full width of the door. Lugged surrounds, at times of some complexity and typical of British architectural practice in the first half of the eighteenth century, regularly survive into the 1790s, and the standard timber stair detail, common throughout all Ireland, will finish in a whorl of banisters. Wainscoting, usually arranged in long fielded panels, survives in many houses, and chimneypieces placed diagonally across a corner of a room are also common.

While these details are generally present, the plans of minor gentry houses are varied. As a general rule those that are only one room deep are the earliest, unless they have been tacked across the end of an earlier house, or else are mere cottages that have grown in consequence in the nineteenth century – in which case they will have none of the features described above. The later houses are normally built on a double-pile plan, and as the century progresses will possess a basement that is usually brick-vaulted under a central entrance hall, to support the weight of stone flags above. The stair in these houses is commonly placed on an axis with the hall at the back, or is set at right angles in the middle of one side. No distinction can be made between the home of a minor landowner, an agent's house, or a glebe house in this period beyond the consideration that the glebe houses, towards the end of the century, may show certain family characteristics in any one diocese.

A note should also be added about the distribution of gentlemen's houses. Obviously they are most frequent in the richer farming areas, most rare in remote parts. They tend, too, to cluster round the navigable rivers that offered in an age of as yet poor roads an easy means of transport. In this respect the estates on Upper and Lower Lough Erne were superior to most others, and it is significant that it is here that by far the largest number of great houses is to be found, as well as an appreciable quantity of better-than-average gentlemen's seats. The Clogher valley, the banks of the Finn and the Mourne, the coastal area round Ballyshannon, and the shores of Lough Swilly and Lough Foyle are all areas that provided good sites for minor eighteenth-century houses.

To start in the Lough Erne area, there is Farrancassidy of 1731, a long, low house with a good cut-stone front only one room deep; Hall Craig nearby of 1721, tall and with a smart stone

pedimented door, but again only one room deep; Dunbar House,
a gentleman's thatched house of about the mid century; and
Dresternan Castle of about 1740, more self-consciously a piece
of architecture, at least on its front, but never quite regular. On the
north shore of the upper lough, Knockballymore, the agent's
house for the Crichtons of Crom to which the family moved
in 1764, following the fire that destroyed the old castle, is one
of the most sophisticated small houses of its date, grandly conceived, with a high symmetrical entrance front and a taller rear
elevation, both gaining height by an attic storey that is hidden
across the front with windows confined to the side gables. Snowhill near Lisbellaw, of about 1760, is essentially similar though
less high, and dignified by a centrally placed Venetian window
above the entrance door. Munville, a Maguire house of 1757, is
unique in these four counties for a feature that is found in the
South and in Scotland: a main front dominated by a monumental
flight of steps and entered at first-floor level. Donagh House, Nutfield, Greenhill, and Drumgoon are all good, substantial buildings
with symmetrical fronts of Mid-Georgian character.

In the Clogher valley the minor Georgian houses are provided
by the Church: the Deanery at Clogher of about 1750 or later,
with a central Venetian window, Errigal-Keerogue Rectory outside
Ballygawley, and Killeshil Rectory, 'nearly built' in 1810, with
two large bows on a symmetrical front. An unusual glebe house,
once again built on a long thin plan and only one room deep, is
Langfield Rectory outside Drumquin of 1742.

The earliest surviving gentlemen's houses (and in some cases
surviving is sadly all too apt a description of their state) are in
Co. Donegal. First in date must be Brown Hall, not for the main
house that dates from about the mid century but for its earlier
wing, long, low, and narrow, with segmental brickwork arches to
the windows, which appears to date from about 1700. Then there
54 is Buncrana Castle, built by Sir John Vaughan in 1718, with long
thin sash windows, forestanding single-bay corner blocks, and a
formal walled forecourt, in all not unlike the regularly massed
fronts of several Scottish houses, but quite irregular at the back.
The house retains some fine bolection-moulded wainscot panelling. Next, up the coast from Buncrana, is Linsfort Castle, built
by Captain Arthur Benson in 1720 and bearing such obvious traits
of influence from the earlier and larger house as to be almost certainly by the same designer. The large plain bulk of Newtowncunningham Castle is similarly detailed inside and may date to
56 about 1730. Then comes Oakfield outside Raphoe, built in 1739

as the deanery for the cathedral. Oakfield is the jewel of its district, perfectly preserved and perfectly unexpected for its date. In England it might have been built at any time from 1630 to perhaps 1680 or 90. It is a square house with a high hipped roof, leaded flat with regular chimneys, and three dormer windows breaking the slope in the middle of each front. The façades are absolutely symmetrical and nicely proportioned, so that however old-fashioned this Artisan-Mannerist-cum-Caroline pattern may seem, the house in fact provided the model for a still later essay in the same manner at Bogay nearby. Redcastle on Lough Foyle of about 1730 must have had a similar old-fashioned appearance, for it used the same hipped-roof-and-dormer formula, though its frontage is far longer and its dormers have now been changed.

An attempt to catch something of the modernity of Palladian ideas appears at Dunmore House of *c.* 1742, where a plain façade of five well spaced bays is invigorated by a largely scaled and well proportioned Venetian window in the centre of the first floor. The house preserves some good if plain Georgian interiors and a parti- 61 cularly handsome main stair. The same sort of awareness of archi- 62 tectural style appears at Brown Hall, a tall cubic house like Oakfield brought up to date and formalized, where the hall is elaborated with a continuous Doric cornice round the room. The Hall, Mountcharles, built by Lord Conyngham, and the agent's house of Salt Hill nearby are two further minor houses that seem to reflect more concern with a classical style than is usual in these parts, but even so their pretensions are modest. One final example of an awareness of Palladian values, not in Donegal but in Tyrone, is Barnhill outside Stewartstown, a delightful small farmhouse with a cut stone doorcase surmounted by a Venetian window under a pediment, the main block linked by quadrant walls to square outhouses like miniature pavilion wings. A similar pattern, though lacking the wings, occurs at the agent's house of Bovagh near Kilrea in Co. Derry. Ballymaclary House, Magilligan, is unique for its fine cut-stone, single-storey façade.

None of the houses mentioned so far is by a known architect, and in many cases even the date is obscure. There is, however, in this period one figure who stands out with an identifiable style and artistic personality: the architect of Lifford Court House, *Michael Priestley.* The court house, one of the finest façades of 55 its date anywhere in Ireland, is a vigorous building of 1746 signed by the architect and so richly endowed with elements of a quirky personal classicism as to make possible the attribution to Priestley of further buildings in the area. He must have had charge of the

remodelling of the Bishop's Palace at Raphoe, for the big pedimented doorcase with Gibbs surround added to the east front of
the palace is identical to the main door of the court house. Similarly, Port Hall, which was built a few miles down the Foyle from Lifford by George Vaughan, one of the directors for the construction
of the court house, repeats many of the features and particularly the high harled parapets that Priestley used there. If Port
Hall is by Priestley, and there seems no reason to doubt that it
is, then the Tomkins family home of Prehen outside Derry built
in the mid 1740s must also be his. It uses the same pilaster quoins
at the corners, the same vigorous Gibbs surrounds to all the windows, and the same gauche though not unattractive central pediment rising from the top of the roof parapet instead of in a more
orthodox way from the main roof cornice. At Prehen the plan is
more sophisticated than in most Irish houses of its size, with its
generous square entrance hall and magnificent timber stair behind
like that at Dunmore, only now more grandly scaled. The roof
of Prehen is in pristine condition, with rafters numbered
apparently as the house was built, some with the monogram MP,
suggesting that Priestley may have come to architecture through
business as a wright. In 1756 he drew up plans for Lord Abercorn
for the layout of Strabane, when he was also employed on the
erection of a market house that has since disappeared.

With Priestley the architecture of the country gentleman's
house reaches a level of achievement so far above the common
run that it may be as well to turn now to the GREAT HOUSES
OF THE EIGHTEENTH CENTURY in this half of the province.
First in importance, though only a fragment now remains, is
Castle Hume in Fermanagh, built in 1728 by Sir Gustavus Hume,
who brought *Richard Castle* to Ireland to work for him and whose
first Irish design Castle Hume once was. Castle had come from
Germany to London and was invited by Hume to Ireland to develop amongst other things the Newry Canal. It was Castle who
naturalized the robust Palladianism first introduced to Ireland by
Sir Edward Lovett Pearce, and though his pedimented main
house at Castle Hume has long vanished, the office range that
remains bears plenty of evidence of his vigorous taste, with its
large, roughly blocked door surrounds, *œil de bœuf*, and elegant
vaulted stable supported directly on columns whose bases are
copied from the unorthodox deep round drums used by Palladio
at the Basilica in Vicenza.

The second great house, now only an evocative shell, is Wardtown outside Ballyshannon built for General Folliot in 1740. For

its date its scale is immense. Its architect is unknown. Anywhere it would be remarkable, but in Co. Donegal it is astonishing, a late Baroque house in the castle idiom of Vanbrugh, absolutely symmetrical and only one room thick, with three round towers across its front and identical matching staircases at either end behind the towers. Not surprisingly, it had no immediate successors in Ulster. A more orthodox solution to the design of a country house, though it was intended only as a place of periodic summer residence, was the first house, now the agent's house, at 57 Baronscourt, begun by the Earl of Abercorn to the general amazement of his tenants just one year after Wardtown in 1741. The architect here was a local mason, *James Martin*, who was employed at Clogher Cathedral at the same time. What the house originally looked like is now hard to visualize, as it subsequently lost its upper floor and has now the character of a large garden pavilion like Gibbs's menagerie at Hackwood.

After these houses, each in its own way of an assured design, the fuss at Florence Court, near Enniskillen, built about 1758 by the 71 first Lord Mount Florence, is something of a shock. Here is *Architecture* with a vengeance, a provincial man run riot with a pattern book to such an extent that even the suave arcades and polygonal pavilions added a decade later, probably by *Davis Ducart*, cannot quite redeem the frontage. Frontage is the proper word, for the back is quite plain, and it is principally for its wayward and charming Rococo interior that the house deserves attention. Two 72 more regular jobs of the period were Stewart Hall by Stewartstown in Co. Tyrone of about 1760 and Castle Archdale on Lower Lough Erne built in 1778. Both were big, plain, rectangular houses without pediments, though with the central hall slightly articulated by a stepped front. Castle Archdale had an interior of considerable quality with an impressive double return stair on an axis with the hall, but the house has recently been demolished; Stewart Hall has been reduced by one storey. More modest houses of a plain Palladian type were Nixon Hall, sometimes called Fairwood Park, south of Enniskillen, burnt out in 1844, and Culdaff House in Co. Donegal of 1779, burnt in 1922. Finally among these larger regular houses comes Moyola Park at Castledawson, built in 1768 and surviving today in pristine condition, with delicate plasterwork cornices in all the main rooms.

CLASSICAL CHURCHES to match these Palladian houses are few. There is *James Martin*'s Clogher Cathedral of 1744 and the very charming church of St John, Ballymore, outside Dunfanaghy 63-6 of 1752 which it is tempting to attribute to *Michael Priestley*. St

Augustine's church in Derry city was rebuilt by Bishop Barnard
with a diminutive pedimented front decorated with a Diocletian
window, but all this was virtually rebuilt as a Victorian Gothic
church a century later. At Lisbellaw the chapel of ease built by
the Earl of Rosse in 1764 survives, with a later transept and Gothic
68 tower; St John, Fivemiletown, built between 1736 and 1740,
retains a good pedimented west door; and St Cones, Castlederg,
rebuilt except for the west tower in 1731, has kept its decorated
doorway into the nave from this period. The list is short partly
because an extensive church building programme after the Act
of Union led to many a modest mid Georgian church being abandoned – places where ruins remain are Derryvullan, Drummully,
Redcastle, and Urney – and partly because the Church of Ireland
clergy already showed by the second half of the century a preference for a primitive Gothic Revival style. Frederick Hervey,
the Bishop of Derry and Earl of Bristol, is pre-eminent among
these EARLY GOTHIC REVIVAL enthusiasts: he added a spire to
the tower of Derry Cathedral in 1776, and built ambitious new
Gothic churches at Ballykelly and Banagher and many more
minor Gothic structures throughout his diocese. In point of style
none of the Bishop's churches is a very sophisticated essay in
gothicism, and this is true of the other Georgian Gothic churches
in the province. There are indeed even some hybrid designs.
Aghalurcher parish church at Colebrooke is a big classical hall
of 1762, with Gibbs surrounds to the windows but a massive
Gothic tower and spire; Cleenish parish church, built about a year
later at Bellanaleck, combines a hall of simple round-headed sash
windows with a neo-medieval west tower of disarming in-
souciance. The best of the early Gothic Revival churches, because
67 it has a glorious site and an unusually elegant spire, is Cappagh
church at Mountjoy Forest built in 1768. Killesher church at
Florence Court of 1791 and 1819 and Inver church of 1807 are
examples of the ambitious scale attempted after the turn of the
century.

LATER GEORGIAN BUILDINGS

The growing sense of a national identity that dominated the
character of Irish political life in the last quarter of the eighteenth
century and culminated in Grattan's parliament is reflected, perhaps, in the sudden increase in the quality of the country houses
erected in this period. That art and political consciousness could
mix is exemplified by a chimneypiece – now sadly lost – designed

for the Earl Bishop by the Cork architect *Michael Shanahan*, with male figures of Liberty and Loyalty supporting an oval relief on which Minerva, aided by Lord Bristol, reveals the arts and sciences to an eager Hibernia whom Britannia tries to keep back. Such flamboyant iconography no doubt appealed to the Volunteer Bishop, but there is nevertheless a real sense in which the resident proprietors of large estates contributed to the culture of the country. Their greater sophistication of taste is reflected in their plantations. Gardens and landscaped parks were laid out at Bell Isle, Castle Caldwell, Caledon, Crom, the demesne at Clogher, the Earl Bishop's park at Downhill, Mountjoy Forest, and – finest of all – at Baronscourt, where the Earl of Abercorn brought a vast tract of country under cultivation, enlarged and altered the pattern of the lakes, and was at pains to establish a herd of deer. Architecture kept pace with landscape improvement. For the first time some of the front rank of English architects visited North West Ulster. *Wyatt* gave advice at Downhill in 1778 and built what is perhaps his masterpiece at Castle Coole, a commission where significantly the Englishman succeeded and replaced the native *Johnston*. Downhill is now a ruin, and a ruin whose appearance is complicated by a fire and Victorian remodelling, but Castle Coole by any standard is a house of European stature, architecturally one of the great monuments of the age of neo-classicism. If the same cannot be said of Baronscourt, it is nonetheless significant that Lord Abercorn employed both *George Steuart* and *John Soane* on the new mansion, whose building relegated *James Martin*'s villa to the rank of an agent's house; and, from 1808, *Thomas Cooley*'s elegant new villa at Caledon, begun in 1779, was to be enlarged and made more obviously classical under the magic wand of *Nash*. These great houses of the late Georgian period – Downhill, Castle Coole, Baronscourt, and Caledon – all had distinguished interiors of which the last three survive intact. Castle Coole and the Cooley rooms at Caledon are decorated in the refined linear patterns established by Adam in Britain and by Stapleton in Ireland; at Baronscourt and in the Nash work at Caledon a more Roman opulence obtains. The work at Baronscourt is by neither Steuart nor Soane but by *William Vitruvius Morrison*, never grander than in the central columnar atrium of the house or (with the possible exception of the dining room at Carton, Co. Kildare) in the great Corinthian saloon that runs across the full width of the main block. Morrison's work at Baronscourt dates from about 1832, but already before the end of the century – in 1798 – another Irish neo-classical architect had made a showing in the North: *Francis Johnston* at Garvey House near Aughnacloy, a house that promised some moments of severe grandeur though in fact it was never to be finished.

By the early nineteenth century other Dublin architects were at work in the north west, notably *John Bowden, John Hargrave, William Farrell*, and, at a slightly later date, *J. B. Keane*. Bowden seems to have confined himself to public and church commissions, but Hargrave, Farrell, and Keane all established thriving country-house practices along with their public authority work. *Hargrave*, who had a weakness for rather shapeless and over-large cottage-style houses, contributed at least one accomplished design in a Greek Revival idiom at Ballygawley Park – the shell of which still stands – and *Keane* enlarged The Waterfoot at Pettigoe, and may well have added the elegant Regency front to Coxtown near Ballintra, also in Co. Donegal. It was certainly Keane who in 1833 rebuilt Castle Irvine at Irvinestown; here, though the house was Tudor, the principal apartment resembled Morrison's south room at Baronscourt, over 80 ft long and divided at its centre by a double columnar screen.

Of all these Irishmen it was *Farrell* who carried off the biggest 80 prize, designing Colebrooke Park in Co. Fermanagh from 1820 and, with the house, the triumphal-arch gate, lodges, classical school, and dower house of Ashbrooke built within the park. His work is competent rather than inspired, and though the interior of the great house has some fine rooms, notably the library, an air of inflated monotony haunts the main front. Farrell was employed by the Marquess of Abercorn to produce a scheme for Baronscourt after Soane's work was finished and before Morrison began, but this came to nothing, perhaps because it too suffered from an excessive scale and bland manner. To judge by the drawings his work at Ely Lodge, on Lower Lough Erne, was perhaps his most elegant design, but that has disappeared except for one pretty gate lodge, and the same fate has overtaken Cecil Manor by Clogher, which can be attributed to Farrell on stylistic grounds. Among the best of Farrell's works in the north west are the large rectories that may be attributed to him – Maghera is a particularly good example – as the result of his close connection with the Church Commissioners in the late 1820s and 1830s. Characteristic is a blockish form, a hipped roof, massed chimneystacks, and a preference for a type of tripartite window with heavy brackets supporting a slab-like cornice running across the top.

Though the houses of minor gentlemen constitute a genre that provides many attractive designs, Farrell is one of the few architects who may be identified as working in this connection a little after 1800. The distinctive feature of the minor late Georgian country house is probably the one that Farrell himself most ignored: the bay window, treated either as a bow or else as a shallow canted bay, to break the frontage of a block. The character of these buildings is otherwise much the same as that of the earlier gentleman's house, built with rendered or harled walls with a minimum of stone detail. Generally, however, from about 1785 or 1790 the bow, which had become the *sine qua non* of the garden front of more self-conscious architectural designs, e.g. Castle Coole or Caledon, is absorbed in the front of a minor gentleman's house. Examples abound: Kildress Rectory and Leckpatrick Rectory, Artigarvan, in Co. Tyrone; White Park outside Lisnaskea in Co. Fermanagh; Tobermore House and Roe Park in Co. Derry; Cavangarden by Ballyshannon; Edenmore and Killygordon, both in the Finn Valley, Co. Donegal. A finer example, with something of the character of a villa by Sir Robert Taylor, was Boom Hall of *c.* 1770 built by the Alexander family outside Derry city with a big canted bay in its garden front. Brook Hall nearby, built about 1790, has one of the most engaging plans of its date that uses not only a central segmental bow but an oval atrium and an oval cantilevered stair as well. Derrybard House by Fintona, Convoy House, and White Castle on the shores of Lough Foyle are three more houses that elegantly adapt the segmental bows of fashionable design to the modest scale of a minor country house. There are still of course numerous plain rectangular houses of this period, usually of three or five bays. Generally they may be distinguished from the earlier houses by their lack of a basement, or use of a basement that is entirely sunk, and by their roofs, which are usually more shallow, usually hipped, and often carried far out over the eaves on brackets or mutules. The tripartite window current in English architectural practice from about 1790 also becomes a leitmotif in Ireland in the 1820s. Minor anonymous houses are too numerous to list, but the small classical Creevenagh House outside Omagh is one of the finest of its date, distinguished by a rich Sienese marble pavement in its hall.

A word must now be said about the GEORGIAN GOTHIC HOUSES in this volume. They are few and for the most part they are late. Only Castle Caldwell on Lower Lough Erne dates from about the mid eighteenth century, and that was a plain rectangular house with a pedimented and battlemented end, Gothicized perhaps because of the presence of two flanking salient bastions left over from the Plantation house of the Blennerhasset family. Earl's

Gift House by Dunnamanagh in Co. Tyrone is a tall Georgian house with a round tower in the centre of its front and simple pointed windows. Like Castle Caldwell it is now only a shell. It is as late as 1792. There is a folly tower in the grounds of Bellarena in Co. Derry, a Gothic lodge at Downhill, and some cosmetic medievalism at Beltrim Castle, Gortin, all of the late eighteenth century. Then nothing more until after 1800.

The new century opens spectacularly with one of the most
81, 84 advanced and freely grouped Regency castles of *John Nash*: Killymoon, built for James Stewart the proprietor of Cookstown, who toyed with a classical scheme by *Robert Woodgate*, Soane's assistant at Baronscourt, before settling for the more metropolitan medievalism of a Norman castle by Nash. The exact date is not clear, but the house was under discussion in 1802 and partly occupied by 1805. Beside Killymoon the symmetrical castle at Portstewart built by Henry O'Hara in 1834 is astonishingly old-fashioned. More accomplished are the additions to Augher Castle by the Sligo architect *William Warren*, who made the old Spur Royal tower habitable again by the addition of two battlemented
38 wings splayed out from the central block. An amorphous jumble of battlements and towers was built at Old Mountjoy as a castle-style house about 1810. In 1839 Robert Ogilby of Pellipar began to rebuild Dungiven Castle as a symmetrical range punctuated by machicolated towers, but lost enthusiasm for the project and never finished the work. Two houses in Co. Donegal have lunatic picturesque gateways in the full-blown picturesque castle idiom:
82 Convoy, a classical house of 1806 already mentioned, and Camlin outside Ballyshannon of 1838, where now only the gate remains. Camlin itself was a trim little Tudor castle by *J. B. Keane*, and it was houses of this type – half Gothic, half manorial – that were most popular in the 1820s and 1830s. Keane himself built two more, at Magheramena Castle, outside Belleek, and at Castle Irvine (already mentioned for its neo-classical interior). *John Hargrave* gave a rich Gothic interior to the manorial Favour Royal in the Clogher valley, and was probably responsible for the Elizabethan-style modification of Ballymacool outside Letterkenny, where he had built the plain little court house. Tudor Gothic houses of late Georgian or early Victorian date were built at Drum Manor outside Cookstown, The Grange, Tobermore, and at Learmount near Park, the last with an unusually fine cut stone front and a dramatic double-return stair inside. The best Tudor houses
85 are both by known architects: *Edward Blore*'s Crom Castle built for the Earl of Erne from 1834, and *Thomas Duff* of Newry's Park-

anaur, a rambling irregular house built in stages from 1820 with 83
crisp Elizabethan detail learnt perhaps from the example of
W. V. Morrison, who is usually credited with the introduction of
revised Tudor and Elizabethan detail to Ireland.

If individual landowners were busy building on Irish estates
in the first thirty years of the new century, the State was also
active. Two factors encouraged government works: the rebellion
of 1798 with its threatened French invasion that alerted the administration to the largely unprotected coast-line of the country;
and the Act of Union, in part a consequence of the rebellion, that
left the landed oligarchy of the established Church of Ireland uncertain of its political future and anxious to assert continued pre-
eminence in a programme of building works. It may well be that
the extensive building and rebuilding on private estates after the
Act of Union sprang from some feelings of this sort too, aided
by a situation in which numerous landed families found themselves unusually if only briefly affluent through the compensation
that was paid to those whose interests were considered to have
suffered by the extinction of the Irish Parliament. Besides the
numerous parliamentary official posts, patrons of boroughs that
ceased to send representatives to Parliament were compensated
at a rate of £15,000 per seat, and the total sum paid to such patrons
exceeded one and a quarter million pounds.

Government work is represented in the north west by a line
of FORTS, MARTELLO TOWERS, AND SIGNAL TOWERS built
round the Donegal coast ostensibly to protect the country and
defend the entry to the natural harbours of Lough Foyle and
Lough Swilly. Elaborate schemes prepared by the Royal
Engineers for massive defence works at Enniskillen and in Co.
Cavan show however that the government had been thoroughly
shaken by the insurrection of 1798, and though plans came to little
– a small square redoubt was built to control the southern
approaches to Enniskillen – the intention at least to supervise and
perhaps to overawe the local population from these stations is
clear. The martello tower at Macamoosh Point dates from 1801 91
and was apparently the first to be extended by a battery and defensive ditch in 1806. Built half-way up Lough Swilly, it was intended to control entry to the upper reaches of the lough, a natural
preoccupation for the government, as it was here that Admiral
Bompard and Wolfe Tone had attempted their invasion in
October 1798. To strengthen the defences of the lough, battery
forts were built soon after at Ned's Point, just north of Buncrana
opposite the martello tower, at Rathmullen, and on Inch Island. 90

Two impressive forts were sited near the mouth and on either
89 side of the lough at Knockalla and Dunree Head, with a final battery almost at the entry to the lough at Lenan Head in Inishowen.
Lough Foyle was less strongly protected, though one of the most
substantial forts of this Napoleonic period was constructed at
Greencastle at the narrowest point of entry to the lough, with a
martello tower to answer it at the tip of Magilligan Strand on the
Co. Derry shore.

Existing barracks between Dungloe and Rutland Island and at
Ballyshannon probably explain the lack of other forts in south Co.
Donegal, where the only new protection was provided by a series
of square signal towers. These occur on prominent headlands
from Malin Head, the northern tip of Ireland, down to the Sligo
coast and beyond. Their design is uniform, and all are now ruined.
Though they are not aggressive structures like the martello towers
and battery forts, they are defended by machicolated bartizans at
their landward corners and by a third above the door. Those at
Malin Beg and Maghery Bay by Dungloe seem especially desolate
and bleak today: abandoned sentinel posts once vigilant and on
the alert for a menace that never came.

The second government activity, less directly the responsibility
of the administration, though supported by large government
grants, was the building of NEW CHURCHES and the modernization of old ones for the established Protestant minority. As a programme it sprang more from political motives than from any real
need of the Irish Church. Ecclesiastical statistics for all Ireland
in 1834, quoted in *The Parliamentary Gazetteer* of 1846, show that
of a population of just under 8 million (7,943,940), some 6½ million
were Roman Catholics, 852, 064 were of the Established Church,
and 646,164 were Presbyterians and other Protestant Nonconformists. Expressed as a percentage, the Established Church in
1834 accounted for little more than ten per cent of the total population, and the proportion will not have been essentially different
at the opening of the century. For this small minority Parliament
provided substantial funds from 1801 to 1821 for a church building programme that has left its mark over the entire country both
in the ruins of older parish churches abandoned in this period
and in the succession of diminutive, toy-like Gothic churches
built with monotonous regularity on a few repetitive plans. The
new churches in many cases pre-date their counterparts in England and Wales erected under the Church Building Commission
which was not set up until 1818. By then the Church of Ireland's
models were already well established, and predictably they are

cast in a rather different and more primitive mould. The need
to accommodate a large congregation, a major consideration for
architects in the growing industrial towns of England, was never
really a problem in Ireland. Here the designer was more concerned to make as imposing a structure as possible with limited
architectural means, and the ubiquitous answer for the first thirty
years of the century was what is perhaps most simply called the
tower-and-hall church: a square tower usually at the west end
(though the clergy were not over-scrupulous about orientation)
with a wider gabled hall immediately behind it. Frequently the
windows would be only on the south side of the building and at
the gable end above the altar, an arrangement that left a good
warm wall bathed in sunlight but far enough from the draughts
of the windows for the quality to sit in comfort on the north side
of a central passageway. Where a resident proprietor had a separate family pew, this was often placed like a miniature transept in
the centre of the north wall, and in some cases two families would
occupy individual transept pews that faced each other across the
body of the church. If there were a chancel, it would usually be
little more than a few feet deep, and was often disguised outside
by the continuation of the rectangular hall walls around it. It
would give these little structures more dignity than they could
ever claim as architecture to call the hall a nave. In consequence
a church described as a hall-church in Ireland will be just that.
The pretensions of Protestant proprietors rose no higher, while
the command of Gothic shown by the architects they employed,
quite apart from their requirements or finances, was far too primitive for an authentic late Gothic 'hall-church', that is a church
with aisles equal in height to a central nave, ever to be proposed
as a proper model for adoption in late Georgian Ireland. In this
sense there are no hall-churches here, though tower-and-hall
churches abound.

The similarity of these small Established churches is in a large
measure due to their common date of origin, and also to a tendency
to centralize the machinery by which they were built. The money
to finance the churches was paid at first through the Board of First
Fruits, and when that board was abolished in 1833, through a
newly established Irish Ecclesiastical Commission. The revenue
deriving from First Fruits was calculated as a proportion of the
benefit of any ecclesiastical living, surrendered by a new incumbent in the first year of his tenure. Obviously the sums available from this source were variable and always modest; yet after
the Act of Union Parliament regularly voted extra support to the

Board of First Fruits to further church building in Ireland. As Dr Scott-Richardson has shown, this support rose rapidly in the first twenty years of the nineteenth century, from £4,850 a year between 1801 and 1808 to nearly £60,000 a year in the years between 1810 and 1816, levelling off at £30,000 a year from 1817 to 1821. The First Fruits' own revenue in the same period averaged about £400 a year, so that by 1821 over a million pounds had been provided for church improvement or replacement and for the building of glebe houses, which was a subsidiary function of the Board. Payments to parishes were made either as direct grants, as loans, or as a combination of both. Inevitably this centralization of resources tended towards a standard end product. Architects were appointed to each Province by the Board, and what was an appropriate Gothic window for one parish was usually thought to be appropriate for another. Thus variety was really only possible when a private patron made a substantial contribution towards the improvement of his church; otherwise one plan might be reproduced in several situations. *John Bowden*, one of the most sophisticated neo-classical architects of the period, whose St Stephen's church, Mount Street, Dublin is a fine if rare example of a new classical church of this date, provided a particu-
86 larly pretty Gothic design for the diocese of Derry that was built in at least five places with virtually no variation. James Pain did the same in Munster and John Semple in Dublin and Co. Kildare.

There are few elements in these early-nineteenth-century Board of First Fruits churches that provide a guide to their date. In an area that was never in the stylistic vanguard, patterns endured for decades, and it was not until the mid 1840s, when the design of the Established Church's buildings fell into the hands of one man, that a decisive change occurred and a development can be seen. Before then only some general points may be noted about the popular plans. In the earliest churches of the rebuilding it was common with the tower-and-hall type for the tower to be incorporated into the rectangular body of the church, with small flanking rooms to take up the spare space on each side, whereas in later designs, generally from about 1812, the tower is usually free-standing. The tower-and-hall type is commonest up to about 1825 or 1830, after which a more elaborately articulated hall with a gabled frontage decked out with finials and a bell-cote becomes an increasingly common alternative. Good examples of the earlier type appear at Tamlaghtard, Inver, and Eglish; and of the later gabled variety at Rosslea, Drumquin, and Sixmile-cross.

CATHOLIC CHURCH BUILDING at the opening of the new century was confronted by a problem that was the inverse of that of the Established Church. Congregations were vast, there were few rich patrons – in the north west virtually none – and little support was available for building from public funds. Acts 'to prevent the further growth of popery' passed from 1704 to 1728 had never forbidden Catholic worship nor the existence of 'mass-houses'. Policy was directed against the Catholic hierarchy, the bishops and regular clergy, who could not continue to act publicly; but the main purpose of the legislation of Queen Anne's reign was not so much to destroy Roman Catholicism as to reduce its adherents to a position of inferiority, and by the mid eighteenth century that purpose had been largely achieved. The relaxation of the penal code that began in the 1770s and continued until the Irish Catholic Relief Act of 1793 provided increasing encouragement for the building of regular churches, especially after 1782, but the population was poor and often dependent on the gift of a Protestant landlord for the site of its church. Even today, the incidence of Catholic churches in many parts of the Ulster countryside is an index of the deprivation that the old faith suffered through two centuries of Plantation policies. Where the land is fertile they are fewest; where it is mountainous or marshy they are at their most frequent. The oldest Catholic churches survive in the poorest districts, where there has been least pressure to enlarge or amend their design. Otherwise the history of Catholic buildings in Ireland is one of constant change as successions of parish priests have sought to improve the churches in their charge, a process that continues down to the present day, often with lamentable results.

The early Catholic churches in North West Ulster were almost invariably rubble-built, with cement-rendered or roughcast walls and simplified pointed sash windows. Two plan types were common: a T-plan copied from the Presbyterian pattern that had developed in the seventeenth century; and a long hall plan that was sometimes converted into a T-shape by the addition of one long arm in the centre of one side of the hall. The most notable example of this is the Long Tower Church in Derry city, begun in 1784 and extended by a new 'nave' in 1810, but the type survives elsewhere in an unaltered form. The characteristic of the early long hall-church is that its altar is set not at the end of the church but half way down one of the longer sides, often with a big window – another Nonconformist touch – flanking the altar on either side. It was this position of the altar that made the church so suitable for conversion to a T-plan type, or alternatively for the incorporation of surrounding galleries on three sides of the basic long hall. The plan survives in its pristine state in at least two instances, 104 at Rosslea in Co. Fermanagh and at Massmount in Co. Donegal, both of which have sufficient merit, architecturally and from a historic point of view, to deserve protection from future change. Early examples of the T-plan occur at Lagg church, Malin, built in 1784, and at Glencross near Rathmullen of 1792, a larger and more ambitious church with a modicum of Gothic detail on its front.

Though it was well suited to the needs of a large congregation and provided a means whereby the majority could easily follow the mass, the long plan seems to have fallen out of favour by the 1840s, when liturgical considerations promulgated by the Camden Society, the Tractarians, and particularly for Ireland by A. W. N. Pugin, were uppermost in men's minds. In this period many an altar was moved from the long wall to a central position at the end of the shorter side; not infrequently, the window lights were at the same time changed from a wide-arched Georgian Gothic or Perpendicular type to the more fashionable narrow lancet that soon became a standard motif of Irish church design – Protestant or Catholic. Today the earlier pattern can usually be detected from the positions of the windows and doors, whatever may have happened to their details or the position of the altar. Apart from the Long Tower Church in Derry there are no elaborate Catholic churches from the early years of the new century in the north west. The earliest that are as rich as the more affluent Protestant churches date from the 1830s: St Mary at Limavady, later improved by the local architect *George Given*, and the de-101 lightful Perpendicular design of St John, Killowen, in Coleraine designed by the otherwise unknown *J. Kirkpatrick* in 1834. But these churches are still exceptional. In 1834 Ireland's six and a half million Catholics worshipped in only 2,105 churches, a figure that works out at an average of something over 3,000 persons for every church in the country. In such a situation structure was bound to take precedence over style.

PRESBYTERIAN CHURCHES up to the early nineteenth century occupied a position midway between the luxury of the Church of Ireland Establishment and the poverty experienced by the Catholic Church. In 1834 there were 452 churches for a population of over 642,000, or one church per 1,500 people. As Protestant Nonconformists, the Presbyterians had been subject to sections of the penal laws. Though they were less stringent and were earlier repealed, these had tended to impede the development of the Nonconformists' social and economic position and had indeed caused them to lose control of their old strongholds, the corporations of Derry and Belfast. The same factors that affected Catholic church building – large numbers and lack of funds – also told, if to a lesser degree, in the design of Presbyterian churches, to which should be added the ethos of the denomination itself, which long abjured conspicuous display. Most Ulster congregations originated in the seventeenth century, but there are now no buildings in the north west that show any evidence of an earlier foundation than the mid eighteenth century, and many of these have been rebuilt. The early churches survive mostly in the countryside as neat plain halls, possibly with corner quoins and big sash windows to light undecorated interiors with box pews. Characteristic examples are at Clogher, Laghy, Malin, the little church at Alt above Castle Finn, and, from a somewhat later period, the now deserted Old Moville church by Redcastle. The big church at Coagh is by far the finest of the eighteenth century, though it is ambitious in scale rather than in detail. A second type of Presbyterian church plan that was popular is T-shaped, usually with a gallery in each arm of the T and with the pulpit and communion table placed axially at the centre of the long wall. Doors are placed in the end of each gable, and sometimes the stair to the gallery is built simply as an exposed outside flight. Examples that remain are the two churches at Clondermott of 1743 and 1744 and Castlederg Old Church of 1739, though none has come down unaltered since the eighteenth century and all are modest.

By 1800 congregations had begun to aspire to more elegant accommodation, and in the first half of the nineteenth century a clear new Presbyterian church type became established throughout Ulster. This is best described as a large meeting-house box: a wide hall, two storeys high, usually with three windows across its gabled front, and with huge galleries arranged in a deep U-shape round three sides of the body of the church, supported on thin columns, often of cast iron. The first Presbyterian church of Derry, begun in 1780, was one of the largest and also one of the earliest of this type. Other examples are the two churches at Cookstown, the first Presbyterian church at Coleraine, and a host 87 of minor Mid-Victorian churches built throughout the countryside. Early in the century Presbyterianism selected the relatively secular forms of classical architecture as appropriate to its form of worship. At its simplest this will mean that a thin pilastered façade crowned by an ungainly gable pediment is laid across one end of the meeting house, degenerating into a plain vernacular hall as soon as the corner is turned. Sometimes architects attempted to ease the transition from front to hall by carrying the architecture round to include the first bay of the side, which usually accommodated the stairs that led to the galleries. This was done at Maghera and on the two late Presbyterian churches at Raphoe that are almost identical. Only rarely are the plan and the façade properly married in a unified architectural concept. 88 *Richard Suitor*'s two churches for the Fishmongers' Company at Ballykelly and Banagher achieve this rare distinction, and *Stewart* 103 *Gordon*'s Great James Street church in Derry of 1835 almost succeeds, contributing a suave Ionic portico to the townscape and one of the most charming galleried interiors anywhere in Ulster as well.

Government concern with law and order is reflected in the PUBLIC WORKS – court houses and prisons – erected in the first decades after the Act of Union. Many are utilitarian, though *John* 95 *Bowden*'s Greek Revival court house at the head of Bishop Street in Derry is a fine design, elegantly detailed and excellently built in imported Portland stone. At Enniskillen, the large late-eight-94 eenth-century court house gained a modish porch with heavy baseless Doric columns designed by *William Farrell*, and at Omagh 93 *John Hargrave* set a massive late Palladian block astride the hill at the top of the high street to express as positively as possible the stability of the new regime. Less spectacular were his designs for Letterkenny and Dungannon. In rural areas a court house could be lost in a village street, tacked on as a balancing wing to a farmhouse, as happened at Letterbreen, or at a later date disguised as a picturesque church, as at Armagh Manor. An interim stage between the grand designs of major towns and these self-effacing buildings is represented by a number of trim façades of a simple classical character at Caledon, Eglinton, Glenties, and Buncrana.

Of the three major prisons constructed early in the century none survives. *Hargrave* designed a large complex convenient to his court house at Omagh, but only the governor's house still stands. *Sir Richard Morrison*, who had worked at Castle Coole, built the prison at Enniskillen, and in Derry extra wings and a new polygonal block were added to the late-eighteenth-century frontage, though all but one tower has now gone. The same fate has overtaken *Francis Johnston*'s lunatic asylum in Derry (1827) and seems likely to claim as well the original Foyle College building, whose main block by *Bowden* at the time of writing stands empty and decaying. Two other old school buildings in these counties are still in use: Dungannon Royal School in its original eighteenth-century building, indistinguishable from a plain country house, and Portora Royal outside Enniskillen, rebuilt in the early nineteenth century in an ample Regency institutional style. The Old Royal School at Raphoe, rebuilt in 1737, should also be mentioned here as it gained extra wings with Venetian windows about the turn of the century.

PUBLIC MONUMENTS, as opposed to buildings, appear in the nineteenth century as an extension of private patronage into the public sector. Lord Bristol erected an obelisk near Castledawson 'to commemorate the virtues and benevolence of the Dawson family', and the Olpherts of Falcarragh lifted the Cloghaneely on to a pillar of stone rubble for all to see in 1774. In Derry, at Caledon, and at Enniskillen, the Rev. George Walker, the second Earl of Caledon, and General Sir Galbraith Lowry Cole were commemorated by giant Doric columns of 1826, 1840, and 1845. Sadly, only the last has survived recent terrorist bombings. Apart from the columns there are few other public monuments: the triumphal south gate of Derry was erected to designs of *H. A. Baker* in 1789 on the centenary of the siege, and perhaps the other city gateways reconstructed early in the next century should be included here. Two Victorian testimonials to the worth of active agents are the Beresford Obelisk and Sampson's Tower of 1840 and 1859, both in the vicinity of Limavady; and in this context the sad monument of Mr Breckenridge, built as a snub to Tyrone society above the Clogher valley, should not be forgotten, though that is really a piece of anti-public architecture.

VICTORIAN BUILDINGS

The accession of Queen Victoria in 1837 was accompanied by no particular change in the appearance of Ulster architecture. For at least the first thirty years of the new reign the Georgian tradition of building survived as the norm in most towns and villages, and the events that marked the country were not aesthetic but political or economic in their origin. In early Victorian Ireland two spirits were abroad: one positive, expansionist, eager for progress; the other suspicious of change, afraid of the mass of the population, and oppressive.

A fearful reminder of the oppressive spirit is embodied in the UNION WORKHOUSES built under the Irish Poor Law Act of 1838 which, despite the report of the Irish Commissioners under

the Chairmanship of the Archbishop of Dublin, Richard Whately,
extended the new English Poor Law into Ireland. Whately had
argued that the English system was quite unsuitable for Ireland,
where poverty was due to a lack of employment which could be
remedied only by a vigorous policy to promote public works and
develop natural resources. The evident success of such a policy
at Sion Mills, where the travelling Halls were so impressed by
the industry and state of the peasantry, is a proof of his argu-
ments, but the government remained implacable and the New
Poor Law received the royal assent in the second year of Victoria's
reign. It brought to the fore *George Wilkinson*, an Englishman and
architect to the Poor Law Commissioners, who left in every
county of the kingdom blocks of a standard Tudor or gable-
fronted design whose repetitive pattern drew immediate criticism
from the Irish and English architectural press. Most were erected
between 1840 and 1846. Taken individually their design is not
unpleasant and, with the limited means at his disposal, a reasonable solution by Wilkinson to the architectural problems a poor
house posed. Many have survived as hospitals, and characteristic
parts either of the governor's house or of the poor-house range,
with paired stair-tower behind, can be seen in the north west at
Ballyshannon, Clogher, Coleraine, Dungannon, Enniskillen, Let-
96 terkenny, Limavady, Lisnaskea, and elsewhere. As architect of
the Poor Law Commissioners, Wilkinson wrote to the various
clerks of works, who were carrying out poor houses under him,
asking them to fill up a paper describing the building materials
of their locality, which inquiry provided the material for his
exceptionally useful *Practical Geology and Ancient Architecture of
Ireland* published in 1845. On the completion of the poor houses
he moved to the Lunacy Board. The largest asylum in the north
west at Omagh is not his, however, but a late job by *William Farrell*. A typical example of Wilkinson's asylum style is the hospital
at Letterkenny of 1860.

The buildings that express the positive spirit in early Victorian
116 Ireland are the warehouses and factories of the expanding linen
industry at Sion Mills, already mentioned, at Caledon, Dungannon, and in the city of Derry. The country was caught too by
the contemporary enthusiasm for RAILWAYS, so typical of the
age, and though this took its origin in other centres – the first
Irish line from Dublin to Kingstown opened in 1834 and the
second from Belfast to Lisburn in 1839 – the north west was not
slow to develop its own network. *The Irish Tourist's Illustrated
Handbook* of 1852, appearing at the height of the railway fever,

did not hesitate to pronounce the whole Irish network one which 'for symmetrical completeness exceeds our English system'. By that year the Londonderry and Enniskillen Railway Company had already a line linking Derry, Strabane, Newtownstewart, Omagh, Enniskillen, Lisnaskea, Newtownbutler, and Clones, a route that was to become the Irish North Western Railway. In the same year the line from Londonderry to Coleraine, which had necessitated the blasting of two long tunnels through the basalt cliffs at Downhill in 1846, was at last opened, and in the next year a new branch line from Cookstown Junction west of Antrim was begun to link Toome, Castledawson, Magherafelt, and Cookstown itself, all on the west side of Lough Neagh. In 1836 the first of the narrow gauge lines in Co. Donegal opened from Derry to Farland Point on Lough Swilly (extended to Fahan and Buncrana the next year), and in 1868 a branch that became the Finn Valley Railway was completed from Strabane to Stranorlar. In 1884 two light railways from Victoria Bridge near Sion Mills to Castlederg and from Tynan in Co. Armagh through the Clogher valley to Maguires Bridge were begun, while the Donegal narrow gauge lines went on expanding until 1909, by which time Burton Port, Letterkenny, Glenties, Donegal, Killybegs, and Ballyshannon were all linked by lines that comprised some of the most remarkable engineering enterprises of railway history.

There remains today one line from Derry to Coleraine and Belfast: the rest have gone, though a number of RAILWAY STATIONS remain to record, with the grass-grown embankments and piers of dismantled bridges, the routes the railways followed. The prince of railway architects in the North was *Charles Lanyon*, county surveyor of Antrim from 1836, Mayor of Belfast in 1862, and a conservative M.P. for the borough in 1866. From 1862 he was president of the Royal Institute of Architects of Ireland and in 1868 received a knighthood. His elegant Italianate station at Coleraine of 1855, doubled in size about 1880 by a replica of itself on the opposite side of the line, captures precisely the spirit of the early railway period, as does his more modest Cookstown terminal, single-storey and Italianate again, of about 1856. Lanyon's son *John* was responsible for the free Lombardic station of the Belfast and Northern Counties Railway at the Waterside in Derry of 1873, and his former pupil and chief clerk, *Thomas Turner*, for the still Italianate brick terminus of the old Irish North Western Railway that became the G.N.R. in Foyle Street, Derry. Small Gothic stations were built at Buncrana by *Fitzgibbon Louch* in 1864, at Stranorlar designed by a Mr *Clayton* of Brixton in 1862, and on the old I.N.W.R. line at Lisbellaw, Lisnaskea, and Newtownbutler, where *Sir John McNeil* was engineer. Here the Gothic stations appear to have been designed by *W. G. Murray*, in the late 1850s, with all the aggressive angularity of his own Gothic idiom. In 1877 *W. H. Mills* became first chief civil engineer of the Irish G.N.R. He added several crisply detailed minor brick stations on the main lines, usually with segment-headed paired windows in polychrome brick and now often derelict.

   The dichotomy of style that is displayed by the railway boards in their stations mirrors closely the two broad alternatives favoured in early Victorian PUBLIC BUILDING AND COUNTRY HOUSE DESIGN. Here *Lanyon* set the pattern for an Italianate palazzo style modelled on the example of the Barry clubs in London and rising in Lanyon's own work to designs of exceptional panache at Dundarave of 1847 and at Ballywalter of 1849, respectively in Co. Antrim and Co. Down, so not included in this volume. But Lanyon's early work is represented here by Drenagh near Limavady of 1836 and by Laurel Hill in Coleraine of 1841. The new Ballyscullion House which *c.* 1850 replaced the ruins of the Earl Bishop's incomplete oval fantasy house is probably also his. He was conceivably responsible too, if the picturesque Italianate gate lodge is a fair guide, for the Italianate remodelling of Cromore outside Portstewart, though 1834 would be early for him to be working in the North. His palazzo style appears most splen-98 didly in a commercial context at the Belfast Bank of 1853 in Derry city, and it is turned to good effect by *Thomas Turner* at the Northern Bank of 1866 in Shipquay Place also in Derry. In addition to his experience in Lanyon's office, Turner, who was the son of the famous ironfounder Richard Turner from Dublin, sought to extend the range of his activity by setting up a partnership with 100 the county surveyor of Derry, *Richard Williamson*, and by establishing a separate office of his own in Glasgow in 1861. The effect was to liberate his Italianate manner from too great a dependence on Lanyon's example, and his Northern Bank shows as clear traces of Glaswegian classicism as it does of his old master. The same 99 is true of his Baroque town hall in Coleraine of 1859, which has more than a dash of James Gibbs in its design, and of his restrained Italianate house of St Mura's at Fahan, or Glenavon by Cookstown, both of which are informed by something of the sensitivity that characterizes the work of the Scottish 'Greek' Thomson. Within the next decade *Sandham Symes* as architect to the Bank of Ireland was to extend the popularity of the palazzo-style

front for commercial premises, and in 1861 a flamboyant private
house was built at The Manor, Killadeas, to designs of a retired [112]
architect and director of the Belleek potteries, *William Armstrong*.
There are in addition to these buildings many minor late Georgian
or early Victorian Italianate houses and town frontages whose
designers remain anonymous. Enniskillen was once well supplied
with sumptuous stucco fronts of this type, and of the houses Ashfield Park, Lizard Manor, Clifton Lodge, the now vanished Dun-
moyle, Rossclare, and the exuberant marine villa of Magheraboy
deserve a mention.

Out-and-out Gothic is rare as an alternative to the Italianate
style. Together *Lanyon* and *Turner* pioneered a curly-gabled Jacobean mansion type of which Tempo Manor of 1862 and Knocknamoe Castle outside Omagh are good examples, and Turner went
on at a later stage to adapt the style baronially at Thornhill near
Derry in 1882. The only truly Scottish Baronial house is Armagh
Manor, which dates from 1865 and may well be by a Scottish
architect, as it is so unlike the work of any local man. Local inspiration supplied the designs for two jagged late Irish castles: Glenveagh begun in 1865 and Lough Eske designed by the Derry [113]
architect *Fitzgibbon Louch* in 1859. Both are hard and unrelenting
in their masonry and totally different from the accommodating
medievalisms introduced to Ireland sixty years before by Nash.
The same hard quality is more appropriately apparent in the
battlemented Royal Irish Constabulary Barracks in Dungannon
built by *J. H. Owen*, the Board of Works architect, which stand in
bold juxtaposition to the Venetian Gothic of the former Belfast
Bank by *W. H. Lynn*.

William Henry Lynn was Turner's successor in Lanyon's
office. He stayed on to become a partner and, in all probability,
took over the more overtly Gothic side of the partnership. The
Dungannon bank of 1855 is one of his most charming essays in
a Ruskinian style, with a pretty cusped *trifora* as the main feature
of its front. *Lanyon* and *Lynn* together designed the vigorous Victorian Gothic almshouses of Shiel's Institution also in Dungannon in 1867, and Ruskinian values appear too in the fine Provincial
Bank at Omagh of 1864 which is probably by *W. G. Murray*.   [97]

During this period of expansion in the railways, in manufacturing industry, and in commerce – an expansion that is interrupted
only slightly by the tragedy of the famine years, 1845 to 1849 –
CHURCH BUILDING AND CHURCH IMPROVEMENT continued
steadily. The Church of Ireland had from 1843 one architect,
Joseph Welland, who catered for all its needs. His qualifications

were impeccable. Welland, a relative of the Bishop of Down, had trained in Dublin in the office of John Bowden, through whom in 1826 he obtained the appointment of architect to the Board of First Fruits in the Tuam Division. In 1839, when the Irish Ecclesiastical Commission replaced the old Board of First Fruits, Welland was appointed one of its four architects (though the older *William Farrell* seems to have retained responsibility for the North), and in 1843 on the reorganization of the Commission he became its sole architect. The post gave him a virtual monopoly of the Established Church's building programme for the next seventeen years, and at his death in March 1860 it passed to his son *William Welland,* who was appointed joint architect in the same year with a Mr *W. Gillespie* also from his father's office. *Welland & Gillespie* continued to act as the Commissioners' architects until 31 December 1870, when, under the provisions of the Irish Church Act of the year before, the Church of Ireland was disestablished and the Commission abolished. Joseph Welland did not necessarily design all the buildings for the Established Church between 1843 and 1860. He worked through local assistants and clerks, and where a large and influential congregation wished to employ a particular architect, that could be done. His son and Gillespie maintained the same approach, but inevitably the bulk of the work came to the Commissioners' architects, especially where church alterations and additions were involved, and their names appear constantly in Irish parish histories. Fortunately both Wellands were gifted men. As architects they showed a happy sense of massing and a knack of economical detail and design that make their smaller rural churches delightful and eminently right for their setting. In large churches their command of the big spare spaces pioneered by men like R. C. Carpenter has left some noteworthy interiors with strong double-chamfered arcades, moulded capitals, and high open roofs that are a perfect latticework of rafters, braced purlins, trusses and struts. Whether William Welland was largely responsible for the stronger character of his father's work from the mid fifties is not clear, but it seems likely that he was, as the office style continued without interruption after the older Welland's death. On the other hand the old man may have acted as a moderating influence, for it was not until the early sixties that the Commissioners' architects began to produce the freely treated Gothic – quite liberated from archaeological restraints – that characterizes the last years of their work.

Good examples of Joseph Welland's work may be seen in the

churches at Creeslough, Derryvullan, Kilmacrenan, and Swatragh. His finest large church is undoubtedly St Swithin at Magherafelt. Continuity in the office style is apparent when the crisp
design of the little churches at Gleneely, Millford, Moville, and
Knocktarna, all dumpy with widely splayed diagonal buttresses, [106]
and all of the 1850s, is compared with a similar series by Welland
& Gillespie at Augher, Mountcharles, and Myroe; and indeed
their big church of the Holy Trinity at Coalisland bears obvious
similarities to St Swithin's, Magherafelt. The wayward side of
Welland & Gillespie's practice is best represented in the north
west by St Margaret, Clabby, of 1864 and by a clutch of three
exceptional churches, all in rural settings near the village of Ballyronan in north Tyrone: St Patrick, Ballyclog, of 1865, and St
Matthias, Ballyeglish, and St John, Woodchapel, both of 1866. [110]
At All Saints, Waterside, in Derry, *W. H. Lynn* of *Lanyon, Lynn* [108]
& Lanyon built a fine 'Middle Pointed' Gothic church in 1864,
and in Dungannon *W. J. Barre*, one of the most original of the
Victorian architects of the North, left a major work in the big,
bold church of St Anne, completed in 1867 just before his death [107]
at the early age of thirty-seven and just before Disestablishment.

If Barre was not quite a rogue architect he was at least a rascal.
Moving easily among the styles and denominations of Mid Victorian Ireland, he left in a short career monuments to an emphatic
taste in Episcopal, Presbyterian, Wesleyan, Unitarian, and Catholic churches. St Anne is in fact really an adaptation of his entry
for the Cork Cathedral competition of 1862 whose printed conditions 'the committee shamefully violated', and it bears evidence
of the care that Barre devoted to his design. At Moy the Church
of Ireland parish church was extended to his plans, though they
were never completed, and the vigorous little Lombardic brick
Methodist church there is also his work. His most jagged Gothic
design, the Adam Clarke Memorial Church at Portstewart, has
unfortunately now been shorn of all its power, but the Corinthian
temple that he designed for the Methodists of Enniskillen in 1865
still exudes an air of brash Victorian confidence. He was, as
C. E. B. Brett has commented, 'amongst the first to cater for the
luxurious tastes of the textile parvenus'. The field of this activity
was in the neighbourhood of Belfast, but Barre also enjoyed the
patronage of Lord Charlemont, for whom he remodelled Roxborough Castle by Moy in a rich François Premier style, normally
the choice of a *nouveau riche par excellence*! Sadly that fantasy
has now gone. Had he not foolishly travelled home in a wet suit
after marking the foundations of a villa by Downpatrick, Barre

might have survived to enjoy a long and successful career. As it is, he has the distinction of being the only Ulster architect on whom a biographical memoir, subscribed to by at least eleven of his professional brethren, was published soon after his death.

In many ways Barre's successor was the young *Timothy Hevey*, a talented architect of CATHOLIC CHURCHES, who shared the same taste for vigorous wall surface and picturesque silhouette, and the same fate. Hevey came from Belfast. He was educated at St Malachy's Seminary School there and then joined the office of the Belfast firm of *Boyd & Batt*. *George Boyd*'s own style has a certain crude vigour, well represented by the heavy Lombardic Gothic of his Presbyterian church at Magherafelt, though by the time that church was built in 1866, Hevey had set up on his own. The clue to Hevey's work, however, lies in his contact with the Catholic High Gothic circle of E. W. Pugin and George Ashlin in Dublin. For three years he worked as a draughtsman for their firm, and through Ashlin made contact with *The Irish Builder*, whose issues were to be frequently illustrated by his drawings – all signed with the monogram T H. In the spring of 1865, when he was twenty, he returned to Belfast, where success in at least three competitions assured him of a growing practice. In 1871 he joined the obscure J. F. Mackinnon in partnership, possibly to overcome the disadvantages with clients that his own youth might cause, for there is no evidence to suggest that Mackinnon contributed materially to the practice, and he disappeared from public notice on Hevey's sudden death at thirty-three in 1878.

Hevey's best work in the north west is represented by two original little churches: St Eunan at Raphoe of 1874, and the closely 119 related Church of the Sacred Heart, Dunlewey, of 1877. Both are clean, clear designs of workmanlike character, and both present at a comparatively early date a type of revived Irish Romanesque with round-tower campaniles off-set on their entrance fronts. A more vigorous Victorian polychrome Gothic appears in Hevey's Hibernian Bank in Letterkenny and in the additions he made to the Catholic churches at Glenties and Gweedore. The Catholic churches at Convoy, Fivemiletown, and Redcastle have many of his characteristic features, though here the architect has not been recorded.

The mainstream of CATHOLIC CHURCH BUILDING followed a different course from Timothy Hevey's work. Early Victorian churches are big and plain, like their Church of Ireland fore-runners, only with much larger halls. All of them are Gothic. Good examples of the scale that might now be attempted are at

Cockhill outside Buncrana of 1848, at Brookeborough and Clogher, both built about the mid century, and St Conall, Glenties, of 1852. Many other churches were, of course, enlarged in the same period rather than rebuilt. Occasionally the builder or architect is known. *Daniel Campbell* built the church at Drumquin in 1832 and the much bigger neo-Norman St Patrick at Ballyshannon in 1842. St Bridget, Ballintra, of 1845 is by a Stranorlar builder, *James McKenna*, though its design is so close to St Patrick, Donaghmore, in Co. Tyrone that it may really be by *John Brady*, the architect of that church. St Catherine, Killybegs, is a unique example of a well known Englishman, *J. B. Papworth*, working for the Irish Catholic Church in the 1830s, though three nice examples of *E. W. Godwin*'s work exist in the churches at St Johnstown, Newtowncunningham, and on Tory Island.

The major figure in Irish church Gothic and champion of ecclesiological principles in Catholic buildings was the Dublin architect *James J. McCarthy*, to whom the job of completing Thomas Duff's Armagh Cathedral was given in 1854. From then until his death in 1882 McCarthy built extensively throughout all Ireland – usually in as massively thirteenth-century a style as his clients could afford. The gigantic spire of his church of the Holy Trinity at Cookstown of 1855–60 is an instance of McCarthy at his best, while the elegance of his detail appears in St Patrick, Dungannon, 109 of 1867 and at St Eugene's Cathedral in Derry erected to his designs from 1851, though the spire here was built in 1900 by the 120, 121 Derry architect *E. J. Toye*, assisted by *George Ashlin*. McCarthy's greatest rival in the North was *John O'Neill* of Belfast, who rose to prominence in the late 1850s. O'Neill took into partnership his principal assistant *William H. Byrne*, after the latter had been injured in a fall from the scaffolding of the new Catholic church in Downpatrick. From about 1870 they practised as *O'Neill & Byrne*. By 1880 Byrne had set up a branch of the firm in Dublin which survived the death of John O'Neill in 1883 and later became *W. H. Byrne & Son*. If O'Neill & Byrne have a weakness it is their tendency to try to make too little go too far. Big French Gothic designs at Enniskillen, Magherafelt, and Falcarragh, though fine in many ways, all suffer from this fault, with their attenuated windows and plans for thin spires, though only that at Magherafelt was ever built. St Patrick, Cross Roads by Killy- 123 gordon, is more successful, with a fine spire which can be seen for miles, and a rich interior that uses the polished granite columns and massive vegetable-type capitals typical of this practice. O'Neill's elegant cruciform design at St Columba, Doneyloop, of 1867 should also be mentioned, as its skilful arrangement of side chapels was much admired and much copied by later architects.

Though O'Neill was succeeded by Byrne, and McCarthy had a son, Charles, in his practice, the death of these two principals within the space of a year left a vacuum in church building in the north west. It was filled by the younger *William Hague*, the son of a Cavan building contractor, who had worked extensively in Co. Fermanagh and Co. Tyrone. In 1863, early in his career, Hague won a competition for the new Presbyterian church in the Waterside district of Derry. Though he later gained pre-eminence as a Catholic church architect, his practice, which was based in Dublin, was never exclusively a Catholic one, and it was to become very large. His career coincides with a period in which the Catholic church had at last the funds to plan and carry through really large building projects, and it is Hague whose work is most often set in a spirit of open competition, inviting comparison with some major Protestant church. This happens with his powerful double-122 spired Church of the Sacred Heart at Omagh of 1893–9 that dwarfs the nearby St Columb rebuilt only twenty years before; at Strabane his Church of the Immaculate Conception, built in 1895, towers over the Bowling Green beside *John Kennedy*'s excellent but modest Christ Church of 1874; and at Letterkenny 124 Hague's new cathedral of 1891 is placed directly opposite Conwall Church of Ireland Parish Church, wider, longer, taller, and richer by far. Hague never swerved from his adherence to an elaborate late Gothic style richly detailed in *real* materials and enhanced by a liberal use of pine and marble, sculptured capitals, corbel heads, spandrels, and bosses. He died in 1899, and with his partner, *T. F. McNamara*, who completed Letterkenny Cathedral, the history of Catholic church building enters the present century.

The later PRESBYTERIAN CHURCHES in North West Ulster tend to be the work of one of two firms. Generally, as their churches had no need of a chancel, congregations were slow to take up a full Gothic style, and when they did it was often a free form of Perpendicular that was employed. In Derry, the Church of Ireland architect *John Guy Ferguson* built a number of simple Gothic Presbyterian churches, but the Nonconformist firm *par excellence* was that established by *Robert Young* in Belfast which soon became *Young & Mackenzie*. Their church work is usually dull. Its development, such as it is, may be traced from their churches at Magherafelt – Early English of 1857 – and Dunfanaghy of 1875, where the Minister insisted on an Early Irish style, to Carlisle Road Church in Derry of 1877 and Ramelton Church of 1906. Both the latter have thin Perpendicular fronts.

As architects Ferguson and Young & Mackenzie each did better COMMERCIAL WORK and contributed factories of some style to the architecture of Derry. In 1863 Young & Mackenzie built the gigantic City Factory, a three-storey block of twenty-118 four bays of rhythmically disposed and vigorously detailed windows, with polychromatic brickwork and stone string courses. Their Bigger's Building in Foyle Street of 1870 is even more vigorous, with a heavy brick frontage that swings gently round the curve of the street. Ferguson's Horace Street Factory of 1872 is in a similarly massive brick Gothic vein, while his earliest factory, dating from 1856, for Tillie and Henderson in Carlisle Square, was still rather Georgian in its character and far removed from his later manner. Best of all, because it is the most completely Victorian, is his Commercial Buildings for Mitchell's in Foyle Street of 1883, enriched with architectural sculpture of a high order. Of Derry's later factories the Star Factory built by *Daniel Conroy* in 1899 and the Rosemount Factory by *M. A. Robinson* of 1904 are the most adventurous.

PUBLIC BUILDINGS of the later nineteenth century are predominantly in a late and free Gothic style. First is *E. P. Gribbon*'s Magee University College in Derry, now a constituent part of the 117 New University of Ulster, but founded in 1853 and built between 1856 and 1865. Gribbon was a Dublin architect, the Presbyterians' chosen equivalent in the South to Young & Mackenzie, though more vigorous in his massing and use of detail. In Derry there is also *J. G. Ferguson*'s Apprentice Boys' Hall of 1873, thinly Scottish Baronial, and by the same architect the Cathedral Schools of 1891, built in red brick and red sandstone in a Netherlandish Gothic idiom. The most ambitious building is the Derry Guildhall, designed in 1887 by *J. G. Ferguson* and restored after a fire in 1912 by *M. A. Robinson* (burnt and restored again after a bomb attack in 1973), free Municipal Gothic once again. Outside Derry only one building deserves especial mention: *Turner & Williamson*'s extraordinary Italianate-cum-Baronial complex designed as a principal new court house in Magherafelt in 1874.

Classical public buildings are, by contrast, few. St Columb's Temperance Hall in Derry by *Croom & Toye* of 1888 is one exception, a swaggering Baroque performance if on a small scale and really only a rich front. Its only rival is *A. Scott & Son*'s new town hall in Enniskillen built in 1898.

Two houses reflecting the later-nineteenth-century interest in
ARTS AND CRAFTS should be mentioned here. One is Bless-
114 ingbourne near Fivemiletown built as a personal form of Elizabethan manor house to designs of *F. P. Cockerell* in 1874. The
other is Sion Mills House, a Lanyon-type Italianate house trans-
mogrified in 1884 by *W. F. Unsworth* into a late Tudor half-
timbered giant that *The Irish Builder* clearly thought half-baked
as well. But black and white Tudor houses had some success about
the turn of the century. There are two lavish remodellings in this
style in Co. Donegal, at Glenmore and Cloughan Lodges, both
in the Finn valley, and at St Angelo, Trory, by Lough Erne and
Annaginny Lodge near Newmills in Co. Tyrone. In 1904 *William
Scott* designed an attractive house in the manner of Voysey at
Killyhevlin near Enniskillen, and about the same time the Hon.
Mrs Phillimore built a witty slate-hung holiday house in the treeless peninsula beyond Tranarossan Bay near Carrigart that is traditionally ascribed to *Lutyens*.

In CHURCH BUILDING the architect who emerged as the
major figure in Church of Ireland circles after Disestablishment
was *Thomas Drew*. A son of the rector of St Anne, Belfast, who
began his career in 1854 as an apprentice in Lanyon's office, in
1861 Drew was briefly associated in partnership with Thomas
Turner. Moving to Dublin the following year to join the office
of W. G. Murray he married his chief's daughter, as Lanyon
had done, and by 1866 was appearing in association with Murray
as the architect of several major Dublin jobs. From then on a constant flow of work kept Drew busy, bringing him an architectural
plum in St Anne, Belfast, in 1896 and in 1900 the distinction of
a knighthood.

Much of Drew's work is confined to the enrichment of Church
of Ireland chancels or the addition of new choirs. In this he
employs a rich yet restrained style: rich in materials – marble,
glass, and tile – yet restrained in the almost obsessive avoidance
of figural sculpture or representational art beyond the non-deno-
minational beasts of the Evangelists and safe forms of vine and
acanthus. Yet Drew had a scholarly knowledge of late Gothic
forms, and where he designed anew could produce churches of
charm and beauty, notable for the delicate elegance of their interiors. Such are his two little Fermanagh churches, both in rural
parishes, at Monea of 1890 and Castle Archdale of 1905. His work
at the parish churches in Coleraine, 1884, and Draperstown,
1888, amounts virtually to rebuilding, and it was Drew who contrived the delicate poise of a restored thirteenth-century chancel

for Raphoe Cathedral in 1892. A fine example of an interior 111 improved by Drew is the little chapel of ease for the Galbraith family at Clanabogan, which he enriched in 1889. Though comparatively late, it is one of the best High Victorian interiors in the north west, equalled only at Castlerock, where *F. W. Porter*, architect to the Clothworkers' Company, designed a new church in 1868, or perhaps by the interior of the church at Killadeas built by *William Armstrong* of Belleek.

CATHOLIC CHURCHES at the turn of the century are often the work of the Derry man *Edward J. Toye*, who also left his mark in a series of jocular classical office blocks in Strand Road, Derry, and at St Columb's College there. Toye had a liking for a very particular wide-plan church that may have been developed by O'Neill or possibly by Toye's older partner, *James Croom*. Its essence is an aisleless nave with transepts divided from the nave by an arcade that continues into the chancel to provide an arched division between the chancel itself and lateral chapels entered from the transepts. This plan first appears at St Agatha, Clar, in 1869 and is taken up by Toye at St Patrick, Gortin, of 1898 and in his stucco-fronted churches at Ardara and Bruckless of 1900 and 1913. It is an original and curiously elegant plan that can stand repetition, and indeed it was copied again by *J. V. Brennan* at Glenmore.

Toye's churches show a marked preference for the round-headed arches and rotund forms of the Irish-Romanesque revival that enjoyed such a vogue at the turn of the century, and in this he is paralleled by the work of the Dublin firm of *Doolin, Butler & Donelly*, whose office designed two spectacular churches at Aughnacloy and Kilcar in 1902 and 1903 respectively. Both have 126 powerful interiors, that at Kilcar as much neo-Byzantine as neo-Romanesque and all the more memorable for its rural hillside setting. *William Scott* used Romanesque in a simple form at Monea and Irvinestown in 1908 and in 1904 in the convent chapel at Enniskillen, where it is tinged with a more Byzantine element that is most strongly expressed in his large, centrally planned pilgrimage church at St Patrick's Purgatory on Lough Derg. *George Ashlin* too has left at least one Romanesque design in Ulster, at the Corr Memorial Church, Lissan, a flamboyant, grand scheme of 1907, filled with a confidence which seems to suggest that the eclectic values of nineteenth-century building might last forever.

And so far as church building in Ulster is concerned that confidence was hardly misplaced. *Ralph Byrne*, in the Church of the Four Masters at Donegal of 1931 and at Carndonagh in 1942, was

still building in Irish and Pisan Romanesque, a style in which the less famous, though hardly less talented, *Padraig Gregory* was happy to work during the inter-war years. His best church is prob-
125 ably St Malachy, Coleraine, of 1937, though here as so often ultra-modern materials of their day, especially cream and green terrazzo, seem now to clash with the concept of a church.

There was no MODERN ARCHITECTURE in North West Ulster until the partition of Ireland in 1922, and little until the end of the Second World War. In Derry, Austin's Department Store of 1906 by *M. A. Robinson* expands a thin Baroque net across a steel frame structure that is principally glass. It could be called *modern*, in as much as nothing of its sort had appeared in this half of the province before. Robinson's Rosemount Factory of 1904, also in Derry, is a restrained red-brick block of simple and massive silhouette, yet it too is articulated in classical terms. So are most of its successors. Emancipation of a kind is expressed in the work of *Vincent Craig*, the elder brother of James Craig, later Lord Craigavon, the architect in a different sense of Unionist Ulster. Craig's main activity centred around Belfast, but there are two examples of his work in the north west: the court house in Cookstown of 1900 and Portstewart Presbyterian Church of 1905. Both are vaguely Art Nouveau and freed from the restraints of historical precedent, though they are too self-conscious to have worn well. In Omagh one small and startlingly modern cinema was built about 1930 adopting the curved glass and linear transoms pioneered by Mendelsohn and Gropius – and that is all until the end of the Second World War.

Since the War, government architects have liked rustic-faced brown-red brick too well to produce much satisfactory modern architecture, and, though the Northern Ireland Housing Trust has fostered plenty of decent schemes, there is none that deserves special mention. SCHOOL BUILDING and MODERN CHURCHES offer the staple of current commissions. The north classroom block at Portora Royal School, Enniskillen, by *Lewis & Baxter* of 1956 is one of the best buildings of its day, substantial and well proportioned, with plenty of interest that is not meretricious. The
129 Collegiate School in the same town extended by *Shanks & Leighton* in 1967 is excellent, and there are other good designs – at Carrickmore by *Patrick Haughey*, at Gortin, and in the Pennyburn district of Derry – that have considered massing and detail beyond the perfunctory repetition of classroom units and flat-ended gables that, sadly, characterizes so much building in the province.
130 The New University of Ulster outside Coleraine, building from

1967 to designs of *Robert Matthew, Johnson-Marshall & Partners*, must be mentioned on account of the sheer size of the undertaking. Its architecture uses the essentially insubstantial materials of many factory sheds and must depend for its final effect on the landscaped setting that has not yet had time to mature. How the buildings will have worn by the time they gain a proper setting remains to be seen. One more gigantic structure is the Coolkeeragh Power Station on Lough Foyle opened in 1960 and designed by *Kennedy & Donkin* with *Sir Alexander Gibb & Partners*.

Church building in the last two decades has contributed positively to the store of fine architecture in the north west. The Presbyterian church at Strabane built by *Thomas Houston* in 1955 is [128] a strong, clean design that handles brickwork well, and there are honest small Church of Ireland churches at Dromore and Brookepark in Derry, both by *A. T. Marshall*. It is however the Catholic Church that has shown most vigour in exploring new forms and in developing a new range of church plans, evident in the work of *White & Hegarty* at Eglinton, of *J. J. Tracey* at Garrison, of *Patrick Haughey* at Sion Mills, Dunnamanagh, and Strabane, and of *Liam McCormick*, the doyen of Ulster church builders, in a succession of inspiring designs. McCormick's church work in Co. Derry and Co. Donegal now ranges through three decades and can be seen in eight churches, at Lifford, Glenties, and Millford, at Desertegney, Cresslough, Maghera, and Burt, and at Steelstown in Derry city. Variety and integrity are the cornerstones of all these designs. It was the church at Burt that won for its [127] architect the Gold Medal of the Royal Institute of the Architects of Ireland in 1971. Its circular form and round rubble wall consciously echo the massive stone fort of Grianan of Ailech beneath [8, 10] whose hill it is set and whose walls take Ulster architecture back to the Irish Early Christian period and perhaps even beyond.

A NOTE ON BUILDING MATERIALS

No area in Ireland is more richly endowed with a variety of building stone than North West Ulster. In contrast to the carboniferous limestone plain that extends across the whole of central Ireland, and indeed covers almost three-quarters of the country, the north west is rich in other stones. The limestone, it is true, covers most of Co. Fermanagh. It extends up into Tyrone in the lowlands around Clogher, Dungannon, Omagh, and in the area of Strabane and Dunnamanagh. Around Donegal Bay from Bundoran to St John's Point is limestone too, and there is more in Co. Derry in the Roe valley. Yet in the geology of these four counties other rocks predominate. The great basalt field that is the essential and most remarkable feature of Co. Antrim expands into considerable portions of Co. Derry. Dipping low, it crosses the whole course of the river Bann. It sends a tongue beyond the western shore of Lough Neagh, and basaltic outliers on Slieve Gallion, west of Magherafelt, prove that it once extended further. The line where it ends provides a dramatic series of escarpments running north from Dungiven to the cliffs of Downhill – Benbradagh, Craiggore, Keady Mountain, and Binevenagh – hill tops that can all be seen to advantage from the little Romanesque churches of Banagher and Bovevagh in the Roe and Owenbeg valleys where other stones take over. These other stones are mostly green mica schist and granite. The schist, mixed near the river Foyle with conglomerate rock and clay slates, is the predominant rock of south Co. Derry and north Tyrone. Between the two counties it rises to form the stark barrier of the Sperrin mountain range and crosses westwards into Co. Donegal, covering most of the country from the In-ishowen peninsula to Malin Beg and Slieve League on the extreme south-west shore. The exceptions are the outbreaks of granite that give to Donegal some of its grandest scenery: the Blue Stack mountains above Lough Eske in the south; Fanad Head and the Atlantic Drive in the north; and the whole extraordinary district of the Rosses from the Bloody Foreland to Gweebarra Bay, a granite coastal plain fretted with inlets, pitted with tiny inland loughs, and littered with gigantic boulders. Behind the Rosses is the line of the Derryveagh Mountains running in a north-easterly ridge and rising to the round-topped Slieve Snaght (683 m). Im-mediately north, towering above the Poisoned Glen, is the dramatic quartzite cone of Errigal – 748 m high and Donegal's highest mountain – with glistening white scree slopes. In the same range is the flat-topped Muckish, that seems always to rise as a purple slab on the horizon of west coast views.

Limestone, granite, quartz, schist, and basalt: to these must be added the old red sandstone that occurs in an extensive area in Co. Fermanagh and Co. Tyrone between the east shore of Lower Lough Erne and Beragh; and the yellow sandstone and sandstone conglomerate that is widely dispersed from Dungiven down the Roe valley on to Magilligan Point and west from Lima-vady towards Derry city. Limestone also occurs in frequent patches throughout the schist regions, and there are small areas of slate near Lisbellaw and Donaghmore. Finally there are the Co. Donegal marbles: grey at Malin Head, bright blue-grey, pink, or white at Marble Hill, yellow-veined and rose at Ballymore, and brilliant white at Dunlewey by Errigal.

For all this wealth of different building stone the Ulster landscape presents in its buildings a remarkable uniformity. As often as not the stone is invisible, hidden behind whitewash or rough harling in the country, or cement-rendered, pebbledashed, or occasionally stuccoed – though this usually means a brick building in the towns. With the exception of the limestones and the sandstone most building stone is rough and hard to dress, so rubble walls are by far the commonest sight. Much of their material has been lifted from fields or from the sides of streams, and large round boulders can be seen in the gables of many farmyard outbuildings and in the walls of the seventeenth-century Plantation castles and bawns built round Lough Erne and in Co. Derry. Boulders always appear in the walls of the whitewashed thatched cottages and the ruins of cottages that together could stand as the symbol of rural Ireland; and they are in the fields too, though field walls in Ulster rarely run far before they are absorbed in the banked-up earth of a ditch or pick up the line of some hawthorn or ash saplings which together with rowan or hazelnut trees may do duty as a hedge. In the rougher pasture in north Tyrone and Donegal where the stones lie most exposed these ramshackle field boundaries are indeed the norm with stone on stone, hedges where the soil is good, and perhaps a piece of new wooden fencing by the side of a recent road improvement, all jumbled together. By the sea a reticulation of pyramidal dry stone walls occurs, haphazardly heaped together and sometimes treacherous to cross. Historically even peat, or the sod from the top of a peat bog, was used for building. Commonly peat sods appeared as roofing materials, and not infrequently they are laid as a coping course along the tops of walls in mountain and coastal areas. Nor is the peat confined to the uplands. Extensive tracts of lowland peat occur from Upper Lough Erne to Belcoo, and around Newtownbutler in Co. Fermanagh; there is more in the flat lands at the south-west tip of Lough Neagh and more west of the Bann a little below Coleraine. In the coastal districts of Donegal large 'beehive' stacks of peat are virtually architectural features built with their sides canted inwards like the dry stone oratories of Early Christian monasteries.

Because so many of the buildings are rendered or colourwashed, the counties do not immediately strike a visitor by the colour of their stones, except that is for north-east Derry and Tyrone, where the ubiquitous black basalt, often stained brown with iron due to humid weathering, makes an unforgettable impression. Otherwise the counties impress by their foliage. Tyrone and Fermanagh are astonishingly green, in high summer almost oppressively so, while Donegal, whose hills and tracts of bog are never far away, is coloured in the minds of most Ulstermen with the palette of Paul Henry, ochre, blue, and Vandyck brown. The building stones do however give their own colour. South Fermanagh is mainly a pale grey, even-textured limestone shading to a slatey blue or cocoa on Devenish Island, where St Mary's Abbey preserves an immaculate piece of fifteenth-century ashlar building. The old red sandstone on the eastern border of the county crops up as the dressed stone in medieval church ruins here. It is used to good purpose in the architectural parts of the Mid Georgian house of Snowhill, and Thomas Drew was historian enough to continue this mixture of limestone with sandstone dressings in his own church work in Fermanagh. In south County Tyrone, in the area of Castlecaulfield, and at Clogher the stone changes again; purplish blue on Clogher Cathedral but warm biscuit on the ashlar façade of the former bishop's palace and creamy yellow at Castlecaulfield on the late-seventeenth-century doors and on the big ashlar piers of the Mid Georgian gates. The basalts of Co. Derry have already been mentioned, but even within this hard unyielding stone variations occur. In seventeenth- and eighteenth-century walls the basalt tends to be used in big rounded lumps mixed with whatever other stones are at hand to create a richly textured surface that might delight a painter – the walls like pieces of plum cake with wide mortar joints for the dough. In the nineteenth century such soft effects were not admired and architects responded to the basalt differently. Its stones were broken and split to flattish angular faces; then built together in hard polygonal pieces with occasionally a white putty pointing to throw up the jagged pattern that was the result. Set with pale ochre Dungiven sandstone, with the brown and old red sandstone that occurs in patches on the north Derry coast, or with red or yellow brick, these hard basalt fronts of Victorian Derry and Tyrone are among the liveliest buildings, if also the most aggressive, in Ulster.

Western Derry and much of Donegal answer the hardness of the basalts with their own green schist, a beautiful building material full of hidden lights that can glisten with colour after rain like the skin of a mackerel. Like the basalt it requires a more accommodating stone for the dressed work at corners, and to frame the doors and windows. It is often found in conjunction with limestone or Dungiven sandstone dressings – green and grey, green and cream, or green and red. The coloristic effects are indeed boldly exploited on the one surviving gate tower of Richard de Burgo's early-fourteenth-century castle at Greencastle, where the old red sandstone dressings of the polygonal tower come from the Derry coast opposite. The schist breaks easily into stones of a long thin form which is its most noticeable characteristic when it is built into a wall. Coursed rubble or coursed faced rubble is the norm, in contrast to the random rubble of the basalts, and fine examples of this built with long thin fillets of stone may be seen in Old Foyle College and St Columb's College buildings in Derry, and mixed with other stone at St Eugene's Cathedral too. Once again the tendency in the nineteenth-century buildings is to be steely and hard, and if an architect wishes, the schist can be used to create aggressive polychrome effects. Near Convoy, on the river Deel, steatite is found in some quantity. It takes a fine and durable edge and can be seen still sharp and crisp at Temple Douglas Abbey. The ruined Protestant church at Dunlewey is built almost entirely of white Errigal marble, and bands of the same white marble were used prominently by Timothy Hevey on his Church of the Sacred Heart, immediately below Errigal's lower slopes.

With such hard stones predominating, ashlar building hardly appears before the nineteenth century. The exception to this rule is at Dungiven, where seams of yellow sandstone provided a tractable material, and at Devenish, which has been mentioned already. At Dungiven Priory and at Banagher Old Church areas of smooth wall were built, particularly at Banagher, where the carefully coursed square blocks of the Romanesque chancel, all of the one yellowish even-grained stone, are in sharp contrast to the irregular massive masonry of the earlier church that mixes schist, sandstone, and limestone in quite irregular shapes. Later church ruins are all rubble-built, though the plum-brown stone surrounding Donegal Bay provided an attractive material that was suited to finely calculated architectural effects, as the sedilia at Ballysaggart and the cloisters of Donegal Friary might show had they been better preserved. Seventeenth-century buildings are all rubble-built, and so too are the early Georgian mansion houses, whose façades are regularly harled or else, where the architectural display is more self-conscious as at Florence Court, rendered in cement. The first regular use of an ashlar freestone frontage occurs where the Earl Bishop set about to encase the front of Downhill about 1784 or 1785, though his garden temples and gateways, beginning with the Mussenden Temple in 1779, are all essentially ashlar work. The Bishop's stone came from quarries at Ballycastle in Co. Antrim and from Dungiven; yet when Wyatt began to build the ashlar façades of Castle Coole for Lord Belmore the stone for the building was shipped from Portland. It is today still wonderfully sharp and clean, though the moist Irish atmosphere has overlaid its surfaces with a delicate bloom of grey and carmine lichen. Portland stone was to be used again later, mixed with an Irish grey limestone, by John Bowden for his Court House in Derry.

An unusual ashlar façade, apparently built of blocks of grey slate, is that of the Regency clergy house at the top of the Diamond in Raphoe; sandstone fronts appear at a number of late Georgian gentlemen's houses. Later in the nineteenth century Thomas Turner erected two large public buildings entirely of ashlar sandstone: the town hall in Coleraine, which was to have been of local black basalt with white freestone chimneys but which was finally built entirely of a warm red sandstone; and the Northern Bank in Derry, whose façades are of an unusually warm deep yellow. Turner, who ran an office in Glasgow for ten years, may possibly have imported the stone for both buildings, a practice which was fairly common and which certainly occurred with McCarthy's first Catholic church in Derry and at the Unitarian church in Coleraine.

Stone is not the only building material of the north west. Bricks have been baked from at least the seventeenth century, with large brickworks using the Loughneagh clays around Coalisland, and others on the flat lands south of Magilligan Point. Seventeenth-century bricks line the bread ovens at Greencastle and at Mongavlin Castle in Co. Donegal, and are spectacularly displayed at Mountjoy Castle in Co. Tyrone, built in 1602, where walls of narrow Tudor bricks built into masses $2\frac{1}{2}$ ft thick tower above a basement rubble wall. Mountjoy is in the heart of the brick-making country, and nearby is an unusual early-eighteenth-century house, Rhone Hill, also brick-built and for once not rendered over but displaying its Flemish bond. More often bricks must be sought out in the basements of eighteenth-century houses, where they are frequently built into segmental vaults to support paved floors above. Many of the smaller country houses in Fermanagh and Tyrone use bricks in this way. Prehen and Creevagh, two eighteenth-century houses outside Derry city, have unusually fine brickwork inside. Culmore House by Limavady and Gortin House near Aghadowey, both in Co. Derry, are good examples of nice early-nineteenth-century country houses with simple brick exteriors. The colour varies. It is reddish in Co. Tyrone and the same shade in the eighteenth-century houses in Pump Street and Shipquay Street in Derry city. In Derry by the 1830s however the typical brick colour is a warm dark brown – well displayed in the fine terraces of Clarendon Street, Great James Street, and Queen Street; later still it becomes a soft pink, as on the Horace Street factory, which contrasts beige sandstone and green schist with its bricks. Elsewhere it can be a bright scarlet, like the interior of Porter's church at Castlerock or the Old Post Office building in Enniskillen which, to borrow a phrase from Capability Brown, sets the whole street in a fever.

THE FUTURE

Two questions which are closely allied must constantly occur to anybody who uses this book: why bother, and what hope? Irish building in the north west is rarely grand and until the early eighteenth century has rarely survived intact. Does it matter if over the next fifty years it should mostly disappear through a combination of neglect and ruthless redevelopment? To this question most people will I hope answer yes. However modest the buildings described in this volume may appear, they are the artifacts of our own history, the roots of Irish culture today. They make up the face of Ulster, combining with the landscape or with other buildings in a street to create effects that are often memorable and sometimes of great beauty. If with rare exceptions they do not measure up to the highest standards of European architecture, that is not a good argument for neglecting them or for sweeping them away.

Neglected ruins have of course a great appeal. People who like the past to be picturesque may well prefer willow-herb and ivy-covered walls to crisp repointed masonry and mown grass; but when the one remaining Norman castle in the north west is left to tumble down with exposed wall heads that small boys can prise to pieces, romantic decay has been allowed to go too far. It is also a pity that the only reinforcement the few surviving medieval and seventeenth-century traceried windows have in Co. Donegal, and in parts of Northern Ireland as well, comes from the ivy branches that so frequently engulf them. Conservation priorities ought surely to bring these buildings forward for government attention, with a modicum of reinforcement and restoration to ensure their continued existence and interest for the future. They are certainly not so common that a number should be allowed to fall down, though this is what is happening now. Candidates for attention are at Balleegham, Cookstown, Fintona, Kilmacrenan, Newtown-cunningham; and the fine lancet at Ballysaggart might also be secured. The old church at Derrygonnelly, technically under Northern Ireland Ministry of Finance surveillance, has lost first one and then both of the mullions that divided its east window into a triple ogee-headed light. They had not been replaced by 1976 simply because there is no administrative structure for the maintenance of monuments that are not wholly in the charge of the State. In the case of such ruins that have no financial value, some remedy is clearly needed.

When work on this series began, there was no official listing of buildings, other than ancient monuments, north or south of the border, and though there now is, a list alone will not in itself save buildings. There are indeed examples in the past where Ministry of Agriculture grants have been paid to remove ruins mentioned in *The Preliminary Survey of Ancient Monuments of Northern Ireland* of 1940, and other cases where an over-zealous and tidy-minded local authority has cleared away the walls of a medieval church or destroyed a seventeenth-century promontory fort. Lists alone will not stop this, nor can they combat the decay which offers the greatest threat to the surviving historic and bigger houses in these four counties. Often a family may inhabit only a few rooms; and even where a property is in reasonable repair, the increasing burden of rates and cost of maintenance must force more and more owners to leave the big house and, as many Ulster farmers have done, build a bungalow which, even if it is more convenient and cheaper to run, hardly makes the same contribution to the landscape or to the stock of Irish architecture as did the older house. If more than a small fraction of the houses mentioned in this volume are to survive, a more generous mentality will have to prevail in the mind of government, with schemes for rate relief on historic properties and grants to assist restoration. Where an owner is determined to leave a house, its potential should not be immediately destroyed, as has happened so often throughout the whole of Ireland, by the granting of planning permission for a new building fifty yards in front of the front door of the old one.

Planning authorities have also a responsibility for the character of Ulster towns and villages. This they have often failed to maintain, partly through a lax attitude to the worth of older buildings, and more importantly through an inability or at least a disinclination – so frequently the great failing in a planner – to think through the effects of their proposals in visual terms. The Co. Donegal

Planning Office in Lifford has butchered the upper windows of a good regular terraced house inconsiderately and apparently without a qualm, while road proposals and minor junction improvements have left a trail of sawn-off house ends and ugly vistas in villages throughout the four counties. New motorways in northern Ireland have in the past decade removed the pressure from many small towns; yet it is sad to note how little of their street architecture is now respected or preserved. Steel-frame windows and setting-sun doors have marred many a village street, and a doctrinaire adherence to planning standards that were designed as a guide to modern development has brought down many more rows of houses which might have been restored and replaced them either with new housing on the outskirts of the town (in which case their site becomes a car park), or else by separate units of semi-detached blocks with small gardens set back from the street, breaking the visual line. The little village of Maguires Bridge is one instance where this has recently happened; here, significantly, the best house in the place, beside the bridge, was standing empty in 1976. Responsible planning should be concerned to find a future for it.

In the larger towns, though none of these Ulster towns is very large, the problem of a decaying centre has still to be tackled properly. The destruction of large areas of nineteenth-century housing, much of it in good structural order, that has taken place in Derry in the name of improvement, and the removal even of clean industry from the city centre, is not the way to tackle urban decay. Cities should be rehabilitated, not redeveloped. Yet the straggling areas of suburban development round Derry, Enniskillen, Omagh, Dungannon, and particularly Coleraine, are proof that planning is failing increasingly to maintain the centre, though it is the centre that is vital to the architectural character of the town. In Northern Ireland the present crisis has accentuated this problem. As commerce is driven to the edges of towns the centres stagnate. But it is a problem that exists throughout the whole country. Who will live in the houses above the shops in the average Irish town in the next century, and if no one wants to, should the streets be retained and converted for other commercial uses such as offices, or may free enterprise take over to redevelop here, and punch holes there, for a petrol station or a car park? These are questions that will affect Cork, Limerick, and Waterford as much as Omagh, Enniskillen, and Derry and they must be answered soon if Ireland's finest provincial capitals are not to lose most of their architectural worth.

The banks too must be persuaded to think again. In the nineteenth century their opulent palaces were built to convince Victorian proprietors of the security of their funds. Twentieth-century man, it is argued, needs a modern equivalent to house his slender resources and is intimidated by the panoply of a classical or a Victorian Gothic front. Such is the psychology of contemporary sales techniques, which bodes ill for the future of many Irish towns. They have lost their railway stations; soon they will lose their banks. Yet people will bank whatever the building is like, and it may be questioned whether the real reason for the new buildings lies rather in the weight of modern computers and business machinery than in the aesthetics of nineteenth-century office buildings. Restoration would be a better and more responsible policy for banking houses to follow than to build anew and leave fine buildings standing empty with no apparent future.

As to churches, the Pastoral Directory of the Episcopal Liturgical Commission in 1972 reports that 'it is extremely rare to find objects of genuine artistic merit in Irish churches' and recommends the reorganization of Catholic churches for modern liturgical purposes. Such a statement seems to prejudge the value of most Catholic church fittings and threatens to destroy much that is aesthetically valuable. Many Irish Victorian churches were designed by men who had made the needs of the church their particular study, and who sought to integrate the building and its fittings into one coherent whole. Their churches are aesthetic entities and are rarely to be improved by the tamperings of a later taste. Yet the churches of all denominations are under attack from clerics who want to make their buildings modern, accessible, ordinary, and seemingly as un-special as possible.

Finally a word must be said about the materials and methods that are currently popular with builders in the north west. Tarmac and reconstituted stone walls with concrete copings, both ubiquitously present, are enemies alike to a historic and to a civilized environment. So too are the metal-frame windows with dimpled coloured glass that seem to be thought so much nicer than Georgian glazing and plain panes by many a church committee in Ulster. The electricity cables which swathe most streets would be better underground or at least off the façades, and in the Republic a stricter control might mitigate the rash of signs and billboards that disfigure many towns. No one who reads the accounts of visitors to Ireland from the seventeenth century to the present day can doubt that the picture presented by the Irish urban scene has always been a mixture of fine old buildings in decay, of modern muddle, and of modern mess. The scene does not change in its essentials; yet a historian of architecture may perhaps be permitted to hope that even in Ireland conservation policies may begin to make some headway and that the inhabitants of the country in the next century will have more than a few photographs to let them know what the Buildings of North West Ulster looked like in 1977.

FURTHER READING

Books on Irish architecture tend to be written for the country as a whole. It is therefore not always possible to give a specifically North West orientation to the list that follows. For the Early Christian and medieval periods there is a wealth of publications starting with the eighteenth- and nineteenth-century antiquarians Mervyn Archdale, Francis Grose, Edward Ledwich, George Petrie, Richard Rolt Brash, and Lord Dunraven. All their work contributed to Arthur C. Champneys' *Irish Ecclesiastical Architecture* (1910, republished 1970), which was in turn followed by Harold G. Leask's *Irish Churches and Monastic Buildings* (3 vols., 1955–60) and *Irish Castles* (1941). Art, sculpture, and architecture from the Early Christian period to the Norman Conquest is fully covered by Françoise Henry's three volumes on *Irish Art* – fifth century to 800, 800 to 1020, and 1020 to 1170 – (1965 to 1970), and there is also her helpful small monograph on *Irish High Crosses* of 1964. Roger A. Stalley's *Architecture and Sculpture in Ireland 1150–1350* (1971) is another short but useful monograph, and John Hunt's *Irish Medieval Figure Sculpture 1200–1600* offers a comprehensive study of its subject. *Images of Stone: Figure Sculpture of the Lough Erne Basin* by Helen Hickey (1976) was published too recently for the excellent accounts of pre-Christian, medieval, and modern sculpture that it contains to contribute to this volume. For figures at Boa Island, Killadeas, and White Island it is essential. Aubrey Gwynn and R. Neville Hadcock's *Medieval Religious Houses Ireland* (1970) is an authoritative account of Irish monastic establishments systematically treated as separate religious orders. The book offers invaluable reference material for the history of any monastic site, though architectural remains are not included by the authors. For the counties of Derry, Fermanagh, and Tyrone (and the rest of Northern Ireland) D. A. Chart's *Preliminary Survey of Ancient Monuments of Northern*

Ireland (1940) is full of factually accurate material, and Peter Harbison's *Guide to the National Monuments of Ireland* (1970) includes condensed notes on the principal monuments in the Republic. Both works deal with archaeological sites as well as historic buildings.

Post-medieval architecture is not so well or so systematically served. There is no Victoria County History for Ireland, no Biographical Dictionary of Irish Architects, and no equivalent of the volumes of the Royal Commission on Ancient and Historic Monuments in England, Scotland, and Wales except the Northern Ireland Government's Archaeological Survey, which has so far published only the volume on Co. Down. Most general works, like the five volumes of the *Georgian Society Records* (1909–13, reprinted in 1969), deal principally with architecture in the South – the first four volumes of the *Georgian Records* are indeed confined to Dublin city – and there is as yet no book that covers Irish classical architecture as a whole, beyond the discussion in Maurice Craig's now celebrated *Dublin 1660–1860; a Social and Architectural History* (1952), which necessarily concentrates on the capital. Two recent surveys of Irish houses and churches are Brian de Breffny and Rosemary Ffolliott, *The Houses of Ireland*, and Brian de Breffny and George Mott, *The Churches and Abbeys of Ireland*: well illustrated though wilful. Dr Maurice Craig's *Classic Irish Houses of the Middle Size* (1976) treats the minor country house in Ireland from the seventeenth century to 1835.

The reader who wishes further to extend his acquaintance with Irish building after 1600 must therefore go to many of the same sources that have been used for this volume. For the seventeenth century there is D. A. Chart's publication of the survey and maps of the London Companies' Plantation submitted to Charles I by Sir Thomas Phillips, published in 1928 under the title *Londonderry and the London Companies 1609–1629*. George Hill's *Historical Account of the Plantation in Ulster* (1872) contains the full text of Nicholas Pynnar's *Survey of the escheated counties of Ulster* made between 1618 and 1619, and the Statistical Surveys of Irish Counties published in 1802 – George V. Sampson, *Londonderry*, James MacParland, *Donegal*, and John McEvoy, *Tyrone* – give a vivid impression of Irish life at the opening of the nineteenth century, though not much architectural information. More use can be made of the two eighteenth-century Irish road books. First is Taylor and Skinner's *Maps of the Roads of Ireland Surveyed in 1777*, which prints the names of country-house and estate proprietors beside the roads shown and sometimes gives an indication of the scale of a building in diagrammatic form. The second publication, W. Wilson's *Post-Chaise Companion or Travellers Directory through Ireland* (1786 and later editions), is sometimes more informative as it has short written descriptions and contains houses that do not appear in Taylor and Skinner. It also plagiarizes large sections of Arthur Young's *Tour in Ireland* of 1776 which contains more architectural comment than the majority of eighteenth-century tours of the country.

For the early nineteenth century there are two indispensable guides: Samuel Lewis's *Topographical Dictionary of Ireland* of 1837 and *The Parliamentary Gazetteer of Ireland* of 1846. Both are arranged alphabetically and treat of towns, villages, and parishes with occasionally some detail on parish churches, ancient monuments, local history, and country seats. Directories can also be useful as sources for building history and for architects. Pigot and Co.'s *City of Dublin and Hibernian Provincial Directory* of 1824 contains entries on many small towns, as does Slater's *Irish Directory* of 1848. There are of course many more; and W. T. Pike & Co.'s *Belfast and the Province of Ulster at the Opening of the 20th century* (1909), in which the architectural descriptions are written by the architect Robert Young, is valuable for the accounts it contains of many country estates.

A mass of information is contained in the form of articles in journals and magazines. Among those that have been read for this volume are *The Dublin Penny Journal* (1832–6), which has articles on ancient monuments and country houses, both often in better repair then than now. The short-lived *Irish Penny Journal* (1840–1) is similar. British architectural journals that have an Irish content are *The Builder* (1843 on) and *The Architect* (1869) and *Building News* (1854–7). In 1859 *The Dublin Builder*, which soon changed its name to *The Irish Builder*, started publication. It is the principal source of information for Victorian and Edwardian architecture throughout the country. From its beginning in 1898 the pages of *Country Life* have carried articles on Irish houses and towns – usually their Georgian aspects.

Antiquarian articles of the greatest value are in the *Journal of the Kilkenny Archaeological Society* (later the *Journal of the Royal Society of Antiquaries in Ireland*) and in the excellent *Ulster Journal of Archaeology*. There is too the *County Donegal Historical Society Journal*, publishing from 1947.

Among the town histories mention must be made of Gilbert Camblin's *The Town in Ulster* (1951), a pioneering work that traces the development of Ulster towns from the seventeenth century down to the present day. Of the older histories of individual towns the first is the single volume produced by Colonel Colby's Ordnance Survey of Ireland on *The Parish of Templemore in County Londonderry* (1835) – in fact devoted to a history of the city. The Royal Engineers under Colby collected much manuscript material on other Irish parishes and counties – notably Donegal, Derry, and Antrim – and though this was never published the memoirs remain with the Royal Irish Academy in Dublin. Other town histories are: Robert Simpson's *Annals of Derry* (1847); W. C. Trimble's excellent three-volume *History of Enniskillen* (1919–21); Hugh Allingham's *Ballyshannon; its history and antiquities* (1879); and J. J. Marshall's *History of Dungannon* (1929). Marshall was a prolific local historian whose specialized small books on South East Tyrone include histories of the villages of Aughnacloy, Benburb, Clogher, Caledon, Charlemont, and Mountjoy Forest. H. P. Swan in Donegal did a similar job for the Inishowen Peninsula with *The Book of Inishowen* (1938), *Romantic Inishowen* (1947), and *Twixt Foyle and Swilly* (1949), the last a collection of essays on antiquities, place names, and folk lore of considerable charm. In church history one name stands out, that of the Rev. James B. Leslie, whose studies on the clergy and parishes of the dioceses of *Armagh* (1911 and 1949), *Clogher* (1929), and *Derry* (1937) contain brief but thoroughly researched articles of a factual sort on the Church of Ireland buildings in each parish. More recently Mr Douglas Scott-Richardson has made a study of the development of the Gothic Revival in Ireland as a doctoral thesis for Yale University. His findings have contributed to parts of this volume. Modern stained glass is covered concisely in James White and Michael Wynne, *Irish Stained Glass* (1963).

Recently a number of guides to Irish architecture have appeared. *Ireland Observed* by Maurice Craig and the Knight of Glin (1970) is much the most generous in its treatment of post-medieval architecture, combining an attractive visual anthology with much useful information. *The Shell Guide to Ireland* by Lord Killanin and Michael Duignan (1961 and 1967) offers plenty of historical material and is an excellent reference guide, though its architectural descriptions are perfunctory and rarely distinguish between ruins where there is something to see and ruins where there is not. The old extra illustrated Automobile Association *Road Book of Ireland* of 1962 is also useful, as is L. Russell Muirhead's *Blue Guide to Ireland* of the same year. Finally, tribute must be paid to the work of the Ulster Architectural Heritage

Society. Founded in 1967 to encourage an interest in Ulster buildings and to campaign for their proper protection, the society, in
advance of government listing, began publishing lists of its own
of historic buildings, groups of buildings, and areas of architectural importance in Ulster towns and parishes. In many instances
its lists overlap with the material in this volume. The account of
the development of Londonderry first appeared in the U.A.H.S.
list for the *City of Derry* in 1973. Other lists are published for
Dungannon and Cookstown, Coleraine and Portstewart, Enniskillen,
and *North Derry* (all areas that appear in this volume) as well as
for other Ulster towns, and there is also a series of hardback mono-
graphs. Four of these are directly relevant to North West Ulster:
C. E. B. Brett's *Court Houses and Market Houses of the Province
of Ulster* (1973); Peter Rankin's *Irish Building Ventures of the Earl
Bishop of Derry* (1972); Homan Potterton's *Irish Church Monuments 1570–1880* (1975); and Jeanne Sheehy's *J. J. McCarthy and
the Gothic Revival in Ireland* (1977). All these publications may
be obtained from the society's office at 181a Stranmillis Road, Belfast.

VERNACULAR HOUSING IN NORTH WEST
ULSTER
BY ALAN GAILEY

The buildings noticed elsewhere in this volume have some
claim – even if occasionally a modest one – to be considered as architecture; the majority of structures in the four counties, however,
fall into a variety of regional vernacular categories. Vernacular
here means the ordinary buildings of the Irish countryside, erected
within the limits of indigenous traditions which changed slowly
until at least the mid nineteenth century. Local designers, using
locally available materials, knew almost intuitively what their local
clients required; indeed designers, builders, and clients were often
one and the same. It is obvious that many rural buildings throughout Ulster are not the work of specialist craftsmen – one reason
among many why few vernacular houses earlier than the late eighteenth century have survived. In a situation where landlord and
tenant relations were often poor, the ordinary folk of the countryside were discouraged from expending much effort in providing

themselves with substantially constructed homes; so that it is more difficult to define what is representative among surviving buildings of any one period than it is at the level of formal architecture.

The case of the one-roomed cottage may make this point. Generally it is associated with the landless cottier population that rose to numerical importance between about 1740 and the period of the Great Famine of the 1840s. The first detailed census of housing in Ireland, taken in 1841, records a great many one-roomed dwellings in parishes all over Ulster; but almost all of these diminutive homes have now disappeared, and we have no way of telling whether the old, thatched, single-storey houses still common in the countryside, and popularly referred to as 'traditional' houses, were inhabited only by cottiers or by other classes as well.

Fortunately, such historical problems do not concern us here. Sufficient is known to recognize that the traditions of rural housing, even that constructed as relatively recently as the mid nineteenth century, go back at least to the late seventeenth century and fairly certainly to about 1600. The generalities of plan types, construction, and local variation are well known and differences can easily be identified.

All vernacular houses in Ulster have some things in common. All are single-storeyed, or have grown (usually in the nineteenth century) from one storey to two. All are one room deep, with the exception that quite often in the later nineteenth century one or more rooms were divided parallel to the long axis of the house, to form front and rear apartments. All have the main kitchen hearth, and usually all other hearths, along the long axis of the structure, and all chimneys are sited on the roof ridge. Windows in gable walls at ground-floor level are rare, and often not part of the original design. Finally, and most importantly, in all vernacular houses the main entrance (or sometimes, for example often in west Donegal, opposite entrances in front and rear walls) is either at the other end of the kitchen from the main hearth – this type predominates in most of our four counties – or beside the hearth, in which case a small screen wall between the two, parallel with the front wall of the house, forms an entrance lobby. It follows that from outside either plan type may normally be identified easily – even in structures that have grown complex through time – by looking at the relationship between the principal door and the main hearth chimneystack.

Houses vary in size from a single room (e.g. Meenagarragh, fig.

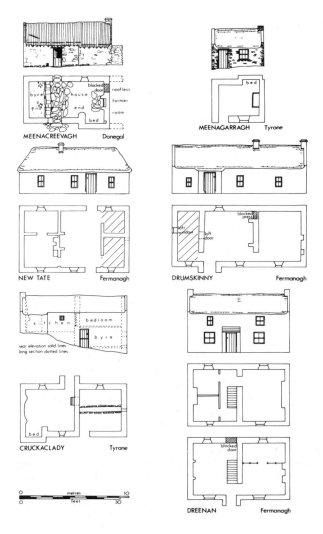

Fig. 1

1) to three or more units (Drumskinny, fig. 1), some of which may be longitudinally divided (New Tate, fig. 1). Survivals of the smallest houses are few, even though on the eve of the Great Famine they were in the majority in some areas, especially in west Donegal, where many took the form of the combined byre and dwelling, the ends open to each other (Meenacreevagh, fig. 1). There seems to have been a greater tendency for opposed entrances in these western areas, including west Fermanagh, whereas most of the houses of this type in Tyrone had but a single door leading into the kitchen from without. Lofted ends were common (New Tate and Drumskinny, fig. 1) and became commoner as the nineteenth century progressed. In the latter half of that century and the early years of this one many houses were enlarged to full two-storey status (Dreenan, fig. 1). Others became two-storey only in part; a fine example is preserved at Dergalt, near Strabane, in the homestead of the forbears of Woodrow Wilson. Today more of the houses of this type remain; the single-storey thatched houses are fast disappearing, deserted in favour of modern bungalows and villas of suburban style, much less in sympathy with their environments.

Two features deserve special mention, for they hark back to earlier forms. Firstly, throughout Donegal, almost all of Derry, north and west Tyrone, and the extreme north-western margins of Fermanagh, many vernacular dwellings include a nook in one corner of the kitchen, almost always beside the fire. Projecting outwards on the rear wall from the basic rectangle of the house, this 'outshot', known in Gaelic as *cailleach* or *cúilteach*, accommodates a bed which traditionally was reserved for the older generation (Meenacreevagh, Meenagarragh, Cruckaclady, fig. 1). By day the bed was usually screened from view with curtains or, less commonly, with timber doors. Sometimes the recess was deepened by a small wall projecting into the kitchen from the rear (Cruckaclady, fig. 1) which also carried the rear end of the roof truss spanning the kitchen. Some bed recesses in west and north Donegal do not constitute outshots, being achieved by building the requisite length of the rear wall thinner than usual. It has been possible to interpret references in early Irish documents as descriptions of forerunners of the outshot. It is not a peculiarly Irish feature; direct counterparts occur in the vernacular housing traditions of Scotland, Wales, the north of England perhaps, and elsewhere in north-west Europe. In Ireland they are confined to the north-west (fig. 2), so rigidly as to represent a distribution broadly complementary to that of the screen wall between entrance and hearth

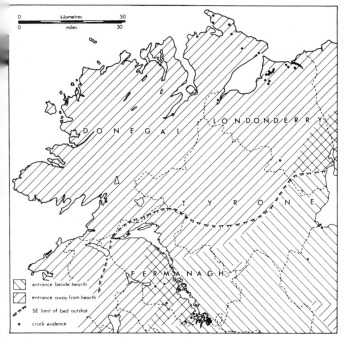

entrance beside hearth
entrance away from hearth
SE limit of bed outshot
cruck evidence

Fig. 2

which is an essential feature of the lobby-entrance house described below.

The other characteristic feature, now almost confined to ruined
dwellings in west and north Donegal, is the combination of un-
partitioned quarters for people and cattle under a single roof
(Meenacreevagh, fig. 1). Byre-dwellings were usually characterized by opposed entrances, the space between them often
flagged because of the cattle entering by either door. Demarcation
between the ends of the house was usually indicated by a stone-
lined drain to remove liquid manure through an opening low down
in one wall, set to the animals' side of the flagged path between
the doors. Ruined remains of these dwellings are now confined
to the far north-west, but oral traditions of their existence are
common more widely, and it is clear that they formerly represented the norm throughout most of our area. Houses like the

Dreenan one (fig. 1), albeit originally constructed as two-storey farmhouses with separate external provision for the accommodation of cattle, are descendants of the byre-dwelling, retaining the centrally situated opposed doorways and the kitchen hearth placed at one gable. A nineteenth-century adaptation of the type is represented by the Cruckaclady house (fig. 1), where the byre was still under the same roof as the living quarters, but now placed under a bedroom, an arrangement possible only on steeply sloping sites. Such houses have been discovered in two areas: in west Tyrone, especially in the lower end of the Glenelly Valley, and in west Donegal. It is unlikely that sites like this were used until population pressure pushed poor farmers into marginal hill land after the late eighteenth century.

The distributional contrast between these north-western vernacular dwellings and the lobby-entrance houses of central, eastern, and southern Ireland is strong. It can easily be observed in travelling across our area from south-east to north-west either over the Glenshane Pass in south Derry, or by the Dungannon–Omagh route by Ballygawley in Tyrone (fig. 2). Transition from one style to the other is usually sharp, especially in Tyrone, but in south Derry, and again in west Fermanagh, there are areas where the two coexist, and where some hybrids have been discovered (fig. 3). Detailed examination of the latter shows that they evolved from encroachment of the lobby-entrance type at the expense of the north-western vernacular model, but the rate at which this change took place is unknown; almost certainly it was very slow.

Lobby-entrance houses are restricted to south and east Tyrone, south-east Derry, and east and south Fermanagh, with a few outlying examples in north Derry. They are usually gabled, although hipped and half-hipped examples occur in south-west Fermanagh, representing the form more commonly known in Leinster. They are usually slightly larger than the vernacular houses of the north and west, and upper floors and lofted areas tend to be commoner. A single entrance is usual; rear entrances in the Drumduff and Killycolpy houses (fig. 4) may merely represent influence from the north-western type. However, in the later part of the nineteenth century and more recently, the insertion of rear doors was not unusual, the secondary nature of which is usually apparent.

The screen wall necessary in this kitchen arrangement, placed between door and hearth, is usually known in rural Ulster as the 'jamb wall', and is normally provided with a small 'spy' window,

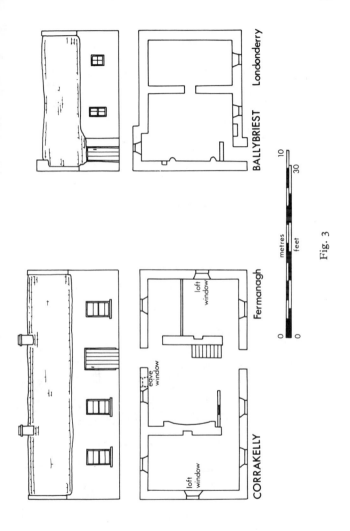

Fig. 3

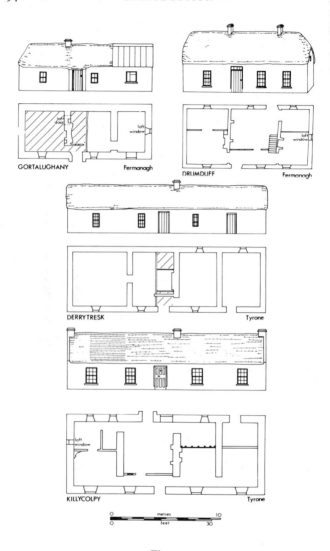

GORTALUGHANY   Fermanagh

DRUMDUFF   Fermanagh

DERRYTRESK   Tyrone

KILLYCOLPY   Tyrone

Fig. 4

probably originally to admit light to the hearth area from the open door. A window in the rear wall lighting the hearth is uncommon. In some old examples, especially in east Tyrone, the jamb wall supported a beam spanning the kitchen, which itself carried the outer edge of the chimney hood. Probably the jamb wall evolved from the simple extension of the side of the chimney hood nearest the door down to ground level. It compares with the 'heck' of many British vernacular houses of lobby-entrance plan. Some old linen weavers' houses in south-east Tyrone had the areas to either side of the chimney hood, and above the transverse beam, boarded to form small lofts or wings, and lofts over hearth areas have also been noted in west Fermanagh. It will readily be appreciated that the lobby-entrance arrangement, involving a sharp turn on coming through the door, is so ill-adapted to the problem of turning a four-legged beast like the cow that derivation from byre-dwelling prototypes is virtually impossible. Lobby-entrance houses represent a different tradition, characteristic of southern and eastern Ireland, a distribution that prompts a search for antecedents perhaps in Britain. Similar houses were coming into existence in parts of western Britain by the late sixteenth and early seventeenth centuries, but whether their appearance in Ireland was due to a direct transference then, or occurred independently but was based upon evolution from some ancestor common to both Britain and Ireland at an earlier period, cannot be said. For reasons based on evidence outside our four counties, the latter proposition is more attractive. Certainly the type has existed in north-west Ireland for some considerable time. On the margins of its distribution in Fermanagh, at Carrickreagh near Ely Lodge, there is a substantial house with this kitchen arrangement, reputedly built for or by a Cromwellian soldier. Its English origin is highlighted by a brick-lined oven placed to one side of the kitchen hearth, for such ovens are rare in Ulster, always occurring in the context of English settlement. The only other example so far identified in our area was in Newlands Cottage in Erganagh Glebe townland to the north of Omagh, although of course non-vernacular examples of built-in ovens are found in some Plantation castles. By contrast, both types of vernacular housing in the four counties are dominated by an ovenless hearth, where baking was done on the griddle or heated hearth-stone, and cooking in pots suspended over or set in the fire, facts reflected in the nature of traditional bread types, including the thin oatcake or oaten bread, known also in Scotland and the north of England, and surely related to the thin, long-keeping breads of northern Europe.

Nineteenth-century development of the lobby-entrance arrangement often involved extension of the jamb wall across the kitchen to form a front passage, or longitudinally placed 'hall' (e.g. Drumduff and Killycolpy, fig. 4), from which stairs to an upper floor (when this was inserted) almost always rose. A less common arrangement, seen in the high limestone plateau to the north of Cuilcagh Mountain for example, dispenses with the passage-like front 'hall', and had stairs rising through a dog-leg bend in one corner of the kitchen. Lofts or upper floors, and often extensive longitudinal subdivision of the basic units of the dwelling, were common in the nineteenth century (Killycolpy, fig. 4), but in the four counties considered in this book, upward extension of lobby-entrance houses to two-storey status was rarer than, for example, in Co. Monaghan.

Superimposed upon the fundamental distinction of plan type, other regional variations may easily be distinguished. Local geological patterns are reflected in the stones used in vernacular buildings as much as in more formal architecture; but if the granites of Donegal, the basalts of parts of north Derry, or the limestones of much of Fermanagh are often to be identified, their detection depends upon the texture of the stonework more than upon the colouring, because the use of whitewash – or of earthen or sand and lime plastering – everywhere imposes a degree of uniformity. Dressed stonework is rare, except about Slieve Beagh on the borders of Tyrone, Monaghan, and Fermanagh. Even coursed worked stone is rare, although coursed rubble is common and random rubble is especially characteristic in the schists and other platy stones of the Sperrins and parts of east Donegal.

White lime-wash accumulated over the years, whether over a skin of plaster or not, subdues the texture of many kinds of stonework. It can conceal too the use of another material, the 'mud' wall, found especially in east Tyrone in the lowland area lying to the west of Lough Neagh and along the Blackwater. The use of solid earth walling, known in parts of England as 'cob', but widely in Ireland as a mud wall, is virtually confined to vernacular building. Mud houses were by no means inferior to stone ones. Many were long-lasting, and, when adequately maintained, were warm, dry, and comfortable. The usual mode of construction involved a course or two of rubble stonework laid direct on the ground surface, upon which the clay, duly worked by trampling, and tempered with chopped straw or rushes, and sometimes animal hair, was laid in layers about eighteen inches thick, until wall heads some six to seven feet high had been attained. The triangular parts of gables and partition walls were sometimes also worked in the same material, but layers of earthen sods laid brick-wise were often substituted. The use of earth walling was not confined to rural areas. Some Ulster towns and villages had rows of small thatched houses constructed in the same manner. A second common material was sod or turf (*scragh*). Surviving now usually in association with other materials, as in clay-walled houses, there is much evidence that sod was used on its own, probably with some system of crude timber framing, to construct many of the houses of the poor in the eighteenth and nineteenth centuries. Occasionally, too, wattle-work has been found, usually in interior, non-load-bearing partition walls.

Brick, fired locally, was widely employed, except in much of Co. Donegal. It was commonly used for external chimneys, and for internal chimney canopies, which often replaced clay and wattle hoods, and this was probably the earliest vernacular use of brick. Thinner, slightly wider bricks indicate that these chimneys could be as early as the latter part of the eighteenth century, but the later 9 in × 4 in × 3 in brick, which is often superimposed, betrays a nineteenth-century alteration and the raising of the roof level, sometimes associated with a change from thatch to slate or, later, to corrugated metal sheeting. Local brick is still commonly encountered in old dwellings in east Tyrone, much of Fermanagh, especially near Lisnaskea and Newtownbutler, and again near the Arney River in the west of the county, in parts of the Mourne–Foyle basin, and in north Derry, where the Myroe brickfields produced materials widely used at vernacular and formal levels. Locally fired roofing tiles have been found in only two places, near Bellaghy in east Derry and near Florence Court in west Fermanagh, significantly restricted to farm outhouses, as if the builders, having little experience of their use, did not trust them for their dwellings. An interesting localized feature survives in the south-western quarter of Fermanagh, where many farmhouses had their kitchen floors laid with locally produced, hollow, fired tiles during the nineteenth century. Insulated flooring like this was used nowhere else in the north of Ireland.

Thatch, made of a wide variety of materials, usually covered the roof. Most recently the golden colour of new wheat straw, which later mellows to a duller grey/fawn, has been common, except in parts of east and north Donegal, where the silver-grey of weathered flax thatch further distinguishes the fine texture of that material when compared with the coarser appearance of wheat or barley straw. In some coastal districts – west Donegal near

Dungloe, Bunbeg and Derrybeg, and again in the Magilligan district in north Derry – another, finer textured material is still used:
'bent' (marram) grass pulled or cut on the sand hills, and always
held in place on the roof by a network of ropes tied to pegs driven
into the wall heads and gables. Other materials formerly used,
sometimes as substitutes for good straw (necessitated either by
seasonal shortages or by the poverty of the house occupiers), were
bracken, the waste product from flax scutching, and even potato
haulms. Heather, widely employed elsewhere in Europe, does not
seem to have been used in Ulster after the eighteenth or early
nineteenth century, before which there are references to its use
on church roofs. Remains of thatched roofs have been found, however, in west Donegal, where heather was used as an underthatch
on a layer of sods or turf.

Regardless of the technique employed, an underthatch of turf
or sods seems generally to have been used. This was laid either
in strips running from eave to ridge where the front and rear strips
overlapped, or in the form of large rectangular overlapping slabs,
rather like enormous slates. Thatchers sometimes say that the sod
underthatch retains the ends of the bent pliable wooden pins,
called 'scollops', which serve to hold the thatch on the roof in
the commonest technique found widely in Derry, Tyrone, Fermanagh, and east Donegal. Yet similar underthatch is just as
normal under the roped thatch in west Donegal, where this
explanation cannot hold good. Furthermore, buildings have been
found elsewhere in Ireland which had an underthatch of straw
roped to the roof timbers. It is best, therefore, to view the use
of sod underthatch as a survival from older housing traditions
where sod was the only roof covering employed, a view that fits
well with other evidence for the consistent use of sod as a building
material in its own right in the past.

In scollop thatching the pins are usually exposed only at the
ridge of the roof. The thatcher begins at the eave, but each scollop,
placed over the upper end of a bundle of straw, is concealed by
the lower portion of the succeeding bundle. Therefore scollops
are exposed only close to the ridge of the roof, where additional
strengthening pins are usually inserted, and also often on the surface of the roof above the eaves. On hipped and half-hipped roofs
in south Fermanagh additional strengthening scollops appear on
the roof surface sometimes at the hip angles, showing that here
also, as at eave and ridge, the thatched roof is most vulnerable
to wind damage. Scollops will sometimes be found all over a
thatched roof surface, which usually betrays extensive repair of

the roof, but occasionally some thatchers purposely left them exposed.

Roped thatch was confined to localities where the possibility of wind damage was greatest, especially along the western and northern coasts of Donegal and in the Magilligan district in north Derry: however, it was normal as far inland as the Blue Stack Mountains. The pattern constituted by the thatch ropes on houses in west Donegal was dominated by transverse elements, across the roof ridge, the ends of the ropes usually being tied to stone 'pegs' built into the wall heads (Meenacreevagh, fig. 1). By contrast, the north Derry tradition demanded as many ropes laid longitudinally as transversely over any area of thatch surface, to give a strictly gridded effect. In both cases the use of the roping technique is clearly associated with a well-rounded, almost 'whalebacked' ridge, quite unlike the sharply defined ridge associated with scollop thatch.

The external roof form reflects, of course, timbering underneath. The rounded ridges in roped thatch areas are achieved by means of 'couple' trusses (i.e. principal rafter trusses) resting on the wall heads. The principal rafters, however, do not meet at the apex, but are joined by a yoke, a horizontal member perhaps one to three feet long, parallel to the collar beam that ties the principals at a lower level. The back of the yoke supports the ridge purlin. Where the rounded ridge predominates, a kitchen usually has at least one, often two, and sometimes three trusses of this kind, although other rooms are not always roofed in this way, having the spans between partition and gable walls traversed only by a series of closely spaced purlins.

Principal rafter trusses are similarly characteristic of scollop thatched roofs with well defined ridges, but the principal members of the trusses often cross, as in houses in south Fermanagh, or may at most be joined by a diminutive yoke, sufficiently long only to form a cradle, together with the projecting ends of the principal members themselves, to hold a fairly heavy ridge purlin in place. This kind of truss commonly survives in old houses in much of Tyrone, Derry, and east Fermanagh.

An alternative system that dispenses with roof trusses altogether is confined to the south-eastern part of our area. In east and south-east Tyrone, where many houses were constructed of earth walls, roofs are carried on heavy longitudinal purlins alone, their ends bedded in the gable and internal partition walls. In some weavers' houses spans in excess of eighteen feet were covered. Purlin-borne roofs were well suited to clay buildings, for the weight and thrust were transmitted through the purlin ends embedded in the walls into downward compressive forces that served to compact the wall material.

The opposite of the purlin-borne roof is the cruck truss, an archaic constructional system that has recently been discovered in a very few houses in north-east Donegal, north Derry, and south-west Fermanagh. An isolated example exists in south Derry. Beyond our area there is another near Toome Bridge in west Antrim, and there are more in north Armagh (fig. 2). Cruck trusses, involving timber blades that may be continuous or composite, in the latter case each consisting of a wall-post scarfed to a principal rafter, rise from or close to ground level to support the ridge and bear the weight and thrust of the roof independently of the side walls. These crucks are related to similar features in western and northern Britain. They have usually been found in buildings whose walls, built of stone, could well have supported the roof with the more conventional 'couple' (principal rafter) trusses already described. As discovered the Ulster crucks are thus anachronistic and must hark back to a time when houses were normally constructed of materials inherently incapable of load-bearing, perhaps sods, turf, or wattle-work. The distribution of discoveries of this feature on Fig. 2 is clearly just that. It does not represent a realistic view of the former existence of the cruck truss. Many more examples will be discovered elsewhere in Ireland. Perhaps the best examples of scarfed, composite-bladed cruck trusses known in Ulster are in the fine thatched house, built in 1691, preserved by the National Trust at Liffock in Co. Derry. Other examples have been dated, like the Liffock house, by means of dendrochronology to the later part of the seventeenth century, including a house now in ruins at Pottagh, also in north Derry, to about 1665. Another house with datable oak timbering (but not crucks) is in the village of Coagh, Co. Tyrone; it was constructed about 1697. If these dates suggest that few if any vernacular houses will be discovered that antedate the turbulent events of mid-seventeenth-century Ulster history, they clearly show that the traditions current until within the present century extend back to at least that period.

Vernacular houses in the four counties are usually gabled, often with gable chimneys. In south-west Fermanagh many houses had hipped or half-hipped ends, while in south-east Fermanagh slated vernacular houses were sometimes half-hipped, giving a distinctive local style, some examples of which may be seen alongside the main Clogher Valley road near Brookeborough.

Only a few of the thatched hipped houses remain (New Tate, fig. 1; Gortalughany and Drumduff, fig. 4); a good example stands on the roadside west of Florence Court at Wheathill.

Gables are treated in two ways. In north Derry, where surviving examples are clustered in the Magilligan area, the thatch is carried out over the skews to overlap the upper edges of the gable itself, so that the facade view reveals none of the gable stonework. Elsewhere a stone edge one-third to half the thickness of the gable wall is left exposed with a step in the skews into which the thatch is bedded. A coping of mortar, or more recently of cement, caps the stonework and is brought to overlap the surface of the thatch by up to six inches. Although the ground-floor level of a gable wall is seldom pierced by windows or doors, small windows set high in the gable ends of houses are common in many parts of Ulster, where the lofting inside was used for sleeping accommodation. The existence or lack of a gable hearth will of course affect the position of these upper lights. Paired windows here may mean that the lofted area has been divided into front and rear portions, though this is not an absolute rule. Gable chimneys need to be interpreted with caution. If smoke is issuing, obviously there must be a hearth below; but houses have been discovered, especially in the east of our area, where dummy chimneys, usually on gables, have been added – to judge from brick sizes normally in the nineteenth century – to give the house a balanced and possibly a more 'genteel' appearance.

Door and window styles are usually modest, sometimes showing ideas borrowed from formal architecture. Panelled doors are mostly confined to more prosperous farmhouses (e.g. Killycolpy, fig. 4), and occasionally eighteenth-century doors can be found. Fanlights are commoner than three-quarter side-lights. Both derive from Georgian styles and were being built into farmhouses until late in the nineteenth century. Older farmhouse doors are usually boarded vertically on three transverse battens on the inside. The wider the boards, usually the older the door. Houses of the smaller farmers and of cottiers or other landless rural dwellers often also had a half-door, hung outside the full kitchen door, so that during daylight hours light and air could be admitted while keeping farmyard animals and fowls at bay. Such half-doors are by no means ubiquitous, and true half-doors, of lower and upper portions, are rarely encountered. The idea was probably borrowed from the stable-yard doors of landed estates, and as used in farmhouses may be no older than the nineteenth century. In some poorer houses, even as late as the mid nineteenth century, there were no properly carpentered doors – only removable hurdles of wattle-work; though evidence for this is solely documentary and no examples have been found in Ulster in recent times.

Window styles vary from two-sash lights, each sash consisting of a single large pane, which are of recent origin, to two-sash lights, each sash having six (occasionally eight) small panes arranged in two rows of three (or four), in the Georgian fashion. Upper floors in two-storey vernacular houses are often lighted by similar windows, either full size, or reduced by the omission of one row of panes from one sash. These older styles of multi-paned openings were still occasionally being built into new dwellings as late as about 1900. Stylistically intermediate between them and the more recent single- and double-paned sashes are four-paned lights of two sashes, each having two horizontal panes one above the other. They obviously evolved simply by the omission of the vertical glazing bars of the Georgian style. In many farmhouses a more recent style characterizes the front of the house, and an older one has been left at the rear, often facing into the farmyard.

It can be difficult to accept that some country houses today truly belong to a vernacular tradition. All too often they are cluttered with discordant flat-roofed porches at front and rear; their outer surfaces are bespattered with modern harling or, worse, with 'decorative' pebbledashing; their thatched roofs are replaced with corrugated metal or asbestos sheeting, sometimes simply laid over the old material. Often chimneys have been rebuilt in modern rustic-finished bricks or other materials, and metal-framed windows of proportions and styles inconsistent with rural housing have been inserted. Yet the vernacular ancestry of these 'modernized' houses is usually unmistakable, even from a cursory inspection of the façade, noting the relationships between main entrance and kitchen hearth, and between length and width of the main rectangular outline of the building, excluding added porches. Many would argue, and with justification, that these recent changes have destroyed the fitness of the older houses for their immediate surroundings. A design dilemma remains to be resolved, between aesthetic fitness and modern living standards – witness the ever-growing encroachment of suburban bungalows and villas into rural settings, a trend that is growing everywhere and seems now, particularly in north-west Donegal, to be regrettably uncontrolled.

Further Reading

There is no general book on Ulster or Irish vernacular housing, or, indeed, dealing with vernacular buildings of any kind. Useful introductions are contained in the relevant chapters of E. Estyn Evans's *Irish Folk Ways* (1957) and *Irish Heritage* (1942), and an interesting, mainly pictorial overview, dealing with housing, is Kevin Danaher's *Ireland's Vernacular Architecture* (1975). Serious study of Irish vernacular housing commenced during the 1930s. A bibliography of some ninety items now exists, mainly studies of specialized aspects in different areas, published in local historical, archaeological, and folklife journals, of which more than half have appeared during the last twenty years. Articles of Ulster interest regularly appear in the Ulster Folk and Transport Museum's annual journal *Ulster Folklife*.

NORTH WEST ULSTER

★

A low-lying rural parish on the w bank of the River Bann.

ST GUARIE, AGHADOWEY PARISH CHURCH (C of I). Built
  c. 1760 and rebuilt by the Earl Bishop with a tower and spire
  in 1797. The spire, struck by lightning in 1826, was taken down,
  and *c.* 1850 the nave gained a Dec chancel and robing room by
  Joseph Welland. Built of rubble basalt with sandstone trim; the
  body of the church of roughly squared blocks. Each part typical
  of its date, but note the mustachioed king as a corbel stop to
  the door moulding.
    The WAR MEMORIAL OBELISK, 20 ft high, is by *J. Robin-
  son.* It cost £700 in 1921.
CHURCH OF OUR LADY OF THE ASSUMPTION, at Agivey,
  3 km E. 1898. A big hall-church in squared rubble basalt, with
  lancets and polygonal apse. Elaborate double pitched pine ceiling and trusses inside. Fine.
AGHADOWEY PRESBYTERIAN CHURCH. Congregation
  founded 1655. This church, a five-bay gabled hall of two
  storeys, looks about 1840.
ST MARGARET'S RECTORY. A waywardly irregular Regency
  house with square and canted bays. Two storeys with Y-traceried windows. Curiously pretty.
AGHADOWEY OLD GLEBE HOUSE. 1791–4, built by Sir Henry
  Hervey Bruce, Bt, for £1,756. A plain Georgian two-storey
  house. Three-bay front; five-bay back.
LIZARD MANOR. 3 km NE. Built *c.* 1860 by the Ironmongers'
  Company for their agent, Sir James Strong. The company's
  crest is a lizard: hence the name. A big stucco house with timber
  corbel brackets to the eaves and canted bay-windows on the
  side elevations.
GORTIN HOUSE. 2.5 km SE. Built about 1830; a neat crisp brick
  house with a high hipped roof that overhangs the eaves, and
  double chimneystacks.
BOVAGH HOUSE. 3.5 km SE. A robust mid Georgian house built
  c. 1750 by the agents for the Marquess of Waterford and looking

a little like an American colonial design. A five-bay, two-storey front, breaking forward in the central bay with a Palladian window on the first floor surmounted by a pediment-shaped gable, filled with a small semicircular lunette. The door with side lights and a wide segmental fanlight is a later alteration. Nice stone eaves cornice. Inside, egg and dart plasterwork, a solid Georgian stair, lugged door surrounds, and five-panel doors.

MONEYDIG PRESBYTERIAN CHURCH. 5 km SE. 1836. A gabled four-bay hall given a cut-price cinema front to celebrate its centenary in 1936 – vertical strips of mannerist cement and futuristic acroteria!

BALLYLAGGAN REFORMED PRESBYTERIAN CHURCH. 5 km NE. A gabled hall of 1840.

F10   AGHALANE CASTLE   FM

On a hillock E of the road by the Woodford River, just before the border with Co. Cavan, the remains of a Plantation bawn built before 1619 by Thomas Crichton and abandoned about 1700. The walls, very much overgrown with brambles and ivy, stand to about 8 or 10 ft. The enclosure is about 30 ft wide, with two round flankers, 12 ft in diameter with walls 4 ft thick, on the S side. There are diamond- and cross-shaped gun loops as well as the more normal rectangular openings.

The Crichtons moved from here to Crom Castle on the opposite side of Upper Lough Erne. For Crom church, NNE on this side of the lough, *see* Crom.

AGHALURCHER *see* LISNASKEA

J7   ANNAGHMORE   TY

ST COLMCILLE. A big church, unusually ambitious, rising up entirely alone in the flat bog-land below Coalisland and Lough Neagh. Chunky late C19 Gothic in painted stucco. Eight-bay hall of tall paired lancets. Short chancel and nice thin geometrical traceried window. Clean and airy inside, with braced portal trusses and hipped panelled ceiling. Erected by the Very Rev. John Roch P.P.O. The Very Rev. Patrick Canavan of the U.S.A. paid the bills, which perhaps accounts for both quality and scale. Perky steel and concrete belfry like an C18 toy fort and finial combined.

ARANMORE ISLAND*   DO *A4*

A large island off the low-lying coast of the Rosses with fine cliff scenery.

LIGHTHOUSE. At the NW tip of the island on Rinrawross Point. The original lighthouse, built by *Thomas Rogers*, was first lighted in 1798. When the lighthouse was erected on Tory Island in 1828 it was decided to do away with that on Aranmore. Protests secured its continuance until 1838, when it was discontinued. In 1865 a new lighthouse was built. The light was replaced by a first order dioptric light by *John S. Sloane* in 1876 and converted in 1953 to a major electric light with a power of three million candles – the second major electric light on the Irish coast and, at that time, the most powerful.

CATHOLIC CHURCH. Foundation stone laid 15 September 1876. A T-shaped rendered Gothic hall.

ARBOE   TY *J6*

The site of an Early Christian monastery on a desolate point in flat pasture on the W shore of Lough Neagh. Founded by St Colman Mucaidhe in the late c6. Burned by Rory O'Morna in 1166.

HIGH CROSS. One of the finest of the northern group of High Crosses. At over 22 ft high, also one of the largest; it is equalled in scale only by the West Cross at Monasterboice, Co. Louth, and possibly by Donaghmore were that complete. The cross bears no evidence of date, and as it is executed in a soft sandstone that weathers poorly, its sculptural style is of little help in this connection. A date in the early c10 is usually agreed.

The cross stands on a double plinth and is made of three pieces with a patterned collar a little more than two-thirds up the shaft, and a separate capstone. The cross head has a pierced nimbus slightly recessed from the face of the arms and shaft with a semicircular cusp within the ring, all the same as at Donaghmore. The capstone fell in 1817 and the whole upper portion in 1846. Both were restored by Col. Stewart of Killymoon Castle, but the upper parts of the nimbus are now missing. The sculptural panels – in some cases open to a variety of interpretations – are on the E face reading from the bottom: 17 Adam and Eve; the sacrifice of Isaac; Daniel in the lions' den; the three children in the fiery furnace – the collar – a pattern of heads and, on the cross, Christ in judgement with Hell's

* Not visited.

flames below his feet. The w face is the New Testament side.
From bottom to top: the Adoration of the Kings; the wedding
at Cana; the miracle of the loaves and fishes (or the Last Supper
or meeting at Emmaus); Christ's entry into Jerusalem – the
collar – a Transfiguration or Arrest scene, and, on the cross,
the Crucifixion with St Longinus piercing Christ's side. The
side scenes represent on the N: the Baptism of Christ; Moses?;
Women before Solomon and the Judgement of Solomon; and
on the s: the murder of Abel; David's rescue of the Lamb;
David and Goliath; and David and Saul.

CHURCH RUINS. Between the cross and the lough. The walls
of a rectangular church, 19 ft by 63 ft, built of boulder rubble
with high splayed window openings. No detailing remains.
There are fragments of moulded brackets and column bases of
the C14, but this church is said to have been rebuilt in 1622.

ARBOE PARISH CHURCH (C of I). 1713. A small harled church.
Two-bay nave with paired lancets, w bellcote, and porch. The
C19 N transept makes the church apparently T-plan. – MONU-
MENT. Plain tablet to Mary Ledlie, the first person buried in
the graveyard, May 1714.

ST PATRICK. 4 km WSW at Mullinahoe. A big rendered hall of
six bays with round-headed Y-traceried windows. Mid C19.

CHURCH OF THE HOLY FAMILY. 1900 by *E. J. Toye*, replacing
a building of 1853. A large rendered and painted church,
vaguely Norman in style. Similar to Bruckless and St Agatha,
Clar, in plan, with nave, pseudo-transepts lit by paired gables,
and side porches in the angles. But this is bigger and more elaborate at the E. Balancing the porches, on the E side of the transepts, are side chapels lit by wheel windows, with the sanctuary
in a semicircular apse between. Large wheel window and lean-
to gabled porch on the w front. The interior is quite impressive, dark and well proportioned. At the head of the nave an
arcade of three round-headed arches screens the transepts and
side chapels. The chancel arch is similarly round-headed, and
its form is successfully echoed in the braced trusses in the roof.
'Extensive improvements' were made in 1936. – STAINED
GLASS. w wheel window by *Evie Hone*, 1954. Christ among
the Doctors in the centre, Erin above, Moses with the tablets
below, the symbols of the Evangelists at the sides. – In the s

transept and E windows, brilliantly coloured pictorial glass of
c. 1900.

ST CONALL (C of I). 1833. A harled three-bay hall with bellcote,
porch, and short stone chancel added in 1908. Stone trim to
the lancets. E window three-light cusped Perp. Panelled trussed
ceiling inside.

Two main streets joining at r. angles with a bridge crossing the
Owentocker River gave Ardara more of the appearance of a real
town than most west coast villages. It is pleasantly maintained,
with rows of substantial two- and three-storey houses. By the
bridge is the former MARKET HOUSE, a two-storey, three-bay
façade, the centre bay set forward, with a segmental archway
below a tripartite window with a gable and clock above. Mid
C19. The NESBITT ARMS in the Main Street is a big stuccoed
hotel. Three storeys with attics and of six bays, with channelled
ground floor, and classical aedicules to the first floor. The
METHODIST CHURCH of 1832 is a plain two-bay lancet hall.

KILCLOONEY CHURCH. 7 km NNW, in open treeless country.
A large mid C19 painted hall and porch, seven bays, with
stepped buttresses and three Y-traceried lancets in alternate
bays. Inside, a very deep gallery. – ALTAR RAIL and BALDAC-
CHINO in marble, 1932.

ARDARA RECTORY. 1875 by *William McElwee*. L-shaped, with
a porch in the corner. Cottagey.

CROSSES. This district is rich in primitive PILLAR STONES and
CROSS SLABS. In a naturally stony terrain they are not easily
located without a map or the assistance of local people.
Loughros peninsula has several: ST CONALL'S CROSS, N of
Lough Aleen (1 km N of Crannageboy and about 4 km W of
Ardara), is a large slab, 5 ft by 2½ ft overall, roughly shaped, with
short arms, inscribed with a Latin cross with serifs drawn
through a circle. At Cloughboy, 2.5 km W of Crannageboy, are
three primitive slabs: (1) S of the road opposite a waterfall,
2½ ft high, inscribed with a Latin cross with serifs; (2) opposite
on the ridge of hills to the N, beside the fence, a trapezium-
shaped slab 3 ft high incised with a Greek cross with serifs;
(3) behind a ruined cottage against a dyke, 4 ft high, an inverted
Latin cross with serifs. Above Maghera Strand, 5.5 km W of
Ardara at Laconnell, a fourth cross cut on a slab boulder N of
the road. Serifs again.

CAPSTONE BRIDGE. 4 km W, crossing the Bracky River, a drystone raised path and bridge with two piers and three slab lintels.

ARDRESS see KESH

ARDSTRAW   TY

An ancient parish with an early C18 BRIDGE crossing the River
Derg. St Patrick ordained Mac Ereae bishop here in the C5.
Annals record the burning of the monastery on several
occasions until 1111, when it became the diocesan centre that
moved to Maghera about 1152 and finally to Derry. No trace
remains of the early Christian buildings. The PRESBYTERIAN
CHURCH, founded about 1656 and rebuilt in 1862, has a stone
gabled façade to a five-bay harled hall with Y-tracery windows.
The CATHOLIC CHURCH, 3 km N, is a three-bay Y-traceried
hall of 1837. *See also* Newtownstewart.

ARTICLAVE   LD

A village founded by the Clothworkers' Company in 1611 but
never more than a straggle of houses over a hill; now with a dull
new housing estate.

ST PAUL, DUNBOE PARISH CHURCH (C of I). Erected on a
new site in 1691, the old church having been destroyed by
James II's army. A small, low hall and tower, all in rubble stone,
with pointed pinnacles to the tower and pretty cast-iron windows. Extensively repaired about 1835. The interior is simple,
with a shallow pointed chancel arch. The chancel is not
expressed outside. Pretty little gallery at the back with big box
pews underneath. Above the S side door a circular window
lights the gallery just like that at Clougherny parish church,
Beragh, also an old foundation. In 1862 Sir Henry Hervey
Bruce of Downhill thought of improving the church but seemingly did nothing. The slate sundial on the S wall with incised
globes and an hourglass is inscribed thus:

> Tis greatly wise to talk with our past hours,
> And ask them what report they bore to heaven.
>   A.D. 1832

FIRST DUNBOE PRESBYTERIAN CHURCH. 1936 by *J. S. Kennedy*. Cruciform last-gasp Gothic with brick quoins and a
vaguely Dutch air.

DUNBOE HOUSE. 1774. A plain three-storey, five-bay glebe
house on a high basement. Designed by *Michael Shanahan* and
restored by Archdeacon Mansell in 1821. The flanking office

wings behind suggest that the house was once entered from the N front.

HEZLETT HOUSE. At Liffock crossroads, 1.5 km NW. A long thatched cottage founded in 1691 and now in the care of the National Trust. From 1690 Bishop King of Derry was providing houses to encourage the clergy to reside in their parishes, and the house was possibly built for this purpose. Dendrochronological tests on some roof timbers have confirmed the date of 1691. The house has rubble walls with a core of earth and sand, roughcast outside, and built with a pronounced batter. The structure, like that of many Magilligan cottages, is framed throughout by fine cruck trusses.

The Hezlett family took over the house in the mid C18, and it was they who in 1823 added the two extra bays at the S end, as a house for Isaac Hezlett's widowed mother when Isaac married. It was presumably he who changed the windows of the main house to their early C19 tripartite form.

ARTIGARVAN   TY F5

A small village with substantial stone and harled mill buildings by the river.

ST PATRICK, LECKPATRICK PARISH CHURCH (C of I). 1.5 km NW. A small T-shaped church built in 1816 and enlarged – probably by the wing that converted it to a T – in 1834. Externally very plain, with four round-headed sash-windows with Gothic glazing bars, a bellcote, and a small W porch, circular inside. The interior of the church is exceptionally interesting as the Ecclesiastical Commissioners never removed its high BOX PEWS or its two-decker PULPIT. – MONUMENTS. Unusually elaborate, if inexpert, and unusually early. Isabella Sinclair †1673, wife of the rector. A large armorial wall tablet with a coat of arms in high relief, flanked by triple-shafted composite columns; salient entablature and obelisks. – The Rev. John Sinclair, rector, † 1702. A similar wall aedicule with hourglass, skull and bones, and angel heads.

LECKPATRICK RECTORY. 1 km N. 1792. A large whitewashed house with more pretensions to architecture than many. Five-bay, two-storey front, with a central canted bay opening into a circular hall. The rooms on either side have segmental bow ends. Front door with a round-headed stone frame set at the top of a flight of semicircular steps.

HOLLY HILL. 1.5 km s. The home of the Sinclair family from
the late C17. A complex house, frequently remodelled, though
part at least seems to date from 1736, when William Starrat
made a survey of the estate. Plain harled front, five-bay, three-
storey, with single-bay screen wings and ball finials. A shallow
canted bay projects irregularly. The architrave to the front door
looks about 1770.

CHURCHES in the area, mostly in the flat land to the N by the
Foyle, are: CLOGHCOR, 3 km N, 1823, a four-bay hall, with
pine-panelled roof of 1896 inside; BREADY REFORMED
PRESBYTERIAN CHURCH, 7 km N, a six-bay classical hall,
built by the Rev. Samuel Alexander in 1786, rebuilt by the Rev.
T. Hanna in 1823; ST JOHN, DONALONY (C of I), 7 km N,
1866, a seven-bay hall with plate tracery and polychrome brick
trim; GULLION, 7 km NNE, mid C19, a four-bay Gothic hall
with a wide gabled front; ST JOSEPH, GLENMORAN, 3 km
ESE, founded in 1792, a five-bay hall with Y-tracery, four-stage
tower with diminutive battlements and pinnacles; DONAGH-
EADY PRESBYTERIAN CHURCH, 3 km NNE, 1855, a six-bay
lancet hall, gable end with tripartite window above the door,
and windows with Y-tracery either side. (For Donagheady *see*
also Dunnamanagh.)

ASSAROE ABBEY *see* BALLYSHANNON

G8   AUGHER   TY

Augher, a simple village at a crossroads, owes its existence to the
Jacobean Plantation of Ulster and particularly to the grants of land
in the Barony of Clogher to the Ridgeway brothers, George, who
had 1,000 acres, and Sir Thomas, who, as Treasurer-at-Wars in
Ireland, ultimately secured an estate of over 4,300 acres. Sir
Thomas is recorded in the Calendar of State Papers as having
built 'a wardable castle' in 1610 and houses in 1611. He brought
materials and men from London and Devonshire: 400 boards and
planks; timber for a watermill and a quantity of stone; twelve carpenters, two masons, and two smiths. In 1613 the town was incorporated and the carpenters Farefax, McLaughton, Robert
Williams, and Henry Holland were freeholders in the new
borough. George Ridgeway also began a bawn in 1611. Sir
Thomas, who was M.P. for Gallen-Ridgeway, Co. Leix, in 1613,
was created Lord Ridgeway in 1616 and in 1622 sold his Irish

estates including Augher to Sir James Erskine in exchange for
the dignity of the Earldom of Londonderry. In 1630, owing to
a flaw in the original grant, Charles I made a re-grant of the lands
to Erskine, which accounts for the epithet Royal attached to both
his houses and to the name of Favour Royal (*see* p. 292).

AUGHER CASTLE or SPUR ROYAL. Immediately NW of the vil- ₃₈
lage. An intriguing Jacobean conceit incorporated as the centrepiece of a modest castle-style mansion. The original castle was
a tower house and bawn erected by Sir Thomas Ridgeway
before 1613, the name Spur no doubt alluding to its unusual
plan, which developed into an eight-point star like the rowel,
or spiked wheel, at the end of a spur. The plan is unique among
Ulster Plantation houses and the detail strikingly more English
than the many Scottish bawns built in the same period. One
side is now embedded in the later house, but three stand almost
clear in the garden front. The tower is 30 ft square, of three
storeys, with a heavy crenellated parapet of characteristic Elizabethan appearance with the tops of the battlements sloping inwards from the top of the wall. The original door – still a two-
centred Gothic arch – is in the E wall. Above is a single section
of machicolation, pierced on the face by a singularly delicate
spiral wheel. The square of the tower becomes a star by the
addition of triangular bays projecting from the middle of each
side, with cross-mullioned windows on the upper floors and
mere slits at ground-floor level. The label mouldings and
chamfered frames of the windows are original. One circular
flanker of the original bawn remains to the E. It is linked to
the later wing of the house by a Renaissance archway with
moulded bases, imposts, and embossed voussoirs – a similar
sort of robust frontiersman's classicism to Derrygonnelly
church.

Spur Royal withstood an attack of Sir Phelim O'Neil in 1641,
but was burnt in 1689 and dismantled by order of the Irish
Parliament. Its state in 1791 appears in an engraving in Grose's
Antiquities of Ireland, with a conical roof still on the flanker
of the bawn. By the C18 the estate had come into the possession
of the descendants of a William Richardson, who had married
one of the two granddaughters of Sir James Erskine (*see* above).
In 1753 Sir William Richardson built a substantial plain Georgian house in the village main street, but between 1827 and 1832
the appeal of Spur Royal, or Augher Castle as it was then
called, induced Sir James Richard Bunbury, Bt., to restore the
old building, adding a new house across one front to the designs

of the Sligo architect *William Warren*. The new house is unusually sensitive and pretty. It has a seven-bay, two-storey elevation with an arcaded central section and gently inclined arms
suggesting the sense of a court on the entrance front, at the
same time leaving the old tower largely unencumbered on the
garden side. Each angle is marked by a dummy bartizan, and
the windows, like those of the original tower, are cross-
mullioned with label moulds. Inside, the Gothic entrance hall
is skilfully planned.

St Mark (C of I). A chapel of ease of 1861–4 by *Welland &
Gillespie*. A four-bay lancet hall, of coursed rubble, with high
pointed gables, splayed base, and offset bellcote half-way down
one side of the gable. Very pretty four-light Dec window. Built
by *Joseph McElvoy* for £686. The church hall is gabled classical
of 1905.

Methodist Church. 1865. A three-bay stone-built hall with
rose windows in the gables.

Somerville House. In the main street. 1753; built by Sir
William Richardson. An irregular six-bay, two-storey house
with steps and Gibbs surround to the front door.

At Knockmary Hill, 4km NW in a state forest, is a
chambered cairn, now buried again under a concrete roof-
light, with the stones arranged according to their possible original alignment. Three carry decoration in the form of scrolls,
snake patterns, and cup marks. The cairn offers a fine vantage
point with breathtaking views over Tyrone to Down and the
Mountains of Mourne.

Aughnacloy is principally one long very wide street, like Cookstown, but unlike Cookstown it runs along a ridge, with big high
houses, mainly of three storeys, lining its length. The town was
developed in the mid c18, largely through the energy of Mr Acheson Moore of Ravella nearby. He rebuilt Carnteel parish church
between 1736 and 1740, and for once a town followed. Though
the place has a derelict air today, it was a thriving community
until the 1880s.

St James, Carnteel Parish Church (C of I). Built by
Acheson Moore from 1736 and dedicated in 1740. A simple
Georgian hall with a tower and slender needle spire added by
Moore's daughter Mrs Malone in 1796. Three-bay nave with

short chancel and pretty double Y-traceried E window. Heavy eaves cornice. The tower is of three stages, forming a vestibule across the original entrance door.

ST MARY. A big hall church by *Doolin, Butler & Donelly*, in a free Romanesque style, with ideas taken from Jerpoint and Mellifont. Designed in 1902. Foundation stone laid on 27 February 1904. As liturgical considerations required the congregation to see the priest officiating, there could be no transepts, so the plan, like that of Kilcar in Donegal, is basilican. Five-bay round-headed arcade, apse, and painted barrel roof. Black granite columns with unsculptured capitals. The gabled façade, with a six-light wheel window and an offset tower and cupola, rises powerfully on steps above the street.

PRESBYTERIAN CHURCH. The first minister was ordained here in 1697. Parts of the present T-plan church are of 1774, though the interior and the big five-light window with intersecting tracery date from an extensive restoration by *John Boyd* of Belfast in 1888.

JACKSON ALMSHOUSES. At the N end of the town. Built between 1851 and 1854 with an endowment of £10,000 from the estate of Dr Alexander Jackson of Dublin. A cottage-like Tudor range by *Sandham Symes* with verandas, half-dormers, and three projecting gables across the main front.

MARKET HOUSE. A little symmetrical group of harled buildings like a gentleman's farmhouse design: three-bay, two-storey centre with segmental arched openings and two-storey gabled pavilions; *c.* 1810.

GARVEY HOUSE. 3 km W. The story of this house is a singular example of Irish folly that saw the creation of a great neo-classical design by *Francis Johnston* and its dismantling within a period of twenty-five years. In 1798 the Bishop of Dromore wrote to his wife that Nathaniel Montgomery Moore of Ravella and Garvey had undertaken to build a magnificent house costing £16,000 with 'mahogany doors, chimney pieces of the finest marbles and a very magnificent gallery to receive a large collection of pictures'. It was habitable by 1812 but by then was said to have cost £70,000, throwing Moore so heavily into debt that he had to retire to France in 1815. By 1821 his agent had been instructed to sell all the woodwork, copper, and lead from the building, leaving only the gaunt cubic carcass of ashlar stone that still stands today.

The house was of three storeys on a brick-vaulted basement, as austere as only Johnston and perhaps James Playfair were prepared to build in the late C18. Six bays on the sides, seven across the front, with nothing as decoration beyond a string course below the first-floor windows and a thin recessed panel round the ground-floor windows. A rectangular entrance hall leads to a central inner hall with segmental apses and paired stairs on either side. Behind is the vast windowless shell that was to be the top-lit picture gallery, now filled only with the sudden alarm of pigeons' wings. The rectangular court of offices s of the ruined house may possibly relate to the spa that existed at Garvey in the late C18 and early C19.

AGHALOO CHURCH RUINS. 3 km N, in Rousky townland. The partial remains of a rectangular church, 21 ft by 66 ft inside, with walls over 3 ft thick. The E and W walls still stand in a circular graveyard. Still in use in 1679, but abandoned when Acheson Moore built St James, Aughnacloy.

CARNTEEL OLD CHURCH RUINS. 4 km NE. The ruins of a rectangular church, 18½ ft by 54 ft inside, with walls 3 ft thick. E window with broken tracery and elaborate hood moulding. Late C16.

KILLENS CHURCH. 3 km ENE. 1826. A rendered five-bay hall with Georgian Gothic sash-windows.

CRILLY. 3 km SE. Two small hall churches: CRILLY (C of I), 1803, five-bay with porch; BALLYNAGRAVE PRESBYTERIAN CHURCH, 1839, a four-bay lancet hall in squared rubble.

BALLEEGHAM ABBEY *see* MANORCUNNINGHAM

The village, no more than 'several miserable hovels' to Jonathan Binns's eye in 1838, is better now. Nice main street of painted two-storey houses with some decent post-war council houses in terraces that preserve a sense of enclosure.

MAGHERACROSS PARISH CHURCH (C of I). Of the church built in 1785 and described by Lewis in 1837 as 'a plain neat edifice in good repair' only the tower fronting the village street remains. Square, in three stages, with pinnacled Irish battlements and stone string courses. The nave behind is early Victorian, four-bay, with round-headed lancets and a big flat wooden ceiling inside. The chancel with its free Dec E window is later still, by *Joseph Welland*, who also proposed a s aisle (not built). – STAINED GLASS. The Boy David by *W. F. Clokey* of Belfast, a frank and steady David in purple and crimson, much the best feature of the church.

METHODIST CHURCH. 1902. A lancet hall of squared rock-faced stone with an offset belfry tower and a Dec w window.

MAGHERACROSS HOUSE. 2 km NE. Formerly Jamestown House, built by the Lendrum family in 1740. Now a pleasant early C19 house on the Ballinamallard River. The front is unusual: two storeys and five bays, but with a projecting central bay with chamfered corners and overhanging eaves on brackets. The gutters have lion masks. Wide segmental fanlight to the main door. STABLES of 1837, a good stone-built court in two storeys, six-bay outside, with a pediment over the central arch entrance.

TULLYCLEAGH HOUSE. 2.5 km W. A square, harled late C18 house built by the Rev. Verscoyle. In 1848 the seat of the Rev. Burke. Two-storey on a basement, with a four-bay front. Inside, a big central hall, two rooms behind and two on either side. Additional s wing. Tuscan stone aedicule to the front door. Symmetrical classical offices to the s.

BALLINTRA

ST BRIDGET. 1845. A big five-bay hall. Lancet windows, three-light E window, and W tower in four stages ending in a gabled parapet, with pinnacles and thin diagonal buttresses – all in grey ashlar limestone. The front is inscribed: 'Rev. Daniel Kelly, Pastor, *James McKenna*, Stranorlar Builder', but its style is very similar to St Patrick, Donaghmore, designed by *John Brady* also in 1845. Large interior, with an enormous back gallery and curious tubular ogee mouldings at the E end.

DRUMHOME PARISH CHURCH (C of I). Built in 1795, with a high elongated harled tower of four stages with clock and stepped battlements, all typical of the Church of Ireland in these parts at this date. Behind is a wide boxy hall of dressed stone, three-bay with groups of triple lancet windows, the result of a remodelling by *Joseph Welland* in 1854. The interior is an extraordinary amalgam. Arcades of four attenuated Doric columns divide the church into nave and aisles. The ceiling height removes all possibility of classical proportion, and the columns look like so many straining elephant trunks marching grimly down the church. Outside them – or better, wrapped round them – is a pine-fronted Gothic gallery by *Welland*, supported on octagonal cast-iron columns. The rest of the church

furnishings are of 1854, including the wells in each aisle, originally for heating stoves.

METHODIST CHURCH. A small five-bay hall. Gable front with
triple lancet window.

DRUMHOME OLD CHURCH. 3 km NW, at the foot of Mullan-
cross Hill. One ivy-covered gable, about 25 ft high, with what
appears to be a bellcote – the late and only remnant of a Colum-
ban monastery where Flahertach O'Maldory, King of Tyrconnell, was buried in 1197 and where St Ernan had been abbot
before his death in 640.

COXTOWN. 2.5 km NNW. Post-1837 and pre-1846, when the *Parliamentary Gazetteer* described it with Brown Hall (*see* p. 151)
as a principal demesne. An elegant classical front, five bays by
two storeys, with a slightly projecting pedimented centre bay.
Pilaster-strip quoins with wide eaves supported on a 'peg' cornice. Tuscan pilasters with laurel wreaths frame a tripartite entrance door. The style is eminently Regency but evidently later.
Inside, all this amounts to is a hall and two spacious rooms,
built across the front of a lower two-roomed farmhouse. The
interior detail is good, with nice Greek key plasterwork and
door surrounds reminiscent of *J. B. Keane.* Pleasant regular
outbuildings and a coach house behind.

BALLYBOFEY *see* STRANORLAR

J7   BALLYCLOG   TY

A rural parish with two churches, a glebe house, and a river, near
Curglasson crossroads.

BALLYCLOG OLD CHURCH. The ruins of a C17 hall and tower
church built of whinstone and red sandstone rubble, with a brick
belfry. The church is 42½ ft by 20½ ft inside. The walls,
recently repaired, stand to full height, with two C17 round-
headed lancets in the N wall and characteristic big buttresses
at the E end. Described by Lewis as a 'small plain ancient
structure', in use until 1865.
   The CASTLESTEWART MAUSOLEUM immediately W of the
church is entered by steps within the ruin. Long rectangular
plinth with central two-stage smaller plinth capped by a concave stone pyramid and ball finial. Similar mausolea exist in
the Presbyterian churchyard at Downpatrick, Co. Down.

ST PATRICK (C of I). Opposite the church ruins. 1865. A roguish
little building by *Welland & Gillespie,* wilfully adapting Irish

architectural elements to jazzy ends. Three-bay gabled hall with a rounded apse built of coursed sandstone rubble enlivened by bands of red stone and touches of yellow and blue brick. Plate tracery and, in the inordinately high w gable, a wheel window. Across the gable a lean-to entrance porch ending in a buttressed finial at one side and a crazy round tower at the other. The tower starts with a steeply battered base round which two bands of red stone spiral, the upper band bumping up over the lancets that light the stair inside. The cap is drawn out to a long thin conical spire. The interior is lavishly polychromatic. Hipped ceiling with braced trusses and exposed rafters. The vestry is apse-ended like the church, with a high slate roof.

BALLYCLOG PRESBYTERIAN CHURCH. Hall and tower type. Three-stage tower with diagonal buttresses. Five-bay hall. Harled, with stone trim. – MEMORIAL STONE in the tower to Mrs John Megaw of Belfast, 1903.

GLEBE HOUSE. 1792 and 1811. A three-bay, two-storey house on a basement. Projecting centre bay with chamfered corners. Older five-bay house behind.

BALLYGAWLEY   TY G8

A plain little C19 village that grew up round a T-junction, the modern centre of the parish of Errigal-Keerogue. As in many Tyrone towns, most of the buildings of interest are dotted about it rather than in it, though it now has three small churches to adorn its streets. At the head of the main street is a three-storey Georgian house of 1780.

BALLYGALLEY CHAPEL OF EASE (C of I). 1831, possibly by *William Warren* of Sligo. A three-bay lancet hall, with a very wide gabled front adorned with a battlemented porch, octagonal corner pinnacles, and a double pinnacled bellcote at the apex of the gable.

BALLYGALLEY PRESBYTERIAN CHURCH. 1883. A five-bay lancet hall in squared rubble with the usual Presbyterian tripartite gable front and wheel window.

CATHOLIC CHAPEL. Much re-worked, though retaining a Georgian three-bay front with Gothic sash windows. Possibly once a Nonconformist chapel of *c.* 1800.

NEIGHBOURHOOD

ST KIERNAN'S CHURCH RUINS. 4.5 km w. The walls of a rectangular church, 60 ft by 20 ft, 3½ ft thick, with a part of the NE gable still standing. These remains are thought to be related to the Tertiary Franciscan monastery founded in 1489 at Ballynasaggart, where the modern Protestant parish church now stands. Traces of a round tower recorded in 1810 link the site with the C6 monastery founded here by St Macartin. – CROSS. A solid cross head with short arms and a longer head, decorated on one face with a circular border, on the other with a raised boss in a square frame. The shaft is mostly missing.

ST MATTHEW, ERRIGAL-KEEROGUE PARISH (C of I). 1831, probably by *William Warren* of Sligo. A stone-built, hall-and-tower-type church. Three-bay nave with Y-tracery. Three-stage tower with very tall upper storey and octagonal pinnacles. – FONT. Stone, possibly C17, with boldly carved formal leaf decoration on the sides. – STAINED GLASS. Nice pictorial windows with clear colours; 1911 and 1933.

ST CIARAN. 3 km N at Ballymackilroy. Described by Lewis in 1837 as 'a small plain edifice'. Now rather an attractive big country church, still in a primitive Georgian Gothic vein but enlivened by additions to make it cruciform with the 'transepts' built as square towers capped by high slate obelisk roofs. Inside, exposed rafters and kingpost trusses. Two side chapels under each tower open into the church through arches. Rich mid C19 materials, dark red granite, marble sanctuary, and old tile floor.

BALLYGAWLEY PARK. 2.5 km NW. Only the shell remains of this substantial Greek Revival house built by Sir H. Stewart, Bt., to designs of *John Hargrave*. The front seems to have been added on to an older house with a forestanding Ionic portico *in antis* surmounted by a square attic and flanked by two bays of two storeys on either side. The whole front of dressed ashlar. Alterations to the farmstead of the estate by *Fitzgibbon Louch*, 1871. Burnt in 1921.

RICHMOND LODGE. 1 km W. Formerly the Rectory. A nice substantial double-pile house of 1780. Two storeys on a semi-basement with diamond-cut stone quoins and basement string course. Three-bay front with steps and a Gibbs surround to the door and lugged surrounds to the windows. Six-panel doors with more lugged surrounds inside.

MARTRAY MANOR HOUSE. 1.5 km NE. The second Stewart house in the parish, enlarged on a similar scheme to Ballygawley Park with a five-bay, two-storey front of dressed stone, with a gabled centre bay and projecting mullioned porch. Inside, the plan is a muddle. C18 offices behind, and on the back door the inscription 'G. V. Stewart 1846 and 1855'.

LISDOART FLAXMILL. 2.5 km S. A large mid C19 mill. Ten-bay and three-storey, with an end stair. Stone-built with brick surrounds. Fine lime avenue with eighteen picturesque workers' houses arranged in a symmetrical group.

BALLYREAGH MILLS. 3 km NE. Water mill and three-storey granary. Harled with dressed quoins. Erected by Harry Crossley in 1838. Builder *John Dunbar*.

BALLYKELLY LD *G₃*

Ballykelly was created by the Fishmongers' Company, to whom the surrounding lands were granted in 1613. Pynnar in his survey of 1619 records a complete township with a church 'neatly made up', fifteen limestone houses, others of timber, and a limestone bawn with a 12 ft high wall, four flankers, and a good house inside for the agent, Mr Higgins. From the late C17 the estate was leased to the Hamilton and Beresford families; then in 1820 the Fishmongers regained possession and set in hand the improvement of the village, building a new Nonconformist church, a dispensary, a school, and a model farm, all to the designs of their surveyor, *Richard Suitor*. His buildings are like the severe, purposeful plates of Gandy and Malton come to life and give Ballykelly, for all its smallness, an exotic air in north Co. Derry.

TAMLAGHT FINLAGAN PARISH CHURCH (C of I). 1795. The most elegant of all the rather primitive Gothic churches erected by the Earl Bishop in his diocese, and probably the result of a collaboration between the Bishop's architect, *Michael Shanahan*, and *John Mitchell*, who superintended its construction. Three-bay nave of slate-like rubble stone, with thin buttresses and battlemented parapet and gables. Three-stage W tower, with very shallow clasping buttresses ending in obelisk-like finials, and a fine ashlar spire with mouldings at its base that are just above the lower parapet. Pretty band of blind Gothic arcading between the second and third stages of the tower. The belfry has circular windows. Short chancel, in a similar style, added by the Fishmongers in 1851. N aisle by *Joseph Welland*, 1859. The church was restored in 1934. – MONUMENT. Mrs Jane Hamilton (1672–1716). The most elaborate early C18 monument in north-west Ulster, based, as Mr Homan Potterton has shown, on Grinling Gibbons's monument to Mrs Mary Beaufoy († 1705) in Westminster Abbey. This Irish version preserves the lines of the design and the concept of the deceased lady kneeling on a hassock with cherubs above and below. The working of the marble is angular and curiously stiff. The aedicule containing the figure supports a Gothic arch with an urn and garlands of flowers.

TAMLAGHT OLD CHURCH RUINS. *See* Limavady.

88 BALLYKELLY PRESBYTERIAN CHURCH. 1827. By the Fishmongers' architect, *Richard Suitor*, and almost identical to the same company's church at Banagher. It cost £4,000, and for Ireland the scale of the building is exceptional. The church is a great hall, 45 ft by 72 ft, covering an area that would be sufficient for almost four Ecclesiastical Commission churches of the same date, and this scale dictates the style. Lewis calls it 'Grecian', but an enormous gable pediment is the only overtly classical reference. The façade below is divided into three bays, the outer very slightly projecting with two storeys of segment-headed windows, and between them a great door in a large relieving arch of ashlar sandstone. Nothing is allowed to interrupt the simple massive form, and the result is very strong. Inside, a gallery runs round three sides, supported on robust square piers. A tablet over the pulpit commemorates the church's foundation:

> By this tablet the Presbyterian Congregation of Ballykelly record their gratitude to the worshipful Company of Fishmongers London, for their liberality in Erecting, completing and presenting them with this Meeting house, March the 7th A.D. 1828.
>
> They are 'worthy for whom' we 'should do this for'
> They love 'our nation and' have 'built us a synagogue'.

ST FINLOGH. 1.5 km SW, at Oghill. 1849. Perched on the side of a hill, a high Gothic hall, rendered, with stone corner finials, timber Y-tracery, and a Dec E window. The only other embellishments are a bellcote and a series of amusingly sham medieval corbel heads beneath the label mouldings.

OLD CHURCH. 0.5 km N of Ballykelly Bridge. The church recorded by Pynnar was 43 ft by 26 ft. These ruins are 37 ft by 21 ft, with a chancel added in 1719. The church is just opposite the bawn of Walworth, and, though dedicated to St Peter, was always known as the Garrison Church. It was ruined in 1641 and again by James II's army in 1689, restored by the Beresfords in 1692, and abandoned only in 1795, on the completion of the Earl Bishop's new Gothic church. In 1849 the S wall was taken down to make room for the MAUSOLEUM of the Cather family, a solid ashlar block with antae and mammoth anthemion acroteria at each corner. The only architectural detail worth note in the ruins is the big semicircular archway opening into the early C18 chancel: stepped in section, with roll mouldings at each corner, and curiously archaic.

WALWORTH. Opposite the old church ruins. A handsome five-bay, two-storey house built by the Beresfords about 1730, though looking now late C18 rather than earlier. It occupies the place of the NW flanker of the bawn built by the Fishmongers in 1613–19. The other three flankers are still intact. Those on the NE and SW are circular two-storey towers; the other is polygonal and seems originally to have been a type of salient bastion. The C18 house is harled, with flat stone quoins and a cut stone eaves cornice. Inside, the original dog-leg stair and banisters remain.

FORMER LANCASTRIAN SCHOOLS. SW of the village. 1828 by *Suitor*, based on an earlier scheme by a local man, *David McBlain*. A charming classical design in local brick with sandstone corner pilasters. The teacher's house is like a minor domestic version of the Presbyterian church, with a big gable pediment flanked by low links connecting to the two-bay classrooms like little pavilions on either side of the house.

CHURCH HILL. Opposite the Presbyterian church. 1824. A model farm built by the Fishmongers at a cost of £900 and charmingly situated at the bottom of a broad paddock. Two-storey, three-bay house of ashlar sandstone, with wide Regency eaves, linked by long rubble walls to single-bay outhouses, also of ashlar stone, with big windows in relieving arches, and shallow hipped roofs.

BRIDGE HOUSE. 1820. A solid five-bay, two-storey house of sandstone, built by the Fishmongers and described by Lewis as an 'excellent dispensary with a very good house for a resident surgeon'.

BALLYMORE   DO D2

A townland between Dunfanaghy and Creeslough distinguished by its C18 church set high above the road.

ST JOHN, CLONDEHORKY PARISH (C of I). 1752. Built to re- 63 place the old parish church at Dunfanaghy and sited in open country for the mutual convenience of the Protestant proprietors in the neighbouring estates. The finest early Georgian church in north west Ulster, though still a simple structure, sticking to the barn-like form of most provincial churches. It is the detail that elevates St John's. Four finely worked segment-headed windows with big Gibbs surrounds in the s wall, and an enormous Venetian window, with heavy rusticated blocks in the place of pilasters, at the E end. The building is harled, with quoins. On the w front a pretty classical ashlar bellcote and a low hipped vestibule with a small Venetian window. N vestry added by *Joseph Welland* in 1853. The interior 65 is charming: a long hall, 62 ft by 26 ft, culminating in the big E window framed in Doric pilasters and frieze. Wainscoting and C18 panelled pews. Gallery at the back. High, coved plaster ceiling. The N wall has segment-headed niches to match the windows opposite. The taste for Gibbs surrounds and the scale and confident handling of this church suggest the hand of *Michael Priestley*.

FAUGHER HOUSE or WRAY CASTLE. 1 km NE. Substantial ruins of a rubble-built house and bawn erected by Tirlogh Oge O'Boyle *c.* 1611. The house, almost square in plan, had an irregular five-bay, two-storey front over a basement with attic windows in the end gables, and big square chimneys rising from corner fireplaces in the main rooms. Central s door with a ruined porch which was possibly defensive. Much of the w bawn wall remains, with two square flankers, battlements, and sixteen gun loops. In the s wall more gun loops and traces of a four-centred archway with a chamfered jamb. After the 1641 rising O'Boyle forfeited the castle to Sir John Stephens and Hugh Hamill who sold it to William Wray of Ards in 1700.*

MARBLE HILL. 2 km NE. An elegant classical villa built by the Barclay family in the early C19. Three-bay, two-storey front on a basement. Stone pilaster quoins with console eaves cornice. Central Ionic porch of cut stone with laurel-wreath garlands and tripartite window above. – STABLES. Mid C18. A big range of coursed stone with brick trim, with curous window patterns. In the centre a pair of coach-house arches under a pediment with three-bay, two-storey sections on either side. Liberal use of bull's-eye windows.

For CLONDEHORKY *see also* Creeslough and Dunfanaghy.

A small village on the edge of Lough Neagh, founded by a Mr Gaussen, who in 1788 built storehouses and a forge for manufacturing spades, and opened up a quarry. A distillery and brewery

---

* I am obliged to Hugh Dixon for an account of this building.

were erected by his descendants in 1824 and 1830, giving the
Salters' Company, to whom the land belonged, the idea of developing the place when the lease they had given of it expired
in 1852. They appear to have done nothing, and the place remains
tiny, with its churches all outside in the country.

St John, Woodchapel Parish Church (C of I). 2.5 km
NW. 1866–8 by *Welland & Gillespie*. The materials are the
usual ones for these architects: random black basalt with sandstone trim. The detail, mainly C13, is not uncommon either, but
the plan and massing are very odd and very personal. St John
is a large sprawling church, delighting in curious collisions and
sharp angular ends representing the new direction that the
Church Commissioners' architects were beginning to explore
shortly before disestablishment. The plan is cruciform, with
a nave, transepts, and a short polygonal apse, and a lopsided
S aisle ending flush with the W gable in a most unorthodox
saddleback tower added two years after the completion of
the church. This has a high applied gable to frame a porch, and
on the W front a massive lancet running right up into the belfry
stage with solid stone louvres. W gable with a big plate-tracery
wheel window. Inside, the principal change is from the play
of exposed trusses and rafters to cheaper panels of tongue and
grooved pine. Clear quarry glass windows. In the porch pretty
Victorian wrought-iron GATES and a primitive carved C17
SLAB of two trees and a sun with a Latin inscription apparently of 1664(?).

St Matthias, Ballyeglish Parish Church (C of I). At 110
The Loup, 5.5 km WSW. 1866–9 by *Welland & Gillespie*, the
foundation stone laid by the agent of the Salters' Company.
A stylish piece of roguery in polygonal white limestone rubble
with red sandstone tracery and trim. Really just a hall with
semicircular apse, but carried off with the same sort of verve as
St Patrick, Ballyclog. The W gable is cross-banded in red, with
a triple lancet window and a sculpturesque flat tower to one
side, ending in a chisel-topped bellcote. High roof with
embryonic transept gables with plate tracery. S porch with nice
boot-scrapers set into the side.

St Patrick. Also at The Loup, 4 km WSW. 1861. A big, ambitious church built by Patrick Quinn P.P. Basalt with sandstone
trim. Nave, N and S aisles, and apsed chancel. Offset square
belfry tower with crenellated and pinnacled parapet.

Saltersland Presbyterian Church. 4 km WSW. Mid
C19. A three-bay rendered hall with round-headed windows.

LAKE VIEW HOUSE. 1.5 km NW. Built about 1800 by the
Gaussen family, who developed Ballyronan. A handsome three-
bay, two-storey house with segmental bows to the outer bays,
tripartite windows throughout, and a pretty fanlight to the front
door.

LISNAMORROW HOUSE. 4 km NW. Built apparently by T.
Dawson in 1835, a charming three-bay cottage with a fanlight
to the central door and tripartite windows each side. Attics in
the gables above. Attractive topiary garden.

GRACEFIELD MORAVIAN CHURCH. 4.5 km N. A five-bay,
single-storey late C18 church, with a single-bay house at the
s end. Forestanding central two-storey tower with stone quoins
and a timber cupola. The church windows round-headed sashes
in stone frames.

BALLYSAGGART FRIARY see ST JOHN'S POINT

BALLYSCULLION see BELLAGHY

C7   BALLYSHANNON   DO

Once an attractive town with a more substantial urban character
than most centres in the north-west. The place owes its origin to
its site, on the N bank of the Erne just before the river widens out
to a broad muddy estuary bounded by immense sand dunes. The
strategic importance of Ballyshannon was recognized by the
O'Donnell Lords of Tyrconnell, who had a castle here that controlled the river crossing until the mid C17. It successfully withstood an English attack under Sir Conyers Clifford during the
great rising in 1597 but was subsequently reserved to the Crown
by James I, who created Rory O'Donnell Earl of Tyrconnell in
1603. Now only its name remains in Castle Street, but the barracks
that took its place in 1700 still stand and are the most interesting
of all the buildings in the town. From the mid C18 Ballyshannon
thrived. The barracks brought business, the harbour was
improved to designs of *Robert Stevenson & Son* in 1834, and the
town grew in importance as a port. In 1860, under the Towns
Improvement (Ireland) Act, it was lighted and paved throughout.
It gained rather swanky bank premises towards the end of the
century and then its development stopped. Today it could be one
of the best towns for architecture in the whole of County Donegal;
its character is still substantially that of an early C19 mercantile

centre, but extensive demolition in the Purt, the suburb s of the river, suggests that it will not remain such much longer.

CHURCHES

ST ANNE, KILBARRON PARISH CHURCH (C of I).* c18, rebuilt in 1841 'in the Saxon style of architecture' by the Rev. G. N. Tredennick to designs of *William Farrell*. A big five-bay, two-storey hall with a high roof that dwarfs the w tower to which it is attached. This, exceptionally tall and thin like the c18 towers at Belleek, Ardress, and Kesh, in Fermanagh, is probably a remnant of the old church of 1745, recently rendered brash with new white harling. Farrell's church is in ashlar sandstone with the windows recessed between flat strips of masonry, a sort of economical Norman originated by Smirke. Inside, BOX PEWS with upper galleries on three sides supported on cast-iron Norman columns. – STAINED GLASS. E window by *Percy Bacon*, 1900, a literal rendering of the Resurrection, the Ascension, and the Sermon on the Mount. – FONT at the E end of the s wall. A primitive stone octagon on a square shaft. – MONUMENTS. Several nice wall tablets at the back of the church: T. W. Crawford † 1842. A weeping figure beside an urn with military trophies. – Captain C. O'Neill, Peninsular War veteran, † 1852. Drums, cannon, and draped urn.

ST PATRICK. A long stone church set sideways to the ridge of the hill. Primitive Norman detailing. Seven-bay, two-storey. In the middle of the N side is a big square tower and spire, inscribed '*Dan Campbell*, Builder 1842'. *J. J. McCarthy* added the polygonal chancel in 1860. The interior seems vast and is a complete volte-face: Lombardic classical in stucco with, to the side altars and chancel, big composite columns supporting arches directly, without an intervening entablature. Shell niches framed in Ionic aedicules to the side walls. The roof is supported on elaborate trusses with wooden tracery infill. *The Dublin Builder* reports this decoration as by Messrs *Barff & Co*. The high altar and windows are by Messrs *Farrell*. But what can McCarthy have thought of such conglomerate effects?

ST JOSEPH, to the s across the river in the Purt. 1886. Builder *James Monaghan*. A five-bay harled hall with round-headed windows with Y-tracery in timber. The altar originally in the middle of the s wall is now in the w chancel. Tower of three stages with pointed slate roof.

PRESBYTERIAN CHURCH. Jumbled Nonconformist Gothic. A

* For Kilbarron, see p. 325.

three-bay hall in stone with Y-traceried windows, built for Dr
James Murphy about 1840, and extended to a T-plan at its W
end. The original hall is eminently 'neat', the extension more
ambitious, with pinnacled gables, big round plate-traceried
windows, and lean-to porch. This was done by the Rev. Andrew
Loung in the mid 1880s.

FORMER METHODIST CHURCH, in the Mall. A crisp Gothic
hall of 1899 with paired geometrical traceried windows in the
gable, like Buncrana and also by *Thomas Elliott* of Enniskillen.
Now a stocking factory.

PUBLIC BUILDINGS

THE BARRACKS. On the N side of the river next to the bridge.
A substantial block, excellent in its setting and bold in its scale.
Dated 1700 on the central archway. The design is presumably
by Col. *Thomas Burgh*, who succeeded Sir William Robinson
as Surveyor General in Ireland that year. Maurice Craig calls
Burgh 'the first indisputably and unmistakably Irish architect';
these would be his first buildings, preceding by a year Collins
Barracks, Dublin, of 1701–4. As such, they deserve a better fate
than to be left to moulder away, as at the time of writing they
are. The plan is a curious one: T-shaped, with a generous two-
storey, five-bay front (partly spoilt by a grocer's shop-front)
with a slate roof, facing the street, and a long four-bay range
on a high basement running back behind it. Brick rendered with
stone quoins. Burgh's detail is restrained: a bold torus moulding above the basement, string course, and eaves cornice. The
front roof has a large leaded flat with big regular chimneys in
the centre. The windows are all sashed and are very widely
spaced. Entrance arch of channelled stone, decorated with arms
and cannon on the keystone. The interior is remarkable for a
long spinal corridor, 8 ft wide and 110 ft long, with elegant
groin-vaulting. An early C18 stair rises in a square below an
octagonal cupola in the NE corner of the building. Some rooms
retain original panelling.

CONVENT OF MERCY. 1880 by *O'Neill & Byrne*. A standard
design of nine bays with projecting gabled ends and gabled half-
dormer windows on the third floor. All in Dungannon freestone.

UNION WORKHOUSE, in the Purt, S of the town. 1842 by *George
Wilkinson*. Now a hospital and still complete. The usual gabled
Tudoresque design.

TOUR

The best houses in Ballyshannon are near the barracks at the bottom of the hill in MAIN STREET and CASTLE STREET: large, comfortable three-storey blocks, of mid C18 appearance, though possibly later. They throw into relief the town's outlandish banks: THE ROYAL BANK OF IRELAND, a good piece of streetscape of a mongrel Scottish Baronial style with clock turret and bellcotes all of 1878, and THE PROVINCIAL BANK next door, a resourceful single-storey Baroque cash office by *T. N. Deane & Son* of *c.* 1885. THE NATIONAL BANK opposite is a more chaste five-bay, two-storey stucco block, spoilt by new windows. In Castle Street MESSRS STEPHENS has a good cut stone aedicule door, Doric with flanking pilasters. Above it the street opens into a steep triangular place with, in the middle, the MARKET AND COURT HOUSE, a utilitarian rendered lump, unworthy of its position. Buildings existed here in 1762, but the present structure is apparently of 1881. MAIN STREET has good Georgian houses. Half-way up the hill on the E side is a big, handsomely proportioned five-bay house with a Gibbs surround and pediment to its door. At the top THE MANOR is a late C18 five-bay, three-storey house. In BISHOP STREET, at the head of Main Street, opposite a pretty thatched pub, SHELL HOUSE, a three-bay, two-storey house decorated with shells and broken crockery.

About 1 km W of the town centre, two bigger houses, DANBY and PORTNASON HOUSE, face each other across the river. They are both early C19 three-bay, two-storey houses, Danby with a pedimented Tuscan porch and cut stone coat of arms.

NEIGHBOURHOOD

ASSAROE ABBEY. 1 km NW. The Cistercian house founded by Flaharty O'Muldorry in 1178 and colonized from Boyle Abbey in Roscommon is now nothing more than two undistinguished walls standing to a height of about 30 ft. Pieces of cut stone remain in the overgrown graveyard; an early C13 stone with a shaft moulding is used as a step into it. The abbey was sacked in 1398; in 1597 it was occupied by English forces, and the community dispersed in 1607.

SMINVER CHURCH. 1 km S by the former railway line. A plain rectangle almost lost in ivy and a rubbish tip.

STONEWOLD CASTLE. 2.5 km ESE. Submerged by the River Erne hydroelectric scheme.

PARK HILL. 3 km NE on the Donegal Road. A charming though

exceptionally modest gentleman's seat, built in the mid C18 for a Mr O'Neill. It lies on low ground down a straight cart track: a little five-bay, two-storey house, thatched within recent memory. Inside, five-panelled C18 doors in lugged surrounds and low, 9 ft ceilings – a rare survival and a salutary reminder of the simplicity of many of the so-called seats that feature in *The Post Chaise Companion*.

CAVANGARDEN. 4 km NE. Built about 1770 by a family called Atkinson, a three-bay, two-storey house on a basement with a canted centre bay, and half-hipped gables, a typical Co. Fermanagh motif that has strayed into Donegal. A porch with columns of a primitive order has been added to the main door. The gable end of farm buildings near the house is brightened up to look like a Gothic chapel.

CAMLIN. 3.5 km ESE on the Belleek road. Once the seat of the Tredennick family, who moved to Donegal after their lands near Bodmin in Cornwall had been confiscated by the Commonwealth. Parts of the C17 house were incorporated by *J. B. Keane* in the pretty battlemented castle that he designed for John A. Tredennick when Camlin was rebuilt in 1838. It had a five-bay, two-storey front with corner towerlets, gabled centre, an upper oriel in the middle, and a toy-castle porch, but all this has gone. Now only Keane's castle-style gate remains, a round folly tower to fly a flag from, with a battlemented Tudor arch beside it and a battlemented curving wall.

BALLYWILLAN *see* PORTSTEWART

BANAGHER *see* FEENY

F6   BARONSCOURT   TY
                     4 km. SW of Newtownstewart

79 Baronscourt is one of the grandest neo-classical houses in Ireland, and also one of the most complicated, with four great classicists each contributing to its appearance. The house was built new between 1779 and 1781 by James Hamilton, the eighth Earl of Abercorn, to designs of *George Steuart*. The Earl, who 'never drank anything but water, nor had more relish for the society of women', died a bachelor in 1782, and within two years his nephew John James, who became first Marquess of Abercorn in 1790, had employed *John Soane* to turn his uncle's sober house back to front and in the process to make it a good deal

grander. But that house was burnt out in 1796 and only partly repaired. In 1818 the first Marquess was succeeded by his grandson James, who about 1831 had schemes for enlargement prepared by *William Farrell*. He did not act on these, however, and subsequently employed *William Vitruvius Morrison* to re-model the house and complete its interior decoration. With Morrison Baronscourt reached its greatest extent, and it was a mixture of Morrison and Soane's work that was removed and the scars tidied over by *Sir Albert Richardson* in 1947.

The architectural history of Baronscourt estate has not been explored in detail,* and only an outline of the development of the house can be suggested here. Steuart's house, which cost the Earl some £8,015 8s. 7½d., seems to be that recorded in the survey made by Soane in 1791. It was a five-bay, three-storey block with window proportions similar to those employed by Steuart at Attingham, Shropshire – that is, with the tallest windows on the ground floor, and those on the second storey very much reduced. The house faced s and had a three-bay loggia of coupled Tuscan columns across the ground-floor centre and a shallow pediment at eaves level. Once again like Attingham, for which Baronscourt might almost be a prototype, the offices were arranged in a wider, lower block behind, projecting E and w, with a colonnaded service courtyard on the N.

Hardly anything is left of this. Soane took off the top storey, removed the entrance loggia, and altered the ground-floor windows to a type with a low panel that he preferred. Inside, Steuart's hall was thrown into the rooms on either side of it to make an immense saloon running across the whole s front. The stairs, which had occupied the usual position within the inner hall (cf. Castle Archdale or Florence Court), were blocked off by a wall and the offices extended and remodelled to create a semicircular N front with a portico and a new hall in the middle. In October 1791 Soane sent over *Robert Woodgate* from his office to superintend the work. The removal of the top storey was probably the result of the fire that began in an attic room and gutted the entire central block in December 1796. Wood-gate's initiative in building up the wing passages with wet sods saved the offices, but a further £4,000 had to be spent on dis-mantling and partly rebuilding the burnt-out shell, work that was begun in July 1798, after a pause of eighteen months, with

* *The Abercorn Letters*, edited by Canon John H. Gebbie (Strule Press, Omagh, 1972), publish many valuable references to architectural work on the estate.

Woodgate in charge. This can have been only a patch-up job as in 1810 a Mr *Turner*, who proved to be rather drunken, turns up to add four feet to the walls and put a new roof on the house. Obviously Lord Abercorn lost a lot of money and perhaps a good deal of his drive through the fire, and it was left to his grandson to complete the house properly.

Before the fire, Soane had experimented with several schemes for Baronscourt, proposing flanking forestanding wings on the s front, and a variety of entrance facades. What was done afterwards is not recorded, though a number of the ideas first experimented with in 1791 were to be explored by Farrell (who proposed squaring off the semicircular N court with a gigantic entrance hall like Kedleston) and by Morrison, who seems to have been responsible for the circular top-lit saloon in the centre of the house where Soane had once proposed an oval billiard room. Soane or Morrison raised the height of the wings behind the main block and remodelled their interiors. The s front remains as they left it: a seven-bay, two-storey façade with a shallow centre pediment and urn finials added by Morrison. The sides and flanking wings are both four bays deep, ending in a single-storey bow on the W, and a Soanic court of offices on the E. Of Soane's semicircular entrance front, nothing remains. The wings were cut down by Richardson, their ends treated as blank arches, linked by a screen of square piers to a Morrison giant-order Ionic portico that now, shorn of its flanking quadrants, seems to project a little too far from the front.

Inside, Baronscourt is entirely Morrison, and Morrison at his most opulent. The *porte cochère* opens into the HALL, a deep rectangle, solemn and high, with widely spaced pilasters and a flat coffered ceiling. Behind, in the centre of the house where the original staircase was, is the ROTUNDA, a dark green pool with eight powerful columns in green scagliola set round the walls. The columns are Greek Ionic, completely free-standing, and support a dome decorated with heavy octagonal coffering. Niches and doors alternate. L. from the hall is the wide STAIR, 30 ft by 24 ft, cantilevered on three sides, with a rectangular roof lantern and square coffered ceiling, and at the upper level quarter-engaged fluted columns with Temple of the Winds capitals. The LARGE DINING ROOM occupies the whole of the E wing, where Soane had planned a parlour and servants' hall. It is a double cube, sumptuous, with a Corinthian order of mustard-yellow scagliola pilasters and half-engaged columns at either end. The ceiling, divided into three panels, has a curious border of angular ribbons. Frieze of winged cupids with garlands over their shoulders. The chimneypiece, a little too chaste for such an emphatic room, is Doric by *Sir William Chambers* and taken from Duddingston House, Edinburgh, once another Abercorn property.

The rooms of the s front, originally three but thrown into one by Soane, were ingeniously divided again by Richardson, and in 1975 were re-instated as Morrison intended them to be. Under Morrison the long s room was subdivided by two screens of fluted Corinthian columns with pilaster responds against the walls. The ceilings are patterned with flowing acanthus borders, deeply undercut, with central bosses and, in the central part of the room, now the SALOON, the added enrichment of a garlanded ring of flowers held in loops by the beaks of fluttering doves. Large plaster figures of winged boys fill the corners. Richardson filled the spaces between the columns with new doors blocked either side by china cabinets and then, with a delightful nonchalance, closed the top with clear glass that permitted a sense of continuity from room to room.

In the w wing the LIBRARY is at least Soanic, with a flat oval ceiling supported on shallow pendentives with consoles (originally columns?) below. A book-door leads to the back stairwell, probably still by Soane, and then the w corridor, a series of clean Soanic arches with a barrel-vaulted cupola lobby on the l. In the RED STUDY a pretty Dublin fireplace by *Peter Bossi* in yellow and white marble, and in the MUSEUM, originally the Music Room, a delightful plaster ceiling with Amor and Psyche and four roundels of billing doves.

BARONSCOURT AGENT'S HOUSE. SE of the house. This 57 charming little essay in rustic Palladianism is one of the most interesting small classical houses in Ulster, architecturally one of the more ambitious and one of the earliest. Begun apparently in 1741 by the seventh Earl of Abercorn, it was finished by his son, who had succeeded to the title in January 1744 and who was corresponding with his agent John Colhoun about chimneypieces 'bespoke in Dublin' in 1745 and about the plasterer's account in 1746. From the agent's correspondence it seems that the designer of the house was the builder/architect *James Martin*, who was also building Clogher Cathedral at this time, and whose opinion was sought on all design and construction problems. It is equally clear from mention of the stair rails and the two large rooms above that the house was not always the single-storey villa it is now, and that it must have had an extra storey above the present eaves cornice. Today it is an unusually elegant small house. Three-bay front, brick-built, with a trim little Tuscan portico *in antis*, and two big wheel windows, such as James Gibbs used at Sudbrook Lodge, Petersham, Surrey, on either side of the door within the portico. The house was originally flanked by forestanding brick wings linked to it by straight brick walls, though unhappily the s wing has recently been removed. The façade as it is now bears a close kinship to Gibbs's Menagerie at Hackwood – plate 84 in *The Book of Architecture* of 1728 – but while Martin no doubt knew Gibbs's book, the similarity must be fortuitous, for the extra storey – an attic on top of the single-storey portico – will have made the original house look very different. The source for this seems indeed to be nearer at hand: in Edward Lovett Pearce's Bellamont Forest, Cootehill, Co. Cavan, also a three-bay design with a central single-storey portico and attic above. It is of course grander, but it too is of brick with the architectural elements in stone. The Agent's House was not a great success as a house – the floors were damp and the wallpaper peeled off the walls almost as soon as it was put on – so it is not perhaps surprising that the Earl decided later to build the new Baronscourt. Indeed he seems to have made more than one attempt, for in 1776 the festivities at the laying of the foundation stone of an Abercorn House are noted, and if this was for Steuart's building, the foundations must have lain unattended for three years before work was continued. When the new Baronscourt was finished the Earl's agent, James Hamilton, wrote in 1781, 'Mr George Steuart the architect ... has made several drawings of the lodges, and for converting the late house (as I may now call it) into conveniences for stables, farming etc., still retaining however a look of the house as it was'. Presumably the top floor came off soon after, for by 1783 the old house is described as 'completely fitted up'.

Inside, the scale of the rooms and the finish certainly suggest that they were meant to be used by a person of quality. The room N of the portico is 40 ft by 17 ft, running from front to back of the house, and has an elaborate cornice with large heavy mutules above an egg and dart cornice. Another room has a substantial dentil cornice, and the main fireplace is in a plain but generously scaled architectural style, like the plasterwork, early C18 rather than late.

STABLES, immediately N of the Agent's House. Scottish Baronial by *Joseph Bell* of Belfast, begun in September 1882. An eight-bay block, one and a half storeys high, with crow-stepped half-dormers and a carriage arch surmounted by a square turreted and gabled tower at the fourth bay. Designed to appear as a romantic outline from the terraces s of the house.

DERRYWOONE CASTLE, N of the house. The shell of a large Plantation castle, L-shaped and of four storeys, with a round tower 12 ft 6 in. in diameter at the point of the L and traces of the dressed stone corbelling of a stair at first-floor level in the re-entrant angle. A dressed round-headed arch here seems to have been the main door. The s gable retains its fireplaces and stout stone chimney head, and also some projecting bonding stones which suggest that an extension may have been planned. The w gable has partly fallen, revealing a curious double chimney presumably for the kitchen below and hall above. The castle is not mentioned in Pynnar's survey of 1619 but must have been built soon after.

MACHUGH CASTLE. On a small island that was probably a crannog in Lough Catherine, the lowest and largest lake in the park. Small stone-built keep about 20 ft high and some 12 ft by 15 ft inside. A door on one side and a small square window with stepped square-corbelled roof on the E. Traces of a small stone-built bailey on the s and E. Traditionally associated with the time of King John, though the late C15 would seem more probable.

ROCK COTTAGE. A picturesque gabled cottage with bargeboards, diamond brick chimneys, lattice panes, and rock boulder walls from which it takes its name. Early to mid C19.

THE PARK at Baronscourt is laid out round a chain of three artificial lakes bearing the names Lough Mary, Lough Fanny, and Lough Catherine and intended to continue the local tradition of giving landmarks women's names, as the two mountains in the area are Bessy Bell and Mary Gray. The Hamiltons were established at Baronscourt by 1566. Improvement in the park was begun by the seventh Earl and continued by the eighth, who sent over a gardener, *James Broomfield*, in 1746 to raise trees, plant clumps of chestnut, beech, and laburnum, and superintend the clearing of the ground and building of the park wall. The planting of Bessy Bell, a bare knoll 1,387 ft high to the E, was begun in the mid C18. In the time of the first Duke, the extensive terraces w and s of the house were laid out and conifers and evergreens introduced, apparently to suit the taste of his mother-in-law Georgiana, daughter of the Duke of

Gordon and wife of the sixth Duke of Bedford. Evidence of her part in the layout of the estate appears in the contemporary doggerel rhyme:

> We pride ourselves on Baronscourt,
> Its Lords, its Ladies fair,
> Its ruins grey, its islands,
> Its lakes, its gay parterre.
> For natural and artistic style,
> Old Erin has few such as
> Its walks for leisure, its grounds for pleasure,
> Designed by Bedford's Duchess.

BARONSCOURT CHURCH (C of I). 2 km SW of the house, above Lough Mary. Consecrated in 1858. A small, essentially English church. Three-bay nave and single-bay chancel with bellcote and side porch. Two-light Dec windows, all with stained glass, making necessary the unusual expedient of four large swept dormer-lights in the roof. – MONUMENT. First Duke of Abercorn † 1885. A large Celtic cross by *Walter G. Doolin* of Dublin. – The LYCHGATE was erected by the second Duke in memory of his mother.

CHURCHES in the area are: ST EUGENE, 1 km S of Baronscourt church, 1846, a four-bay harled hall with sandstone trim, bellcote and porch; DRUMLEGAGH PRESBYTERIAN CHURCH, 1.5 km WSW of Baronscourt church, a mid-C19 three-bay rendered hall; CAVANDARRAGH METHODIST CHURCH, 4 km NW of Baronscourt church, a mid-C19 three-bay hall with Dec W window.

D9   BELCOO   FM

A tiny village in attractive countryside, between Upper and Lower Lough Macnean, and on the border with Co. Cavan. The ruins of a medieval church are by each lough.

TEMPLERUSHIN CHURCH, Holywell. 1 km NW. The ruins of a very small church, 39 ft by 16½ ft inside. Early C15. The E gable, N wall, and part of the W gable, rebuilt, remain. Credence cavities in each wall and a delicate cusped lancet in the E gable. Window reveals spanned by straight lintels stepping down to the window frames. 'Entirely restored' in 1931 at a cost of £41 1s. 3d.

TEMPLENAFFRIN CHURCH. 2 km E. This small rectangular church served as a chapel of ease to the medieval parish of

Cleenish. It stands on a hillock N of the lough, surrounded by a graveyard wall, and set on a plinth. The w gable is intact, with a late C17 round-headed window. Inside, the church measures 20 ft by 58 ft, divided, with a small room at the w end. Two narrow slit windows in the nave, one with a round head and widely splayed reveals. The setting is pretty, but there is little of interest here now.

THE COTTAGE. A picturesque shooting lodge at the w end of the lower lough. Exceptionally long and low, with wiggly barge-boards and a myriad of diamond-shaped chimneystacks. Originally of c. 1830; extended in a similar style with double wings round a central yard in the later C19.

GARDEN HILL. 2.5 km NE. A complex of mid to late C17 buildings enlarged into a gentleman's residence by the Hassard family in the late C18. Now ruinous. Of the C17 are two enormous chimneys at the w end of the building and the crow-stepped outbuildings in the yard. The original house was a two-storey double pile set end on to the hill and extended as a single-storey cottage at the upper level, more than doubling the length of the front. The approach is by a rock-hewn drive through the remnants of a miniature park.

CREENAHOE HOUSE. 3 km E. A large two-storey, four-bay Georgian farmhouse, thatched, with four ample chimneystacks along the ridge of the roof.

BELLAGHY LD *J5*

A village that was the centre of the lands owned by the Vintners' Company after the Jacobean Plantation of 1607. It was settled by one Baptist Jones, who built his community on a very slight rise of land in the flat ground w of Lough Beg. The settlement as described by the *Calendar of State Papers* in 1622 is typical of many, with a fortified main house with two round towers of red brick and, an unusual feature, convex dome-like roofs. There was a gatehouse and sallyport and, beside the castle, 'fourteen framework houses', each with its field and garden; also a stone or wooden cross with stocks beneath it and eight circular thatched dwellings – the last for native inhabitants. The castle was taken and burnt by the MacDonnells in the 1641 rising and not repaired. In the C18 the decision of the Earl Bishop of Derry to build a large neo-classical house at Ballyscullion nearby no doubt brought improvement and work to the village. Today it is a small rural community with little architectural focus.

ST TIDAS, BALLYSCULLION PARISH CHURCH (C of I). 1794, replacing a church built on the site in 1625. Three-bay nave, now pebbledashed, with round-headed windows. Three-stage tower with cheese-like block pinnacles and a freestone octagonal spire added by the Earl Bishop, who preferred steeples to plain towers. Lewis talks in 1837 of a proposed new aisle, but this was never built. Inside, a small, low-fronted gallery supported on cast-iron cluster columns. Restored by *Welland & Gillespie*, who added a robing room in 1868. – MONUMENTS. A crude classical tablet of 1712 with open pediment and angels' heads instead of capitals, erected by Simon and Anna Rowe to their children. – In the churchyard the square stone DOWNING MAUSOLEUM dates from 1776.

ST MARY, 7 km N and 2 km W of Portglenone, Antrim. A big late C19 hall of black basalt. Five bays, with paired lancets. High double-hipped roof inside. The tower with double-louvred belfry stage by *J. V. Brennan*, 1912.

BELLAGHY PRESBYTERIAN CHURCH. A four-bay hall of 1819 virtually rebuilt in 1969.

CHURCH ISLAND RUINS. 3 km S. The ruins of a rectangular pre-C17 church, built of shore boulders, in a little yew-planted graveyard. Plain nave with the side walls and gables almost entire, a door and window on the S, an opening where the E window was, and a N window. To this in 1788 the Earl Bishop added a square battlemented tower, detached and just outside the W gable, also of boulder stone, with short corner pinnacles and a slender needle spire of ashlar granite blocks. The spire now leans crazily at the top, for the whole steeple was added merely as a decorative object to be viewed from Ballyscullion House and has not been maintained since the early C19. The island, anciently associated with St Tida, has now become a peninsula attached by sodden fields to the mainland.

BELLAGHY CASTLE. Late C17, extensively restored in 1791, a long two-storey house, rendered, with quoins. Porch with a pretty fanlight door inside. The octagonal brick tower to the SE may relate to the C17 house.

BALLYSCULLION HOUSE. 1.5 km E. The Ulster estates of the Earl Bishop (Downhill and Ballyscullion) were left on his death in 1803 to Harry Bruce, his cousin, who in June 1804 became a baronet, Sir Henry Hervey Aston Bruce of Downhill. It was one of his younger children, Admiral Sir Henry William Bruce (1792–1863), who built the present palazzo-style house about 1850, probably to designs of *Sir Charles Lanyon*. It is a square block, two storeys on a sunk basement, with a five-bay front, four-bay side, and four-bay rear elevation. Stuccoed, with a bracketed eaves cornice, shallow hipped roof, and regular massed chimneys. The windows on the first floor have shallow segmental heads, and more Lanyon features are the four-columned Doric porch in sandstone on the front and the paired Doric columns flanking an asymmetrical tripartite window (at the end of the drawing room) on the garden front. Alterations in 1939 were by *R. T. McGuckin*.

Of the BISHOP'S PALACE only the foundations remain in a wood N of the present house. It was built from 1787 to designs of *Michael Shanahan* of Cork, assisted possibly by *Francis Sandys*, as a great oval house to be linked by quadrant wings to flanking pavilion buildings that were never finished. The main block of the house was based, according to Lord Bristol, on John Plaw's circular house of Belle Isle, on Lake Windermere, though to accommodate more rooms the plan was changed from a pure circle to an oval; it is the oval that can now just be traced in the woodlands, with diameters of 84 and 94 ft. It stood three storeys high, with a giant order of twenty-two Corinthian pilasters supporting a rectangular entablature with an attic storey and domed roof above. On the entrance front was a four-columned portico, the only substantial portion of the house to survive, as it was bought in 1813 by Dr Nathaniel Alexander, then Bishop of Down and Connor, and presented to St George's Church, Belfast, where it still stands.

BELLANALECK FM E9

CLEENISH PARISH CHURCH (C of I). A quite perfect mid Georgian toy Gothic church of *c.* 1763. Tower and hall type, with only the three-stage tower with monstrous and curiously 'soft' pinnacles attempting a Gothic idiom. The nave is a plain four-bay hall with big round-headed windows decorated with keystones and stone imposts all rather too close together. E window with double Y-tracery. The church was reseated by *Welland & Gillespie* in 1869.

SKEA HALL. 3 km W. A stylish late Georgian villa built for George Hassard *c.* 1830. Long and low, of seven bays, single-storey at the front, with a primitive Doric porch of four columns and a Doric eaves cornice. Inside, a nice original fireplace with figures of Music and Painting and Ceres (but surely it should be Ariadne) on a leopard. Early C19 wallpapers of a naval engagement and an Indian battle.

CLEENISH ISLAND. 2.5 km E. A large triangular island in the reaches between Upper Lough Erne and Enniskillen remarkable for a succession of nine abandoned single-storey cottages built for ex-servicemen after the First World War, and for the ancient graveyard by the N W point of the island. The monastery founded here by St Sinell in the C6 was succeeded in 1100 by the church of St Sinell. References to a religious community continue until the C15. The ruins were used as a quarry in the C18.

CHURCHES near here are DRUMRAINEY CHURCH, 3 km WNW, a three-bay hall and porch; and ARNEY CHURCH, of hall and tower type, early C19, with a pinnacled tower and Y-tracery windows.

CLEENISH. *See also* Lisbellaw.

A large square house of coursed basalt and sandstone, with an architectural development that is not easy to unravel. The land was settled in the mid C17 by a Northamptonshire man, William Gage, who bought the lease of the estate, then called Ballymargy – the dwelling in the fen – from the Bishop of Derry. It was baptized Bellarena – the beautiful strand – in the later C18 by that cosmopolitan traveller Lord Bristol. The Gage family remained the owners of Bellarena until 1851, when the sole heiress, Marianne Gage, married Sir Frederick William Heygate. About 1860 the Heygates added a bay-window on the E side of the house, to make room for a billiard table, and built a wing at the back on the W side; but the principal changes to the house were made earlier, by the Gages.

The main front is a five-bay, two-storey block with a hipped roof behind a stone cornice and blocking course raised over the central bay to suggest a pediment. Inside, the pediment at first-floor level is an enormous and disproportionate Venetian window, with a bowed freestone porch below it. This front, which accommodates no more than a hall with two rooms 30 ft by 20 ft on either side, is laid across a haphazard suite of rooms that is said to incorporate parts of the oldest house, dating from 1690. Upstairs there are still several doors of the mid C18 with six panels and lugged surrounds. Behind, on the N, is a curious four-bay, two-and-a-half-storey façade with flat half-dormers and all the windows of the tripartite Regency type. There are therefore three piles of building one in front of another with the central pile the oldest and now completely obscured from outside. The N front is said to have been built by Marcus McCausland (who took the name of Gage) about 1797, and he may also have added the s entrance block. His son Conolly introduced the dormers at the back in 1822 and at the same time opened up two floors of the old house on the W side to accommodate a fine library made up, as Mr Donald Girvan has shown, with windows and fitments bought at the dismantling of Ballyscullion House.

A plan made for insurance purposes in 1824 shows the late Georgian arrangement of the ground floor with a simple dog-leg stair in the hall. This was replaced to accommodate the notions of grandeur of Marianne Gage's mother, a rich Miss Tindall from Bristol whose sister was Mrs McCausland of Drenagh and who seems to have employed *Charles Lanyon* about the time that he was designing Drenagh. In place of the dog-leg stair came a gargantuan double return flight shooting up from the centre of the hall between bloated Corinthian columns and then curling back on itself round the capitals to the landing above: cramped grandiloquence like the saloon stair of an Edwardian liner. On the half-landing is a deep niche that communicates with the library and the older part of the house. At the time the stair was built the front porch was added to the house.

STABLE COURT. Opening from the N front of the house, a wide cobbled courtyard with single-storey offices, pre-1823, and in the centre opposite the house a symmetrical two-storey coach house with a central carriage arch surmounted by a timber clock tower and spire.

FOLLY TOWER. 0.5 km N of the house on the edge of a belt of trees. An C18 folly that would delight Miss Barbara Jones. Pure nonsense and very evocative. A stout stone drum winds as an exposed staircase round a circular brick belvedere only 5 ft in diameter inside, with four Gothic arches, a corbelled course, *œil de bœuf*, and drum above, in all about 25 ft high, sprouting very effectively from a stone wall at its base. The field the folly overlooks was said to have been used for horse racing in the C18.

A nice village just beyond the w end of Lower Lough Erne on the border with Co. Donegal. Celebrated now both for trout and for the porcelain factory that manufactures a fine cream lustre ware.

BELLEEK PORCELAIN FACTORY. By far the largest building in the village. Begun in December 1858 and robustly commercial, the factory is of local limestone, a solid rectangular block thirteen bays long and three storeys high. The centre three bays project slightly, with the ground floor treated as a triumphal arch with a segmental carriage entrance and doors at either side. Above, pilaster strips without capitals support a pediment with central oculus. The windows are segment-headed except on the top floor, where paired round lancets are used. In the central bay there are three instead of two. By *William Armstrong* (?).

ST PATRICK. Erected by the parish priest in 1892, a large six-bay hall and tower built in squared rock-faced limestone with lancet windows. E window a triple lancet. The tower was evidently intended to have a spire, but this was not built.

BELLEEK PARISH CHURCH (C of I). A stone-built hall with bellcote and porch. Round-headed windows. The parochial hall until 1909, when it became the church.

METHODIST CHURCH. Mid c19. A tiny rendered three-bay hall with porch. Quoins the only decoration.

FORT. On the crown of the hill immediately w of the bridge the walls of the N side of an c18 artillery fort built by General Knox. Star-shaped on the river side, with gun loops and brick vaulting.

POLICE STATION. Seven-bay design with red-tiled roof and dormers by *T. F. O. Rippingham.*

TIVEA LOUGH FRIARY. 4 km E, on the s shore of Keenaghan Lough. Ruins of a rectangular church with a thin cusped lancet in the E gable and a small square-headed opening in the s wall. Said to have been a Franciscan foundation. Late medieval, with details comparable to Templerushin Church, Belcoo.

BELLEEK OLD PARISH CHURCH. 5.5 km E. A splendid landmark and a monument to c18 isolationism, built between 1788 and 1790 to save Protestant proprietors the inconvenience of going to Templecarne parish church. Thirty-two townlands were disunited in 1792 to form the new Belleek parish. But this isolated hilly site was not really convenient for many. The church held two hundred and rarely had a congregation of over eighty. By 1846 'evening service was performed during summer in a rotation of private houses', and by 1875 Belleek school house had been licensed for public worship. Now the church stands abandoned and lonely on its hill. The fittings have been removed, but the hall and tower remain, visible for miles around. Inside are four Y-tracery windows in timber and a delicate cusped and crocketed trifora in plaster at the E end, framing the Ten Commandments. Outside, the whole church was given crenellations c. 1830 to hide the roof. The tower, unnecessarily elongated, is three storeys high with thin corner buttresses. The Ordnance Survey memoirs give the original architect as a *Mr Boggs*.

BELLEEK RECTORY. 5 km E. 1826. A large late-Georgian-style rectory, three bays by two storeys, with relieving arches to the central door and ground-floor windows. Outhouses in a rectangular block to the E.

FARRANCASSIDY HOUSE. 2.5 km SSE. A fine old Irish farmhouse built by the Dundas family in 1731. Long and low, originally thatched but now with a corrugated iron roof. Seven bays and two storeys, though the upper floor is really an attic with the windows very low, almost at floor level, and of only six sash panes. The walls are rendered and whitewashed. Cut stone Gibbs surround to the central door and stone sills to all the windows.

MAGHERAMENA CASTLE. 3 km E. The ruins of an Elizabethan-style house built by James Johnston to designs of *J. B. Keane* between 1835 and 1840. Mr Johnston married in 1838, so the new house perhaps marked a new stage in his life. Now all that remains is the walls. The building became a temporary parochial house and was unroofed and partly demolished in the 1950s. It makes a good ruin. The house faced S across the River Erne. The entrance was to the N, a conservatory to the E, and a small kitchen court to the W – an oddly back-to-front orientation for the last two. The main façades are quite irregular, with big octagonal turrets and haphazard breaks from room to room. A corridor running E–W connected the five main rooms on the S front. The building was of cut stone. Some details, notably the pointed machicolations at the W end, were copied from Irish castles such as Termon at Pettigoe. As in so many Irish Georgian houses, the servants were not to be seen. A covered passage led W from the house to the C18 stable court and offices left over from the older buildings of Leuare House.

ROSSCOR HOUSE. 5 km E, on the s side of the river Erne. A large rendered mid C18 house, much altered.

ST MICHAEL. 6.5 km E, at Muleek, below the former parish church. A four-bay rendered hall with a short sanctuary and a pine gallery at the back. Rebuilt in 1912 by the Rev. C. McMeel P.P., *John Reid* of Enniskillen builder.

ROSSCOR CHAPEL OF EASE (C of I). Early C19; a plain three-bay hall and porch with Y-tracery windows.

ST JOHN THE BAPTIST. 3 km ESE. Built about 1880. Crisply detailed stone with yellow brick trim and carved details. Nave and chancel with asymmetrical s porch and sacristy. Modern free-standing bellcote in concrete.

BELL ISLE

BELL ISLE HOUSE. The core of the house, whose brick-vaulted basement offers a guide to its original extent, is a seven-bay, two-storey block facing s across a beautiful lakeland view. This is probably a vestige of the original Bellisle House described by Arthur Young in 1776 as 'the charming seat of the Earl of Ross', i.e. Sir Ralph Gore, Viscount Bellisle and Earl of Ross, whose family had been established here in 1629. By 1837 the place had become dilapidated and was 'about to be rebuilt' by the Rev. J. Grey Porter, whose son, John Grey Vesey Porter, added the stable court in 1856 and some time before 1890 recast the entire house in a free manorial style, with a multi-gabled entrance front, large mullioned bays, and a high five-storey tower at the SE corner to command a view of the lough. The architect was *Morley Horder*. The effect is grand enough in places, but incoherent.

ST MICHAEL. 1 m NE, at Derryharney. Built by the Rev. John Grey Porter of Bellisle, a moderate-sized three-bay lancet hall with porch and bellcote. Squared quoins. Chancel added in 1883. Curiously simple, with a brick vault and a brick chancel arch.

BELTRIM CASTLE *see* GORTIN

BENBURB

This tiny place on the banks of the Blackwater is celebrated in Irish history for the spectacular defeat of the Ulster Scots under

General Munro by Owen Roe O'Neill in 1646. The battle was hailed as a decisive victory, and when the news reached Rome, Innocent X attended a Te Deum in S. Maria Maggiore. Architecturally the village still has strong links with the C17, for its church and castle date from this period.

CLONFEACLE PARISH CHURCH (C of I). It is a measure of the destructive talents of the Irishman that this small hall built by Sir Richard Wingfield between 1618 and 1622 should be the oldest church in North West Ulster still in use for regular services. Repaired in 1815 and 1837, in 1892 it gained a belfry tower added by the local landlord, James Bruce, probably to designs of his architect, *W. H. Lynn*. The church is still a typical Planter's Gothic structure: a long hall, 24 ft by 70 ft, of four bays, with characteristically massive double-stepped buttresses and primitive Jacobean Gothic tracery. Pointed E window of four lights, with a cusped vesica motif on the point introduced in an ungainly provincial way. The side windows, flat-headed under label mouldings, are three-light with a single transom, set in segmental arches inside. Notice the odd outward-curling label stops to the door and E window. The interior is plain save for a large wooden gallery of 1837. – FONT. Late C17; a fluted bowl on a stumpy Tuscan pillar, all in sandstone. – STAINED GLASS. In the E window, medium-sized figures of 1893. – MONUMENT. Captain James Hamilton † 1646. A sandstone aedicule with an open pediment and armorial bearings. – BELL. 1688. Bought by Lord Charlemont for Clonfeacle, though intended for Limerick. Inscribed I.H.S. MR. P-FRS-LAUDATE IN TYMPANO ET CHORO: FR: X: MATHEW MCMAHON CAPUCINORUM LOCI: LIMERICENSIS SUPERIOR ME FIERI FECIT DIE 8 IULY ANNO DO. 1688.

BENBURB CASTLE. In the grounds of Benburb Manor, below the main street of the village and set on a cliff some 36 m (120 ft) above the Blackwater River. A large planter's bawn built by Sir Richard Wingfield, who had a grant of 1,000 acres here from James I. An earlier castle belonged to Shane O'Neill in 1556. This building, with detailing like Spur Royal and Castle Archdale, is said to have been begun in 1611. There is no main house, but the bawn measures 110 ft by 130 ft, enclosed by a 16 ft high wall with musketry loop-holes and a sloping cope. The door is on the N, and the bawn is flanked at either end by two square towers with large six-light, two-mullioned windows and label mouldings. A circular flanker on the NE contains a spiral stair. The castle is regularly described as 'badly built' despite its impressive size. Today it is overgrown, and a C19 house replaces the fourth flanker.

BENBURB MANOR. In 1887 James Bruce of Belfast purchased Benburb from the Wingfield family and began this big red-brick house to designs of *W. H. Lynn*. Sold on Bruce's death in 1917, in 1948 it was dedicated as the first Servite priory in Ireland. The style is similar to Lynn's Campbell College, Belfast, with high, clean walls, sandstone trim, and big gables with squared corners. Two-storey with high attics and dormers. Stable court and clock tower on the w. The ballroom has become a chapel, and the priory has added a decent modern range behind the stables. SCULPTURE introduced by the community includes St Joseph by *Seamus Murphy*; Our Lady of Benburb – iconographically a female St Christopher – by *Gabriel Hayes*; and in the chapel a mannered Crucifixion by *Peter Dowd* and a Via Matris by *Muriel Brandt*.

SCOTS CHURCH. 1839. A stone-built hall with pinnacles and machicolated gable eaves. Lancet windows.

BRANTRY CHURCH (C of I). 6.5 km w, by Hollands crossroads. A plain little church built of quality materials by the Countess of Caledon in 1844. Ashlar hall with w bellcote, side porch, and three-light lancet window. The L-shaped GLEBE HOUSE with Elizabethan porch was also built by the Countess.

A village in one long street, with some substantial houses that give it a sustained architectural effect. About the middle of the N side is the NORTHERN BANK, two-storeyed like its neighbours but twice their height, with a big sandstone Doric porch, stone string courses, and a dentil cornice. On the s side No. 37 is a three-bay, two-storey house with mid Victorian fancy stucco in a vaguely classical style.

ST PATRICK, CLOUGHERNY PARISH (C of I). 1.5 km NW. Reputedly on the site of a C13 church burnt in the Williamite wars and restored about 1691, the date of the Communion chalice that is inscribed 'Teampul mael na Cloighearriach'. The present church, incorporating the side walls of the old one, was built in 1746 by the Rev. Richard Dobbs. The gallery was added by John Lowry in 1775 and the tower by James Lowry, who succeeded his father as rector in 1794. In 1855 the nave was extended, a new chancel built, and paired stone lancets fitted throughout by *William Fullerton*, the diocesan architect.

Modest interior with exposed trusses and rafters. – STAINED
GLASS. E window in memory of James Lowry, 1875; seven
small scenes in vesica-shaped frames by *Hardman & Co.* –
MONUMENT. George Perry † 1703. A slab carved with a skull
and crossbones and a free coat of arms.

CLOUGHERNY GLEBE HOUSE. E of the church. A substantial
double pile built by the Rev. John Lowry in 1778 at a cost of
£2,167. Two storeys with a three-bay rendered front with
central gable pediment above a Venetian window. The design
is spoilt by an ugly new front door and porch. Five-bay garden
façade.

DONAGHANIE OLD CHURCH. 4 km W. The site of a medieval
church with an old graveyard. Little remains.

CHURCHES in the area are: BERAGH CHURCH, at the W end
of the street, mid C19, a simple T-plan building with timber
galleries in each arm and box pews upstairs; CLOUGHERNEY
PRESBYTERIAN CHURCH, 3 km WSW at Dervaghroy, 1902,
refaced in 1963, a hall with brick pilasters and pediment; and
KILLARAINE CHURCH, 4 km N, a late C19 six-bay lancet hall
with porch and bellcote.

BLESSINGBOURNE *see* FIVEMILETOWN

BOA ISLAND   FM *D7*

FIGURE SCULPTURES. In Caldragh graveyard, on the S shore
of the island about 1.5 km E of Inishkeeragh Bridge, and down
a cart track leading across a field. The walk is worthwhile, for
the graveyard contains two upright stone effigies, idols of a pre-
Christian Celtic religion. Both have been re-erected on different base stones. The smaller, brought from Lustymore
Island, faces E and is sculptured to represent a little man with
hunched shoulders and hands held across the lap. The sides
of the block show traces of modelling, especially at the front
shoulders, and even suggest crossed legs. The back is plain. The
large figure has two faces, that on the E a little shorter than that
on the W but closely similar. The chin and eyes are pointed
like a child's drawing of a Chinaman, and the arms cross each
other in an X immediately below the pointed chin. One side
is sculptured with crisscross patterns between the two heads
(to suggest plaited hair?), and a deep slot has been hollowed

out in the top of the stone to connect it with an upper piece
now lost. Pre-c5.*

A parish celebrated for its underground chambers and caves.

BOHO HIGH CROSS. By the SW corner of the Catholic church
the base and shaft of an 8 ft High Cross of the C9 or C10,
decorated with rectangular panels of interlace, spirals, and
figure scenes: the Fall of Man, with a curly serpent between
Adam and Eve; the Virgin between two saints; the Baptism
of Christ.

AGHANAGLACK CROSS. 2.5 km SW of Boho crossroads. The
base and shaft of a plain High Cross, almost 9 ft high, with the
mortice at the top of the stone for the head still intact.

BOHO PARISH CHURCH (C of I). Built in 1777 and restored
c. 1830. A small, three-bay tower and hall church with round-
headed windows. Inside the vestibule, the arch of the door to
the church is from the site of the medieval church 1 km N.

CHURCH OF THE SACRED HEART. Built by the Rev. Nicholas
Smith in 1832. 'Renovated' in 1913. A four-bay hall with a
squared rubble gable and bellcote.

A parish in upland pastoral country N of Dungiven where an early
Christian monastery was founded in 557 by St Colmcille.

BOVEVAGH OLD CHURCH. 0.5 km N of Bovevagh New
Bridge. The ruins of a rectangular church spectacularly situated on a high spur, skirted on two sides by a stream. 48 ft by
18 ft inside, with walls approx 3 ft thick and standing, in the
side walls and part of the gables, to a height of 10 ft. There
are three windows and a door on the S side and a W window,
but no architectural details. The church is set on a steeply raked
podium. The ruins are thought to be C13 or C14. An earlier
oratory here was burned by Norsemen in 1100.

At the SW corner is a MORTUARY HOUSE, a small church-
shaped stone tomb about 9 ft long, 6½ ft wide, and 7½ ft high,
similar in form to the larger Tomb of St Muriedach O'Heney
at Banagher, though earlier and said to date from the C12.

* A detailed discussion of these figures and of their significance is given in
Helen Hickey, *Images of Stone: Figure Sculpture of the Lough Erne Basin* (Belfast, 1976).

Recent removal of soil has revealed at the s w angle a facing stone with coarse diagonal tooling. The chief interest of these little shrines is that they preserve in miniature the form of early Christian Irish oratories long after full churches had ceased to be built in this manner.

BOVEVAGH PARISH CHURCH (C of I). 0.5 km W of the bridge. 1823. A pretty example of the tower and hall type as designed by *John Bowden*, identical to churches at Faughanvale and Eglinton. Three-stage tower, tapering to the top, with large corner finials. Three-bay nave with cusped Y-tracery in timber. The entrance is through a circular vestibule in the tower.

SCRIGGAN PRESBYTERIAN CHURCH. 1.5 km SE of the bridge. Originally of 1791. T-plan Gothic, with cusped lancets and double bellcote.

ST MATTHEW. 5.5 km NE, at Drumsurn. Mid C19 six-bay lancet hall with short chancel and bellcote. Stuccoed. The interior panelled in pine. Simple but nice, with an avenue of trees leading up to it.

STRAW HOUSE. 1 km N of the bridge. Originally late C18. Three-bay, two-storey front, now stuccoed, with aedicule windows and a porch.

BOVEVAGH BRIDGE. 1816. Three segmental arches in dressed sandstone.

BROOKEBOROUGH   FM *F9*

AUGHAVEA PARISH CHURCH (C of I). 3 km SW. Burnt in 1806 and rebuilt 'under the direction of the Rev. R. Webster and Henry Leslie Esq.'. Four-bay hall with a tower added in 1810 – a pretty design in three stages with quoins and a round-headed belfry window. In 1855 the windows of the church were altered to paired lancets and a small N vestry was added by *Alexander Hardy*.

CATHOLIC CHURCH. A little E, above the village. Building in 1841. An enormous, rather dull hall, 42 ft wide inside, with six lancet windows down each wall. The outside, of squared coursed stone with buttresses between each window, is saved from dullness by a delightful square three-stage tower which must be early Victorian, yet manages to look exactly like a Sanderson Miller product – perhaps Wroxton – with small spiky pinnacles and Y-traceried stone mullions.

METHODIST CENTENARY CHAPEL. 1839. A large three-bay

hall with a two-bay chancel. Cement-rendered paired round-headed windows.

Brookeborough is a C19 village of painted, cement-rendered houses along one main street. It would be improved by tree planting. At the N end of the street the SOUTH AFRICA WAR MEMORIAL, a limestone plinth covered with delightful arabesques and surmounted by a lively lion carved by a local sculptor, *Harte*, in 1901. Beside this is the LADY BROOKE MEMORIAL HALL of 1891, a single-storey hall with a high-pitched roof and a gabled two-storey central bay with a louvred bell tower on the ridge above. Further down on the l. is the MARKET HOUSE, now the Orange Hall, with its three segmental arches to the ground floor blocked up, and beyond is the former POLICE BARRACKS (now a private house) of *c.* 1830, in a gabled Tudor style with high chimneys.

GOLA HOUSE. 0.5 km SW. A neat, symmetrical farmhouse of *c.* 1780, with a three-bay, two-storey front and single-storey wings on either side. Diamond-cut quoins and simplified Gibbs surrounds to the windows and door. The wings are later but follow the central block in style, with high pitched roofs and attic rooms lit through the end gables.

GREENHILL. 2.5 km NW. A gentleman's solid, mid C18 house, built by the Irvine family. Three-bay, two-storey, the centre bay very narrow and slightly stepped forward, with a small pediment. Quoins and a flat-headed main door with Gibbs surround. Later in the century a second floor was added – slightly detracting from the proportion and dominance of the pediment. The plan is symmetrical, with a brick-vaulted basement below the hall. Lugged door surrounds and C18 balusters to the stair. Coat of arms in the pediment with the motto 'Dum memor ipse nei'. The gates to the stable yard on the l. are surmounted by splendid carved lions like those at Rash House, Old Mountjoy, and Clover Hill, Inver.

WHITE PARK. 2 km NW. 1790. A three-bay, two-storey house with a canted central bow and a pretty fanlight. Six-panelled doors in lugged surrounds inside.

SKEOGE HOUSE. 1 km N. A substantial farmhouse of Regency appearance with a shallow hipped roof and wide overhanging eaves on consoles. L-shaped, of two storeys, with three windows across the entrance front and a square stone porch.

TATTYKEERAN CHURCH (C of I). 5 km N. 1814. A pretty three-bay hall, harled, with quoins and stone surrounds to slender Georgian Gothic lancets. Bellcote and porch. Finials on the gables. A stone on the E gable is inscribed: 'Erected by the Rev. B. Brooke 1814'. Pretty miniature gallery inside, and E window with red, white, blue, and yellow glass in square panes.

BROWN HALL   DO C7

A big C18 house built by the Hamilton family and basically of two periods: a low, eight-bay, two-storey wing – the original house of John Hamilton and his son James, who moved to Brown Hall from Murragh in 1697 – and the main block, a regular four-bay, three-storey cube. Exact dates are not known. A weathervane in the yard behind the old wing is initialled J.H. and dated 1710. This must be James, who succeeded his father in 1706 and died in 1755. The big house was probably built by his son John (1735–1811) and was certainly complete by 1789, the date of an estate map in the house. Brown Hall is an unpretentious yet substantial country house, built in straightforward materials. The wing is harled and has widely spaced segment-headed windows, framed in brick – typical of its date. The roof is of heavy Boylagh slates, supported by massive trusses that appear in the yards and in the two-storey kitchen in the NW corner. Typical, too, are the squat, fat chimneystacks in brick.

The main house, more than twice the height of the wing, is also harled, with stone quoins to the front, a plain eaves cornice, and a high hipped roof with a regular central chimney – all in an old-fashioned style. The only unusual feature is the porch, an odd addition, supported on four square stone pillars with primitive abacus tops and plain entablature. In 1794 *Robert Woodgate*, who had been superintending work at Baronscourt, wrote to Soane that he was taking plasterers to work at Mr Hamilton's at Brown Hall; so the porch may be by Woodgate, who was presumably also responsible for the extension of the ground-floor windows on the N and S sides and for enlarging the dining room. Inside, the best feature is the hall – a rectangular space with a continuous triglyph frieze and big lugged five-panel doors. The staircase behind (remodelled in the C19) leads to a large upper hall, now two rooms, with a bold egg and dart cornice. To the N of this was the original drawing room, with a panelled dado. In the park to the S are the remnants of an extensive lime-tree avenue, planted in the early C19, and a natural limestone bridge where the River Ballintra suddenly flows underground, passing through several caves. In one of these, the rock formations resemble piles of sheepskins – hence the name 'Ballintra'.

BUNBEG

This part of Donegal between the Rosses and Gweedore, though popular with holidaymakers, is one of the poorest areas of Ireland. Between its serrated coastline and bare mountain ridges the land is a table of rock-strewn acres broken and pitted with small lakes. There are no trees, few crops, and no buildings of much quality beyond the vernacular whitewashed cottages that, in this wind-swept district, tie down the thatch of their roofs to rows of stout pegs along the eaves. Bunbeg is a centre for those interested in walking, bathing, or fishing. It enjoys a remarkable situation, but at the time of writing a complete lack of planning control threatens to turn the area into a rural holiday slum. Apart from the folly-like SIGNAL TOWER at Bunbeg and the empty two-storey HOTEL at Gweedore, built by Lord George Hill about 1840, there are only some churches to note.

ST MARY, Derrybeg. 2.5 km N, in Gweedore. An ambitious T-plan church with tall Y-traceried lancets framed by stone quoins. 'Recently consecrated' in 1860 and altered by *Timothy Hevey* in 1874. His is the sanctuary gable with a big rose window and a round sacristy behind.

GWEEDORE PARISH CHURCH (C of I). Tiny tower and hall built as a dual-purpose church and school in 1844. Restored as a church only in 1914, when the tower was added. Miniature two-light Tudor windows in wood.

MAGHERAGALLON CHURCH RUINS. 3 km NNW in the sand dunes. Two gables of a small rectangular church built of pink granite. Traces of an E window, walled up, and a W oculus.

CARRICKFIN CHURCH (C of I). 2.5 km SW, on a little peninsula. Early C19. A diminutive rendered hall with miniature Georgian Gothic windows and a porch. If it were thatched it could be a cottage. The seaside setting with wild flowers all round and a little low cottage behind is very memorable.

ANNAGARRY CHURCH. 5 km SSW. A seven-bay rendered mid C19 Gothic hall with a big pine gallery. W gable with a wheel window.

BUNCRANA

Of some importance in the Middle Ages, with a small harbour on the Crana River and an O'Doherty castle on its W bank, Buncrana declined after the Plantation of Ulster. From 1717, under Sir John Vaughan, Governor of Co. Donegal, the place was largely rebuilt. Sir John founded a new castle w of O'Doherty's keep, built a handsome bridge across the Crana to connect it with his park, and laid out the town in a long curving street running roughly N–S with a market square on the E side. One road runs roughly parallel to the Main Street between it and the shore where a C19 promenade now is. The town is bounded at its S end by mills and the course of the Mill River.

Like Moville, the other seaside resort of Inishowen, Buncrana's best years were in the C19 and early C20, when it became a popular holiday town linked to industrial Derry by the Londonderry and Lough Swilly Railway. This opened as far as Farland Point in 1863; a junction to the town was added in the next year. Prior to the partition of Ireland Buncrana was Donegal's biggest town, with a population of over 2,200. Now at 3,300 it is second in size to Letterkenny, which has grown in importance since Derry, the natural focus of northern Donegal, has been separated politically from the country surrounding it. Buncrana is still Derry's resort. In August 1938 a 'sixpenny train' carried 1,350 passengers for a day by its sandy beach – a record addition of more than half the population – and after the war similar numbers travelled before the line was closed. Guest houses, fairground, putting green, and fish and chips show that the place still thrives. But a typical C19 resort with railings and stucco, promenades, paths, and shrubberies goes quickly to seed when a C19 labour force is withdrawn. Buncrana has lots of open spaces that are dog-eared and not as trim as Victorian proprietors would have liked, lots of street signs and too much tarmac. Swann Park, the former demesne of Sir John Vaughan's castle, at the time of writing badly needs attention and a policy for its replanting.

O'DOHERTY'S CASTLE. In a curiously indefensible position below the w bank of the River Crana. A rectangular keep, 33 ft by 28 ft. Roofless, of three storeys, with harled gables on the N and S sides. The first two floors with walls 6 ft to 8 ft thick are possibly C14, built by the O'Dohertys after 1333. Inside is a single chamber, 14 ft by 18 ft, with wide loophole recesses on each side. A slab-roofed mural stair runs round the S and W sides. The floors were not vaulted.

The top storey dates only from 1602, when the keep was repaired by Hugh Boy O'Doherty as a base for Spanish troops. After Sir Cahir O'Doherty's rebellion of 1608 it was leased by Sir Arthur Chichester to Henry Vaughan, who altered it

further. (The big windows are mid C17.) Vaughans lived here
until their new castle was built in 1718, when the bawn round
O'Doherty's keep was taken down to provide materials. The
entrance to the keep is now walled up and the interior difficult
to see.

54 BUNCRANA CASTLE. Built by Sir John Vaughan in 1718 – the
date inscribed on the main doorcase – this house is the most
important and also the earliest of all the big houses in Inishowen. It occupies the site of the former township that had
grown up round O'Doherty's keep which Vaughan re-sited
beyond the river. The castle is approached grandly across the
C18 CASTLE BRIDGE, stone-built, of six arches, with cutwaters
and pedestrian recesses. Bridge and house are on an axis with
a formal walled court between, terraced on the N and S and
closed by the tall façade of the castle on the W. Plain but impressive, the frontage is of 86 ft, broken back in the centre, a seven-
bay, two-storey block on an unusually high basement with
flanking single-bay pavilion wings, the same height but thrusting forward and given hipped roofs to distinguish them from
the main block. Harled, with stucco quoined strips to the wings.
The window proportions are long and thin: eighteen sash panes
on the main floor, twelve above. Refinements are the bolection-
moulded frame to the door with open scrolled pediment and
niches set in the sides of the wings. The house, two rooms thick,
has no other regular elevation. Inside are wainscoted rooms,
tall eight-panelled doors, and a handsome stair with fluted
balusters and acanthus-scrolled tread-ends. In the forecourt a
modern MONUMENT to Sir Cahir O'Doherty, last Lord of Inishowen, and a PLAQUE to Wolfe Tone, who landed here on
3 November 1798 as a prisoner from the French warship 'La
Hoche'.

CHRIST CHURCH, LOWER FAHAN PARISH CHURCH (C of
I). In the centre of the town, a small tower and hall church
of 1805. Built of harled rubble. Enlarged in 1816, 1837, 1867,
and 1902, and now cruciform, with a long N transept and a
heavy chancel which was the last part to be added. The interior
is dark, late C19 in appearance, with a coved timber ceiling supported on bracketed trusses. – MONUMENT. Rear Admiral
George Hart † 1812. Faith taking the hand of a weeping female
who leans on a broken anchor.

ST MARY'S ORATORY. A big stucco hall of c. 1890 with an elaborate classical front that would look well enough in a street but
here, with space all round it, is revealed as the sham it is. A

free-standing Corinthian portico sits directly on the ground with pilaster responds extending to short single-bay wings on either side. The interior is still classical, with pilasters in green and red scagliola framing the altar wall. – STATIONS OF THE CROSS. 1896 by *A. Mariani*; dramatically Tiepolesque.

PRESBYTERIAN CHURCH. 1861 by *J. G. Ferguson*. A five-bay lancet hall in local stone, with buttressed porch and quatrefoil above.

CONVENT OF MERCY. 1952–9 by *Simon Leonard*. Neo-Georgian.

OTHER BUILDINGS. Buncrana lost its best secular building, MOUNT TILLY, a brick terrace of four C17 houses with curving Flemish gables and alternating pediments, between the two World Wars. The COURT HOUSE erected by Mrs Todd of Buncrana Castle in 1830 had to be enlarged or replaced by 1839, when the present design was procured. It was executed by 1842. Five-bay, two-storey front recessed in the centre three bays, stucco, with horizontal rustication on the ground floor and pedimented ends above the doors – a simplified version of *William Caldbeck*'s court houses at Monaghan and Glenties. In 1864 the STATION, to the s, beyond the Mill River, was built in a vigorous railway Gothic style to designs of *Fitzgibbon Louch*. The LOUGH SWILLY HOTEL, on the point opposite the coastguards' houses, followed the next year, at a cost of £3,000. Twice extended, in 1890 by *James Croom* and in 1892 by *William Barker*, both architects from Derry, it is a solid, no-nonsense stone-built hotel with an Italianate tower over the door.

NEIGHBOURHOOD

ST MARY. At Cockhill, 1.5 km NNE. Built in 1848 in open country to replace an earlier chapel. The Board of Works contributed to its completion and the church is unusually big for its date, with a satisfyingly solid square stone tower, and a six-bay hall behind. Timber Y-tracery. The interior is enriched with a good deal of carpenter's Gothic, notably the reredos, which has triple-shafted cluster columns. Flat ceiling with C19 Jacobean panelling decorations.

NED'S POINT BATTERY. 1 km w of Buncrana Castle. An 1812 battery and ordnance ground with stone revetments, ditches, and a low tower. Derelict at the time of writing but still complete. The name of the place is a corruption of the earlier and more classical Niad's Point.

ST MARY OF THE IMMACULATE CONCEPTION. 1859. A straightforward cruciform church with gabled transepts, W front, and an offset NW tower and spire. Built for the Rev. Francis Kelaghan by local builders – the *Gilroy* brothers. Rendered except for the front, which is of ashlar stone. Lancet windows and diagonal corner buttresses. The interior is remarkable for the intersecting cross-braced trusses at the crossing, the white marble altar, and the bright, clearly coloured E window.

CHRIST CHURCH, FINNER PARISH CHURCH (C of I). 1839–40. Built by the Ecclesiastical Commissioners for £2,150 – a nice church that sits unusually high by the side of the road. The detail is in the typical C13 style of Welland's office, though this design is by *William Hagerty*, who, by adding extra height,
105 gave some grace to the interior. Four-bay nave with double-chamfered arcades to N and S aisles, set on single round columns. A shallow chancel is balanced at the W end by an extension of the nave through an arch, one bay beyond the aisles. Paired lancet windows in the aisles, a three-light E window, and single lancets in the clerestory. The nave roof of open rafters has Welland's usual alternation of cross-braced and kingpost trusses.

CAMPBELL MEMORIAL METHODIST CHURCH. 1888 by *Thomas Elliott*. A four-bay hall in the centre of the town, of squared sandstone, with paired Gothic windows with hood moulds facing the street.

OLD CHURCH RUINS. 2 km NE of the town bridge. The walls remain of a rectangular church, 18 ft by 55 ft, built in 1600 and now subdivided into burial plots. A brick-arched opening takes the place of the E window. Further W, traces of other buildings.

PRESBYTERIAN CHURCH. A four-bay rendered hall of 1865.

Lewis described the village as one long street on the road from Ballyshannon to Sligo, 'a favourite place of resort for sea bathing during the summer'. By 1846 it was the most celebrated watering place 'in the whole of the north west coast', and it has retained this popularity. The setting on a rocky coast with grand views of the Leitrim hills is fine, but the town today is squalid and of little interest. Its heyday is symbolized by the big GREAT SOUTHERN HOTEL, built by the Irish Highlands Hotel Company in 1894 on the golf links N of the town. The original design by *Sir Thomas Drew*, three-storey, with two floors of dormer windows in big roofs and many gables and verandas, is now disfigured by illiterate additions. Several THATCHED COTTAGES remain at the E end of the Main Street. The PROVINCIAL BANK is late C19 Italianate, a sandstone ashlar front with segment-headed windows, heavy eaves, and stumpy Tuscan pilasters to the ground floor. The CONVENT OF ST LOUIS, near the town centre, is of 1891 by *C. J. McCarthy*, and of a standard Gothic design: a seven-bay, two-storey front with a projecting central bay surmounted by a gabled statue niche.

BURT   DO *F3*

Three churches on an open hillside that slopes NW from Grianan Hill to Inch Island. Grianan with its circular stone fort (*see* p. 312) is the inspiration of the most interesting of these, which is also the most modern.

ST AENGUS. 1965–7 by *Liam McCormick*. An eclectic building, 127 unashamedly Romantic like Frank Lloyd Wright's 'prairie' houses but, unlike them, and like Gibberd's Liverpool Cathedral, a round structure with a high conical lantern. Wright, Gibberd, and the Grianan of Ailech are all present in this church, but only as starting points for the design, which must be judged on its own, and which must be judged a success.

Externally the church is a circular ring of stone, massively secure, with battered walls of finely pointed squared rubble masonry. Above this is a continuous glass clerestory carefully detailed to continue the line of the wall from which project the eaves of a roof sweeping like a coolie hat up to a lantern above the altar. On the entrance axis when the lantern is seen centrally above the main door it gives the building a scale and formal quality that is hardly equalled by other recent church designs. But this is not a static formal roof from all angles. The lantern is axially, not centrally, placed, and it moves as we move round the church, providing a varied and constantly changing silhouette with a slow slope rising over the body of the congregation on the E, and a steep plunging roof to the offices on the W.

This is the surprise that the interior holds. Outside, the church appears a single-cell design. Inside, the circle becomes an irregular oval with the church offices accommodated in a crescent of space behind the altar wall. On the N, this space appears clearly where it is broken into to provide a small baptistery. This spatial play, which might be called baroque, is emphasized by the ring of white columns, circular like the outside walls, which supports the whole of the roof and adds an effect of optical movement to the interior as the columns step closer and closer to the altar wall.

Finally, there is the detailing: heavy, primitive, like the single slab of stone with the sign of a fish that is the altar, or the brown bricks on end that pave the floor. Everything is co-ordinated into a consistent and very expressive conception of what a modern church in a rural and an ancient community should be.

CHRIST CHURCH, BURT PARISH (C of I). 1868. A standard Gothic church by *John G. Ferguson*, of local slate rubble with sandstone trim, high roofs, and a yellow brick turret and spire. Four-bay lancet hall, single-bay chancel, with s vestry. All with diagonal buttresses. Porch, tower, and spire offset at the w end of the N wall. w gable with three lancets. E window with three-light geometrical tracery. Plain inside. The contractor was *Alexander McElwee*.

BURT PRESBYTERIAN CHURCH. 1895. A five-bay harled and rendered Gothic hall with a fancy buttressed front. Pine detailing and a big gallery within.

BURT CASTLE. *See* Newtowncunningham.

A harbour and fishing village directly opposite Rutland Island (*see* p. 480), developed as part of the fishery there by Colonel Conyngham in later C18. When the herring left this part of the coast the island industry and Burton Port dwindled in importance. There is a seven-bay, three-storey stuccoed classical HOTEL and a large late C18 grain store of four storeys, derelict at the time of writing.

ST COLUMB. 1898–1908 by *E. J. Toye*, a six-bay lancet hall with granite trim. Gabled w porch and rose window above. Polygonal apse.

TEMPLECRONE PARISH CHURCH. 4km NNE. A big T-plan Gothic church, wonderfully situated on the shore opposite Cruit Island, erected by the Rev. D. O'Donnell in 1856 and restored in 1929. It is the perfect seaside Catholic church, brightly painted in black and white, with big Y-traceried windows. The inside is simple but light and airy. Intersecting queenpost trusses at the crossing and a gallery in the longest arm. Altar in white marble with three pinnacled niches, with a rose window above filled with colourful STAINED GLASS by the *Eardly Studio*.

ARDLANDS CASTLE. 3 km NW, on an island N of Castle Port bay. Hard to find and just a piece of wall.

For TEMPLECRONE *see also* Dungloe.

CALEDON   TY *H9*

This little town wears the appearance of a thriving small community of the early C19: trim and tidy, with long terraces of two-storey stone houses and, at its southern end, a group of gabled houses and cottages 'in the Picturesque Old English style'. It owes its good looks to the Alexander family, merchants from Londonderry, who bought the Caledon estate in 1778. James Alexander was created Baron Caledon in 1790, Viscount in 1797, and Earl in 1800. He began the great house at Caledon, whose gates stand just s of the town. His son Du Pre, the second Earl, enlarged the house, and as a resident proprietor began the process of rebuilding and enlarging the town that his son and grandson continued. From 1816 onwards written accounts of Caledon are full of praise for the Earl's exertions, and until its demolition by a bomb in 1973, a monumental column by the gates to the house stood witness to the appreciation of his tenants.

In the Middle Ages, Caledon, then called Kinard, was a strategic military position held by a sept of the O'Neill family. In 1498 Mac Art O'Neill was driven out by the Earl of Kildare, who re-settled the place on the pro-British Turlough O'Neill. His descendants owned Caledon until the Ulster Rising of 1641, which began with the murder of Lord Caulfield by Sir Phelim O'Neill at old Kinard Castle, and ended only after the battle of Benburb in 1646. Cromwell confiscated the property, granting it to a branch of the Hamiltons, from whom *c.* 1735 it passed by marriage to the fifth Earl of Orrery. Lord and Lady Orrery apparently liked Caledon and spent a good deal of time here, but their son Edmund, who became eighth Earl of Cork and Orrery in 1764, was a spendthrift – 'devoted to the most wretched voluptuousness' – who lived largely in Gloucestershire and sold the place to the Alexanders about 1770.

ST JOHN (C of I). The principal interest of the church is its needle spire, designed by *John Nash* in 1808, when Lord Caledon's agent, John Pringle, thought it 'very pretty'. Originally of timber, it was replaced after 1830 with one of stone. The church is otherwise a plain five-bay hall and tower, with a short chancel and s aisle added later. Originally the windows were round-headed; they were altered to a Gothic form in a remodelling by *Joseph Welland* in 1848. The earlier building of about 1682 was destroyed by James II's troops, and repaired in 1698–1712. The present church, built by Primate Robinson, dates from 1768 and the tower from 1785. – PULPIT. 1890, of carved stone, with a marble prayer desk and reredos, designed for the fourth Earl of Caledon by *Thomas Drew*, sculptor *A. P. Sharp*. – MONUMENT. In the graveyard, a large Vanbrughian pyramid on a stepped base to Galbraith Lowry Corry † 1769.

ST JOSEPH. 1849. A four-bay hall with lancet windows. Three together in the nicely built cut stone front. Consecrated 1855.

Caledon is one of the few places to merit exploration on foot, though it is simply one main street. Architecture begins at the N end with the curious NATIONAL SCHOOL of 1907 by *Doolin, Butler & Donelly*, cottagey and vaguely like Mackintosh, with big swept dormer windows to the classrooms. Uphill in the street proper is a nice two-storey stone house with a segment-headed door and flanking Doric columns. Opposite on the E the MARKET HOUSE of *c.* 1830 is set in a grass court behind the PUBLIC WEIGHBRIDGE, a diminutive but vigorous Gothic hut erected in 1873 as a memorial to Henry Leslie Prentice, for forty-one years the agent to the Caledon estates, Close by, on the turning for Aughnacloy the former CALEDON PARISH SCHOOL, built by the Countess Dowager in 1852, is in a similar brutally Picturesque idiom. The two-tier Lombard Gothic FOUNTAIN beside it is the memorial to the fourth Earl put up in 1901 by *W. Costigan & Co.* of Belfast. The COURT HOUSE further s is the most conscious piece of architecture in the town. Two storeys, with a projecting central bay open as a segmental arch on the ground floor, surmounted by a squat tripartite window, an ashlar pediment, and a square timber cupola with a clock and an ogee lead dome. An extension on the N, under the same roof, makes the front asymmetrical. Mr C. E. B. Brett quotes a payment of £46 to '*Johnston* Architect' in the Caledon journal account book of 1815. This may however relate to the layout of the town developed in the following year, and it seems likely that the Court House, which is of *c.* 1822, is by *William Murray*, who prepared a plan of an inn, market house, and linen market for the Earl in April 1821. Opposite and just s from the Court House, a street lined with picturesque cottages runs down to CALEDON MILLS, built from 1853 for flax spinning at a cost reputedly of £30,000, a huge five-storey range with attics, L-shaped and now ruinous. The stone plinth in the middle of the street opposite the gate to the mills was once the base of a chimney treated architecturally like a column. The METHODIST CHURCH of 1864 and the PRESBYTERIAN CHURCH, on the Glaslough Road, are both plain Gothic halls.

The lane running w, immediately s of the town, leads to the NORTH LODGE of Caledon House, picturesque mid C19 with high gables, and, just inside the gates, the DORIC SCHOOL, an exercise in very primitive Doric with four-column portico, square block capitals, and no bases to the shafts, presumably by *Nash* and dating from 1815. Back on the main road by the BRIDGE GATES, the CALEDON MONUMENT was a Greek Doric column on a high plinth designed by *William Murray* in 1840, surrounded by four weeping lions and surmounted by a statue of the second Earl by *Thomas Kirk*. That has now gone, but the impressive avenue of enormous monkey-puzzle trees and the railings with faces remain. Coming immediately before the bridge across the Blackwater – the boundary between Tyrone and Armagh – the gates are properly speaking the last feature of the town. A pair of single-storey pedimented lodges of 1820 flank large flat panelled piers, surmounted by sphinxes of *Coade* stone.

ANNAGHROE HOUSE. 2.5 km wsw. A small two-storey, three-bay house of the early C19, cube-like, on top of a gentle hill, with a Regency-type roof.

CALEDON HOUSE

The present late Georgian and Regency house is probably the 73 fourth great house on the estate. First was the castle of old Kinard, destroyed by the C17 and replaced by a bawn of lime and stone and a strong house built by Turlough O'Neill about 1619. That was overrun after the battle of Benburb and replaced by a late C17 house of the Hamilton family described by Lord Orrery, its proprietor, in 1738 as 'old, low and, though full of rooms, not very large'. The Orrerys, according to Mrs Delany, planned to build a new house about a mile away where there were 'all the advantages of water, wood and diversified grounds'. This was in 1748; but the core of Caledon House today was begun, not by the Orrerys, but in 1779 by James Alexander, who had recently bought the estate. The architect was *Thomas Cooley*, and the house was at first a two-storey villa on a half-basement. The entrance (N) front was of seven bays with a pedimented centre and Diocletian windows a little like Wyatt's Newtown Mount Kennedy. The garden front (S) had an elliptical drawing room in the centre. The original axis of the house runs N–S, with a large square entrance hall on the N, connecting through the traditional columnar screen of Irish Georgian halls – the same occurs at Castle Coole, Castle Archdale, Slane Castle, and Castle Ward – with the drawing room on the S. The main stair is to one side, on the E.

Additions for the second Earl of Caledon were made in several stages. First came *John Nash*, who like Wyatt at Frog-
77   more ran a screen of coupled Ionic columns across the entire N front, ending in blank terminal pavilions, projecting beyond the house and decorated with niched recesses and shallow saucer domes. The domes and the plaster composition for this work were shipped from London in June 1808. The pavilion on the W side became one great library; the columns and glass for its cupola light were sent from England in June and November 1809. Nash visited Caledon at least twice, in 1808 and in 1810. He advised that the area round the old house should be arched over and filled in to hide the basement, that an extra storey could be added to the main house, to increase the accommodation, and that the interior should be enriched by extra plasterwork. John Pringle, Lord Caledon's agent, obviously found Nash an extravagant architect to employ: 'we are certainly at his mercy as to ornaments' he wrote in September 1810, when the contracts for the alterations had risen to £9,537 2s. 6d. Perhaps this was why the addition of the attic storey was delayed until 1825, long after Nash had lost interest in Ireland. Though low in itself, it has the effect of making the main block rise rather too high above the colonnade. The final addition was in 1833, when the area behind the E pavilion was filled in with a new sequence of hall, octagonal inner hall, and passage, to link an Ionic *porte cochère* on the E front with the stair hall and the main house. These additions are by *Thomas Duff* of Newry and, unlike the rest of the house, which is stucco, are of dressed ashlar sandstone.

The interior of Caledon offers a neat contrast between the refined manner of the earlier neo-classical rooms by Cooley and
78   the heavier opulence of Nash. Of Cooley's rooms the SALOON (the original entrance hall) is 34 ft deep by 27 ft wide with apsed recesses behind the yellow scagliola column screen and delicate

Adamesque plasterwork with paired sphinxes and a tripod
above the drawing-room door. The Doric frieze and central ceiling roundel seem later than 1780 but can hardly be Nash's
work, though the chimneypiece with a satyr and nymph draping
garlands along its transom is probably his. The OVAL DRAW-
ING ROOM, with paired segmental apses to answer the windows
of the bow, has marvellously delicate panelled shutters and
doors and a frieze of gilded dolphins above the doors. The
STAIRCASE on the E preserves the C18 wrought-iron banister
rail of alternating straight and acanthus-scroll supports, and
opens on the upper floor to an elegant gallery articulated with
pairs of delicate Ionic pilasters. The BOUDOIR, S from the
stair, has one of the finest neo-classical ceilings in Ireland, a
shallow square saucer, prophetic of Soane, with diaper borders
in black and white above the spandrels, and roundels by *Ange-
lica Kauffmann*. The chimneypiece is of piping and lyre-playing
nymphs, and the walls retain a pretty C18 Chinese paper. In
the W pavilion Nash's LIBRARY is divided by a screen of two
red scagliola columns with an octagonal coffered dome light in
the centre and coved ceilings at either end – grand, but lacking
the delicacy of Cooley's work.

Immediately N from the main house stand the STABLES, late
C18 and presumably by *Cooley*, with a spacious cobbled court
surrounded by two-storey ranges with six arcaded coach
houses facing the entrance arch. The S front, facing the house
but sunk below the lawn and screened by trees, is a nine-bay
block of coursed rubble with ashlar quoins and architraves. The
centre three bays project, with a large arch, pediment, and bell
cupola above. As at Castle Coole, an underground service
tunnel connects the stables with the basement floor of the main
house. On the W side of the stable façade the DAIRY is a low,
single-storey block with a pedimented centre flanked by short
Tuscan colonnades and recently converted into a house. The
building looks *c.* 1820 and could well be by *William Murray*.

The PARK at Caledon was first developed by the fifth Lord
Orrery, whose improvements are described delightfully by Mrs
Delany in 1748:

It is a fine place by nature, and they [the Orrerys] are both fond
of the County. She delights in farming and he in building and garden-
ing, and he has very good taste.... Nothing is completed yet but an
hermitage, which is about an acre of ground – an island, planted with
all the variety of trees, shrubs, and flowers that will grow in this
country, abundance of little winding walks, differently embellished

with little seats and banks. In the midst is placed an hermit's cell, made of the roots of trees. The floor is paved with pebbles; there is a couch made of matting, and little wooden stools, a table with a manuscript on it, a pair of spectacles, a leathern bottle; and hung up in different parts, an hourglass, a weather glass and several mathematical instruments, a shelf of books, another of wooden platters and bowls, another of earthen ones, in short everything that you might imagine necessary for a recluse. Four little gardens surround this house – an orchard, a flower garden, a physick garden and a kitchen garden ... I never saw so pretty a whim so thoroughly well executed.

The Rococo garden here described has vanished, for the park was later landscaped and the terraces on the s front added on the advice of *William Sawrey Gilpin*. What does remain from Lord Orrery's day is the BONE HOUSE, an unusual mid C18 conceit of four square piers formed of knuckle bones and built into a brick loggia. The bones were supposed to have come from the midden of an encampment of Shane O'Neill. Near the Bone House is a small IRON SUSPENSION BRIDGE by *Dredge* of Bath. To the N is a square WALLED GARDEN planted with a crossed yew walk.

CAPPAGH *see* MOUNTJOY FOREST

CARNDONAGH

A small C19 market town, regularly built, with a large triangular Diamond laid out in the centre on rising uneven ground. Today Carndonagh is dominated physically by its big new Catholic church, set on a hill just s of the Diamond, but culturally by another church: the monastery of Donagh, founded by St Patrick for Bishop MacCairthen in the C6, from which the Carndonagh cross and pillar stones derive.

MONASTIC SITE AND CROSSES. 1 km W of the Diamond, by the Protestant church. ST PATRICK'S CROSS, re-erected facing down the road and flanked by two short stelae, is one of the most elaborate early crosses in Ireland, dating possibly from the mid C7, when the plaited ribbon work with narrow borders that decorates its W face was briefly in favour. The cross, 10 ft high, is cut from a thin slab of sandstone formed with primitive arms and head that mark, according to Françoise Henry, the victory of the cross shape proper over the slab. The E face, with an interlace Greek cross at the head, has triquetra and birds in the spaces between the arms, and a panel on the shaft representing Christ in glory with three small figures below, all – head, body, and feet – seen in profile. Similar incised figures seen full face with folded arms stand one above the other at the s side of the shaft. The STELAE have spiral patterns and more profile figures: a warrior with his sword on the E, King David with his harp and a bishop with a bell on the W. The style of these figures is closely similar to those at Killadeas and White Island in Co. Fermanagh.

The CROSS SLAB in the churchyard is rectangular, 5 ft high and carefully shaped, with a protruding knob at the top. This contains the head of Christ in a Crucifixion scene on the W face, with two warriors and a plaited cross below. The E face bears a stylized 'marigold' or mirror pattern flanked by two figures that face each other. Below, a large triquetra inscribed in a circle.

DONAGH PARISH CHURCH (C of I). A harled two-bay hall of 1769, re-using a C15 double-chamfered doorway, the hood moulding ending in tapering prisms with foliated vine tendrils that are typical of this period in Ireland (cf. Raphoe Cathedral). By the door a medieval LINTEL with central Celtic cross, traces of figure sculpture, and a mortice joint in the top.

CHURCH OF THE SACRED HEART. 1942–5 by *Ralph Byrne*, replacing the original building of 1826 (which had a tower by *William McElwee*, 1875). The ultimate source of the new building, vast but dull neo-Romanesque, is Pisa. Long cruciform plan, aisled nave, transepts with a domed crossing, and an offset attenuated campanile tower. Built of coursed squared granite, boulder-faced and regularly irregular. Even with these real materials the church manages to look like a cheap reconstituted stone job. The granite statues on the drum of the dome are by *Albert Power*. The interior gains by its scale. Reassuringly solid piers in granite with foliated capitals support a round-arched arcade with a lancet clerestory above. But the ceiling is poorly contrived, with nasty plaster panels. Apse-ended and plaster-vaulted chancel. The church could be improved if its pink plaster were painted white and its ceilings darkened.

OTHER BUILDINGS in the area are DONAGH RECTORY, 2.5 km NW, of 1776, a five-bay, two-storey house with a projecting two-storey centre porch; TERNALEAGUE HOUSE, 1 km NW, C18, but enlivened by Victorian bays, a battlemented porch, and a spiky roof; the COURT HOUSE, 1873 by the County Surveyor, *William Harte*, C.E., two-storey, five-bay, with a classical rendered front rusticated on the ground floor – a watered-

down version of William Caldbeck's model; the former
UNION WORKHOUSE, seven-bay, two-storey Tudor of the
1840s; and the PRESBYTERIAN CHURCH, a stucco hall with
pediment of 1886.

A small village on the Glen River above Teelin Bay. A fertile oasis
among many bare hills.

ST COLUMBA. A long mid C19 tower and hall type church, built
of sharp, dark stone with sandstone quoins and window surrounds. Five-bay nave with pointed lancets; single-bay
chancel. The tower, with stepped Irish battlements, was raised
by an extra storey early this century. The interior is memorable:
all that Pugin would have wanted a remote country church to
be, with a nice solid roof panelled in pine and braced with heavy
trusses, clear, clean walls, and a spiky HIGH ALTAR of 1883
by *George Ashlin*, the type of design that is now so often reso-
lutely cast aside without a thought for the workmanship or care
that has gone into its design. It is of Caen stone with a Puginesque pinnacled centre flanked by triple arcades on green
marble colonnettes, and octagonal terminal piers crowned by
angels. Sculptured reredos panels are set within the arcades:
Christ appearing to Mary, and the Good Shepherd.

CHURCH RUINS. 4 km s, by Teelin Bay quay. Said to have been
a Spanish foundation. A small rectangular structure of huge
boulder stones. Part of the E gable is built into the sheds by
the quay.

SLIEVE LEAGUE CHURCH RUIN AND WELL. On the bare
mountain top at about 550 m (1,800 ft), a group of low dry stone
walls, 4½ ft thick, forming a rectangular building, 11 ft by 22 ft
inside, with a small cell to the N. Such bleak sites are typical
of the hermitage cells of the early Christian church. Slieve
League is approached by a road running w, 2 km s of Carrick,
and then on foot. The prospect from the church site in any
direction is truly awesome. A few yards to the s is ONE
MAN'S PASS, a rock path along the top of a sea cliff that rises to
a height of 601 m (1,972 ft).

CARRICK LODGE. A ruined mid C19 house, two-storey, with
crow-stepped gables and a monogram MH.

CARRICKABRAGHY   DO *F1*

CASTLE. On a rocky promontory by the N point of Pollan Bay. An O'Doherty castle, probably of the mid C16, though the place appears in the *Annals of the Four Masters* from the C9 to the C12 as Carraic-brachaidhe. Sir Cahir O'Doherty, normally resident at Burt, selected this remote spot to plan his revolt in 1608. Phillips's map of 1690 shows it as an oval bawn with seven round towers surrounding a square keep. Only traces of the bawn remain. Part of the square keep of battered rubble stone, 9 ft by 11½ ft inside, still stands to a height of two storeys. At the SE corner the remains of a circular flanking tower, 11 ft in diameter, with gun loops. Inside, the keep checks back at the first floor to take joists. A large segment-headed recess on the upper floor still bears clear traces of wattle shuttering. Mural stairs that led to the second floor remain in the upper section of the N wall.

CARRICKMORE   TY *G7*

A small upland village set on a wooded hill-top in the parish of Termonmaguirke. Little more than a T-junction with houses.

ST COLUMB, TERMONMAGUIRKE PARISH CHURCH (C of I). Built between 1787 and 1792 to replace the C17 church at Ballinacreg, which had become ruinous. Small three-bay nave of rubble stone, short chancel, and pretty rendered tower with blind arcading below the battlements. The Y-traceried windows in stone were added with the chancel by *Joseph Welland* in 1851. The ashlar needle spire on top of the tower was erected ten years later in memory of the Rev. Charles Cobbe Beresford, Rector from 1817 to 1861. Attractive interior with an elaborate Gothic gallery at the back supported on clustered columns.

ST COLUMBA. Built in 1846 on the site of the ancient and C17 churches, incorporating medieval sculptural fragments. Big, cruciform, with a three-stage W tower with gabled parapet and corner pinnacles. Spoilt inside by modernization and a new flat ceiling.

CREGGAN CHURCH. 6 km N. 1930s neo-Norman in artificial stone. Nine-bay hall with barrel-vault inside, apsed baptistery, and zigzag decoration.

ST TERESA. At Loughmacrory, 5 km NW. 1833, rebuilt in 1916. A plain cruciform church with a wagon roof inside. The modern

PRIMARY SCHOOL by the church, an elegant, simple design in brick with higher central hall, is by *Patrick Haughey*, completed in 1967.

CARRICKMORE HOUSE. A trim late Georgian house with a walled yard behind. Built by Sir John Marcus Stewart and enlarged and improved for Lady Ann Stewart about 1840. Front of three bays; two-bay sides. Shallow hipped roof and dressed sandstone ashlar front.

TERMON HOUSE. A startling instance of the grandeur, at least in terms of scale, that the Church of Ireland clergy conceived as being appropriate to their status. Termon was built in 1815 by the Rev. C. C. Beresford at the then considerable cost of £3,293. It is a huge, plain rendered cube set in its own well-wooded park with a tall three-bay, three-storey front, a shallow hipped roof, and a massive range of eighteen chimneys grouped in the centre of the house.

LOUGHMACRORY LODGE. 5 km NW. A pretty Regency lodge overlooking this small inland lough. Five-bay, apparently single-storey front with a central square porch projecting forward, and two ample tripartite windows on either side. There is in fact an upper storey, but this is not expressed on the front. Shallow Regency roof and overhanging eaves.

DEAN BRIAN MAGUIRE SECONDARY SCHOOL. A subtle design, with single-storey flat-roofed blocks forming a court round a central two-storey hall built in soft fawn-red bricks. 1966 by *Patrick Haughey*.

CARRIGANS *see* ST JOHNSTOWN

D2   CARRIGART   DO

A nice small village on a windy isthmus between Sheephaven and Mulroy bays. The beaches here are spectacular, with Tra More Strand on the W stretching in a shallow silver crescent for over five kilometres. The sands, as at Horn Head to the W and at Ballyshannon further S, can become a menace. The dunes are in places enormous. At ROSAPENNA, 2.5 km N, Dark Age habitation floors are marked by dark peaty stratifications well below the tops of the dunes. What is perhaps of more concern to architectural enthusiasts is the fate of ROSAPENNA HOUSE, an early C18 house built by Lord Boyne and gradually engulfed by sand until 1808, when its then owner, the Rev. Mr Porter, who had retreated to the first floor, abandoned it. Late Georgian travellers reported enthusiastically, if fancifully, on its chimneys sticking through the sand. The ATLANTIC DRIVE N from Carrigart round the Rosguill Peninsula is a route that is noted equally for its striking coastal scenery and the many Donegal cottages that it passes.

HOLY TRINITY, MEVAGH PARISH CHURCH (C of I). 1895, replacing a church built on the same site in 1675. This is a good design, E.E. Gothic but villagey in character, with a big strong tower N of the nave, to which it is linked by a short passage, and a low N aisle. The church proper is a narrow gabled nave and chancel with a three-light E window and paired lancets in the W gable, S porch, and an exposed round stair-turret at the SW corner of the tower. Squared grey stone walls with red sandstone details and trim. The architect must be *Thomas Drew*, whose plan of St Philip, Miltown, Dublin, of 1866–79 is closely similar and who was working in the diocese at Raphoe Cathedral from 1892.

ST JOHN THE BAPTIST. 1 km S, at Umlagh. An ambitious cruciform gabled church founded in 1868 and dedicated in 1886. The most lasting impression will be of the extraordinarily gaily patterned masonry, in squared rubble stone from at least four quarries: brown, grey, white, and biscuit-coloured. Robustly buttressed nave and transepts, with freely flowing Dec tracery and a big rose window in the W gable. The obvious care and expense of the exterior continue inside with a lavish hammerbeam and cross-braced roof whose trusses intersect at the crossing. The spandrel panels are filled with filigree woodwork. The modern reredos cutting off the chancel is a pity.

CARRIGART PRESBYTERIAN CHURCH. 1806. A harled and rendered hall, brightly painted. Gothic, with a buttressed W gable and an offset stumpy N tower with a broach-spire.

MEVAGH OLD CHURCH. 4 km N, on the Atlantic Drive above the W shore of Mulroy Bay. The ruins of a small rectangular church, approximately 16 ft by 43 ft. The E wall stands to the start of a gable, and sections of the S wall remain to almost 12 ft. Traces of a window and door in the S wall. The E window is complete almost to the top. The reveals are widely splayed and built of thin brick-like stones. Said to be C12.

Opposite the lane leading to the old church is a CROSS SLAB fragment 2½ ft high with r. arms and part of a top.

TRANAROSSAN HOUSE. 6.5 km N, beyond Tranarossan Bay. A witty holiday house, built apparently by *Lutyens* for the Hon. Mrs Phillimore and now a youth hostel. Two gabled granite blocks like staggered triangles set on the hillside and linked by a short arm. The larger is surrounded by a veranda of fat granite piers, one of which stops short about two inches below the beam it is meant to support – a typical Lutyens joke. The roofs are huge unbroken slopes of heavy local slates, and the gables are slate-hung. Inside the veranda an exposed granite stair leads, ranch style, to the attic bedrooms. In the common room a big slab fireplace with a cobbled hearth.

MULROY HOUSE. 2.5 km E. A gabled Elizabethan-style house built by the third Earl of Leitrim in 1865. Two-storey, in squared sandstone, with a mixture of mullioned and sash windows. A little hard and institutional for a private house.

CASTLE ARCHDALE

A low-lying, wooded estate on the E shore of Lower Lough Erne.

ST PATRICK (C of I). A small cruciform church built between 1905 and 1908 to designs of *Sir Thomas Drew*. Like Drew's other Fermanagh church, Monea, the building replaces a late Georgian one, but here no use was made of any part of the old structure, which was abandoned for a new site to the S. Drew's church is of dark plum-coloured stone with grey limestone trim, Perp in style, with a slightly odd – not to say mean – tower built over the N transept. Inside, everything changes. The walls are a pale biscuit sandstone, complemented by a generous amount of warm unvarnished oak, and the hesitant nature of the exterior is resolved into a clear, unified expression. This is an extremely attractive church with workmanship of great quality: a perfect, if late, example of an Arts and Crafts taste. The nave and chancel dominate, with high wagon roofs panelled in oak squares, and big Perp windows at the E and W ends. The chancel arch springs from a C14-style cluster pier, with smaller arches opening to the transepts: vestry N, and organ S. – PULPIT. Carved with panels of vine leaves, barley, lilies, apples, and a fig tree. – The sanctuary has dragons in encaustic TILES.

FORMER CHURCH TOWER. Built by Mervyn Archdale c. 1770, a three-storey square tower, harled, with stone quoins and Irish battlements at the top. Derelict at the time of writing.

OLD CASTLE ARCHDALE. 2 km N of the church. In Castle Archdale Forest, the ruins of a bawn built by John Archdale in 1615, destroyed by Rory Maguire in 1641, but rebuilt and inhabited until 1689, when it was burnt out and abandoned.

Pynnar's survey of 1619 described 'a bawn of lime and stone with three flankers 15 ft high' and a house in the bawn 80 ft long and three storeys high. The house is set on the edge of a short steep hill, with the bawn to the w before it. It must have seemed an impressive place, and can still conjure up a momentary picture of Jacobean Ulster with its high E gable and three storeys of mullioned windows with label mouldings. But a momentary picture is all the ruins afford. The flankers and almost all of the house have gone, and what remains seems to date from the rebuilding, as the area of the enclosure is now only about 58 ft by 62 ft – less than Pynnar described. The arched gate, 7 ft wide with traces of a lean-to covered area inside, is still apparently of 1615, with an Italianate Latin inscription above: *Data Fata Secutus Johannes Archdale Hoc Edificium Struxit Anno Domini Millessimo Sexcentessimo Decimoquinto.*

CASTLE ARCHDALE. The largest Palladian house in Co. Fermanagh, built by Col. Mervyn Archdale in 1778, unroofed and partly demolished in 1970. Its interior is a great loss, for the workmanship was of high quality, especially the hall and staircase. The house was a rectangular stone-built block, three storeys on a low basement, and six bays wide. The centre two bays projected slightly, as at Brown's Hill, Co. Carlow. The end elevations were unusual, three bays wide, with Venetian windows on the ground floor on the outer bays. The rear (E) elevation was completely flat, overlooking a stable court of which it formed one side. Convex quadrants connected the house to the yard behind.

Inside, the plan was perfectly symmetrical, with one large room either side of a square entrance hall. The hall, with two grey marble chimneypieces facing each other, led through a screen of fluted Corinthian columns to a corridor running the length of the house, that is, N–S. More columns divided the staircase from the corridor, so that on entering the front door one looked straight through a double screen to a majestic double return stair. Wrought-iron S-shaped rails with brass medallions and carved acanthus scrolls to the stair ends. The stair, lit by a huge Venetian window on the landing, connected only with the first floor. The attic was reached by a secondary stair in the NE corner.

CASTLE CALDWELL   FM *D8*

This estate on a peninsula at the w end of Lower Lough Erne was granted at the Plantation to Sir Francis Blennerhasset, who

also developed Belleek. Pynnar's survey records a 'strong bawn'
and 'stone house' built here by 1619, apparently on the site of
an earlier religious foundation. In 1671 the estate was sold to Sir
James Caldwell, a wealthy merchant of Enniskillen, created a
baronet in 1683. By the c18 Castle Caldwell had a reputation as
one of the most beautiful country houses, in point of situation,
of any in Ireland. Arthur Young, who visited another Sir James
here in August 1776, describes its beauty in detail but is content
to characterize the house as 'almost obscured among the trees'
and 'a fit retreat from every care and anxiety of the world'. It had
been called Rossbeg House, after the townland, but was by now
Castle Caldwell. On the death of Sir John Caldwell, the sixth
Baronet, in the early c19, the house passed by marriage to his
son-in-law, J. C. Bloomfield, in whose family it remained until
it was burnt out early this century. Since 1913 the estate, which
contains four ruined buildings, has been owned by the Forestry
Commission.

CASTLE RUINS. At the head of a long avenue facing w. The
   ruins incorporate the flankers of a bawn first built by Francis
   Blennerhasset in 1612, though these look later. In 1792 the
   building was extended and regularized as a Gothic country
   house, though even before that it had evidently been much
   rebuilt. The walls are now so overgrown with ivy that it is difficult to distinguish the various parts. In the c18 the w elevation
   became the entrance front, set between the c17 flankers. These
   are square in plan, two storeys high, with five gun slits on the
   three exposed sides on each floor. The harled walls end in Irish
   battlements that are probably c18 romanticism. The house
   extends across the full width behind the flankers and is linked
   to it, in true Gothic/Palladian fashion, by low quadrant walls
   that spring from two thin square towers projecting a little from
   the main front. Between these is a two-storey, three-bay range
   with Gothic windows and battlements, and on either side the
   high gables of the old house. In all, a very pretty build-up at
   the head of the long main avenue.
      The main rooms were to the r. along the s front. Here was
   a seven-bay, two-storey house on a high basement, divided into
   three principal rooms on the main floor, with a corridor and
   courtyard behind. Beyond it, further E, and checked back from
   the s front, is a late Georgian wing, three bays on the s and
   eight bays on the E. It appears to have contained a long gallery
   with a double return main staircase between it and the courtyard on the w. The interior was classically treated, with semi-

circular niches in the corridors and stairwell, and the rooms
planned symmetrically with balanced doors and fireplaces.

CHURCH RUINS. N of the main avenue. A rectangular rubble-
built church, 19 ft by 50 ft inside, was begun by Sir Francis
Blennerhasset in 1641 and completed as a private chapel by the
Caldwell family. No details remain. The windows appear to
have been all round-headed with segmental reveals inside.

BELVEDERE. At the end of Ross-a-goul Point. The foundations
of an octagonal belvedere built by Sir James Caldwell about
1770. Misleadingly called an out-look in the Forestry Commission's plan for visitors.

LODGE AND FIDDLER'S STONE. A ruined Gothic gate lodge,
and a dismantled castellated railway bridge. Mid C19. A giant
stone fiddle, 5 ft high, is set against the lodge and inscribed:

To the
memory
of
Denis McCabe
Fiddler
who fell out of the
St Patrick Barge belonging
to
Sir James Caldwell Bart.
and Count of Milan, &
was drowned off this
Point August Ye 13
1770

Beware ye fiddlers of the fiddlers fate,
Nor tempt the deep lest ye repent too late,
Ye ever have been deemed to water foes,
Then shun the lake till it with whiskey floes,
On firm land only exercise your skill,
There you may play, and drink your fill.

As well as Denis McCabe the stone accidentally records the
most common mode of transport for the C18 proprietors around
Lough Erne – the family barge. When Young had absorbed
all the beauties of the estate, and the details of Sir James's hus-
bandry, he left in the customary style:

Take my leave of Castle Caldwell, and, with colours flying and his
band of music playing, go on board his six-oared barge for Inniskilling;
the heavens are favourable, and a clear sky and bright sun gave me
the beauties of the lake in all their splendour. Pass the scenes I have

described, which from the boat take a fresh variety, and in all pleasing.
Eagle Island first salutes us, a woody knoll. Others pass in review;
among the rest, Herring Island, noted for the wreck of a herring boat,
and the drowning of a fiddler; but the boatmen love herrings better
than music, and gave their name to the isle, rather than that of the
Son of Apollo.

St John, Muckross Parish Church (C of I). 6.5 km ENE.
1868. A small High Victorian country church, built for a new
perpetual curacy established in 1865 and endowed by John and
Armar Lowry. The church has a nave and short chancel, with
a bellcote asymmetrically placed on one side of the w gable,
seeming to grow out of the porch at the side. Nice details, such
as the boot-scrapers in cusped recesses on either side of the
door.

This small Plantation village was founded by Sir Toby Caulfield,
afterwards the first Lord Charlemont, who was granted the townland of Ballydonnell by James I in 1610.

St Michael, Donaghmore Parish Church (C of I).
Built under the auspices of the Rev. George Walker, later the
redoubtable defender of Londonderry, about 1680. Originally
a plain hall, now cruciform, with a w tower of three stages with
stepped battlements. The church presents today an intriguing
mixture of c17 Gothic and the newfangled classicism of Lord
Charlemont. The s porch, dated 1685, has crude Tuscan
columns on high plinths, a salient entablature (that shrinks to
just a cornice above the door), and two cherubs holding the
Bible open at Psalm 24. Beside it is a quite charming Gothic
Survival window, cusped Perp with a wheel at the top, surmounted by a hood mould ending in corbel-stop heads like cari-
catures of Charles I. This, with other similar windows and label
stops, comes from the old Protestant church at Donaghmore
built c. 1622 and destroyed in the war of 1641. Originally these
early c17 bits seem to have been concentrated on the s wall,
the other windows being round-headed, like the belfry openings and the w doorway in the tower. This doorway is classical
like the porch, flanked by more crudely worked Ionic columns,
and surmounted by Lord Charlemont's crest.

The transepts, chancel, and robing room date from 1860.
What apparently happened then was that the s windows of the
original nave provided the pattern for the end windows of each
transept, and the old E window was copied and replaced at the

end of the chancel with an authentic C17 angel with floppy wings and the Bible set above its apex. For contemporary ideas on tracery see the elaborate Dec windows on the w wall of each transept where, with no pattern to follow, mid C19 flamboyance takes over. MEDIEVAL FRAGMENTS are built into the quoins of the nave below the eaves at the NW and SW corners: relief figures of beasts and an angel. The SUNDIAL on the s side of the tower is dated 1485.

The interior is attractive, with a pretty w gallery supported on slender fluted columns. Coved plaster ceiling to the nave. Single-chamfered arches to chancel and transepts. – MONUMENTS. Classical wall-tablets to the Rev. George Evans † 1804 and to Sarah Maria Evans † 1844. – In the churchyard, handsome early C18 GATES with ball finials and a large BURGES FAMILY MAUSOLEUM with a tetrastyle Tuscan temple front erected after the death of John Henry Burges of Parkanaur in 1822.

CASTLE CAULFIELD. To the s of the village, opposite a new housing estate. A three-storeyed mansion of the early C17 built by Sir Toby Caulfield on the site of an Irish chieftain's bawn. Caulfield came to Ireland in 1598 in command of a troop of horse, was in charge of Charlemont Fort, Co. Armagh, in 1602, and administered the O'Neill lands in Co. Tyrone after the Flight of the Earls in 1607. The castle was built between 1611 and 1619, when Pynnar described it as 'the fairest building in the North'. Burnt in 1641 by Patrick O'Donnelly but restored and lived in by the Caulfields in the 1660s. St Oliver Plunket used the courtyard for ordinations in 1670 and Wesley preached here in 1767, though the castle was by then a complete ruin.

The ruins are in two parts: the L-shaped house of Jacobean character built by Sir Toby, and at its NW end a squat and more substantially built gatehouse that may have been part of the earlier Irish bawn. This is a separate block, 22 ft by 40 ft, with a vaulted entrance passage running the depth of the building with small chambers on either side and a round flanker at the NW corner. In the tunnel at the E side are the gaps of three murder-holes and the hole for the draw-bolt of the door. The door to the s chamber from the tunnel is a single-chamfered Tudor arch in sandstone.

The main house is built of coursed limestone rubble with sandstone string courses between each floor and sandstone mullioned and transomed windows with flat heads. The main entrance was in the re-entrant angle within the courtyard leading to the E range, 76 ft by 22 ft inside. The most substantial remains are here, with two tall chimneybreasts, capped with octagonal stone chimneys, rising the full height of the building. The ends of both ranges to the N and W had large four- or five-light windows, but apparently no bays or oriels.

CASTLECAULFIELD HOUSE. N of the church. A generous seven-bay, two-storey house with brick chimneys and high curved flanking walls with battlemented tops. Mid C18. Harled wing in the middle of the back. Stables to the N dated 1785.

LAURELDENE HOUSE. 1 km NE. Former rectory of 1737 built by a Mr Vincent. Originally a five-bay, two-storey, double-pile house. To this, two-bay, two-storey wings were added on the front. Then about 1800–1820 the old centre was changed into a three-bay front with tripartite windows throughout.

PRESBYTERIAN CHURCH. 1842. A four-bay lancet hall and single-bay chancel. Harled, with stone quoins. – MONUMENT. A massive pink granite obelisk to Samuel Clark, a native of Castlecaulfield who died in San Francisco in 1882.

METHODIST CHURCH. 1886. Small gabled hall.

E9   CASTLE COOLE   FM
                        2.5 km ESE of Enniskillen

This house is *James Wyatt*'s masterpiece, built for the first Earl of Belmore from 1790 to 1797, as perfect in its workmanship and preservation as in its design. Just before it was completed, the old Castle Cool, a Queen Anne house of 1702 designed by one *John Curld*, burnt down, so the furnishings of the house are of the period and in keeping with its austere style. In front of Castle Coole Wyatt's complaint that at first he had been obliged to follow the Adam brothers may seem to have a good deal of force, for the house is very different from the early Wyatt, more massy, more masculine, and more totally liberated from Palladian practice than anything he had done before.

75   Like all truly neo-classical houses Castle Coole sits directly on the ground. Its basement is sunk completely, and three steps are all that is required to take the visitor from the gravel to the entrance hall. The house is nine bays by two storeys, a plain rectangular block scrupulously detailed in Portland stone, with only a balustrade and Ionic cornice at the eaves, a string course, and a dado on the ground floor to relieve the smooth ashlar walls. The windows are just voids in the wall
74 without any surrounds. In the centre of the entrance front is a four-columned Ionic portico with pilaster responds. It is

answered by a segmental bow with fluted giant columns on the 75
park side of the house. The roof is unusually high, rising in
a clear slope from just above the level of the top of the balustrade – not hidden behind it – and adding considerably to the
weight and severity of the house. Straight colonnaded wings ending in single-storey pavilions flank the main block. The
columns are an elongated fluted Doric type – perhaps Wyatt
thought of them as Etruscan, for they are rather too tall to be
Greek Doric and have no frieze, though they are without bases,
which is normally an indication of a Greek intention: they die
as half-columns against the pavilion walls, and then reappear
flanking big tripartite windows in the centre of the pavilions
themselves. Within the colonnades square- and round-headed
niches alternate along the back wall. On the park front the wings
are treated as smooth walls, five-bay in the place of the colonnade, with a pretty Venetian window, decorated with oval
medallions in the spandrels, in the middle of the pavilion
blocks.

There is a rightness about Castle Coole that is immensely
satisfying. None of Wyatt's lines is superfluous: all are carefully
calculated, with a few chosen to run right through the design.
Notice, for example, the string course below the first-floor windows that continues as the blocking course – that is the top
stones – above the entablature of the colonnade, and ends as
the plinth on which the balusters of the pavilions stand. That
is one continuous line. The dado level and the bases of the
niches on the ground floor is another.

The perfection of Castle Coole's façades, remarkable in any
house, is particularly striking here because Wyatt did not
apparently have a free hand. Before he was consulted Lord Belmore had commissioned, in October 1789, a design from the
Dublin architect *Richard Johnston*, who proposed a plan very
similar to what Wyatt was to build. Johnston's scheme was for
a nine-bay, two-storey house flanked by arcaded wings rather
in the manner of John Carr and ending in pavilions that owed
a good deal to Sir William Chambers's Casino at Marino. It
was Johnston who proposed a four-columned Ionic portico for
the house, Ionic of a curiously old-fashioned Roman type, with
big curly volutes pitching out at 45 degrees from the corners of
the capitals, and curiously it was this sort of capital – not at all
a type to recommend itself to Wyatt in the normal run of events
– that found its way into the executed design. But the house
as it is today is indisputably by Wyatt. He changed the

proportions of Johnston's house (the oval saloon became 37 by
31 ft instead of 40 by 30 ft) and improved parts of the plan,
tightening up and pruning its design as he did so.

The building of Castle Coole began in June 1790 with the
long arched tunnel running upwards of 50 yds from the E end
of the house to the stable and office buildings on lower ground
to the NE. It is 14 ft wide, 12 ft high, and stone-vaulted, with
periodic grilled light wells along its length. It became the
kitchen passage, but was used first to bring the stone in carts
right into the foundations. Work began in the W wing, which
was roofed by 1791, the main house by 1792, and the E wing
by July 1793. The portico was up by 1794 and the main stairs
and paving laid by 1795. Lord Belmore acted as his own contractor, importing the Portland stone for the house via Lough
Erne and Ballyshannon, and the final cost was said to be
£54,000. *Alexander Stewart* acted as clerk of works or resident
architect, and the craftsmen whose names are known are
William Cane, master mason; *Domenico Bartoli*, the scagliola
worker; and *Joseph Rose*, the London plasterer much used by
both Wyatt and the Adam brothers.

The interior is coolly elegant and restrained. The HALL,
square with a Doric frieze, is screened at the back, as so many
Irish houses are, with a colonnade of red scagliola Doric
columns by *Bartoli*. A double door leads through to the SA-
76   LOON, by far the richest apartment in the house. Twelve scagliola pilasters flecked with grey and black are set round the
oval walls worked by *Bartoli* in July 1794, with Corinthian capitals sent over from London by *Rose* in March 1795. The mahogany doors painted with arabesques in the panels are by
McBrien and *Barnaby McGer*, and the cast clay and iron stoves
set in the niches are by *George Burns* of Dame Street, Dublin.
Wyatt intended the walls to be worked in yellow scagliola, but
this was never completed. One may note here nonetheless the
admirable coherence of his decorative schemes, with the garlands surrounding oval paterae in the ceiling, repeated in the
frieze and again in the architraves above the doors. This form
of decorative continuity from one part of a room to another
occurs throughout the house: there are oak and strawberry-leaf
garlands in the DINING ROOM; anthemion and palmette
friezes in the DRAWING ROOM; fluted reeds in the BREAK-
FAST ROOM; and laurel wreaths in the LIBRARY. Here the
pièce de résistance is the enormous chimneypiece by *Richard
Westmacott*, carved as marble drapery with great knots caught

up at each corner. The bookcases, pretty tripartite designs, are by *Peacock & Berry*.

The STAIRCASE, a double return flight opening on the W of the hall, leads to a colonnaded screen and then to a remarkable two-storey BEDROOM LOBBY, Wyatt's adaptation of a common Irish idea, lit by an oval oculus and surrounded at the attic level by a gallery on paired Adamesque columns of no particular order. *Rose*'s plasterwork here is very fine.

Opening off the E colonnade on the ground floor the second Lord Belmore installed a ROMAN BATH, apparently the first piece of private plumbing introduced into the house!

Lord Belmore's family have been associated with Castle Coole since 1655, when the estate was bought by a Scottish planter, John Corry, who had first settled in Belfast. In 1740, on the death of his great-grandson, Leslie Corry, the estates passed to Leslie's second sister Sarah, who had married Galbraith Lowry of Ahenis, M.P. for Co. Tyrone. It was their third son, Armar Lowry-Corry, who succeeded to Castle Coole in 1769 and who became the first Lord Belmore in 1781, Viscount in 1789, and Earl in 1797. The fourth Earl, who succeeded in 1845 at the age of ten, later wrote the delightful *History of Two Ulster Manors*, which includes many family records. Early this century his grand-daughter Lady Dorothy Lowry-Corry contributed the careful Fermanagh entries to the *Preliminary Survey of Ancient Monuments of Northern Ireland*. In 1951 the property was purchased with a grant from the Ulster Land Fund. It is administered by the Northern Ireland Committee of the National Trust.

STABLES. 0.5 km NW of the house. A rectangular two-storey courtyard of rendered rubble stone, nine by eleven bays inside, by *Sir Richard Morrison*, 1824. The HEAD GARDENER'S HOUSE nearby, a charming Gandyesque design of three bays with segmental windows, oversailing roof, and curious corner pilasters, is presumably also by Morrison. Further S there are more walled courts and offices of a vernacular character.

GATE LODGE. By the main road. A Lombardic Victorian design in ashlar, with incised stone bands and paired round-headed windows. It looks about 1880.

RUSTIC LODGE. 1.5 km S of the house at Derryvore. A picturesque thatched cottage, L-shaped, with lattice panes, bay-window, and rustic veranda.

CASTLE CURLEWS *see* DRUMQUIN

A village by the Moyola River, once called called Dawson's Bridge after the single arch erected by the Dawson family, who bought an estate here in 1633. The present appearance is of the early C19, though the wide street and square green indicate an earlier origin. The place was in fact developed in the early Georgian age by Sir Joshua Dawson, Chief Secretary for Ireland in 1710, who built the present Mansion House in Dublin and after whom Dawson Street in Dublin is named.

CHRISTCHURCH, CASTLEDAWSON PARISH CHURCH (C of I). In the grounds of Moyola Park. Built in the late C18 by G. R. Dawson. Four-bay hall with round-headed windows but triple lancets in the gables, a new overhanging roof with Tudor-esque bargeboards, and a side porch that all look late C19 and probably date from the creation of the parish (out of a perpetual curacy) in 1875. – The interior is memorable for two MONU-MENTS. The first is to Captain Harry Brereton Trelawny † 1851, signed by *J. Bedford* of London. A single white marble figure of an officer stands, head bowed, beside an Etruscan sarcophagus, a bearskin and gloves at his feet. – The other, to
70   the Rt Hon. George Robert Dawson (1790–1856), is one of the most astonishing monuments in any church in the British Isles, as it is made out of a huge Rococo chimneypiece and overmantel elaborately carved in dark oak with memorial inscriptions set in brass above and below the transom in the space where the fire should be. Where did it come from? The quality of the carving is as exceptional as the extraordinary use to which it has been put. More imported swags of flowers and cupids' heads frame a panel with the Ten Commandments.

ST JOHN. 2.5km SW. 1831. A three-bay rendered hall with Gothic windows. The old type of Catholic church, with the altar in the middle of the N wall.

CASTLEDAWSON PRESBYTERIAN CHURCH. 1700, largely rebuilt by *T. Houston* in 1903. T-shaped, with a three-stage tower at the W end. Harled, with stone quoins and odd semi-circular buttresses between the windows.

METHODIST CHURCH. 1838. A three-bay Georgian-glazed hall with round-headed windows.

MOYOLA PARK. 1 km N. Set in lovely parkland to the E of a curve in the river, a stylish though severe Georgian block built in 1768 by Arthur Dawson. The front is five bays by two storeys, though with the outer windows widely separated from the centre, where two windows are set close on either side of the front door. The central section is faced in ashlar stonework with a plain pediment above the main cornice that continues round the whole house, with a heavy blocking course above. The outer bays, in contrast to the ashlar, are of boulder basalt. The garden front, also of five bays, appears now (through the removal of a bank that had concealed the basement) to be three storeys high. Only the middle bay is of ashlar work, and canted bay-windows project from the sides at either end of this front. On the N is a harled service wing of 1929.

Inside, the glory of the house is the series of rich architectural cornices, finely incised and for once not clogged with paint but retaining the crisp sharpness that Rococo detailing admired. The finest are in the library, the drawing room, and richest of all in the dining room. The hall has a black and white marble floor and nicely detailed five-panel oak doors with inlaid borders to the panels. In all, a house of unusual finish and quality.

The Maghera Road GATE LODGE is a very pretty Pictur-esque cottage, L-shaped, with exceptionally high gables and bargeboards. The OBELISK erected by the Earl Bishop of Derry to the virtues of the Dawson family is, sadly, no more.

GLENBROOK HOUSE. 3 km SW. An attractive Tudor-style house of c. 1830, stuccoed, with octagonal corner turrets ending in finials, oriel windows, and panels of inset quatrefoils. Two storeys, with an H-shaped gabled front blocked in the centre by a big canted bow. Nice.

CASTLEDERG   TY E6

A market town on the River Derg in west Tyrone founded by Sir John Davies, Attorney General for Ireland to James I and Speaker in the Irish House of Commons in the Parliament of 1613–15. Davies, who received a grant of 2,000 acres in 1609, had laid out the town and built the first bridge across the Derg and a castle by 1619.

ST CONES, DERG PARISH CHURCH (C of I). One of the most interesting early churches in North-West Ulster. Tower and hall type, with a N aisle and a small chancel. The nave, built in 1731 by Hugo Edwards of Castle Gore, is a plain barn-like hall with five round-headed windows on the S side. The door-way inside the church leading into the nave is a round-headed archway with a cut stone surround, dated at the impost and patterned with a panel of floral bell drops down the architrave and acanthus leaves on an ogee moulding. This detail is important, for, though crude, it is clearly derived from a different pattern-book source and executed by a different hand from the classical doorcase outside on the s side of the tower. The tower itself has the high proportions and minimal openings character-istic of Elizabethan and Jacobean churches in Ulster. It is in-deed said to remain from the earlier church, and its classical doorcase must do so too. That makes it one of the oldest as well as one of the most accomplished pieces of classicism in this culturally remote province. Like Sir John Davies's Castle Curlews at Drumquin, its taste is English of the late C16. It is an aedicule of free-standing Tuscan columns set on charac-teristically high plinths with an inordinately high open pedi-ment above. Inside, the N aisle, by *Welland & Gillespie*, 1866, is joined to the nave by a robust arcade of four arches. Its w window is a big plate-tracery wheel. – MONUMENTS. Agnes Dovey † 1699, a primitive inscribed slab in the tower porch. – Robert Kyle † 1759. Sophisticated classical tablet and frame built into the s wall of the chancel. Exceptionally primitive carved angel underneath.

St Patrick. A cruciform church of about 1850, with a three-bay nave and triple lancets in each gable. Rendered, with stone trim, and greatly enhanced by a masonry tower between the nave and s transept with a belfry and an elegantly detailed broach-spire. The plan of the interior is one much used by E. J. Toye (cf. Gortin and Ardara), with an arcade across the tran-septs ending in small side chapels that flank the chancel. The proportions of this design are excellent: the concept clean, neat, and clear. – FONTS. In stone, taken from the previous Catholic church (1790–1846).

Castle. Just w of the town on the N bank of the river. Built by Sir John Davies before 1619. A square enclosure of approxi-mately 100 by 115 ft. The N wall remains almost to its full height, though much battered, with forestanding square flankers at each end. Behind this wall was a two-storey house, 15 ft wide, of which the E gable still stands. The N wall is pierced by eight musketry loops with flat lintels and splayed on the interior. Towards the middle is a part of a brick-lined oven. The flankers, 13 ft square inside, have two slot holes to cover each exposed face and were apparently added after the first structure was built, as was the bawn to the s, now marked only by a rise in the grass. The castle withstood the attack of Sir Phelim O'Neill in 1641, but the damage it sustained then was not repaired.

OTHER BUILDINGS. Castlederg is a pleasant little town to walk
about, laid out on a triangle of streets, though with little of
architectural value. The first monument is undoubtedly the
NEW BRIDGE, at the S of the town, built in 1835 to replace
the C17 structure of Sir John Davies. Four segmental arches
in dressed ashlar masonry. In an entry off BRIDGE STREET,
by the old church, is a NICHE with a vigorously carved bearded
head on an octagonal shaft; mid C19. The SCOTS CHURCH is
a four-bay pinnacled hall of 1858, the NATIONAL SCHOOLS,
double-gabled with plate tracery, are of 1868, and the crenellated ST PATRICK'S PAROCHIAL HALL is of 1907. The
ULSTER BANK is Italianate Gothic. The old STATION, in red
and black brick with segment-headed windows, served the
Castlederg and Victoria Bridge tramway.

NEIGHBOURHOOD

CASTLEDERG FIRST PRESBYTERIAN CHURCH. 2.5 km SSE,
at Garvetagh. The old church, now converted to a dwelling
house, is T-plan with stone quoins. Plaque inscribed 'This
House was Built 1739 chiefly by means of the Rev. Mr Nehe-
miah Donaldson'. The congregation dates from 1700, and Mr
Donaldson was minister from 1716 to 1747. The present
church, of the early C20, looks like a design by *McIntyre* of
Letterkenny. White-harled Presbyterian Gothic with red
sandstone string courses and trim to windows and buttresses.
A big hall with short transepts and offset tower with slate spire
at the gable front.

SPAMOUNT. 3 km E. A group of factory workers' COTTAGES
built for J. G. Smyly Q.C., apparently to designs of *John
McCurdy*, in 1863. Also a fine C18 BRIDGE of four arches.

CREW BRIDGE. 5 km E. A fine, low, rubble-built bridge on five
semicircular arches with pointed-cap abutments. Mid C18.

DRUMCLAMPH PARISH CHURCH (C of I). By Crew Bridge.
1846. A two-bay lancet hall with a W bellcote and porch.

CASTLE FINN   DO *E5*

A village built round a big triangular Diamond with an unusually
fine terrace of eight late Georgian houses along the length of its
N side. All are three-storey and were once quite grand. They still
look splendid from the fields S of the town, but at the time of
writing the locals don't care and many are derelict. There are a
number of minor churches in the vicinity, the best furthest away.

ST PATRICK, DONAGHMORE PARISH CHURCH (C of I). 1 km

w. Early C18. A plain four-bay hall with a bellcote and a dumpy Georgian porch. Apsidal E end added *c.* 1865. – MONUMENTS. Captain Newburgh. A late C17 armorial floor tablet. – Rev. John Nicholson † 1729. Grey and white marble tablet with armorial coat and *memento mori.* – Mary Hamilton Lighton † 1826. A large white marble wall obelisk. – The Rev. Sir John Lighton Bt., 1827. A grey and white marble sarcophagus.

SCHOOL. E of the church. Mid C19. A small, symmetrical Gothic design with gabled porches.

DONAGHMORE PRESBYTERIAN CHURCH. 3 km w. A big stuccoed hall of 1875 with four Tuscan pilasters and a gable pediment. Pretty three-bay, two-storey early C19 MANSE next door.

DONAGHMORE HOUSE. 1 km w. A large High Victorian house of *c.* 1880 in a free Artisan-Mannerist vein with a high hipped roof and regular dormer windows. Enormous conservatory immediately to the E.

ALT PRESBYTERIAN CHURCH. 4 km s. Early C19(?). A simple rendered hall in a tree-bordered graveyard. Four-bay on one side, two-bay on the other, with Georgian glazed Gothic windows. A surprise entrance front that is simple but robustly classical with Tuscan corner pilasters, a high gable pediment, aedicule bellcote, and a perfect pattern-book Doric porch with triglyph frieze mutules and a high pediment. The interior has box pews, oil lamps, and blue and orange glass borders to the windows behind the pulpit.

ST COLUMBA, DONEYLOOP. 3 km SE at the border by Clady. 1867 by *John O'Neill.* A fine cruciform Gothic Revival church, with a handsome tower and broach-spire added in 1891 at the SW angle. The chancel is apsidal, with a high half-conical roof outside, and side chapels with separate gabled roofs linked to the sanctuary by single side arches supported on polished stone columns. The detail is all E.E. Built for the Rev. James Connolly to replace a thatched church.

CASTLE FINN CATHOLIC CHURCH. In the village. Originally of 1822; now cruciform and rendered in cement.

CASTLE FINN CONGREGATIONAL CHURCH. Mid C19. A four-bay buttressed stone hall with a projecting porch.

CASTLE FINN BRIDGE. Late C18. Of seven arches, built by a Mr *Mason* with stones from a ruined O'Donnell castle nearby.

CASTLE HUME

Castle Hume holds an important place in the history of Irish classicism, for it was here that *Richard Castle,* who was to become one of the principal protagonists of Irish Palladian architecture, made his debut. The son of Huguenot parents, born in Hesse Kassel – hence the surname that he adopted in Ireland – by 1725 Castle had come to London, where in 1728 he met Sir Gustavus Hume, Bt., who brought him to Ireland that year. He became a draughtsman with Pearce in Dublin and embarked in the same year on his career as an Irish country house architect. Castle Hume was his first work, built for Sir Gustavus from 1728 and burnt out by accident the next year but completed again. An estate map of 1768 shows it to have been a small classical house of three storeys with a pedimented centre and with pineapples and other sculpture along its stone balustrade – in all similar to Castle's other small house at Hazlewood in Co. Sligo. By 1793 it was again in ruins. All that remains today is a long avenue of about thirty beech trees leading up to where the house stood, and a courtyard of stable offices.

The STABLES are typical of Castle's robust manner, beautifully built in harled brick with cyclopean stone dressings such as the granite slabs above the doors and the heavy frames to the circular upper-floor windows that he so frequently used. The present court contains two main blocks, linked by a range of seven arcaded coach houses. The large block, L-shaped, contained the stables, with an exceedingly fine elliptically vaulted ceiling in cut brick supported on an arcade of six Tuscan columns. The vaults spring from the capital without any intervening entablature, while the base of the column sits on a stumpy rounded drum instead of the more usual square, a feature perhaps derived from Palladio's Basilica at Vicenza, and one that the Knight of Glin points out as a *leitmotif* of Castle's work. The PIGEON HOUSE nearby is c18, a harled octagonal tower, brick-lined, with holes for about 600 pairs and a wooden octagonal cupola.

DUNBAR HOUSE. 2.5 km S, on the Enniskillen-Belleek Road. Mid c18, originally thatched. Now a small two-storey square house with overhanging eaves. Three-bay main front with segment-headed central door flanked by Ionic columns. Built for the Dunbar family.

CASTLE IRVINE see IRVINESTOWN

CASTLEROCK   LD *H2*

A railway halt on a breezy bit of coast just E of the mouth of the Bann. Two straggling streets between the railway and the sea are stopped at one end by the strand and at the other by the cliffs of Downhill, where the railway runs into a tunnel. Two churches, a terrace of early Victorian basalt houses, and a big brick villa with gables and bargeboards make up the architectural sum.

CHRIST CHURCH (C of I). An unusually ambitious little church of 1868–70 by *Frederick William Porter*, architect to the Clothworkers' Company. Built of the usual black basalt, with weathered cocoa-coloured sandstone dressings. The church is cruciform, with a polygonal spire, E.E. lancet windows, and an offset NW tower with a broach-spire that is a little too big and looks, not inappropriately for a seaside resort, like an ice-cream cone upside down. Mrs Alexander composed a hymn for the dedication of this church.

The interior is a pleasant surprise. Little has been altered, and instead of the usual plain plaster, the walls are lined in a warm red brick. Ten brass candelabra, with twisted stems and ivy-leaf sprouts, step down the nave, and above glows a varnished pine roof supported on braced trusses. Note too the blue stencil patterns inside the S transept arch. – PULPIT. Caen stone octagon with symbols of the Evangelists. – STAINED GLASS. In the chancel, bright reds and blue contemporary with the church's foundation. – W window by *Wailes & Strang* of Newcastle. – MONUMENTS. Many brass plaques to the Bruce family of Downhill.

CASTLEROCK PRESBYTERIAN CHURCH. A rendered Gothic hall, mid C19, with an offset buttressed tower erected in honour of Samuel McCurdy Greer in 1885. *J. Kennedy* of Coleraine builder (and architect?).

STATION. Red and yellow brick by *John Lanyon*, 1873–5.

MILLTOWN CATHOLIC CHURCH. In a rural setting by a small housing estate 2 km SW. A diminutive Gothic hall of *c.* 1830, rendered, with three lancet windows, porch, gallery, and timber chancel arch. The windows have cut stone voussoirs – the building's only enrichment.

Described in Pynnar's survey of 1619 as a village of twenty families founded by Sir John Hume. It is now a haphazard street of small houses. The original church was rebuilt in 1688 and again on a new site at Inishmacsaint in the C19.

INISHMACSAINT PARISH CHURCH (C of I). 1 km E. Built in 1831 and enlarged in 1871. Hall and tower type, of stone, with delightfully elongated Dec windows in timber. Two pinnacled porches with separate roofs project on the N and S sides and provided individual family pews. The enlargement, externally rather a clumsy one, consisting of a raised chancel approached through a C13-type arch, gives considerable life to the interior.

METHODIST CHURCH. 1878. A high stone hall with yellow brick trim. Five bays, with a triple window in the gable.

BENMORE RECTORY. 1 km E. Built in 1829 for the Rev. H. Hamilton, a square, three-storey house, four bays on the front, three on the side, with a heavy stone porch. Two extra bays were added to the side by Dean Tottenham c. 1880. Inside, a remarkable double return stair in wood rises steeply in a narrow hall, repeating itself completely on the second floor.

TULLY CASTLE. 2 km NE, on a point above Lough Erne. That sense of isolation which the early C17 planters in Ulster must have known is immediately excited by the sight of the roofless ivy-covered mass of Tully Castle, rising from its knoll above the lough. Its isolation was its downfall, for the castle, a fortified bawn founded by Sir John Hume before 1619, surrendered to Captain Rory Maguire in 1641 and was burnt with its inhabitants. It has since remained a ruin.

According to Pynnar's survey it was 'a bawn of lime and stone, 100 ft square, 14 ft high having four flankers for defence' with 'a fair strong castle, 50 ft long and 21 ft broad'. Of all this there remain the castle walls and one salient angled flanker that extends about 25 ft from the NE corner with traces of a second flanker further S. The castle entrance was within the bawn, in a square wing projecting from about the centre of the S side. This contained a spiral stair leading to the main apartments on the first floor. The ground floor was given over to an impressive barrel-vaulted room, 48 ft by 15 ft, with a fireplace and deep chimney at the E screened by a large semicircular arch. Stone shelves at either side inside the fireplace. The first floor is divided into two rooms, each with a fireplace, and with windows only on the S and E sides, i.e. within the bawn. A second, smaller spiral stair, corbelled out in the SE angle in the traditional Scottish fashion, led to the top floor. Traces of wattle centering are on the ground-floor vault; the draw hole at the main door remains, and a shot hole on the first floor in the SW corner.

INISHMACSAINT ISLAND. See p. 318.

CLABBY

ST MARGARET, CLABBY PARISH CHURCH (C of I). A striking church by *Welland & Gillespie*, but by now (1864–70) it is

William Welland and not his father Joseph, so the style is even more personal, more wayward and roguish. Local lore says that the plans of Clabby were muddled with those of a city church and that the wrong building was erected on each site. The story – a common one often told of old buildings and never really true – makes its point at once, for the church is unusually large and ambitious for a small country parish, reflecting the generosity of the Rev. J. G. Porter, who made the original endowment. Land was appropriated for the church and its glebe in 1864 and the building was consecrated in September 1870. The first impression is one of many gables, the second of fine punched stonework and plate tracery. The S wall, facing the road and therefore the most important, has five gables, a porch with a smooth stone spire springing from a gabled tower above it, then three bays of gable-topped paired lancets that light the body of the church, and finally, to end, a taller gable with a three-light plate-traceried window, suggesting the embryo of a S transept. The N wall follows the same arrangement without the spire, and the 'transept' projects N to accommodate a vestry. The chancel also projects. The E window is remarkable, five lights, ending in plate tracery, a sexfoil, two quatrefoils, six trefoils, and twenty-four tiny studded circles.

In invention the interior fully matches the outside. The church is really no more than a vast rectangle with a shallow chancel end, but that feeling of uncomfortable width and bleakness so common in late C19 churches in Ireland is entirely overcome by a rich and unique roof structure. Braced trusses are grouped in pairs between the windows, with exposed pine panelling on the inside of the gable roofs between them. The effect is low and warm, suggesting the character of an aisle. Then from the ends of the braces of each truss the roof rises high above the centre of the church in a two-centred arch, vaulted in plaster; only the tie-beams of the trusses continue across the width under the vault with lively contrapuntal effect. – STAINED GLASS. E window 1885. The Resurrection: Christ in white, pale pink, and golden robes. Angels either side. In the outer windows, the Nativity and Christ with children, both against leafy backgrounds. The rest is set against a brilliant cerulean sky. Above, the plate tracery is wonderfully effective, with angels, the Paschal lamb, lilies, and pure colour all twinkling in the thick dark stone.

METHODIST CHURCH. 1885. A gabled hall and porch of two bays. Paired round-headed windows and brick trim.

CLADAGH   FM *D9*

ST LASAIR'S CHURCH RUINS. 0.5 km W of Cladagh Bridge. Of a small C17 church, a long hall about 18 ft wide, only a simple cross-mullioned window with two round heads in the E gable remains. In an old oval-shaped graveyard, girt with trees and beautifully sited on a slope between Clogan Hill and Lough Macnean Lower.

MONEEN HOUSE. A stone-built gentleman's house of *c.* 1830 but looking curiously C17, with an unusually tall slated hipped roof. Two storeys. Segment-headed door flanked by tripartite windows.

SCHOOL. By Cladagh Bridge. 1880. A pretty gabled hall built by Lord Enniskillen's family, with patterned tiles, bargeboards, and ridge finials.

CHURCHES. On the road SE to Florence Court are: WHEATHILL METHODIST CHURCH, a small stone-built hall of three bays with paired round-headed windows, and WHEATHILL CATHOLIC CHURCH of 1874, a four-bay lancet hall built by the Rev. J. Cleary P.P.

CLANABOGAN   TY *F7*
6.5 km SW of Omagh

A typical gentleman's estate in mid Victorian Ulster, created by Samuel Galbraith Esq., with house, family church for a specially created curacy, and a modern rectory.

CLANABOGAN HOUSE. A large, plain double-pile house with unusually widely spaced windows and small porch-like wings at either end. Mid C18. Inherited by Samuel Galbraith from his uncle in 1819.

CHURCH (C of I). 1861 by *Welland & Gillespie*. A standard design with nave, chancel, N robing-room, and S porch surmounted by an octagonal tower and spire. Much enhanced by a High Victorian interior designed by *Thomas Drew* in 1889. Chancel arch supported on short black marble columns on brackets; walls lined with Bath stone with bands of red marble; alabaster REREDOS, encaustic tile floor. – PULPIT. Of Irish marbles and panels of alabaster inlaid with marble. – STAINED GLASS. E window to Samuel Galbraith † 1864. Heraldic. – MONUMENT. James Galbraith, killed in action in Maiwand in 1880. High relief plaque of military officers by *T. Brock*, 1885.

RECTORY. 1887, grotesquely picturesque. L-shaped, with hipped gables and hipped dormers, fleur-de-lys ridge tiles, and elaborate bargeboards with pendants at each end.

ST PATRICK. A largish early Victorian Catholic church. Plain T-plan, stuccoed, with Y-tracery windows and a nice buttressed tower in three stages. The interior has a panelled plaster ceiling, two galleries, a choir loft, and grandiose timber aedicules to the three altars.

HOLY TRINITY, CUMBER LOWER PARISH CHURCH (C of I). 3 km NW. 1796. A large tower and hall type church. Originally classical, with a three-bay S side with round-headed windows in relieving arches and a shallow pediment over the middle bay. Paired plate tracery now fills the windows, and the tower is surmounted by a later C19 Norman belfry of a good scale. – MAUSOLEUM of the Acheson Lyle family, a square sandstone block of 1870.

CUMBER UPPER PARISH CHURCH (C of I). 1 km S. 1860 by *Joseph Welland*. A tall three-bay hall, rubble-built, with side porch and offset square tower with a copper spire added in 1960. Three-bay arcade to the N aisle. Polygonal apse.

CUMBER PRESBYTERIAN CHURCH. 4 km NW. 1884. A large gabled hall of stone with five bays of geometrical tracery.

BRACKFIELD CASTLE. 4 km NW, by the Presbyterian church. A simple enclosure, about 70 ft by 70 ft, with walls varying between 6 and 10 ft in height, built by the Skinners' Company about 1615. The gable of a long-house within the bawn remains, and parts of two circular flankers at diagonally opposite angles.

KILCATTEN HOUSE. 2.5 km NW. A pretty, single-storey Regency lodge. Five-bay front with porch. Blank recessed tablets above the windows. Shallow hipped roof, and double segmental bows at the back. GATE LODGE. A rock-faced extravaganza with a pyramid roof.

COMBER HOUSE. 0.5 km S. A seven-bay, two-storey house with tripartite centre door. It looks about 1820, though the lower floor was built earlier by William Ross, who lost his money in the American War of Independence and sold the house in 1785.

CUMBER OLD CHURCH. In Claudy. The ruins of a rectangular church, 24 ft by 63 ft, with both gables standing and a small W porch and bellcote. Ruined in 1689, repaired in 1693, rebuilt on the old site in 1757, and replaced in 1860 (*see* above).

GLENALLA HOUSE. 2.5 km S. Built by the Rev. Francis Brownlow. A tall two-storey house with tripartite windows throughout. Large extensions. Nice bow-fronted GATE LODGE.

NORTHERN BANK. 1898 by *G. W. Ferguson*. A free mixture of
Dutch gable, Palladian window, and pagoda-roofed Tuscan
porch.

CLOGHER   TY *G8*

Clogher is a tiny inconsequential place. A row of houses lines the
road as it climbs a slow hill. They look across fields with a dis-
ordered jumble of a few buildings at the bottom, then the vestiges
of an C18 park, a big classical house, and a big plain church with
a square tower in a graveyard at the top. Beyond the church the
place ends, and the crisscross of Tyrone hills and fields takes over.
There is not much to indicate the history of the place, but history
it has. The big church and the big house are a cathedral and a
bishop's palace. If their appearance today is of the early C19, that
need not obscure the origin of the see: it goes back to the C6 when,
according to tradition, St Patrick consecrated MacCairthinn first
bishop of Clogher. Clogher still gives its name to a Protestant and
a Catholic diocese, though the Catholic cathedral and bishop's
palace are in Monaghan.

ST MACARTIN'S CATHEDRAL (C of I). The early Christian and
medieval predecessors of the cathedral have vanished. A fire
in 1396 reputedly destroyed the cathedral, two chapels, an
Augustinian abbey, the bishop's court, and other buildings. In
the mid C15 Abbot Patrick rebuilt the abbey, but was accused
of misrule. By 1622 the cathedral was 'altogether ruinous' and
the walls of the abbey church would 'beare noe roofe'.
    The church that stands today was built by Bishop John 64
Stearne in 1744, apparently to designs of the architect builder
James Martin. The design was once said to have been in the
E.E. style, which would make it among the first attempts at
a serious Gothic Revival style had not Dean Bagwell decided
in 1818 to recast the building in a plain classical garb. But this
now seems untrue. The church looks C18: cruciform, with pedimented gables to the transepts and chancel. The broad W front,
wider than the nave, also has a pedimental gable but is topped
by a solid, square belfry tower with a balustrade and obelisk
finials. All the windows are round-headed except the E Venetian
window, Tuscan outside, Scamozzian Ionic within. The entrance vestibule, panelled in deal for the Countess of Ennis-

killen in 1885, is a miniature portrait gallery of the Bishops of
Clogher from the c16 Miller Macgrath to the snobbish Robert
Clayton whom Mrs Delany visited here in 1748. The church
interior is bare and plain, with a modillion cornice, flat plastered
ceiling, semi-circular arches opening into the short transepts,
and a w gallery supported on fluted Ionic columns that look
more like 1745 than 1818. The seating dates from c. 1865.

SCULPTURE. In the porch is part of a lintel thought to come
from an c8 or c9 church, 5 ft long and 2 ft high, with a recessed
rectangular panel on both sides; an old circular font stone perhaps of the c16; and a date-stone from the first Protestant
church of 1628. – CLOGHER CROSS has also been erected here.
It is a slab cross similar to the crosses at Carndonagh and Fahan,
Co. Donegal, with a broad half-round edge moulding and broad
interlace patterns on each face. The shaft widens to include
stumpy arms at the top decorated with an inverted 'protractor'
shape almost like a sundial. The s face has a small naturalistic
fish at the base and a short rectangular block of interlace at the
top. The n face (less well preserved) has a simplified head projecting from the top block with a semicircular cope or breast-
plate decorated with triquetrae below it. Stylistic parallels
suggest the mid c7. – FONT. c18, in polished black marble,
with a fluted basin and a gadrooned baluster base. – STAINED
GLASS. Narrative E window of c. 1870 with the Baptism, Ascension, and Last Supper, in memory of Lord John George Beresford, 1862. – Note also the splendid pageantry of the Revelation
window (nave s side) to Moutray Gledstanes, 1917. – MONU-
MENTS. James and Thomas Gledstanes, 1778, an elegant urn
against an obelisk. – The Rt Rev. John Porter D.D., 1819, a
sarcophagus with bishop's mitre and crozier.

In the churchyard to the SE are the remains of two other plain
CROSSES with solid recessed rings.

CONVENT OF THE SISTERS OF ST LOUIS. Immediately E of
the cathedral. Formerly Clogher Park and before that the Protestant bishop's palace. A plain ashlar block, built into the
hillside, so that the entrance front is three storeys and the garden
side four. Seven-bay front with three-bay pediment and single-
storey Doric porch. Six-bay garden front with a high arcaded
terrace across the ground floor flanked by recessed two-storey
wings with canted bay-windows. The house overlooks a miniature park. Mrs Delany describes it in 1748 as 'pretty with a fine
large sloping green walk from the steps [fifty, which she thought
intolerable] to a large basin of water, on which sail most grace-

fully fair beautiful swans. Beyond the basin of water rises a very steep hill covered with fir in the side of which Mrs Clayton is going to make a grotto. The rest of the garden is irregularly planted.' The landscape still bears traces of Bishop Clayton's planting, but the house is a more recent one, begun in the late C18 by Bishop Lord John Beresford and completed by Bishop Tottenham in 1823. Square entrance hall with drawing room and dining room *en suite* across the garden front. Mahogany doors in fine late neo-classical architraves. The drawing-room ceiling painted by *A. S. Rogerson*, 1905. There is a small Doric gate lodge.

ST MACARTEN. 2.5 km E. A large, bare, T-plan church of 1846 in squared rubble with elementary Gothic detail. Altered by *J. L. Donnelly* in 1921. – STAINED GLASS. St Patrick window, Celtic type, by *J. Clarke & Sons*, 1922.

LONGRIDGE PRESBYTERIAN CHURCHES. 2.5 km NW. The congregation was founded here in the later C17. Of the two churches CLOGHER PRESBYTERIAN CHURCH is a long, six-bay harled hall with round-headed windows with quoin surrounds and Y-tracery sash-windows. Probably late C18. Crantall Old School, a long low row of cottages, is beside it. LONGRIDGE PRESBYTERIAN CHURCH is of 1843, a wide gabled hall with four round-headed lancets and a porch.

CATHOLIC CHURCH. At Aghadrummond, 3 km NW. A four-bay Georgian glazed hall with buttresses; early C19.

FORMER UNION WORKHOUSE. 1842. The standard Tudor design of *George Wilkinson*. Now the Clogher Valley Home and Council Offices.

DEANERY. 1 km W. Mid to late C18. A square rubble-built block with a three-bay, two-storey front and a hipped roof. Tripartite pedimented door with Tuscan pilasters and primitive Venetian window above. Lugged door surrounds with irregular six-panel doors inside.

KILLYFADDY. 3 km NW. Cecil Manor, built for the Rev. Francis Gervais near Clogher by *William Farrell*, has gone. Killyfaddy, which belonged to R. W. Maxwell in 1837, must also be a Farrell house. Bare and cubic, but with Farrell's typical attempts at style: a tripartite window with heavy consoles above the central Greek Ionic porch; recessed panels to the windows at either side; and a shallow mutule cornice at the eaves. Two-storey, three-bay front on a hidden basement. Shallow hipped roof.

CORICK. 1.5 km NNE. The seat of the Story family since 1697, almost completely rebuilt in a plain minimal Italian style by

Lanyon, Lynn & Lanyon in 1863. It is a large-scale rendered villa L-shaped. Three-storey tower in the angle with an Italianate hipped slate roof. The old house had a five-bay, two-storey front of which Lanyon kept two bays, building the tower and s wing before the rest. Canted bay-window in the middle of the long s front. The yards behind the house have handsome BARNS of 1748 and 1858, one with a late C18 brick-vaulted end.

FARDROSS. 3 km SW. Reputedly 'an ancient seat of the Gladstane family', though now not looking much earlier than Regency. The lines are long and low and the windows much wider apart than usual. The house is now extended at one end with a five-bay, two-storey garden front, the central bay taken up by a large canted bay-window with recessed segment-headed panels and wide overhanging eaves. Lion mask gutters and big square regular chimneys.

ASHFIELD PARK. 2 km S. A pleasant mid Victorian Italianate villa. Single-storey, but set on a high basement, with a grandiose double perron approaching the front door. The style is very much that of a railway station in a prosperous provincial town: dressed ashlar walls, paired round-headed windows with big keystones, and console-bracketed eaves. Inside, a central hall with dome light. The builder was a Mr Breckenridge, never accepted by the county families, but revered locally as a patron of William Carleton (1794–1869), the Irish novelist, born in the townland of Prillisk nearby.

BRECKENRIDGE'S MONUMENT. 3 km S. On a bare hill above the Clogher valley and visible for miles. Mr Breckenridge of Ashfield Park never forgave the local society that had refused to accept him as one of their number and had this monument built where he was interred so that those who looked down on him in life would look up to him in death. It is a very plain telescopic square stone tower in three stages with an iron rail at the top; in all about 30 ft high. The lowest stage has four round-headed windows with the remains of metal frames and a stair in the thickness of the wall. Sadly, the mausoleum in the basement was broken into by troops stationed in Northern Ireland in the 1940s.

A parish on high ground immediately to the SE of Derry city.

ALTNAGELVIN GENERAL HOSPITAL. By *F. R. S. Yorke, E.*

Rosenberg, and *C. S. Mardall*, 1949–60, the first general hospital to be completed after the Second World War, at a cost of £2,680,000. Brutally inconsiderate on its hill-top site with the wards in a twelve-storey tower and the operating theatres and administration in a lower seven-storey block. – SCULPTURE. By the entrance Princess Macha by *F. E. McWilliam*.

GLENDERMOTT PARISH CHURCH (C of I). Tower and hall type in primitive Georgian Gothic. The four-bay body of the church, described rather perplexingly by Lewis as 'a handsome building in the Grecian style', dates from 1753. The three-stage battlemented tower was added in 1789. In 1794 it gained a wooden and copper spire, but that was blown down in 1831. High N aisle of 1861. – WAR MEMORIAL, 'The Last Post', by *J. Robinson*.

GLENDERMOTT PRESBYTERIAN CHURCH. The congregation dates from 1696. This T-plan gabled hall is basically of 1743, built by the Rev. William Haire, reworked in 1939 by *I. W. Lynch* of Derry. Three galleries inside with porches at the end of each arm.

FORMER SECOND PRESBYTERIAN CHURCH. 1744, built by the Rev. Mr Holmes, a smaller T-plan church just E of the other with an outside stair to the gallery in the leg of the T.

ARDMORE CATHOLIC CHURCH. 2 km SE. Red brick Romanesque of *c.* 1910. Stepped arcading on the gable and a central octagonal tower. The unusually rich interior contains a gilded oak *baldacchino* supported on four columns with trumpet-playing cherubs; and praying angels sculptured in wood on either side of the sanctuary.

From Altnagelvin the back road to Claudy runs along the w bank of the River Faughan, passing a series of minor country houses almost like suburban villas, to late Georgian Derry.

ASHBROOK. 1.5 km SE. Reputedly built in 1686 by John Ash. No old work can now be seen behind the robust but gauche front of perhaps 1760 that turned the house into an irregular double-pile plan, with a strongly projecting semicircular bow in the middle of the front. The fenestration is odd, with single windows either side of the bow on the ground floor and two windows above (cf. Cloncallick in Fermanagh). This was obviously meant to be a smart job, for the architraves to all the windows and the front door are lavishly treated with dressed stone Gibbs surrounds. There are eagles in niches on the gables; the hall is paved in grey stone slabs with black marble inset diamonds, and the doors have lugged surrounds. All this looks like the work of George Ash, who owned the house in 1777.

BEECH HILL. 2 km SE. A complex and very curious jumble dating apparently to 1729 at its SE end, where three old Georgian sash windows and a side door have convincing early C18 proportions. From this, which must have been the regular and simple front of the Skipton family house, projects a massive late C19 *porte cochère* with heavy oriel windows on three sides above the carriage arch and a hipped slate roof with a timber clerestory. On the other side of the *porte cochère* the continuation of the C18 house front, with bigger windows, dates from 1851, with a still later picturesque Italianate addition behind. The house was bought in 1875 by Edward Nicholson and altered by his son Thomas in 1898 to designs of *R. E. Buchanan* of Derry, who added the attic floors at the E end. Inside, the library of 1851 is a gargantuan classical hall arcaded down each side with heavy Doric pilasters and a monster frieze filled with very lifelike and large ox-heads taken no doubt from Stuart and Revett.

The house is set in a formal avenue, partly remaining, with limes to the S and beeches to the N. GATE LODGE of the 1870s, heavily Picturesque, with a slated rubble tower.

ARDMORE HOUSE. 2 km SE. A three-bay, two-storey Regency villa, with tripartite windows on the ground floor and a veranda that breaks forward to form a glazed octagonal porch. Exceptionally pretty Tuscan conservatory. Built for John Acheson Smyth c. 1810.

GLENKEEN HOUSE. 2.5 km SE. An ample four-bay, two-storey house of about 1790, the middle two bays curving in a segmental bow. Tuscan columned entrance in the centre.

THE OAKES. 6 km SE, across the river. A large-scale stuccoed house built by the Lyle family and remodelled, as it now appears, to designs of *John McCurdy* for Acheson Lyle in 1867. Two-storey, with a three-bay entrance front with an Ionic columned porch, and a five-bay garden front with central pediment. Big plaster ceilings inside.

GORTNESSY LOWER PRESBYTERIAN CHURCH. 4.5 km ENE. 1841. A five-bay gabled hall with round-headed windows. Flat pine ceiling and box pews inside.

GORTNESSY CROSSROADS SCHOOL. 4.5 km ENE, on Gorteen Hill. 1831. A plain harled building decorated with a lively sculptured panel of a camel with a wool pack. Built by whom?

CLONFEACLE

TY J8

The site of an early Irish monastery of which St Lugad was abbot in 597. The name – church of the tooth (*fiacul*) – is traditionally associated with one of St Patrick's teeth that was preserved here. The monastery was later vested in the Culdees and granted to Primate Hampton in 1614.

CLONFEACLE CROSS. In St Patrick's churchyard. This cross, some 4 ft high, may be unfinished. It is of an unusual pattern, with the ring recessed on one face and attached to the arms by short brackets. The workmanship is crude and the base shaft fatter than the head.

ST PATRICK. Mid C19. A three-bay rendered hall with timber Y-tracery windows. Gable façade. Kingpost trussed roof. – GRAVESTONE. In the churchyard a curious stone shaped like a bow tie on its end, with a bell and a face on the back. To James Givern. IHS 1688.

TULLEYDOEY HOUSE. A not quite regular façade of seven bays with a projecting centre bay. Built by the Jackson family. Of various dates: parts are possibly late C17 or early C18. Lugged door surrounds inside, brick-vaulted basement in parts, and a substantial stair with three banisters per tread. A lead Phoenix Assurance plaque of 1783 is affixed to the old part of the house. – GATE LODGES. One dated T.J. 1793, the other a picturesque cottage of 1843 with large bargeboards inscribed 'Let us watch and be sober', 'Welcome and God speed', 'John Lawson 1844'. *See also* Benburb.

CLONMANY

DO F1

A parish and small village remotely situated near the top of the Inishowen peninsula. Memorable for its trim C19 houses and tapering Diamond, closed by a charming Market House.

ST MARY. A big T-plan building, painted and rendered, with a square stone tower asymmetrically placed at the s end of the T. The church appears to date from *c.* 1810 and was enlarged in 1833; the tower was added in 1843. The earliest stone in the churchyard is the grave of the parish priest, Charles O'Haggerty, who built the church and who died aged twenty-nine in 1820.

MARKET HOUSE. A nice little building that deserves to be better looked after than it was at the time of writing. Chaste yet robust, with a three-bay, two-storey front. The roof is hidden behind a parapet. Built of local coursed rubble with red brick trim, the ground floor is of five arches with a wide one in the middle and paired narrower ones on either side. The outer arches both contain doors with stairs inside leading to the upper floor. Note too the horrid detail of cast-iron hands that grasp the outside bar and thus provide hinges for the gates in the central arches. Date: about 1850.

CLONMANY PARISH CHURCH RUINS (C of I). 1 km W, at Straid. A diminutive tower and hall church built by the Earl Bishop of Derry in 1772, dismantled in 1927, and now roofless.

GLEN HOUSE. 1.5 km W. A five-bay, two-storey house with a segmental fanlight. Late C18.

CROSS STONE. 1.5 km NNW at Bunacrick farm. An irregularly shaped slab stone incised with a Latin cross. Associated with an early Christian monastery founded here by St Colmcille.

COAGH   TY J

A small village with a big bridge over the Ballinderry River, the boundary between Co. Derry and Co. Tyrone. There are four plain hall churches here, and a weird modern one nearby. Cloghtoyle is a dolmen on the Derry side of the river.

PRESBYTERIAN CHURCH. Very much a meeting house, set above the road with an avenue of beech trees, flanked by symmetrically disposed outbuildings. A big square hall, 54 ft by 56 ft, with box pews inside. Five round-headed sash-windows at the sides and front, with a central round-headed door. Half-hipped roof with the ridge running parallel to the front. Coagh congregation was established in 1711, but the present church is probably late C18.

ST PATRICK. A large five-bay hall of 1843, modernized in 1966, with segment-headed windows and grey brick baptistery and campanile.

ST LUKE (C of I). 1782. A small harled hall with bellcote and porch built by Primate Robinson as Tamlagh Parish Church. Two BULLAN STONES are in the churchyard by the porch.

ST JOSEPH AND ST MALACHY. At Drumullan, 3 km W. By *John S. O'Doherty*, 1958. A utility portal-frame church with upstanding roof at the altar end and a high entrance tower like those attached to fire stations. Will this weather into an endearing freak? At present it looks a little like a gigantic old steam engine modelled in Meccano.

COALISLAND   TY J7

In the C19 a centre of Ulster rural industry, with limeworks and brick kilns. Population 2,500. Now run down, with few buildings of interest.

HOLY TRINITY, BRACKAVILLE PARISH CHURCH (C of I). A moderate-scaled Ecclesiastical Commissioners' church, built for a new parish and consecrated in 1865. Nave, s aisle (actually E), and chancel. Tower and spire offset beside the side porch. Built of brownish basalt with sandstone trim. The nave is lit by three windows, each of three slender lancets; the choir by paired cusped lancets. Four-bay single-chamfered arcade inside on round piers with moulded capitals. Exposed braced trusses and braced purlins make an effective open roof. Presumably by *Welland & Gillespie*.

CATHOLIC CHURCH. 1857. A big stone hall and chancel with a high roof and a curiously wide bellcote with three finials. Four-bay nave with Y-traceried windows and thin buttresses. Single-bay chancel. E window with intersecting Y-tracery.

EDENDORK CATHOLIC CHURCH. 3 km sw. Dated 1814 on the E gable. Rebuilt as a small cruciform church with s porch and w bellcote. Harled, with stone dressings. Interior with exposed cross-braced beams. – STAINED GLASS. An attractive E window of five lights: The Last Supper very graphically shown with Judas tiptoeing out. Brilliant blues, greens, and purples. Of *c.* 1920.

EDENDORK PAROCHIAL HALL. 3 km sw. 1963. Possibly the ugliest building in Ulster and an astonishing example of how not to build in open countryside. A sea of tarmac and an inane facade like a 1930s fireplace.

POLICE STATION. A nice brown brick building with diamond-cut stone quoins and handsome proportions. Eight-bay, two-storey front with a segmental arch on the ground floor below the central two bays. Early C19.

ST MICHAEL, CLONOE PARISH CHURCH (C of I). 2.5 km ENE. Founded in 1431. A tiny rubble hall with w bellcote and porch. Sandstone surrounds to the windows. Three-bay nave with paired round-headed lancets. Three-light E window with round-topped C17 tracery. The church was not in use in 1622 because it was too far from Mountjoy Fort, but it was restored in 1699. The windows are said to be of that date, but this is doubtful. – MONUMENTS. Tablets to Thomas Morris of

Mountjoy † 1712 and to Cornet W. Clements and Lettice his wife, 1752.

GLEBE HOUSE. By the church. 1810. Three-bay, two-storey on a high basement. Harled.

CLONOE CATHOLIC CHURCH. 2.5 km ENE. A rendered T-plan church of the mid C19, with a shallow segmental sanctuary. Gallery facing the altar inside. – MONUMENT. Framed slab to the Rev. James Derlin, thirty years P.P., † 1816.

F9   COLEBROOKE PARK   FM

Colebrooke Park takes its name from Major Thomas Brooke, the great-great-grandson of Sir Basil Brooke, the governor of Donegal in the early C17, and from Catherine Cole his wife. Thomas and Catherine were the first of the Brooke family to make their permanent residence in Fermanagh, though the family had held property here from about 1666, when a large portion of the confiscated lands of Conor Macguire was granted to Sir Henry Brooke in recompense for his activity during the 1641 rising. There are two houses on the estate, a church, and minor buildings.

80 COLEBROOKE. A large classical house of 1820 by *William Farrell*, incorporating earlier parts. Farrell's work, for Sir Henry Brooke Bt., consists of a big new block added to the E and N of an earlier U-shaped house. This has the characteristically inflated scale of early C19 neo-classicism. It is all two-storey, while the buildings to which it is joined – under the same roof – are three-storey. In the SE corner, where the junction of the two scales is most apparent, the effect is not very happy. The entrance (E) front is a nine-bay, two-storey design with a free-standing Greek Ionic portico of four columns rising from a base of only two steps. The walls should have been rendered but are now of exposed rubble that is a good deal at variance with the fine ashlar work of the window architraves and the portico. The N front is of nine bays, with string courses continued round from the entrance façade. All quite grand but lacking in finesse and, as so often with Farrell, careless of proportions.

Round the corner on the S, something of the older house appears, described in the *Post Chaise Companion* of 1786 as 'a very fine and delightful seat'. This may have been built for Sir Arthur Brooke about 1770, but was much reworked by Farrell. Nine-bay, three-storey front, breaking back after the fourth bay and coming forward as an extra wing two bays before the end. Part is screened off by a garden wall. The contractors for Farrell's work were *Colborne & Richards* and the stone came from Altabrook quarry.

Inside, a square hall with niches leads through to a double return stair, with a large three-light landing window filled with classical stained glass of figures in niches and Corinthian pilasters, the colours predominantly blue and gold. The window is in odd contrast to the shallow Gothic vaulting in the passage crossing in front of the stairs. The plasterwork throughout the house is wonderfully crisp and generously detailed. It is perhaps at its best in the library which has a high segmental ceiling with shallow octagonal coffers.

Double STABLES AND OFFICES, of vernacular character, to the SW behind the house.

ASHBROOKE. 2 km W of the main house. Built as a dower house presumably also by *Farrell*, and not unlike Killyfaddy near Clogher. A five-bay, two-storey front with big windows and a projecting solid porch with Tuscan columns. Above, a tripartite sash window. Shallow hipped roof, like the big house, but here supported on an eaves cornice with projecting stone mutules. The house has only one regular front, with a long wing behind. A plaque, in the stable yard behind, has the legend 'Built by Sir Henry Brooke Bt. for the use of his tenants in the year 1830'.

In the park is a CLASSICAL BRIDGE of *c.* 1820 and the GARDENER'S COTTAGE, a pretty three-bay picturesque design of *c.* 1830 with gabled centre and bay-windows either side. The AGENT'S HOUSE is an L-shaped, plain Elizabethan design of *c.* 1850, and the TRIUMPHAL GATE and LODGE on the Fivemiletown Road is three arches wide with Tuscan pilasters. The lodge has a central bow. Opposite the gates, COLEBROOKE OLD SCHOOL, a long, low, five-bay, single-storey block with a squat Tuscan portico in the centre and pilaster quoins at the corners. All presumably part of *Farrell's* original commission.

AGHALURCHER PARISH CHURCH (C of I). 3 km NE of Brookeborough at Coletrain, set on the crown of a hill backed by trees. Erected in 1762, and constituted the parish church, to replace the old one near Lisnaskea, in 1767. An unusually large four-bay hall, 34 ft by 64 ft inside, with simplified Gibbs surrounds to the windows similar to those at Lisbellaw church. At the W end (actually S) a tower in three stages, each one stepped back slightly, with a parapet of blind Gothic arcades, spiky finials, and a slender octagonal spire. The Brooke family pew is accommodated in an extension like a vestry on one side of the nave.

Inside, the church owes its appearance to a refitting of 1873. Segmental wagon roof pierced by braced trusses, and a short coffered chancel with triple round-headed E window. – P U L P I T. The base of a late Georgian Gothic double- or triple-decker. – M O N U M E N T S. Lieut. Francis Brooke, 1st Dragoon Guards, † 1815 aged 22 'when gallantly charging the French in the ever memorable battle of Waterloo'. A fallen horse in high relief against a heavy Greek aedicule with torches and palmettes. – Sir Henry Brooke Bt. † 1834 by *Thomas Kirk*. Allegorical figures of Hope and Charity, on either side of a plinth supporting two urns. Middling relief and quality. – Captain Thomas Brooke of Colebrooke † 1838. A Greek sarcophagus surmounted by a helmet and sword.

COLERAINE

INTRODUCTION

With a population of nearly 13,600 in 1971 Coleraine is now the largest town in north-west Ulster, excepting only Derry city. Even so the growth rate is not of that spectacular sort known in other parts of Europe. Coleraine has not quite doubled since 1837, and for a town of its size hides both its history and its modern importance behind a modest architectural dress.

There are two distinct Coleraines, built on the E and W banks of the Bann just before the river takes its last turn into the broad reach that flows out at the mouth of Lough Foyle. The W bank in the parish of Killowen has an older history of settlement. A monastery was founded here by St Patrick of which Carbreus was bishop in 540. Coleraine was burned in 731, and there were several later raids by Norsemen, who slew the abbot, Airmedach, in 932. There was great destruction in 1171 and 1177 and what was left, apart from the church, was demolished when a castle was built there by Thomas MacUchtry in 1214. In 1244 St Mary's Friary was founded on the E bank and in 1484 it became a regular Dominican house. In 1543 Shane O'Boyle, the last prior, surrendered the building to the Commissioners of Henry VIII and, though the community continued until the early C17, a massacre of the friars took place in Antrim in 1559. There is a story that two men died in 1611 when they touched a famous statue in the friary which they had been ordered to destroy by the Protestant Bishop Babington of Derry, who also died soon afterwards, but such tales did nothing to preserve the medieval fabric of the place. Monastery, castle, and friary have left no trace today.

The earliest visible remains in Coleraine are now of the C17. At the Jacobean Plantation Coleraine was, like Derry, granted to a group of London merchants who, as the Irish Society, had collective responsibility for founding and fortifying the town and 'planting' it with a Protestant population. Of this town only the plan remains, with a main street running uphill from the E bank of the river to a rectangular central square – the Diamond – and continuing in approximately the same line E to the parish church. The rather half-hearted grid of streets opening off the Diamond to the s is also a legacy of the C17 planters. Thomas Raven's map, prepared about 1622 as part of Sir Thomas Phillips's survey of the London Companies' estates, shows Coleraine with a five-arched fortified bridge, an embattled river frontage, a surrounding ditch, and a stone-faced wall strengthened with bastions and fortified gates. But this was an expression of the ideal rather than the real. The fortified river front and bridge – despite a specific grant of land by King James to pay for it – remained unexecuted. The ramparts were only of earth and the town gates of timber. Most of the houses too were half-timbered and were imported in frames from London as C17 precursors of prefabricated building construction. They survived into the early C19, but their appearance is now known only from the plans and from stained-glass picture windows in the town hall. The large three-storey gabled house built by the Clothworkers' Company on the w bank has also long since gone.

Coleraine survived an Irish attack in 1641 but was taken by General Monck in 1648. Its state in 1662 is recorded by Major Legg as 'pretty well fortified in the late troubles with earthen walls but neglected and decayed'. There was 'a fort of stone begun and raised to the 10 or 12 foot height upon the River side, but the walls neither finished or ramparted, which either ought to be done or else the thing demolished'. As so often, the fort disappeared. The foundations of a medieval bridge over the Bann were in existence in 1611, but it was not until 1716 that a new bridge was built in wood, and that was washed away in 1739. Four years later it was replaced by a new stone and timber bridge, and in the same year, 1743, the Irish Society erected a Market House in the centre of the Diamond to designs of *George Dance* the elder, of London. Both the bridge and the Market House have been replaced, the bridge in 1844 and the Market House by the Town Hall in 1859. By the mid C19 Coleraine had assumed much of the appearance it has today. In 1855 the railway arrived, and by 1860 the town was connected with Belfast. The same year saw the completion of another typical Victorian structure, the Academical Institution, and nine years later the picturesque Irish Society Schools went up. If the villas that marked 'suburban progress' to the *Irish Builder* were the first steps on the road to the characteristically undistinguished housing sprawl of the post-war period, two new initiatives, the County Hall on the w bank and the New University of Ulster N of the town, mark a substantial C20 contribution to the architecture of the neighbourhood.

CHURCHES

ST PATRICK, COLERAINE PARISH (C of I). Erected by the Irish Society in 1614. s aisle added in 1684, and a spire of short duration (1714–19). Allegedly on the site of St Patrick's monastery, though Lewis states that this was in Killowen on the w bank of the Bann. The church is set back from the road in a graveyard, skirted on its N side by the traces of the earth ramparts of the Plantation town.

The fabric has been so worked over and extended that apart from some wall tablets it is now all Victorian: black basalt walls, hard sandstone gables, and cusped Dec tracery have replaced the curved and ogee gablets and mullioned windows of the C17. In 1851 *Joseph Welland* added a new chancel, s aisle, and porch and replaced the window of the s transept. In 1866 *James Alison* of Limavady added a N transept, and in 1875 an organ chamber and NW vestry were built to designs of *J. H. Coyle* of Coleraine. He also put encaustic tiles into the chancel. Then in 1884 under the rector, Henry O'Hara, the church was virtually rebuilt by *Thomas Drew*, who took down the old tower and replaced it by a massive and scholarly C15 design that soars above the church at the w end of the s aisle. At the same time he extended and raised the nave, adding a clerestory and a N aisle, and to adjust the proportions of the church rebuilt the nave arch and chancel. The decorative carving by the Coleraine craftsman *Charles Magowan* is best seen in the Perp belfry of the tower and in the gable of Drew's elaborate entrance porch.

The interior is spacious and nicely detailed, with a double-chamfered arcade down each side of the nave, six bays on the N, five on the s. The piers alternate between keel-moulded quatrefoils, octagons, and circular shafts, all with deeply undercut foliate capitals. Single-bay chancel, built in sandstone, with an enriched wagon roof and a Perp E window. – PULPIT. 1894 by *R. Caulfield Orpen.* – STAINED GLASS. In the N transept brightly coloured mid Victorian scenes of 1854. – In the S transept by *J. Clarke & Son*, Dublin, 1919. – MONUMENTS. Elizabeth Dodington, wife of Edward Dodington, Captain of Dungiven Castle, † 1610. Slate tablet flanked by pilasters with arabesques and surmounted by a strapwork achievement. – Ann Munro, wife of Col. George Munro, † 1647. Slate tablet set in alabaster surmounted by a curved pediment with cherubs at the corners. – John Rowe † *c.* 1660. A slate tablet in an alabaster frame wrongly remounted, with death's head Ionic supporters. – Sir Tristram Beresford Bt., M.P. for Londonderry 48 and first Mayor of Coleraine, † 1673. An elaborate strapwork panel in three stages surmounted by a crowned and winged death's head. – Mary Heslett † 1627, Stone slab with *memento mori.* – Ensign William Hamilton † 1716. An armorial slab.

ST JOHN, Killowen. Late Georgian Gothic of 1834, ambitious 101 for its date and denomination, and well set on high ground on the W bank looking across the river to the rest of the town. The architect, *J. Kirkpatrick*, otherwise unknown, signed the building. It is unusually elegant, a long five-bay hall with pinnacled and buttressed corners, crenellated parapet, and tall octagonal shafts flanking a large central window marked by a shallow gable. The end elevations are three-bay, with a central gable bay buttressed like the corners. The style is reminiscent of the work of Thomas Duff of Newry or of Archibald and James Elliott in Scotland, so perhaps Kirkpatrick trained with one of these architects. Sandstone and basalt as usual in this area. The interior originally had an altar in the centre of the W wall, but it has been rearranged with three timber arcades screening the N wall instead.

ST JOHN (C of I), Killowen. The first church here was founded in the mid C13 for the castle soldiers. Decayed in 1616, it was renovated in 1690 and 1767. The present church is of 1830, remodelled in 1875 by *J. G. Ferguson*, who heightened the pitch of the nave roof and added the chancel and side porch. Gothic. Of rubble black basalt, with a low gabled S aisle. Vestry of 1927 by *Blackwood & Jury.*

In the churchyard to the N is the cell-like MAUSOLEUM of John Dunlap, erected in 1731. The doorway is round-headed with a moulded surround and keystone, and a tablet inscribed to the many sons, daughters, wives, and children-in-law there interred.

FIRST PRESBYTERIAN CHURCH, Abbey Street. 1827. A large

two-storey hall. Six-bay sides and three-bay entrance front enhanced by a single-storey Doric portico to the middle bay added in 1833. The scale of the portico is really too small, like a garden temple come to town. The interior has its original gallery supported on fourteen Corinthian columns. Ionic niche at the pulpit end. Drastically 'modernized' in 1966 and painted blue and white.

TERRACE ROW PRESBYTERIAN CHURCH. A simple two-storey hall of 1834, with a flashy classical front of 1892 by *W. J. Given*. Stuccoed Italianate towers flank a three-arched loggia centre. The whole now floats in a sea of asphalt.

METHODIST CHURCH, Circular Road, 1853 by *Isaac Farrell*, the main Methodist architect of the day. A serious Corinthian temple design in stucco, flanked by quadrant walls, with the minister's house on the s. The portico is hexastyle with the outer columns as pilasters filled in between with channelled stone and blind niches. The classicism peters out, as does the paint, just behind the façade. The entablature has lost its mouldings, which is a pity.

NEW ROW PRESBYTERIAN CHURCH. A two-storey, six-bay hall of 1832 with an Italianate front in stucco added by *W. J. Anderson* in 1891. The gallery inside is supported on Tuscan columns.

CONGREGATIONAL CHURCH, New Row. 1862 by *R. M. Smyth*. A wide Gothic hall of basalt and Glasgow sandstone with an offset gabled tower and paired side porches. The church halls below the body of the church.

125 ST MALACHY, Nursery Avenue. 1937 by *Padraig Gregory*. Last in date of the Coleraine churches, but by no means least. A powerful neo-Romanesque composition with an offset stumpy tower, reminiscent of St Albans, half-way down one side. Seven-bay nave with paired clerestory windows and a big wheel in the entrance gable. The interior, though not helped by its cement walls lined to imitate masonry or its terrazzo floors, is an interesting design, with corridor aisles lining the nave and the clerestory windows cut into the sides of a barrel-vaulted roof.

PUBLIC BUILDINGS

99 TOWN HALL. Pride of place among the buildings of Coleraine must go to *Thomas Turner*'s town hall. Set in the centre of the Diamond, it dominates the views from all the main streets, while its slender w tower and cupola still ride comfortably

above the roofs of the rest of the town. In massing it has just
a hint of St Mary-le-Strand in London, with the same capacity
to surprise like a Baroque island in the centre of a stream of
traffic. Erected in 1859 at a total cost of £4,146, the building
replaces the earlier Market House and Town Hall by Dance.
It has many typical Turner features: horizontal rustication on
the ground floor; a subtle use of curved elements; Baroque
features in the big Gibbs surrounds to the windows, the massive
oculi that join the chimneys in a way that Hawksmoor would
have approved of, and the elegant clock cupola with concave
chamfered corners. Inside, a circular hall in the centre of the
building is lit by a memorial window to commemorate the ter-
centenary of the Irish Society (1619–1913) with three inset
sepia views of old Coleraine and one of Turner's Irish Society
Schools. Above is a large public hall approached by a double
return stair at the E end of the building tactfully added by
W. J. Given in 1902. Busts of Edward VII and Queen Alexandra
in the stair hall are by *W. Merrett*, 1904.

COURT HOUSE, Castlerock Road. 1852. Not very large and probably by the County Surveyor of the time, *Stewart Gordon*,
whose Presbyterian church in Great James Street, Derry, this
closely resembles. A tetrastyle Greek Doric temple – the
columns too widely spaced for comfort – at the head of a flight
of steps with large scrolls at the sides. Pilastered side elevation
extended in 1908.

COLERAINE ACADEMICAL INSTITUTION. One of Northern
Ireland's major schools, opened in 1860. The first building by
Isaac Farrell is a plain two-storey block with projecting two-
bay ends and a single-bay centre in an eleven-bay façade. The
dressed corner quoins, stucco, and Georgian sash-windows all
belie the real date of the building. To this *Young & Mackenzie*
added a Genoese palazzo opened in 1894 as the 'Old Boys'
Wing'. It was a four-storey block on a high basement with a
rusticated ground floor, a Tuscan giant order, and a high attic
with a decorative parapet. Today the attic floor has gone and
a suburban hipped roof overhangs the tops of the giant order
capitals. With a little more care it would have been possible
to reduce the block and yet leave it with something of the style
of an Artisan Mannerist house. What has been done here
merely spoils an attractive older design. The Dumfriesshire red
sandstone memorial arch to Maud Houston is by *Vincent Craig*,
1906. The post-war building at the school, though extensive,
never rises to the level of architecture.

NATIONAL SCHOOL. Opposite the Academy. 1847 by *George Wilkinson*. Irregular for once; otherwise the usual sandstone and basalt Tudor Gothic of this architect.

COLERAINE HOSPITAL, Mountsandel Road. The 1841 Poor Law Union Workhouse, by *George Wilkinson*. The five-bay, two-storey gabled governor's house remains.

IRISH SOCIETY SCHOOLS. 1867–9 by *Thomas Turner*. Picturesque and chunky brick Gothic: irregular gables, bay-windows, fish-tail slates, sculptured sandstone panels, and octagonal bell-turret. Enlarged in much the same idiom by *Malcolm McQuigg* in 1935.

THE MARKETS. 1830 by '*Mr Alex Mitchell, Arch^t and Builder*'. A large open area bounded by a coursed basalt wall with two segmental sandstone arches on the N and a vernacular pedimented archway flanked by single-bay pavilions on the S. The old curfew bell hangs in the arch.

RAILWAY STATION. 1855 by *Charles Lanyon*. A long, low stucco block in Lanyon's Italianate station style. Central forestanding arcaded portico with Tuscan piers flanked by four-bay wings with round-headed windows each side. A second platform with a similar building was added in the 1880s. Both platforms remain unaltered, with reticulated brick pavements, cast-iron columns, curly brackets, and frilly eaves boarding.

TOWN LIBRARY, Queen Street. 1969 by *John Neil* of Coleraine. Circular, entered on the first floor, with the ground floor recessed into a falling site. The frame is of concrete with six slightly projecting piers to support it, with a zigzag of window and panels arranged within the first and second floors. Too cramped in its site for the concept to read clearly.

COUNTY HALL. 1967–70 by *Smyth, Cowser & Partners*. A large, ill-mannered complex, out of scale with Coleraine and with the surrounding countryside. It is possible to get good views of the building, as for example from the entrance drive, where a long, two-storey curving wing screens the main office tower. Walk round about and this appears for what it really is: an ill-proportioned long block, seven storeys high, with a banal sequence of twenty-six repetitive windows.

THE MANOR HOUSE, in the County Hall grounds. Originally called Jackson Hall. A six-bay, two-storey house with hipped roof and attic domes. Built by the Jacksons in 1680 and improved in 1773, after which it became in the words of the *Post Chaise Companion* 'the noble and beautiful seat of the Rt. Hon. Richard Jackson'. It is neither noble nor beautiful now.

Cement-rendered and stripped of most of its detail. The plaque above the door inscribed MY TRUST IS IN GOD 1641 is taken from the old Clothworkers' building that occupied a site nearby.

TOUR

Coleraine is a place which people with a taste for architecture and old buildings will not want to walk round. At the opening of this century it had considerable, if modest, quality as a nice C19 Ulster town. That quality has been systematically eroded by needless road widening, the uncontrolled creation of car parks, the shoddy modernization of shops and offices, and a seeming lack of concern for the fate of its older buildings. If there are still attractive groups of buildings and areas of considerable architectural potential, there is no sign that they are valued locally and no security that, in the general exodus to the growing country suburbs, they will not soon be thought of as redundant and be demolished. The route suggested here, starting at the gates of the parish church in MAIN STREET, passes most of what there is to be seen in the town. Little comment is required.

From the church E to BROOKE STREET (l.), which marks where the old East Gate was. Further E from here is WATERFORD TERRACE in LODGE ROAD, a long, rendered terrace of three-bay, three-storey houses of about 1860 though still Georgian in appearance. Victorian villas beyond. Back by Main Street, largely lined by stuccoed three-storey houses of various roof levels, to THE DIAMOND, dominated by the Town Hall in the centre. In the C19 the Irish banks built their offices here. Almost all have been spoilt recently with bad ground-floor fronts. The former NORTHERN BANK in the centre of the N side still has a handsome Italianate appearance. Four-bay, three-storey façade in brick and stone. Ground floor in arcaded ashlar with stone architraves to the windows above and a bold roof cornice. It has been vacated by the bank, who have built, next door to it, a concrete and dark-glass cage which would be ill-fitting in any urban context and which fails entirely to cope with the problem of its corner site. Round this corner QUEEN STREET, now wider than it once was, leads N, with a view of the tower of the New University of Ulster in the distance, to the County Library (see p. 208). Here turn l. into CIRCULAR ROAD, skirting the quays along the river and passing the Methodist Church, to BRIDGE STREET. From the Bridge,

STRAND and WATERSIDE, the W parts of the town, appear with, in the distance, the new by-pass road bridge, and then two churches to the S, the County Hall and Manor House to the N. Bridge Street is flanked by substantial mid C19 terraced houses of a Georgian character, those on the S with a nice curved 'nose' to the corner by the river. The street is dominated by the spire of the Town Hall.

Back in the Diamond turn r. into ABBEY STREET, off which to the r. is the attractive little courtyard of WATERFORD PLACE, a U-shaped C19 group which was once the Linen Hall. The side wings date from 1817; the middle with a central pedimented porch of two storeys supported on Tuscan columns is of about 1850. Just beyond, No. 23 is a High Victorian two-storey shop with the improving text 'The hand of the Diligent worketh Right'. Next in the short street running back down to the river is a good two-storey stucco-fronted house, with Tuscan aediculed doorcase. Beyond, the Presbyterian and Baptist churches, both recently spoilt, face each other. The former MANSE has a fine Ionic porch. S from here the townscape disintegrates into a succession of dreary car parks, with BANNFIELD HOUSE, a pleasant classical house of about 1840 with an ashlar sandstone front and elegant Ionic porch, rising out of a sea of asphalt. (It is now used as District Council offices.) A little E from here NEW ROW, a long street running N–S, retains something of the scale and character of the C19 town. Off to the r. are the City Markets (see p. 208), and further N two churches before the row returns to Main Street.

NEIGHBOURHOOD: EAST DISTRICT

ST JOHN, BALLYNASHANE PARISH CHURCH (C of I). 4.5 km ENE. 1826. A tiny tower and hall type church. Very pretty, toy-like, and unaltered since it was built. Three-bay nave with lancets with quarry glass and hood moulds. The tower has diagonal buttresses converted to octagonal shafts at the belfry stage and ending in tall pinnacles with battlements between. In a little churchyard filled with cawing rooks. – MONUMENT. The Rev. Thomas Cupples † 1854, by *Francesco Ceccarini* of Belfast. A weeping angel with an extinguished torch.

BALLYNASHANE PRESBYTERIAN CHURCH. 4.5 km ENE. Founded by the Rev. Robert Hogsherd in 1657. Rebuilt in 1846 and renovated in 1886. A four-bay Gothic hall with timber Y-tracery. Box pews inside, with later gallery round three sides.

War Memorial tower of 1924 by *George Watt* of Aberdeen. Triple-louvred belfry and short copper spire.

BROOKE HALL. 4.5 km ENE. Built in 1827 for S. Boyce, a five-bay, two-storey house with a pretty segmental fanlight. Gatepiers with ball finials.

ST PAUL, KNOCKTARNA PARISH CHURCH (C of I). 5 km SSE. 106 1851–5 by *Joseph Welland*. A perfect small Tractarian church, chunky, honest, and making a little go a long way with its high nave lit by lancet windows, separate lower chancel, side porch, and two-bay s aisle differentiated by an altered pitch to the roof. Black basalt with sandstone trim. Note on the N gable the lean-to bell-ringers' chamber from which a rope passes to the bellcote on the gable. – MONUMENT. Fanny de Neufville Given † 1863. A sculptured angel in a vesica-shaped recess.

KNOCKINTERN HOUSE. 4 km SSE. A largish, two-storey, cement-rendered house, with shallow canted bays and a square front porch. Built in the early C19 by Hugh Lyle, Mayor of Coleraine, and now the Vice-Chancellor's Lodge for the New University of Ulster. Beautifully situated in mature grounds above the river Bann, with woodlands and drifts of bamboo running down to the water's edge.

CLOONAVIN. 1 km N, on the Portstewart Road. A Victorian Gothic villa in brick and sandstone built for John Huey by *Young & Mackenzie* in 1870. Half-hipped gables, C12 window details, and a heavy square sandstone bay-window with pierced balustrade. Pine stair inside. Converted as a hotel in 1968 by *G. A. Kelly*, whose grey brick extensions treated the old building with some tact. Now council offices.

NEW UNIVERSITY OF ULSTER. 3 km NNW. 1968–77 by *Robert Matthew, Johnson-Marshall & Partners*, who had just completed designing Stirling University, on which much of the design brief and building programmes – if not the appearance of the buildings – was based. The university occupies an elevated site on the E bank of the Bann between Coleraine and Portstewart. In open, even bare, countryside with only distant views across the river to the housing estates of Coleraine, it does not, like so much modern architecture, have to compete or to marry with any building of an earlier age and taste: it can be 'read' on its own as the expression of a later C20 ideal. The planning, conceived as a series of complex rectangular areas overlapping and interlocking, is typical of the design processes of Sir Robert Matthew. There is a generous provision of enclosed circulation space – the planner's 'microclimate' which on this exposed site is probably justified – and there are some moments of a certain architectural grandeur, as in the entrance foyer and the extravagant double-return staircase that leads to the library. The elevations and cubic massing of the buildings are also typical of this office. There is a preference for horizontal emphasis, with long three- and four-storey buildings whose floors are marked by bands of concrete or glazed brick, with continuous ranges of windows between, and with the top band usually deeper than the rest. (A similar elevational system characterizes Matthew's work for the universities of Edinburgh and Stirling.) Above the roof line slanting wedge-shaped towers, for roof lights and for stairs, add extra modelling.

The formal problems of the creation of a large architectural complex, more or less in a vacuum, become evident here. Is there a specifically appropriate form for the arts, the sciences, music, a library, or a student refectory? No. Yet the architect, afraid of the charge of monotony, feels he must change his form of expression from time to time and so, in contrast to the familiar Matthew stress of the horizontal, we are given the international office block – here called the Humanities Tower and made functionally expressive by steel chimneys at one end and a ten-storey staircase shaft in glass at the other. The refectory and student societies are housed in another sort of modern architecture – a steel-framed box with continuous glazed curtain walling and a zigzag glass roof. And this is surely the most mistaken part of the design; for such modern architecture already has a personality and a context, the factory and the aeroplane hangar, and whatever a university dining hall may be, it is certainly not these. Music and exhibitions are accommodated N of the refectory in a more comfortable and homely octagon of red-brown brick. Phase I, 1968, the crispest and most self-sufficient of the university buildings, is a separate small group to the s. Its scale is modest and its style, which contrasts white glazed fascias and glass stair towers, is more coherent.

Beyond the formal and aesthetic problems posed by these buildings is the matter of their practicability. Costs have been pared to a minimum and there is insufficient provision for maintenance. The grandiose, and largely useless, flight of steps approaching the concourse before the main building (what is meant to happen here?) had already begun to break apart by 1976. So too had the desolate flight of steps connecting the student societies' building to the terrace overlooking the Bann. Roof systems of exposed space frames, or steel joists, and hung ceilings of slatted timber, become traps for dust and dirt that cannot be cleaned, and the endless areas of glass are rendered almost constantly opaque by salt-laden winds. Functionalism as an architect's creed has failed here.

NEIGHBOURHOOD: WEST DISTRICT

LAUREL HILL HOUSE. Now within the town, just s of St John's Catholic church. A restrained Italianate villa with a five-bay, two-storey front built to designs of *Charles Lanyon* for Henry Kyle in 1841–3. Lanyon's front is added to an older building that faced E to the river. It is in Roman cement with vermiculated corner quoins and a slightly projecting centre marked by a wide Corinthian porch, with three round-headed lancets above – a motif much used by Lanyon – and an eaves pediment. A column screen in the hall and nice plasterwork to the main rooms.

SOMERSET HOUSE. 1.5 km S. A Richardson family house, originally 'Summer Seat'. It now looks early C19, with a two-storey, three-bay front with a central canted bay and a round bow on the E façade.

CAMUS HIGH CROSS. *See* Macosquin.

CONVOY   DO E5

A pretty little village by the river Dell with four churches, a big house, and a factory. And the remains of a nicely planned square.

ST NINIAN, CONVOY PARISH CHURCH (C of I). On the S side of an open square with old thatched cottages on the E side. A charming hall and tower type church built in 1821–4 in squared coursed rubble with diagonal buttresses to the tower, ending in plain finials. Three-bay nave and a short chancel, added in 1901. Two original windows in the nave with pretty Dec tracery in timber. Inside, Gothic piers with odd cluster columns at the ends.

CATHOLIC CHURCH. 1790 in origin. A rendered T-plan church with a long six-bay front to the road. Georgian Gothic glazed and enlivened by a big buttressed bellcote in stone, added *c.* 1860 in the middle of the long front.

CONVOY PRESBYTERIAN CHURCH. 1903 by *J. McIntyre*, who took the design from Vincent Craig's First Presbyterian Church in Omagh. Four-bay rendered hall with a big Dec window in the gabled front and offset octagonal stair-turret. Church hall of 1910.

REFORMED PRESBYTERIAN CHURCH. Pre-1837. A long six-bay Gothic hall by the river.

CONVOY HOUSE. Immediately w of the village. 1806. A substantial nine-bay, two-storey house on a low basement with shallow segmental bays of three windows on either end of the main façade. Built of squared rubble stone with red brick trim to the windows and finely drawn sandstone detail. Thin entablatures to the windows, string course, and cantilevered eaves cornice. The interior was destroyed by fire in 1971 but has now been partly restored.

The house was built by the Montgomery family, parts of whose C17 house – primitive carved faces, coats of arms, and date-stones – are incorporated in the main GATE LODGE. This is a nice piece of castle-style nonsense in the manner of Francis Johnston with a turreted Tudor arch set between battlemented quadrants. At one end is a two-storey Gothic tower with pepperpots. It is approached by curving steps behind the quadrant wall. The whole is very similar to J. B. Keane's gate to Camlin outside Ballyshannon, though too early to be by him.

CONVOY WOOLLEN CO. 1883. A battlemented stucco factory with an Italianate tower in brick and one Venetian window.

GREEN HILLS. 2 km SE. Described in the *Post Chaise Companion* as the seat of Mr Hamilton, so this house is presumably pre-1786. The plain five-bay, two-storey brick front looks early C19, but the wainscot panelling and five-panel doors inside are earlier. A primitive carving of a dragon(?) and two people is built into the outbuildings. Extensive stabling with segmental brick arcade, now ruinous.

ARDVARNOCK. 1.5 km NE. An attractive three-bay, two-storey house with a handsome doorcase and a nice hall. Early C19.

Cookstown is remarkable for its one main street that runs N–S in a straight line for over a mile and a quarter, rising to a gentle hill in the middle and again towards either end. The town was founded about 1609 by a Protestant planter, Allan Cook, who leased the land from the Bishop of Armagh. He was granted a patent for a market and fairs in 1641. The present great street is the product of C18 ideas of improvement and of the enterprise of William Stewart of Killymoon (*see* p. 334), who, impressed by the contemporary schemes in Dublin, resolved, about 1750, that he 'would build a new town on his Tyrone estate, which would rival even the new avenues of the metropolis'. His great street is 130 ft wide and was to be planted with an avenue of hardwood trees, though only a few, notably a big copper beech near the hill in the middle, relieve its monotony today. A street that is over a mile long may suit Dublin or Edinburgh, where Princes Street is about the same length: it is too large for a remote, if fertile area of Tyrone. Cookstown prospered but, like Aughnacloy further s, it has never been able to fatten out on its linear origins. The cross streets to E and W soon peter out into insignificant lanes or minor suburban developments, and the one street is all there is to offer as architecture. Even this is largely vernacular; modest and unmemorable, with only the churches and a few bigger houses in the vicinity worthy of note.

ST LAURENCE, DERRYLORAN PARISH (C of I). 1822. Built [87] to replace the old parish church of Derryloran, reputedly to designs of *John Nash*. Repaired in 1837 and rebuilt in 1859–61 'to designs by the architect to the Ecclesiastical Commissioners', presumably *Joseph Welland*. The plan of the church associated with Nash had a W tower and spire and a three-bay nave with projecting flat-roofed side chapels at the centre of each side containing a pew for the Stewarts of Killymoon and a recess for the pulpit opposite. The same plan appears in the original C19 churches at Irvinestown and Inishmacsaint in Fermanagh. Of this only the tower and spire, with the first bay of the nave, remain. Childishly simple Gothic and built in a soft whitish-pink sandstone with diagonal tooling. Three-stage tower, with diagonal buttresses, double-lancet belfry, corner pinnacles, and solid octagonal spire. The Welland addition is a straightforward large cruciform church, spacious inside, with intersecting kingpost trusses at the crossing. Single-chamfered arches to choir and transepts. Four-light Dec E window. – FONT. 1684; inscribed 'He that believeth and is baptised shall be saved'. Stone shaft decorated on three sides with a rose, lily, and thistle. – MONUMENT. Mrs Anne Maughan † 1861. An unusually elaborate wall tablet quoting the biblical texts of which the deceased was last conscious. A sculptured dove ascends from a vacated death bed with allegorical figures each side.

HOLY TRINITY. 1855–60 by *J. J. McCarthy*. Textbook late C12, and wonderfully impressive in an obvious kind of way. The church is on the W of the main street near the central hill, though only its huge tower and spire can be seen from the main street. Behind is a large five-bay nave with aisles and chancel.

Competent Gothic with straightforward but well detailed tracery, and a big Frenchified altar window in the sanctuary – three
rosettes in wheels above five lancets. The interior is unusually
lofty, with moulded chamfered arcades supported on round
piers. Hipped nave ceiling with braced trusses, panelled in
squares with stencil painting in mustard and black. The organ
gallery, under the tower, is supported on one massive single-
chamfered arch. – ALTAR. White Caen stone, triple-pinnacled
niche type.

FIRST PRESBYTERIAN CHURCH. A large, five-bay, two-storey
hall with round-headed upper-floor windows 'of recent erection' in 1886. The front, with its high gable pediment supported
on Tuscan pilasters, looks later C19. Built of ashlar freestone,
but too thin to be effective. The interior is a pleasant large hall
with box pews and galleries on three sides supported on cast-
iron Ionic columns. Built by the Rev. Hamilton Brown Wilson.
Church hall behind of 1875. The congregation was founded in
1646 and met in a meeting house in Killymoon demesne from
1701 to 1764.

MOLESWORTH STREET PRESBYTERIAN CHURCH. 1835. The
model no doubt for the later and larger church of the first congregation. Once again a five-bay, two-storey hall with classical
undertones. A high gable pediment, but no pilasters, and this
time of stucco. The interior is not original.

METHODIST CHURCH. Built c. 1860. A jaunty little Lombardic
hall in freestone, the twin of the Methodist churches at Donegal
and Ballymoney.

OTHER BUILDINGS. With its linear layout, Cookstown is not
an inviting place to walk around. Other buildings worth a mention are as follows. In MOLESWORTH STREET, near the N end
of the main street, the two former railway termini: the BEL-
FAST AND NORTHERN COUNTIES STATION of c. 1856 by
Charles Lanyon, a long, low Italianate block of ashlar stone,
seven bays with a central porch, and the GREAT NORTHERN
STATION, seaside Italianate in polychrome brick, by *William
H. Mills*, 1899. Opposite the stations is the entrance to COOL-
NAFRANKIE HOUSE (formerly Loymount), built before 1868
for J. B. Gunning Moore, a square two-storey house, rather
grim despite its Italianate Baroque ashlar porch. The COM-
MERCIAL BUILDINGS before the stations are red brick
Gothic, modest but vigorous, and described in the *Tyrone
Directory* of 1889 as 'a masterpiece of art'.

Cookstown main street is one of those streets that changes its name needlessly. From N to S it starts as MILLBURN STREET, becoming OLD TOWN, WILLIAM, JAMES'S, LOY, CHAPEL, CHURCH, and KILLYMOON STREETS in turn. Between Loy Street and Chapel Street, ST BRIGID'S CONVENT and the Court House face each other. The convent house is a seven-bay, three-storey block of 1891, standard for its date and purpose but now totally changed by a new CHAPEL OF THE ANNUNCIATION built in front of the old block in 1965. This, by *Laurence McConville*, is a square two-storey block set at 45 degrees to the line of the old front with the leading corner thrusting forward as a salient towards the street. The chapel is on the first floor and is entered by the space that was the middle first-floor window of the old convent front. Whatever the quality of McConville's architecture, the collision of the two forms of chapel and convent is a mistake. Sculptural panels on and in the chapel are by *Patrick McElroy* and the glass is by *Patrick Pye*. The COURT HOUSE opposite is of 1900 by *Vincent Craig*. Decidedly odd and decidedly ugly. Its turn-of-the-century mannerisms – double sashes under single segment heads and big oversailing eaves – have not worn well. Four-bay, two-storey, with a broad pyramid-roofed tower at one corner. The banks have all been modernized or rebuilt. *Thomas Jackson's* ULSTER BANK of 1852 is now almost unrecognizable. The TOWN HALL, in a thin 1930s cinema style, is of 1953 by *G. G. Birthwell*, rendered, with a rustic brick podium, coy iron porch, and balancing public lavatory wings for ladies and gents!

NEIGHBOURHOOD

DERRYLORAN OLD CHURCH. 1.5 km SW of the town. The church, by the bridge over the Ballinderry River, marks the site of the medieval community from the C14, and indeed of Cook's plantation town. The ruins are fairly complete: a long church, 20 ft by 62 ft inside, with gabled walls 3 ft 6 in. thick, and side walls of 3 ft. The gables stand entire, with traces of a W bellcote and a fine three-light E window with intersecting Y-tracery, all of early C17 appearance. The church is described as 'almost finished' in 1622, but this must be a rebuilding, witness the moulded Gothic jambs built into the N wall, evidently from a previous structure, and the C16 corbel stop to the label moulding in the SE window. The church was damaged in 1641 and in 1689 but continued in use until replaced by the Nash building in Cookstown proper. The porch is mid C18, as are the stone gatepiers to the graveyard. – MAUSOLEA. In the church ruin one to Henry Lewis von Stieglitz † 1824. – N of the church, Stewart of Killymoon vaults, erected 1680, repaired 1840. Stone-slated with pedimented front.

DERRYLORAN HOUSE. S of the church ruins. The former glebe house. A tall rendered Georgian house, originally of 1709, remodelled in 1820. Three storeys on a half-basement. Three-bay front and four-bay back with a side bow. Overhanging Regency eaves. C18-type six-panel doors inside and finely detailed stair treads.

GREENVALE. N of Derryloran Bridge. The C18 home of the Adair family, who developed extensive flax-spinning mills here powered by the Ballinderry River. The house is a five-bay, two-storey rendered block with Ionic columns to a segment-headed front door. Its lodge is identical, which may be significant, to *William Farrell*'s gate lodge at Ely Lodge, Fermanagh.

GLENAVON HOUSE. Opposite Greenvale Lodge. The big house into which the Adairs removed in the early Victorian period. Now a hotel. Built by Thomas Adair in 1855, to designs, to judge by its appearance, either by *Lanyon* or by *Thomas Turner*, once his principal clerk. Chaste Italianate in style. Nicely built of local sandstone, with window details and ashlar banding reminiscent of Alexander 'Greek' Thomson. Two-storey, with a corner campanile above the entrance and, on the garden front, an offset segmental bow balanced by a curvilinear glass conservatory and office wing. The interior has an ingenious plan that almost dispenses with any corridors. Some nice plaster ceilings. The grounds, stepping down to the river, are handsomely landscaped with plantations of conifer laid out to Mrs Adair's designs.

GORTALOWRY CHURCH. 1824. Now disused. A pretty little Catholic church. Five-bay, with a central gable pediment and crisscross window glazing-bars, like those of a Regency cottage. It deserves a better fate than to fall down.

LOUGHREY AGRICULTURAL COLLEGE. 2 km S. A sprawling, ill-assorted complex of modern buildings. Mostly two-storey. The core of the college is a large, two-storey, five-bay stucco house, with a Doric porch. The GROUNDS provide a pleasant pastoral setting, improved by early C19 planting with several clumps to accentuate the shallow hills.

ST ANDREW, ARDTREA PARISH CHURCH (C of I). 5 km ESE. 1830. A spiky late Georgian Gothic church in whinstone with cocoa-coloured sandstone trim. Three-bay hall, with double-chamfered, cusped Y-tracery (a later C19 improvement). Very pretty w front with octagonal shafts, porch, and pinnacled bell-cote. – STAINED GLASS. E window of 1878. Pretty scenes in panels.

E of the church the small SCHOOL was built in 1860 by Primate Beresford. Five-bay, single-storey, with mullioned windows.

COONEEN   FM F9

A parish for the most part in bleak upland country.

COONEEN PARISH CHURCH. 1871–3. A dour little church in coursed squared rubble with ashlar buttresses and mullions in sandstone. Nave, polygonal chancel, porch and sacristy positioned like transepts, and an offset w tower with an octagonal spire rising from a battered base so that it looks like an inverted ice-cream cone. Cusped lancets and Dec windows. Patterned slate roof.

ST JOSEPH. 1939–42 by *J. L. Donnelly*. A rendered hall with round-headed windows. Asymmetrical N tower in three stages, ending in a vaguely Moorish cupola described in the *Irish Builder* as 'Irish Romanesque'. Ogee-domed apse.

GROGEY METHODIST CHURCH. 1 km SW. 1884. A medium-sized three-bay hall and porch. Minimal Gothic with quoins. Extraordinary for its date.

DOOCARN HILL. 6.5 km S. A spectacular viewpoint overlooking Upper Lough Erne, South Fermanagh, Cavan, and Monaghan, with access roads supplied by the Tourist Board.

CREESLOUGH   DO D3

ST MICHAEL. 1970 by *Liam McCormick*. A white-harled modern church built to reflect the form of Muckish mountain whose humped mass, rising to a flat summit of 2,197 ft, is the dominant feature in the landscape. The church, roughly fan-shaped, has all the slow subtle curves of which its architect is a master. Computer-card windows in the E wall facing the road may seem unnecessarily reminiscent of Ronchamp: indeed to some the whole building will appear derivative, but it works admirably, and the notion of integrating the church with the surrounding landscape comes into its own inside, from where Muckish's distinctive profile is always seen through a range of clerestory windows in the roof.

33 DOE CASTLE. 3 km NE. Beautifully situated by the upper reaches of Sheephaven Bay, Doe Castle is built across a narrow promontory called Cannon Point. It is fortified on three sides by sea, shallow shingle, and boulders, and on the W by a rock-cut ditch. The castle consists of a C16 tower keep surrounded by an irregular bawn with low bartizans corbelled out at each corner and a battered round tower at the NE angle, the area most open to a land-based attack. The entrance on the W side, originally defended by a square internal tower, has had a barbican (C19?) added to it across the ditch.

Doe is first mentioned in 1544. Built by the Quin family, it passed soon after to the MacSweeneys of the Tuatha and became their chief seat. It provided a refuge for Spanish sailors wrecked after the Armada of 1588, and was the place that welcomed Owen Roe O'Neill on his return to Ireland in 1642. Much fought over in the C17, it was used as a garrison for Charles II and William III before being abandoned in the C18. The *Post Chaise Companion* mentions its 'magnificent ruins' in 1786, but early the next century these were acquired by the Hart family and restored as a private residence by Captain George Vaughan Hart of Kilderry House, Muff, whose arms and initials are set over the door of the building before the keep. Today Doe is once again a magnificent ruin, though an interpretation of its walls is confused by Captain Hart's work.

The KEEP is the core of the castle. Four storeys, to a height of 55 ft, with an attic floor above, originally accommodated within a gabled roof. The wall head is now level and the interior of the tower much altered, with C19 arched recesses, fireplaces, and plastering. The internal dimensions are small, 16 ft by 14 ft. Like other C16 towers in Donegal, e.g. Inch and Buncrana, the stair runs in straight flights within the thickness of the walls, using a spiral turn only at the corner. Some original openings, including a cross-mullioned window, remain at the top of the tower. The rest of the castle is not easily interpreted. It was taken and retaken so many times between 1600 and 1650, when it was finally surprised by Sir Charles Coote and captured for the Cromwellians, that the details of its bawn walls, with wall walk and big high battlements, can hardly be earlier than the C17. Nevertheless the beehive-roofed casemate inside the walls, NE of the tower, must be Elizabethan. It has musket loops to cover the N and E sides and firing platforms at two levels. The similarly roofed round tower at the NE angle of the bawn is likely to be C16 also.

Most of Hart's work is on the s side of the keep, but to what extent it is a rebuilding is not clear. The main gate in the w wall is obviously widened and modern, and a vertical joint between the square tower and the barbican shows that it is an addition. But what of the flight of steps that curves down just inside the enclosure and leads out into the s side of the ditch? And what is the fat round tower immediately facing the barbican: late C17 or by Captain Hart? On the wall of the tower is a tapered C16 CROSS SLAB. Eight-point cross carved in shallow relief with an interlaced centre and twisted stem like a basketwork carpet beater. On the r. side of the stem interlace knots and on the l. four creatures, one a bird, the third a bull – perhaps the symbols of the Evangelists. The inscription on the border has been read as MADONIUF ORAVAITY ME FECIT 1544. Beyond the gate on the E, a late C17 ravelin in rubble and earth may be made out.

CASHEL CHAPEL OF EASE (C of I). 3 km NE, by Doe Castle. Built in 1852 by the Ecclesiastical Commissioners. A simple hall of dressed stone, five bays, with a s porch, lancet windows, w bellcote, and diminutive capped buttresses. – FONT. 1684. Octagonal basin of white limestone on a grey slate shaft.

OTHER BUILDINGS by Creeslough are CLONDEHORKY OLD CHURCH, 1.5 km N, a C17 wall with a splayed window in a graveyard; and the OLD CATHOLIC CHURCH, 1 km N, a T-plan church, harled, with Georgian Gothic sash-windows. Built by the Rev. Peter Gallagher in 1830 to replace a chapel erected in 1784 by the Rev. Bernard Rodan. The two-stage Gothic tower on the hillock to the N may be part of the older church. Father Gallagher's church was extremely simple, with a flagged floor, exposed trussed roof, rafters, and slates. The altar had an ambitious timber tabernacle with palmette columns on the s wall.

For CLONDEHORKY see also Ballymore and Dunfanaghy.

CROM   FM F10

In 1764 when the Crichton family of Crom, later to become Earls of Erne, were celebrating with the housewarming party at Florence Court a glow in the sky to the SE told them that their own house at Crom was on fire. As a result there are now two castles on this beautiful water-locked demesne: the old Plantation castle and the new C19 house.

CROM OLD CASTLE. On the shore 1 km SE from the new castle.

Begun by the Scottish planter Michael Balfour, laird of Mount-whinney in Fife, in 1611 and sold by him to Sir Stephen Butler in 1619. The castle is described by Pynnar as 'a bawn of lime and stone', 60 ft square and 12 ft high, with two flankers, 'with a house of lime and stone' inside. In 1665 or 1666 it was sold again to Abraham Crichton of Aghalane Castle (q.v.). It was twice besieged in 1689 (by Lord Galmoy and General Macarthy) and burnt out accidentally in 1764.

The ruins today are little more than a romantic ensemble running in a line E from the shore, and much 'improved' by C19 gates and steps to make the old castle a garden feature. In the centre of the main wall are two towers, one square, the other round, with traces of brick and stone vaulting inside and a decorated diamond-faceted gun loop on the s face of the E tower. These towers presumably define the area of the main house and seem to be answered by traces of towers further s. The bawn extended W and E, ending in round flankers.

Beyond the ruins, to the s, is the layout of the C18 FORMAL GARDEN and BOWLING GREEN. A large square lawn is retained by a battlemented haha along the shore and lined at the s and W sides by an avenue of lime trees round a raised walk. On the N and E sides the avenue is replaced by box hedging. The area thus enclosed is about 100 by 80 yds, open at the NW corner to a view back to the old castle with an enormous yew tree, said to be the largest in Ireland, in the corner of the lawn. With the gardens of Antrim Castle, this must rank as one of the most important pieces of C18 formal planting to remain in Ulster.

CROM CASTLE. 1834–6 by *Edward Blore*. A large Elizabethan-style house of dark local limestone with sandstone dressings, boulder-faced, and a little forbidding on all but the finest days. The drawing-room front, overlooking a terraced garden to the s, is symmetrical, with two-storey wings, with gabled bay-windows in the middle of each, flanking a tall four-storey tower with octagonal turrets – like a gatehouse. Behind this front the house extends in two deep wings round a courtyard. The drawing rooms continue on the W front, and the entrance is on the E under a *porte cochère* tower with oriel above – a motif pioneered in John Nash's castles – treated much more heavily here by Blore. The front is one storey higher, as it is below the level of the garden terraces, but this allows for a dramatic staircase entrance rising in a straight flight to the central hall of the house behind the main façade. The hall is certainly the

85

grandest moment at Crom, with a double return staircase –
rather like Smirke's Lowther – rising behind a late Perp arcade
crisply detailed in timber and plaster. Above is a galleried upper
hall lit by an octagonal 'Elizabethan' roof lantern.

For a comparatively modern house the history of Crom is
complicated. The first Earl of Erne left £20,000 to build the
new castle in 1820. The contractor was *Charles Macgibbon* of
Edinburgh, who had been building Brownlow House, Lurgan,
for W. H. Playfair when Crom was proposed. He replaced *J.
Henry* of Dublin, whose offices built in 1833 had caused a lot of
trouble. Macgibbon's contract for £8,655 was completed by
October 1836, and Blore visited the house three times while
it was building. In 1838 a conservatory pavilion and arcade in
stone were added to the w wing. When three years later, in 1841,
the new house was almost completely burnt out, the restoration
was given not to Blore but to *George Sudden* of Dublin, a contract worth £11,710. In 1890 a billiard room was added and
a number of the interiors altered, notably the yellow drawing
room, which gained a beautiful late c18 chimneypiece in white
marble by *Peter Bossi*, and the library, which was classicized
and turned into a drawing room with scagliola columns. The
original library fireplace with Jacobean panelling was moved to
a room in the w range. The furniture for the house before and
after the fire came from *William Trotter* of Edinburgh.

CROM CHURCH (C of I). 200 yds across the Lough on Derryvore
peninsula. 1840–4. A four-bay Gothic nave with a single-bay
chancel. Dec windows and buttresses. Not apparently by Blore;
possibly by *J. S. Mulvany*. The showy belfry tower with octagonal stair-turret is of 1885 in memory of Selina, Countess
of Erne, by *William Fullerton* of Armagh.

CROM DEMESNE. The grounds of the estate have many picturesque small buildings. On the w shore peninsula s of the
church, THE COTTAGE, a long, low gabled design with cross-
mullioned windows of *c.* 1840, was built as the original rectory
(bombed and burnt out 1972). CROM OLD SCHOOL HOUSE
nearby is a pretty Tudor cottage with curly bargeboards and
an arcaded veranda. The TOWER on the island between the
cottage and the old castle was built in 1847 as an observatory.
On the e shore are INISHERK LODGE, a single-storey cottage
with bargeboards and fancy lattice window panes; the hexagonal Gothic SUMMER HOUSE, a mid c18 stone building perhaps adapted from the 'hexagonal island gazebo for Mr Creigh-
ton' designed by *Sir Edward Lovett Pearce*; and the BOAT

HOUSE, a complex little structure with bargeboards and battlements designed about 1850 by *George Sudden*. As at Caledon nearby, the grounds of Crom were landscaped by *W. S. Gilpin* c. 1838.

A pretty little village on the Culdaff River sw from the sandy Culdaff Bay. Just a church, a two-arched bridge over the river, and a few large houses. This was the birthplace of Charles Macklin, author of 'The Man of the World', 'Love in a Maze', and other c18 comedies. As an actor he last appeared as Shylock in London in 1789, when at ninety years of age he forgot most of his part.

CULDAFF PARISH CHURCH (C of I). 1747. A two-bay hall with a tall four-storey tower with harled battlements and square finials. This is possibly of 1828, though its appearance is c18. The E window has double Y-tracery with quarry glass.

ST CONGAL'S CHURCH. 1.5 km SE. A T-plan Gothic church with a tall belfry tower at the head of the T. Originally a hall of 1824. In 1848 the Board of Works granted £300 to finish the chapel – presumably the finely detailed four-storey tower and possibly the aisles. The tower is the *chef d'œuvre*, with diagonal buttresses rising continuously through three storeys before sprouting unaccountably into short colonnettes to support the final belfry stage. Date-stones in the graveyard wall read 1836 and 1846.

CULDAFF HOUSE. E of the village in handsome plantations. Built for George Young in 1779 and burnt out in 1922. Rebuilt in 1926 and remodelled c. 1950 by the removal of the main front. Now only the service wing that ran in a T from the back of the house remains. It is still substantial, a five-bay, three-storey house with quoins and a high roof. Of the old front only a tripartite doorway in freestone with Tuscan aedicule is left.

CARTHAGE HOUSE. 1 km N. A large, plain house. Five-bay, two-storey front of late c18 appearance. Five-panel doors and lugged surrounds inside.

CLONCA CHURCH AND CROSS. 2 km S. The church abandoned in 1827 stands almost complete, though roofless. A single hall, 20 ft by 47 ft inside, with high gables, a round-headed E window, and two windows on the S wall with segment-headed reveals, all early c17. The door lintel, re-used from an earlier church, is clearly checked to fit a narrower opening and was apparently once sculptured, though nothing can now be read. Inside, the slab TOMBSTONE of Magnus MacOrristin, well preserved, with a divisional cross breaking into elaborate foliage at its base. Double anthemion motif along one side, and a broadsword with decorated pommel, a hurley stick, and a ball on the other. The inscription says it was made by *Fergus MacAllan*. Probably mid C16, and similar to the dated slab at Doe Castle.

ST BUADAN'S CROSS in the field in front of the church is a beautifully carved green slate shaft 10 ft high. It is decorated with panels of double banded plaiting and with scenes of St Paul and St Anthony in the desert (w face) and the miracle of the loaves and fishes (E face). C8 or later.

CARROWMORE CROSSES. 4 km SSW. The site of the monastery of Bothchonais said to have been founded by Chonas, second husband of St Patrick's sister Darerca, and recorded until the C11. Three crosses remain: E of the road a tall cross slab about 10 ft high rising out of a pile of stones with an impish angel carved in low relief at the head of one side; w of the road a tall cross pillar with stumpy arms 12 ft high; and NE of it a slab stone incised with a circle, a cross, and zigzag.

CULMORE *see* LONDONDERRY, p. 403

DERRY *see* LONDONDERRY

DERRYGONNELLY   FM D8

DERRYGONNELLY OLD CHURCH. A little N of the village. A small rectangle, 19 ft by 50 ft inside, built in 1627 by Sir John Dunbar, whose coat of arms with that of his wife Catherine are set in a plaque above the w door. This church seems caught in a moment between Gothic and Classical ideals. The E window is a triple light with sandstone mullions and miniature nodding ogee arches. The details of lateral windows have gone, but the w door, set centrally under a common Scottish vernacular bellcote, is a vigorous exercise in Renaissance work: a semicircular arch studded with regular diamond-cut voussoirs and imposts *à la* Serlio or perhaps, more likely, copied from the doorways of the Old College at Glasgow.

CARRICK CHURCH RUINS. 3 km NW. A small late C15 church in an idyllic setting on the s shore of Carrick Lough, remote and magical. Founded by Gilbert Ua Flannagain and his wife Margaret Maguire who died in 1498, the church measured 60 ft by 18 ft inside. Though only parts of the two gables remain, much of the E window is preserved: two-light Dec with splayed window reveals and a supporting single-chamfered arch inside. The island in the lough by the church is a CRANNOG.

ST PATRICK. S across the river. A three-bay Gothic hall of c. 1830 with a short chancel and N tower. E window of three lancets. Exposed kingpost truss roof with a gallery at the back. Reconstructed at a cost of £10,000 in 1940, when the tower was rebuilt with an egg-shaped cupola on top.

Derrygonnelly village was new built by its proprietor, General Archdale, in the early 1830s and has on that account an apparent unity rare in this part of Ulster. A street of substantial, brightly painted houses, mostly two-storey, with some attractive fanlights and early Victorian shop-fronts. At the N end, breaking forward to terminate the street, is the former MARKET HOUSE of c. 1830, with two round-headed arches to the street (now filled with windows). Three-bay above. Beyond, the POLICE STATION by *T. F. O. Rippingham*, c. 1930. The ORANGE HALL of 1889 is a heavy cement block with pediment gable and classical porch.

DERRYLIN

KINAWLEY PARISH CHURCH (C of I). 1825. A pretty little hall and tower type church in coursed rubble with Y-tracery timber windows to the three-bay nave, and a double Y-tracery E window in a tiny chancel. Diagonal buttresses at all the corners. The tower in three stages with spiky pinnacles. To this in 1860–1 *Welland & Gillespie* added a N aisle, opening into the nave through a two-bay double-chamfered arcade.

CATHOLIC CHURCH. 1.5 km NW of Derrylin crossroads. The core of this church is C18, founded by Michael Wynne P.P. in 1797. It is a long rectangle, like Massmount in Co. Donegal or Rosslea, but unlike those churches the altar has been moved from the long S wall to the E end. This was done in 1870, when the church windows were refitted with stone mullions and a W bellcote and porch were added. – STAINED GLASS. Brilliantly coloured 20 E windows representing the Virgin and Christ with the Sacred Heart.

CORRATRASNA. 2 km N, on the slope of Knockninny Hill. The ruins of a rectangular, two-storey gabled house, 36 ft by 16 ft inside, built of local rubble stone, perhaps by a member of the Balfour family before 1611. Only the massive gables and the lower part of the W wall that connects them remain. Each gable embraces a square chimneystack with fireplaces at ground- and first-floor level. Gun loops on the first floor of each gable. Traces of an earth rampart or terrace survive S of the house.[*]

CALLOW HILL GRAVEYARD. 1 km SW. Here are the walls, now very low and of little interest, of a C17 church, 21 ft by 44 ft externally. The window openings are all that can be seen. In the graveyard are three ARMORIAL GRAVE SLABS, one dated 1707, the other two also early C18. The flanking primitive columns are similar to those found at Pettigoe, at Leckpatrick, and in Enniskillen Cathedral.

KINAWLEY RECTORY. 3 km SSW. 1822. Typically Regency in appearance, with a shallow overhanging slate roof and long, low proportions. Two storeys on a basement. Three-bay front and back, with a three-bay extension to the E. Pretty fanlight to the central door with windows on either side in segmental relieving arches.

DRESTERNAN CASTLE. 2 km E. A small mid Georgian country seat built by Daniel Winslow about 1740, with a large yard, a walled garden, and a haha. The house itself is a typically Irish, almost cubic block, two storeys high on a half-basement, with a not-quite-central entrance door enhanced by a Gibbs surround. Inside is a simple hall with doors with lugged surrounds leading to the main rooms and the stair in the front l. corner. In the front E room a window-pane is engraved 'W. M. Nixon dined here July 10th 1779'. The house originally had two thatched cottage gate-lodges, of which one remains.

ST MARY. 5 km SE by Teemore crossroads. 1893. A plain, stone-built lancet hall with bellcote and buttresses. Three-light E window (actually S).

DERRYVULLAN   FM E9
2.5 km W of Lisbellaw

This is a parish name, not a place. Even as a parish it is confusing, for Derryvullan consists of four detached pieces of land between Lisbellaw and Irvinestown. It is this, the S end of the 'parish', that is its old centre, with a church and the ruins of two others, all near Tamlaght Bridge.

DERRYVULLAN PARISH CHURCH (C of I). 0.5 km SE of Tamlaght Bridge. 1852 by *Joseph Welland*, extended to the W in 1866 by *Welland & Gillespie*. The fourth Earl of Belmore from Castle

[*] I am obliged to Hugh Dixon for an account of this building.

Coole laid the foundation stone, and no doubt it was his energy that had the church enlarged fourteen years after it was built. The design is modest, but quite perfect of its sort: typical Welland, with firmly handled stone details, nice strong buttresses, and paired lancets under relieving arches. To the original three-bay hall and chancel the 1866 extension added an extra bay on the W, and a porch, tower, and spire grouped asymmetrically on the S side. Welland was fond of this sort of irregular accent and used it here with particular charm. – FONT. Gothic type, taken from the medieval church.

DERRYVULLAN OLD CHURCH. 1 km SW of Tamlaght Bridge. The ruins of a big hall, 28 ft wide, rebuilt in 1776. The E gable with its round-headed window and some 30 ft of the N wall still stand. In the gable a carved head taken from the medieval church on the same site.

DERRYBRUSK OLD CHURCH. 2 km S of Tamlaght Bridge. An interesting little church, modest, like most of the medieval remains around Lough Erne, but preserving the only authentic Perp window in these four counties. The church, in a burial ground, is rectangular, 21 ft by 51½ ft inside, of squared coursed rubble with sandstone corners and details. The gables are better preserved than the side walls. At the W end two tiers of slit windows and beam holes inside suggest that this part of the church was divided into two storeys, perhaps as a priest's house. The E gable has a pronounced batter on the lower 6 ft where the ground falls away from the end of the church. A gargoyle-type head projects from the wall. The window is an elegant paired cusped light, square-headed, with blind panels above and a label moulding ending in carved kings' heads. Inside, the reveal is spanned by a single segmental lintel – almost flat, and presumably late C16. Note too the sockets for metal reinforcements for the window glazing. The church is mentioned in the Ecclesiastical Taxation of 1302–6 and by the Four Masters as a parish church in 1384. It was sacked by O'Neill and Con Maguire in 1536; so the E window is presumably part of a repair after that attack. The W gable shows traces of an earlier arch above its existing window.

DERRYVULLAN NORTH. *See* Irvinestown.

DERRYWOONE CASTLE *see* BARONSCOURT

DESERTCREAT   TY J7

A rural parish some 4 km s of Cookstown situated around the
meandering Killymoon River.

DESERTCREAT PARISH CHURCH (C of I). The church dates
from the early C17 (it is described as 'in building' in 1622), but
its appearance today is Victorian, with a three-bay nave of
paired sandstone lancets with quarry glass and a three-lancet
E window. The porch keystone is inscribed RD 1735.

In the churchyard to the SE are two MAUSOLEA: a small
gabled structure of ashlar sandstone built for the Rev. Lowry
in 1787, and the grander mausoleum of the Greer family of
Tullylagan House nearby (see Sandholes). This is almost
Piranesian, a stone cube with battered sides, an overhanging
Egyptian cornice, and a double-stepped cope above supporting
a broad masonry obelisk with a sarcophagus before it. Now
swathed in ivy and creeper. Erected about 1840 and last used,
apparently, in 1907.

s of the church by the vestry door is PHELIM BRADY'S
GRAVE, an early C18 stone slab with raised crozier and mitre,
recording the burial place of the Catholic Bishop of Armagh
who, after the act of 1697 outlawing bishops, carried on his episcopal duties while disguised as the harper Phelim Brady.

ROCK LODGE. 0.5 km NW of Desertcreat church. A three-bay,
two-storey house with bargeboards and high paired brick chimneys. Tripartite windows to the outer ground-floor bays.
Further E is a row of picturesque COTTAGES built by Captain
Daniell of Rock Lodge. Exceptionally pretty, with paired brick
chimneys, bargeboards, and hooded dormer windows. They
look about 1840.

THE PRIORY. 1 km NE. A large, multi-gabled, picturesque
house of about 1850. Seven-bay, with square projecting centre
porch. Stuccoed, with label mouldings.

SHERIGRIM HOUSE. 3 km S. Late Georgian. A pretty three-bay
cottage with a segmental central door flanked by Ionic
columns. Gable pediment above and bracketed pediments over
the windows.

BLOOMHILL. 3½ km S. Pre-1837. A square two-storey house with
a big yard at the back. Altered in the late C19 to a grand stucco
villa with three bay-windows across the whole front – canted,
bowed, and canted. Door in the middle with monster bracketed
pediment and ball finials. – GATE LODGE. Grotesquely pictur-

esque Gothic of a High Victorian sort. All in cut sandstone, with many half-hipped gables.

This parish is the essence of a rural Irish backwater. In its history is an early Christian monastery founded by Colmcille of which no trace remains. It has a big new Catholic church and several buildings of the Protestant ascendancy all dotted about in peaceful fields at the edge of Lough Swilly. The church is a good one, and the other buildings are all interesting.

STAR OF THE SEA. 2.5 km ESE from Dunree Head. 1964 by *Liam McCormick*. A long, low hall shaped a little like an upturned boat, with a gently curving sanctuary end and a peaked gable. The orientation is N–S rather than E–W. Harled, with high square windows with curved tops and bottoms and overhanging eaves. The entrances are at the S and W under an oddly urban belfry tower.

After the clean lines of the outside the mysterious, almost primeval quality of the interior is a surprise. At the back, by the entrances, a broad curving gallery sweeps forward with all the style and functionalism of the bridge of an oil tanker. The gallery is supported on two tapering pilotis, and the pilotis continue down the sides of the church and behind the altar to provide a type of continuous ambulatory skirting the walls of the church. There are in all thirteen complete arches moulded in a single surface with the shallow vaulted ceiling over the body of the church and the steeper cove over the ambulatory. McCormick delights in slow irregular curves. There is nothing trite or mechanical about these lines: seen in perspective, with the uneven lighting of the windows, the forms seem to alternate and shift, and the arcades take on a sense of direction pointing towards the altar. As usual the furnishings are austere: the altar of local granite with an enamelled bronze fascia strip; walls white; the floor of red and dark blue tiles. The seats are of solid pine, but nicely shaped and comfortable, not modern stylish instruments of torture.

BAPTISTERY in a white grilled cage below the choir, with a window of Christ's Baptism in the end wall.

DESERTEGNEY PARISH CHURCH (C of I). In Linsfort townland. 1779. Described by Lewis as 'a neat little edifice with a square tower'. Tower and hall type, replacing an earlier Protestant church of 1666. The tower has stepped high battlements at the corner like Trory church in Co. Fermanagh, and a Gibbs surround to the door. In the E window three-light plate tracery of 1884. All very charming.

LINSFORT CASTLE. A handsome two-storey, seven-bay house, 80 ft long, and earlier than is usual in this remote part. The outer bays project at the front and back. The chimneys are regular and the roofs have shallow hips. Nicely proportioned windows with fifteen-pane sashes in the ground floor, nine-pane above. A coat of arms and date-stone over the door reading: 'This house was built Capn Arthur Benson in Ye Year of God 1720.' At the back is a big yard. The interior has lugged door surrounds, six-panel doors, some good classical cornices, diagonally set fireplaces, and the original primitive kitchen on the SE. Late C19 stair. The use of advanced end bays and the general character of the house are reminiscent of Buncrana Castle nearby.

OTHER BUILDINGS here are LINSFORT HOUSE, a plain square block of the mid C19, built for Thomas Baldrick, agent to Lord Donegal, and since 1928 a house of Loretto Convent, Omagh; LINSFORT COTTAGE, a charming Regency cottage, minimally Gothic, with portholes to lighten the upstairs rooms; the GLEBE HOUSE, 1827, L-plan, a three-bay, two-storey harled front with dummy centre windows identical with the Glebe House at Lettermacaward; and the PAROCHIAL SCHOOL, 1829, a five-bay, single-storey Tudor hut with label moulding, now a byre.

DUNREE FORT. At Dunree Point. An artillery station and battery erected by the Royal Engineers in 1812 to control, with Knockalla Fort opposite, the Lough Swilly sound. The contractor was a Mr Edgar of Buncrana, who built all the forts on Lough Swilly, and the work was superintended by a Captain Spicer.

DESERTMARTIN   LD J5

A small village where a fort was built in 1611. There is no proper centre now, and the churches are set in countryside.

ST COMGALL, DESERTMARTIN PARISH CHURCH (C of I). 1820. Hall and tower type. Four-bay nave with Y-tracery windows with quarry glass. The tower is a pretty, small-scale design in three stages ending in high battlements with cheeseblock pinnacles. Wide N transept with a big four-light Dec window added by *Welland & Gillespie* in 1869. Inside, nice old oil lamps and a stone Gothic dado at the altar end.

St Mary. Mid c19, a four-bay nave and short sanctuary built
of square basalt with sandstone quoins, plate tracery, and an
iron bellcote. The interior is modest in its materials but very
pretty and beautifully maintained. Trussed pine-panelled roof,
and an arcaded pine altar rail. Pine too is the reredos, with
arcading made of simulated marble and white-painted colonnettes with cusped arches. – STAINED GLASS. Of c. 1870.
Strong blues and reds in vesica-shaped windows behind the
altar.

St Patrick. 3 km w, at Gortahurk. A four-bay, Y-traceried
rendered hall with porch and gallery. Improved by *J. P.
McGrath* in 1913.

Desertmartin Rectory. 1831. Regency-style, with arcaded
relieving arches to the ground floor and a shallow hipped roof
projecting beyond the eaves. Three-bay, two-storey front on
a high basement. Four-bay behind. STABLES. A whitewashed
regular eight-bay block with pediment over a two-bay carriage
arch.

E9   DEVENISH ISLAND   FM
            3 km below Enniskillen in Lower Lough Erne

Devenish Island may be visited by launch from Enniskillen or
from the e shore of Lough Erne, near Trory, where a ferry oper-
ates. It is one of the most important and interesting monastic sites
in Ulster.

History. The name Devenish – Daw-inis – means Ox Island
and was probably given to the place because it provided fairly
extensive and safe pasture for cattle. The island, about a kilometre long and a little over half a kilometre at its widest point,
is a shallow ridge in the narrows between Upper and Lower
Lough Erne and commands a clear uninterrupted view across
the country on both sides. For this reason it was often used
as the setting for parleys between hostile parties from Con-
naught and Ulster, as it could not be taken, at least during daylight, by a surprise attack. Its Christian origins can be traced
back to St Molaise, or Laisre, who founded a monastery here
in the c6 and died in 564 or 571. By the c10 the monastery
had been taken over by the reforming anchorite sect of the Culdees, who remained at Devenish after the general suppression
of monasteries until at least 1603. In 1130 the Culdees were
joined by the Augustinians of a new foundation, St Mary's
Priory, that appears to have been colonized from the abbey of

St Peter and St Paul at Armagh and that continued here, like the older community, until the early C17. Devenish was raided several times by Norsemen, its abbots being killed in 869 and 896. The churches were burnt in 1157 and in 1360 and were described as 'almost ruined' in 1622. The parish church was moved at this time to Monea on the mainland, and the E window of the priory church was re-erected there (*see* p. 423).

In the C17 and C18 the buildings were totally neglected. The nadir of their proper conservation came in 1807, when a certain Captain Fitzmaurice of the Artillery at Enniskillen stole the inscribed foundation stone of the priory and set it up, to add 'insult to sacrilege, above the common privy house door at Enniskillen Barracks'. Pressure from the local archaeologist and schoolmaster 'Frith the Philomath' and from the Bishop of Clogher, and finally the threat of prosecution, secured its restoration to the island in 1808. In 1835 the round tower was restored at the instigation of the rector of Enniskillen, the Rev. J. C. Maude, and between 1874 and 1877 all the ruins were repaired by the Irish Board of Works. Further restoration and re-pointing was carried out in 1970.

ROUND TOWER. One of the finest in Ireland, built of coursed 20 ashlar, 81 ft 4 in. high, with a circumference at the base of 49 ft 9 in. tapering to 42 ft 7 in. under the cornice below the conical roof. The tower is sited W of St Molaise's church, whose door is protected by its position. It is entered by a plain round-headed door some 10 ft up from the ground and is of five storeys, the first four lit by single-slit windows and the top by four larger windows placed just below the cornice on the cardinal points of the compass. Inside, each floor was supported on a check in the masonry, and 'hook' stones are provided to attach ropes or rope ladders. At the cornice level are four finely carved faces set in an enriched band with beards and moustaches flow- 21 ing in elaborate interlace patterns. The tower is sometimes dated to the C10, though most authorities argue that the carved faces suggest a date in the first half of the C12 and compare them to those in the chancel at Kilteel church, Co. Kildare. D. M. Waterman has found traces of a footing of a second round tower which this may have replaced possibly after destruction in 1157.

ST MOLAISE'S HOUSE. A small Romanesque oratory, 19½ ft by 11 ft inside, standing between St Molaise's church and the round tower. Until about 1830 the building was still covered with a high-pitched stone roof vaulted inside in a manner

similar to that of Cormac's chapel at Cashel or to St MacDara's
Island church, Co. Galway. Unfortunately a c19 Bishop of
Clogher made use of the cut stones to flag the church at Enniskillen, so now little more than the base courses of cyclopean
22 masonry remain. On the w front the corners project in *antae*,
with bowtell roll mouldings as shafts, and bases that are finely
sculptured with volute and anthemion motifs that reflect some
knowledge of European Romanesque sculptural decoration and
are ultimately of classical derivation. On account of them the
building is usually dated to the late c12.

TEAMPUL MÓR or ST MOLAISE'S CHURCH. A long, rectangular church, 80½ ft by 17½ ft, Transitional Romanesque, with
23 one fine round-headed lancet remaining in the s wall, widely
splayed inside, with bowtell and beak moulding at the edge of
the reveals similar to those in the chancel of Banagher church,
Co. Derry. Similar mouldings outside, with a hood with long
horizontal stops characteristic of mid c12 work in the North.
Little more than the s wall is now standing. ST MOLAISE'S
BED is a stone coffin in the NW corner of the church.

30 ST MARY'S ABBEY. The largest and the latest ecclesiastical
building on the island, w from the other ruins. Mid c15, built
according to the inscribed stone now in the tower by *Matthew
O'Dubigan* in 1449, when Bartholomew O'Flannagan was Prior
of Devenish. One long church, 94 ft by 24 ft inside, divided after
the Irish fashion, a little w from the centre, by a crossing tower
supported on two double-chamfered piers. The arches, crossing
tower, and N wall of the choir stand complete. The other walls
are only a few feet high. The conventual buildings were, as
usual, on the N, arranged as a court round an enclosed cloister:
sacristy and chapter house in the E range, refectory on the N,
and the guest house on the w. The E window of the abbey is
now at Devenish parish church, Monea, but there is still some
fine stonework to see: the pinnacled and foliated doorway of
the sacristy in the N wall of the choir; the crossing arches with
triple-chamfered voussoirs, the innermost supported on a short
prismatic bracket similar to, but finer than, those at Rathmullen
Friary Co. Donegal; and the fluted chamfer dying to a point
by the doorway on the s side of the tower that leads to a circular
staircase and the belfry. The ceiling of the tower is cross-
vaulted, with intermediate tierceron ribs. It is pierced by two
rope holes. The stair gives access to two doors on the w face
of the tower looking into the nave. Stone brackets here evidently
supported a timber gallery or rood screen. The masonry of the

church, especially the internal faces of the tower, is of unusually high quality.

HIGH CROSS. In the cemetery s from the abbey. A flamboyant late C15 cross, 7 ft high, discovered during the clearance by the Board of Works in 1874 and re-erected. One cusped Perp panel on each face of the shaft, with crocketed corners for the upper third. Plaited work and a Crucifixion on the E face. The head is made of four intersecting half-circles with an open diamond shape in between and the half-circles cusped like a fragment of reticulated tracery.

MUSEUM. Here are collected a number of Dec tracery fragments, capitals from cluster columns, pieces of zigzag moulding from Teampul Mór, and a label moulding with the head of the Virgin or a female saint with pigtails.

DOE CASTLE see CREESLOUGH

DONAGH   FM F10

A collection of houses by an ancient burial ground with some traces of the walls of a medieval church. A new housing estate has been built here to designs of *Storie, Lynch & Partners*, 1969.

ST PATRICK. 1824. A large hall and tower type church, the nave four bays long, the tower in four stages with a leaded pyramid roof, all in an elementary Gothic style, rendered and with quoins. The tower is presumably of *c.* 1860.

DONAGH HOUSE. A handsome mid Georgian farmhouse. Five-bay front of two storeys on a semi-basement. Gibbs surround to the door and eaves cornice, both of dressed sandstone. The interior preserves a good C18 stair with Tuscan newel posts and an original lugged corner fireplace. The additional wing behind is of the early C19.

ARMAGH MANOR. 3 km E. 1865. A small Scottish Baronial manor house, beautifully sited, with an extensive view s to Newtownbutler and Co. Cavan. The design is asymmetrical and depends for its effect on two round towers with high conical roofs, one attached to a crow-stepped outbuilding, the other in the centre of the main front, providing the hall entrance. The house was built for James Haire, a barrister with a taste for improving inscriptions. The best is in the dining room:

> He that sittis down to the buirde to eat,
> Forgetting to gif God thanke's for his meit,
> Syne rysis up and lettes his grace ower pass,
> Sittis down lyk ane ox and risis lyk ane ass.

MANOR COURT HOUSE AND COTTAGES. By the road below
Armagh Manor three highly picturesque gabled and mullioned
buildings, erected by Mr Haire. Furthest up the hill is the Court
House, 1853, with a slender square tower and a lavish supply
of bargeboards. Its E end is a two-storey cottage. Next a twin
two-storeyed cottage with four gables to the road, and, at the
bottom, the most elaborate of all, a *cottage orné* of 1857, worthy
of Nash, with grouped high chimneys, winking oriel windows,
and a timber veranda at the front.

SALLAGHY CHURCH (C of I). 1.5 km WSW. 1840. A medium-
sized, three-bay lancet hall and porch. Quoins, label mouldings,
and cast-iron trusses inside. Surrounded by beech trees.

MANOR WATER HOUSE. 2.5 km WNW. An interesting early C19
coaching hotel half-way between Derry and Dublin, as the
milestone opposite records. Classical façade of two storeys and
five bays with tripartite windows throughout except on either
side of the central door, where Diocletian windows are used.
The outer bays step forward slightly with shallow gables. The
eaves throughout are supported on long console-shaped
mutules in pairs. A stylish design, but by whom?

ROOSKY MILL. 2.5 km WNW. A large complex of corn mills,
derelict at the time of writing. 'Erected by James Clarke AD
1833.' Mostly five-storey, rubble-built, in three distinct sections.

HIGH CROSS. The only survivor, but a spectacular one, of an
early Christian monastery founded by St Patrick for St Colmcille and recorded in the Taxation of Pope Nicholas in 1291,
when it was said to have had costly shrines. Later the monastery
belonged to the Culdees. The cross, one of the northern group
of carved crosses, is C9 or early C10. Re-erected in 1776, it stands
15 ft high, but is obviously – because of the step half-way up
the shaft and the truncated panel scene on the W side – either
incomplete or else a compound of the base of one cross and
the head of another. The head has a pierced ring with cusps,
the nimbus missing on the upper half. The carving in fine sandstone is now much eroded but is notable for the combination
of figure panels with abstract patterns of lozenges and bosses
in relief. The beaded borders are also worth note. The scenes,
to be read from bottom to top, have been identified by Françoise
Henry as from the Old Testament on the W side: Adam and

Eve, Murder of Abel, Sacrifice of Abraham, Daniel in the Lions' Den (broken short); and on the E from the New Testament: the Angel appearing to the Shepherds (one shepherd and three sheep), the Adoration of the Magi, the Baptism of Christ, the Wedding at Cana, the Miracle of the Loaves and Fishes, the Transfiguration or Arrest, and within the cross itself the Crucifixion.

ST PATRICK. 1845 by *John Brady* of Dungannon. A big T-plan church with a W tower rising to a battlemented gable, rubble-built, with cut stone trim and thin battlements and pinnacles. Timber Y-traceried windows. Interior with three galleries and recessed sanctuary almost converting the plan to a Greek cross. – STAINED GLASS. Three-light E window by *Mayer & Co.* of the Nativity, Crucifixion, and Ascension.

DONAGHMORE CHAPEL OF EASE (C of I). A four-bay lancet hall of 1826. Rubble with dressed sandstone surrounds. Extended by a semicircular apse and squat S tower by *Welland & Gillespie* in 1867.

ST JOSEPH'S CONVENT. Originally the Rev. George Walker's house, built as the glebe house for St Michael's Castlecaulfield in 1683. Demolished and rebuilt by John Walker in 1707 as a tiny four-bay, two-storey ashlar house now tucked in behind the early C19 mansion of Mullagruen that was built for the local industrialist and patriot, Alexander Mackenzie. The house has a five-bay, two-storey front, with a forestanding two-storey central porch. Ground floor channelled, with ashlar above and paired giant order pilasters at the corners. The Ionic order of the porch is unusually correct archaeologically. Inside, a domed oval hall with pilasters, and alternating doors and niches, leads to a shallow double return stair with an oval dome light. The detailing looks of about 1830–40. There is too much tarmac round the house and not enough trees, but the additions by *W. J. Gregory* of 1935 happily left the house unspoilt. – LODGE. A dumpy classical block with four free-standing Ionic columns along the front.

ST JOSEPH. 5 km W, at Galbally. A four-bay rendered hall of 1841 with Y-traceried windows. The old type of plan, with galleries round three sides and the altar on the S wall. Old Tyrone tile floor. Gabled entrance in squared rubble with Gothic bell-cote of 1927, probably by *W. H. Byrne & Son.*

ST MARY. 8 km WNW, by King James's Well. 1870. A three-bay harled hall. Stone Y-tracery, W bellcote.

See also Castlecaulfield.

Donegal, which gives its name to the most northerly Irish county, and gave the titles of Earl and Marquess to the Chichester family that owned much of the city of Belfast, is an unimpressive little place. The wide but shallow estuary of the Esk opening into Donegal Bay made it a stopping-place for Viking raiders – its name means Fort of the Foreigners – but its history is limited and more recent.

In the Middle Ages Donegal was an O'Donnell stronghold with a castle and two religious houses in the vicinity. O'Donnell opposition to Elizabethan policy at the end of the C16 caused the town to be taken by English troops in 1591; it was liberated in 1592 and retaken in 1601. In 1610, three years after the Flight of the Earls, the town was granted to Sir Basil Brooke, a captain in the English army who had been selected to take reinforcements to Ulster in 1598. He laid out the town Diamond, similar to those at Castle Finn and Raphoe. In 1651, when the Brookes supported Parliament, the Marquess of Clanricarde took and tried to hold the castle against a Cromwellian army, but had to give it up. In October 1798 a French frigate of thirty guns anchored near the town, but failed to make a landing. Such is Donegal's history.

Her historians are more celebrated: four monks, Michael O'Clery, Peregrine O'Clery, Peregrine Duignan, and Fearfeasa O'Mulconry, from the Franciscan friary at Donegal, whose *Annals of the Four Masters* was compiled between 1630 and 1636, and whose work is commemorated in a sandstone monument in the middle of the Diamond and in the Church of the Four Masters, a little to the E. Since Sir Basil Brooke's plantation, Donegal has grown little. In 1846 it was described as 'not bulkier than a mere village' with 'scarcely an edificed alignment which can be called a street', and the same is true today.

DONEGAL PARISH CHURCH (C of I). 1825–8. A pretty tower and hall type church, built with Board of First Fruits money to designs of 'Mr *Graham* of Donegal, Architect'. Simple Gothic. Cut stone ashlar tower and spire with a three-bay harled hall lit by Y-tracery timber windows. The interior has a gallery and a chancel entered through a chamfered arch added in 1890.

ST PATRICK (the Church of the Four Masters). Neo-Irish-Romanesque by *Ralph Byrne*, 1931–5. An ingenious plan with double transepts expressed as high-pitched gables with an offset round tower in the NW angle. Solid enough outside, but woefully stagey within: cement-rendered walls, unconvincingly lined with masonry joints, flimsy barrel-vaults inches thin, triangular-topped lancets, colonnettes with cushion capitals, and zigzag galore. It is a pity the materials are so shoddy and so clumsily handled. – Irish marble ALTAR and altar rail.

METHODIST CHURCH. Across the river, W of the Diamond. An entertaining design and a favourite one with Ulster Methodists, appearing in the late 1850s and early 60s at Ballymoney, Cookstown, and Newtownards as well as here. It always has the same plan: a diminutive four-bay, two-storey stone hall with an emphatic Norman-style front – a derivation of Farrell's neo-Norman but given an extra twist – that ends in a machicolated bellcote like a Victorian country-house chimney.

PRESBYTERIAN CHURCH. W from the Methodist church. A harled T-plan hall of 1886.

CASTLE. By the W corner of the Diamond. One of the most interesting ruins in the whole county, unusually large and unusually well preserved, though the conservation with concrete beams and cement copings is hardly sympathetic. This was the great house of the O'Donnells, erected first in 1474, though the existing detail seems to date from a rebuilding or remodelling of c. 1563. Hugh Roe O'Donnell burnt the castle in 1595 to prevent it falling into English hands. In 1616 it was granted to Sir Basil Brooke for twenty-one years, and in 1623 the grant was made permanent.

Two dates of building appear clearly: the O'Donnell tower, a massive rectangular block at the N end of the enclosing bawn wall; and a manor-house wing added by Sir Basil, running SW 35 from the longer side of the tower. The O'Donnell castle is largely overlaid by Jacobean rebuilding, though its mass completely overpowers the wing at its flank. The ground floor – vaulted with corbel brackets to support a loft floor – is original. So, too, is the spiral stair in the S angle leading to the great hall. On the SE side, the shorter, was the original entrance, now blocked by the solid stone base of a canted bay-window added by Sir Basil to the great hall. The doorway from the stair into the hall is C16 and nicely detailed, with single-chamfered reveals, a Tudor arch, and spandrels filled with shallowly sculptured ferns. A fireplace floating in space on the N wall is similarly treated.

The rebuilding by Sir Basil has radically altered the exterior of the tower. From the great hall up, all the architectural detail is Jacobean. A great mullioned and transomed window breaks into the s w side just beside the wing he added. Above it are two more storeys attempting the regularity of a three-bay façade, with similar six-light mullioned windows on each floor, the upper rising as three gables through the roof. Note the water spouts between that still stick out like cannons. The shorter end of the tower is single-bay but similarly treated. At each corner is a square cap-house or bartizan, supported on heavy clumsy brackets that lack completely the elegance of those at Termon Castle, Pettigoe.

The manor-house wing, despite the same mullioned windows and flat hood mouldings, has a completely different air – very much a house, even if it is still inside a defensive bawn. Again, the roof line is the most regular part of the façade – a succession of five gabled bays with two-light windows. Where the wing joins the tower, the end bay is stepped forward. Otherwise the façade is flat. The wing, now only a shell, was of three storeys. It has two doorways, evidently older work, with chamfered jambs and pointed arches, one in the projecting bay and the other below the second gable from the free s w end. The contrast of the up-to-date in architecture is provided by a big Renaissance archway inserted at first-floor level – its stairs are now missing – between the third and fourth bays; round-headed with pilaster shafts, imposts, and scrolled keystone, all decorated with restless strapwork patterning. Similar patterning covers the jambs of a small fireplace in the tower, although the profile of its arch is still Gothic: C16 or C17(?). But there is no doubt about the principal fireplace in the great hall – a sophisticated piece of Mannerist decoration, carved in freestone, with an overmantel divided by paired consoles and filled with the coats of arms of Sir Basil Brooke (r. hand side) who died in 1633 and his wife Anne Leycester of Chester. In the complete house, when this fireplace rose uninterrupted from the floor to ceiling – as it obviously did – the effect will have been magnificent. The square angle turret with a corner arrow slit by the gate and the wall are C17: the western wall turret is C16.

FRANCISCAN FRIARY. On an open site by the mouth of the river, s w from the Diamond. The friary, founded in 1474 by the first Red Hugh O'Donnell and his wife, Nuala O'Brien, was apparently complete by 1488. The four masters, members of its community, wrote their Annals in 1630–6, but by then its buildings were already shattered by an explosion that occurred

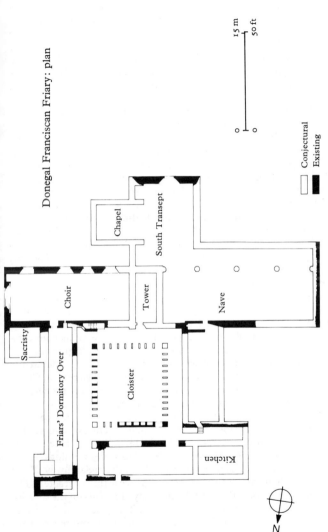

Donegal Franciscan Friary: plan

Sacristy

Choir

Chapel

South Transept

Tower

Friars' Dormitory Over

Cloister

Nave

Kitchen

N

15 m

50 ft

0

0

☐ Conjectural
■ Existing

Irish Office of Public Works, National Monuments Branch, redrawn by Stephen Gage

in September 1601, while the house was a garrisoned fortress
held for the English by Niall Garbh O'Donnell against his cousin Red Hugh. The property was confiscated and granted to
Sir Basil Brooke in 1607.

Little is now left, and what there is is buried several feet deep
in the graveyard. The plan is that of a long church, approximately 22 ft wide, extending through the nave and choir in a
straight line for 146 ft. s of the nave were an aisle and transept,
with a large chapel on the E side of the transept. The domestic
buildings were arranged round a cloister on the N side of the
church. The junction of the nave and choir was probably
straddled by a tower. In other words, a usual Franciscan layout.
The gables of the choir and transept, standing intact, allow a
visitor to visualize the extent of the church among the long grass
and tombstones of today. The most substantial remains are of
the N wall of the church and the E and N sides of the cloister.
The latter are unusual and curiously different from each other.
The cloister was small, about 31 ft by 34 ft in size. Six arches
of the N arcade remain, small-scale, with their piers at no more
than 30 in. centres. They are crudely fashioned with long thin
shafts of stone – eight-sided slabs – that flow upwards through
weakly moulded capitals to single-chamfered arches. All this
contrasts strikingly with the crisp, firm modelling of the nine
remaining arches of the E side, where the piers are cut like paired
octagonal shafts, linked by a web, which is extended and
expressed as a nib on the exposed cloister face. This plan continues round the soffit of each arch to give a deep modelling
to the arcade that is the stronger for its tiny scale. The arcade
was buttressed on the cloister side, as at Quin Friary, Co. Clare,
though here only between the sixth and seventh arches, i.e.
in the middle of each side: see the projecting stones above the
arcade, where the buttress died into the wall. Paired shafts by
the SE corner beside the round-headed archway suggest that
the same arcade system continued along the S side of the
cloister, which was the only side not to have buildings above
it – see the marks of a lean-to roof above the big archway. What
other detail can be seen is consistent with this character. The
main windows of the church had splayed reveals on the interior
and double-chamfered trim outside. The piscina and aumbry
in the SE corner of the choir have single-chamfered reveals.
Note also the primitive construction of the roofed passage in
the nave N wall with massive stone beams and the paving of
a corridor(?) above.

MAGHERABEG ABBEY. 1.5 km SSW, in the countryside. These remains of a small C15 Franciscan Tertiary friary retain walls to a height of about 12 ft. The church has the usual elongated proportions, 22 ft by 95 ft. The whole is ivy-covered, and there seems to be little to see save a credence cavity, a piscina or lavabo, and a splayed door opening in the E end of the N wall. Traces of vaulted domestic buildings to the NE.

FORMER UNION WORKHOUSE. 1842. A standard design by *George Wilkinson*. Five-bay administrative Tudor block with a nine-bay, two-storey block behind. Now pebbledashed.

ROYAL BANK OF IRELAND. In the Diamond. A handsome mid C19 classical façade of two storeys and five bays.

ST AGATHA. 3 km NNW at Clar. 1869–71 by *O'Neill & Byrne*. An unusually large cruciform church, dropped in open country, at first perhaps not much to look at, yet honest and curiously satisfying as a design – perhaps this is architects' architecture. The whole building is in stone, mildly polychrome, with clean, simple lines. The basic plan is similar to that used by *E. J. Toye* for the church at Ardara and later by *J. V. Brennan*, and with reason, for it works well. Paired lancet windows to nave and transepts with porches tucked into the SW and NW corners, leaving the lancets to be replaced by tiny quatrefoils. At the E end a big semicircular apse with flanking chapels. The interior is as clean and crisp as the exterior, sympathetically restored with white walls and a clear varnished roof by *Bernard Rhatigan* in 1967.

KILLYMARD PARISH CHURCH (C of I). 2 km NW. 1830 by *Mr Graham* of Donegal. A three-bay harled hall with buttresses and a pinnacled bellcote in granite. Short chancel of *c.* 1860. – SCULPTURE. In the porch a carved bishop's head taken from the old church.

KILLYMARD GLEBE HOUSE. 2 km W. A long, low harled house of late C18 character. Symmetrical three-bay section with stone quoins and central porch with tripartite window over. Two-bay extension on the S.

ST MARY. 2 km N, at Killymard. 1858. A harled T-plan church with three galleries, the altar on the long S wall. Additional stone tower of two stages, with finials and a slate spire.

ST ERNANS. 3 km SW. This was the island retreat of John Hamilton of Brown Hall (1800–84), the author of *Sixty Years Experience as an Irish Landlord*. Mr Hamilton took a romantic fancy to the island, laid out a pretty garden on it, with a wall round the shore, and built a two-storey Regency-style cottage there between 1824 and 1826. It is five windows long with a continuous veranda running the length of its front across canted bays at either end.

The setting is indeed glorious, but the romantic whim of a young and newly married proprietor proved inconvenient. For most of each day the island was cut off either by the tide or, worse, by impassable shallows of mud. The construction of a causeway, despaired of by professional engineers, was achieved by Hamilton with free labour from the surrounding country, as an inscription on its retaining wall records:

This causeway stands to commemorate the great mutual love between John Hamilton and the people of Donegal, both his own tenants and others. Through a time of bitter famine and pestilence, John Hamilton, not for the first or last time had stood between them and death. Knowing that his great wish was to build a road joining the island of St Ernans, his favourite dwelling place, with the mainland, and that owing to the Atlantic tides he could not achieve this without expenditure far beyond his means, the people, Roman Catholic and Protestant, came in their hundreds with spade, pick and barrow to build this causeway, refusing all recompense. John Hamilton J.P., D.L., of Brown Hall and St Ernans was born in the year 1800. He succeeded his father in 1807 and died in 1884.

SCULPTURE. In the rockery before the house a complete carving in low relief of a pair of sitting dogs or lions joined by a single head with a crown. Brought by John Hamilton from Donegal Abbey and possibly C10 or earlier.

DOON FORT see PORTNOO

Of all the building ventures of Frederick Augustus Hervey, Bishop of Derry and Earl of Bristol, Downhill, though now only a gaunt ruin, is still the most complete. Hervey owed his connection with Ireland, as Ireland owes her most flamboyant Georgian bishop, to his elder brother, the second Earl of Bristol, who for a period of less than a year, from September 1766, was Lord Lieutenant of Ireland. Five months after this appointment, Bristol raised his younger brother to the first Irish see that fell vacant, the bishopric of Cloyne, and soon after, having served his family's interests as best he could, resigned the Lord Lieutenancy without ever setting foot in Ireland. Fortune or interest continued to follow the new bishop, for in just over a year Hervey was translated from Cloyne, worth about £2,500, to the very rich bishopric of Derry, valued at £7,000 a year. In 1779 he succeeded to the earldom of Bristol, and from that year until his death at Albano in Italy in 1803 he ruled both his ecclesiastical principality in Ulster and his estates in England, worth £20,000 a year, as the Earl Bishop. In his later years, as he spent little time in Ireland, his estates were administered by an agent and distant cousin, Henry Hervey Aston Bruce, who succeeded the Earl Bishop at Downhill and Ballyscullion (see Bellaghy) and who in 1804 was created a baronet. Downhill remained in the Bruce family until 1918, when it was sold by the fifth Baronet. The house was subsequently dismantled. In 1950 portions of the estate including the glen and the Mussenden Temple were conveyed to the National Trust.

DOWNHILL CASTLE. The history of the Earl Bishop's house at Downhill is complex but, thanks to extensive documentation and the work of Mr Peter Rankin, reasonably clear. In 1775 the Bishop started to build a 'cabin', intended at first to be no more than an C18 villa, and it was this that brought Arthur Young to Magilligan the following year 'for the sake of seeing a new house building on the sea coast by the Bishop of Derry, the shell not finished'. It stood on a bold shore, but in a country where a tree was a rarity. Built in the rough local basalt, it can hardly have been elegant. Perhaps it was the desire to improve it that led the Bishop, as soon as he succeeded to the earldom, to encourage *John Soane* to cut short his study in Rome in the summer of 1779 and come to Ireland to redesign the house. The Earl Bishop has gained many a black mark from English art historians for misleading poor young Soane, who spent six weeks at Downhill from July to September 1780 to no purpose. But Soane was not alone: in the same year *Robert Adam* made designs for a new dining room and other additions and, if the mason who executed all the decorative carving and much of the subsequent building for the Earl is to be believed, *James Wyatt* made designs in 1778 which, though they may have provided the basic elevations of the house in its final form, were not to be superintended by Wyatt in their execution. Whatever may have happened at the Earl's houses of Ballyscullion and of Ickworth in Suffolk, Downhill Castle was to be an Irish job.

While Bishop of Cloyne, Hervey had made contact with a Cork architect, *Michael Shanahan*, who later accompanied him on one of his frequent visits to Italy. It was Shanahan who was to superintend the construction of the new house and who designed most of the garden buildings that decorated the grounds. The mason employed from 1784 to reface the house in Dungiven and Ballycastle sandstone was a local man, *James McBlain*, whose son *David McBlain* carried on work at Downhill after his father's death in 1792 and became a local architect in his own right.

In 1851 the mansion, with the exception of the E wing, was gutted by fire. It was not restored until January 1876, when *The Irish Builder* carried a long article on the work that had just been completed. The arrangement of the interior was completely altered. The entrance was moved from the S front to a ground-floor porch in the middle of the long W side with a vaulted hall supported on coupled Tuscan columns and a new stair leading to the winter garden above, which had been the Earl Bishop's gallery. The architect was *John Lanyon*.

Downhill can never have been an easy house to live in. Like Robert Adam's Culzean, Ayrshire, begun just two years later in 1777, it is perched on the edge of a cliff, but unlike Culzean it took no advantage of the views its situation offers: it turned its back to the sea with the main front facing S, extended in two long wings that run back behind it on the E and W, making the plan a deep U. The dressed ashlar front, faced by *James McBlain* from 1784, was unusually sophisticated: two storeys on a rusticated basement with ashlar walls above divided by pairs of fluted Corinthian pilasters between the windows. The centre is of three window bays, with a double perron to the door, flanked by wide canted bays on each side, each with three windows. The pilaster system is continued round the sides, where a pair of segmental bows project, not quite in the middle of the façade. Beyond, a basalt wall, battlemented in the C19, runs N, almost to the cliff edge, shielding the domestic offices from view.

MUSSENDEN TEMPLE. 1783–5 by *Michael Shanahan*. This domed rotunda on the cliffs below the house is named after the Bishop's cousin, Mrs Mussenden, who died in 1785 shortly before its completion. Its scale and proportions link it more clearly than the house itself with the style of international neoclassicism emanating from Rome in the later C18. Sixteen half-engaged Corinthian columns support a continuous circular entablature, with a stepped blocking course above and a semicircular dome ending in a stone finial. The contrast, typical of the C18, between the logic and reason of the architecture of the temple and the rude grandeur of the natural setting is also made within the structure itself, where a rough plinth of basalt blocks contrasts at once with the finely fluted plinth of the base course of the temple itself, the Vitruvian scroll at dado level, and the carved drapery swags between the capitals. The inscription in the frieze, SUAVE MARI MAGNO TURBANTIBUS AEQUORA VENTIS, E TERRA MAGNUM ALTERIUS SPECTARE LABOREM – 'Tis pleasant to watch from land the great struggling of others when winds whip up the waves on a mighty sea – is from Lucretius, *De Rerum Natura* (II, I, 2.) It was cut by *David McBlain* and originally gilded. Shanahan wanted the dome to be of gilt-metal to match: the Bishop wanted slates and got them. The roof is now lead. The temple was used as a library and once had scagliola columns and a coffered ceiling, now gone.

MAUSOLEUM. A ruined stump, standing in the fields in front of the house. Built in memory of the second Earl of Bristol, who had introduced his brother to Ireland. *Shanahan*'s estimate in 1779 was for £426 0s. 9d. Building continued until 1783. It is based on the monument of the Julii at Saint-Rémy in Provence, though Shanahan's architecture is a good deal more refined than its CI B.C. model. The extravagant form – square plinth, arcaded first stage, drum, colonnaded rotunda, and cupola – is of the sort to appeal to a patron who had known Piranesi's Rome. Today the upper half is missing, for the cupola, the rotunda, and the statue of the Lord Lieutenant that it contained were blown down in a gale in 1839. The statue, by *Van Nost*, has been put up headless by the Bishop's Gate. The inscription 'He gave me his word that my oxen should roam, as you see, while I myself play what I please upon my rustic reed-pipe' is from Virgil's *Eclogues*, *I*, 9–10.

WALLED GARDEN. 1778, extended in 1783. High basalt walls, coursed in brick inside, and divided into no less than six compartments, each of considerable size. One contained a formal pond.

DOVECOTE AND ICEHOUSE. Built by *David McBlain* in 1786 in the NW wall of the estate. Coursed rubble basalt, brick-vaulted, with a tiled dome.

LION GATE. A sophisticated Adamesque design of about 1780. Paired gatepiers treated as Doric aedicules with quarter-engaged columns flanking a blind niche and supporting a salient entablature with bucrania where the triglyphs ought to be. All in finely carved sandstone. The lions, more like mastiffs, though the Bishop's crest was an ounce or lynx, were carved in Cork in 1787. Only one remains *in situ*.

BISHOP'S GATE. 1783–4, probably by *Shanahan*. A regular pattern-book arch surmounted by a mutule pediment with flanking Doric columns and outer wings with blind niches and thin pilasters that line in with the curve of the imposts of the arch. Quasi-Gothic gate lodge outside on the E side.

DUNBOE CHURCH RUINS. Only the side walls remain of a C13 church, repaired by the Clothworkers' Company in 1622 and abandoned for the new church at Articlave in 1691. The Earl Bishop intended to build a folly spire here but never did so. In the S corner of the graveyard is the MAUSOLEUM of the Hervey-Bruce family, built in 1810, an odd composition with an octagonal vault supporting a panelled shaft with an urn on top and a pineapple.

Anciently Cross, until 1818, when the Drapers' Company, who owned the place, decided to take an interest in it, changed the name, and drew up plans to rebuild it round a triangular green. The present layout is by the company's surveyor, *W. J. Booth*. His plan dates from 1827 and was carried out about three years later. Its effect has been ruined by the lax attitude of the local authority that allowed a shop, a garage, and a pebbledashed house to be built on the green.

ST COLUMBA, BALLYNASCREEN PARISH (C of I). 1888 by *Thomas Drew*, replacing a Georgian Gothic church built by the Earl Bishop in 1760. Of this the tower and spire, added by Sir William Rowley in 1792, remain. The tower is plain, of three stages, with wayward battlements; the stone spire is octagonal. Drew's church is long and low, with a broadly buttressed porch and cusped lancets. The E end is given an unusual profile by the treatment of the transepts as separate gabled additions with their roof ridge running parallel to the nave-like aisles. Arcades inside divide the transepts from the chancel.

PRESBYTERIAN CHURCH. Built *c.* 1840. A severe hall, of ashlar, with a pedimental gable and three shallow recessed panels across the windowless front. Presumably by *W. J. Booth*.

ST EUGENE. At Moneymena, 4 km NW. 1898 by *E. J. Toye*. A big sandstone Gothic church on a typical Toye plan with arcaded transepts, semicircular apse, pine ceiling, and paired lancets.

COUNTY LIBRARY. Formerly the Market House, built in 1839 to designs of *W. J. Booth* as the centrepiece of the main side, across the top of the hill, of the Diamond. A three-bay, two-storey front with pedimental gable with oversailing eaves and extended mutules. Flanked by a regular row of two-storey houses that ended originally in a dispensary and an inn.

THE GLEBE. 2.5 km NE. 1794. A substantial late Georgian house of five bays and two storeys with segmental bays immediately at the corner of each side elevation. Harled all over, with a dressed stone door surround identical to one at Fort William, Tobermore.

DERRYNOYD HOUSE. 3 km NW. Demolished save for the vernacular classical stable block. The estate is now a government forest.

CHURCHES in the area include: ST COLUMNKILLE, STRAW, 2 km SW, a seven-bay sandstone hall with a small square tower, built in 1853, improved by *W. J. Doherty* of Derry in 1926; ST ANNE (C of I), CAVANREAGH, 6 km SW, of 1840–3, a small tower and hall type church with lancet windows, box pews, and oil lamps inside; and SIXTOWNS LO CATHOLIC CHURCH, a six-bay lancet hall of 1835. Of the ruined church at Sixtowns Lo only the E gable and parts of the walls remain. No details.

DRENAGH LD *H3*

Drenagh, originally Fruit Hill, has been McCausland property since 1729, when the estate was inherited by Robert McCausland, along with that of Roe Park, from Speaker Conolly. Robert built a house here, but the present building is the work of his great-grandson, Marcus Conolly McCausland, who succeeded in 1827.

Some time before that the architect *John Hargrave* had been asked to prepare plans for a new house. These, which still survive, show a tall, three-storey Regency design with a shallow roof behind a cornice and blocking course, and wide canted bays at either end of the main elevation. Though nothing came of Hargrave's plans, the idea of the bays was taken up again in 1836 when *Charles Lanyon*, the newly appointed surveyor of Co. Antrim, was engaged to build the house. Scrupulously detailed and of fine ashlar sandstone, Drenagh stands at the

beginning of a succession of large-scale country-hous
commissions to be executed by Lanyon's office. He was neve
to be so chaste again or, one might add, so careful.

The house is planned round a large central hall and has, a
a result, three main façades with a lower service wing on the
N. It is two-storeyed throughout, with a balustraded parape
hiding the roof. The entrance front is of five bays with a
recessed central bay and a six-columned Ionic porch; the side
elevation (S) of six bays indulges in the curiosity of a central
pediment supported on three giant pilasters which, perhaps
because of the careful spacing of the windows, does not look
as gauche as it should. The W front has paired canted bays taken
over from Hargrave's design, with a central French door.
Though the scale is large, the detail is refined: note, for
example, the dentil cornice below the balustrade and the odd
mannerism of the square corner to the leading face of the bay-
windows on the W front.

The interior is typical of the plans of many large early C19
classical houses, with portico, entrance hall, and central hall
arranged on a straight axis. The central hall communicates with
all the public rooms and is itself on a heroic scale, with large
fluted Corinthian columns screening rectangular recesses on
the W and E and an impressive double return stair opening
behind the columns on the N. It is lit by a circular dome now
filled in with an early C20 flat leaded light.

The STABLE COURT, N of the house, is symmetrical, with
space for six carriages.

In the glen NE of the house are the ITALIAN GARDEN, a
big flight of steps that ends on a balustraded platform above
a niche, and the MOON GARDEN made in the walls of an
old pigeon house to designs of *Francis Rhoades* in 1968. This
is a little in the style of Lutyens, with twin tiles pavilions
looking down a court to a brick and stone 'O' that overlooks
the glen.

GATE LODGES. Classical with a tetrastyle Ionic portico at
the main gate; simple Gothic at the Coleraine gate.

DRUMACHOSE CHURCH RUINS. 1 km SE of the house, in the
demesne. On a mound are the ivy-clad remains of an unusually
long rectangular church, 25 ft by 88 ft inside, dating apparently
from the C13. Both gables are standing and substantial parts
of the side walls, with a consecration cross cut on the N wall.
Sections of the single-chamfered sandstone dressings of the E
gable lancet remain. The church was dedicated to St Cainnech,

born in the neighbourhood in the C6. It was in use until 1749, when the new church was built at Limavady.

'TREEVE HOUSE. 1 km NW of the house, in the demesne. Originally the home of the Gage family later of Bellarena. A three-bay, two-storey brick house of 1735 that now looks more like 1800; very wide windows that may well have been built as narrow pairs. Remodelled 1967.

DROMORE   TY *F7*

A village with some late C18 and early C19 houses in terraces round a T-junction. St Patrick arranged for Cinnia, daughter of King Echaid, whom he had raised from death, to take the veil here; so Dromore was the first place in Ireland where there were any nuns.

DROMORE OLD CHURCH. WSW of the village on an elevated site between two roads. The ruins of a church built in 1694, probably on the site of a Plantation building. The nave is 20 ft wide, with a big S transept. Round-headed windows, that on the E with a central mullion replacing an older one.

CATHOLIC CHURCH. 1835. *E. M. Guigan*, builder. A big five-bay hall. Windows with provincial Gibbs surrounds and Y-tracery. The interior is a surprise, with an arcade of three arches across the E end and a heavy Byzantine-style altar behind. Square bell tower with cupola cap.

HOLY TRINITY, DROMORE PARISH CHURCH. 1957 by *A. T. Marshall*. Five-bay white-harled nave on a stone podium. Chancel with modern stained glass in mahogany frames. Asymmetrical square gabled tower with a slight batter like a round tower. The church replaces one of 1839 by *William Farrell & Son*.

PRESBYTERIAN CHURCH. Mid C19. A three-bay, Y-traceried hall.

RECTORY. Opposite Holy Trinity. Built *c.* 1830 by the Rev. H. Lucas St George. Generously scaled, with a three-bay, two-storey Regency front held between projecting end bays that are emphasized by quoins and gabled pediments. The windows are recessed in segmental relieving arches.

DRUMHALLAGH   DO *E2*

CROSS SLAB. 5 km N of Rathmullen in Drumhallagh townland. (Take the road inland by Drumhallagh bridge for 1 km to the first group of cottages. The cross is about 300 yds SE from the turn in the road, by a river.) A small but unusually fine cross slab, 8 ft 6 ins by 2 ft 1 in, with carving on both sides. On the NW face is a Latin cross with a raised border and circle in the centre, the ends of the arms slightly splayed out. The SE face is a similar shaped cross ornamented with double ribbon interlace of a simple pattern in a raised border with figures of bishops below the arms and seated figures 'sucking their thumbs' above. Like Carndonagh and Fahan crosses, the arms are marked with slight protuberances on the sides. Probably C8.

91 MACAMOOSH FORT. 5 km N of Rathmullen. One of the earliest martello towers to be erected in Great Britain or Ireland. Built in 1801 on a peninsula jutting N into Lough Swilly and reinforced in 1806–7 by a rock-cut ditch, a drawbridge, and three gun emplacements below the tower. The superintending engineer was *Colonel Fisher*. Now a private house, though clearly seen from Macamoosh golf course.

DRUM MANOR *see* KILDRESS

F10   # DRUMMULLY   FM

An old parish in the uppermost reaches of Upper Lough Erne. Mrs Delany visited Dr Madden at the Rectory here in 1748 and reported enthusiastically on the plantations and situation of the house. It is between two BRIDGES: Gortnacarrow Bridge, a fine mid C18 design of seven stone arches, and Wattle Bridge. DRUMMULLY OLD CHURCH, 1 km E, has gables on the N and S walls of a rectangular church already 'ruinous' in 1622. Now almost 8 ft high and covered in brambles. At DRUMCRIN, 1.5 km NW, standing on a hill are the ruins of an C18 church with a battlemented tower of two storeys; round-headed windows.

CLONCALLICK. 4 km E of Gortnacarrow Bridge. An attractive Irish variant of a gentleman's farmhouse, built *c.* 1760. Central block flanked by quadrant wings that terminate in gabled office blocks. What is Irish here is that the wings flank *the back* of the house, forming a convenient yard – not a forecourt. The front is odd, too, for the ground floor is of five bays, the first floor of only three, with the bedroom windows over the spaces between the windows on the floor below. Tiny eaves pediment over the central bay. The front door, obscured by a conservatory porch of 1870, has a robust Tuscan aedicule surround. Inside is a pretty stair (turning in a bow in the middle of the rear elevation). The stair rail is decorated with Rococo vine-leaf carving, and the dining room has a delicate plasterwork frieze of flowers and garlands. The doors are of an unusual seven-panel design with lugged surrounds.

DRUMQUIN   TY *F7*

This country village, closed in on three sides by high bare hills, was founded *c.* 1617 by Sir John Davies, who also built Castle Curlews nearby in the manor of Cloghmore. It is little more than a straight street, crossing a river at its w end by a double-arched bridge built in 1787.

DRUMQUIN OLD CHURCH. The ruins of a rectangular church, 19 by 52 ft inside, with a round-headed E window. Ruinous in 1695, rebuilt *c.* 1740 by Dr Benson, and in use until 1842. Described by Lewis as 'a small ancient edifice surmounted by a cupola'.

LANGFIELD UPPER PARISH CHURCH (C of I). 2.5 km ESE. 1803. A diminutive tower and hall type church set on a hillside in a pretty little churchyard. Interior by *Welland & Gillespie*, 1863.

LANGFIELD LOWER PARISH CHURCH (C of I). 1 km w. 1842. A spiky little façade with pinnacled porch, gable, and bellcote. The chancel was built in 1867, re-using the old E window. Surveyor *A. Hardy*. Restored and improved by *James Reid* of Derry, 1916.

ST PATRICK. 2 km s. A big, plain, barn-like church with a stone recording its date, 1832, and its builder, *Daniel Campbell*, who was no doubt also the architect. There is something very appealing about these solid, honest Catholic churches of the early C19. Five-bay hall with Y-tracery timber sashes and provincial Gibbs surrounds. The interior is a remarkable survival, with a big gallery supported on quatrefoil columns at the back and an elaborate display of Gothic joinery on the altar wall. The parish hope to build a new church to designs of *Frank Corr* on a new site. It is to be hoped that this will not toll the knell of the present St Patrick. – BELLCOTE TOWER in the churchyard, a two-storey belfry with round tower corners and an arched bellcote. Mid C19?

METHODIST CHURCH. 1878. A small gabled hall, and the only church in the village.

PRESBYTERIAN CHURCH. 1 km s. 1860. A six-bay lancet hall built by the Rev. John Davidson.

RECTORY. 1 km W. 1762. A large and unusually early rectory, built into the side of a hill in park-like surroundings below the church. Five-bay, two-storey, with a two-storey central pedimented porch. Only one room thick. Five panelled doors in lugged surrounds inside. The date-stone is inscribed

> AD MDCCLXII REV
> Ar BENSON DD PAROCHIAE
> RECTOR SUET RECTORIBUS
> SUCCEDENTIBUS POSUIT.

BURREL'S FOLLY. 2 km S. Despite its promising name, this is just a ruined farmhouse of 1779 with extensive outbuildings, once the home of a family called Sproule.

CASTLE CURLEWS. 2 km NNW. Built by Sir John Davies before 1619. The little that remains suggests an ambitious and emphatically English house, conceived in the manner of Robert Smythson, with a long range ending in a rectangular room. This has wide cross-mullioned windows arranged in canted bays on three sides, E, S, and W, and was at least two storeys high. The base of the E window stands entire, with two musket holes in the face and narrow chamfered slits in the splays of the bay. The room appears to have had three fireplaces.

KIRLISH HOUSE. S of the castle. Early C19. A perfect cube of ashlar stonework with a stone eaves cornice, a slate pyramid roof, and central chimneystacks. The front a door with a window above it. Built into a hill and three-storey at the sides. Decidedly odd.

An attractive small town situated by a broad inlet W of Sheep Haven Bay and sheltered from the Atlantic by Horn Head. The town was noted as a fishing community, and after the reconstruction of its quay in 1831 as a port exporting corn. It consists almost entirely of a main street running E–W. About the middle this opens to a square bordered by the quay on the N, with in its centre a sedate two-storey MARKET HOUSE 'lately built' in 1847. There are more substantial two- and three-storey houses and stores here than is usual in a remote Irish town, but the salt air and the fish and chips of the place are still more likely to leave a greater impression than are its buildings.

CLONDEHORKY OLD CHURCH. 1 km S. The ruins of an early

C17 rectangular church, 56½ by 18½ ft, the walls, gables, and W bellcote still entire. Built of rubble stone with segment-headed windows – rather Scottish in appearance. – MONUMENT. On the N wall inside remains of an inscribed classical tablet to William Wray of Castle Wray † 1710. Aedicule surmounted by a coat of arms – the columns now missing.

DUNFANAGHY PRESBYTERIAN CHURCH. A little before the town on the E, set on a terraced grass bank. Built in 1875–8 to designs of *Robert Young* to replace the old meeting house of 1750 opposite the Market House in the town. In May 1875 the Rev. William Kane, minister here from 1869 to 1905, wrote to Young stressing that 'Romanesque is the early Irish type of church building and therefore to be chosen in preference to the pointed style'. He got what he asked for. The church is a simple stone-built hall with high equilateral gable and offset tower and spire to the W. In the gable a big pierced tracery rose window in a round-headed arch. The tower, which is the porch at its base, tapers abruptly at eaves level to an octagonal belfry topped by a limestone spire. Church halls and sexton's house balance each other at the back.

HOLY TRINITY, CLONDEHORKY PARISH CHURCH (C of I). W of the town. Of 1873, a lean little church of squared rubble with diagonal buttresses and plate-tracery lancets. Nave with chancel, S transept, and N porch. Wilfully grouped in a way that is very reminiscent of E. W. Godwin. High panelled ceilings in pine.

HOLY CROSS CHURCH. A six-bay gabled mid C19 hall with a seven-sided apsidal sanctuary. The parochial house of 1874 was built for Father Diver by *Timothy Hevey*. Plain.

HORN HEAD HOUSE. On the N shore of Dunfanaghy Bay in the remnants of a park. A substantial, plain house, harled, of two storeys and five bays, with a central porch and tripartite window above. Square hall with big rooms either side, 18 by 25 ft, and a broad central stair. Pretty stone fireplaces with fluted keystones upstairs. All mid C18, the seat of the Stewarts of Horn Head from *c.* 1700 to 1935. At the time of writing derelict. – SIGNAL TOWER, 4 km N of the house, on Horn Head Cliffs. Early C19, one of several ruined towers on the Donegal coast. – McSWYNE'S GUN, 2½ km W, in the cliffs N of Tramore Strand. According to Lewis 'a perforation in the rock through which the sea is forced during or immediately after a storm from the north-west, to a height of between 200 and 300 ft, with so great a noise as to be heard for 10 miles'. A fine cliff path leads

from here to TEMPLEBREAGA ARCH and other rock formations.
FORMER WORKHOUSE. On the Falcarragh Road. Two rubble
buildings with Elizabethan gables set side by side.
For CLONDEHORKY *see also* Ballymore *and* Creeslough.

INTRODUCTION

According to the Four Masters, the name Dungannon records the
fort or strong place of Geanaun, the son of Gathbhadh, a druid
priest who lived here about the C1. Nothing else is known of the
site until the C13, when the O'Neills moved from their great fort
of Grianan near Derry and made the place the heart of their
medieval kingdom, building a fort on the castle hill, which is still
the centre of the town. From here Donald O'Neill wrote to Pope
John XXII to complain of Norman depredations in Ulster in
1329, and to Edward III in 1364. About 1489 his descendant Con
O'Neill founded a monastery for Tertiary Franciscans at Dungannon; but the O'Neill power was in decline, and by 1498 the castle
had been taken by the forces of the Crown under the eighth Earl
of Kildare and two years later was demolished by the O'Donnells.
In 1542 another Con O'Neill was the first of his line to submit
to the English, accepting from Henry VIII the title of Earl of
Tyrone, while his heirs Shane and his nephew Hugh were to prove
formidable antagonists of Queen Elizabeth. It was Hugh O'Neill
who with the O'Donnell Earl of Tyrconnell fled from Ireland in
1607, leaving Ulster open to the Protestant Plantation of James I.
    Dungannon, like so much land in Ulster, was granted to Sir
Arthur Chichester, whom the *Calendar of State Papers* records
as building a new castle of limestone with 'a strong stone wall
and deep ditch with a counter scarp of stone to hold up the earth'
set round it. Masons and workmen were then removing the ruins
of the old castle still standing in 1611. Pynnar's Survey of 1619
found the fort existing as a 120 ft square with four half-bulwarks,
nine stone houses built on a good scale, five more in progress,
six timber-frame houses up, and six more under erection. A large
stone church and steeple had also been completed by this date.
Chichester obtained a charter of incorporation, and the re-grant
of a weekly market and two annual fairs – held in the central Market Street below the castle – already granted to Con O'Neill by
Elizabeth in 1587. All this thriving plantation community came

1. *Landscape:* The Sperrins, Co. Tyrone

2. *Landscape:* Slieve League, Co. Donegal, view from the summit with church ruins in the foreground

3. *Landscape:* Co. Tyrone near Fintona, air view

4. *Landscape:* St John's Point

5. *Townscape:* Londonderry, Clarendon Street

6. *Townscape:* Dungannon, Northland Row

7. *Townscape:* Enniskillen from the west, air view

8. Greenan, Grianan of Ailech, probably fifth or sixth century

9. Portnoo, Doon Fort, fifth or sixth century

10. Greenan, Grianan of Ailech, probably sixth century, restored 1874–8

11. Carndonagh, St Patrick's Cross, perhaps mid seventh century

12. Clogher Cathedral, slab cross, probably mid seventh century

13. Fahan, St Mura's Cross, probably late seventh century, east face

14. White Island, sculpted figures, perhaps ninth or tenth century

15. Maghera Old Church, sculpted lintel, c. 1100

16. Raphoe, St Eunan's Cathedral, sculpted lintel fragment, late ninth or early tenth century

17. Arboe High Cross, probably early tenth century, east face

18. Dungiven Priory, north-east corner of the nave showing timber-style construction in stone, late tenth or eleventh century and later

19. Feeny, Banagher Old Church, tomb of St Muriedach O'Heney, later twelfth century

20. Devenish Island, round tower, probably twelfth century

21. Devenish Island, round tower, sculpted head on the roof cornice, probably twelfth century

22. Devenish Island, St Molaise's House, carved *anta* base, eleventh century

23. Devenish Island, St Molaise's Church, south window, twelfth century

24. Feeny, Banagher Old Church, chancel window, c. 1150

25. Kinawley Old Church, east window, mid-fifteenth century

26. Derryvullan, Derrybrusk Old Church, east window,
late sixteenth century

27. Dungiven Priory, O'Cahan Tomb, late fifteenth century

28. Raphoe, St Eunan's Cathedral, sedilia and piscina, thirteenth century

29. Donegal, Franciscan Friary, cloisters, later fifteenth century

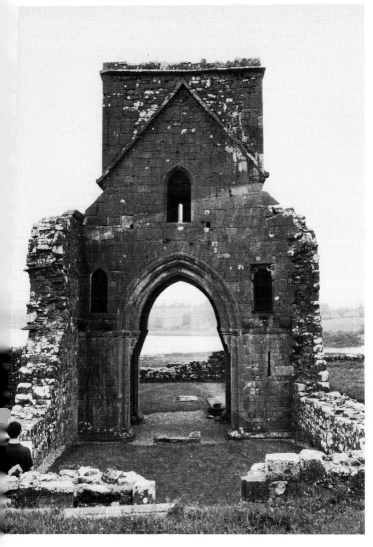

30. Devenish Island, St Mary's Abbey, Matthew O'Dubigan, master mason, 1449

31. Greencastle Castle, 1305 and fifteenth century

32. Pettigoe, Termon Castle, *c.* 1610

33. Creeslough, Doe Castle, sixteenth and seventeenth centuries

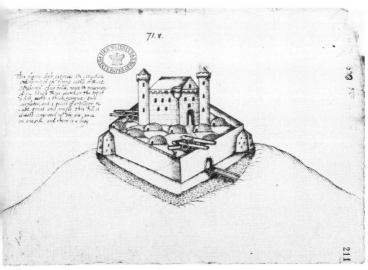

34. Newtowncunningham, Burt Castle, drawing dated 1599

35. Donegal Castle, Sir Basil Brooke's wing, *c.* 1616

36. Rathmullen, St Mary's Friary, fifteenth century and later,
converted to a fortified house *c.* 1617

37. Monea Castle, begun 1618

38. Augher, Spur Royal Castle, before 1613, with additions
by William Warren, 1832

39. Newtownstewart Castle, early seventeenth century

40. Newmills, Roughan Castle, 1618

41. Raphoe, Bishop's Palace, 1636, mid eighteenth century, and later

42. Donegal Castle, chimneypiece in the great hall, c. 1620

43. Londonderry, St Columb's Cathedral, William Parrott, builder, 1628–3 spire perhaps by John Bowden, 1822, chancel by J. G. Ferguson, 1885

44. Benburb, Clonfeacle Parish Church, 1618–22

45. Londonderry, St Columb's Cathedral, nave 1628, roof 1885

46. Castlecaulfield, Donaghmore Parish Church, nave window,
early seventeenth century

48. Coleraine Parish Church, monument to
Sir Tristram Beresford and his

47. Castlederg, Derg Parish Church, doorcase on the
tower, early seventeenth century

50. Artigarvan, Leckpatrick Parish Church, monument to Isabella Sinclair † 1673

49. Lifford, Clonleigh Parish Church, monument to Sir Richard and Dame Anne Hansard † 1619

51. Londonderry, the city walls looking from the double bastion down Grar
Parade to the Royal Bastion and Walker Memorial Column: walls 1613–18, colum
1826, blown up 1973

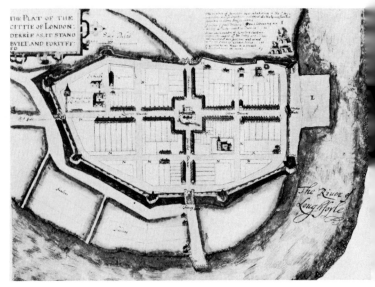

52. 'The plat of the Cittie of Londonderrie' from Sir Thomas Phillips's
Survey of 1622

53. Enniskillen Castle, Watergate, probably after 1607

54. Buncrana Castle, 1718

55. Lifford Court House, by Michael Priestley, 1746

56. Raphoe, Oakfield, 1739

57. Baronscourt, Agent's House, by James Martin, begun apparently in 1741, reduced by one storey *c.* 1781

58. Moneymore, Springhill, entrance front late seventeenth century, wings main house *c.* 1775

59. Moneymore, Springhill, staircase, perhaps late seventeenth century

60. St Johnstown, Dunmore House, *c.* 1742

61. St Johnstown, Dunmore House, five-panelled Georgian doors and lugged architraves

62. St Johnstown, Dunmore House, detail of the stair

63. Ballymore, St John, Clondehorky Parish Church, perhaps by
Michael Priestley, 1752

64. Clogher Cathedral, by James Martin, 1744, recast in 1818

65. Ballymore, St John, Clondehorky Parish Church, perhaps by
Michael Priestley, 1752

66. Clogher Cathedral, by James Martin, 1744

67. Mountjoy Forest, Cappagh Parish Church, 1768

68. Fivemiletown Parish Church, 1736–40

69. Ballykelly, Tamlaght Finlagan Parish Church, monument to
Mrs Jane Hamilton † 1716

70. Castledawson Parish Church, timber chimneypiece of *c.* 1750
re-employed as a memorial to George Robert Dawson † 1856

71. Florence Court, 1758 or 1764

72. Florence Court, Rococo plasterwork on the staircase

73. Caledon House, by Thomas Cooley, begun 1779, top floor and pavilion by John Nash, 1808–25

74. Castle Coole, by James Wyatt, 1790–7, entrance front

75. Castle Coole, by James Wyatt, 1790–7, garden front

76. Castle Coole, by James Wyatt, 1790–7, Saloon

77. Caledon House, colonnade by John Nash, 1808, portico entrance
by Thomas Duff, 1833

78. Caledon House, former front hall, by Thomas Cooley, begun 1779

Baronscourt, entrance front, by William Vitruvius Morrison, *c.* 1832, colonnades and reduced wings by Sir Albert Richardson, 1947

80. Colebrooke Park, by William Farrell, 1820

81. Killymoon Castle, by John Nash, *c.* 1802

82. Convoy House, 1806, gate lodge

83. Parkanaur, by Thomas Duff, 1802–48

84. Killymoon Castle, by John Nash, *c.* 1802, staircase

85. Crom Castle, by Edward Blore, 1834–6, main stair

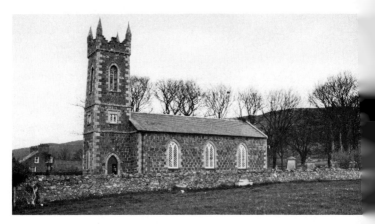

86. Limavady, Aghanloo Parish Church, by John Bowden, begun 1823

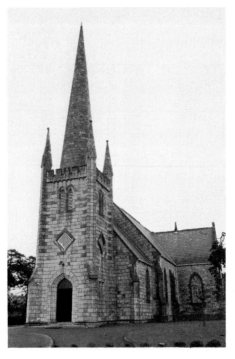

87. Cookstown, Derryloran Parish Church, tower and spire by John Nash,
c. 1820, church rebuilt 1859–61

88. Ballykelly Presbyterian Church, by Richard Suitor, 1827

89. Portsalon, Knockalla Fort, *c.* 1810

90. Rathmullen Fort and Battery, *c.* 1810

91. Drawing of martello tower of 1801 and battery of 1806–7 at Macamoosh Point,
Drumhallagh

92. St John's Point, lighthouse, by George Halpin, begun 1829

93. Omagh Court House, by John Hargrave, 1814, portico
1820, wing by W. J. Barre, 1863

94. Enniskillen Court House, c. 1785, portico by William Farrell, 1822

95. Londonderry Court House, by John Bowden, 1813–17

96. Limavady, Roe Valley Hospital (former Union Workhouse),
by George Wilkinson, 1841

97. Omagh, Provincial Bank of Ireland, probably by
W. G. Murray, 1864

98. Londonderry, Belfast Bank, by Sir Charles Lanyon, 1853

99. Coleraine Town Hall, by Thomas Turner, 1859

100. Magherafelt Court House, by Turner & Williamson, 1874

101. Coleraine, St John, Killowen, by J. Kirkpatrick, 1834

102. St Johnstown, St Baithen, by E. W. Godwin, 1857–60

103. Londonderry, Great James Street Presbyterian Church, by Stewart Gordon, 1835–7, remodelled by Boyd & Batt, 1863 (*Copyright Country Life*)

104. Rosnakil, Massmount Church, *c.* 1810 and later

105. Bundoran, Finner Parish Church, by William Hagerty, 1839–40

106. Coleraine, Knocktarna Parish Church, by Joseph Welland, 1851–5

107. Dungannon, Drumglass Parish Church, by W. J. Barre, begun 1865

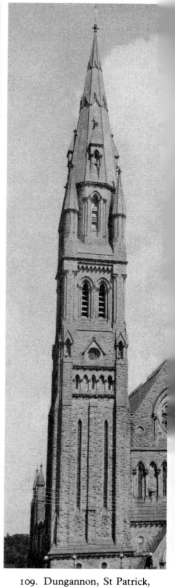

108. Londonderry, All Saints,
Waterside, by Lanyon,
Lynn & Lanyon, 1864–7

109. Dungannon, St Patrick,
Northland Row, by
J. J. McCarthy, begun 1867

110. Ballyronan, Ballyeglish Parish Church, The Loup, by Welland & Gillespie, 1866–9

111. Raphoe, St Eunan's Cathedral, chancel, restored by Thomas Drew, beginning in 1892

112. Killadeas, The Manor House, by William Armstrong, 1861–8,
entrance hall ceiling

113. Lough Eske Castle, by Fitzgibbon Louch, 1859–61

114. Fivemiletown, Blessingbourne, by F. P. Cockerell, completed 1874

115. Kildress, Wellbrook Beetling Mill, 1768

116. Sion Mills, Linen Spinning Mill, by W. H. Lynn, *c.* 1860

17. Londonderry, Magee College, New University of Ulster, by E. P. Gribbon, 1856–65

118. Londonderry, City Factory, by Young & Mackenzie, 1863

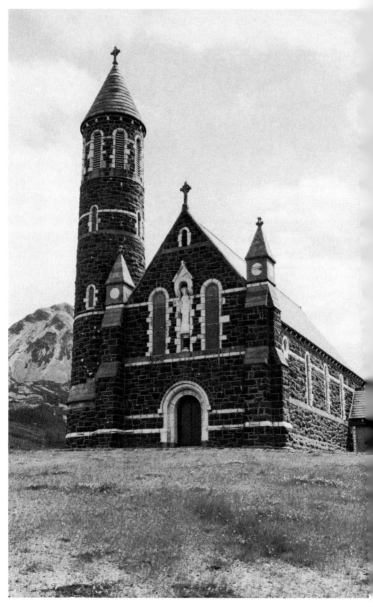

119. Dunlewey, Church of the Sacred Heart, by Timothy Hevey, 1877

o. Londonderry, St Eugene's Cathedral, by J. J. McCarthy, completed 1873,
spire by George C. Ashlin and E. J. Toye, 1900–3

121. Londonderry, St Eugene's Cathedral, interior

122. Omagh, Church of the Sacred Heart, by William Hague, 1893–9

123. Killygordon, St Patrick, by O'Neill & Byrne, 1893–5

124. Letterkenny, St Eunan's Cathedral, by William Hague and T. F. McNamara, 1891–1901

125. Coleraine, St Malachy, Nursery Avenue, by Padraig Gregory, 1937

126. Kilcar, St Cartha, by Doolin, Butler & Donelly, 1903–4

127. Burt, St Aengus, by Liam McCormick, 1965–7

128. Strabane First Presbyterian Church, by Thomas Houston, 1955

129. Enniskillen Collegiate School, extension by Shanks & Leighton, 1967

130. Coleraine, New University of Ulster, first phase, by Robert Matthew, Johnson-Marshall & Partners, 1968–77

o an end with Phelim O'Neill's rebellion; the town was seized
n 1641 and burnt in 1646.

Though the church was repaired in 1656 and again in 1671,
he reconstruction of Dungannon did not properly begin until the
Chichesters had sold out to a new owner of Scottish stock,
Thomas Knox, in 1692. The church was rebuilt in that year, and
the Knox vault that still remains in the churchyard was put up
in 1696. Towards the end of the next century a new and powerful
political force, the Ulster delegation of the Volunteers, met twice
in Dungannon, in 1782 and 1783, and in 1791 it was proposed
to erect a column both in honour of Lord Charlemont and to
record the volunteer meetings held in the town. Nothing came
of this proposal, and in the end the architectural development of
Dungannon was to be more indebted to the growing importance
of its linen and brick-making industries, and to the coal found
to the E near Lough Neagh at Drumglass and Lurgaloy, than to
political events. The assets of the town were all developed by the
Knox family. At first they lived in a town house by the market
square, but about 1740 (apparently because one Mrs Knox had
been horrified by the spectacle of a public execution carried out
opposite her drawing-room windows) they moved to Farm Hill,
now in Dungannon Park, to the SE, and towards the end of the
century settled in the newly built Northland House on the E edge
of the town. Neither house remains today, and the family who
rose through the Irish peerage to become Earls of Ranfurly by
1831 left Dungannon in the 1920s. Though intended in the time
of Chichester to be the county town of Tyrone, Dungannon had
by the early C19 surrendered this claim to Omagh. The population
throughout the C19 remained surprisingly static: 3,800 in 1841;
3,694 in 1901. By 1971 it had almost doubled to 7,535.

CHURCHES

ST ANNE, DRUMGLASS PARISH (C of I). 1865. Rebuilt on the 107
site of Drumglass parish church to designs of *W. J. Barre* of
Belfast, whose masterpiece this is. Any views of Dungannon,
but especially those from the S and W, will be dominated by
the lumbering mass of this bulky Gothic church rising above
the roofs of the houses, and closing the view up Perry Street
and Church Street with an emphatic gable window, tower, and
broach-spire. Barre was one of the best and most vigorous High
Victorian architects working in Ulster, and this design, completed just before the disestablishment of the Church of Ireland
in 1869, is both full of confidence and unimpeded by financial

restraints. It cost £8,500, and because of the weight of the
materials makes extensive use of inverted relieving arches under
the traceried windows and buried in the ground between the
aisle and the transept piers.

The plan is that of a large cruciform church (liturgically reversed) with four-bay nave, two-bay transepts, and a short
chancel. On the N (street) side is a lean-to aisle with a double-
gabled porch, in front of an offset belfry tower with an elaborate
broach-spire. The material is squared rubble sandstone with
generous E.E. Gothic detail: clustered columns and keel
mouldings.

The best impression of the rich interior comes on entering
through the N transept, where the view through the E.E.
column piers of the arcade to the balcony across the back of
the nave is highly promising – a mixture of warm round shafts
of sandstone, bright accents of light from the nave windows,
high dark arcade arches, and a glistening pine-fronted gallery
glowing aggressively in the distance. Walk into the nave itself
and this Burges-like vitality is somehow diminished. The lack
of an aisle on the S side creates a rather bare space, though the
asymmetrical plan is by no means a visual failure. Barre has
used the high braced trusses with exposed purlins common to
Welland & Gillespie and has supported the trusses themselves
on polished stone colonnettes that come down to clerestory
level. The transepts and chancel open through moulded
chamfered arches on half-columns. Note Barre's wilful details
in the cramped stair to the gallery and the clumsy trefoil-arched
entrance in pine that opens into the side aisle. The chancel furniture is of 1910 by *Purdy & Millard*. Panelling of 1933. –
FONT. 1876. Chamfered marble octagon on colonnettes. –
PULPIT. 1874. A Caen stone octagon with an open arcaded
front on pink and black colonnettes. – STAINED GLASS.
Chancel E window to the third and fourth Earls of Ranfurly:
Christ healing, teaching, risen, and triumphant. Almost Pre-
Raphaelite in brown, grey, and olive green. – Stevenson
memorial window by *A. K. Nicholas* of London. – Second
World War window by *James Powell & Sons*. – Also windows
by *W. F. Clokey* and *A. E. Child*. – MONUMENT. An inscribed
slab of Penelope Knox † 1696 aged 7.

109 ST PATRICK, Northland Row. An ambitious design of 1867 that,
if it were not on a lower site at the end of Northland Row, might
vie with Barre's St Anne for the dominance of the town. By
J. J. McCarthy; it took a long time to build and was completed

by *Charles J. McCarthy* in 1889. Not as solid as Barre's church or McCarthy's own design at Cookstown, yet enhanced by a noble C13-style spire, 195 ft high, that contributes notably to the skyline of the town. The proportions are a little attenuated, in a way that is typical of McCarthy, but the main front is good. Gabled, with a solid porch surrounded by a slant podium, a seven-bay arcade with plinths for three statues, and above this a wheel window in an ashlar frame flanked by colonnettes. An aisle to the E and an offset tower, belfry, and spire to the W. The door is a double design with shoulder arches supporting a carved tympanum of St Patrick preaching. Notice the neat detailing that incorporates holy water stoups in the reveals of the entrance arches.

The interior is lofty and generously provided with sculptural detail. Five-bay arcaded nave with round piers and deeply undercut foliated capitals. Clerestory of paired sexfoil windows alternating between pine shafts that brace the high hipped roof. Chancel lit by paired lancets with wheel window above. Elaborate choir gallery at the back, in pine, supported on paired granite shafts as in St Eugene's Cathedral, Derry. – ALTAR. Elaborate pinnacled reredos in Caen stone by *C. J. McCarthy*. – The LADY CHAPEL, carefully detailed in a French Gothic style, has good modern STAINED GLASS by *D. I. Branie*.

FIRST DUNGANNON PRESBYTERIAN CHURCH, Scotch Street. 1854–8, with transepts of 1870. Built by the Rev. Dr Morell. Lumpy Gothic in style, in polygonal basalt with sandstone trim. Three-stage, much stepped offset tower. Plate-traceried windows in the transepts.

Despite appearances the church is historic, for it re-uses the walls of the C18 Presbyterian meeting house. This was a long six-bay hall with galleries at either end and paired round-headed windows flanking the pulpit in the centre. The General Assembly of the Presbyterian Church in Ulster held its meeting here on no fewer than twenty-five occasions in the C18, and it was here that the Volunteers met in 1783, when the Bishop of Derry and fifteen members of the Irish House of Commons attended the meeting at which the Rev. Dr Black of Derry 'electrified the auditory' with his patriotic speech.

METHODIST CHURCH, Perry Street. 1850. A five-bay hall with lancet windows and a Gothic gable front divided into three parts by pinnacled flat buttresses – lancet, door with three lancets over, lancet.

PUBLIC BUILDINGS

DUNGANNON ROYAL SCHOOL, Northland Row. Founded b
letters patent of Charles I in 1628 and first based at Mountjo
Fort. By 1726 it had transferred to a lane near the High Stree
and in 1786 was established on the present site in a buildin;
erected by Primate Robinson that cost £4,626 8s. 2d. It look
very much like an ordinary Irish country house of the period
a five-bay, three-storey, cement-rendered Georgian bloc
with corner quoins, later central porch, and two-store;
gabled wings on each side, flush with the front, but extending
behind the main block to enclose a garden court. The back end;
of the wings were joined in 1850 by an open arcade of ten four-
centred arches, built by the Lord Primate to provide coverec
recreation space. The large-scale Italianate extensions to the
s, including a hall and square tower with corbelled eaves, are
by *John McCurdy*, 1860–1.

The STATUE before the school of an old boy, Brigadier
General John Nicholson (1822–57), by *T. Brock*, 1905, was
brought from the Kashmir Gate, Delhi, in 1960.

COURT HOUSE, George Street. 1830 by *John Hargrave*. Curiously small and insignificant, a three-bay, two-storey ashlar
front with a long eight-bay side, projecting on the second and
seventh bay, built down the slope of the hill to become three
storeys with cells in the bottom. The front has four pilaster-
like buttresses, a salient cornice – but no entablature – and a
heavy block balustrade with plinths above the pilasters. Central
royal coat of arms flanked by 'G' and 'IV' in wreaths. Later
projecting porch. Astylar, like Smirke or Robert Reid.

CHARLES SHIEL'S INSTITUTION. 1867 by *Lanyon, Lynn &
Lanyon*. An attractive group of almshouses, symmetrically laid
out, in a chunky Gothic idiom. Two-storey, with gabled ends
and half-dormers in the links between. Central louvred clock
tower above a bold Gothic doorway with colonnettes. Built of
local sandstone rubble with bright red sandstone and green slate
bands. High Victorian taste.

TOUR

The character of Dungannon, though recently much battered by
bombing and ill-conceived improvements, is still perhaps sufficient to justify a tour on foot. The centre of the town is the
MARKET SQUARE, a broad street, lined by plain Georgian-
type C19 houses, that runs down from the castle hill in a SW

direction. It opens at its lower end to the cross streets of IRISH STREET on the w and CHURCH STREET on the e, while the narrower SCOTCH STREET runs steeply on downhill in the same line as the Market Square. These three streets composed the core of the town until the mid C19, with a limited growth of gentlemen's houses to the E in PERRY STREET and NORTHLAND ROW that led to the Royal School and to Northland House. Industry is represented by a brewery, distillery, linen mills, and bleaching greens developed in the broad curve of low-lying ground to the SW, where the streams associated with Ballysaggart Lough provided a convenient source of power.

Starting at the top of Market Square, Dungannon presents one of the most striking architectural combinations to be met with in all Ulster: the Venetian Gothic former NORTHERN BANK and the Baronial fortress of the POLICE BARRACKS. The first, built for the Belfast Bank in 1855 by W. H. Lynn, in a Ruskinian Gothic very similar to that used again by him for the same bank in Newtownards, Co. Down, is of squared rubble, with an emphatic corbel eaves cornice, and slender colonnettes running up the whole height of each corner. Two-storey façade, divided in traditional Venetian Gothic pattern in an a–b–a rhythm. Outer single windows with cusped heads. A *trifora* between on the first floor with *quadrifora* below to light the banking hall. The barracks to the r. was built for the Royal Irish Constabulary in 1871 by the architect to the Board of Works, *James H. Owen*: 'Following soon after the Fenian Rising scare of 1867–8 it owes its semi-castellated style,' according to J. J. Marshall, 'to the endeavour of the authorities to combine both a defensible post and a barracks.' Hence no doubt the exposed outer stair to the door at first-floor level, and the drawn-up crow-stepped tower with aggressive machicolation that overrides the tops of surrounding buildings in the corner of the square.

CASTLE HILL runs N from the side of Lynn's bank to a fine late Georgian house on the l. – five-bay, two-storey, with pedimented doorcase – and on the r. to the grounds of O'NEILL'S CASTLE, where the O'Neill stronghold and Chichester's fort were and where one folly-like round tower still remains of the mansion built by Thomas Knox Harrington about 1780 or 90. The castle was a square with a round tower at each corner and a central entrance bow. Its style was old-fashioned for its date, and by 1856 it was already a ruin. The tower has an ashlar stone top with bracketed machicolation, and is of rubble

stone below, with brick dressings to the pointed windows. Back
in the MARKET SQUARE, No. 7 on the W side is a handsome
three-storey house with wide tripartite windows and segmental
arches on the ground floor. Below Thomas Street in the square,
the ULSTER BANK of 1921 is by *Blackwood & Jury* in an irre-
verent classical style with paired sash-windows between meanly
scaled Ionic giant columns. Not a serious design. The First
World War Memorial – a statue of a soldier with gun and flag
– is by *F. W. Pomeroy*.

Now r. into CHURCH STREET, with the massive modelling of
St Anne's faced across the street by modest two-storey houses.
E of the church the big brick terrace of shops with Gothic
dormers is of 1878. Straight on down PERRY STREET and
NORTHLAND PLACE to NORTHLAND HOUSE LODGE – all
that remains of the Ranfurly house, an elegant Greek Revival
lodge of ashlar sandstone (as was the house) with pedimented
central bay flanked by pseudo-peripteral Ionic loggias, possibly
by *Robert Woodgate*. Banal new buildings of the Royal School
by *Hobart & Heron* appear behind.

Back at the E end of Perry Street, NORTHLAND ROW runs N,
past DRUMGLASS PARISH HALL of 1884 with its big geometric tracery window, to the spire of St Patrick's church. The
Royal School (p. 260) is on the E, and opposite Nos. 12–26 form
6   one of the most handsome Georgian terraces in the North of
Ireland, eight houses, each of three storeys on a basement,
mostly four-bay, but with three five-bay houses, one with a carriage archway. Each has a substantial stone doorcase with Gibbs
surround. The interiors have six-panel doors of *c.* 1760 and
timber stairs with Tuscan column newels. The stables of No.
26 are dated 1762. Beyond the classical terrace is HOWARD
TERRACE, a row of nine Victorian Gothic houses of ashlar
sandstone with alternate arcaded mullioned windows and
canted bays, and big gables and sandstone dormers at roof level.
As fine in their way as the Georgian work that precedes them.
Notice the French Gothic detail round the doors and the polychromatic bands in the slate roofs. The CONVENT OF MERCY
opposite and ST PATRICK'S ACADEMY further E are both of
squared rubble in a traditional Catholic Institutional style,
severe and purposeful. 1893 and 1907.

Beyond St Patrick's church the CIRCULAR ROAD leads past
some recent and some early C19 houses to DUNGANNON
TECHNICAL COLLEGE of 1879, a three-bay, two-storey
square of brick with stone quoins, string courses, and window

surrounds, and a hipped mansard roof with French attic dormers. Beyond is Shiel's Institution (p. 260), and then, turning w, at the junction of CARLAND ROAD and THOMAS STREET, to the N, SOUTH TYRONE HOSPITAL, built on the site of the 1841 Union Workhouse of *George Wilkinson*. The usual five-bay Tudoresque front survives, with a later s wing ending in a tall gabled tower. The modern buildings are by *Huston & Beaumont* of 1962. From here THOMAS STREET leads back to the MARKET SQUARE, passing the ornate yet diminutive RESERVOIR GATE of 1931 – a miniature folly castle, worthy of Claude Lorraine were it not in cement, with one round and one square tower linked by a balustraded arch. Beyond, the MASONIC HALL, early c20, has fluted Corinthian pilasters in stucco and a central pediment. And so back to the Square.

The w sector of the town can hardly be arranged as a consecutive tour. There are some nice c18 houses still in SCOTCH STREET, notably No. 36, a big five-bay, two-storey house with a good pattern-book pedimented door surround. Remnants of a similar house opposite. The PROVINCIAL BANK OF IRELAND is of *c.* 1890, a two-bay block of rock-faced sandstone rubble with shoulder-headed arch and triangular dormer pediments. The NORTHERN BANK is 1920s classical in brick and Portland stone. IRISH STREET is pleasantly scaled, with stepped and curving two-storeyed houses. It leads to ANNE STREET, at the head of which stood GORTMERRON HOUSE, latterly the Technical College but at the time of writing derelict. This late Palladian house was once the most sophisticated piece of architecture in the town. Built about 1780 by John Wilcocks, a local bleacher, it had a five-bay sandstone front with a rusticated ground floor, corner quoins, and a fluted string course below the first-floor windows. Round-headed ground-floor windows with cobweb-pattern glazing bars. The central doorcase, a tripartite design with Tuscan columns and broken pediment, is surmounted by a Venetian window with a Diocletian window above. In BROOKE STREET the pretty row of forty-six Victorian cottages was erected by the Board of Public Works in 1872 at a cost of £1,650.

NEIGHBOURHOOD

The loss of Northland House and of the castle has removed the two great houses in the town. Those that remain are more modest.

MILLTOWN HOUSE. Below Brooke Street on the southern outskirts. Early C19. An unusual symmetrical stucco block. Three-bay, two-storey centre with a segmental-arched doorcase approached by a wide flight of steps and flanked by long single-storey wings of two bays. All on a semi-basement. At the back is a more substantial four-bay, three-storey addition joined to the old house by a wide corridor with an attractive double return staircase.

Milltown belonged in 1841 to John Falls, owner of the distillery, who was the first man to stand as a Liberal in the election that year in opposition to the Knox family interest. With only 167 voters out of a population of 3,800 he was not returned, but his successors in the house, T. A. Dickson and James Dickson, successfully opposed the Ranfurly ascendancy in 1874 and 1880.

KILLYMEAL HOUSE. To the NE, off Killymeal Road. A nice five-bay, two-storey house on a high basement with flanking bow-fronted single-storey wings. Late C18. The door is approached by a flight of stone steps and framed by a good sandstone aedicule of pattern-book type with three-quarter Tuscan columns and broken pediment. Eaves cornice of stone. The proportions rather high. The thin fluted columns attached to the sides of the windows in the wings are an odd feature. A lease of the house was granted to William Murray, headmaster of the Royal School, in 1791, and it may have been he who added the wings.

DUNGANNON PARK FARM. 1½ km SE. An attractive mid C18 stable court. Two storeys of rubble sandstone with some brick trim. The E front appears outside like the façade of a country house, with a five-bay, two-storey centre with projecting single-bay wings, that to the N with a round bow of three windows. Within the courtyard the carriage arch and coach houses have round heads with circular *œils de bœuf* to light the lofts.

DUNGIVEN

ST MARY'S PRIORY. 1 km S. Approached by a lane from the E entrance to Dungiven village. There is believed to have been an early monastery here whose C7 church is traditionally associated with St Naechtain. The present ruins, like the nearby church of Banagher, are originally of two periods: an early rectangular nave, some 43 ft by 21 ft, of the late C10 or C11; and a chancel, 23 ft by 17½ ft, added in the early C14 and now approached through a yet later C17 semicircular arch. The priory was suppressed by 1603 and was subsequently adapted as a Protestant church until the building was abandoned about 1720 for a new church in the village.

Constant reworking and adaptation have made the building remains complex. The earliest details are to be seen at the outside NE and SE corners of the nave and the base courses of the 18 S wall, all of which project to copy in stone the earlier post-and-transom patterns of the timber-built churches of central Ireland. These 'timber' corners, and a small round-headed window on the S wall of the nave (which has inclined jambs and a broad flat projecting border like Banagher), are the only elements of the C10 church.

About 1140 the Priory became Augustinian, at the instance of the O'Cahans, who on becoming lords of the district also became its benefactors. Some time after this change to Augustinian rule the E wall of the church was rebuilt to incorporate a sequence of colonnetted niches, portions of which have been exposed inside the nave at the NE and SE corners. This work must have been largely obliterated by the creation of the chancel arch when the church was enlarged in the early C14, though the base course for the arch can still be traced on the S side, built into the wall of the narrow Jacobean archway. The chancel itself is lit by the usual paired lancets in the E wall and was apparently intended to be stone-vaulted, as capitals, rings, and bases remain in the corners. The line of the vault has been suggested on the restored E gable wall.

On the S wall of the chancel the O'CAHAN TOMB preserves 27 the finest piece of late medieval tracery in North West Ulster, with beneath the only complete sculptured effigy in the four counties. The canopy of the tomb, the effigy itself, and the figures in the arcaded face of the tomb front have been restored. Identifications of the main figure have included Cumhaighe O'Cahan, who flourished around 1260, and Cooey na Gall O'Cahan, who died in 1385. Neither is satisfactory. A C13 date is stylistically too early and, while the late C14 would be possible for the flowing curvilinear tracery of the wall canopy, the cusped elliptical arch below is more like late medieval work; the bowtell-moulded frames round the eight figures of the tomb front are debased and equally late. John Hunt (in *Irish Medieval Figure Sculpture*) argues for a date in the late C15 and points out similarities between this figure and that of a Burke knight at Glinsk, Co. Galway, of the early C16. In 1970 the

chancel was roofed and the arch filled in with a rather blank
timber partition to protect the tomb.

ST PATRICK'S WELL. N of the church by a hawthorn tree.
Apparently an old font stone used now to charm away warts.

DUNGIVEN PARISH CHURCH (C of I). 1816. Cruciform, and
expensively built of coursed squared ashlar sandstone with dia-
mond-jointed quoins and simplified Gibbs surrounds to the
Gothic windows. Tower in two stages with octagonal finials
at the W end. Thin and not effective. The interior is very
curious, with segmental plaster ceilings on flat arches. Renovated in 1891. – STAINED GLASS by *Mayer & Co.*

ST PATRICK. 1877 by *O'Neill & Byrne.* A high and hard French-
style hall with arcaded aisles and a semicircular chancel. Six-
bay, double-chamfered arcade on columns, with paired quatrefoil clerestory windows above and a panelled wagon roof. The
pastel painting scheme does nothing for this fine High Gothic
interior.

PRESBYTERIAN CHURCH. A six-bay gabled hall, in course of
erection in 1837. Front rebuilt in a Flamboyant Gothic vein by
Samuel McCartney in 1908.

DUNGIVEN CASTLE. Built on the site of the Skinners' Bawn
in 1604–11. The E and W walls remain, with two big Gothic
gateways knocked through them at the S end. This was the
largest Plantation bawn – 150 ft by 200 ft. It had a platform for
defence carried on an arcaded basement, two of whose arches
survived at the N end of the E wall until 1972. There are also
cross-shaped gun loops in the E wall and remains of the square
NW flanker.

Between the two walls at the S end is the early C19 house
built by Robert Ogilby of Pellipar in 1839 and never completed
inside. The façade towards the bawn is dull except for a small
round tower in the centre that carries the stair. The front overlooking the Roe Valley is more self-consciously architectural,
a long, castle-style façade with two five-bay, two-storey ranges
connecting three towers. Those at the end are circular, that in
the middle is octagonal with heavy machicolations, and all have
stepped Irish battlements. The style is identical with the additions made to the now demolished Derry prison; so the castle
is probably by the same architect, the then County Surveyor,
Stewart Gordon.

PELLIPAR HOUSE. 1.5 km N. A big Frenchified mansion of the
Ogilby family ingeniously contrived in 1907 out of an earlier
house. There are at least three buildings here. The first is a

small gentleman's house, late C18, of two storeys, with a central hall and a room lit by two windows on either side. Then about 1800 this house received additional single-storey wings, nicely built of dressed ashlar blocks with big Georgian relieving arches, and, behind the E addition, a two-storey servants' wing. The front door was also enlarged. Further work was undertaken in 1866 to designs of *Fitzgibbon Louch*, but this has largely been submerged in the grandiose remodelling of 1907 which added an extra storey to the wings with bay-windows below, and re-roofed the entire house with high mansard roofs pierced by pedimented stone dormers and enriched by high chimneys. In the centre of the back of the house a round stair tower was added with a high conical roof that rises high enough to be felt on the entrance front.

GATE LODGE. A pair of three-bay, single-storey lodges of *c.* 1800, of dressed sandstone, with pediments over the central bay and windows in relieving arches.

DUNGLOE   DO B4

A long street running N–S and crossing the Dungloe river by a narrow bridge at the middle. 'It is small', says the *Parliamentary Gazetteer* of 1846, 'and signally sequestered but possesses a sort of irksome importance from being the only apology for a town within an extensive range of dreary and island flanked sea-board.' Architecturally this is still true, but we have learnt in the C20 to value sequestered settings. The only building of any value in Dungloe, the Northern Bank office by the bridge, built in 1886 by *G. W. Ferguson*, has recently been demolished. It had a bold slate pyramid roof and was boldly detailed in granite. The castle near which Spanish cannons were found in the C18 has long disappeared.

TEMPLECRONE PARISH CHURCH (C of I). To the N, by the shore. Built in 1760 at a cost of £400. A small stone hall with three round-headed windows in the s wall, one in the N. The chancel is formed inside the rectangle of the church. w porch. All whitewashed.

ST PETER. Crowning a hill at the s end of the street. A big, airy T-plan church. Mid C19. Whitewashed, with Y-tracery lancets. Pine-panelled inside, with high galleries in each arm. This is probably the improvement made by *E. J. Toye* in 1895.

TEMPLECRONE OLD CHURCH. 5.5 km WSW, on Termon peninsula, N of Maghery Bay. The rubble walls remain of a rectangular church, 45 ft by 18½ ft inside, with a stone partition forming a vestibule at the w end. Both gables are almost entire, and the e window is of an interesting early type, late C12 or early C13, narrow outside, widely splayed within, with a double roll and cavetto moulding at the edge. There are credence cavities in the s and e walls. Ruined by the early C17, the church was repaired about 1622 and continued in use until 1829. The site is connected with Cróine, a Christian virgin and a relative of St Colmcille. Her festival and *turas* is performed here on 7 July. The present church was built by the O'Duffy family, the medieval superiors of the lands. Today it is surrounded by a high wall and is full of gunnera and cow parsley.

SIGNAL TOWER. 6.5 km wsw on Crohy Head. One of the more accessible of the early C19 coastguard towers that dot the Donegal coast. A grim, square block, the wall to the landward side formed into a slight salient (is this because it has the fireplaces and chimneys inside?) and protected at the corners by machicolated angle bartizans. The entrance is one floor up. The w face is also protected by a corbelled central bartizan. (The gabled buildings with square chimneys N of the tower by the shore are the ruins of a C19 distillery.)

For TEMPLECRONE *see also* Burton Port.

A village consisting of one long street of substantial houses in open fertile countryside. Early C19.

KILLAGHTEE OLD CHURCH AND CROSS. 1.5 km wsw, in an old graveyard. A rectangular church, 19 ft wide inside. Little remains except the e gable and half the s wall, all ivy-covered. The e window has interesting later Romanesque detail: a round-headed lancet with a roll moulding outside and widely splayed inside, with a moulded frame of three rounded shafts, one a keel moulding, but treated like a bundle of sticks. Probably mid C12. Later segment-headed window on the s wall.

s of the church is an interesting early CROSS SLAB of *c.* 650–700. Shaped circular head, very slightly wider than the shaft on which it is set, with a Greek cross with splayed arms set in relief in a circular border. A triquetra in raised work is carved a little to one side on the shaft below. The cross is small, yet possesses a distinctly monumental quality representing a transition from the early inscribed slabs, that are mere engraving, to the more fully developed shaped high crosses.

RAHAN CASTLE. 2 km SW. On a narrow promontory with the
sea on three sides, like Kilbarron Castle further S. Possibly C15;
built by the McSwiney Barragh. Little now remains beyond
one section of high wall curved at its E end to take a stair, and
a vaulted chamber with one single-chamfered slit window
further W.

KILLAGHTEE PARISH CHURCH (C of I). 1827. A pretty
miniature tower and hall type church. Two-bay rendered hall.
Tower of squared coursed stone unusually elongated and
breaking into very unorthodox corbels, battlements, and shafts
above the belfry. Interior little changed since the church was
built.

BRUCKLESS CHURCH. 2.5 km NW. 1913 by *E. J. Toye* of Derry.
A large cruciform church similar to Ardara, with simple Norman detailing. Three-bay nave with round-headed paired lancets. The transepts are lit by paired gables with porches in the
angles. E window of three round-headed lancets. Rose window
in the W gable. – ROUND TOWER. Four-storey, rebuilt on old
foundations in the C19.

BRUCKLESS HOUSE. S of the church. A substantial three-bay,
two-storey house with hipped roof and central chimneystacks.
Built by two Cassidy brothers *c.* 1760, though it looks at present
more like 1830. Late C18 doors inside and a fine cobbled yard
behind.

KILLAGHTEE GLEBE HOUSE. A tall, regular-fronted three-
storey house of *c.* 1790.

DUNLEWEY   DO C3

CHURCH OF THE SACRED HEART. There is something almost [119]
threatening in the juxtaposition of this church and the huge
humped form of Errigal behind it. Apart from the church with
a few white gravestones round it the landscape is bare, stony,
and treeless. It was built in 1877 at the cost of William Augustine Ross of Curzon Street, Mayfair, who had recently bought
the Dunlewey estate. The architect is *Timothy Hevey*, elaborat-
ing here on a formula he had already tried at St Eunan's,
Raphoe: that of a long church with a semicircular sanctuary
end covered by the one high roof. An offset round tower 95 ft
high is on the N side of the W gable. The scale is just right –
big enough for the grandeur of the setting but not overblown
– and because there was money for this commission there is
more enrichment than at Raphoe. The walls of rock-faced

basalt rubble are trimmed with bands of grey stone and loc.
white marble. A statue of Christ is set in a hooded canop
between the w windows over the main door, and the roof, her
a prominent feature, is enlivened with two bands of paler slate:
Inside, the chancel is framed by paired colonnettes supportin
a semicircular truss. The ceiling is panelled in pine.

DUNLEWEY CHURCH. At the head of the lough, a roofles
chapel of ease of 1844. Once rather pretty. Four-bay lancet ha
with short chancel and delicate tower of white limestone witl
grey stone trim. It was only used for a few years while its firs
and only rector resided here. Unroofed in 1955.

DUNLEWEY HOUSE. By the church ruins on the s side of the
lough, a five-bay, two-storey house with a battlemented wing
and Tudor label mouldings. Early C19; built by the Dambrene
family.

DUNMORE HOUSE see ST JOHNSTOWN

DUNNAMANAGH

A village in well wooded rural surroundings, founded by Sir John
Drummond, who was granted the greater part of the parish of
Donagheady by James I.

ST JAMES, DONAGHEADY PARISH CHURCH (C of I). Built
in 1877 to replace a classical church of 1788. Cruciform, with
three-bay nave and a tower and octagonal needle spire between
the N transept and the chancel. Walls of dressed rubble stone
with sandstone trim. Remarkably bare, with no buttresses or
superfluous detail. Geometrical tracery, and quatrefoil parapet
to the tower. – STAINED GLASS. E window: the Ascension,
1894.

ST PATRICK. 1968 by *Patrick Haughey*. An impressive if relent-
less modern church, the prototype for the same architect's work
at Strabane. A five-sided polygon, with polygonal rubble-stone
walls interrupted only on one side, where the walls turn out
to flank a wide row of glass doors. The walls rise well above
eye-level and support a continuous clerestory, seven rectangular windows to each side, faced in sheet aluminium and recessed
with sloping reveals and a high upper fascia that gives a perspective effect. The roof is a very shallow pyramid and the whole
building sits on a gently sloping paved base, like the glacis of
a star fort or the stylobate of a Greek temple, with a stone cut
drain in a channel all round. The mass of the building, as un-

compromisingly pure as a centrally planned Renaissance church, seems almost to benefit by the sea of tarmac that surrounds it. The interior is theatrical: literally in the arrangement of its seats as if round an apron stage, and emotionally in the way that light is focused on the altar. The windows are filled with stained glass to suggest the rippling lines of the hills in the surrounding country.

DONAGHEADY FIRST PRESBYTERIAN CHURCH. 1876 by *William McElwee*. A five-bay stone hall with plate-tracery rose window and bellcote. The congregation dates from 1658.

CASTLE RUIN. On the s bank of the river, the shell of an interesting C18 Gothick castle built by the Hamilton family on the site of Sir John Drummond's bawn. The plan was apparently a double pile with a five-bay, three-storey s front with arched windows to the top floor and a forestanding round tower in the central bay.

EARL'S GIFT RECTORY. 1792. A large whitewashed Georgian house with sash windows. Five-bay, two-storey, with a two-storey porch and classical doorcase.

OLD CHURCH. 2 km NE. Only the blank gables of a rectangular church, 19 ft wide, survive.

MOUNTCASTLE. 3 km NW. The ruins of a Plantation castle built by Sir Claude Hamilton in 1619 on his estate of Eden. A fragment of one corner remains, about 18 ft high, with the corbelled courses for a round, typically Scottish angle bartizan. The walls are 3 ft 3 in. wide on a base of huge boulders.

ALTNACHREE CASTLE. 4 km E. Built by C. W. L. Ogilby, a scion of the family of Ardnargle and Pellipar House. The gaunt ruin of an enormous late Victorian castle, staring blankly across a denuded park. A seven-bay, three-storey block with central four-storey turret. Two rooms deep, with a wide corridor running from one end of the house to the other. Hall in the middle with the stairs behind. Built of regular boulder-faced stone with all the courses the same. Boxy, and probably better as a ruin. GATE LODGE, E of the house. A machicolated archway.

DUNNY BOE BRIDGE. 1831. A single-arched masonry bridge built by *Edward Shearer*.

For DONAGHEADY *see also* Artigarvan.

EDERNY   FM *E7*

This village is no more than a group of houses round a cross roads with a modern development of grey brick council housing. At

the cross roads is the MARKET HOUSE, built for the Rev. Wes
about 1838, a three-bay, two-storey stone front in the same
simplified Classical style as Lisnaskea and Newtownbutle
market houses.

ST JOSEPH. By *J. A. Tynan*, Romanesque of 1954, in artificial
stone, with a short green slated tower and an asphalt car park
before it. The interior is surprising, bathed in yellow light with
yellow terrazzo floors and a five-bay round-headed arcade on
each side of the nave. E end elaborately decorated with mosaic.
Two mosaic apses, top-lit through flat oculi, terminate the
aisles. Sanctuary square with more mosaic and fifteen vesica-
shaped tile pictures of the life of Christ round the walls.

There are three tiny rural CHURCHES nearby: the Catholic
church at DRUMSAWRA, 3 km ESE, 1929, Gothic Revival survival; COLAGHTY Parish Church (C of I) at Keeran, 5 km
ENE, a four-bay lancet hall of 1845; and TIRWINNY Methodist Church, 3.5 km NE, a two-bay hall with Y-tracery, built in
1870.

KILTIERNEY GRANGE RUINS.* 2.5 km S, in Castle Archdale
Deer Park, the foundations of three buildings of a grange of
the Cistercian abbey of Assaroe. This is thought to be the site
of an early monastery, and the earthen circular enclosure that
once surrounded it can still be traced.

G3   EGLINTON   LD

A scattered village in the parish of Faughanvale with an unusually
elegant Court and Market House at its centre.

OLD COURT HOUSE. Built for the Grocers' Company in 1823–
5 to designs of *Michael Angelo Nicholson*, son of the well-known
early C19 writer of architectural handbooks, Peter Nicholson.
Up-to-date in its reticent detailing, but then it should be, coming from London. A stone cube, ashlar throughout, with
dressed quoins and big mutules to the overhanging eaves cornice. The roof is slated and rises as a shallow pyramid to a
central chimneystack. Two-storey, three-bay on each side. The
ground floor originally open arcades; the upper-floor windows
round-headed and set in relieving arches. Blank arches at the
sides.

ST CANICE, FAUGHANVALE PARISH CHURCH (C of I). 1821.
Originally a typical and rather pretty tower and hall type

* Not visited.

church, built to *John Bowden*'s design, with a tapering belfry stage to the tower and big overhanging finials. The materials are slate with sandstone trim. In 1853 transepts were added, ostensibly to designs of *Joseph Welland*, but probably by *Alexander Hardy*, the surveyor of the area. – MONUMENT to Sarah Spencer, 1766, in the churchyard. An open classical enclosure made up of four arches with Gibbs surrounds surmounted by a cornice and corner pyramid finials.

OLD CHURCH RUINS. In St Canice churchyard. Only the E gable with typical large clasping buttresses and the arch of a large pointed window remain of the Plantation church of 1626.

MEDIEVAL CHURCH RUINS. 5 km E, by Faughanvale Bridge. The ivy-covered remains of a rectangular church of some 17 ft by 60 ft, with walls $2\frac{1}{2}$ ft thick. Only parts of the gables remain to any height.

ST MARY, STAR OF THE SEA. 2.5 km E. 1969 by *White & Hegarty* of Derry. Carefully detailed, cream-rendered outside and of brownish brick with cedar wood within. Though in a modern idiom, the building is accidentally historical, like some of the oldest Catholic churches, in placing the altar at the centre of its longest wall. Basically a portal-frame structure, nine bays long, with the middle three rising higher and spanning a greater width than the rest. This creates the modern equivalent of a cruciform plan, while the extra height of the middle sections allows for a band of clerestory lighting between the centre and the wings of the church; this is continued down the sides of the 'sanctuary' and the 'nave', creating in the interior the effect of an arch of glass. A very neat solution to modern church design, with plenty of hall and community space in the podium below the church itself.

FAUGHANVALE PRESBYTERIAN CHURCH. 1 km E. Late C19. A gabled Gothic hall with sandstone traceried central window, and buttresses and finials at the corner.

WILLSBOROUGH. 3 km NW. A big, long, low, Regency-style stucco house facing W across flat land to the River Foyle. The house has its back to a plain vernacular courtyard, but the front, now sadly derelict, has some pretensions to style: six bays, two storeys, flanked by projecting canted bays at either end, with the whole roof hidden behind a cornice and parapet. The estate of Willsborough was bought in 1696 by the Rev. Gideon Scott, Chaplain to William III's army in 1688. His son, William, who became a Baron of the Court of Exchequer, is said to have built the first house here, but the present building looks more like the work of the Baron's grandson, Thomas Scott, who succeeded in 1820.

Little more than a rural crossroads and a focus for three modest country churches.

ST COLUMBA, DERRYGORTREVY PARISH CHURCH (C of I). 1.5 km N. 1815. The old-fashioned type of Protestant church built for a new parish, with a thin W tower of three stages with stepped Irish battlements clasped *within* the roof of the three-bay hall. Stone Y-tracery with an intersecting four-light E window. Flat ceiling and small gallery inside.

ST PATRICK. 1834. The early long type of Catholic church with a U-shaped gallery focusing on the altar on the N wall like Massmount and Rosslea. Harled, with stone quoins. Five-bay front with projecting centre bay and crow-stepped gables. Designs for a new church at Eglish were made by *F. O'Connor* in 1891.

PRESBYTERIAN CHURCH. Established 1769. A four-bay hall with Georgian Gothic glazing.

GLEBE HOUSE. 3 km W of St Columba. 1822. A very small glebe house built for a perpetual curate. Two storeys on a semi-basement; two rooms and a hall on each floor. The whole house is of ashlar stonework. Ground-floor windows recessed in segmental arches. Porch and stair an irregular appendage that almost looks as if for once they really were forgotten by the builders.

SWEAT HOUSE. A tiny stone-built chamber of beehive construction, about 5 ft high, now incorporated in the corner of the bank of a field by the road. Local directions had best be followed. From Eglish churches take the road NW to Pluck Bridge over the Oona Water, turn l. over the bridge, and follow the road roughly SW for 2 km. Here a lane runs sharply back on the r., passing two cottages on the l. with outhouses on the r. The Sweat House is about 100 yds further on the r., where the road runs straight. It is marked by a big hawthorn but still takes some finding.

'What a spot to build on and form a retreat from the business and anxiety of the world': such were the thoughts of Arthur Young as he was rowed past Lord Ely's wooded estate in Sir James

Caldwell's barge in 1776. He envied the proprietor, who then used the estate simply to derive a periodical profit, felling the trees with 'sacrilegious axe' and ignoring its picturesque potential. His heirs however thought differently. In 1824 Pigot's *Irish Directory* reports that the Marquess of Ely is building a residence on an island in Lough Erne to be seen from Church Hill. This was Ely Castle, a large classical house for which *William Farrell* prepared a number of schemes before the house was begun. The main front was a five-bay, two-storey, stuccoed block with Tuscan pilasters and a central columned porch. On either side were single-storey bowed wings. In 1870, pending, according to legend, (i) an un-welcome visit from Queen Victoria, (ii) the discovery of the agent's fiddling, and (iii) the building of a bigger and better house, it was blown up as the climax of the festivities that marked the coming of age of the fourth Marquess, who had succeeded to the estate as a boy of eight. However that may be, the Marquess still gave his principal seat as Ely Castle in the later C19 peerages.

Of Farrell's work only two lodges remain. The GATE LODGE is an exceedingly pretty classical design, single-storey, with a central circular recess that forms part of the same space as the bowed porch, supported on two short Tuscan columns. Two niches on either side of the door with classical goddesses. BRIDGE LODGE, a three-bay single-storey cottage, has label mouldings, twin-light lattice windows, and quatrefoil-shafted columns to its porch. Also pretty.

ELY LODGE, the present house, is a modest low range looking SW, converted from a stable block in 1965. The garden front is nine bays long, with a central bell-shaped gable and project-ing wings. The entrance is in one of the wings. Three-bay front with central columned porch supporting a gabled projection.

ENNISKILLEN FM *E9*

Enniskillen, the county capital of Fermanagh, occupies a long 7 island in the reticulated web of land and waterways between Upper and Lower Lough Erne. It is an island with two slight hills in its length across which the main street of the town is threaded, linking the stone bridges at its E and W ends. Inniskillen, the name of the island, is still also the name of a celebrated Irish regiment, though the town has now changed the I for an E. It is a C17 foundation, taken in 1608 by Captain William Cole, whom the Calendar of State Papers for 1611 records as having built 'a fair strong wall newly erected of lime and stone, 26 ft high with flankers, a parapet and a walk on top of the wall'. Cole also built a house on the foundations of the old castle, excavated ditches, and erected a large half-timbered house for himself and his family 'after the English fashion'. The old castle, which still remains in part, was a Maguire stronghold, but there was no town here until the Protestant Plantation.

Enniskillen held out against the uprising of 1641 and played a prominent part in the war of 1689 and 1690 between William III and James II, the population rising dramatically on both occasions, as this was the only town in the county to escape devastation. In 1705 an accident wrought what the forces of war had failed to effect when over eighty houses were destroyed by fire. Most were probably little more than cabins, for as late as the 1760s there was apparently only one two-storey house in the town. With the alarmed state of Irish affairs during the Napoleonic wars, proposals were made for gigantic artillery forts to command both the E and W bridges, though the redoubt that was built at the W edge of the town was in the event quite modest. In the late Georgian period Enniskillen extended beyond the limits of its island. The account given by Lewis in 1837 testifies to its increasing importance, and the good influence of trade, with 'a range of respectable houses' building on the W shore, in Brook Place and Willoughby Place, likely to 'add much to the beauty of the town'. Victorian extensions tended to concentrate on the N and E, where the workhouse, railway, and prisons were all built, and the C20 has covered the surrounding islands and hillsides with housing estates of varying quality. Queen Elizabeth Road, a new loop road, now skirts half of the northern bank of the island, and a second by-pass cutting across the S side of the island is under consideration. However it may relieve congestion in the main street, its impact on the townscape must do considerable damage.

CHURCHES

ST MACARTAN'S CATHEDRAL (C of I). Really a large parish church, but still the principal architectural feature of the town, set, with its graveyard round it, high in the centre of the island. Under the terms of the grant from James I, Sir William Cole founded the church early in the C17, but of this Planter's Gothic building only a small N extension, the remodelled square tower, and traces of a double-chamfered arch on its E side remain. The main church door is C18, with a small three-light Gothic window above, and a stone sculptured with the Paschal Lamb and the date 1637.

The rest of the church dates from 1841 and is in an old-fashioned, naive Perp style first introduced into Ireland by the Paine brothers thirty years before. The design for St Macartan is either by a local architect, *Thomas Elliott* of Ballygonnell, or by the regional architect to the Ecclesiastical Commissioners, *William Farrell*, with Elliott acting as contractor. Clerestoried nave with N and S aisles, six bays long, with Y-tracery windows between shallow buttresses that end in simple square finials. On the N aisle, where the buttresses would not normally be seen, they are omitted. At the time that the church was rebuilt the tower was encased in thin Perp work and given a parapet of quatrefoil banding and a thin octagonal spire.

The cathedral vestibule is now more like the hall of an Edwardian house, with tiled floor, panelled walls, and a staircase leading to the gallery. The church itself is entered not centrally but in the corner of the S aisle. The interior, light and delicate, is characteristically late Georgian rather than early Victorian. Quatrefoil cast-iron columns support a gallery round three sides, with shallow four-centred arches stepping rhythmically along the nave. Sexpartite rib-vaults in plaster float lightly above the airy arches. The chancel extension of 1889 respects the original character of the building and retains the E window. When the church was raised to cathedral status in 1923 the chancel was refitted as a First World War memorial. Since 1970 the N aisle has been set apart as the IN-NISKILLING REGIMENTAL CHAPEL, with wrought-iron screen and cedar coffering by *John Storie*. – FONT. Presented by the rector, William Vincent, in 1666. Octagonal, with dog-tooth decoration, set like a sundial on a turned baluster. – STAINED GLASS. E window 1856 by *William Warrington* of London. Predominantly blue, yellow, and crimson, with four Resurrection subjects. – ORGAN. 1830 by *John Smith* of Bristol, enlarged in 1888; still in a pretty Gothic Revival case. – MONU-MENTS. William Pockrich † 1628. A stone tablet with half the inscription upside down, originally set into the floor. – Elisabetha Vincent and Margaret Ryno, 1673. Two crudely classical wall tablets with quarter-columns flanking coats of arms. – David Eccles † 1707. A rustic classical tablet with scroll top, cherub's head, a skull, crossbones, hour-glass, and coffin. – In the chancel, John Willoughby, second Earl of Enniskillen, † 1840, a life-size statue in peer's robes with the order of St Patrick, set on a bracket sarcophagus. – General the Hon. Sir Galbraith Lowry Cole, 1842, facing the Earl across the chancel arch and brandishing his sabre. – Bust of the Rev. J. C. Maude, the rector responsible for rebuilding the church, 1860. – Bust of the Rev. W. E. De Burgh by *Robinson* of Belfast, 1902.

ST MICHAEL. An ambitious design by *O'Neill & Byrne*, 1870–5, C13 in style, with a gabled façade looking incredibly tall and thin even without its intended broach-spire, which would have made it even thinner. Front of smooth grey stone wedged into a narrow space and much enriched. Two elongated windows with geometrical tracery surmount an entrance porch with a roundel in the top of the gable. The porch is sculptured with a Judgement subject: the blessed and the damned with Christ enthroned between them.

Inside, scale has outrun invention. Details are solid and good, and the whole construction is clear, but the volume enclosed is banal. Six-bay nave with fat round columns with foliated capitals; narrow aisles with sloping roofs either side. Two-centred arches, with a high clerestory and exposed trussed roof above. The pitch is very steep, the effect dark. The apse, externally a tall strong feature on the slope of the hill, is polygonal. Elaborate Caen stone reredos of 1882 with pinnacled central statue of St Michael. – PULPIT. Celtic Romanesque, by Professor *William Scott*. – STAINED GLASS. Nativity window by *Michael Healy*.

METHODIST CHURCH, Darling Street. 1865 by *W. J. Barre*. A full-blown Imperial Roman temple front in stucco with a tetrastyle Corinthian portico set across its five bays; pilaster responds and corners. The whole is surprisingly orthodox for Barre, with only the balustrade and tall keystones to the first-floor windows departing from classical textbook standards. The interior of the church is more personal, with a curving U-shaped gallery opening through an arcade of three arches to the space above the entrance vestibule.

The church halls in Wesley Street, built in stone with round-headed traceried windows, date from 1887 and occupy the site of the Wesleyan Chapel of 1849.

PRESBYTERIAN CHURCH, East Bridge Street. 1897. A Gothic gabled front with a low lean-to vestibule and false flying buttresses to dress up the architectural end of a wide hall behind. The interior is surprisingly dramatic, with a hipped timber roof supported on a series of elaborate hammerbeam trusses in dark pine. – STAINED GLASS. Pulpit window: First World War memorial, 'The White Comrade' – Christ appearing to two soldiers on the battlefield – by *G. H. Swinstead* copied by *W.*

Morris & Co. – MONUMENT. Wall tablet to William Trimble, 1888, the father of twenty-five children, of whom William Copeland Trimble, the historian of Enniskillen, was one.

CONVENT OF MERCY, Belmore Street. The original building here is a trim three-storey stucco block, seven bays wide, the middle bay emphasized by a wide blank wall space on either side. The first floor is decorated with pilasters that sprout from tiny brackets and support a continuous enriched entablature. All this looks mid C19, but it can hardly be by *J. J. McCarthy*, who was reported to have made designs for the convent in 1851. These presumably were never used. The building is now part of a large school complex, rather squashed on its riverside site and, though decent, undistinguished. Only the CHAPEL is of note. It is of 1904 by *William Scott*, a neo-Byzantine hall with apsidal E end (actually S) and semi-dome. – STAINED GLASS. The chapel has many good windows. By *Michael Healy*, a Good Shepherd with the four evangelists in the apse, and the nave windows with the Annunciation, St Patrick, St Brigid, St Columcille, St Benignus, St Benedict Labre, and St Anthony; others, by *Lady Glenavy*, are the Immaculate Conception, St Macarten, St Margaret, the Sacred Heart, St Joseph and St Mary; and by *Sarah Purser*, St Michael and St Elizabeth.

PUBLIC BUILDINGS

CASTLE. Situated at the W end of the island to control the widest passage between the two parts of Lough Erne, the castle has been three things: a Maguire stronghold in the C15 and C16; a Plantation strong house rebuilt by Sir William Cole *c.* 1607; and an artillery barracks from the late C18. Most of its buildings have now the matter-of-fact appearance of early C19 vernacular offices, arranged in an irregular court of two-storey buildings round the Maguire keep. The keep is now truncated, and has a roof like a Regency rectory replacing its battlements and caphouse. Beyond to the S, best seen from outside by the river's edge, is the watergate.

The KEEP is said to have been founded by Hugh Maguire 'the Hospitable', who died in 1428. It is mentioned in 1439 in the *Annals of Ulster*, and a map drawn *c.* 1550 shows a plan bearing a close resemblance to the present building. In 1594 it was taken by Captain John Dowdall. The drawing made of Dowdall's siege shows it as a four-storey square block with a pitched gabled roof within a battlemented parapet. After the

grant to Captain Cole in 1607 the *Calendar of State Paper.*
reports in 1611 'a fair house begun upon the foundations of
the old castle with other convenient houses for store and muni-
tion'. So the keep was presumably rebuilt by Cole. Today it
is a rectangular rubble-built block of three storeys with large
sash-windows dating either from 1796, when £7,000 was spent
on the castle barracks, or else from the restoration carried out
in the reign of William IV. The pronounced batter to the base
is all that can be linked now with the Maguire building.

53   The WATERGATE is the most prominent and evocative
feature left of the old castle. It has a high three-storey façade
with stepped Irish battlements, supported on square corbelling
and flanked by two unusually tall round bartizans corbelled out
from the first-floor level and roofed with conical stone caps.
If it were in Scotland this could be work of the later C16, when
such tall bartizans were much employed. The gate is supposed
to have been built by Chonnacht Og Maguire, who owned the
castle from 1566 to 1589, but it does not appear in the views
of Dowdall's siege, though something like it was shown in John
Speed's view of Enniskillen Castle in his *Theatre of the Empire
of Great Britain* of 1610. The details of the corbelling and
chamfered square window reveals with label mouldings over
look C17 and probably date from Cole's time, when he built
'a fair strong wall ... 26 ft high with flankers, a parapet and
a walk on the top'.

Until the late C18 the castle was cut off by a ditch on its N
and E sides. It is entered today from Wellington Place between
two two-storey ranges of *c.* 1830, of squared rubble with brick
and stone trim. Inside the court the W range backing on to the
river is of 1796, with an arcaded ground floor and C18 sash-
windows above. The castle complex now houses a museum of
local antiquities and of the Royal Inniskilling Fusiliers.

FORMER INFANTRY BARRACK. At the head of Queen Street.
Of 1790 – next in order of antiquity after the castle – built to
accommodate 21 officers and 547 men. Now a police college
and depot. It is a big late Georgian block, functional, but handsomely arranged in a shallow U. Three-storey, with a central
eleven-bay block flanked by projecting three-bay wings, all
stuccoed and painted white. The centre three bays with a pediment and clock, the ground floor here in dressed ashlar with
three semicircular relieving arches across the front. The back,
exposed to the river, is protected by gun loops from the corridors, 4 ft apart. SCHOOL BUILDING. 1831, two-storey,

irregular. RECREATION CENTRE. 1939 neo-Georgian, seven-bay, two-storey.

COURT HOUSE. In East Bridge Street. Built c. 1785, remodelled in 1821–2 by *William Farrell*. The most distinguished façade [94] in the city, but now no more than that, as the interior has been gutted and the whole building is at the time of writing under threat of needless demolition. It is essential to the streetscape. A handsome five-bay, two-storey block on a lavish scale, it has big round-headed windows on the first floor, four sash-panes wide. The pattern of the top of the glazing bars is quite delight-ful, with a line of bars, like the loops of a spider's web, curving round the top of the arches. In complete contrast to this delicacy is the single-storey portico of massive and primitive pro-portions added by Farrell to the middle of the block. Unfluted Doric with four stumpy columns and an entablature of gargan-tuan weight half the height of the columns. The building is rendered, with stone quoins and trim, and strategically placed at the curve of the street as a focus both from the bridge and looking back from the town hall.

TOWN HALL. At the top of the more eastern hill of the island, dominating the Diamond, with fronts to Town Hall Street and Water Street. A competition was held in 1897 for a new building to replace the C18 Market House that had been built on the site of Sir William Cole's old market. Thomas Drew, P.R.I.A.I., was the assessor, and the prize of £50, out of nine-teen entrants, went to *A. Scott & Son* of Drogheda. The build-ing, begun in 1898, was to be erected for £7,500, but by January 1901, when it was opened, it had cost £13,000. According to Scott the style is 'a free treatment of the Renaissance'. There are two main halls at first-floor level, the smaller behind a five-bay front on the main street, the larger assembly hall lit by big windows at the side. Between is the clock tower, a six-storey campanile set on the corner, with opulent classical detail that seems to reflect the influence of William Young's Municipal Chambers in Glasgow, completed a decade before: here is the same Flemish-Baroque-cum-Wren amalgam, with a statue niche, clock, belfry stage, and cupola set one above the other. The swags and flower drops round the clock were carved by *Hart* of Brookeborough. The interior has a heavy top-lit Renaissance staircase with stone balusters and pink marble rails.

ORANGE HALL. By the East Bridge. A jaunty Italianate block of 1872, probably by *Thomas Elliott*, the local contractor turned architect in the later C19. A four-bay, two-storey front to the

river, with patterned stone quoins and a modillion bracket
eaves cornice set rather high and giving the building the raised
eyebrow look that first appeared in European architecture a
the Palazzo Strozzi. Sadly dilapidated at the time of writing

NEW MODEL PRIMARY SCHOOL, Dublin Road. 1975 b
Shanks & Leighton Partnership. A strongly modelled grou
with clean lines and an 'expressive' assembly hall roof ligh
funnel.

OTHER SCHOOLS. *See* Tour, East Bank, and West Neighbourhood.

TOUR

Enniskillen is a very rural county capital. Its buildings concentrate
almost exclusively on the main street, running in a slow S-curve
across the island from the East to the West Bridge; in the Middle
Ages, there were two fords. The street crosses the two hills of
the island at their highest points, with a dip about the centre –
'the hollow' – in between. Turn to r. or l. from this main street
and there is little left to look at but the water and island-set reaches
of Lough Erne, now rather spoilt by utilitarian modern buildings
and housing schemes. What was a comfortable cluster of small-
scale C18 and Victorian housing is rapidly being cleared away by
traffic engineers who want roads at any price. Hence on the N
Queen Elizabeth Road, 1954, skirts round the riverside to a new
bridge crossing N to the Erne Hospital and modern housing
estates. It has brought demolition in its wake, and at the time of
writing more is proceeding on the S in preparation for a new
through-pass scheme. The best way to see the town is to start
at one bridge and walk to the other. The route adopted here moves
from E to W.

The core of the EAST BRIDGE dates from 1688. It was widened
in 1832 and again sixty years later. Originally of at least five
arches, but the mainland shore has encroached on at least two,
one is filled up, and only two now span the river. Moving W
from the Orange Hall (*see* p. 281), EAST BRIDGE STREET
focuses on the Court House façade (p. 281) with the Presbyterian church (p. 278) opposite. From htere the street rises in
a slow curve past two- and three-storey C18 and C19 stucco
houses. On the l. the COUNTY BUILDINGS by *Harry Gibberd*,
1958, an abject symmetrical block in rustic brick, out of scale
and dingy before its time. Beyond on the r. the C19 did better
with a handsome group of banks and a big Georgian hotel. First
the FORMER POST OFFICE of *c.* 1890, a solid brick block with

a pyramid roof. Two storeys and five bays, the middle three slightly projecting. A strong design, bright red, and probably by *J. L. Donnelly*. Next three stucco houses, with segmental consoles to the first-floor windows, and a dummy fourth floor. The robust little Tuscan porch straddling the pavement, for all its appearance, is later C19. The buildings, once the Royal Hotel, are now the MUNSTER AND LEINSTER BANK. Further uphill on the same side is the NORTHERN BANK, in rosy-brown sandstone, recessed behind railings. A firm palazzo design, it has three central arcaded windows to the banking hall, doors either side, and five segment-headed windows above, all below a big Ionic cornice. Built for the Belfast Banking Co., probably by *S. P. Close*, c. 1880. Beyond is THE FERMANAGH TIMES, a vigorously stuccoed mid Victorian front, recently mutilated by the removal of its balustrade. Opposite, the new POST OFFICE is not as good a neighbour as the old one was. Next to it the BANK OF IRELAND, a handsome brick and stone front, neo-Palladian, five-bay, three-storey, by *A. G. C. Millar*, 1922.

The DIAMOND must be one of the smallest in Ulster, nothing more than a check back in the façades of the buildings where the main street is crossed by WATER STREET to the N and EDEN STREET – formerly Pudding Lane – to the s. It is dominated by Messrs Scott's town hall tower (*see* p. 281). Down Eden Street on the l. is a small two-storey house with the plaque 'Built by L.H. 1731'. From the Diamond the road runs down and up again to the churchyard and cathedral, whose elementary tower and spire close the view. The street has two names now, HIGH STREET and then CHURCH STREET, but in the C18 and early C19 it was known simply as The Hollow. Its architecture is modestly substantial rather than remarkable, though the curve of the C19 façades is undeniably pleasant. Half way down on the r. in MIDDLETON STREET is a curiously elaborate cottage house of 1877 with mullioned windows, big gables, and exposed bracketed rafters in the eaves. Odd rather than picturesque. Further N, near the new road, are the CORN MARKET and BUTTER MARKET, nice two-storey ranges of coursed rubble stone, with segmental arcades to the ground floor, erected in the 1830s by the architect builder *William Frith*. Climbing Church Street, the last house on the r. is a good early Victorian block with a five-bay, three-storey front, stucco, with moulded architraves to the first floor. Opposite, BLAKE'S is a fine Victorian bar with a nice shop-front and atmospheric

interior with tall pine-boarded snugs. Then the ENNIS
KILLEN SAVINGS BANK, a tall classical block of *c.* 1900, followed by a vigorously stuccoed mid C19 terrace house with rusticated quoins, oak-leaf garlands, and Ionic doorcase. The
PROVINCIAL BANK of 1858, opposite the cathedral gateway,
is of three storeys, stone and cement, in a commercial Lombardic style; possibly by *W. G. Murray.*

Three churches are at the top of this hill: the cathedral, O'Neill's
St Michael, squashed into two house plots and completely hiding the immense depth of its nave, and beyond it Barre's Methodist church with its big Roman portico. From here DARLING
STREET and ANN STREET complete the course of the main
road to the W end of the island. Little of note beyond the nice
haphazard rhythms of stepped two- and three-storey houses
curving along the street. On the l. ULSTER BANK HOUSE,
a substantial early C19 front of five bays, is the former infirmary.
Further on, on the r. Nos. 19 and 21, a nice pair of mid Victorian
stuccoed houses, set back, with a segmental carriage arch in the
centre. No. 19 housed the original Royal School for Girls. The
WEST BRIDGE is at least the third to cross the river here. A
light arcaded bridge of *c.* 1698 on diamond-pointed piers was
replaced in 1773 by a wider bridge of three segmental arches
– the piers with domed caps. The present bridge on two wide
segmental arches, each with a span of 70 ft, is dated 1885,
though the work was not completed until 1892. The castle lies
s from this bridge, the George III barrack N, in the western
point of the island.

EAST BANK

Beyond the East Bridge the buildings of note hardly group into
a coherent pattern. The town here consists largely of small-scale
houses, thatched until the late C19, flanking Belmore Street,
the road leading to the bridge and curving N up Fort Hill Street.
The start of the town proper is marked by the INNISKILLING
SOUTH AFRICAN WAR MEMORIAL of 1904, a pink granite
obelisk now in the centre of a roundabout. s of this was Gaol
Square, so called from the County Gaol erected between 1812
and 1815 to designs of *Sir Richard Morrison.* That has now been
replaced by a massive TECHNICAL COLLEGE of 1969 by
H. A. Patton & Partners. Much the largest building in the town,
but happily far enough away from the centre not to be dis-
ruptive; a bit boxy, but a decent clean design in an honest

modern idiom. Fort Hill above Belmore Street is a public garden, the site of an earth fort of 1689, 170 ft square, with salient angled bartizans, built to defend the E approach to the town by Majors Hart and Rider, 'good mathematicians'. About 1800, after the redoubt above the West Bridge had been built, the fort was reinforced with masonry walls, though plans by the Royal Engineers in the first decade of the C19 to turn them both into batteries were not carried out. The fort, shorn of its stone cope, is now the base for the COLE MEMORIAL COLUMN erected between 1845 and 1857 to the memory of General Sir Galbraith Lowry Cole, the second son of the first Earl of Enniskillen, who 'received the repeated thanks of both houses of parliament for his eminent and gallant services during the Peninsular war' and who died in 1842. A fluted Doric column on a high plinth. Inside, 108 steps take the visitor to a giddy abacus where, protected by a flimsy rail, he may gaze down on the town and islands or up to *Terence Farrell*'s heroic giant statue. Beside the Cole Memorial is a splendid BANDSTAND erected about 1895 in memory of Thomas Blanchett, Chairman of the Town Commissioners. Cast-iron with octagonal pagoda roof, pierced by a cupola and clock. Dragons, filigree ridges, and curly brackets.

On the main road at the junction of DUBLIN ROAD and CASTLECOOLE ROAD is the MASONIC HALL. 1930 by *Benjamin Cowser* and *John MacGeagh*. Nicely massed, with a symmetrical front. Rustic brick and tile with re-cast stone trim – sub-Lutyens. Further S is the NATIONAL MODEL SCHOOLHOUSE, a vigorous institutional building in bright red brick by *J. H. Owen*, 1865–7. Five-bay, two-storey, with big sandstone keystones to paired round-headed windows. Most of the modern schools are on this side of the town on hilly sites to the N and E, and most are dull, planned without any imagination as large ranges of two-, three-, and four-storey blocks with big windows, brick walls, and concrete lintels. ST MICHAEL'S COLLEGE and SCHOOL of 1957, 1961, and 1970, is such, by *Brian Gregory* of Belfast; ST JOSEPH'S SECONDARY SCHOOL and ST FANCHEA'S SCHOOL FOR GIRLS, both of 1960 by *John White* and *D. L. Martin* of Drogheda, are similar, lacking real style or any overall design. ENNISKILLEN AGRICULTURAL COLLEGE by *H. A. Patton*, 1968, has a discreet, clean look about it, two- and one-storey boxes in white wood and glass, but only the COLLEGIATE SCHOOL in COOPER CRESCENT is really worth attention: miniature neo-

129   Georgian of 1931, ably extended in 1967 by *Shanks & Leighton* of Belfast in a crisp modern idiom that manages to give style and an intimate scale to the school. The materials are concrete, wood, square-set cobbles to the various courts, with slate-hung classroom blocks, chamfered at the corners to give a sense of weight to the design. The concert hall, a small irregular octagon with cowl-like roof-lights, is a feature in one court.

EAST NEIGHBOURHOOD

HOLY TRINITY (C of I), GARVARY. 5 km ENE. A lonely little church on an open site. 1865 by *Welland & Gillespie*, a tall rubble-built hall with a high gable and a boldly faceted porch and spire in the middle of the N side. – STAINED GLASS. Resurrection window by *Mayer & Co.*, 1910.

DERRYGORE HOUSE. 2 km NW, on the Derryinch peninsula opposite Portora Castle. Derrygore is a large rambling house with big chimneys and many gables built in 1856 by Edward Irwin J.P. His son John Arthur Irwin added a nice U-shaped court of stables some time later, and a splendid stone-built barn in 1881. In 1938 the house was burnt out and rebuilt. The shell of the Victorian house was preserved in the rebuilding, but it lost its gables and high chimneys.

CHANTER HILL. 1.5 km NE. Pre–1780; built as a glebe house for the Rev. Thomas Smyth on the crown of a hill in a delightful miniature park. Like most C18 glebe houses, the building is of two storeys on a basement, but the usual three-bay front is here replaced by paired canted bays that rise to a parapet and flank the central porch held between them. Round-headed windows to the ground floor. Inside, the rooms in the bays are treated as segmental apses.

KILLYHEVLIN HOUSE HOTEL. 2 km SE. 1904 by *William Scott*, a nice whitewashed house, two-storey, with a stone base, service tower, and gently sloping low slate roofs, all in the manner of Voysey. Extended recently, on becoming a hotel, by *F. A. Sweeny* of Enniskillen.

BELLEVUE. 3 km SSE. A comfortable late Georgian and early Victorian house by the shore of Upper Lough Erne. Three-bay, two-storey front on a basement, with terracotta balusters at the roof line, extended at the SE by an additional wing ending in a large canted bay-window with a pyramidal slate roof. The stucco classical mouldings to the windows look *c.* 1850, which is presumably the date of the large cast-iron and curvilinear glass CONSERVATORY beside the house.

WEST NEIGHBOURHOOD

Beyond the West Bridge the ground rises steeply and is under-developed apart from the C19 houses lining the two roads that lead to Belleek and Belcoo. Above these is the REDOUBT, a square fort of 1796 with ashlar walls 142 ft square, protected by a ditch 15 ft wide with an even glacis all round. Inside the walls are gun emplacements at each corner (with a cover of 270 degrees). Two blocks, built as a hospital for the garrison of Enniskillen in 1829, are now adapted as a school house. Both are seven bays long, one single- and the other two-storey.

PORTORA ROYAL SCHOOL. 1 km NW of the bridge. Established by James I in 1608 and first built by Lord Balfour at Lisnaskea in 1618. In 1777 the school moved to Portora Hill, and the core of the present buildings dates from then: a seven-bay, three-storey block with shallow roof, dressed quoins, and flat architraves to the ground-floor windows. About 1837 this was extended, on the pattern of Bowden's Old Foyle College, Derry, by the addition of large single-bay, two-storey wings, joined by Tuscan colonnades to the main block. At this time the middle entrance door of the main block was removed. The tripartite windows with console-bracketed architraves in the wings have the air of *William Farrell*, but no architect is recorded for the main school. In 1859 *John McCurdy* of Dublin filled in the space behind the colonnades with two-storey blocks and built the STEELE HALL, W of the main building.

The C20 has added pleasantly to the buildings in the school grounds. First MUNSTER HOUSE, 1936 by *R. H. Gibson* in a symmetrical Mediterranean-villa style with round-headed windows, shutters, and hipped eaves covered with green pantiles. Then the WAR MEMORIAL GATES, 1945 by *Robert McKinstry*, re-using the Corinthian columns from the demolished Inishmore Hall, and the N CLASSROOM BLOCK of 1956 by *Lewis & Baxter*, extended by *McKinstry* in 1965. The idiom here is unusual, a two-storey range with long wide windows, ending on the W in a galleried tower with lines that recall naval architecture. The extension stands on the fashionable pilotis of the 1960s. GLOUCESTER HOUSE, the Junior School, of 1963 is largely single-storey, in brick, with a butterfly roof over the central assembly hall. It is also by *McKinstry*.

PORTORA CASTLE. 1.5 km NW, by the shore of the lough. Built by Sir William Cole, who purchased the land in October 1612, Portora Castle remained the residence of the Cole family, later

Earls of Enniskillen, until about 1764, when it was abandoned for the newly built Florence Court. Schoolboys 'playing' inside it blew a part of it up in 1859, and gales in 1894 completed its ruin. Today it is much overgrown, but the plan and some features can still be made out.

In 1619 Pynnar describes it as 'a bawn of lime and stone, 68 ft square, 13 ft high, with four flankers and a stone house or castle three storeys high, strongly wrought'. Three of the flankers remain, round towers approximately 10 ft in diameter inside, the two on the w flanking the walls of the castle itself. There are several gun loops in the flankers, and inside the castle proper fireplace chimneys in the w and N walls. Like all the C17 Plantation castles, the house was only one room thick and the walls were harled.

Rossory Parish Church (C of I). 1.5 km w. 1839–43 by *William Hagerty* of Derry. Cruciform, but the chancel is so short that the church appears to be T-plan. Thin Norman lancets to the nave, paired in the transepts. The tower added in 1915 has stepped Irish battlements and elaborate tracery at the belfry stage. Inside, a curious roof with segmental vaults cantilevered from the walls. – STAINED GLASS. Te Deum window by *Sarah Purser*.

Lenaghan House. 3 km wNw. A square-built, two-storey house of c. 1850, pebbledashed, with a porch and a segmental bow to the ground floor on the E front.

The Graan Passionist Monastery. 3 km wNw. Now an extensive U-shaped three-storey complex, the centre dating from the late C18, with a broken pedimented Tuscan doorcase and fanlight brought forward on a new porch in the centre. The eight-bay s wing is probably also Georgian, with tripartite windows at either end. The interior preserves some C18 door surrounds. In the N wing the CHAPEL OF ST GABRIEL, by *R. M. Butler*, 1917–21, is a long, barrel-vaulted, pine-panelled hall broken by seven windows down each side. Low chapels open through fluted Tuscan screens on either side. – STAINED GLASS. Stations of the Cross by *Mayer & Co.*

The site of a monastery founded by St Colmcille, possibly also called Clonenagh.

Catholic Church. Mid C19. A modest hall with Y-traceried windows with timber colonnettes. – STAINED GLASS. E window by *Mayer & Co.* – MONUMENT. The Very Rev. William McLaughlin † 1856 by *J. Core* of Derry. A rarity: C19 Provincial Baroque in black and white marble with a pedimented niche supported by consoles *seen side on*. A statue of the Virgin in the niche: adoring angels above.

CHURCH RUINS. Opposite the present church. Late medieval on a rectangular plan. One segment-headed opening and an ivy-covered W gable.

FAHAN   DO F3

Here was one of the most influential early Christian monasteries of the North, founded in the late C6 by St Colmcille, with his disciple St Mura as first abbot and patron. Mura was of the O'Neill family and became the patron saint of the northern branch seated at Grianan. Though Fahan was sacked by Danes in the C9, its community survived and is still referred to in records as late as 1136, while secular abbots are recorded into the early C17, inhabiting no doubt the castle described as 'ruinous' in 1609.

ST MURA'S CROSS. A magnificent example of early Irish art,[13] dated usually mid or late C7. Carved on both faces are Greek crosses set on stems and woven in broad ribbon interlace with narrow borders similar to the plaited cross at Carndonagh. The slab here is 7 ft high by $3\frac{1}{2}$ ft wide and carefully shaped with a gently pitched 'gable' at the top (filled by the head of the cross on the E face) with short arms like tenon joints protruding from the sides. These are rare but may be compared with a small cross slab at Kellegar, Co. Wicklow, and with the 'knob' on top of the 'marigold' cross-pillar at Carndonagh. A raised border surrounds both crosses, and on the W face two small figures face each other on either side of the stem of the cross. On the N edge is a Greek inscription – the only early example in Ireland – which has been taken to reflect a connection with Spain, as it appears to be derived from a doxology in the Acts of Toledo of 633. This and stylistic comparisons of the ribbon work with the Book of Durrow provide the evidence for a C7 date.*

A small rectangular stone carved with a CROSS in a square border is built into the outside face of the old churchyard wall just S of the S gate. N of this gate is a stone with a bore hole.

OLD CHURCH RUINS. In the graveyard the gable and some 12 ft of the N and S walls of the parish church replaced in 1820. In

---

* R. B. K. Stevenson argues that Carndonagh and Fahan Crosses are later, describing them as decadent works of the C10.

the E gable a perfect C17 round-headed window. Double Y-tra
cery with irregular octagonal stone shafts.

In the NE corner of the graveyard is a MEMORIAL SLAB to
Horatio Nelson, a midshipman on H.M.S. Endymion, who
died at Fahan House in 1811, aged 18.

ST MURA, FAHAN PARISH CHURCH (C of I). A particularly
pretty tower and hall type church built in 1820 from a design
by *John Bowden*. The same plan is used for the churches at
Aghanloo, Eglinton, and Bovevagh in Co. Derry, but it is never
prettier than here, where the design stands out to advantage
against a wooded setting. The tower is of three stages, with hood
mouldings and a pinnacled and crenellated parapet. The top
stage has a slight batter that gives the pinnacles a pronounced
piquancy. Three-bay nave with cusped Y-tracery in stone, and
a single-bay chancel added in a congruous style by *S. P. Close*
of Belfast in 1897. Circular vestibule in the tower. Gallery at
the W end of the church. Chancel arch with half-colonnettes
on brackets supporting an inner moulding. – STAINED GLASS.
N window in memory of Mary Dickson: St Elizabeth of Hun-
gary by *Evie Hone*, 1941. Luminous velvety colours in a somewhat primitive composition. – E window: the Resurrection, by
Mayer & Co., 1900. – MONUMENTS. Rev. Josiah Marshall
† 1794 by *T. King* of Bath. Tablet with coat of arms and nice
verses. – Agnes Elizabeth Jones † 1868. Primitive wall tablet
with weeping classical figure.

CHURCH SCHOOL, at the bottom of the graveyard. 1876 Victorian Gothic with slated bellcote.

FAHAN HOUSE. A long, low C18 house by the shore, said to have
been built by an English Captain Heath who didn't want to
go back to England. Five-bay, two-storey, harled, with overhanging eaves and a two-bay extension to the S. The interior
with wainscoting, lugged door surrounds, and turned balusters
to the stairs looks about 1740.

ST MURA'S HOUSE. A reticent classical block with two segmental bows, one at the front and one at the side. Two-storey,
rendered, and now a convent. Built for D. M. Colquhoun in
1870 to designs of *Turner & Williamson*. The idiom owes something perhaps to Greek Thomson of Glasgow.

C₂   FALCARRAGH   DO

A straggling village in the heart of the Donegal Gaeltacht, with
an Irish summer college.

▸T FINIAN. 1877 by *O'Neill & Byrne*. A big stone church, rather
more thinly detailed than the engraving in the *Irish Builder*
shows and lacking the tower, broach-spire, and clergy house
of the original scheme. Four-bay nave with paired cusped lancets extended by a N porch inside the stump of the spire. The
sanctuary end semicircular, with N robing room. Inside, the
high roof with exposed trusses and rafters is characteristic of
O'Neill. The trusses are alternately large strutted kingposts and
a simpler, smaller design. Moulded chancel arch with clustered
columns and E.E. detail.

ST ANN, TULLAGHOBEGLY PARISH CHURCH (C of I). A tiny
tower and hall church of 1792. Harled walls, three very narrow
lancets, and a stumpy two-stage tower in elementary Gothic.
Double Y-tracery in the E window. Vestry added in 1886. Note
the ventilation holes under each lancet and the big coke stove
in the middle of the aisle!

BALLYCONNELL HOUSE. Built by the Olpherts, a Dutch family
who settled here about 1633, the house is C18, enlarged *c.* 1840.
The main front faces E: a plain two-storey, five-bay façade with
gabled single-bay projections at either end. Label mouldings
and cross-mullioned Elizabethan windows. Now part of the
Irish College, with many modern additions.

CLOGHANEELY. 1 km NE of the Catholic church. A huge lump
of white limestone with crystalline red veinings turned into a
folly monument by Wybrants Olphert who, with Sarah, his
wife, set it on top of a pillar of rubble stone in 1774. The Cloghaneely that gives its name to the whole district is said to be
stained with the petrified blood of Faoladh, whose head was
cut off on the stone by a one-eyed giant, Balor, who lived on
Tory Island and had stolen one of Faoladh's cows. Faoladh's
grandson, like Ulysses, got his own back by piercing the giant's
eye with a red-hot iron. The name is a corruption of *Cloch*
(stone) *ceann* (head) *Faoladh*.

TULLAGHOBEGLY OLD CHURCH RUINS. 1.5 km S of Falcarragh crossroads. Part of an E gable and N wall remain, built in
rubble with huge boulders on a high site surrounded by a circular wall like a fort. Traces of windows with very wide splays
built at the head with very small shallow stones. An early
medieval technique?

FANAD HEAD   DO E1

LIGHTHOUSE. A three-storey round tower, with a corbelled

gallery round the light. Gabled single-storey buildings groupe
round the base. A sea light to mark the entrance to Loug
Swilly. In April 1812 a ship was wrecked here, in consequenc
of which the lighthouse was built. The buildings designed b
George Halpin were erected at a total cost of £5,756 1s. 10d.
and the light was first exhibited on St Patrick's Day 1817. Th
lighthouse was electrified in 1974. The station is now the shor
helicopter base for the relief every fortnight of Tory Island an
Inishtrahull lighthouses.

St Patrick's Well. 1 km w of the lighthouse, near the roac
to Portsalon. A small cairn well, about 4 ft high, built of dry
stones.

FAVOUR ROYAL

Favour Royal. Sir James Erskine, who bought the Augher
estates of Sir Thomas Ridgeway, had two grand-daughters,
between whom the estates of Augher and Favour Royal were
divided (*see* Augher). One married John Moutray and settled
here in a house built in 1670. It burnt down in 1823 and was
replaced by the present house, built for John Corry Moutray
in 1824 to designs of *John Hargrave*. The Elizabethan Manorial
style is meant no doubt to refer to the early C17 origins of the
grant of the land, but like so much of Hargrave's work the house
lacks definition or any real sense of proportion. Though of only
two storeys with gabled attics, it is on a large scale, of ashlar
throughout, with flat-headed windows filled with the Perp
timber mullions introduced to Ireland by John Nash. Three-
bay entrance front with a central castellated *porte cochère*, five-
bay garden side with a single-storey bay-window. Shallow
stepped gables at all the corners. The interior is predominantly
Gothic, with a big central staircase.

In the rock garden in front of the house some late medieval
carved stones: two faces, a bishop's head, and a ram skull.

Favour Royal Bawn. 2.5 km NE of St Mary's Portclare, and
SE of Lismore Bridge. The ivy-covered walls of a large bawn,
75 ft square, with rounded corner towers. Begun by George
Ridgeway in 1611.

St Mary's Portclare, Errigal-Trough Parish (C of
I). A small cruciform church built by Mr Moutray of Favour
Royal in 1834 at a cost of £1,000. The square, single-chamfered
windows and the pretty NE tower are reminiscent of work at
the house; so the design could be by *Hargrave*, who had died
in a yachting accident the year before.

KILLYBRICK HOUSE. Opposite St Mary's Portclare. A five-bay, two-storey house with a hipped roof. Early C19, with older yards behind. Built by the Moutray family. The tenants' cottages nearby, all of cut stone with unusually high picturesque gables, date from 1859.

KILCARNAN LODGE. 1 km SW from Killybrick House. A rather sinister multi-gabled villa dated 1859, with sheer high roofs built of coursed rubble with sandstone mullions. On the road further S a tiny lodge of the late C18 with remarkable rustic 'log cabin' quoins.

FEENY   LD G_4

A village round a T-junction between Claudy and Dungiven in the historic parish of Banagher.

BANAGHER OLD CHURCH. 5 km ENE. One of the most important early medieval buildings in Ulster, preserving an imposing W portal of a characteristic early Irish form. The church is said to have been founded by the obscure local saint, Muriedach O'Heney. It consists of a rectangular nave built of large blocks of rubble stone and a later chancel of finely worked ashlar sandstone. The nave is 33 ft 4 in. by 19 ft 10 in.; the chancel 20 ft 6 in. by 15 ft 10 in. All the walls are 3 ft thick. The nave was assigned to the C8, though a foundation date no earlier than the C10 is usually accepted now. Its N wall was evidently rebuilt in the later Middle Ages.

It is the W door that gives rise to the disputed date: this is an impressive ancient design, a flat-headed door with sharply inclined jambs (such as Vitruvian manuscripts describe as suitable for temples) set within a recessed square panel and framed by a projecting square border. A massive lintel almost 6 ft long fills the space of the frame above the door, though inside there is a round-headed arch. This form, though unsculptured, is closely similar to the doorway at Maghera and has been interpreted as an immediate precursor of the fully developed Irish Romanesque round-headed door with inclined jambs of which the doorways at Inchagoill and Clonfert are the most complete examples.

Two windows in the church are round-headed: the first, in the nave, is bordered on the exterior by a square section that links it in date to the doorway; the second, in the chancel, dates from about 1150 and is broadly splayed with a more elaborate architrave frame, moulded with triple rolls both inside and out. 24

Outside, the quoins at the E end of the chancel are treated as three-quarter-round shafts with late Romanesque type capitals carved in low relief with foliage and animals. The base of the chancel arch is also moulded to take detached colonnettes that are now missing. The inscription 'This church was built in ye year of God 474' was cut on the building in the 1730s when it was believed to have been built by St Patrick, whose *Tripartite Life* records the foundation of a church in the area.

19   TOMB OF ST MURIEDACH O'HENEY, outside the church. A mortuary house built in the form of a miniature church with a high-pitched roof of stone blocks. Of the same date as the chancel of the church, i.e. later C12. 10 ft long, 4¾ ft wide, and 8 ft high. At the W 'gable' is a worn figure sculpture of the saint set within a chamfered frame surround. Similar tombs are at Bovevagh (Co. Derry) and at Cooley (Co. Donegal).

CROSS. A plain slab cross some 4 ft high stands E of the church.

ST MORESIUS, BANAGHER PARISH CHURCH (C of I). 3 km ENE. Built by the Earl Bishop in 1780–4 in a characteristically plain Gothic style. Coursed rubble walls. Tower and hall type with a three-bay nave with delightful iron tracery in Y-shaped timber frames and an octagonal spire on a two-stage tower. Renovated by *William Hunter* in 1869, when the plaster ceilings were replaced by the present wooden roof. E window 1889.

BANAGHER PRESBYTERIAN CHURCH. 2 km W. Built by the Fishmongers' Company to designs of *R. Suitor* in 1825. Plain but very bold, like the church at Ballykelly, or, further afield, the W side of Inigo Jones's St Paul, Covent Garden. A huge high hall with a pediment roof running the length of the building and deeply overhung at the eaves. Two colours of stone: a green schist and brown sandstone. Five windows down each side, round-headed and recessed in big relieving arches. Just for its scale, one of the grandest buildings in the area. The CHURCH HALL is of 1900 by *M. A. Robinson* – a cruder miniature version of the church.

FEENY FORMER CHURCH (C of I). 1861. A miniature hall with a high gable, three lancets, and a bellcote.

DRUMCOVIT HOUSE. 1 km E. A big two-storey, five-bay Georgian house of rubble stone, with freestone quoins and brick trim to the windows. Shallow bow at the S end placed across an earlier part of the house. Mid C18?

KNOCKAN HOUSE. 2 km ENE. A handsome five-bay, two-storey

house, with single-bay, single-storey wings built about 1790. Dentil cornice. Buildings in the yard dated 1721.

ASH PARK. 2 km ENE. A five-bay, two-storey house of 1796 with half-hipped gables and centrally massed chimneys. Eight-panel doors inside.

FINTONA   TY *F8*

An attractive small town built over the top of a hill. Founded by John Leigh in the early C17.

DONAGHCAVEY OLD CHURCH. At the E end of the town the ruins of a mid C17 church built after an older church, 2 km N, had been destroyed in 1641. The E window, a row of fine round-headed lancets surmounted by intersecting Y-tracery, is an interesting example of the continuity of Gothic forms in the mid C17. At the time of writing held up by ivy, it deserves a better fate than to be left to fall down. The tower was added in 1818, only twenty-two years before the whole building was abandoned. – MONUMENTS. On the S wall to Gilbert Eccles of Shanock in Co. Fermanagh † 1694: a large slab, primitively carved, with an aedicule of Corinthian columns containing a coat of arms and a skull and crossbones below. – In the grave-yard to the N the monument to John Stewart Eccles † 1886 has a collie dog set in the grass, looking up alertly at his master's tombstone.

DONAGHCAVEY PARISH CHURCH (C of I). 1840. A primitive neo-Norman five-bay hall with bellcote and three porches grouped together on the W gable. Colonnettes and cushion capitals flank the doors. Probably by *William Farrell.*

ST PETER. 1 km S. A large Catholic church, characteristically outside the town, and for once provided with a dated sequence for its development. The GATES and presumably the first proper building 'Built in the year of our Lord 1823'. Classical, with urn tops, and a tablet carved with IHS and relief figures of St Peter and St Paul. Erected by the Rev. Patrick Conran P.P. The big four-bay Gothic hall of the church is of 1841, erected by the Rev. J. Kelly P.P.; and the tall square tower, of dark red stone with belfry, Irish battlements, and slate spire, is of 1872, erected by the Rev. Jas. Cassidy P.P. The chancel, with windows like those at Maguires Bridge, was added in 1925 and must be by *R. M. Butler.*

OTHER BUILDINGS. The character of Fintona depends on one handsome street running across the top of a hill. The houses step up the slope nicely, with varying levels and roof pitches. Half-way up on the s side is ST PATRICK'S HALL, set back from the road, with a showy classical front. It has a pediment with a musical cartouche mixed up with shamrocks in the centre, coupled Corinthian pilasters at the corners, and a projecting Corinthian porch, all of *c.* 1880. At the crown of the hill the NORTHERN BANK, the one piece of street architecture in the town, tall, of two storeys, with an Italianate façade in cut sandstone. A blind arcade runs to the first-floor windows, and two pedimented dormers break through the roof balustrade. Opposite, No. 70, a large stuccoed house with a shop-front with cast-iron Corinthian columns. The PRESBYTERIAN and METHODIST CHURCHES are both simple gabled halls.

ECCLESVILLE. 0.5 km s. The big house of Fintona, in a park, now part golf course and part Forestry Commission. Above the door is the Eccles coat of arms of crossed halberds with the initials C.E., for Charles Eccles, and the date 1703. The house, altered and extended by Daniel Eccles, now looks *c.* 1795, with two facades to tidy up appearances. These are low, of two storeys, with rendered walls and stone quoins. Five-bay E front with a slightly recessed centre and shallow relieving arches to the ground-floor windows on the outer two bays. On the N front only the end bays have relieving arches and the centre three are recessed. The kitchens and offices are (oddly) on the s and w sides. Inside, heavy mid C19 plasterwork, mahogany doors, and marble fireplaces. The NE corner room is earlier and more graceful, with a delicate plasterwork frieze of crossed cornucopias twined with garlands of roses.

DERRYBARD HOUSE. 3 km E. The ruin of a once elegant late Georgian house built about 1830 by the Rev. George Vesey, Rector of Mansfieldstown, Co. Louth, and Reader at the Royal Hospital Kilmainham. A square two-storey block with a shallow segmental bow on the s front in the manner of the Wyatts and a single-storey Ionic porch on the w. Late C18 stables behind. Partly dismantled in the 1930s and now beyond recall.

GLENGEEN.* In 1864 the *Dublin Builder* reports this house in progress: Italianate, by *Fitzgibbon Louch.*

FIVEMILETOWN   TY

A small village consisting of one principal street with a few three-storey houses and several nice two-storey designs with character-

* Not visited.

istic tripartite windows above shops. The mid CI9 NORTHERN
BANK has a five-bay, two-storey façade in ashlar limestone, with
segment-headed windows and a central balcony. The MODEL
SCHOOL is of 1881. At the E end of the town is a small picturesque
brick building, originally the terminus of the Clogher Valley Railway. The town, once called Mount Stewart, was founded by the
Jacobean planter Sir William Stewart early in the CI7.

ST JOHN (C of I). 1736–40. Built by Mr Margetson Armar at 68
a cost of £392. A small rectangular church of rubble stone with
a pretty quasi-classical tower with finials and a good Gibbs surround and pediment to the door. To this in 1863 *Welland &
Gillespie* added their usual N aisle, a high gabled block connected by a three-bay arcade to the nave. – STAINED GLASS.
Pictorial windows of 1887, 1910, and 1924.

CHURCH OF MARY IMMACULATE. Built *c.* 1871 and robustly
Victorian. Heavy Gothic with a vengeance: a five-bay hall with
paired cusped lancets, a semicircular apse, and an arcaded
three-bay porch laid across the entrance gable with a wheel window above. Offset double belfry with chisel-shaped stone roof.
Inside, a big bowed gallery and elaborately braced trusses to
the roof. The church was restored in 1910 by *J. V. Brennan*.

METHODIST CHURCH. A mid CI9 T-shaped hall of rock-faced
stones with a three-light lancet E window.

BLESSINGBOURNE. 0.5 km NE of the village. A large Elizabethan 114
manor built to designs of *F. P. Cockerell* for Hugh De Fellen-
berg Montgomery and completed in 1874. The view of the
house in *The Architect* (1878, p. 8) shows the entrance front
with a tall collegiate tower, a *porte cochère*, and an oriel above,
none of which was built; but the house still groups well and
is one of the most sophisticated for its date in Northern Ireland.
This is Elizabethan of a whimsical yet scholarly kind, nicely
varied in texture between the squared rubble of the walls and
the finely worked dressings of big mullioned and transomed
windows. At roof level the fancy erupts in tall finials, turned
knobs, strapwork brackets to the dormer windows, and applied
Ionic balusters in stone. Only the garden front is symmetrical:
five bays on the ground floor, two-storeyed with attics, and
big gables at either end. Perhaps there is an echo of Burford
Manor here. The pleasantly irregular interior is entered by a
large hall with a huge fireplace of medieval proportions. The
stairs are off to one side behind an arcade of banded columns.
Drawing room in the SW corner, with a large ground-floor bow-
window and an elaborate Jacobean fireplace. Nice Arts and

Crafts fireplaces in the other rooms, *Morris* papers, and original pine bedroom furniture. Much of the interior work is by *Howard Bros.* of Old Quebec Street, London. – SCULPTURE. Medallion of F. P. Cockerell by *E. D. Ford*, 1890.

AUGHENTAINE. 3.5 km NNE. The large, dull Italianate house with an asymmetrical service wing and two campanile towers built to designs of *William Farrell* by Thomas B. Browne in 1860 was replaced in 1958 by a long, low house by *Claude Phillimore*, pseudo-Regency, just not symmetrical, and sadly not much better than its predecessor. The situation is splendid.

OLD AUGHENTAINE CASTLE. 6.5 km NE. Built by Sir William Stewart about 1620, destroyed by Sir Phelim O'Neill in 1641, and apparently not restored. L-shaped, with rubble walls 3½ ft thick and a corbelled stair of Scottish character in the re-entrant angle one floor up. Three storeys. The W gable stands, including a square chimneystack, but little else remains. (N.B. The farmer often keeps a bull in the field.)

CHURCHES in the area are KILTERMON CHAPEL OF EASE, 3 km E, early C19, a plain five-bay hall with arched bellcote and porch; AUGHENTAINE PRESBYTERIAN CHURCH, 5 km NE, late C18, a three-bay Georgian Gothic hall with church offices at r. angles at the W end; and AUGHENTAINE CATHOLIC CHURCH, 5 km NE, mid C19, a tall slated hall of four bays, with wooden Y-traceried windows.

FLORENCE COURT

71 FLORENCE COURT is the great house of the Cole family, who came to Enniskillen with Captain (later Sir) William Cole, the governor of the town and grantee of surrounding lands under James I. He repaired the castle at Enniskillen and built the tower and strong house at Portora. In 1710, on the death of his grandson, Sir Michael Cole, the estates passed to the first of the family to live at Florence Court, John Cole, M.P. for Enniskillen, whose wife, Florence Wrey from Trebitch in Cornwall, gave her name to the house. John Cole is called 'of Florence Court' and is said to have begun 'very costly and sumptuous buildings' on his estate before he died in 1726, but the bulk of the present building is the work of his son, another John, who in 1760 was raised to the Irish peerage as Baron Mount Florence of Florence Court. A memorandum of 5 November 1767 added to Lord Mount Florence's will shortly before his death directed that his eldest son William should in-

herit 'all the marble chimney pieces and cut stone for the colonnades at Florence Court'; so the wings of the house must have
been projected in that year. William Cole was created Earl of
Enniskillen in 1789, and the title has remained in the family
ever since. In 1955 the main block was partly destroyed by fire.
It was restored by the National Trust, to whom the house had
been made over by the fifth Earl two years before. Much of the
fine Rococo plasterwork in the interior was saved by the fore-
sight of the then Countess, who had holes bored through the
surviving ceilings to let the water drain away.

The house is then of two, if not three, periods and restored
in this century. It occupies a magnificent site on a shallow ridge
looking E across pastoral country towards Lough Erne and W
to the Leitrim hills, with Cullcagh, an escarpment of over
608 m where the Maguire chiefs of Fermanagh were anciently
crowned, behind the house to the SW. Further S is the bold
outline of Benaughlin rising as a great humped cliff out of the
trees of the park. The Irish Georgian Society volumes describe
the house as the finest early Georgian house in Co. Fermanagh.
It is in fact the finest in all the counties dealt with in this volume,
but its architecture is endearing rather than fine, with a showy
façade that degenerates into a very plain rendered box at the
sides and back. The main house, dated variously around 1758
to 1764, is a tall three-storey block, three rooms wide and two
rooms deep, with a central hall opening directly to a staircase
behind which projects as a narrow canted bay in the middle
of the rear façade. All round, the roof is hidden by a high parapet, balustraded at the front but solid at the sides and back,
so that the house from the W has a blank, bald appearance
similar to Mountcharles Hall in Donegal.

The wings added about 1768 have improved the house
immeasurably, for it is now impossible to walk round the main
block and experience the architectural disintegration just described. Extending in a straight line with the front and ending
in irregular octagonal pavilions, the wings expand the show
façade to a frontage of 260 ft, so that the exterior must be judged
as a front. The wings, a good deal more sophisticated than the
main block, are attributed by the Knight of Glin to *Davis
Ducart*, the architect of Castletown, Cox, the Customs House,
Limerick, and Lissan House near Cookstown in Tyrone. Their
straightness, extent, and terminal pavilions are all unusual,
recalling, if anything, the younger John Wood's wings at Buck-
land in Berkshire of 1757. The arcades are open, of seven bays,

Doric, with a triglyph frieze and rusticated pilasters; the pavilions with high leaded roofs have shallow pedimented centres with windows flanked by niches between plain Doric pilasters.

In detail the main front is quite crazy. Seen in perspective from the entrance drive it masses grandly enough, but anyone who stands opposite the front door and looks at the facade will soon detect the vaingloriousness of a provincial hand. Rustication, keystones, and lugged surrounds run riot. The window surrounds are not the same on any two floor levels, and those on the ground and first floors are of a curious Gibbs type gone wrong, with the rusticated blocks moved sideways, set beyond the edge of the architrave surround and not over it. Each floor is marked by a string course and cornice, and all the corners have rusticated quoins. The centre, projecting slightly, is a welter of jumbled scales. First the main door, flanked by side lights and surmounted by a big Doric pediment supported on illiterate rusticated pilasters that shrink to a thin line between the rusticated blocks. Above, a rusticated Venetian window with blind balustrading almost sits on the point of the pediment and is flanked by two niches in aedicules different in scale from anything else on the façade. A third, fatter niche, flanked by paired rusticated pilasters, is squashed in between the two attic windows on the top floor. What is one to make of this front? Richard Castle, who designed the now vanished Castle Hume nearby, has been proposed as architect, but the design, for all its charm, is far too gauche for him, though it does seem likely that the plan to judge by its old-fashioned style might have been drawn up a good many years before it was built. The mason for the wings was a man called *Andrew Lambert*, who incorporated plain office buildings behind them, with a plain quadrant wall curving away from the w front.

Inside it is the plasterwork and woodwork that are the best features. One would not look for ingenious planning. The HALL, almost square, is Doric, with a nice sandstone Doric fireplace surmounted – unusually for a chimneypiece – with a raking pediment. The front-door pediment is repeated inside and bumps awkwardly into the ceiling cornice. The doors are a curious seven-panel design that is used throughout the house. The STAIR, opening off the hall through a segment-headed arch, is particularly fine. Three fluted banisters per tread, with a mahogany rail and a pine floor. It is lit from the half-landing by two tiers of windows (making the centre of the rear façade have four storeys while the bays on either side are only three) and has fine Rococo panels in plasterwork, similar to those in [72] Trinity College Common Room in Dublin, and a Gothic plaster cornice of alternating cusped and ogee arches in brackets round the walls. The best surviving ceiling is in the original DINING ROOM, where birds, acanthus scrolls, and cornucopias in high relief fill the frieze of a rich Corinthian entablature; the ceiling itself is filled with scrolls, shells, and rocaille work round a circular panel with Jupiter's eagle hovering over the hook for the chandelier, surrounded by the four winds. The chimney-piece is a nice mid C18 design – perhaps one of those mentioned in Lord Mount Florence's will – with consoles and a central Apollo mask. On the first floor beyond the stair is a charming VAULTED LOBBY and then the VENETIAN WINDOW ROOM with another cornice of birds and flowers worthy of Dublin craftsmen, and restored Rococo ceiling that just lacks the edge of the original work.

ST JOHN, KILLESHER PARISH (C of I). An attractive and un-usually complete late Georgian Gothic church, well sited on the brow of a hill, with the body of the church running N–S. The original building – a simple, almost barn-like hall – dates from about 1791. It is of a decent size for its period: about 30 ft wide and 64 ft long. By 1819 this hall was considered too plain; so a pair of transepts, a chancel, and a four-storey tower and spire were added to turn the building into a textbook cruciform parish church. The detail is all of a simplified Gothic sort, with pointed windows, and in the W transept an adventurous timber-traceried window, possibly taken from the altar window of the original design. In the later C19 the chancel and E transept win-dows were replaced by more orthodox sandstone Dec tracery, but the nave retains its double Y-tracery windows with lattice panes, and a delicate trefoil cornice in wood reminiscent of the plaster cornice in Florence Court staircase. The tower and spire with crenellations and diagonal buttresses is one of the most attractive in the county.

ST PATRICK. A four-bay lancet hall of 1857 with an asymmetri-cal N tower (altered in its top stage to become a modern belfry). Exposed kingpost roof inside.

DRUMINISKILL CHAPEL OF EASE (C of I). 5 km E of Florence Court. 1855 by *J. M. Derrick*. A small but characterful church in red brick with grey stone trim. Boldly offset bell pinnacle. Four-bay, Y-traceried hall with a double Y-tracery W window in a high gable. Not completed (despite the date-stone) until 1860 – an odd delay for such a small design.

KILLESHER RECTORY. 1.5 km E. Built about 1855, with out houses dated 1858. Elizabethan, with a symmetrical double gabled front, lavishly provided with label mouldings and cross mullioned windows.

FORT STEWART *see* RAMELTON

GALLOON ISLAND*   FM
5 km SW of Newtownbutler

In Galloon churchyard are two sculptured CROSSES, one at the E, the other at the W end of the graveyard. Both consist of a base and sculptured shaft terminating in a socket. The sculpture is much worn. The E cross, 5 ft 3½ in. high, has the following subjects: N side, the Last Judgement, Jacob wrestling with the Angel; E side, Moses, Aaron, and Hur, and the sacrifice of Isaac; W side, St Paul and St Anthony receiving bread from the raven, the Baptism of Christ, and the Adoration of the Magi; S side, a flat spiral design. The W cross is 6 ft high. On the E side, the Fall, Daniel in the Lions' Den, the Temptation of St Anthony; W side, Noah's Ark?, Sacrifice of Isaac, and the three children in the Fiery Furnace; S side, zoomorphic figures, an animal head, and a spiral pattern with an inscribed prayer.

A broken CROSS HEAD seems to be the centre and N arm of the E cross. On one side the Crucifixion with the Arrest of Christ on the arm; on the other, Daniel in the Lions' Den with another figure scene. The figure holding a sceptre and cross at the end of the arm is thought to be Christ in Judgement, which would complete the judgement scenes on the N side of the E cross. A section of the nimbus from the head of the cross, 1 ft long, with interlaced knots, is also here. The date of these crosses is possibly late C10.

See also Newtownbutler.

GARRISON   FM

A haphazard village at the mouth of the River Roogagh by the shore of Lough Melvin. Houses grouped loosely round the early C19 BRIDGE, a strong design in cut stone with rounded parapets and abutments.

CHAPEL OF EASE, DEVENISH (C of I). 1827. A pretty, tiny

* Not visited.

church on a hillock. Tower and hall type. Two-bay nave with
Y-tracery windows. The tower in three storeys with thin pinnacles. Harled.

St Mary, Queen of Peace. 1973 by *J. J. Tracey* of *Liam
McCormick & Partners*. A boldly simple design.

Former Catholic Church. Pre-1837. Harled, simple
Gothic, T-shaped, with a rubble-built square tower placed not
quite centrally at the head of the T. The interior had tiny angels'
heads above each window. Now roofless.

Melvin Cottage. 1.5 km N. A charming Ulster cottage of
c. 1820. Single-storey, with half-hipped gables, a local feature.
Three-bay, with big tripartite windows either side of a
segment-headed door with fanlight.

St Joseph. 5.5 km SE. 1873. A hall in stone with brick trim,
round-headed windows, and decorative bargeboards. Kingpost
trussed roof and gallery inside.

GARTAN   DO

St Colmcille was born in this parish and founded a monastery
here in the early C6. The site is marked now by two small medieval
ruins on a hill facing E, a little to the N of Gartan Lough, commanding lovely views over a lake-studded pastoral landscape.

St Columba's Church. The ruins of a tiny rubble-built
chapel apparently still in use in 1810. 20 ft by 13 ft inside. Doors
in the S and W walls have single-chamfered arches that are probably late C15. The E window, a single round-headed lancet with
widely splayed reveals, is possibly late C12 or early C13, as too
is the single lancet in the S wall. Credence cavity in this wall
at the altar end. The 'ABBEY' is a rectangular plan of stones,
mostly modern. Two PILLAR CROSS SLABS mark the boundaries of the holy ground. Both are very roughly shaped and
stand little over 4 ft high.

Temple Douglas Abbey. 4.5 km SSW of Gartan Bridge. St
Colmcille was believed to have been baptized at the church of
St Cruithnechan here. Little is recorded of the present rectangular church. It is 21 ft by 64 ft inside. The high E gable is
intact, with its fine C13-looking plate-traceried lancet of two
lights with a single transom and a top circular light – the only
example of its sort remaining in Donegal, with a characteristic
widely splayed reveal, topped by a single-chamfered arch inside. The hood outside is curiously built up of cavetto and right-
angled mouldings. No other windows remain beyond the trace

of one on the S wall and a large gap – presumably the door. Credence cavities at the E end of the N and S walls. – MCDAVIT TOMB. A vaulted cell-like structure E of the church ruins.

ST COLUMBA, GARTAN PARISH (C of I). 1 km S of Gartan Bridge, at Church Hill. 1819. A simple tower and hall type church, appropriately set on a hill. For once the architect's name is recorded on a plaque on the tower: *George Grier*. Nothing else by him is known, but the disarmingly childish harled Gothic tower hardly suggests more than a competent builder giving himself airs. The S aisle and short chancel in squared whinstone were built in 1895 in memory of Canon Edward Dougherty. – STAINED GLASS. E window: Life of St Columba by *Heaton, Butler & Bayne*.

GARTAN GLEBE HOUSE. Built in 1828. A characteristic early C19 Irish rectory, with a wide three-bay front and a pretty segment-headed entrance. Overhanging eaves. At the back, an elaborate cast-iron conservatory-cum-veranda of *c.* 1840 recently brought here by Mr Derek Hill from Clontibret in Co. Monaghan.

LOUGH VEAGH HOUSE. 1 km SW of Gartan Bridge. An overblown Picturesque villa built for Daniel Chambers to designs of *John Hargrave c.* 1825, a five-bay, two-storey stuccoed block with attics, label mouldings, fancy chimneys, and overhanging bargeboards with timber drops. Too big to be really pretty. The stable offices behind are more honest and nicer.

J4   GARVAGH   LD

A village granted to the Canning family in the C17 and laid out by them round a crossroads with one long main street. George Canning, the British Prime Minister in 1827, was of this family, who became Lords Garvagh in the C19. But the family seat has been demolished and its grounds planted as a government forest. The place lacks the focus of its big house, and none of the many churches in the area can supply it. The Main Street has some good C19 houses in brick and basalt; a stuccoed ULSTER BANK of 1873 by *Thomas Jackson*; and a WAR MEMORIAL battlemented clock tower at its S end.

ERRIGAL PARISH CHURCH. In Lewis's day 'a low plain building adjoining the town' and still that today. Three-bay harled hall with short chancel and bellcote. Timber Y-tracery and hood moulds – all looking early C19, though the walls are said to date from 1697.

MAIN STREET PRESBYTERIAN CHURCH. Mid C19, a stuccoed gabled hall with a gallery round three sides inside.

FIRST GARVAGH PRESBYTERIAN CHURCH. Congregation founded in 1641. A small C19 hall with round-headed windows was replaced in 1971 by the present design by *Gordon McKnight*, Romanesque, in reconstituted stone. A cloister links church and church hall.

ST JOSEPH. At Glenullen, 4 km SW. 1879. A high nave and short chancel. Rubble stone with sandstone trim. Lancet windows.

GARVAGH OLD CHURCHES. There remain the N wall and one corner of the E gable of a church at Ballynameen, 1.5 km SE; and the grass-covered foundations of another at Errigal Bridge, 3 km W.

BALLYNAMEEN CHURCH (C of I). 4 km SE. 1784. Primitive tower and hall type Georgian Gothic church. Windows in the S wall only.

BOVEDY PRESBYTERIAN CHURCH. 6.5 km SE. A mid C19, four-bay, Y-traceried hall of coursed black basalt.

ST MARY. 5 km NW at Ballevin. A five-bay harled hall of the mid C19 with Y-tracery in timber. The large square tower of sandstone and basalt in three stages was built for Bernard O'Kane of Mobuoy in 1899. – STAINED GLASS. Eight brilliantly coloured windows by *Clokey* of Belfast and *Mayer & Co*.

GLENCOLUMBKILLE   DO A6

This narrow valley with a village at the bottom has long been a place of habitation. It is remote, exposed to the Atlantic on the W, and cut off from the rest of Donegal by high, unproductive moors. Like Malin More and Malin Beg, coastal slopes further S, the valley is rich in prehistoric remains, though it takes its name now from St Colmcille, who founded an early Christian monastery here in the C6. There were also earlier foundations associated with St Fanad and St Conall. Glencolumbkille is famous for the *turas* or penitential pilgrimages that are made round the various stations on 9 June, the saint's day. The circuit takes over three hours and should be completed before sunrise. Many of the stations are marked by pillar stones or slab crosses associated with the early monastery, but there are no significant architectural remains. The only prominent buildings in the village are the churches.

CATHOLIC CHURCH. Mid C19. T-plan, with Y-tracery windows in timber.

GLENCOLUMBKILLE PARISH CHURCH (C of I). Originally a four-bay nave with plain pointed windows of 1828. About 1890 this gained a single-bay chancel and big buttresses, and in 1913 a tower by *R. M. Close* in three stages with a pyramid roof set inside stepped Irish battlements. The tower was paid for by Henry Musgrave, whose family had owned the Glencolumbkille estates from 1867.

CROSSES AND STATIONS. The *tura* begins just in front of the door of the Protestant church at a SOUTERRAIN which may be entered by a trap door in the graveyard and which appears to have been used as a place of concealment from Viking raids. The principal chamber, almost 5 ft high, is roughly rectangular, 19 ft by 7 ft. The decoration of concentric circles on one of the passage lintels is similar to that on the pillar stones of the stations and has been taken to be of the C9. A further passage runs beyond the main chamber. The *tura* route takes in fifteen cairns (not listed here). The best PILLAR STONES are: (1). In the churchyard, the last station, about 50 ft E of the church, pieces of two pillars (or two pieces of one) with incised circular cross patterns on a stem. The short 'head' has a compass-drawn three-point star. (2). Station number 12, 1 km NE of the church, a fine pillar above the road decorated on two faces: one with patterns of three rectangles on a stem, the other more flowing, with cups, circles, and knots on the stem and a square head. (3). Perforated cross in Farranmacbride townland about 0.5 km NE of the church, three ring patterns on a stem. The top is perforated in the centre with a cross pattern made up of rectangles inside the circle. Pilgrims peeping through the hole get a view of heaven. (4). By the T-junction, W of the church, a broader slab with a similar sequence of three round patterns on a stem. The top circle has a plain cross of two intersecting diameters laid over a Greek cross plan. These pillar stones have been dated C9.

ST COLUMCILLE'S CHAPEL AND WELL. Almost 1.5 km NW of the church, across the river. A small rectangular dry stone structure, 11 ft by 20 ft, the walls only a few feet high. Here are three cairns with primitive cross slabs.

At Doonalt, 1.5 km W, to the N of the road above Glen Bay is a CROSS SLAB 4 ft high incised with a Latin cross with a circle at the base associated with St Conall's *tura*.

GLENDERMOTT *see* CLONDERMOTT

GLENEELY   DO *G2*

ALL SAINTS CHURCH (C of I). 1856 by *Joseph Welland*. Said
to have been built by Miss Catherine Bell of Grouse Hall. A
pretty little hall with a bellcote and bold diagonal buttresses.
Side door, four bays, lancets, and a thin five-lancet E window.
Provision was made for a chancel – its arch can be seen outside
at the back – but it was never required.

GROUSE HALL. A surprisingly complete gentleman's house of
1735, built apparently by the Butler family. Single-storey on
a high basement, with segment-headed windows like the old
wing at Brown Hall and a corbelled brick eaves cornice like the
Agent's House at Baronscourt. Big steps to the front door;
otherwise a plain harled elevation. Seven-bay front – the windows flanking the centre door narrower than the rest – with
a single-bay extension to the N and a long wing to the S, almost
as long as the house itself. Inside, a square hall with corridor
behind, five-panel doors with lugged surrounds, and double-
lugged frames to the fossil marble fireplaces. A pleasant surprise
in empty country.

GLENMORE   DO *D5*

A district in rich farming country in Kilterogue parish at the
upper end of the Finn Valley between Ballybofey and the mountain
passes to the W. Two churches and two country houses are in the
valley.

ST JOHN (C of I). 6.5 km WNW of Ballybofey. 1877–9. An attractive small church with a cut stone tower and broach-spire; the
rest harled. Four-bay nave with cusped lancets and prettily patterned quarry glass. Short chancel with a three-light Dec window. The tower is offset at the W end, providing a picturesque
accent and a porch in one. – DONALDSON MEMORIAL HALL.
Chunky E.E. revival of 1901.

OUR LADY OF PERPETUAL SUCCOUR. 5 km further W. 1925–
8 by *J. V. Brennan*. A large cruciform church in boulder-faced
squared stone with cast cement details that cheapen it. Big buttresses and reduced Norman detail. The plan is essentially the
same as those of Toye's church at Ardara and St Agatha, Clar.
Transepts screened by arcades – here supported on quatrefoil
shafts of polished grey granite – with side chapels opening

through arches to the transepts and the sanctuary. Lofty pine-panelled roof with cross-braced trusses. Opposite the church by the river the RUINS of the medieval church restored in 1733. Little remains.

The two estates belonged to the Styles family. Both houses were rebuilt early this century.

CLOGHAN LODGE, by the salmon leap where the rivers divide, was burnt down about 1911 and rebuilt as a black and white Tudor Revival house. Five bays with gabled ends and a colonnaded ground floor between. Black and white work above.

GLENMORE LODGE. 5.5 km WNW of Ballybofey. The core of the house is a three-bay, two-storey Georgian block, two rooms deep, with an extensive late Georgian yard and offices behind. Mid to late C18. This was re-worked for Sir William Styles early this century and is now, like its neighbour, half-timbered. Rather more stylish, with a projecting central gable over the porch, supported on four Ionic columns, and pretty quatrefoils below the gables. Pleasant panelled hall inside.

B5   GLENTIES   DO

A prosperous inland village. Small (population 734) but of a good appearance, with one main street, tree-lined and closed by the well proportioned GARDA HOUSE of the mid C19 at its E end. Two public buildings on the Ardara Road are of more consequence than most Donegal towns can boast.

COURT HOUSE. 1841–3. A stylish little two-storey block with an ashlar sandstone front of five bays, the middle three slightly recessed. Railed area before the building with the Bridewell cells underneath. The ground floor has doors in the end bays framed in heavy stone surrounds but is otherwise plain. The first floor has five round-headed Georgian sashes in similar frames set in a rhythm of 1–3–1. Single shallow-pitched slate roof, hipped, and coming to a fine line on the eaves cornice. The building costs of £700, which the Donegal Grand Jury were loath to pay, were contributed by the Board of Works. The design may be attributed to *William Caldbeck* of Dublin, who did several court houses in Ulster in this period, on this pattern. The interior fittings are original.

MARKET HOUSE. Built about 1840 for the Marquess Conyngham, a nice two-storey block, harled with stone quoins and trim, and a central segmental archway flanked by doors.

ST CONALL, OLD CHURCH. 1852. A very large T-plan church.
Rendered, with stone quoins, and given timber Y-tracery sash-
windows, three to each gable. The basalt and sandstone porch,
in chunky style, with a round plate-traceried window and
stepped buttresses, is an addition by *Timothy Hevey* of 1866.
The *Irish Builder* in November that year reported a projected
Italianate Gothic residence to be built opposite the church for
D. McDevitt, also by *Hevey*. The CLERGY HOUSE to the NW
seems to be the outcome of this, sadly remote from the splendid
intention.

ST CONALL. 1975 by *Liam McCormick & Partners*. Two high
slated slopes overlap to provide a continuous clerestory at the
ridge. Elegantly simple, like the same firm's church at Steelstown, Derry.

GLENTIES CHAPEL OF EASE (C of I). A trim but tiny tower
and hall church with a short chancel. It looks about 1810 but
is certainly post-1846 and is said to be of 1860. Even so it has
sash frames to its four lancet windows and box pews inside.

ST COLUMBA'S COMPREHENSIVE SCHOOL. On the site of the
old workhouse, at the W end of the town. A long, low modern
block in grey brick, mostly two-storey. By *Bernard Rhatigan*,
1968.

FINTOWN CHURCH. 14 km NE. A mid C19, cruciform rendered
church with a short sanctuary end. Two-bay nave, single-bay
transepts.

GLENVEAGH CASTLE   DO D3

The Glenveagh estate, a deer park of some 25,000 acres with the
long finger of Lough Veagh lying in a gully between steep
granite mountains, was bought in 1857 by an ill-starred proprietor, John George Adair. The foundations of his castle, set
at the edge of the water half-way down the S side, were laid
out in 1865, and the house was complete, with the exception
of the round tower to the E, by 1870. Its principal feature is
a large keep tower of four storeys with a boldly crenellated parapet of stepped Irish battlements, all detailed in a hard un-
weathering shiny granite. Two-storey wings running NE and
SE from the tower form an entrance court of a haphazard sort.
The architectural detail is minimal, as one would expect with
granite: paired round-headed windows to most rooms, 'peg'
corbelling, and a big tube moulding ending in upturned round
knobs over the main door. This may all be the work of *I. T.*

Trench, Adair's cousin, whose pencil plan of Glenveagh is the only architectural document relating to the castle. Mr Adair did not get on with his tenants and disappeared one night on the lough, never to be seen again.

GARDENS. The gardens of Glenveagh, largely the creation of Mr Henry McIlhenny, the present owner, are in sharp contrast to the rough style of the castle and its more rugged mountain setting . Immediately beside the castle below the keep is an elegant Italian garden with shady laurels, pines, busts, sphinxes, and a pair of STATUES of Ceres and Bacchus flanking a marble bench. To the NE, on the one piece of flat ground above the shore, is a magnificent lawn belted by conifers and dotted with specimen flowering trees. To the s is the walled garden with a charming Gothick CONSERVATORY and beyond, on rising ground to the sw, a heather garden with whimsical rustic seats conically roofed with shingles, the southernmost commanding a spectacular view to the end of the lough and the Derryveagh mountain range.

_{C3}   GORTAHORK   DO

CHURCH OF CHRIST THE KING. 1950–3 by *W. J. Doherty* of Derry, a big, symmetrical-fronted church in a style somewhere between a 1930s cinema and a pebbledashed garden castle by Vanbrugh. Not very promising outside. The interior is a great square hall flooded with light. The N and s aisles, which open through exceptionally wide segment-headed arches, are lit by paired round-headed windows, and so is the clerestory, two pairs per arch. The sanctuary end has the same arches only higher. The finishes are uncommonly rich: marble-panelled walls inset with gold mosaic, and the sanctuary, in contrast to the open airy church, glowing with stained glass, the central subject the Nativity in brilliant colours, purple, emerald, crimson and orange.

_{G6}   GORTIN   TY

A small village set amongst green fields in a shallow valley between the Sperrins and Mullaghcarn. The contrast between the fresh grass and hedges and the bleak heather-topped hills is remarkable, and especially so if one arrives from Gortin Glen Forest Park or the lakes in the bald hills above the valley. Gortin is one long, wide street with a hump-backed bridge in the middle and two churches, one at either end.

ST PATRICK, LOWER BADONEY PARISH CHURCH (C of I).
1856 by *Joseph Welland*, replacing the first Lower Badoney
church of 1730. A standard, stone-built hall with short sanctuary, end porch, and bellcote. Short paired lancets, seven
down each side, with quarry glass, and a nice braced truss roof
inside, high and a little richer than usual. – STAINED GLASS.
Second window N by *J. B. Capronnier* of Brussels, 1872.
Delightfully fresh with smallish figures and vine patterns at the
top and bottom. – Second window S: Baptism of Christ and
the Last Supper, 1868.

ST PATRICK. An attractive stone church by *E. J. Toye* of Derry,
well placed just E of the village. Foundation stone 1898, the
interior finished by April 1902. Church and setting have
matured together. There is a rookery behind and a grove of
sweet-smelling tall cypresses in front. The whole façade is now
only seen from close to and seems therefore more impressive.
Nicely designed C13 with just the right amount of detail. Well
proportioned tower to the N, with a niche for St Patrick, and
a smooth broach-spire with tiny crockets at the very top. Broad
gabled front with a blind arcade running across about 10 ft up,
and a rose window above. In the tympanum a modern primitive
design of Christ with two angels. Toye's standard plan inside,
the nave, possibly too wide, opening at the altar end through
arcades to side chapels. The sanctuary is apsed; columns of
polished granite and pine-panelled roof.

BELTRIM CASTLE. 0.5 km NW. Granted in the early C17 to
William Hamilton, who erected a house and bawn here on a
steep bank S of the Owenkillew River. Parts of the bawn remain
in the garden wall E of the house: the curving shell of a flanker,
and a round tower of rubble and lime. Beside these is a more
picturesque C18 turret with pointed windows dated 1785; so
the other bawn remains were possibly 'improved' as well. By
1815 the house had become L-shaped, with a long thin wing
running W from the ruins, probably along the line of the original
bawn, and returning at r. angles to the S. The main front faced
W, with two round turrets near the middle and an oval-shaped
tower at the S end. About 1820 the house was given its present
appearance: a second range of rooms was added on the inside
of the shorter arm of the L, and the turrets and tower were removed to leave a pleasant Georgian five-bay, two-storey front
with overhanging eaves. At the N a brief section of wall with
crow-steps may remain from the C17. The windows throughout
are Georgian-glazed, but wide, with four panes instead of the

usual three. Simple interiors. Grooved cornices and two whit
marble Tuscan chimneypieces in the drawing room.

GRAAN, THE, *see* ENNISKILLEN, p. 288

8 GRIANAN OF AILECH. This grand stone fort, at the summi
of Greenan mountain, 808 ft above Lough Swilly and Lough
Foyle, is one of the most impressive ancient monuments of Ireland. A good deal that is imposing about the cashel is only a
hundred years old – the result of an enthusiastic restoration
carried out between 1874 and 1878 – but this need not detract
from the evocative power of the structure as a whole. If Dr
Walter Bernard, the citizen of Derry who rebuilt the walls from
about 6 ft to the present level of 17 ft, comes first to the minds
of archaeologists, the average visitor will still find it easier to
picture the place as the stronghold of the ancient royal house
of O'Neill, seated here perhaps from the C5 to the C12.

The origin of the fort, mentioned in legend as a sacred meeting place, is presumed to lie in the Early Iron Age. Traces of
three concentric earthworks at distances of about 80, 130, and
230 ft from the walls are said to be of this period. The fort itself,
at times cheerfully ascribed to the Middle Bronze Age, i.e. 1000
B.C., is probably little earlier than the C6. It is built of un-
mortared dry stone, with walls some 13 ft thick, roughly circular, with an internal diameter of about 77 ft and an outer circumference of 240 ft. The upper sections of the walls have a
pronounced batter, but no other feature beyond a single entrance on the E side. This runs as a passage 15 ft through the
wall and has inclined jambs and a roof lintelled in stone. On
the N side is a small recess. On N and S, entrances to narrow
galleries, 2 ft wide and 5 ft high, running round inside the walls
to low openings within the enclosure at points approximately
10 S and NE. The interior, stepped in three terraces with four
flights of irregularly disposed steps, arranged in V-shaped
flights, is largely Dr Bernard's work, carried out on the advice
of George Petrie.

Grianan was plundered several times by rival kings and
Norsemen. The *Irish Annals* record that it was destroyed by
Finshnechta, the son of Donough, King of Ireland, in 674, and
by the Danes in 937. The worst destruction came in 1101, when
in revenge for the destruction of his own royal seat at Kincora,

in Co. Clare, Murtogh O'Brien demolished the fort and, according to the Four Masters, ordered every soldier to carry away one stone for every sack of provisions he had.

GREENCASTLE

DO H2

A haphazard holiday village with a fishing harbour and villas like Moville. The point about Greencastle is that it commands the straits between the Inishowen shore of Lough Foyle and Magilligan Point on the Co. Derry side. It controls the entry to the lough, and through that to Derry, Tyrone, and inland Donegal. Hence the fortification that gives it its name, its Napoleonic fort, and the martello tower at Magilligan on the opposite shore.

CASTLE. Here, on the site of an ancient fort, traditionally Danish, 31 are the shattered remains of the principal Norman castle in North West Ulster, built by the 'Red' Earl of Ulster, Richard de Burgo, in 1305. De Burgo chose a strong position on a prominent rock close to the shore immediately opposite Magilligan Point, where the Manor of Roe was also in his hands. The castle, called Northburg or Newcastle, was intended to subdue the O'Neills and O'Donnells and to check the incursions of the Scots. Following its erection the Red Earl received, about 1311, a grant of Derry and Inishowen from the King, but with the advent of Edward Bruce, Earl of Carrick and brother of Robert Bruce, King of Scots, it fell in 1316 into enemy hands. The same year Bruce was invested King of Ireland at Dundalk, only to be killed two years later. Northburg then reverted to the de Burgo, who held it until 1333, when the murder at Belfast of Richard de Burgo's grandson, William, the 'Dun' Earl, brought an end to Norman power in the north west. From then until the C17 the castle was held by the O'Dohertys, vassals at one time of the O'Neills and at another of the O'Donnells. In 1555 the *Annals of the Four Masters* record its destruction by Calbhach O'Donnell who, having quarrelled with his father, ravaged the whole peninsula with Scots auxiliaries. It was repaired and garrisoned by the O'Dohertys until the Plantation when – in 1608 – it was granted with the rest of Inishowen to Sir Arthur Chichester. Chichester had further repairs made, and the place remained in use for the rest of the century.*

* In 1600 the *Calendar of State Papers Ireland* described the castle as 'seated in O'Dohertys country within four miles after you have entered the Lough. It stands within good musket shot of the channel but cannot be made of any strength to the landward. It is all ruined and not much material to be rebuilt though it might a little annoy the ships that come by it.'

Greencastle: plan

D. M. Waterman, Ulster Journal of Archaeology, vol. 21, 1958, redrawn by Richard Andrews.
Note: the plan to the left of the line AB is taken at a lower level than that of the upper ward.

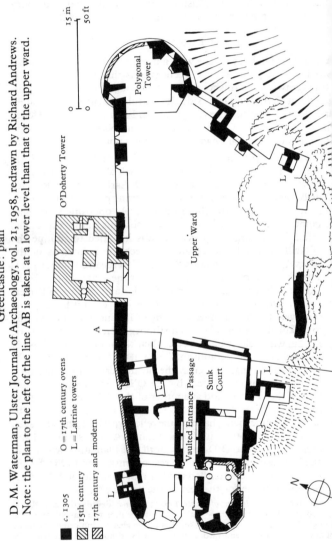

O'Doherty Tower

Polygonal Tower

Upper Ward

Vaulted Entrance Passage

Sunk Court

O = 17th century ovens
L = Latrine towers

■ c. 1305

▨ 15th century

▨ 17th century and modern

15 m
50 ft

N

The castle has not been excavated, and a description of the ruins in their present state is not easily made. The castle is covered with ivy and small trees; farm buildings now themselves derelict are built up against the N side, and great mounds of rubble covered with grass impede progress. The buildings are set parallel to the shore about 100 yds inland, running in two wards from NE to SW for about 280 ft. The UPPER WARD on the NE is on a bluff of rock that presents a face about 20 ft high on the shore side of the castle, with the walls rising above; the LOWER WARD, physically lower because it is below the level of the rock, is to the SW, with a sunk court and extensive vaulted basement. The upper ward is about 100 ft wide: the lower ward more like 60 ft. This causes a step in the wall between the two wards in the middle of the shore side. Three substantial and easily identifiable structures remain: the gatehouse; a massive polygonal tower at the N angle of the upper ward; and a heavy square tower built into the N wall of the upper ward.

The GATEHOUSE TOWER, patently C14, is at the extreme SW end of the castle, with a seven-sided turret standing S of the entrance. (There was an answering turret further W on the other side of the entrance, but only a faint trace of a splayed wall at ground level now remains.) A vaulted passage led between these towers with chambers to l. and r. The standing polygonal turret, three storeys high on a battered basement, is similar to the contemporary towers of Caernarvon and makes notable use of polychrome stonework of boulders and slate with red sandstone long and short work at each of the angles. Delicately cusped lancets light the top floor, with two levels of arrow slits below. Immediately l. of the entrance at the boundary wall of the castle is a square interval tower with the remains of a circular stair with a garderobe on the second floor. A vertical joint with the N wall proves that it is an addition. On the r. within the gatehouse the unvaulted chamber on the ground floor served as the kitchen for Chichester's garrison in the C17. Its chimney, with brick-lined ovens on each side, is on the NE wall.

The POLYGONAL TOWER at the N corner of the upper ward is set on a massive round drum of rubble masonry that bevels out towards its base. Though three sides have fallen away, there remain four deep segment-vaulted recesses opening to narrow slit windows. This tower is also of polychrome stonework, with walls from 10 to 12 ft thick. On the shore side is a mural chamber 6 ft wide and, in the SE corner of the ward at the edge of the rock, the base of a square angle tower.

The SQUARE TOWER on the N wall of the upper ward is usually described as a C15 O'Doherty addition. It is not built with the aesthetic consideration of the polygonal towers and is simply massive. Walls 10 ft thick surround a square of some 27 ft with a masonry pillar 9 ft square in the centre that rises to the height of the first floor. The tower was apparently always entered at this level. Window embrasures (now inaccessible) contain a garderobe on the NE side and apparently a well hole in the opening opposite. The dating and purpose of the tower require further investigation: it appears to have been self-sufficient and may have been maintained by the O'Dohertys after other parts were abandoned.

GREENCASTLE FORT. Immediately E of the castle. Dated 1812 on its entrance arch, though the guns had still not been mounted when Sir Walter Scott visited Greencastle in September 1814. The fort is on two levels: a barrack-yard with officers' and men's quarters ending, by the gate at the W, in a sullen masonry tower of oval plan with steeply battered sides. Inside, a large brick-vaulted hall with one window, two fireplaces, and a spiral stair leading to the platform roof with mountings for two guns. Below the yard is an extensive battery, protected by flanking walls to E and W, with a magazine under a mound of earth in the middle. By the time the fort was ready for action the war that made it necessary was over: it is now a hotel.

ST FINNIAN, LOWER MOVILLE PARISH CHURCH (C of I). 1781. A diminutive tower and hall type church built by the Earl Bishop of Derry. Tiny mid C19 chancel.

ST MARY. 2 km W, at Ballybrack. Another tower and hall church, this time of c. 1840, bigger and a bit more Gothic.

TEMPLEMOYLE CHURCH RUINS. 0.5 km N of Greencastle harbour, in a field. Massive dry stone walls of a rectangular church, 25 ft by some 48 ft long. Impressive angle buttresses about 5 ft thick. Sedilia recess in the S wall. The whole is now covered in a luxuriant growth of ivy.

OLD COASTGUARD STATION. Opposite the harbour. A nice row of eight two-storey cottages arranged as a symmetrical block, with pedimented porches and a big roof pediment over the centre two houses. Built about 1850 and presumably designed by *Jacob* or *James Owen*.

GREENCASTLE MANOR. Early C19 T-shaped villa by the shore.

Six-bay front on a shallow basement, the centre two bays in a segmental bow.

GRIANAN OF AILECH *see* GREENAN

GWEEDORE *see* BUNBEG

HALL CRAIG *see* MONEA

HARRY AVERY'S CASTLE *see* NEWTOWNSTEWART

HEZLETT HOUSE *see* ARTICLAVE

INCH ISLAND   DOF3

A small, well cultivated island, 3 km wide and 5 km long, set in the upper reaches of Lough Swilly and now attached to the mainland by a causeway 2.5 km s of Fahan. Inch, which could be easily reached by sea and which connects by an isthmus of low land to the city of Derry, saw its share of fighting in the C16 and C17. The island, an O'Doherty stronghold, was laid waste by the English in 1600 during the campaigns against Hugh O'Neill. Subsequently it was granted to Sir Arthur Chichester, but was won back by the Irish in the rising of 1641. In 1689 General Kirk with two English supply ships waited here before the relief of Derry, and during the Napoleonic wars a battery was erected and a garrison installed.

INCH CASTLE, though much ruined, is the most interesting of the architectural remains. It stands across corn fields on the edge of a rubble cliff about the middle of the s shore and is protected by the cliff to the s and w, and by a steep incline on the other two sides. The castle, first mentioned in 1454, was already ruinous in 1600 and is not recorded after that date. In plan it was a rectangular tower house with a vaulted basement and mural stairs running straight within the N and E walls. The entire w wall and part of the s wall have disappeared, but a room 20 ft by 14½ ft remains on the E side of the tower, with a high vaulted ceiling and clear marks of the joists that once subdivided the space. A second vaulted room evidently existed on the w. The principal chamber above was also stone-vaulted. The walls are generally 7 ft thick. Details that still exist are a murder hole above the first-floor stairs in the NE corner, and a garderobe in the thickness of the wall to the SE over the cliff.

Inch Castle is associated with a famous Donegal incident when the Lordship of Tyrconnell was disputed by two cousins, Donnell O'Donnell and Rory O'Donnell, in 1454. O'Doherty as Lord of Inishowen had arrested Donnell and lodged him in Inch Castle when Rory arrived and camped outside. The garrison however rallied to the imprisoned O'Donnell, and in the ensuing siege Rory was killed when Donnell threw a stone down from the battlements. Donnell then became Lord of Tyrconnell, but only for two years; he was killed by Rory's brother Turlough.

INCH FORT, at the opposite NW point of the island, is a battery erected in 1813 to control, with Rathmullen Fort opposite, the passage to upper Lough Swilly. The mid C19 garrison block is now a private house.

INCH HOUSE. A big seven-bay, two-storey house, now of Regency appearance with overhanging eaves, which seems unusually substantial for such an island. Moreover its interior looks older and has many early C18 characteristics: angled fireplaces in all the rooms, bolection-moulded panelling, and a spacious upper hall the depth of the whole house. Perhaps this property was connected with the Alexander family of Boom Hall, Derry, whom Arthur Young records as establishing a fishery at Inch and building a salting house between 1773 and 1776.

FORMER CHAPEL OF EASE, near Inch House. 1776. A two-bay hall with stone dressings and round-headed Gothic-glazed windows. Its extension is of 1869.

CHURCH OF OUR LADY OF LOURDES, near the middle of the island. 1922 by *J. P. M. McGrath* of Derry, a seven-bay neo-Norman hall in rendered cement, but pleasantly proportioned inside, with a canted beamed ceiling and a little pine gallery at the back.

INISHKEEL *see* PORTNOO

E8   INISHMACSAINT ISLAND*   FM

An island off the W shore of Lower Lough Erne, 5 km E of Derrygonnelly, where an early Christian monastery was founded in the early C6 by St Nennid, a disciple of St Fiacc and a contemporary of St Brigid and St Finnian of Clonard.

CHURCH. The ruins of a rectangular building, 60 ft by 23½ ft. The
* Not visited.

gables have fallen, though the side walls remain. At the E end of the S wall a small pointed window of the late C13 or early C14.

CROSS. Plain, on a base, 14 ft high, the shaft a broad thin slab. The arms and top are made of one stone, and splayed towards the ends. The date is uncertain – C7 to C10.

See also Church Hill.

INISHOWEN HEAD   DO *H2*

The most easterly tip of Donegal.

DUNAGREE POINT LIGHTHOUSES. Two lights, first applied for in 1832 and first exhibited on 1 December 1837. The use of a pair was suggested by *George Halpin*, engineer to the Ballast Board, who also designed them. The lights with houses were built by James Pettigrew of Dublin and cost £17,055 including lighting to the end of 1839. In 1870 the W light was raised, and in 1961 the E light abolished. Compact functional buildings of whitewashed squared rubble with stone copes to the walls. The towers originally slate-hung, short, and with corbelled galleries round the light.

INISHTRAHULL*   DO *G1*

A small granite island, over 1 km long, about 15 km E of Malin Head.

LIGHTHOUSE. Designed and erected under the supervision of *George Halpin*, the Ballast Board engineer, November 1811 to March 1813. The light, first exhibited on the night of 17 March 1813, was originally catoptric but altered to dioptric in June 1863. The cast-iron stair, floor, and lantern were made by Messrs *Edmundson* of Dublin. Lighting apparatus by Messrs *Chance* of Birmingham.

In 1958 the lighthouse was abandoned and replaced by a new electric light and diaphone fog signal in a new tower at the W end of the island. Designed by *A. D. H. Martin*.

INVER   DO *B6*

A district rather than a village proper, centred on Inver Bay and Eany Water. A pleasant row of fishermen's houses on the shore.

INVER PARISH CHURCH (C of I). 1807. A nice church, ample

* Not visited.

rather than big, set on a hill with a commanding view. Tower
and hall type, enhanced by a cut stone front with Gothic
porches either side of the tower itself to screen the nave behind.
Three-stage tower – door, oculus, and belfry – with square
corner pinacles and an elegant octagonal spire. The nave of
three bays with Dec windows was remodelled in 1861 by *Welland & Gillespie*, who added the short chancel at the same time.
Perp E window.

INVER CHURCH. A six-bay harled lancet hall of *c.* 1900. Circular
apse. Wheel window in the w gable. Pine-panelled ceiling.

INVER OLD CHURCH. An old site, picturesquely situated by the
last curve of the river before Inver Bay. There was an early
Christian monastery here of which St Natalis, who later transferred to Devenish, was abbot in the mid C6. It seems doubtful
whether there was a Franciscan Tertiary house here later, as
is sometimes stated. The present ruins of a rectangular church
are C17 at the earliest. No details are visible save a sculptured
head above a round-headed entrance arch on the N wall and
the remains of an C18 eaves cornice. The massive buttresses
to the w gable are typically C17. The building was abandoned
when the present church was built.

CHURCH OF OUR LADY OF THE VISITATION. 2.5 km NE, at
Frosses. A large T-plan church, harled, with Georgian Gothic
windows. Built *c.* 1840. The three-stage sandstone tower with
gabled and pinnacled battlements dates from 1892. – STAINED
GLASS. Modern windows by *J. Hogan*.

CLOVER HILL. Across the river from the old church ruins, a
two-storey, three-bay house with tripartite windows on the
ground floor and a classical central porch in sandstone. Built
by the Rev. Montgomery *c.* 1800. Large in scale and Regency
in feeling. The gates are earlier, or at least the lions on top of
them are: two robust, cocky little animals holding shields in a
posture like supporters but here free-standing. Similar lions at
Old Mountjoy, Co. Tyrone, were brought from Clonleigh, by
Lifford, also in Donegal.

DERRYVULLAN NORTH PARISH CHURCH (C of I). 1828 by
William Farrell. Built to replace the old church in the centre
of the town. Hall and tower type. Simple Gothic, harled, with
stone trim. About 1831 two porch-like extensions were added
half-way down each side of the nave, with big finials and Tudor

windows. These became private pews like boxes for the gentry; that on the r. was appropriated by the Irvine D'Arcy family of Necarne Castle. This germ of a cruciform plan became a grander reality in 1860 when *Joseph Welland* extended the church through arches at the E end and in the side walls beyond the family pews, creating new transepts and a chancel with a Perp E window. – STAINED GLASS. In the E window geometrical patterns by *F. Wilkinson & Co.*, Liverpool, 1894. – MONUMENT. William Robert Judge D'Arcy and Maria Brooke his wife, 1857. A large marble tablet with two urns.

CATHOLIC CHURCH. 1908 by *William Scott*. A very odd design, built in a massive granite style. A hall widening to the E through a three-bay granite arcade, N and S. Polygonal sanctuary with a wide chancel arch on round columns with smaller arches to the side chapels. Perp dormer windows light the nave half-way down each side.

OLD CHURCH TOWER. The most conspicuous monument at the head of Main Street. The standard square tower, of rubble, in three stages, with cut stone trim, pinnacled Irish battlements, and a clock. This is all that is left of the new church built by Patrick Delany, the rector, in 1734. Delany went on to become Dean of Down, and in marrying Mary Granville brought one of the most delightful diarists and letter-writers to C18 Ireland.

Irvinestown is obviously thriving and has the makings of an attractive centre, with a good MAIN STREET broadening to market-place width at its S end. MARKET HOUSE on the W of *c.* 1830, two storeys, with a segmental central archway flanked by narrower round-headed ones on either side. Rebuilt 1914. The METHODIST CHURCH in PUMP STREET is a small three-bay hall with a side porch, all harled. Recent improvements have not helped the scale of the town. The NORTHERN BANK and SUPERMARKET both ignore their surroundings and are intrusive. Traffic is also a menace: Pump Street at the N end has been widened into a yawning gap, and Main Street is divided by concrete-edged flower beds and a big concrete and cobble roundabout at the S end with more flower beds and a fountain. Trees and some lawn would have been more effective.

CASTLE IRVINE. 1 km S. By *J. B. Keane*. A romantic Gothic house of 1833 incorporating earlier parts. The gothicization was carried out for Judge D'Arcy (1783–1857), after which the house became known as Necarne Castle. The original seems to have been a rectangular block between 50 and 60 ft across

with two substantial round towers at the back on the NE and
NW corners. It had four floors. Keane and Judge D'Arcy almost
completely enveloped it in new building. Across the front a five
bay, two-storey range was built in a Tudor Gothic style with
octagonal turrets at the corners, buttresses ending in curious
round pinnacles, and an arcaded central porch with a balcony
above. The scale is lavish, measuring over 90 ft. The front
returns by a corridor round the E side to the edge of one round
tower, where a large Gothic dining room was built as a separate
wing at r. angles. After this work the only part of the old house
that could be seen was the W side and tower, which remained
tucked in behind Keane's new front. From here another wing,
designed to imitate a C13 peel tower, with big crenellations and
two-centred arched windows, extends to balance the dining
room. Further battlemented walls link it to the stables behind,
from where the old towers are best seen. Their form and massing, with two great ranges of chimneys rising between, suggest
a C17 date at least. The state of the castle, last inhabited by
hens and at the time of writing with collapsed and collapsing
floors, does not permit a proper examination.

The interior of Necarne must have astonished visitors. It was
completely classical, and its classicism had a crisp precision and
grandeur that is equalled only at Colebrooke. The hall, in the
centre of the new front, was flanked by free-standing Corinthian columns in blood-red scagliola with pilaster responds in
the corners. Behind the columns double doors could fold back
for the entire width of the wall, throwing both rooms and the
hall into one vast apartment, 86 ft long. Behind the hall, a lobby
with a staircase lit by a stained glass window, and in a room
to the l. a large white marble fireplace with dancing nymphs
and garlands on a gargantuan scale. The plasterwork throughout is elaborately undercut, almost free-standing, with great
twisted snakes writhing about the roundel in the centre of the
drawing-room ceiling.

STABLES. Immediately behind the castle. Two courts of vernacular buildings in stone with brick trim. Elegant classical
cupola in stone over the N entrance arch. In the first court, on
the gable of an outhouse abutting the castle, is a stone with the
D'Arcy crest of a bull on a cap and the date 1833.

GATE LODGE. On the Enniskillen–Irvinestown road. A neat
three-bay Elizabethan house with label mouldings and diagonally set chimneys. The gatepiers are Greek stelae with semicircular coping stones carved with anthemion motifs on top.

Lodge and gates reflect in miniature the mixture of styles at the house.

ᴌISNARRICK. 4 km w, by Castle Archdale. A tiny village noted by Lewis in 1837 for its triangular village green. It is still triangular, and, though on one side the buildings have been replaced by local authority housing, the green is as delightful as ever, with a double row of horse-chestnuts along each side. The houses are unremarkable.

KERRYKEEL   DO *E2*

Two churches in the countryside on the edge of a small village.

ꜰANNET PRESBYTERIAN CHURCH. 1913 by *J. M. M'Intyre* of Letterkenny. An entertaining way to treat the gable end of a cement-rendered hall. The result is stagey but effective, divided into three sections with a castellated w side, a middle gable with two traceried windows surmounted by a trefoil, and a big s tower with a pyramid slate roof and curious blind cusped corbelling that is almost Gothic.

CHURCH OF OUR LADY OF LOURDES. 1958. Exceedingly messy. Like a vulgar bungalow gone wrong. A gabled hall with out-of-scale monopitch entrance porch on the N side. Red brick, stone, concrete, and sculpture all mixed together by *J. O'Doherty*.

ST MARY, Glenvar. 4 km NE. Late C19, a four-bay harled Gothic hall with cement quoins and a short chancel. – STAINED GLASS. E window, the Assumption of the Virgin, in sumptuous peacock colours by *Earley Studios*, 1943.

KESH   FM *E7*

A scattered collection of houses at the meeting of several roads by the bridge over the Kesh river. Two parish churches and a Plantation castle are in the vicinity.

DRUMKEERAN PARISH CHURCH (C of I). 2.5 km N. 1774. A tower and hall type church built as the chapel for George Vaughan's charity. The tower is characteristically tall and thin, of three stages, with Irish battlements at the top. Between 1857 and 1859 the church was more than doubled in size by the Ecclesiastical Commissioners who, to the design of their local surveyor *Alexander Hardy*, added a N–S transept cutting right across the old nave. The whole roof was rebuilt at this time with high braced trusses that cross diagonally in the middle.

VAUGHAN SCHOOL. A charitable Charter School erected an
endowed under the will of George Vaughan, who died in 1758
The school hall stood N of the church and is now incorporate
in farm buildings. Only a cut stone tablet on one gable record
its previous use. A house and offices were added in 1862. Th
road from Kesh to the school is remarkably straight, and at th
church end is still planted with a beech avenue, presumabl
part of Vaughan's endowment.

DRUMKEERAN RECTORY. N of the Kesh River Bridge. A larg
late C18 house. Two storeys on a basement. Two overlappin
wings with a pedimented porch in the angle.

MAGHERACULMONEY PARISH CHURCH (C of I). 3 km ESE, a
Ardress. A hall and tower type church dating from c. 1767 or
the site of a C17 building. The tower is exceptionally tall and
plain, in three stages. It must have been built after the three-
bay nave as it runs across part of the dressed stone surround
of the door leading into the nave. The N aisle, entered through
a four-bay single-chamfered arcade on octagonal columns, is
of 1863 by *Welland & Gillespie*. Dec windows. – MONU-
MENTS. On the E wall worn C17 slabs to the Humphrys family.
– STAINED GLASS. Christ, St John, and St Luke, by *Mayer
& Co.*, 1899.

ARDRESS HOUSE. Opposite the church and originally the glebe
house for Magheraculmoney, built in 1780 for £808. 4s. On
a hill. Two storeys on a basement with a four-bay front to the
W, and a three-bay entrance front, with a curving flight of steps
leading to the door. A stone porch that looks about 1820
obscures the original Venetian door with Tuscan pilasters.

ARDVARNY HOUSE. 3 km W. A small farmhouse Elizabethanized
about 1850 by Edward Atthill, the agent for the Killadeas estate
and son of the Rector of Magheraculmoney. The design is
asymmetrical, with four rooms arranged along a front. The
second projects as a big gable with a stone porch beside it. The
walls are harled. Stone buttresses, gables, and finials. The
whole is reputedly copied from Brandiston Hall in Norfolk. –
CROSS. In the garden W of the house. The shaft and imperfect
head of a plain High Cross.

CREVENISH CASTLE. A ruined Plantation castle built by
Thomas Blennerhasset before 1618, when it is described by
Pynnar as a bawn of lime and stone 75 ft long by 47 ft broad
and two and a half storeys high. The remains suggest that it
was enlarged later. A salient angle tower in the NW corner is
now four storeys high, with gun loops on each face. The main

range, of which the N and parts of the E and W walls remain,
has fireplaces through three storeys. Part of the NE flanker
balancing the NW tower is built into a farm shed. Wood was
used to form the lintels of wall openings, and the fireplace
arches are of brick. Crevenish was occupied in 1641 by Lady
Deborah Blennerhasset and her second husband Captain Rory
Maguire, who played such a prominent role in the destruction
of Plantation houses in the Irish Rebellion of October that year.
It was while dining here that Sir William Cole and other Protestant gentry received warning of the danger threatening them
and made good their escape. In the later C17 parts of the castle
were used as a church and the bawn as a graveyard. Some early
C18 monuments remain.

OTHER BUILDINGS in this area are a mid C19 SCHOOL like a
Methodist chapel at LETTERKEEN, 1 km N; BARNAGH
CHURCH, 3 km NW, a four-bay lancet hall; MONTIAGHROE
CHURCH, 5.5 km NNE, another four-bay hall; and a stone
circle and alignment at DRUMSKINNY, 6.5 km NNE, exca-
vated in 1962 and restored with thirty-nine upright stones.

KILBARRON   DO C7

ST BARRON'S CHURCH RUINS. The ruins of a simple rectangular building of squared boulder rubble. The walls stand
to eaves level; the W gable, almost entire, has a small slit window, widely splayed inside. Typical small-scale doors each side,
hardly 5 ft high, Gothic-arched on the exterior and with single-
slab lintels above the reveals inside. All this points to a late C15
or C16 date, but there are no ornamental or moulded sections
to help further. The church was founded in the C6 by St Barron,
a kinsman and contemporary of St Colmcille and St Brendan
the navigator. It later came under the patronage of the O'Clerys
of Kilbarron Castle.

KILBARRON CASTLE. On the cliffs 1 km W of the church. The
seat of the O'Sgingins and their O'Clery successors, where
Michael O'Clery, the principal author of the *Annals of the Four
Masters*, was born about 1580. The castle, built on a rocky promontory 15 m (50 ft) above the sea, is cut off from the landward
side by an artificial ditch that runs N–S. Apart from two parallel
walls to the SE, the ruins do not survive to any great height,
though the plan may still be traced in its walls. The principal
accommodation was in the gatehouse facing the ditch and running in an angled line to a further block on the SE. The castle

appears to have had some form of drawbridge and was entered
by a passage 7 ft wide and about 35 ft deep. The site is still
impressive.

See also BALLYSHANNON, p. 126.

ST CARTHA. 1903–4 by *Doolin, Butler & Donelly*. After endless
tower-and-hall or T-plan churches with minimal detail inside
and out, St Cartha's seems wonderful. Of course it cannot really
merit such an adjective but it *is* good, especially inside. The
church sits high on the side of a valley E of the village and looks
perhaps too big. It is a long rendered hall with a boulder-faced
stone front in what the *Irish Builder* calls a Romanesque style:
that means it has three round-headed lancets in the gable above
a round-headed door with a tympanum. Offset bellcote and
aisles. Inside, Byzantine might be a better description, for the
church has a basilican plan with four arcades on weighty
Tuscan columns stepping down the aisles, and a powerful
barrel-vault in cedar (cross-braced with timber stretchers) running 128 ft, the whole length of the church. The space feels big,
metropolitan, and perhaps again too grand for the countryside,
but grand it certainly is, solid and satisfying. What is the source
of Butler's design? The *Irish Builder* cites Jerpoint, but that
can hardly be all. Does the roof go back to Deane & Woodward's
great barrel-vault in Trinity College Library, and is the Byzan-
tinism a reflection of the taste of J. F. Bentley's newly completed Catholic cathedral at Westminster? If it is, there are not
close parallels; but the ALTAR in marble and mosaic is patently
a product of the same spirit, with domed central and corner
canopies. The patterns however are a subtle blend of classical
and Celtic motifs. – STAINED GLASS. E window dedicated in
1927. Celtic again, in dark olives, reds, and green: the Adoration of the Shepherds, Crucifixion, and Pentecost, set over the
Flagellation, Last Supper, and St Mary Magdalene.
FORMER PROTESTANT CHURCH. 1828. Two-bay hall with
tower. Now roofless.

A rural parish in the shallow valley of the Ballinderry River some
6 km W of Cookstown with a very characteristic assembly of Irish
buildings dotted among its fields.

KILDRESS OLD CHURCH. By Kildress Bridge. The ruins of a
rectangular church, 50 ft by 20 ft, with gables 3 ft deep. Now
heavily restored, with a segment-headed E window and one
single-chamfered round-headed lancet in the N wall. 'In building' in 1622, burnt in 1641, restored in 1698, and used until
1818, when the new church was built.

ST PATRICK, KILDRESS PARISH (C of I). 2 km w of the old
church. 1818. A pretty hall and tower type church that cost
£1,296. Three-stage tower with quoins, a big louvred belfry,
battlements, and plain pinnacles. Three-bay nave and short
chancel. Five-light Perp tracery in the E window. Nave ceiling
plastered in cusped Perp panels.

ORRITOR PRESBYTERIAN CHURCH. 1.5 km N of the old church.
1825. A pleasant five-bay hall with big round-headed windows,
Georgian-glazed, and a porch.

ST JOSEPH. 4 km w of the old church. Built by the Rev. B.
Murphy P.P. in 1855. A four-bay stuccoed lancet hall with high
gables, diagonal buttresses, and a small bellcote, set in an attractive old graveyard with flat-topped yew trees. Queen-post
trusses inside. Painted and panelled sanctuary. – STAINED
GLASS by *Clokey* of Belfast, and a modern lancet by *McClure*
of Ballyclare dedicated to St Oliver Plunkett.

ST MARY. At Dunnamore, 8 km WNW of the old church. A large
stone-built church of *c.* 1870, T-plan, with high gables and a
slender Perp tower in one corner of the T. High cross-trussed
and braced roof inside. Arcade at the E end supported on round
columns with granite cushion capitals.

DRUM MANOR. The demesne, opposite the road to the old
church, is now owned by the Forestry Commission, who maintain the C19 pleasure grounds of the house and keep a caravan
park within its former walled garden. In the C18 this was a
Richardson house. It was rebuilt in 1829 by Major Richardson
Brady, in a flat Regency Manorial style, with symmetrical S and
E fronts. Big gables, stepped buttresses, and battlemented bay-
windows. In 1869 it received further additions in the form of
a new N front with a massive outlook tower – four storeys with
an extra turret – and a serious Gothic porch added by Viscount
Stuart to designs of *William Hastings* of Dublin, assisted
apparently by *Timothy Hevey*. The interior was re-planned
round a great central hall which – as the house is now only a
picturesque shell – cannot be seen. The castle-style GATE
LODGE of 1876 in the Cookstown Road is also by *Hastings*.

KILDRESS HOUSE. By the old church. 1861. A three-bay, two-storey front with central porch, flanked by single-bay recessed wings. Stone quoins to the corners of the main block, and horizontal glazing bars.

KILDRESS RECTORY. A big vernacular house of 1791. Two-storey, with central semicircular bow and tripartite windows on the ground floor at either side. Six-bay side elevation, all rendered and whitewashed. Pretty timber stair.

WELLBROOK. Built by the Faulkner family near the linen mills founded by Hugh and Samuel Faulkner in the C18. The present three-bay, two-storey house, with slightly projecting central bay, has almost lost its C18 appearance under late C19 mullioned windows and square suburban bay-windows. But inside are nice lugged door-frames, three typical C18 country Georgian chimneypieces with basket grates, and an original stair. Outbuildings before the house are dated 1764.

115 WELLBROOK BEETLING MILL. A whitewashed, two-storey slated mill and cottage built by J. Faulkner in 1768. Fully restored with its original machinery, mill lade, and water wheel by the Northern Ireland Committee of the National Trust and open to visitors.

MAGHERAGLASS PRIORY. 1½ km S of Corchoney Crossroads. The ruins of a rectangular Augustinian church founded by Terence O'Hagan in 1242 and fortified by the O'Hagans in the wars against Elizabeth I. No details remain.

THE PRIORY CHURCH, KILLADEAS PARISH CHURCH (C of I). 1864. A long, large church designed apparently by *W. Armstrong* of Belleek and built for J. G. Irvine of the Manor House on the site of the ancient Yellow Church of the Culdees (or Ceile-De) of Devenish. The local diocesan architect *J. F. Fuller* claims the church as his design in his autobiography, *Omniana*, of 1916. Of dark red stone, apparently asymmetrical. A high slate roof is the dominant impression. Gabled porch and transept facing the road, and a rather small tower behind. The tower looks, and is, an addition, dated 1881. The windows have plate tracery, except the N transept, which is Dec. Inside, the church is more traditional: a cruciform plan with a polygonal apse and a curved plaster ceiling set between widely spaced pine ribs. The W end projects in a gable with an elaborate window lighting a baptistery.

CARVED FIGURE AND STONES. In the churchyard, opposite the porch, a sculptured stone 3½ ft high, possibly of the C9 or 10 and similar in style to the White Island figures and the pillar stones at Carndonagh. On the s side, a low relief of a bishop or abbot carrying a crozier and bell, with a faint inscription in Irish on the back of the bishop's cloak. The w side has a grotesque head above a body of interlace pattern. Nearby is a stone SLAB, 3 ft by 5 ft, carved with a cross and circles, and another stone with a small Greek cross.

THE MANOR HOUSE. Overlooking Lower Lough Erne. Now a hotel. A modest five-bay, two-storey C18 house converted by Colonel John Gerard Irvine between 1861 and 1868 into a gargantuan Italianate stucco palace. The original w front can still be discerned, under stucco aedicules, and the Venetian window motif applied to its main door. At the s, a new front was added, taller, wider, and much more gross, with a central arcaded porch of pink fossil marble columns and a heavy tower to the E. The top floor of the tower has arcaded, almost Lombardic, windows, and these are repeated above the porch. The rest are square-headed, with curious garlanded surrounds which suggest that *William Armstrong*, the architect, had exhausted his Italianate vocabulary and turned to French Renaissance examples to finish the façade. Inside, nothing is more remarkable than the hall, rising through a square oculus on an upper floor and laden with plasterwork. Three spandrels along each wall support the floor of a gallery with bead and fillet, laurel bands, and Greek key all set round the square opening. In the upper hall the ceiling is supported on great consoles like an in- 112 flated version of Kent's cabinet at Chiswick. By comparison the other rooms seem tame. A long corridor runs from the hall along the back of the original main rooms to the staircase at the N end of the house with Armstrong's *pièce de résistance*, the Choragic Monument of Lysicrates, turned outside in, on the landing. Nice late C18 chimneypiece in grey and white marble in the SE room.

ROSSCLARE HOUSE. 1.5 km w of Killadeas church. A large Italianate villa of *c*. 1840 on a promontory above Lough Erne. Symmetrical, with a pleasing preponderance of wall over window and very wide eaves sitting directly on top of the first-floor windows. A two-storey, three-bay block flanked by two-bay, single-storey wings with flat roof and cast-iron balustrades. Considerable additions behind to convert the house to a special-care hospital.

A country parish between Dungannon and Ballygawley, created by order of council in 1732. The church sits on a hillside just s of the main road.

KILLESHIL PARISH CHURCH (C of I). 1732, rebuilt in 1768, and enlarged by *Welland & Gillespie* in 1861. A nice old church. Harled, originally tower-and-hall type, the tower with squat Irish battlements and a provincial Gibbs surround to the door. Three-bay nave, to which transepts were added on the last bay, and a polygonal apse.

KILLESHIL RECTORY. 5 km s of the church. 'Nearly built in 1810'. A big double-bow-fronted house, cement-rendered, with diamond-cut quoins and a Gibbs surround to its door. Two-storey on a high basement, with nine steps to the central door. The bows look rather odd with two windows each, not three.

MANOR OF CASLAN. 5 km SSE. A trim white villa of Regency appearance, five-bay, two-storey, and regularly planned, with a three-storey wing behind and a square central porch. Sometimes called The Bawn from the reputed existence of a C17 bawn on the site.

CHURCHES in the area are: UPPER CLONANEESE PRESBYTERIAN CHURCH, 3 km SE, a five-bay rendered hall of *c.* 1830 with quoins and Y-traceried sash windows and box pews inside; CHURCH OF OUR LADY OF THE ASSUMPTION, Tullyallan, 4 km E, 1952 by *Padraig Gregory*, in rustic brick Norman style (its predecessor, a plain six-bay hall, was built in 1768, rebuilt in 1830); AGHAGINDUFF CATHOLIC CHURCH, 1 km NE, 1862, a high, four-bay harled hall with buttresses and a tower added in 1905; and AGHNABAR CATHOLIC CHURCH, 3 km N, 1861, a three-bay harled hall with a hideous zigzag chancel arch.

A small village SW of Castlederg with a fine big hump-back BRIDGE of four arches probably dating from about 1750.

ST BESTIUS, TERMONAMUNGAN PARISH CHURCH (C of I). 1822, though looking older. A four-bay harled hall with round-headed classical-type windows. W porch and bellcote. N aisle added by *Welland & Gillespie* in 1870, a separate gabled extension with a large plate-traceried window, linked by an arcade of three round arches. The window tracery was changed at this time. The contractors were *G. & R. Ferguson* of Derry, who went on to design similar work at Seskinore three years later. – OLD FONT. C17. Tulip-shaped octagon. In the graveyard.

ST PETER. At Aghyaran, 2 km WNW of Killeter Bridge. A wide five-bay hall with Y-tracery, begun in 1840, dedicated in 1844, and enlarged in 1856, when a tower was added at one end and the orientation changed. Gallery inside, and an elaborate white marble canopied altar.

AGHYARAN METHODIST CHURCH. A tiny stone-built hall with grouped lancets and a side porch.

MAGHERAKEEL OLD CHURCH. 2.5 km WSW of Killeter Bridge, in an old graveyard, the walls of a church of 57 by 22 ft stand to about 4 ft.

LISLEEN PRESBYTERIAN CHURCH. 4 km E of Killeter Bridge. A small four-bay harled hall with cast-iron columns down the middle. There is a plaque inscribed: 'This House was Built AD 1789 For the Worship of God by the direction of Mr Nebu Lee, Founded upon the ground of Mrs Margaret Johnston's Dwelling House in Compliment to her memory.'

KILLYBEGS

A small straggling town centred on a natural harbour and supporting a small fishing fleet. A 'rigmarole looking' place in 1842, Killybegs is still the same today, with narrow streets, an untidy cluttered quayside, and a few big buildings heaving up here and there out of the roofs. Everything apart from the ruins of the C17 church and a cross slab at the Catholic church looks C19, but the place is older. The harbour, according to the Four Masters, was saved by the intervention of St Catherine, the patron saint of the town, in 1513. There were churches here before that, and in 1616 King James granted burgh status to the town, then newly planted under Roger Jones.

ST CATHERINE. A big cross-shaped church, unusual in its size, its substantial materials, and its plan. This is still the 'spacious and neat building' of Lewis's Dictionary, designed by *J. B. Papworth* for Alexander Murray of Broughton (Kircudbright-shire), an absentee proprietor who nonetheless set up two public schools in Killybegs. Designs were made for the church between 1834 and 1839, and it was built a little more simply than Papworth intended by the Rev. William Drummond P.P., who died in 1863. Solid qualities are admirable on the exterior – a big tower, large lancet windows, stone buttresses, and stone trim. What is exciting inside is the volume – one great high hall, 100 ft by 46 ft, opening through arcades of three immensely slender arches in the middle of each long side to airy transept-like extensions of the hall. The arcades are of dressed stone with octagonal shafts and big capitals like a Gothic version of a primitive Paestum Doric, so large is the overhanging moulding at the top. Pine-panelled ceiling. – Outside, N of the tower, is the C16 TOMB SLAB of Niall Mór MacSweeney. The gatepost to the garden opposite is a shaft from the SEDILIA of Ballysaggart church, St John's Point.

ST JOHN, KILLYBEGS PARISH CHURCH (C of I). On the Ardara Road. A plain two-bay rendered hall of 1829. Y-traceried timber windows. W porch supporting a bellcote spire. Polygonal chancel in stone by *Welland & Gillespie*, 1856–62, superintended by *A. Hardy*.

Victorian schools, a bank, and a coastguard station make up the PUBLIC BUILDINGS of Killybegs. The COASTGUARD STATION, E of the town above the estuary, is a six-bay, two-storey block, aggressively picturesque, with a tower at the W end enlivened by a machicolated upper window, and bracketed eaves cornice throughout. It was built in 1866 by *E. Trevor Owen*, assistant to his brother at the Board of Works. Nearer the town centre are the MURRAY MALE NATIONAL SCHOOL, 1850, and the MURRAY FEMALE NATIONAL SCHOOL, 1861, decent U-shaped groups of gabled houses and schools with label mouldings, mullioned windows, and bellcote. Grander but also bleaker by far is the former INDUSTRIAL SCHOOL, now the Killybegs Hotel, sticking up on the W shore beyond the town: a three-storey, twelve-bay block with projecting gable ends in the Convent style of *W. H. Byrne*, 1894–8. Not improved by pebbledash.

ST CATHERINE'S GLEBE HOUSE. S of the town. A pleasantly proportioned three-bay, two-storey house with wide eaves. Built about 1830 with a prospect E to the site of Killybegs Castle.

CHURCH RUINS. Below the Glebe House. The ivy-covered remains of a nave, 53 ft by 17½ ft, with a N transept 25 ft by 17 ft, opening through a double-chamfered segmental arch of the early C17. Though the walls are almost intact, no detail survives save a pointed door with a hood moulding on the S wall.

FINTRA HOUSE. 1.5 km N. A plain rendered block built for a

family called Hamilton. Early C19. In 1896 it gained more enterprising stables, a low five-bay design in hard squared rubble with a central clock tower ending in an engaging concave slate pyramid.

KILLYDONNELL FRIARY see RAMELTON

KILLYGORDON   DO E5

A village in an open rural setting on the banks of the River Finn.

ST PATRICK. 1 km s at Cross Roads. 1893–5 by *O'Neill & Byrne*. An ambitious stone-built church with a great expanse of roof emphasizing the horizontality of the whole and, at its w end, a charming slender spire, the church's principal feature that makes it a landmark for miles around. The tower is very thin and elongated in a Puginesque way: entrance porch, canopied statue niche, oculus, double louvred belfry, corbelled parapet, and spire. But it is carefully integrated too, with a half-round stair-turret tying it to the w gable, though this can hardly be appreciated today as the graveyard trees grow so close.

The interior is uncommonly rich and is visually rewarding. 123 Arcaded nave of four two-centred arches with N and S aisles. At the w end a solid half-bay to accommodate the entrance porch and space for the choir gallery. Short single-bay chancel, opening through side arches to side chapels. The detail is bold: polished pink granite shafts for the piers; deeply undercut capitals revelling in vegetable forms; corbel stops of singing angels to support the chancel arch, and above all a rich, exuberant roof – the exceptional feature of the church – very high and richly panelled in three different colours of wood.

ST ANNE, MONELLAN PARISH CHURCH (C of I). 1 km s at Cross Roads. A simple hall and tower type church, built apparently as late as 1858 by *William Armstrong* of Belleek. Square three-stage tower with timber Y-tracery. Old-fashioned for its date.

KILLYGORDON HOUSE. Built by a family called Bonar in 1652. What is there today is a late C18 five-bay, two-storey house with a central canted bay acting as a front porch and with a Diocletian window to third-floor attics.

KILLYGORDON BRIDGE. A handsome late C18 bridge of seven arches with angle-faced abutments.

81 Killymoon is one of the most brilliant examples of the Picturesque
castle style evolved by *John Nash* and it is also one of the earliest.
Begun by at least 1802, it is preceded in its irregular plan and
bold groupings only by Luscombe in Devonshire begun in
1799, and Luscombe is Perp Gothic whereas Killymoon is a
fully-fledged essay – and once again an early one – in a revived
Norman style. Set close over the N bank of the Ballinderry
River, the house employs an elaborate variety of features – all
typical of Nash castles: a two-storey *porte cochère* flanked by
octagonal Tudor turrets, a large round tower with machicolated
crenellations and a stair-turret rising higher beside it, and a
second octagonal tower at the end of the main elevation that
seems to owe its inspiration to Payne Knight's Downton Castle
in Herefordshire. The S side of the ground floor of this tower
has a unique six-light window of Norman interlace arcading.
The garden door is recessed in a 'Saxon' arch framed by zigzag
mouldings and colonnettes. On the W front a short two-storey
wing with Perp windows and pinnacled buttresses looks like
a chapel but is really kitchen offices. Part of a former house
destroyed by fire about 1800 exists behind this façade.

   The interior is contrived to provide a dramatic entrance with
a narrow flight of steps connecting the *porte cochère*, the main
hall, and the stair hall on one axis. All have elaborate tierceron
84 plaster vaults. The stair is Nash's usual double return design
set in a square space with a pendant vaulted lantern of a gross
Tudor character providing top lighting. The main rooms on
the S offer a succession of square, oval, and octagonal shapes,
classically detailed inside. The house was built for James Stewart of Killymoon, whose family had come to Tyrone in the
Jacobean Plantation and had built Cookstown. His son, Colonel
William Stewart, was responsible for the restoration of Arboe
Cross.

   The STABLE and farmyard N of the house include a mid C18
two-storey block with Gibbs surrounds. The PARK, now partly
planted with conifers or farmed, was much approved of by Sir
Joseph Paxton, who wrote: 'I have visited most of the celebrated country seats in the Kingdom and a very large number
on the continent, and I have never seen one – for the extent
of it – more compact, more perfect in itself, or where the highest
natural beauties have been more aided by refined taste and
judgment, than Killymoon.'

KILMACRENAN   DO D3

A crossroads, a street of houses, and a bridge in a green valley.
St Colmcille spent part of his youth here, fostered by a priest
called Cruithneachan, and later founded a monastery that was
captured and burned in 1129. The lands of this monastery were
taken over by a Franciscan house of the Third Order founded
probably about 1537 by Magnus O'Donnell. In 1603 the friary
lands were granted to James Fullerton by James I, and the
Calendar of State Papers records a bawn built by Captain William
Stewart in 1611. He had also built three 'English style' houses
and was to build more.

CHURCH AND FRIARY RUINS. NE from the crossroads. The
grass-grown ruins of a C17 church with a harled square tower
with battlements that looks mid C18. Described by Lewis as
'a very old structure', it was wainscoted throughout and given
a marble floor at the altar end in 1733. The ruins of the friary
to the E, though large, preserve no architectural detail. The nave
wall on the S, part of the E, and a corner of the W wall remain.
The dimensions are approximately 70 ft by 20 ft.

KILMACRENAN PARISH CHURCH (C of I). A strong little
church in a chunky Gothic idiom built for the Rev. A. Hastings
in 1840–6 almost certainly to designs by *Joseph Welland*. Three-
bay hall and single chancel, with porch tower and octagonal
bell-turret squashed together at the W end of the S side. The
interior unaltered since the building went up. The cost of the
church was £1,220. – STAINED GLASS. Pretty patterned E window of the 1840s.

DOON ROCK. 3 km W, by Kilmacrenan old station. The site
where each succeeding O'Donnell was inaugurated by the
Abbot of Kilmacrenan.

OTHER CHURCHES near Kilmacrenan are ST COLUMB, 3 km
N W, of 1903, a simple gabled hall, vaguely Norman, with a porch
and a polygonal apse; LEITER PRESBYTERIAN CHURCH,
1.5 km E, a harled Gothic hall of 1846 with monster concrete
detailing on its front, but the interior suitably rural, with box
pews, oil lamps, and diagonal pine-panelled ceiling; and
TRENTAGH PRESBYTERIAN CHURCH, 5 km SW, a gabled
hall of 1836 with Y-tracery windows.

Granted to the Mercers' Company in the Jacobean Plantation and
laid out by them on a rise by the w bank of the bawn with a central
square at the top of the hill. The present small town is all C19,
the result of the Company's intention from 1830 'to carry on
extensive improvements in the town, and in the large tract of
dreary, wild and uncultivated country around'. Their efforts are
more obvious in Kilrea than in the countryside, which is still bleak
today.

ST PATRICK, KILREA PARISH (C of I). 1841 by *George Smith*,
   surveyor to the Mercers' Company. Clumsy Norman Revival,
   very like an English Commissioners' church of twenty years
   before. An ashlar box with grouped round-headed lancets,
   three at a time, and thin buttresses. Set at the head of the main
   street leading out of the square, with a tower-cum-flèche across
   the gable end. Gallery inside by *Wm. Barnes* of London, 1862.
      The OLD CHURCH RUIN in the graveyard is pre-Plantation,
   built of boulders, and measuring 56 by 19 ft inside. It was
   repaired in 1613 and in 1690, burnt in 1780, and restored in
   1799. Traces of the C17 bellcote remain on the w gable.
PRESBYTERIAN CHURCH. Built *c.* 1845 by the Rev. H. W.
   Rodgers on a plan similar to those pioneered by the Scottish
   architect William Burn. Basalt and sandstone, vaguely Romanesque, with a very jagged main door and hard angles everywhere.
SECEDING PRESBYTERIAN CHURCH. 1838. A rubble-stone
   Gothic hall with timber Y-traceried windows.
NORTHERN BANK. A two-storey ashlar block on a corner site
   with wayward Italianate detail that could be by *Thomas Turner*.
The siting of Kilrea, together with its planned layout and a
   number of substantial two- and three-storey 'Georgian' houses,
   makes it more memorable than many Ulster towns of a larger
   size. ALBERT PLACE in East Street is a detached six-bay,
   three-storey ashlar block, and the CONVENT further E is
   another large and regular early C19 design, stone, with a five-
   bay, two-storey front and a pedimented central bay.
MERCERS' BAWN. 3.5 km N, on the edge of the River Bann. Of
   the strong castle and bawn built by the Mercers' Company in
   1615 only the polygonal NW flanker and part of the bawn wall
   remain among farm buildings.
CHURCHES in the area are: ST MARY, DRUMGARNER, 2.5 km
   SW, 1842, a five-bay lancet hall with little square tower and

octagonal cupola; TAMLAGHT O'CRILLY PARISH CHURCH, 7 km S, 1775, rebuilt in 1815, tower and hall type, with chancel of 1859 by *Joseph Welland & Son*; and at DRUMBOLG, 7 km S, two PRESBYTERIAN CHURCHES, both gabled halls of 1836.

KINAWLEY

ST NAILE'S CHURCH RUINS. Of the simple rectangular late medieval church that stood on the site of a monastery founded in the C6 by St Natalis no more remains than the E gable, 19 ft 6 in. high inside, and a part of the N wall. In the gable is a two-light mid C15 traceried and cusped window with the usual single-chamfered relieving arch across the reveal inside. The hood moulding on the exterior ends in sculptured heads, a king and queen at the bottom and a bishop above. Two shelf brackets and a credence cavity remain inside.

ST NAILE. Erected through 'the zeal and exertions' of the Rev. Peter Whelan P.P. in 1867–76, large, of stone, too wide for its narrow tower and too much dominated by the smooth grey slopes of its roof, yet curiously successful inside: light and nicely articulated, with a five-bay arcade on cast-iron E.E. columns stepping rhythmically down to the apsed E end. The window detailing is curious, with thin lancets surmounted by circles and triangular plate-traceried E windows at the end of each aisle. The roof is a hipped pine vault. Elaborate wooden chancel arch. Paid for largely by the Maguires of Gortoral House nearby.

ST PAUL, KINAWLEY PARISH CHURCH (C of I). 1857. Hall type, with a buttressed four-bay nave and a two-bay chancel. Round-headed windows. The church is harled and whitewashed outside, making it look like a 1930s hall. Exposed kingpost trusses inside.

GORTORAL HOUSE. 3 km SSW. An early C19 two-storey house with a large semicircular bow in the centre of the main front. Vernacular behind, with a gabled central bay above the door and low hipped-roofed extensions on either side. Built by a branch of the Maguires.

CHRISTCHURCH (C of I). A chapel of ease, 2.5 km NE at Drumany. 1844 by *Joseph Welland*. Three-bay lancet hall with buttresses and a tiny single-bay chancel.

See also Derrylin.

KNOCKALLA FORT *see* PORTSALON

KNOCKBALLYMORE   FM

An unusually perfect mid Georgian house built by the Earl of Erne for his agent probably about 1740 and certainly before 1764, when the old castle at Crom burnt down and the family moved here. The house, though much smaller, has features in common with Mount Ievers in Co. Clare of 1736: that is to say, it is an unusually tall, almost cubic block, 40 ft by *c.* 40 ft, with a high hipped roof and a flat leaded platform in the centre. Five-bay, two-storey on the entrance façade, with a shallow pediment springing from the eaves at the centre three bays. The rear where the ground falls away is three-storey without a pediment, and it is here that the house most resembles Mount Ievers. The attic floor is lit only by windows at the sides, leaving a high band of undecorated wall between the string course above the top-floor windows and the roof line which adds much to the impression of height. The house is rendered, with stone quoins and string courses.

Inside, a big scale-and-platt stair rises directly from the entrance hall, with a moulded handrail and three turned balusters per step. The hall has a good, large-scale modillion cornice. Six-panelled doors set – unusually for this date – in architraves without any lugs.

Attached to the house on the N is a low STABLE COURT of brick and rubble with stone-framed doors. Bellcote on the N side.

OAKFIELD. 1 km S. Lord Erne's second agent's house, built after the family moved to Knockballymore. A low, square block with a shallow hipped roof returning to a central chimneystack with the pots of no less than ten flues lined up in a row. Two-storey with a three-bay front. Ground-floor windows and central door recessed in segment-headed relieving arches. Said to date from the late 1790s.

KNOCKCLOGHRIM   LD

A crossroads in S Co. Derry, with two primitive little churches at hand, the four-storey stalk of a basalt and brick windmill tower, and also a big basalt house for the miller.

KNOCKCLOGHRIM CHURCH (C of I). 1801. Hall and tower type, harled all over. Tower of three stages with pinnacles like blocks of cheese. The nave is three-bay on one side, two- on the other!

CURRAN PRESBYTERIAN CHURCH. 1833, rebuilt 1866, a three-bay rendered hall. Big sandstone porch decorated with ball finials.

LAGHEY   TY J8

A cluster of minor churches s of the Dungannon–Lurgan motorway.

ST ANDREW, KILLYMAN PARISH CHURCH (C of I). A pretty church of 1823. Three-stage tower with pinnacles and battlements. Three-bay hall with Y-traceried windows. Undulating plaster cross-vault inside like a drawing-room ceiling in a Gothic mansion. Polygonal apse, PULPIT, and seating by *Welland & Gillespie*, 1868. – STAINED GLASS. Geometrical patterning by *Mayer & Co.*, 1892. – MONUMENT. Sir William Edward Hercules Verner Bt., 1886. Tablet with Gothic canopy over an elaborate carving of the Entombment.

CATHOLIC CHURCH. Originally of 1786, and unusually early. A long, low, six-bay hall, converted to a T-plan church in the mid C19.

METHODIST CHURCH. 1904. A four-bay hall, plain pointed, with a rock-faced stone gable front.

RECTORY. Opposite St Andrew. Built by the Rev. R. Crump in 1748, though it looks later. Plain, harled, two-storey, on a basement. Ground-floor string course and flush stone surrounds but no quoins. Charles Wesley preached here in 1775 and 1789.

RHONE HILL. 1.5 km s. An unusual house that is not easy to disentangle, built for the Greer family apparently in 1724. Irregular six-bay, two-storey front with the door in the third bay from the E and a miniature pediment and attic window squashed above it. Two rooms deep, with an ample scale-and-platt stair behind the hall. A two-bay, two-storey wing to the N is of diaper stonework. Later or earlier? The house itself has early features: it is of brick laid in Flemish bond, and the sash-windows and boxes are almost flush with the front. Offices behind are dated 1729.

TAMNAMORE HOUSE. 3 km E. A biggish classical villa of two and a half storeys with overhanging eaves on paired bracketed consoles. Shallow hipped roof and grouped chimneys. Rendered in stucco, with rusticated ground floor and Tuscan porch. Lewis mentions the house, so it is pre-1837. The plan looks older, but the stucco front could be mid Victorian.

C7   LAGHY   DO

A pretty group of houses by a river and bridge between Donegal and Ballintra.

LAGHY PARISH CHURCH (C of I). 1837. A diminutive two-bay hall erected by private subscription. Pretty, toy-like architecture: windows with timber Y-tracery and quarry glass, and a gabled front with diagonal buttresses and bellcote, all capped by obelisk-like finials. Restored in 1911–19. N addition and short chancel.

RATHEENY PRESBYTERIAN CHURCH. 1 km N. Built c. 1800. Originally the first Donegal town congregation. A simple harled three-bay hall with a huge Georgian glazed round-headed w window and porch. Inside, original box pews and two-decker PULPIT.

BROOKFIELD. 3 km N. The seat of Mr Bird in the *Post Chaise Companion* of 1786. A small, plain, three-bay, two-storey stone house, very modest and used at the time of writing as a hay loft.

LEARMOUNT *see* PARK

E1   LENAN   DO

A remote plateau below the Urris Hills, rich in unspoilt thatched houses, peat stacks, and strip cultivation, reached either from the N via Clonmany or by the dramatic GAP OF MAMORE, a straight ascent to an 827 ft pass commanding, in the words of the *Parliamentary Gazetteer*, 'a sublime view of the rugged shores and far away expanse of the Atlantic, and of close scenes of Alpine precipice and cloud-cleaving cliff'. The view is truly impressive. Below at LENAN HEAD is a C19 BATTERY and – at the time of writing – all the mess of a derelict army camp. To the NE is ST MICHAEL, Urris, a trim whitewashed hall with a high roof and a multi-gabled porch.

E9   LETTERBREEN CROSS ROADS   FM

METHODIST CHURCH. 1885. A surprisingly picturesque High Victorian church by the crossroads. Squared and coursed

rubble walls with heavy pierced bargeboards, asymmetrical
porch, and polygonal apse. Something of an asset in this area.
SUNNYBANK. 1 km w. Early C19. A stylish three-bay farmhouse,
two storeys high, flanked by single-bay projecting wings with
label mouldings. One was built to serve as a court room!
CORNAGEE CHAPEL OF EASE (C of I). 3 km w. 1817. Built at
a cost of £1,125. A nicely detailed tower and hall type church.
Slender square tower in three stages with battlements. Three-
bay nave.
ST JOSEPH. At Mullaghdrum, 3 km w. 1873. A four-bay nave
with chancel and three-stage tower ending in finials, all curiously naive for its date. Interior with exposed kingpost trusses
and trefoil patterns bored in the timbers. – STAINED GLASS.
E window very bright in scarlet, blue, green, and gold. Symbols
of the Evangelists in quatrefoils.

LETTERKENNY   DOE4

'There is a town called Letterkenny wch hath a Markett evry ffry-
day and two faires in the yeare, with a large stone house, a bawne
of fower flankers, a faire Church, and a Bridg at the E end over
the River Swolly.' Such is the account in the Civil Survey of 1652.
The town remains, but these buildings have all gone. The *Post
Chaise Companion through Ireland* of 1786 has nothing to say of
the place, but by the mid C19 its 'expansive prosperity' was the
subject of comment: Letterkenny was 'fast becoming a place of
importance and wealth'; three banks in the town 'spoke of its
growing trade and commerce'; in the summer there was 'a weekly
communication by steamer with Glasgow'; the cross-channel
trade was 'considerable and increasing'. It had gained a new
lunatic asylum which, with other buildings, marked it out 'as the
county town of the future'. It has grown steadily ever since. The
partition of Ireland has given Letterkenny much of the local trade
that used to be channelled through Derry. It is the centre for con-
sumer durables for most of northern Donegal and the largest town
(pop. 4,930) in the county.
    Set in a peaceful landscape of lush meadows backed by moun-
tain screens, the town still has the air of a big village, and rather
an untidy one, lacking architectural accents. It consists principally
of one main street straggling up the side of a steep hill and down
again. From a distance the impression is one of a ribbon of grey
slate roofs with the needle of a white French spire marking the

highest point. Letterkenny is the seat of the Catholic Bishop c
Raphoe, whose cathedral and palace are here.

ST EUNAN'S CATHEDRAL. The architectural rivalry that de
veloped between the Catholic Church and the Church of Ireland in the later C19 is nowhere better demonstrated than here
The cathedral faces Conwall parish church across the road. Its
site is slightly lower; yet, like St Eugene's Cathedral in Derry
it completely dwarfs the little Protestant church beside it. This
sort of architectural oneupmanship was possible for the Catholic Church only by the end of the last century, and indeed
the cathedral is very late, building from September 1891 to May
1901. The style is a rich one, French Gothic of a late C13 character – that is *the* French Gothic style – crisply handled by
William Hague and after his death in 1899 by *T. F. McNamara*,
his junior partner. St Eunan's is possibly Hague's most faithful
Gothic exercise: a large cruciform church with a polygonal
choir, ambulatory, lady chapel, and an offset S spire flanking
the side of the choir. The orientation is reversed; otherwise the
building is an orthodox cathedral design: a five-bay nave with
aisles and two-bay transepts.

124   EXTERIOR. Built of Mountcharles freestone, a pinkish
biscuit colour, banded at the window levels in green slate. The
walls of squared coursed rubble. Tracery and quoins smooth-
faced. Architectural display is concentrated on the spire and
at the main front, though the transept gables with large wheel
windows and transitional Irish Romanesque doors below are
worth attention. The best view of the cathedral, rarely obtained,
is in fact from the SW. The front is composed round a large
gable window with flanking towers ending in miniature spires
buttressing the ends of the nave wall. Similar towers are at the
ends of the aisles. Between are three doors, deeply recessed, with
colonnettes to the reveals. Flying buttresses and an arcade of
four cusped arches link the aisle towers to the nave walls. On
the main towers statues of St Eunan and St Colmcille in
canopied niches. In the tracery of the window St Michael below
the central rose, and the Crucifixion in the gable. The sculptural
work is by *Daniel Gilliland* of *Purdy & Millard* of Belfast. The
spire is particularly elegant, octagonal, rising from a base with
crocketed corner pinnacles and itself banded and crocketed increasingly towards the top.

INTERIOR. Solemn and rather murky owing to the quantity
of stained glass and liberal use of gilding and stencilling. Nave
with classic French geometrical tracery to the clerestory and

a lierne-vault. Aisles and transepts similarly vaulted, with a pendant star-vault at the crossing. The chief interest of the interior is in the elaborate crossing arch, carved in a continuous ribbon, 3ft wide, contained between the colonnettes of the piers. This is by *Purdy*. In the centre of the soffit, God the father is flanked by long figures of St Eunan and St Colmcille on s and N respectively. Each figure is supported on a cloud of cherubs' heads. From here down, scenes from the lives of the two saints mixed with emblematic creatures are intertwined in corded ropes whose tasselled ends come to the bottom of the arch where the saints' names are inscribed. The choir is richer than the nave and transepts, flanked by an ambulatory and side chapels. Note the curious double width of the first bay – not quite resolved in the vaulting above. The vaulting is enriched with gold and green stencilling; the spandrels of the arcades are painted with arabesques of vine leaves and birds on a gold ground. The LADY CHAPEL behind the high altar is lit by an oculus in the top of the vault. – BAPTISTERY. A theatrical space in the base of the tower. – FONT. A sculptured marble octagon supported on eight green marble colonnettes with an oak 'dome' cover. – PULPIT and ALTAR RAIL by *Pearse & Co.* of Dublin. – STAINED GLASS. Transepts by *Michael Healy*, 1910–11; clerestory by *Harry Clarke*, 1928–9.

CONWALL PARISH CHURCH (C of I). Mid to late C18, described by Lewis as 'a small plain structure with a spire'. Minimal Gothic. Tower and hall type, rubble-built, with an octagonal ashlar spire. s aisle, treated in elevation as three sharp gables with plate-tracery windows, of 1865 by *Welland & Gillespie*, contractor W. McClelland. The interior retains its early C19 cast-iron circular roof trusses and a short gallery. Red sandstone arcade to the s aisle. Nice twisted brass light brackets.

ST EUNAN'S SECONDARY SCHOOL. Prominently set in open ground above the cathedral. 1904–6 by *T. F. McNamara*. The one obvious piece of architecture after the churches in Letterkenny: a big three-storey castle, heavily picturesque, rectangular, with a round tower at each corner, like Inveraray or Kinloch on the Isle of Rhum. One tower has a conical roof; the others are battlemented. Rich Irish Romanesque arcading across the ground-floor windows, with interlace and zigzag patterns to the column shafts. The interior is impressive. Large granite shafts with Celtic capitals flank the door in the vestibule that leads straight to the main stair. On either side doors open to a cloistered courtyard. Massively solid, drum columns with cushion capitals, broken into on the E side by the drum of the staircase tower. The wing of 1930 is by *W. H. Byrne & Son* – NEW CHAPEL. Double-gabled, with triangular-topped windows.

BISHOP'S PALACE AND PAROCHIAL HOUSE. N of the cathedral. A substantial three-storey stone block built in 1900 in squared boulder-faced sandstone. Segment-headed windows and gables.

LORETO CONVENT. SW of the cathedral and older than it, a small rubble-stone complex. The chapel has a short campanile and plate tracery. The original group was built in 1860 by *Hadfield & Goldie* at a cost of £1,600. Extended in 1897.

TOUR

Most of the town's buildings can be taken in by a walk along the main street from E to W. First, opposite the Kilmacrenan Road, the COURT HOUSE by *John Hargrave*, 1828–9, a two-storey, three-bay classical front with a gable pediment and aediculed windows to the first floor. Blank ground floor with flanking single-bay porches on either side. Galleried court room inside with cells below. Immediately E the TAX OFFICE – a five-bay, two-storey late Georgian house with overhanging eaves, a porch, and pretty cast-iron Gothic railings.

From here on all the good buildings are on the S side of the street. No. 61, the ROYAL BANK, has a wide Italianate classical front in stucco. Channelled ground floor with carved keystone heads and pedimented windows above. Next to the bank TRINITY PRESBYTERIAN CHURCH. A date-stone declares the origin of the congregation in 1640. This building is of 1907, personal Perp in slate and sandstone, with a gable to the street, an E porch, and a S tower all squashed together. Four-bay galleried hall behind. The MUNSTER AND LEINSTER BANK is late C19 stuccoed Italianate classical with a Mannerist ground floor.

Now half-way down the main street on the edge of Market Square the HIBERNIAN BANK of 1874 by *Timothy Hevey*. Local rogue architecture: aggressively ornate Gothic, with attached columns in polished granite, red sandstone trim, and squared blue rubble walls. Two-storey, four-bay, with doors with heavy balconied porches at either end. Paired windows between. The MARKET SQUARE is on a sloping site dominated at the top by a big polychrome terrace, MOUNT SOUTHWELL PLACE. It could have townscape value, with the spire of the cathedral rising to the N, but is messy, spoilt by an ugly shelter and a tele-

graph pole swathed with wires. Half-way down Lower Main
Street is the LITERARY INSTITUTE of 1876, also by *Timothy
Hevey*, a modest red-brick Gothic façade of two storeys. Not
as grand as it was intended to be.

On the KILMACRENAN ROAD are the former UNION WORK-
HOUSE of 1843 by *George Wilkinson*, a standard Tudor design,
and further up the hill, out of the town, the DONEGAL MEN-
TAL HOSPITAL, also by *Wilkinson*, 1860–5. The usual succession of plain institutional buildings, enlarged in 1872, 1876,
and 1886 by *John Boyd* of Belfast and in 1893 by *William McElwee*. The hospital CHAPEL, nine-bay neo-Norman with an
apsidal E end, is of 1935 by *C. McLoughlin*.

NEIGHBOURHOOD

CONWALL OLD CHURCH RUINS. 3 km WSW. The site of an
early Christian monastery of which St Fiachrius was abbot
about the early C7. The ruins are of a rectangular church, 56 ft
by 22 ft, the walls standing only to about 5 ft, except on the
S, where they are much rebuilt. Fragments of cut stone and
single-chamfered arches of late medieval and C17 date. The
church was apparently divided into two cells at the W end. To
the S on a raised rubble plinth are several SLABS AND PILLAR
STONES. The finest is an elaborate slab with a High Cross pattern in shallow relief and bands of interlace on either side of
the shaft, said to have been carved for the grave of Godfrey
O'Donnell, who died in 1258. Beside it is a small pillar stone,
3 ft high, with swastika and spiral decoration at the top. Other
smaller stones include five with simple line crosses, one circu-
lar-pattern cross, set up at the extreme end of the plinth, and
one Greek cross. The incised pillar with primitively carved crucifix (date?) was discovered here in 1968.

CHURCH RUINS. 3 km NE. The walls of a rectangular church
of the C17, 19 ft by 43 ft. Segment-headed window openings.
W gable slate-hung.

BALLYMACOOL. 1.5 km WSW. The estate belonged to the Boyd
family, who are said to have built the present house about 1770.
If that is true it was probably a five-bay, two-storey design with
a break forward in the middle bay like Killygordon House not
far away. Early in the C19 Ballymacool went Elizabethan, gaining an extra storey and three unequal gables across the main
front and an oriel window over the main door. Gabled dormer
windows to the sides. Cross-mullioned windows with label
mouldings in the stucco. The interior detail, all rather gross,

suggests *John Hargrave* as the architect of this transmogrifica-
tion.

ROCKHILL HOUSE. 2.5 km SW. In a mature park across th
River Swilly, a big classical house of three distinct periods. Th
main front is the most recent part of the house: a five-bay, two-
storey block, two bays deep, with a big Doric porch with a triglyph frieze in the middle of the main front. Stucco with sandstone trim and quoins. Console brackets to the eaves. All b
John Robinson and built in 1853. The s end of this block is
segmental bow that connects to a long façade of nine bays an
three storeys, with a slate-roofed bow in the centre three bays
built by *John Hargrave* for John V. Stewart some time afte
1823. The three bays between Robinson's segmental bow and
Hargrave's semicircular bow are the end of an c18 house whos
façade is completely obliterated by the front of 1853. Insid
on the site of this house is a vast square hall, top-lit, with ar
arcade and balcony running round at first-floor level.

LECK PARISH CHURCH (C of I). 3 km SE. About to be rebuil
in 1837. A three-bay lancet hall with double-chamfered stone
reveals to the windows, double Y-tracery E window, and W bellcote.

LECK GLEBE HOUSE. 3 km SE. 1820. A typical two-storey
three-bay Regency glebe house with a shallow hipped roof and
overhanging eaves.

LECK OLD CHURCH. 1 km S. In a graveyard, the ruins of a rectangular c17 church measuring 20 ft by 60 ft. W bellcote. Three
windows down each side (one on the S was a door) and segment-
headed E and W window openings. No details remain.

BALLYRAINE HOTEL. At the E entry to the town. 1968 by
Michael Scott. A long, low building in grey brick, straddling
a shallow hill.

CHAPEL OF EASE (C of I). 4 km ENE. Mid c19. A three-bay
harled hall with narrow lancets and a fancy W bellcote.

CHURCH RUINS. 2.5 km ENE. The walls of a rectangular church,
19 ft by 43 ft. c17 segment-headed window openings. W gable
slate-hung.

KILTOY LODGE. 2 km ENE. A nice three-bay, two-storey house
of *c.* 1820 with tripartite windows to the outer bays. Pretty
thatched lodge opposite the gates.

GORTLEE CATHOLIC CHURCH. 1 km ENE. 1785 and 1904. A
four-bay rendered hall with round-headed windows.

LETTERMACAWARD   DO B5

, remote coastal parish by Gweebara bay and river.

LD CHURCH RUINS. 0.5 km W of Gweebara bridge. No more
than some low walls of a rectangular building, 30 ft by 19 ft.

LETTERMACAWARD PARISH CHURCH (C of I). 1788. A three-
bay hall with bellcote and Y-traceried timber windows built
beside the old church ruins.

GLEBE HOUSE. 1 km W. 1828. A pretty three-bay, two-storey
house, nicely proportioned and L-shaped behind. The middle
window on each floor is a dummy.

CATHOLIC CHURCH. 1 km N. A six-bay harled mid C19 Gothic
hall.

At DOOCHARY, 9.5 km NE, a surprisingly substantial group of
slated terraced houses by a bridge and some pretty thatched
cottages. The CATHOLIC CHURCH is a five-bay mid C19
Gothic hall.

LIFFORD   DO F5

A small town (pop. 1,121) pleasantly situated on the W bank of
the Foyle opposite Strabane. The situation is important, for it
is here that the Foyle begins, formed by the meeting of the
Mourne and Finn rivers. Hence the towns on either bank. Lifford
is the older and historically the more important, but it lost out
to Strabane in the C19, and is often referred to in older guide books
as a mere suburb of the Co. Tyrone town. Characteristically, the
canal proposed to bring prosperity to Lifford was never built –
that to Strabane was.

Nothing remains of the Irish castle where Red Hugh O'Donnell
entertained Don Alonzo Copis, the ambassador of Philip II of
Spain, in 1596, nor of 'the good strong fort of lime and stone'
that succeeded it, built in 1611 by Sir Richard Hansard, the grantee of the Jacobean Plantation. By 1607 Sir Richard, a Cambridge
graduate and soldier, had built up the town with twenty-one
houses 'of good timber after the English manner', and thirty-
seven cottages of one hearth each were added by others at the same
time. £400 was settled from his estate with an endowment of £86
a year to build the church and found a free school – but of all
this activity only a monument in the church remains today. By
English standards this is not particularly notable; yet it is the
finest Jacobean monument in North West Ulster and worth a visit
to the parish church.

CLONLEIGH PARISH CHURCH (C of I). Erected under the wil
of Sir Richard Hansard, the foundations laid by 1622. A
simple tower and nave type church, now of late C18 appearanc
– described in 1768 as 'in good repair'. The tower, very thin
of coursed rubble with clasping buttresses and Irish steppe
battlements, was added c. 1800 by the rector, Mr Daniel. N aisl
and interior arrangement by *Welland & Gillespie*, 1863. Nav
with exposed kingpost trusses; wagon roof to the chancel. E
window triple-light Dec type. – MONUMENT. Sir Richar
49 Hansard Kt. † 5 October 1619 and Dame Anne his wife † 2
October 1619. Two kneeling figures in Jacobean costume facing
each other across a draped reading-desk. Sir Richard is in
Cavalier armour with moustache, beard, and curly hair radiating from the crown of his head. His lady wears a long veil.
The group, with a tablet inscription behind, is recessed inside
a primitive segmental arch.

55 COURT HOUSE. A handsome building that may soon be added
to an already long list of Lifford losses. Brett calls it 'one of
the finest buildings in the north, and one of the most neglected'.
For Ulster court houses both remarks are true. The building
forms the SE side of a once attractive square, a long, low classical
design in the Board of Ordnance idiom coined by Vanbrugh
and Gibbs. The architect here is *Michael Priestley*, the date 1746.
Both are inscribed on a panel with the arms of George II above
the door, and the grand jury lists record a payment in 1754 of
£23 4s. 6d. 'to Mr. Mick. Priestley to reimburse him for building the Sessions House and Gaol'.

Only the front is architecturally conscious, but that is good.
Seven bays (with an extra bay on the l.), stepped out slightly
over the middle three bays. Dressed sandstone quoins and
string courses; the walls harled. The windows have Gibbs surrounds and segmental heads. Central door with pulvinated
frieze and a bold pediment. A screen wall hides the basement
that once contained the gaol. The roof is hidden behind a parapet, described in 1757 as battlemented – did Priestley get these
Vanbrughian ideas through Pearce? – but now plain. Tall
Venetian windows on the river side. The interior, altered in
1830, is virtually derelict at the time of writing, though the hall
retains a big bold plaster cornice, characteristic of the provincial
classicism of this period.

To the l. of the court house at r. angles to it and closing the square
was the COUNTY GAOL, a cardboard-castle-style design like
a folly, identical with Derry Old Gaol, with square and octa-

gonal towers flanking a central gate. The architect was apparently *Edward Miller*; the date 1793.

In the vicinity of the court house are some pleasantly scaled vernacular classical buildings. First, DONEGAL COUNTY COUNCIL OFFICES, late C19, a seven-bay, two-storey block with a Tuscan aediculed door. To the w a pair of mid Victorian rubble and brick houses. JOHN DEVINE & CO. has a vaguely Lombard tower, the GARDA STATION is of *c.* 1850, Tudor, with label mouldings. The COUNTY PLANNING OFFICE, a decent five-bay, three-storey house, has been abominably treated on the top floor by the local authority architects.

BALLYDUFF HOUSE. On the Raphoe Road, pleasantly situated in a garden. A five-bay, two-storey rendered house, reputedly C17 in origin. It now looks late C18 at the earliest. Off-centre porch with Doric pilasters.

PORT HALL. 5 km NNE. One of the finest small houses in the area, built in 1746 for John Vaughan of Buncrana Castle, presumably by *Michael Priestley*, the architect of the court house. The style is similar: a little old-fashioned, with narrow windows and rusticated stone bands running up the front to contrast with the harling. The front, nicely set at the end of an avenue of trees, is of five bays and two storeys, with a high parapet stepped into a pediment over the centre three bays, which project slightly. As at the court house, the basement is hidden by a parapet wall. Gibbs surrounds to all the windows on the front and to the door surmounted by the coat of arms of George II. In the pediment a small Diocletian window. The plan is of double-pile type, with paired chimneys appearing at the sides. The back of the house facing the river – the port part rather than the hall – is a straightforward harled block, with no quoins or Gibbs surrounds. Three-storey, as the basement is now exposed. Two warehouse wings of two storeys flank the main block to form an 'office' court.

ST PATRICK. 2 km NW. The site of one of the first Catholic churches built since Penal times, on land given by Lord Erne in the late C18. A three-stage Gothic tower of about 1820 has been kept as a feature isolated from the new church, 1963 by *Liam McCormick*, on a cruciform plan, but with blunt-nosed gables and canted side walls to give more space in the middle and a better view. Nicely detailed, though the idiom is possibly more that of a school or concert hall than a church.

BALLINDRAIT. 3 km WNW. A village round a triangular green with pollarded sycamores. The plan is presumably C17. Some thatched houses. The PRESBYTERIAN CHURCH, an early C19 harled hall, has double Y-tracery windows. CAVANACOR HOUSE is late C18, five-bay, two-storey, with a porch.

LIMAVADY

Limavady, in the fertile countryside at the foot of the Roe valley, was until the Plantation of Ulster the seat of O'Cahan power. Its name, meaning 'dog's leap', is taken from the O'Cahan castle that was built with the river as a natural moat over which a dog with a message in its collar is said to have leapt to get aid from Dungiven when the castle was attacked. From here the O'Cahans sent an army to Scotland to help Robert the Bruce at Bannockburn in 1314. At the Plantation of Ulster in the early C17 the castle and some 3,500 acres around the Roe valley were taken by Sir Thomas Phillips, the overseer of the London Companies' estates. By 1611 he had reinforced the castle with a subsidy of £200 from the Crown, and by 1622 had established a Newtown of Limavady about a mile from the castle, with eighteen small houses set round a crossroads, and a stone cross at the centre. Sir Thomas was attacked in the castle in 1641, and, though the garrison held out the first year, the building and the town were ultimately taken and burned. Limavady was again destroyed in 1688, and though it was rebuilt after 1690, its appearance now is of the later C18 onwards. Indeed, in the Georgian period the town enjoyed considerable affluence, benefiting no doubt from the periodic visits of Speaker William Conolly, who purchased the estate from the Phillips family and built Roe Park just S of the town. After the Act of Union, when it lost two Members of Parliament, it seems to have declined in civic status.

CHURCHES

CHRIST CHURCH, DRUMACHOSE PARISH CHURCH (C of I). A tower and hall type church of the mid C18 – the tower is dated 1749 – enlarged by the addition of a N transept in 1824 and reconstructed by *Turner & Babington* of Derry in 1881, when a chancel and S transept were added. The church is visually dull except for the four-stage harled tower; this has a certain stocky vigour, with each stage just a little narrower than the one below, making it look as if it could pack up like a telescope. The interior is dark and rich, the roof panelled and supported on braced trusses with wall posts. Fussy Bath stone chancel arch with bosses set in the cove by *R. E. Buchanan*, 1913. (For Drumachose, *see also* Drenagh.)

ST MARY. 1836, on the site of a chapel of 1783. A long five-bay hall of coursed rubble with battlemented gables and pinnacles. 'Repaired and improved' to designs of the local architect *George Given* in 1846, which probably means the E and W porches, the pretty cusped lancet windows with quarry glass, and perhaps even the N and S transepts that cross in the middle of the third bay. The tall belfry tower at the N end was added by a Dr O'Brien in 1896.

LIMAVADY FIRST PRESBYTERIAN CHURCH. In Rathmore Road. 1856. A hard little design in basalt and sandstone with minimal Tudoresque detail. Three-bay front with forestanding two-storey gabled porch, single-bay side gables, and a four-bay hall behind. Like one of the nastier illustrations out of Loudon's *Architectural Magazine*, though apparently this is an adaptation of *Charles Lanyon*'s design for the Church Accommodation Society at Hollymount, Co. Down, and at Carrick Rocks (*see* p. 355).

LIMAVADY SECOND PRESBYTERIAN CHURCH. 1840. A five-bay hall with a sandstone temple front of dressed ashlar. Big gable pediment supported on four Ionic pilasters that are rather too thin. Interior with a gallery round three sides.

DRUMACHOSE PRESBYTERIAN CHURCH. 1877. A harled and sandstone cruciform church with flamboyant tracery windows and a thin belfry-tower-cum-porch, set in the angle between nave and N transept. Reputedly a design by the incumbent, Dr *N. M. Brown*.

METHODIST CHURCH. 1877. A black basalt hall in rudimentary Gothic.

GOSPEL HALL. 1830. Formerly the court house and probably by *Robert Given*, a tall, ashlar-fronted hall erected by the local landlords, with gable pediment and three-bay, two-storey front. Ground floor plain, first floor with a large Tuscan aedicule flanked by blank niches.

PUBLIC BUILDINGS

TOWN HALL. 1872. An unusually tall, three-bay classical block, free-standing, with a big gable pediment and a late Baroque bowed balcony on consoles to distinguish the middle first-floor window. Ground floor rusticated. An earlier proposal for a town hall was reported in *The Builder* in February 1858. This building was reconstructed in 1953 by *I. W. Lynch*.

COURT HOUSE. 1914. Not everybody's idea of a court house,
for this is surely the architecture of Toytown: a red-brick
single-storey hall with a high gabled roof and a dinky two-storey
tower in the middle, square, with a pyramid roof like a hat.

POST OFFICE. 1952 by *T. F. O. Rippingham*. Orange brick and
concrete trim with fussy tile-hung stepped gables and other
outdated gimmicks. A sad falling-off from earlier and better
work by this architect.

96 ROE VALLEY HOSPITAL. The former Union Workhouse. By
George Wilkinson, 1841, the standard large design, unusually
complete and in good order. The Tudoresque five-bay gabled
governor's house has a fifteen-bay, two-storey block behind
ending in double-bay three-storey towers with paired gables
and square stair-turrets behind.

TOWN TOUR

The centre of Limavady has more to offer in terms of good street
architecture than many Ulster towns and preserves still a fragile
idea of its C18 and early C19 appearance. As all the modern
straggle has been kept to the E and s, the most evocative views
may be had from the w, where the River Roe is still, as it was
in Phillips's day, the natural boundary of the town. The slightly
elevated site of Limavady is best seen from Roe Bridge, which
leads E into CATHERINE STREET. The entry here used to be
marked on the r. by the handsome frontage of the War
Memorial Building, a long two-storey house ending in segmental bays, erected by the Boyle family about 1735, bombed and
demolished in 1974. Its Tuscan aedicule porch had close similarities with the work of *Davis Ducart* at Lissan House.

Catherine Street appears on the earliest plans as The Green. It
is partly tree-lined and has a quantity of nice early C19 terraced
houses, several with coach arch pends leading through to
gardens at the back. No. 44, the ORANGE HALL, is of 1890
by *R. E. Buchanan*. Nos. 30–34, including the ULSTER BANK,
was once a fine three-storey terrace, and No. 34 the finest house,
with a fanlight door framed by Tuscan columns set in a recessed
segmental arch. The POLICE STATION, a fine four-bay, two-
storey house with tripartite windows throughout, is of *c.* 1840.

At the E end of Catherine Street IRISH GREEN STREET runs
r. (s) and MARKET STREET l. (N). The pedimented coach arch
facing down Catherine Street is the old CORN MARKET, built
by Edward Boyle about 1822. Further N is a Victorian red and
yellow brick terrace, Nos. 41–47, and then the street joins

MAIN STREET about its middle. The parish church is at the head of the street to the NE (r.), and at the other end is THE LODGE, a nice five-bay, two-storey house with a central eaves pediment and an *œil de bœuf*, dating from 1782, and said to occupy the site of C17 defence works. Main Street deserves its name, with a quantity of good terraced houses, nicely detailed, and partly screened by trees. It would benefit, as would the whole town, from a more responsible attitude on the part of the local authority planning department that has permitted appalling devastation in the name of modernization to many shop-fronts and houses. Some of the nicest blocks remaining are Nos. 13 and 15, a pair of four-bay, three-storey houses, one red brick, one cement-rendered; Nos. 21 and 23, with pretty early Victorian doorcases; and Nos. 14 to 18, which make up a grand four-storey brick block, No. 14 – Moffat Donaghy & Co. – preserving a fine late Georgian shop-front flanked by Greek Ionic columns. At its SW end the street turns l. down LINENHALL STREET, predominantly C19 Georgian vernacular, with ALBERT TERRACE, Nos. 28–46, late Victorian, with bay-windows and nice iron railings; and the MASONIC HALL (No. 48) by *W. J. Given*, built in 1900 to an irregular off-beat classical design in red brick. Linenhall Street leads back into the SW end of Catherine Street. Oddly, the churches of Limavady (*see* above) are all outside its main rectangle of streets: four are dotted about the S end of Irish Green Street, and two more are in Church Street, almost in the country, well E of the parish church, which is itself on the edge of the old town.

NEIGHBOURHOOD: WEST DISTRICT

ROE PARK. 1.5 km SSW. The estate was purchased about 1700 by William Conolly, M.P. for Co. Londonderry and Speaker of the Irish House of Commons from 1715. Subsequently he built a house called Daisy Hill, the core of the present mansion, a seven-bay, two-storey range with the middle three bays in a boldly projected semicircular bow, and a Tuscan aedicule door in the middle. On Conolly's death his estates in the North of Ireland passed to the McCausland family, under whom the house was extended by the addition of a dining room. Then in 1826 it was bought by Sir Francis McNaughton, who added a drawing room. The new rooms are apparently the four-bay and three-bay extensions to the N and S that end in wide canted bays. Their rooms are higher than the rest and have some vigorous C19 classical cornices.

The STABLE COURT, s of the house, is a finer piece of architecture. Seven-bay, two-storey coach-house block of *c.* 1740, Palladian in style, with the three middle bays higher than the rest, the middle with an eaves pediment and the building line stepped forward at each bay. In the walled garden on a hill behind the yard an irregular two-storey battlemented GAZEBO.

ARDNARGLE. 1.5 km N. A plain square house built about 1780 by James Ogilby and improved in 1855 by Robert Leslie Ogilby, who added an ashlar stone porch, aedicules to the windows, and a big modillion cornice in stucco. The house has irregular fenestration with a five-bay, two-storey front that suggests that he may have enlarged the building as well. The stucco improvements were removed in 1966, leaving the place a little bald.

SAMPSON'S TOWER. 1.5 km WNW in a strip of woodland. A square battlemented tower with a circular stair-turret and a battered base built of sandstone and slate rubble. A plaque bears the inscription 'Erected by public subscription in memory of Arthur Sampson, for nearly forty years J.P. for the counties of Londonderry and Tyrone, and Agent of the Worshipful Company of Fishmongers. He died on 22nd January, 1859 in the 64th year of his age.' Forty-eight steps lead to the top, very narrow and not recommended for fat people.

CULMORE HOUSE. 4 km N. Dated 1805 on a brick. An excellently finished late Georgian brick house, five-bay, two-storey, on a semi-basement, with a broad flight of steps in the middle leading to the front door. The central bay – wider than the rest – is nicely treated with niches either side of the door and thin blind windows on the floor above repeating the pattern. Inside, a nice circular staircase, and some rooms with more niches.

ST JOHN, MYROE CHAPEL OF EASE (C of I). 3.5 km NW. A tiny hall of 1863 in polygonal black basalt with diagonal buttresses bellcote, and side porch. By *Welland & Gillespie*.

MYROE PRESBYTERIAN CHURCH. 3 km N. 1832. A six-bay hall with round-headed windows.

LARGY PRESBYTERIAN CHURCH. 4.5 km S. 1831. A stuccoed L-shaped gabled hall.

TAMLAGHT OLD CHURCH RUINS. 2 km WSW, by Tamlaght Bridge. A small rectangular structure, 18 ft by 54 ft inside, the remains of the medieval predecessor of the Protestant garrison church, itself now a ruin, at Ballykelly. Ivy-covered, with the E gable still standing.

NEIGHBOURHOOD: EAST DISTRICT

AGHANLOO PARISH CHURCH (C of I). 4.5 km N, on the Down- 86
hill road. One of the prettiest Board of First Fruits churches,
begun in August 1823 to a frequently used design by *John
Bowden*. Tower and hall type. Three-stage tower sharply
tapered at the belfry stage before big pinnacles and Irish battlements. Three-bay nave with pretty cusped Y-traceried windows in timber. Built of big blocks of squared basalt partly gal-
letted with thick mortar joints contrasting in a lively way with
the sandstone quoins, mouldings, and window frames. Inside
is a false chancel accommodated within the last bay of the nave
with little rooms on each side – just the thing Tractarians would
hate. The grass-grown mound immediately to the N is the site
of the former church.

BALTEAGH PARISH CHURCH (C of I). 4.5 km ESE, at Ardmore.
1815. A standard tower and hall type church built of slate
rubble with sandstone trim. Three-stage tower with battlements and pinnacles; four-bay nave with short chancel. Originally the church had windows only on the S side. Those on the
N were added in 1894.

BALTEAGH PRESBYTERIAN CHURCH. 6 km SE. 1823. A six-
bay hall with battlemented porch.

BALTEAGH OLD RECTORY. N of the church. Mid to late C18.
A tall, almost gaunt old house, three-storey, five-bay, with diamond-cut quoins and round-headed door. Later porch. Lugged
door surrounds.

ARDMORE LODGE. N of the church. Early C19, a haphazard
jumble of classical character with two plaster plaques and a bay-
window.

CARRICK CHURCH (C of I). 5 km S on the E bank of the Roe
by Carrick Rocks. An 'improved' church of 1846 with a spiky
Gothic front of three bays. The central gable and gabled porch
mask a three-bay nave and chancel behind.

CARRICKMORE OLD RECTORY. By the church. An irregular
Elizabethan group with stepped gables, label mouldings, and
diagonal chimneys, like Florence Court Rectory, and of about
1850.

BERESFORD OBELISK. 6 km SSE at Ballyquin. 1840. A sandstone obelisk set on two steps on a high plinth, in all about 40 ft
high. A plaque bears the inscription: 'This pillar was erected
by the tenants of the Estates of the Most Noble Marquess of
Waterford in this county to commemorate the virtues and

talents that distinguished and adorned their late Agent, Henry Barre Beresford Esq. Born 1784 at Walworth in this county. Died 1837. 7th son of the Rt. Hon. John Beresford.'

LINSFORT see DESERTEGNEY

LISBELLAW

CHAPEL OF EASE, CLEENISH PARISH (C of I). The church is the principal feature of this village, set on a little hill behind the main street and, since the addition of a late Victorian bell-tower, seen from everywhere. It is of three periods: first the nave and shallow chancel built in 1764 by the first Earl of Ross, who is buried in a vault below; then a wide N extension of *c*. 1793 that makes the church L-shaped; and finally the vestry and the three-stage W tower of coursed rubble stone with a clock and open belfry above. The church apparently always had a tower but the present design is late Victorian. The extension must have followed the original building fairly soon, as the cut stone eaves cornice and segment-headed mullioned windows are the same. The windows of the original church were given rather widely spaced provincial Gibbs surrounds, and the corners have diamond-cut quoins. Both these features are omitted on the extension. The arrangement inside dates from 1853, but the E end, opening through a segmental chancel arch, still has a pretty vine and grape motif in plaster in the ceiling and a robust Venetian window with quarter-engaged Tuscan columns in the centre and World War I memorial glass. (For Cleenish, *see also* Bellanaleck.)

CATHOLIC CHURCH. A large mid C19 stone-built hall of six bays, with long lancet windows and buttresses. Four-light E window with geometrical tracery. The W gable is completely blank, with a chunky bellcote, empty statue niche, and blank stones protected by label mouldings but lacking any inscription.

PRESBYTERIAN CHURCH. At the bottom of the hill. A four-bay lancet hall of the mid C19. Elaborate four-light geometrical E window.

METHODIST CHURCH. The standard Co. Fermanagh two-bay hall and porch.

This village, in the C17 and C18, was the property of the Gore family seated at Bell Isle. In the early C19 both house and village passed to the Porter family. The main public building, half-way down the central street, is the COURT HOUSE, a small three-bay, two-storey structure with an arcaded ground floor (originally open) facing down the road to Bell Isle (*see* p. 144). The only other building of note was the small Gothic RAIL-WAY STATION, a delightful symmetrical design of 1861 by *William G. Murray*, with high gables and curiously spiky plate-traceried windows – at the time of writing derelict.

SNOWHILL. 2.5 km ENE. A handsome minor country house built by James Johnstone of Snowhill, probably about 1760. The house sits well in a lovely park of undulating country with specimen trees, ilexes and maples. The front is consciously architectural: a five-bay, two-storey design on a high basement with a tall band of wall between the top of the first-floor windows and the eaves, as at Knockballymore. Pedimented door in the central bay, approached by a high flight of steps, with a Gibbs surround and a small Venetian window above. Lugged architraves to the other windows and cut stone quoins at the corners. Double-gabled sides and a totally irregular rear elevation. A hall runs through the house. Lugged six-panel doors.

GATE LODGE. A pretty, five-bay Regency Gothic cottage with the motto 'Nunquam non paratus'. Built opposite the gate because it was nice for visitors to know who owned the land on both sides of the road!

KILLYREAGH HOUSE. 3 km WNW. A five-bay, two-storey late Georgian house of *c.* 1830 in a beautiful situation commanding wide views. In the centre is a two-storey projecting porch with coupled sash-windows under label mouldings. Quoins to all the corners.

COOLBRUCK CHURCH (C of I). 3 km NNE. Early C19. A tiny hall with coupled round-headed lancets, benches inside, and a wooden altar rail. Built by a Mr Ford as a school on his own land and handed over to the Rev. J. G. Porter for a church.

LISGOOLE ABBEY   FM *E*9

A charming early C19 Gothic villa built by a Mr M. Jones on the site of a celebrated monastery. Plain, of two storeys, nicely proportioned but quite standard, with a three-bay front marked in the centre by a segment-headed door with side lights and with big tripartite windows on either side, it sits on a little podium and is attached, on the N, to a nice fat tower, square, with Irish stepped battlements that rise a little higher than the eaves of the villa proper. The tower, with perhaps some of the range of buildings extending behind it, is all that remains of

the abbey – much re-worked. It contains one large square room
lit by an enormous tripartite window on the main front. The
interior is a surprise, for the house was decorated *c.* 1910 by
Waring & Gillow, who provided elaborate plasterwork, a curving main stair, and an Elizabethan-style fireplace. At the same
time battlements to match the tower were added across the front
of Mr Jones's villa, making it even prettier.

The ABBEY BUILDINGS, now represented by the tower
alone, had an involved history. The first monastery here, an
early Christian foundation associated with St Aid of Lisgovel,
was succeeded in 1106 by a monastery of St Mary that became
an Augustinian house about the middle of the C12. By 1485
the full dedication is given as SS. Peter, Paul, and Mary. In
the time of Abbot Cahill MacBrian the buildings were ruinous
and divine service was neglected to such an extent that the Lord
of Co. Fermanagh, Cuchonnaght Maguire, made an agreement
to have the buildings restored and to introduce Franciscans to
take over the abbey. This was done about 1580–3, though the
friars apparently did not complete their work before being
driven out in 1598.

HOLY TRINITY (C of I). 1852–65. Lord Balfour of Clanawley
built a church here about 1622, intending that it should become
the parish church of Aghalurcher. That never happened (*see*
Colebrooke Park), though the building was used throughout
the C18, when the handsome sandstone gatepiers to the present
churchyard were built. Lord Balfour's church was replaced by
a chapel of ease in 1814, and that by the present big church
designed by *Joseph Welland.* Five-bay nave with N and S aisles
of four bays. Two-bay chancel and offset square tower at the
W end between the N aisle and the nave (the orientation is actually N–S). Dec windows, with quatrefoils in the clerestory. The
walls are rather sheer and boxy-looking, perhaps because the
buttresses seem too small. Inside, double-chamfered arcades
on octagonal columns link the aisles to the nave. Open trussed
timber roof and oak-panelled chancel.

CHURCH OF THE HOLY CROSS. On a hill to the E, overlooking
the town. 1902–7 by *T. F. McNamara*, six-bay Gothic hall with
lancet windows, a shallow polygonal apse, and an offset tower
by the main gable, four-storey, with double louvres at the top
and a thin broach-spire. The interior has braced crossed

trusses, marble shafts to the chancel arch, and a marble-panelled apse.

CASTLE BALFOUR. In Holy Trinity churchyard, on the edge of a low limestone cliff, the ruins of a T-shaped tower house built by Sir James Balfour about 1618 within a 70 ft square bawn. The building was refortified by Ludlow in 1652 but dismantled in the wars of 1689 and abandoned in the early C19. The present entrance on the E front is through a canted bay porch of late date. This admits to the leg of the T, where the main hall of the castle was accommodated at first-floor level. On the ground floor are the usual barrel-vaulted chambers with a big kitchen with a fireplace and a small brick-lined oven. In the return, on the NW side, a spiral staircase corbelled out from the wall at first-floor level connects with the bedrooms at the top of the castle. The corbelling is characteristic of C17 work in Scotland, as are the steps themselves, whose ends project through the wall, and also the row of small square corbels below the parapets. The ruins today, unlike Monea, do not readily engage the imagination.

TOUR

In 1837 Lewis described the town as 'consisting chiefly of comfortable houses and shops', and much the same applies today. It is one long street with a curve half-way up, lined by stone-built houses with just sufficient of three storeys to give the place a distinct, if brief, urban air. Near the N end of the town the OLD HOTEL, latterly a police station, on a scale that far exceeds anything else, with a high three-storey front ending in a Doric eaves cornice, the block flanked by a low wing on one side and a carriage arch on the other. Opposite, the gabled T-plan METHODIST CHURCH and hall, mid C19. Next the PRESBYTERIAN CHURCH, gable end to the street with a modest W window, also mid C19, and then the MARKET HOUSE of about 1830, apparently by *W. D. Butler* of Dublin (bombed in 1971), a fine building, erected at the expense of the Earl of Erne and similar to the Market House of Newtownbutler, with two rows of segmental arcades of four bays across each floor. Here the central two bays step up to a gabled pediment surmounted by a cupola with a clock below. From 1837 a court house was accommodated on the first floor. Almost opposite, at the curve in the street, the CORNMARKET of 1841 with the motto 'Live and let Live' is apparently by *George Sudden*, who was working for Lord Erne at Crom. The market consisted of a courtyard framed by two Tudoresque three-bay cottages with a small central building at the back of the courtyard like a Tudor church porch. Since 1970 the N lodge has gone – demolished to make way for a dismal modern shop. Between the two gates to the market is LISNASKEA CROSS, the base of a late High Cross carved with Adam and Eve on one side and a panel of thirty-two boss-knots on the back. Further down the main street on the opposite side is the third market, the BUTTER MARKET, designed in 1856 by *John S. Mulvany*, another court of U-shaped buildings opening off the street. Now in a more severe Gothic style, with a solid two-storey range at the back of the court, relieved by narrow arcades and a projecting central arch with plate-tracery window and gable above. The banks in the street are the ULSTER BANK, a two-storey, five-bay stuccoed classical block by *Thomas Jackson*, 1873, and the BANK OF IRELAND, 1924 by *A. G. C. Millar*.

Further s, beyond Holy Trinity church and Castle Balfour, down a side road to the r. is the former UNION WORKHOUSE, now a HOSPITAL, with the monogram VR and the date 1851. Opened in 1853. One of *George Wilkinson*'s standard Elizabethan designs, unusually well preserved. The governor's house is a five-bay, two-storey gabled block before a wide court. Behind is a long fifteen-bay, two-storey range, terminating in projecting three-storey pavilions with paired gables and cross-mullioned windows.

NEIGHBOURHOOD

THE MOATE. 1.5 km N. The hill-fort that gives this place its name is a circular earthwork consisting of a bank and low ditch of a diameter of about 400 ft. Inside is a large mound, now grass-grown, but apparently composed of stones, which are exposed at the top. Traditionally this was the inauguration mound of the Maguire Lords of Fermanagh and is an early Celtic site.

MOATE HOUSE is an early C19 T shaped villa with Tudor detailing. MOATE OLD SCHOOL, a little to the N, originally Moate Catholic Chapel, is a modest harled six-bay hall of about 1820 with four big Gothic sash-windows and doors in the end bays. Primitive Gibbs surrounds in stone – rather more like long and short work than Renaissance rustication. This sort of detail is very characteristic of the work of *Robert Shepherd*, who may well have designed the building.

LISNASKEA RECTORY. 1.5 km NW. 1829. A small two-storey,

three-bay house with a central fanlight door and a short service wing.

CLIFTON LODGE. 0.5 km E. A big classical villa of about 1830, three-bay, two-storey, with a Tuscan aedicule to the main door, flanked by a square and a canted bay-window on the ground floor. Low hipped roof, supported on large mutules at the eaves. GATE LODGE with lattice panes and diagonal chimneys.

MUNVILLE. 2 km NNE. An unusual small Georgian house of two storeys entered at first-floor level by a grand flight of sixteen steps rising to a central door like a Palladian window with the inscription 'DUX FOEMINA FACTI M^{N}M. This then is the Georgian seat of the Maguires, between Maguires Bridge and the Maguires' Moate, and it is still a Maguire house. The big stair is more common in C17 Scotland than in C18 Ireland, but it gives the house a certain grandeur that a two-storey, three-bay design could not otherwise have. In keeping with the stone stair are the stone quoins and cut stone cornice. Otherwise the house is plain. Both windows on the first floor have been replaced by large 1930s metal French windows with shutters and balconies.

NUTFIELD. 4 km NNE. A substantial mid to late C18 farmhouse, built by the Brooke family. Three-storey, three-bay front, the windows diminishing nicely on the upper floors. Venetian window on the first-floor central bay, with a somewhat suspect stone surround (mid C19?). A big stone porch sticks forward from the front as a canted bay. This was obviously a rich house with an ashlar stone front, and a substantial newel stair inside similar to Donagh House nearby. The grounds still have the clumps and belts of C18 planting.

AGHALURCHER OLD CHURCH. 2.5 km S. The meagre remains of an old foundation dedicated to St Ronan in the C9. A Thomas Maguire put a 'French roof' on the church here in 1447, and another Maguire killed a kinsman on the altar in 1484, which act of sacrilege may have led to the abandonment of the church. What remains is the end of a rectangular structure with a small pointed barrel-vaulted chamber on the r. This was used as a Balfour and Galbraith mausoleum and may well be of the C17, re-using earlier worked stones. No old details remain save a carved head, possibly a corbel, in the arched gateway leading to the graveyard.

A rural parish N of Cookstown.

CORR MEMORIAL CHURCH, CHURCH TOWN. 1907 by *George A. C. Ashlin* of Ashlin & Coleman. Well sited on the crown of a hill, a large Romanesque design with nave, aisles, choir, side porches, and offset round tower belfry on the entrance front. Built of coursed squared sandstone rubble with corbelled arcading on the gables at the eaves. The doors are flanked by colonnettes with cushion capitals, but the nicest detail is reserved for the belfry, which has a light arcade on slender shafts and a candle-snuffer roof – more like Pavia than provincial Ulster. Inside, a four-bay Norman arcade on clustered piers of four shafts. Polished granite colonnettes.

LISSAN PARISH CHURCH (C of I). Described by Lewis in 1837 as a 'plain and very ancient structure'. A long harled hall with a W bellcote and a deep S porch. Two round-headed lancet windows at the E end. Gallery inside on cast-iron Gothic columns. 1861.

LISSAN HOUSE. 1 km SW of the churches. A large and rather confusing house, basically of the early C18 but dull in appearance. A nine-bay, three-storey front tucked into the side of a valley with river, bridge, and ornamental lakes to the E of the main front and a stable yard, at a high level on the W, attached to the upper floors of the house. In the centre bay a monster *porte cochère* ending in a mullioned bow-window obscures the original entrance door, with its sturdy Tuscan columns with salient entablatures and higher framing pilasters on each side. The house must once have been quite grand and may be by *Davis Ducart*, a Scandinavian architect who settled in Ireland about 1760 and whom Lewis credits with the design of the ORNAMENTAL BRIDGE and presumably also the lakes and layout of the grounds. An early C19 octagonal single-storey drawing room overlooks the river. The rear of the house looking back to Ducart's lake is three storeys by seven bays, all very plain. The interior appears to be all C19. Lissan was developed by the Staples family, descended from Sir Thomas Staples, created a Baronet of Ireland in 1628. Ducart's improvements were carried out for Sir Robert Staples, the seventh baronet.

LISSAN RECTORY. 3 km SE. By *John Nash*, who built it in 1807 for the Rev. John Staples at a cost of £1,313 14s. 5d. Nash designed this house as a picturesque Italianate villa, a little like Cronkhill, but with a square entrance tower and a long six-bay loggia on the garden side surmounted by a wrought-iron veranda. Beyond, a long line of offices extended to an asymmetrical round tower that was essential to the composition. Unhappily the church authorities in 'restoring' the rectory decided this wing was ugly and demolished it, turning the long straggling composition into a lopsided lump. They also cut down trees to let in light, removed the creeper and climbing roses that once covered Nash's arcade, and laid a concrete path all round the house to make sure that none can grow again. The slated roof of the square tower has been replaced by a flat coping, and a sea of tarmac flows up to the front door. A sad instance of misapplied zeal and the consequences of inadequate state protection of Irish monuments.

CLAGGAN PRESBYTERIAN CHURCH. 2.5 km NW. 1840, rebuilt in 1872. A four-bay hall with round-headed lancets. Gable front with five lancets over the door.

CREEVE HOUSE. 1.5 km W. Late c18. A five-bay, two-storey block, harled, with a Gibbs surround to the front door.

DUNMORE HOUSE. 2 km NW. Late c18. A five-bay, two-storey block, harled, with a Venetian window in the middle of the first floor.

INTRODUCTION

The city of Londonderry, rising on the banks of the River Foyle, is bounded on its east side by the broad curve of the river, not quite five miles upstream from its estuary and the broad reaches of Lough Foyle. It is set on a roughly regular hill whose axis runs from north-east to south-west, and on the west, bounding the city on the other side from the river, lies low marshy ground, known as Bogside. The name of the city, always popularly called Derry, is taken from the Irish *Doire* which means 'a place of oaks'. The oaks, or at any rate a thick wood, grew naturally on this mound between bog and river, with wide views across the rising country towards the Sperrin mountains, the hills of Donegal, and the Inishowen peninsula. It is fertile country modelled with broad, sweeping contours, and it was here on the firm dry hill crowned with trees that St Colmcille founded his first abbey in 546. Derry's history goes back at least to that date.

The architectural monuments in the city hardly suggest its antiquity. St Colmcille's monastery was on too crucial a site to develop indefinitely in peace. It was immediately accessible from the river and estuary, and as long as it remained the centre of a religious community it was the first place to be attacked by any ambitious invader. When in more modern history Derry became a town and centre of commerce, its position commanding the river crossing and with easy access to the sea gave it a strategic importance that inevitably brought further attacks. As a result the history of the city is one of recurrent destruction from 783, when the Danes burnt the abbey, to the end of the c17. The Great Siege by James II in 1689 is no more (and no less) than the final period to a pattern that had lasted for a thousand years. Despite this history of intermittent attack, the religious community at Derry thrived. In 1162 a new abbey church, 240 ft long, was begun by the Augustinian Bishop Flaithbertach O'Brolcháin (Bradley), and from then on the old church of St Colmcille became known as the Black

Church. In the C13 Derry gained a Cistercian nunnery, in 1274 a Dominican abbey, and at an unrecorded date a Franciscan friary. The resulting notable collection of medieval architecture survived the Middle Ages intact. The raids of local chiefs and opportunist English adventurers brought havoc but rarely did long-term damage: walls might be 'slighted' but they would not be demolished, and so the church architecture was maintained.

It was the Tudor reassertion of English power in Ulster that brought an end to the medieval appearance of Derry. In 1565, on Shane O'Neill's rebellion, seven foot companies and one troop of horse were sent to the town as garrison. The year following, however, an accidental explosion of gunpowder in the cathedral, which the English had converted into an arsenal, rendered the town untenable. Elizabeth's troops withdrew, leaving the medieval buildings largely in ruins, and so they remained until the end of the century. Then in 1599 the strategic position of Derry forced the government to re-occupy and fortify the city, and on 22 May 1600 it was taken by Sir Henry Docwra, who, like most previous commanders, came up Lough Foyle to the head of the river estuary and then marched on the town. Docwra, to obtain materials to fortify Derry, demolished the ruins of its medieval buildings, leaving only the long, tall tower to the cathedral belfry that was to give its name to the Long Tower district of the town. Through this act of what must have seemed legitimate destruction, Docwra became both the founder of modern Derry and the eradicator of its past. Of the Gaelic community and medieval city nothing now remains.

In many ways Docwra's city suffered a similar fate to that of its predecessor. The earthwork fortifications he erected were overrun by Sir Cahir O'Doherty in 1608. Then in 1613, under Charter from James I, the city of London became responsible for the settlement of Derry, which gained the prefix 'London', and between 1614 and 1618 Londonderry's walls were built. The plan 51 & 52 of the city had the functional simplicity of a Roman military camp, with four streets leading to a central square, The Diamond. By 1622 over a hundred houses existed within the walls and a small T-shaped market house had been built in the central Diamond. The community within the walls had to make do with a patched medieval fragment, St Augustine's Abbey, for its church, but between 1628 and 1633 a new cathedral was built, in Planters' 43 & 45 Gothic style, at the head of the town in the south-east corner of the defence work.

It was this city with its new-built cathedral that was attacked by the Irish in 1641. Seven years later during the civil war it declared, not surprisingly considering its London bias, for Parliament. On each occasion the siege that followed was unsuccessful, though in 1648 the city was saved from starvation only by a supply of food sent from Scotland. The last siege of Derry began on 26 April 1689 and was to continue for 105 days. This time the besieging army of James II had taken the precaution of throwing a boom across the river to prevent the approach of relief ships to the town. As James did not have enough engineers to storm the walls, the city was to be starved out. Yet once again the siege was unsuccessful. The boom across the Foyle was broken by the supply ship Mountjoy, and two days later James raised the siege. In August 1689 Derry was still victorious, but the effect of the three sieges was to reduce the town's buildings to rubble. The market house in the Diamond was destroyed by shells; the cathedral tower, commandeered as a gun emplacement during the siege, was hit and had to be rebuilt; the walls and gates were severely damaged.

An architectural history of Derry cannot really begin until after the siege of 1689, when the city settled down to a less stirring era of reconstruction. The first building of significance, the New Market House, was built in the Diamond on the site of its predecessor in 1692. It was a rectangular structure with short cross arms at the south end, dignified by an attempted classical order with an open arcade on the ground floor and assembly rooms above. Meal and potatoes from the surrounding area were bought and exchanged within its open arcades, and it continued as the exchange for over 130 years. Through the c18 Derry was to suffer the economic stagnation that a system of absentee owners imposed. The city was tied to the London Companies through the Irish Society that owned the land. The corporation was self-elected and self-perpetuating. Development was partial and slow, and for the first half century all the main functions of the town were easily contained within its walls.

The quays at this time were much closer to the city, for the shallows created by the bend in the River Foyle before the northeast face of the walls had not been filled in. An irregular pattern of wharves and jetties, and the shipquay itself, stuck out into the river, gradually filling up the shallows as the century progressed; but this process too was slow. In 1788 the river still came up to the East Water Bastion, in front of which 'The New Walk', ultimately to become part of Foyle Street, had just been constructed. For most of the c18, Shipquay Street, the steep hill leading from the quays up to the Diamond, was the centre of the city's trade.

In its lower section, conveniently near the wharves, what seems to have been a Customs House was erected in 1741, and this was the most ambitious building to be put up in Derry to that date. It is a tall brick house whose scale and character compare with early C18 architecture in Dublin, and indeed it would not even seem out of place in the contemporary Cavendish-Harley and Grosvenor estates in London. The rest of Shipquay Street is a little later, but the high plain façades of many of the buildings, and their fenestration, even where the walls have been stuccoed over, proclaim their C18 origin. Indeed this one street preserves more precisely than any other in Derry the character and sense of mercantile enterprise that was so much part of the mid Georgian town.

Bishop Street, leading to the high south end of the walled city and to the cathedral, was less concerned with trade. Its development was less compact, with haphazard openings behind the street frontages to the Bishop's house and garden, the free school, and St Augustine's Chapel on one side and to the cathedral and churchyard on the other. By 1788, however, the cathedral side of the street from the Diamond to Bishop's Gate had been filled in completely and its gate was in process of being rebuilt.

1768 marks a change in Derry's architectural history, for it was then that Frederick Augustus Hervey, later to be the fourth Earl of Bristol, was translated from the see of Cloyne to the very rich bishopric of Derry. Hervey spent much of his money in the city and county, and both benefited. He had already travelled widely, especially in Italy, and his advent brought a new conception of the role of architecture to the city by the Foyle. His predecessor, William Barnard, had rebuilt the chapel of St Augustine as a small classical hall with a Diocletian window and pediment. Hervey proceeded to restore the cathedral, to build a tall ashlar spire on the tower, completely to redesign the Bishop's palace, and to erect many new churches throughout the diocese. He had, too, a firm grasp of what would now be called Political Economy. He advocated religious freedom, and his schemes for agricultural improvement and for new roads, and his extensive search for coal, were all calculated for the good of Derry. Not surprisingly, in 1770 the corporation presented the Bishop with the freedom of their city.

By the 1780s Derry had expanded beyond the walls. Colonel Campsie's orchard below the east wall, whose pear trees had provided a route for the escape of the traitorous Governor Lundy during the siege in 1689, still remained an open space, now belonging to a Mr Patterson. But the triangle of land between

it, the walls, and the river had been built up, with a curving street
of houses and shops stepping down to the ferry crossing. This
became Bridge Street, the centre of the town's skilled trades, with
printers, dyers, cutlers, glaziers, and cabinetmakers working
there. A row of cottages now skirted the lower slopes of the west
wall, running down from Butchers' Gate to the 'Gullet' Dock
(long since built over by Waterloo Place); and another line ran
back into the Bogside. Here linen industries were established,
with clothes-brokers and ropemakers all concentrating in the west
of the town. Ribbons of development had begun to fringe the main
routes out of Derry: the Long Tower, Howard Street, and St
Columb's Wells, with from 1788 a line of cottages, Nailer's Row,
hugging the w walls. A substantial part of Bishop Street Without
was developed now as far at least as the Bishop's own gardens
on the level of the hill. Here, on the site of the present St Columb's
College, the Earl Bishop had laid out a bowling green with walks,
lawns, and a grove of Spanish chestnut trees. The stump of an
old round windmill was converted into a pigeon house, and on
the brow of the hill a small Ionic casino was built overlooking
the meadows to the west, in front of Creggan's 'Bluebell Hill' –
a hill that was to become a century later the inspiration for 'the
green hill far away' of Mrs Alexander's famous hymn and more
recently the site of a huge housing estate.

   In August 1776 Arthur Young visited Derry. He came from
Limavady, reached the city at night, and waited two hours in the
dark before the ferry boat came over for him. Fourteen years later
he would not have been thus inconvenienced, for Derry had
gained a bridge.

   'A very curious and handsome wooden bridge has been erected here,
   which was opened for foot passengers in the latter end of the year 1790.
   This plain and elegant structure (the first of the kind introduced into
   Ireland) was framed in America and transported from thence across
   the Atlantic. It was built in 13 months at the expense of the corporation
   by Messrs. Lemuel Cox and Jonathan Thompson, natives of America.'

So ran the account of the greatest novelty in the city, in the *Post
Chaise Companion Through Ireland*. To it might be added that the
Bishop contributed largely to the cost of the bridge, that it brought
£34,253 in tolls in twenty-three years, that it contained a swivel
lock at the town end, and that the corporation went bankrupt in
1832 through borrowing too heavily to repair it after ice and floods
in 1814. Despite the bankruptcy the bridge, by connecting the
city with the whole county, brought vital trade to Derry as a port.
It marks the opening of an era of expansion. By 1799 the street

pattern of lanes running down from the ridge of the hill to the water's edge had begun to emerge. Carrigan's, Ferguson's, and Bennet's Lane had all come into being. Wapping Lane, Hakins Lane (now Hawkins Street), and the Fountain Street area had been developed beneath the city walls, and in Bogside, William Street and Fahan Street had been laid out. As the c19 opened Derry was laying the foundations of its present plan.

The waterfront too was changing. The new bridge brought a new faith in woodwork, reflected in the rapid extension of the wooden quays. The corporation erected a long timber wharf sticking straight out into the river opposite Shipquay Gate. More of the shallows were reclaimed in front of the Water Bastion; and at the foot of Sugar House Lane, Mr Robert Alexander, one of the principal merchants of the city, who had entertained Arthur Young in 1776, built his own great square quay. By 1835 others had followed his example and a continuous line of quays extended from the bridge almost to Shipquay Place. As London was later to do, Londonderry had pushed the river away from its walls to gain an extra strip of land about 150 yards wide – a strip of land that in 1976 was designated to take through traffic that must cut the city off from its river, which seems a wrong thing to do.

Two changes occurred in the architectural pattern in the early 1800s. In the first place the density of building within the walls increased. Every street was fully built up, and the back gardens between blocks disappeared under new wings and extensions. At this time Pump Street, the houses facing the ramparts in the east wall, and the fine brick groups in Magazine Street gained their present appearance. Under the pressure for sites the orchard below the east wall was finally built over, at first only a part as Orchard Lane, and then after 1845 the rest as Orchard Street. The second change was in the quality of the new work. The city had become architecturally conscious, and its new buildings were self-assertive both in style and scale. Between 1805 and 1808 Shipquay Gate and Butchers' Gate were both rebuilt. Then at the end of the Napoleonic wars fresh capital and a larger labour force were available for building. Derry celebrated peace in a spate of public works: a new free school (Foyle College), a new Greek Revival court house, extensions to the castellated gaol outside the walls; and the new Bishop, William Knox, found Lord Bristol's cathedral spire unsafe and replaced it by a new one. In 1826 the Exchange shared with most Irish arcaded markets the indignity of having its arches built up to accommodate a Public Reading Room. In 1828 Walker's Testimonial, a robust Doric column, was erected by subscription, with the vigorous cleric more than life size at its top. On the north side of the town stood the city's infirmary, built in 1810, and in 1828 the new lunatic asylum, to serve Derry, Donegal, and Tyrone, was put up beside it to designs of *Johnston* and *Murray*, architects to the Board of Works.

This spate of building activity just at the end of the Georgian era set the pattern for Victorian development. Housing for the merchant and professional classes developed to the north along Strand Road by the bank of the river, with a criss-cross of regular streets running uphill to the infirmary: Great James Street, Princes Street, Queen Street, and Clarendon Street. Asylum Road marked the limit of this northern expansion, and the well-to-do then moved uphill behind the mental hospital to Crawford Square, the speculative development of a Mr Samuel L. Crawford, begun in the late 1850s and completed in the early 1870s. Large Victorian houses in their own grounds – Aberfoyle, Dill (formerly Talbot) House, and others – extended the suburbs of the town further north, where the new Presbyterian college, Magee College, went up in spiky institutional Gothic in 1856. Other smaller residential schemes of streets and individual houses had been begun by the early 1830s across the bridge at Waterside.

The polarization of more wealthy citizens N and SE left the Bogside, Bishop Street Without, and the south slopes of the town hill to industrial development and to houses for the workers. A huddled confusion of small stepped roofs and chimneys sprang up below the southern walls and on either side of the Bishop Street line. Shirt factories, rope works, and a brewery were grouped round William Street, with flour mills and warehouses in Prince Arthur Street. Gas works, replacing an early building in Foyle Street of 1829, went up in Bogside in 1866. Most of the housing was drab, but in places, such as St Columb's Walk, Fountain Street, and Albert Street, the development achieved a picturesque miniature scale that was architecturally valuable and alive, though it has now been ruthlessly cleared away.

The most significant addition to Derry's street pattern in Victorian times was caused by the proposal to replace the 1790 timber bridge by a new steel structure 200 yds upstream. Plans and estimates for this had been prepared in the first year of Victoria's reign, 1837. In 1852 it was reported in *The Builder* that the work was to begin at a cost of £60,000, a third being paid by the Londonderry and Enniskillen Railway Co., but it was not until 1863 that the project was finally realized and the bridge declared open at a ceremony performed by the Lord Lieutenant, the Earl of Carlisle. The cost was £100,000. The bridge with its approaches opened up the area at the foot of Wapping Lane just below the cathedral precinct, and it also led to the construction of two new roads in Waterside, Duke Street and Spencer Road. On the city side Carlisle Road, running in a dog-leg from the bridge end up to Ferryquay Gate, replaced the older Bridge Street as the thoroughfare into the town. In the same year, 1863, a new line of quays was completed, extending from the old bridge end to the Strand opposite the mental hospital. The city's rail connections were now extensive, with lines via Strabane, Omagh, and Enniskillen to Dundalk and Dublin, and via Coleraine and Antrim to Belfast. One was also in course of construction to Buncrana, 'a fashionable watering place on Lough Swilly'.

The period from 1863 to the end of the century was one of the most prosperous for Derry. As a brisk commercial city, it enjoyed an extensive coastal trade, and there were as well weekly sailings carrying emigrants to America and Canada. As the economy of the city expanded, three new building types came to express its 98 & 118 commercial buoyancy: warehouses, banks, and factories. Like the late Georgian public buildings they stand out clearly in the city and are identifiable immediately by their size. Great brick and timber warehouses and mills are still the dominant feature of the waterfront. Often they are now decayed or derelict, but they still have a solid functional grandeur, and in Foyle Street, where they tower above the curving street line, they create a particularly impressive effect, turning the whole street into a deep canyon of buildings. The banks also are larger than the surrounding architecture, impressive classical façades in stone or stucco that either impose their new scale on the houses in Shipquay Street or are found in the new open spaces at the foot of the North Wall, Shipquay Place, and Strand Road. The factories of Derry bring its architectural history up to the C20. The Victorian ones are all in the centre, in Abercorn Road, Foyle Street, and Horace Street, or else off the Strand Road in Sackville Street and Patrick Street. Later factories are sited in a more haphazard manner, isolated blocks in the suburbs, at the end of Strand Road, in Rosemount Avenue, and in Foyle Road.

While the laws of commerce largely dictated the expansion of Victorian Derry, the laws of human nature affected its appearance. Whatever trouble was caused, the difference in religion within the city had one good effect. Architectural design is stimulated by rivalry, and the Victorian churches of Derry were never dull. Approaching from any direction the spires of the city are always

120 & 121 prominent. On the hill near the entrance to Brooke Park, the soaring walls, tower, and spire of St Eugene's Catholic Cathedral seem
to accuse the Planters' Cathedral, on the other side of the valley
108 of undue modesty. The Church of Ireland's answer is All Saints
Waterside, dramatically set at the apex of Bond's Hill with a solid
broach-spire rearing high above the road. St Columb's Roman
Catholic Church in the Long Tower more than doubled its size
in the early C20 and came out of the ordeal if not the best proportioned at least the most sumptuous church in Derry. Presbyterians were early and late in the field: early in Great James Street
103 – the most elegant church interior in the town – and late in Magazine Street, where their first church was ennobled in 1903 with
an Imperial Roman portico. It is this massive, imperturbable
church, staring out from the top of the wall, that provides the
most effective counterweight to the Gothic drama of St Eugene's.
The Methodists too contributed buildings of some style. They
began on the East Wall with a Greek Revival Church that has
now been demolished, and then in 1901 did a *volte face* by moving
to an awkward site on Carlisle Road where they stole St Columb's
thunder in a flurry of flying buttresses and a C15-style spire.

MODERN REDEVELOPMENT

Throughout the 1970s plans have been prepared, and in part
implemented, to modernize the city. This initiative, from a historical point of view, has not been good for Derry. In terms of
urban conservation the proposals are poor, limited by a doctrinaire and unimaginative approach to the problems of old buildings, and seemingly discounting the value of the Victorian contribution to the appearance of the city. Wholesale clearances have
been carried out, and the sense of the place as a built environment
which has developed through the centuries has been sacrificed
to two notions, both equally misconceived: of stripping the C17
walls bare to reveal their original appearance (and remove thereby
all the picturesque organic city growth that had accumulated
round them in a century and a half of life); and of ringing the
central city with a belt of roadway which both cuts an alien swathe
through Bishop Street Without and the hillside to the E, and –
for the length of the quays – sets the barrier of a motorway
between the city and the river that has always been its life-line.
    Unhappily the recent history of terrorism and civil disorder
militates against the organization of effective public pressure that
might, in normal circumstances, be brought to counter such
official insensitivity, and officials, to be fair, are themselves under

a different sort of pressure to proceed at all costs, none of which makes for good planning. New housing, built in the Bogside from the mid 1960s and more recently in the redeveloped Fountain Street area, makes no attempt to relate to the fabric of the town as a whole. The first, conceived as multi-storey blocks, is too large and too aggressive in character, the second too small, set out on a plan that bears no evident relationship to the streets or walls round it and made up of white, slab-like units that are in sorry contrast to the older architecture round about that still remains. A zoning policy for factories has also begun to threaten some of the oldest and best industrial buildings of the past. Only two zones are treated as conservation areas: the old town within the walls and nearby streets including the Long Tower and river front to the E (though here rather too great a degree of redevelopment is intended), and the area of late Georgian and Victorian terraced housing to the N bounded by Strand Road, Great James Street, Francis Street, and Asylum Road, with later housing in Crawford Square also included.

THE WALLS

Derry's first walls were earthwork defences thrown up in 1566 by Colonel Edward Randolph and again in 1600 by Sir Henry Docwra. They were not sufficient to withstand the attack of Sir Cahir O'Doherty in 1608 and in consequence were rebuilt with a stone face between 1613 and 1618. In 1619 Captain Pynnar records the city surrounded with a strong wall 'excellently made and neatly wrought' of rubble limestone. Its circumference was 284⅔ perches, its height 24 ft, and there were four battlemented gates, two of which had drawbridges but no portcullises and were not normally used as entrances to the city. What Pynnar describes is shown in 'The plat of the Cittie of 52 Londonderrie' prepared with other plans of the London Companies' estates by their overseer Sir Thomas Phillips for his Survey of 1622, and what Phillips's map shows is still, with the exception of a part of the East Wall and the exact gates, intact. Derry's walls are the most extensive early C17 fortifications in the 51 British Isles. They were designed by *Captain Edward Doddington* and built by *Peter Benson*, a grantee of 1,000 acres in Co. Donegal. The core of the rampart is of earth, faced with split-stone rubble laid in lime mortar. The height varies from 20 ft to 25 ft and the breadth from 14 ft to 30 ft. The faces of the walls have a steep batter rising usually to a string course, above which a straight wall-head with embrasures for artillery rises to breast height. The copings are often of dressed sand-stone. The town has long ago encroached on all these walls, built up now on the inside and now on the exterior. Something of the historic huddle can still be appreciated on the lower sections to the NE from Butchers' Gate down Magazine Street to Shipquay Place, but the nicest and in many ways the most evocative sections about the wall – Fountain Street, Albert Place, Bishop Street Without, and Nailer's Row – have now been ruthlessly cleared of their little streets and houses as part of an ill-conceived redevelopment plan for Derry.

The walls at the top of the hill today stand bleak and exposed. If this is a questionable way to treat a historic fabric, it does at least serve to emphasize the danger inherent in manning the walls in the C17. They withstood three sieges: first in 1641, next in 1648 and 1649, when the Parliamentarians held out against the Royalists, and lastly in the famous siege of 1688–9 that lasted 105 days against the forces of King James II.

BASTIONS AND GATES

Until 1970 visitors to Derry could walk the entire circuit of the parapets. At the time of writing, though access is restricted, it is still convenient to describe the gates and bastions as if seen in a clockwise circuit. There were originally nine bastions and two platforms of which five remain intact with portions of another two. The four original gates are all rebuilt, and three more have been added.

Starting at the head of the old town at the S end of Bishop Street is BISHOP'S GATE, so called since the early C17, though rebuilt as a triumphal arch by *Henry Aaron Baker* in 1789 on the centenary of the siege. The style has the blockish cubic quality associated with French neo-classical designs. A high central arch flanked by flat-headed pedestrian passages with channelled horizontal rustication and exaggerated flat voussoirs. There is no attic – only a heavy dentil cornice set above the two side passageways and breaking into a solid block of masonry (intended to be carved but never finished?) above the keystone of the central arch. Martial trophies on each face were carved by *Edward Smyth* of Dublin, who also did the keystone heads of the River Foyle looking SW and dated 1689 and of the River Boyne looking NE and dated 1690. Steps at the side of the gate lead up to the ramparts. W from here is the DOUBLE BASTION, a salient square corner at the highest point above the Bogside, known in the early C17 as Prince Charles's Bulwark. A wall that ran from its salient angle, dividing the outer ditch in two, accounts for its name. During the siege, enemy prisoners were hanged here in the sight of besiegers as a counter to the practice of driving captives under the walls to distress the defenders.

N from here the ROYAL BASTION, a salient interval bastion, was originally Lord Docwra's Bulwark and until 1973 supported the Walker Memorial Pillar (*see* p. 394). Further N is a shallow artillery PLATFORM and then BUTCHERS' GATE, called New Gate in 1625 and rebuilt in 1805–8 as a narrow elliptical archway, like a piece of early C19 canal building, with dressed imposts, continuous voussoir band, and parapet string course in rubble sandstone. An iron railing as parapet. N from here was the Gunners' Bastion, originally the Mayor of Londonderry's Bulwark, now gone completely, and then CASTLE GATE, built in 1803 in a style similar to Butchers' Gate. Beyond is part of the HANGMAN'S BASTION, a square platform built into the backs of houses in Waterloo Street, opposite which the old O'Docherty castle, converted by Docwra as a magazine, once stood.

At the N corner of the walls, projecting in the C17 into the shallows of the river, was Lord Chichester's Bulwark, known from 1689 as Cowards' Bastion, as it was the least dangerous place on the walls. It has gone – demolished in 1824 to make way for a butter market – and immediately E of its site is the new MAGAZINE GATE, very wide and spanned by a single segmental arch with V-jointed voussoirs, a central keystone face, and quoin piers at either side. Designed by *Fitzgibbon Louch* in 1864.

The section of wall running SE from here is the only part that has always been exposed. It is lined with cannon. Though now fronting the C19 Shipquay Place, it once bordered the river, and was not at first considered necessary as a defensive work – the original agreement with the London Companies being to wall the city on three sides. At its centre is SHIPQUAY GATE, originally Water Gate, rebuilt from 1805 to 1808 in the same style as Butchers' Gate, though wider and dignified by ashlar sandstone facings with decorative roundels in the piers above the imposts of the arch. Like Cowards' Bastion, the answering salient-angled bastion on the river side at the NE of the city has virtually disappeared. Only a stump remains. It was originally the Governor of the Plantation's Bulwark and later the Water Bastion, as its foundations were covered at high tide.

East Wall begins again a little before the London Bulwark or
NEWGATE BASTION, a salient-fronted defence work breaking
forward dramatically amongst a line of little red-brick houses
in Orchard Street. Climbing uphill again to the SW is FERRY-
QUAY GATE, rebuilt as an ambitious triple-arched gateway to
designs of *Robert Collins* in 1866. Carlisle Road had by this date
become a principal thoroughfare leading up from the bridge
to the centre of the old town, and the gate is self-consciously
intended as the main entrance to the city. Built of red-brown
ashlar sandstone, the central high arch is flanked by two smaller
round-headed arches with rusticated masonry above, and piers
with coupled Tuscan pilasters set above the outer imposts of
the arch. The parapet is balustraded. It was this gate, once also
called New Gate or Ferry-port Gate, that the Apprentice Boys
closed before the Earl of Antrim's troops on 7 December 1688,
thus setting in motion the events that led to the siege in 1689.
Further uphill again is the ARTILLERY BASTION, formerly the
Lord Deputy's Bulwark, or the Ferry Bastion during the siege.
Beyond it is the third NEW GATE or Hawkins Street Gate and
really a *new* gate, opened in 1787 but closed again by 1799 –
perhaps to prevent people from outside the town making a dis-
turbance at the New Theatre just inside. Reopened in the later
C19. It is a small arch with sandstone facings and moulded voussoirs – possibly by *Collins* who was the city engineer. Past New
Gate the ramparts skirt the churchyard of the cathedral, with
a small corbelled circular SENTINEL HOUSE added about 1627,
to CHURCH BASTION at the S corner of the city, originally
King James's Bulwark, a broad salient-angled bastion now
cleared of the little houses in Fountain Street that once nestled
round it and looking out instead to nondescript local authority
housing. The clearing has revealed a small round-headed door
at the base of the wall. Beyond the bastion is one more small
sentinel turret of 1627, and then on the inside of the ramparts
a short terrace of small red-brick Georgian-style houses, sitting
up proudly as a modest but essential element in the historic
townscape just before the wall returns to the Bishop's Gate.

ST COLUMB'S CATHEDRAL

INTRODUCTION

The dedication to St Columb recalls the ancient Christian history
of Derry. Colmcille founded a monastery here in 546 and made

it his base until 563, when he left Ireland to found Iona. In the
C12 Derry became an important centre of monasticism – so much
so that in 1254 the see of Maghera was transferred here. The
church that then became the cathedral, the great church or Templemore, had been built in 1164 by the abbot Flaithbhertach
O Brolcháin and King O Lochlainn. *The Annals of the Four
Masters* and the *Annals of Ulster* record much of its history but
little of its form beyond its over-all dimensions of 80 ft. It stood
largely complete in 1520 but was desecrated with other churches
by an English force that occupied Derry in 1566. Adapted as an
arsenal, it was destroyed a year later by the explosion of gunpowder stored within the building, and in the C17 its ruins were
dismantled to provide materials for the new cathedral and for the
city walls. The tall tower attached to the old Irish monastery
remained a feature of Derry until the years of the siege. Its site
is marked today by the Long Tower church, half-way down the
hillside, s w from the present cathedral and outside the city walls.

The present church, built near the site of the Cistercian nunnery,
is entirely new – a fact that is proudly proclaimed on the famous
inscription preserved inside the porch: 'If stones could speake
then London's prayse should sounde who built this church and
cittie from the grounde'. The stone is signed 'Vaughan aed.', for
Sir John Vaughan, Governor of the City of Londonderry, under
whose direction the cathedral was built; but the real builder was
William Parrott, who in 1628 contracted with the London Irish
Society to erect a fair church for £3,400. It took five years to complete and ultimately cost £4,000. It was of course not much larger
than a moderately scaled English parish church, with an arcaded
nave, aisles, short chancel (accommodated within the body of the
nave), s porch, and stumpy w tower. The detailing was of an Elizabethan Gothic type with grouped cusped lancets under segmental
hood moulds. The tower, before the siege, had a wooden spire
covered in lead, but the lead was used for bullets in 1689 and the
spire was converted to provide a platform for artillery and subsequently dismantled. It was not until 1776 that the Earl Bishop
provided £1,000 to add an ashlar spire of his own that rose to
a magnificent 228 ft, with a gilt copper ball on the top. Alas, it
proved too heavy for the old C17 steeple tower. Tower and spire
were demolished in 1802, to be replaced by the present reassuringly solid structure with its pretty two-light cusped Dec windows
on each storey. The bells were re-hung in 1813 and the present
ashlar spire was added for Bishop Knox, possibly to designs of
John Bowden, in 1822. Its overall height is 191 ft.

Victorian architects did not approve of the cathedral as it had come down to them, and thrice remodelled its appearance. First in 1859 *Joseph Welland* removed the Georgian galleries from the aisles, refitted the entrance porch in the tower with oak panelling and *Minton* encaustic tiles, and removed the box pews from the body of the nave. The *Dublin Builder* congratulated the restorers in May 1862 on their 'correct and cultivated taste', but by 1885 the same journal reported that the cathedral was to be enlarged and again 'restored'. This time the local C of I architect *John Guy Ferguson* got the job of extending the nave by an extra bay into the space of the old chancel, which he rebuilt further E on an enlarged plan, re-using Welland's E window. Ferguson also took out plaster vaults from the nave and aisle roofs and replaced them with the present Perp trusses. Finally, in 1889, as Ferguson's chancel was thought to be rather cold, *Thomas Drew*, the rising star of late C19 church building in Ireland, was called in to design the reredos and pulpit, and it was Drew who in 1910 added the rather hard chapter house and choir vestry in the S W corner below the steeple.

EXTERIOR

43 The different periods of the parts of the cathedral can all be distinguished on walking round the outside. Rising up powerfully above the steps of St Columb's Court where the cathedral comes close to the walls of the court house, it can be seen best as a whole from the S W, where its churchyard runs unimpeded by buildings up to the southernmost stretch of the city walls. For all the different dates the materials are the same: rubble schist walls with sandstone trim. The tower and steeple are typical of their date, though more lavish in scale than usual. Four-stage tower with thin clasping buttresses, regular string courses, and odd octagonal pinnacles that seem to be an early C19 attempt to catch the style of the original C17 church. The spire too has an odd feature in the roll mouldings of the arrises.

Beyond the green gabled projections of Drew's chapter house and vestry – the latter on the site of the original S porch – the S aisle wall of 1628 takes over, with late Gothic windows and curious quasi-classical buttresses. The windows are in groups of four lights, cusped, and set within a shallow segmental arch with a segmental hood mould above. In the clerestory they are three-light, and both aisle and clerestory end in crenellated parapets. The ambivalence of the mason Parrott's taste is nicely shown by the contrast of these windows with the regular *cyma recta* base-course moulding on which the whole wall is set, and the classicizing profiles, especially the finials, of the buttresses. The best preserved without restoration is the second on the s aisle.

The original church stopped at the half-round turret towards the E end of the aisle. This is C17, though its crocketed dome finial is by *Ferguson* and the window immediately before it, i.e. on the w side, is also his, as in the original scheme this was a blank wall to a chancel side-chapel. Past the half-round turret everything is by *Ferguson* until the corresponding half-round turret is reached on the N side. The foliated tracery of the E window is however what *Welland* provided in his restoration of the chancel in 1859, re-erected by *Ferguson* in 1885. It probably preserves the pattern of the C17 Planters' Gothic E window. The smaller Dec windows to the side chapels are Ferguson's own design: the originals were low groups of cusped lancets like those in the aisles and clerestory. On the N side note how the aisle windows are only of three lights – not four – and also how the buttresses lack the elaborated finials of the s side. The two-storey arrangement of the windows at the w end of the N aisle dates from the insertion of the galleries in the C18 and records the arrangement of the windows of the aisles at the E end before the Victorian extensions.

INTERIOR

For the time that it was built Champneys considered the nave 45 arcade at Derry Cathedral to be 'rather good work'. It is certainly the most elegant feature of the interior: seven double-chamfered and moulded arches stepping rhythmically down the nave and springing from octagonal piers with almost classical capitals and bases. The last arch before the chancel occupies the place of the old C17 choir and was copied by Ferguson from the others. The aisle and clerestory windows, set in deep segmental reveals, are original, but everything else in the cathedral dates from the C19 restorations. The nave and aisle roofs with open Perp timber trusses were inserted by Ferguson in place of C18 plaster vaults, as were the uncomfortably realistic heads of bishops connected with the diocese that act as corbel stops for the main trusses in the nave. The new chancel arch and two-bay chancel arcade is richer and earlier in style, with applied half-round columns and bell capitals. E wall faced in ashlar sandstone.

FURNISHINGS

The changes to the interior of the cathedral are conveniently
charted in drawings and photographs hanging in Drew's
chapter house. Of the C18 there remains the ORGAN CASE, now
only a case, whose body acts as a draught-proof lobby to the
gallery at the W end of the nave. The gift of Primate Stone when
Bishop of Derry in 1747, it is a magnificent Baroque design
carved in mahogany with musical trophies and corbel brackets
of winged cherubs' heads of an early C18 type. – Also of the
C18 is the BISHOP'S CHAIR, set inside the C19 pinnacled
THRONE, an ample Chinese Chippendale seat with an inset oval
plaque bearing a mitre. The canopy and filigree spire above the
bishop's throne were designed by *Welland* as the pulpit in 1862.
– The PEWS with poppyheads and the LECTERN, a brass eagle
of 1861, are also *Welland*'s. – The octagonal Caen stone PULPIT
with brown marble shafts, dating from 1878, and the REREDOS
are by *Drew*. – STAINED GLASS. All post-1860 and in general
of a realistic pictorial type. In the E window the Ascension, with
Christ's charge to the Apostles below, *c.* 1865. – Signed windows are by *Charles A. Gibbs*, 1874, four children in Gothic
canopies, the third window in the S aisle; by *A. L. & C. E.
Moore*, 1924, St Columba in the S chapel; and by *E. W. Murray
Marr*, 1947, in the N baptistery.

MONUMENTS

Derry's London connections are nowhere more obvious than in
the liberal peppering of its cathedral walls with memorial plaques
and monuments. There are more here than in any other church
in Ulster. The most interesting artistically and historically are the
late C17 Elvin and Edwards monuments in the N aisle, the C18
Tomkins monument in the S aisle, and the C19 sculptural groups
to Bishop Knox and to Captain Boyd. The monuments listed here
are in the sequence vestibule, N aisle, S aisle, S chapel, and gallery.

VESTIBULE. James Gregg † 1812, signed by *W. Spence* of Liverpool. Allegorical figure of Hope on a square tablet. – Francis
Rogan M.D. † 1854, signed by *Kirk* of Dublin. Cross-legged
sinuous figure leaning on an urn above a pedimented tablet.
– James Major Boggs of Belmont † 1841. A heavy Greek stele.
– Hugh Chatham Lyle of Tamnagh † 1897. A tripartite crocketed Gothic tablet. – Thomas Bunbury Gough † 1855 at Sebastopol. Marble stele surmounted by an urn with martial trophies.
– Benjamin Bloomfield Gough † 1893. Small roundel. – The

Venerable John Hayden † 1855. Crocketed ogee Gothic aedicule. – Richard Wells Lloyd † 1874. Oval marble plaque surrounded by an ivy wreath. – Lt. Col. William Holland Lecky Daniel Cuddy † 1855 at Sebastopol. Marble shield on crossed flags. – David Cairns † 1688. A Grecian tablet replacing an old monument in the graveyard erected by the Hon. the Irish Society in 1841. – Bishop William Higgin † 1865. Aberdeen granite sarcophagus by *Frederick H. Smith* of Belfast, the sculptured crozier and mitre by *Kirk* of Dublin. – (The cannon ball in the vestibule has been preserved from the days of the siege of Derry. Other tablets here record the rebuilding of the tower and re-hanging of the BELLS in 1813, and the re-casting in 1929 of the bells given by the Irish Society in 1614 and 1630, and by Charles I in 1638.)

NORTH AISLE. Croker Miller † 1857. A marble Gothic shield. – Kerr McClintock † 1899 in South Africa. Square marble tablet – John Elvin † 1676, 'Alderman and sometime Mayor of this citty, who came over on the first plantation thereof and departed this life on 29 Day of December in the year of our Lord 1676 and the 102 of his age'. An ambitious and wonderfully barbaric classical mural tablet, dated 1678 and probably copied from a French source. The inscription, surmounted by two coats of arms, is flanked by spiral columns with gilded fillets set on bases that are decorated with interlace patterns, with three bucrania below separated by hanging garlands. Here is all the pomp of death in the age of Le Brun and Bérain translated into near-nonsense by an ambitious Ulster mason. Above the entablature obelisks impaled with late C17 heads flank an ogee garlanded pediment with a winged cleric's face in the centre – a cross between a putto and Apollo. – First World War Memorial. A Rickmanesque Gothic canopy. – Hugo Edwards † 1667. Erected by Edward Edwards in 1675. Another ambitious classical tablet, carved and gilt, and every bit as crude as the Elvin monument. The inscription is flanked by triple-shafted, fluted and banded columns, so tapered that they look like the trunks of palm trees. Salient entablature above with a central coat of arms flanked by leafy scrolls. The base panel is filled with *memento mori* motifs: hourglasses on their sides, bell, book, coffin, spades, skulls and crossbones, and – incongruously – winged heads of cherubs holding acanthus fronds between their teeth. – Adam Schoales † 1803. A slim classical aedicule in grey and white marble. – Thomas Bewley Monsell † 1846. A flat Baroque marble tablet. – Captain John McNeil

Boyd R.N. † 1861, signed by *Thomas Farrell*, R.H.A. Life-sized figure of Hope, her l. arm raised to Heaven, her r. round an anchor, set above a sarcophagus tablet that shows Captain Boyd surrounded by four sheet-pulling sailors battling against the elements that overwhelmed H.M.S. Ajax in a hurricane on 9 February 1861. – Mary Anna Chambers † 1879. A marble scroll. – Douglas Bateson, magistrate, murdered by Ribbonmen near Castleblayney, 4 December 1851.

SOUTH AISLE. Letitia Munbee † 1859. A marble scroll. – Frances Kennedy † 1840. A Greek tablet. – Valentine Munbee McMaster † 1872. High Victorian Gothic aedicule with sumbols of the Evangelists. – Anne Scott, daughter of Robert Alexander of Boom Hall, † 1865. Bombée marble shield with draped urn above. – Robert James Scott † 1864. Bombée shield with palm-branch base. – Margaret Maxwell † 1862. Oval marble plaque with palm surround. – John Hickman † 1703. A black marble inscription with now only a fragment of its original aedicule of white and green fossil marble. – John and Rebecca Tomkins † 1741. An unusually sophisticated mid C18 aedicule, Rococo in its elaboration though not in its forms. Lugged and draped architraves frame a black marble inscription, with consoles canted outwards at 45 degrees supporting an open scrolled pediment. The whole tablet set in an inverted fluted dome base. High quality. – Archibald Boyd † 1825. A claw-footed sarcophagus against a grey slate obelisk. – William Knox D.D., Lord Bishop of Derry, † 1831, by *William Behnes*. A large-scale neoclassical sculptural monument in the Canova–Flaxman tradition with full-sized figures of Faith and Charity, the latter with three small children, the eldest a boy dressed in formalized contemporary clothes, flanking a tomb in the centre surmounted by the bishop's mitre. – William Hogg † 1770. A large slate slab attached to the wall.

SOUTH CHAPEL. Richard Ponsonby, Lord Bishop of Derry and Raphoe, † 1853. A heavy marble sarcophagus tablet. – Ensign John Gay Leathem † 1830 at Madras. Greek tablet. – Sir Hugh Hill † 1795. Plain tablet. – Jane Lady Hill † 1836. A marble profile head surmounting a heavy tablet. – Louisa Rea † 1815. Shield and armorial coat on an oval plaque. – John Rea † 1832. A square tablet with rosettes in its cornice. – Alderman John Crooksham † 1704. New stone of 1914. – Bishop the Rt Rev. Charles J. Tyndell D.D. † 1971. – Daniel C. Jones † 1911. A coloured tile and mosaic tablet to the cathedral organist with a tile picture of Asaph, the chief musician.

GALLERY. Harvey Nicholson † 1865. A Gothic niche.

In the CHURCHYARD are many slab stones from the late C17 to the C19. Many were once of the raised sarcophagus or table type, and their balusters have been used to edge the paths. On the S side one large MAUSOLEUM remains, the burying-place of the Manghan family, 1810. Beyond the E end of the cathedral the APPRENTICE BOYS' MOUND was made to contain the bodies of people buried in the N aisle of the cathedral during the siege which were discovered during the restorations of 1861.

ST EUGENE'S CATHEDRAL

Built on a triangular site at the head of Great James Street, the Catholic cathedral is conceived in the hard, spare Gothic introduced to Ireland in the early 1840s by Pugin. Unadorned wall surfaces and sheer height create its effect. Moreover the elaborate spire, planned with the original though not built until the C20, is 256 ft high, a full 65 ft higher than its Protestant rival on the hill of the old city and said to be 8 ft higher above sea level. It is certainly much higher than the little C of I Christ Church beside it, whose tower it completely dwarfs.

The decision to build the cathedral was taken in 1838 and the foundation stone laid thirteen years later, on 26 July 1851. The first architect, who 'made grave errors in building the foundations', is unknown. He was soon superseded by *James J. McCarthy*, under whom the building (except the spire) was completed by 1873. McCarthy's assistant in charge of the job was *Charles Whelan* and the builder was Robert Maxwell. The spire, designed jointly by *George C. Ashlin* of Dublin and *E. J. Toye* of Derry, was begun in 1900 and completed in 1903.

The plan is straightforward, almost a copy of the older cathedral, with six-bay nave arcades supported on octagonal shafts, a clerestory, aisles, and a short chancel flanked by N and S side chapels. The walls are of green schist with Mourne granite trim and geometric tracery in deep double-chamfered reveals. McCarthy's detailing, plain to the point of severity, is relieved outside only by buttresses and paired octagonal finials at the E gable, to which *Toye* added cusped and crocketed canopies for six statues in 1904. His spire is in a C14 style, with twelve crocketed pinnacles and diaper stone panelling in bands across the needle.

Inside, the nave has a hipped panelled ceiling, with the shafts of the roof trusses running down the clerestory wall to twenty-six corbel heads. Choir gallery supported on cluster columns at the W end.

FURNISHINGS. The PULPIT, FONT, and REREDOS in Caen stone with Middleton red and Clifden green marbles were supplied by *Earley & Powells* of Dublin in 1878. The spire and canopy over the pulpit were executed in Austrian oak by *Ferdinand Stufflesser & Co.* to designs of *Toye* in 1906. All these elements survive in part, after the introduction of a new freestanding altar and rearrangement of the pews designed by *Liam McCormick & Partners* in 1975. – STAINED GLASS. All the aisle windows and those of the side chapels and chancel are by *Mayer & Co.*, dating from 1880 to 1902. The E window, showing the Crucifixion with seven Irish saints below, was installed as a memorial to Bishop Francis Kelly D.D. † 1889, under whom the cathedral was built. His MONUMENT is in the S side chapel with a portrait bust in profile.

In the CATHEDRAL PRECINCTS the BISHOP'S PALACE of 1873, also by *McCarthy*, a big three-storey, five-bay block with gabled ends and quatrefoil pierced balconies over square bay-windows. All in green schist. Below the cathedral ST EUGENE'S CATHEDRAL SCHOOL is a long nine-bay, two-storey block with gabled ends and towered centre, built for the Christian Brothers in 1852, in Institutional Gothic style. The gabled gate lodge of 1905 is by *Toye*, who also added to the schools in 1895.

CITY CHURCHES

CHURCH OF IRELAND

ST AUGUSTINE, on the West Wall fronting Grand Parade. This little chapel of ease occupies the site of the Augustinian abbey that was repaired and used by the original planters until their cathedral was built. It was rebuilt as a small Palladian chapel by Bishop Barnard about 1750, with a pedimented W front of three bays with a Diocletian window set over the entrance door and segmental windows down the sides. All this disappeared in 1872, when the present diminutive Gothic church by *J. G. Ferguson* took its place: a three-bay gabled hall with a W bell-cote, geometric wheel window, and lean-to slated porch across the entire front with a gabled door in the centre. Built of whinstone with sandstone dressings. Hammerbeam roof inside. – In the CHURCHYARD numerous late C18 'table-top' tombs and some late C17 slabs.

CHRIST CHURCH, Infirmary Road. A small tower and hall type

church built by Bishop Knox in 1830 to designs of *John Ferguson*. Refitted by *Welland & Gillespie* in 1862 and enlarged in 1881 by the addition of transepts and a chancel to designs of the original architect's more famous son, *John Guy Ferguson*. Built of rubble schist and whinstone with a battlemented three-stage tower in primitive Gothic style. Two-bay nave, single-bay transepts and chancel.

ALL SAINTS, Waterside. Dramatically set at the junction of Bond's Hill and Clooney Terrace, making good use of its steeply banked hairpin site. Built by the Ecclesiastical Commissioners in 1864–7 to designs of *Lanyon, Lynn & Lanyon*, with more of *W. H. Lynn* in its design than anyone else. Cruciform, with short transepts contained within the line of the aisles, polygonal chancel, s porch, and offset w steeple built for maximum effect to tower above the lower side of the site on Bond's Hill. The materials are whinstone with sandstone dressings: the detail heavy E.E. with red granite colonnettes. Single-chamfered arcaded aisles inside on round column piers. A good, solid design.

ST PETER, Culmore Road. 1963–7 by *A. T. Marshall*. A modern harled hall with canted heads to the windows and wide shallow eaves.

ST COLUMBA (THE LONG TOWER CHURCH). In 1802, when Sampson wrote the *Statistical Survey of Co. Derry*, the stump of the round tower that gives this church its name still survived, converted into an icehouse. It was the only medieval fragment left from the historic monastery founded by St Colmcille in 546 and was itself probably of C10 origin.

The large T-plan church of today, with its double gabled transepts and steeply stepped galleries, has evolved out of and incorporates the oldest Catholic church of Derry, built by Bishop McDevitt from 1784 to 1786. It was a long hall built on a NW–SE axis with the altar at the SE gable end. To this a large nave was added in 1810 at r. angles to the long NE wall, with four round-headed Georgian-glazed windows on each side. Galleries were fitted in the nave and at both ends of the old church, and the altar moved to a position on axis with the nave. The church had no seating on the ground floor and could then accommodate 2,000 people. Decorations and improvements, including the BALDACCHINO, which incorporates marble capitals brought from Naples by the Protestant Earl Bishop, were carried out from 1820 to 1829. Then in 1908 *E. J. Toye* restored the whole fabric, adding the extra gabled transepts on the far side of the nave – a motif that he often used in his own designs – replacing coping stones and porches, and building the copper cupola over the crossing.

The interior, though not particularly well proportioned, is in an ornate neo-Renaissance style with paired marble columns supporting the valley in the centre of the church caused by Toye's second transept plan. – SCULPTURE on the high altar and side altars is by *Edmund Sharpe*. The original altarpiece by *B. R. Haydon* has been lost.

ST COLUMB, Chapel Road, Waterside. A Gothic hall by *J. J. McCarthy*, begun in 1838 and completed in 1841. Enlarged in 1887 by the addition of transepts, united to the nave through a triple arcade, and a chancel. McCarthy's original front has a gabled battlemented parapet with a corbelled central tower and spire. The later C19 transepts have Dec sandstone mullions.

ST PATRICK, Buncrana Road, Pennyburn. 1932. A large cruciform church in red brick with sandstone dressings by *E. J. Toye*, completed after his death by *J. P. McGrath*. Except for the offset front tower that ends in a squared onion-shaped dome (copied from Ashlin & Coleman's Church of the Sacred Heart at Newry), the detail is Celtic-Romanesque, with a big wheel window, blind arcading, and cushion capitals to the nave and transept columns inside. Toye's usual double transepts, though the chancel here has shrunk to a mere semicircular apse. The roof is shaped as a coved barrel-vault.

ST MARY, Fanad Drive, Creggan. 1959 by *Corr & McCormick*. T-shaped, with the low-pitched copper roofs fashionable in the fifties. Walls of rock-faced Dublin granite.

OUR LADY OF LOURDES, Steelstown. 1975 by *Liam McCormick & Partners*. A very basic building, but none the worse for that: a slate-hung tent stepped in three stages with a bivouac porch offset at the end. The windows are where the flaps would be, right down at ground level. A timber-lined triangular space inside.

PRESBYTERIAN CHURCHES

FIRST DERRY PRESBYTERIAN CHURCH, facing Magazine Street Upper on the West Wall. Possibly the most wholehearted of the many temple-fronted Presbyterian churches in

Ulster and unusually late, for this big Roman Corinthian portico in reddish sandstone dates only from 1903 and is by *W. E. Pinkerton*. Tetrastyle and textbook. Built on a generous scale with pilaster responds and flanking single bays, it masks entirely the front of the earlier church built in 1780. This was a plain, rectangular, two-storey hall with a gallery round three sides. In 1828 it was given a new five-bay front with a central three-bay pediment and round-headed windows to the first floor which can still be discerned as the bones of Pinkerton's design. Inside is a rich coffered ceiling, and behind the pulpit late C19 STAINED GLASS of the Four Evangelists. – MONUMENT. The Rev. William McClure † 1874 by *William McElwee*.

The first Derry congregation was founded at the time of the original Plantation and, though persecuted in the 1660s, was firmly established by the ministry of Robert Craighead *c.* 1680. When the steeple of St Columb's Cathedral threatened collapse about 1800 the churchmen used the Presbyterian church until the cathedral tower had been dismantled.

STRAND ROAD (SECOND) PRESBYTERIAN CHURCH. 1847 by the County Surveyor, *Stewart Gordon*. A plain Gothic hall built in rubble whinstone with an ashlar sandstone front. Gabled, of three bays, with buttresses. Octagonal central tower ending in thin pinnacles. Hardly an accomplished design.

GREAT JAMES STREET PRESBYTERIAN CHURCH. Built from 1835 to 1837 as the third Presbyterian Church, though also known as the Scots Church. By *Stewart Gordon*. An unusually ambitious classical design with a tetrastyle Greek Ionic portico flanked by single bays with large aedicule windows. The portico is set at the top of a broad flight of steps with gigantic scrolled edges. Behind is a regular four-bay, two-storey hall lit by large round-headed windows, with a gallery round three sides supported on sixteen slender fluted cast-iron columns that run through to the ceiling in a segment-headed arcade. A segmental barrel-vault in plaster spans the central space. The window behind the pulpit is of Venetian type with Corinthian columns and pilasters, though the centre is now filled with a lumpish organ. Box pews throughout. Perhaps the unusual quality of the interior sustained the first members of the congregation through a dedication service that lasted from eleven a.m. to nearly four o'clock in the afternoon! The interior, including the mahogany-fronted galleries, was remodelled by *Boyd & Batt* in 1863.

REFORMED PRESBYTERIAN CHURCH, Clarendon Street. A

doughty piece of rogue architecture, probably by *J. J. Stevenson* and *Campbell Douglas*, who designed a church in Derry carried out between 1860 and 1868. This fits the bill best. T-shaped, with three gables, paired slated porches with hipped roofs, such as a Voysey house might have, and a side porch in the angle of the T with a wide but very thin stone tower ending in a chisel-shaped slate roof above a timber belfry. A curious companion for the late-Georgian-style brick terraces round about it.

WATERSIDE PRESBYTERIAN CHURCH, Clooney Terrace. Won in competiton by *William Hague Jr.* in 1863. Hague, the son of a Co. Cavan builder, was to become a major Catholic architect in the later C19. This was an early success, built by *Alexander McElwee* and superintended by *J. G. Ferguson.* E.E., of local blue rubble stone with Glasgow sandstone dressings, skilfully accommodated to a sloping site, with gabled front, transepts, and tower and broach-spire. Alterations were made in 1924 by *R. B. Roe*.

CARLISLE ROAD PRESBYTERIAN CHURCH. 1877–9 by *Young & Mackenzie*. The fourth Presbyterian church, prominently sited at the foot of Carlisle Road facing Craigavon Bridge. Large but dull, with a mechanical three-bay gabled front divided by octagonal pinnacles with a big Perp window in the middle of the front and paired doors below.

EBRINGTON PRESBYTERIAN CHURCH, Limavady Road. 1897 by *William Barker*. A showy but ill-proportioned stucco temple-fronted church. Three-bay pedimented centre with half-engaged Corinthian columns and lower balustraded wings. The usual three-sided gallery inside. The church halls were completed by *M. A. Robinson* after Barker's death in 1899.

CLAREMONT PRESBYTERIAN CHURCH, Northland Road. 1905 by *M. A. Robinson*. A big hall in neo-Gothic style with a clean-cut, wide brick gable divided into three by square corner turrets and polygonal shafts flanking a central Perp window with a gabled porch below.

OTHER NONCONFORMIST CHURCHES

FORMER COVENANTERS' CHURCH, Bond's Hill, Waterside. 1857–8 by *W. Raffles Brown* of Liverpool. A thin Commissioners'-Gothic church, four-bay, with a gabled front and narrow buttressed central tower. Derelict at the time of writing.

CARLISLE ROAD METHODIST CHURCH. 1901 by *Alfred For-*

man. A clever design in an enriched late Gothic style that contributes generously to the townscape on its narrow street frontage. The façade combines a delicate steeple above an entrance porch, a side of four gables stiffened by flying buttresses, and a projecting polygonal baptistery with a pointed slate roof. The side of the roof of the church rises high above this with a ridge finial. The spire of the steeple is supported by more flying buttresses. The interior, all in timber, has a high gallery and is accoustically excellent – a quality for which Forman was noted.

PUBLIC BUILDINGS

COURT HOUSE, Bishop Street. 1813–17 by *John Bowden*. A scrupulous Greek Revival block with a tetrastyle central portico linked by narrow single bays to slightly projecting ends – also single-bay – flanked by coupled pilasters. The order of the portico is a very pure Erechtheum Ionic with almost as pure antae capitals on the pilasters. The building is of two storeys, though on the front only the upper floor is expressed by windows – seven across the whole front. The wall is rusticated below and ashlar above. Generally in Dungiven sandstone, with the orders, cornices, and string courses in a whiter Portland stone. The royal coat of arms above the pediment and figures of Peace and Justice – set on a recessed blocking course in the middle of either end bay – are by *Edward Smyth* of Dublin. The two-storey brick-built Council Office to the S is by *Thomas Turner*. Further additions and remodelling to the courts were carried out in 1896 by *A. C. Adair*, who apparently added the square lanterns that light each of the two courts.

GUILDHALL, Shipquay Place. Derry's first two town halls were in the Diamond, within the walls. This building, twice burnt out (in 1908 and again in 1972), was designed in 1887 by *John Guy Ferguson*. It was rebuilt, retaining its basic outline (though with an elaboration of the fenestration and window tracery typical of its time), by *M. A. Robinson*, who completed the reconstruction in 1912. Under reconstruction again in 1975–7. Of rubble sandstone with red sandstone dressings, conceived in the loose Tudoresque Gothic vein of S. P. Close. Gabled front flanked by thin octagonal turrets with an elaborate arched tracery window that lit the main hall. The tall belfry tower at the SE corner remains from Ferguson's building. More solid and firmly detailed than the rest. The building occupies an island site and groups well from Foyle Street and as seen from the quays to the N, where more of Ferguson's work remains.

OLD JAIL, Bishop Street Without. Of the former castellated prison built in 1791 to designs of *Edward Miller* and extended between 1819 and 1824 only one octagonal machicolated turret has been permitted to remain, inanely attached to the corner of a flimsy housing block.

HARBOUR COMMISSIONERS' OFFICE, Harbour Square. 1882 by *John Kennedy*. A trim Italianate block of boulder-faced sandstone, with ashlar cornices and window architraves. Two-storey, the front of seven bays not quite symmetrical, with a narrow central pediment beside a square clock tower which forms the fifth bay, with an aediculed door at ground level. Four-bay sides. A nice design.

OLD FOYLE COLLEGE, Strand Road. 1814 by *John Bowden*. A handsome Regency-style group not unlike a severe neo-classical country house. A tall centre block, five bays and three storeys with wide overhanging eaves, is flanked by slightly projecting single-bay, two-storey wings with pedimental gables and tripartite windows at ground-floor level. The wings and centre are joined by single-bay links each with a tripartite door surmounted by huge fanlights. In 1968 Bowden's building was closed when the college moved to a new site at Springtown. The buildings there are by *A. T. Marshall*. The statue in front of the college (which moved with it) is of John Lawrence, Viceroy of India from 1864 to 1869, brought from Lahore in 1903. It is by *Sir Joseph Edgar Boehm*.

117 MAGEE UNIVERSITY COLLEGE, Northland Road. 1856–65 by *E. P. Gribbon*, completed following disagreement with the architect by the County Surveyor, *Stewart Gordon*. Institutional Gothic in Scottish sandstone enlivened by a welter of Gribbon's Presbyterian church detail: two-centred mullioned windows, pinnacles with gablets and crockets, and some unusual two-sided salient oriels in the projecting end blocks and over the door of the central tower. The elevation not quite symmetrical, though the plan is. The groups of two-storey red-brick houses for professors were added in 1881, 1895, and 1911 to designs of *Young & Mackenzie, W. A. Barker*, and *Robinson & Davidson* respectively.

ST COLUMB'S COLLEGE, Bishop Street Without. The school occupies the site of the gardens of the Earl Bishop's Casino, which was adapted as a chapel until it was replaced by the present building on the same site. The first of the school buildings was the JUNIOR HOUSE, S of the chapel, 1877 by *O'Neill & Byrne*, a good, solid Victorian block in coursed green schist, three-storey, seven-bay, with a forestanding Venetian Gothic porch and two tiers of gabled dormer windows in its high roof. In 1892 the SENIOR HOUSE was added N of the Casino, designed by the locals *Croom* and *Toye*, based on the earlier O'Neill & Byrne design. Same materials, same style. Toye is more like himself in the rendered classical MUSEUM BUILD-ING of 1897 which, rather surprisingly, lifts the Protestant Bishop's C18 Casino up a storey to set a replica of this small Ionic temple on a high rusticated podium with salient plinths beneath the columns. A versatile essay that deserves to be well painted. CHAPEL of 1936 by *W. H. Byrne*, a long, high rubble-built hall with a semicircular apse. N of the school the remains of a C17 WINDMILL TOWER converted into a pigeon house in the early C19.

MUNICIPAL TECHNICAL COLLEGE, Strand Road. 1908 by *E. J. Toye*. Out of scale with its surroundings but good in itself. A very tall four-storey block in brick and cement. Nine-bay, with gables over the outer three windows at each end, and a central ridge cupola. The window spacings subtly grouped. Massive additions of the late 1960s in the grounds of the demolished asylum by *Francis Johnston*.

LONG TOWER SCHOOLS, Long Tower Street. INFANTS' SCHOOL of 1825, remodelled in 1894, GIRLS' SCHOOL of 1893 by *E. J. Toye*, BOYS' SCHOOL of 1912 by *Daniel Conroy*, the last with a grandiose pedimented classical gateway in cement.

ST PATRICK'S SCHOOLS, Pennyburn. 1955 by *Corr & McCormick*.

APPRENTICE BOYS' HALL, Society Street. *See* p. 394.

EBRINGTON BARRACKS, Limavady Road. *See* p. 405.

GWYN'S INSTITUTE, Brook Park. *See* p. 398.

IRISH SOCIETY HOUSE, Bishop Street. *See* p. 393.

MASONIC HALL, formerly BISHOP'S PALACE. *See* p. 393.

OLD INFIRMARY, Infirmary Road. *See* p. 398.

ST COLUMB'S HALL, Richmond Street. *See* p. 396.

WALKER TESTIMONIAL, Grand Parade. *See* p. 394.

WATERSIDE STATION, Bond's Hill. *See* p. 405.

INDEX OF STREETS

Bold numbers indicate reference in Tours, pp. 393–401

TOURS

The pressures of modern redevelopment, mentioned on p. 372 are likely to make too detailed tours rapidly out of date. What is indicated here are two walks in areas that should not change significantly for some time: (a) a circular tour within the walls of the C17 city, and (b) from SHIPQUAY PLACE, N to the C19 suburbs, and back by STRAND ROAD. Commercial and factory buildings, which do not come together into an easy promenade, are given in two further groups: (c) those between FOYLE STREET and ABERCORN ROAD, E and S of the old town, and (d) suburban developments. THE WATERSIDE is included in the East Neighbourhood, *see* p. 405

(a) Inside the Walls

The obvious place to start inside the walls is at Bishop's Gate (*see* p. 374), which closes the S end of the spinal street that runs through the old town. In BISHOP STREET on the r. is the Court House facing the former BISHOP'S PALACE, the MASONIC HALL since 1945, a grandly scaled five-bay, three-storey block, free-standing, with the remnants of the bishop's garden to l. and r. (l. now all tarmac). Several palaces are supposed to have stood here; one, of *c*. 1753, was rebuilt by Bishop Barnard (1747–68) and largely reconstructed by his successor the Earl Bishop (1768–1803) (*see* p. 367). In 1798 the palace was used as a barracks. It was repaired by Bishop Knox (1803–31) after its use by the military, and what is here now must be Knox's work – distinctly Regency in character, with shallow hipped roofs and overhanging eaves. The centre three bays are recessed to give the building a typically early C19 duality with paired projecting ends that have a look of *Bowden* about them. Limited traces of C18 detail remain inside.

Diagonally opposite the palace is ST COLUMB'S COURT, leading into the cathedral churchyard. IRISH SOCIETY HOUSE, on the corner, is a plain rectangular Georgian block, three-storey like most of the street, dated 1768 on one of the SW quoins. Five-bay front to Bishop Street with a handsome doorcase at the side. The window glazing bars were replaced about 1820, though one old window with thick bars remains at the back. Solidly mid Georgian inside, with a good staircase – three banisters per tread – and Tuscan pilasters. Lugged door-frames with six-panel doors and nice C18 polychrome marble fireplaces. Next, No. 3, a big five-bay brick house slightly recessed from the street. Opposite, PALACE STREET leads l. down to

ST AUGUSTINE'S SCHOOLS, late Victorian red-brick Gothic with freestone details and gables. Next is St Augustine's church set in a triangular graveyard with some C17 and C18 grave slabs.

51   From the graveyard the remains of the WALKER TESTIMONIAL can be seen in the GRAND PARADE on the W face of the wall. The testimonial was a 90 ft Doric column in Portland stone erected in 1826 to designs of *James Henry* and surmounted by the lively figure of the Rev. George Walker, governor of the city during the siege of 1689. The statue was by *John Smyth* of Dublin. The column was blown up by terrorists in 1973 and only its square Portland stone plinth remains.

In SOCIETY STREET, on the N, the Baronial APPRENTICE BOYS' HALL of 1873 is by *J. G. Ferguson*, rather flat, with monotonous large mullioned windows and a corner tower. All but the first bay on the l. is in fact an extension by *Robinson & Davidson* of 1937. Ferguson's façade faces MAGAZINE STREET and looks W across the wall. Down Magazine Street past the First Presbyterian Church and some Georgian houses to BUTCHER STREET with its gate opening l. to the Bogside.

In Butcher Street turn r. into THE DIAMOND, the central square of the C17 town. Here the site of two earlier Market Houses is marked now by the FIRST WORLD WAR MEMORIAL, though the basement of the C18 Market House remains below ground. The memorial, with a winged figure of victory flanked by a soldier and a sailor, is of 1927, the sculpture by *Vernon March*. In the S corner of the Diamond, diagonally opposite Butcher Street, AUSTIN'S DEPARTMENT STORE, 1906 by *M. A. Robinson*, is by far the largest building in the square and memorable for its free-wheeling Edwardian Baroque frontages with more than a hint of C18 Austria and Art Nouveau. Turn l. round the Diamond past No. 15, a nice Victorian stucco block in an Italianate style, and l. into SHIPQUAY STREET, which runs steeply downhill. The terraced block on the r. is the DERRY JOURNAL OFFICE, originally of 1772 though much reworked, with further downhill the flamboyantly stuccoed six-bay Italianate ALLIED IRISH BANK by *Croom* and *Toye* of 1890. No. 6, on the l., is a fine four-bay, three-storey mid C18 house, brick with a stone eaves cornice and a handsome segmental pediment on console brackets over the door. The interior has robust contemporary detail including lugged door-frames, big solid cornices, and a generous timber stair, set at right angles across the back, with paired Tuscan columns as newel posts, and a splendid banister whorl at the ground floor. No. 8, next door, is also four-bay, three-storey, in brick but later, with a tripartite Adamesque door similar to those of Merrion Square, Dublin. Beyond a four-bay brick and stone block, later C19 and reminiscent of *Thomas Turner*, is the HIBERNIAN BANK, 1896 by *E. J. Toye*, an Italianate stucco block with central pedimented aedicule. From here CASTLE STREET leads l. back to the wall, passing on the r. the frontage of the OLD LIBRARY of 1825 with three high round-headed windows framed in diamond-faced quoins of dressed sandstone.

At the wall turn r. down MAGAZINE STREET, lined with late Georgian brown-brick houses and warehouses. No. 14, MAGAZINE HOUSE, built as the Bank of Ireland's agent's house, is of four bays and three storeys with a horizontal channelled ground floor in sandstone. Nos. 18, 19, and 20 form a good group: two three-storey houses in brick, with offices in schist and brick further uphill, the houses with elegant Ionic doorcases. No. 19 has bold early C19 plasterwork in the hall. Now down to Magazine Gate, with its big keystone face, and r. along the return of the wall to the bottom of Shipquay Street. (Turning l., through the gate, SHIPQUAY PLACE is the start of the second tour.)

Now back up Shipquay Street. Immediately on the r. the BEL-[98] FAST BANK of 1853 is one of *Charles Lanyon*'s most confident Renaissance designs, high and massy like a Genoese palazzo, only three windows wide and three storeys high but big in scale, with a rusticated central archway surmounted by a Corinthian aedicule so large that it erupts into the attic window of the floor above, like Gibbs's pediment at King's College, Cambridge. A similar fine preponderance of wall over window is here. Mid C19 stucco and brick blocks of three storeys run up the street. No. 40 is a big six-bay design with opposite on the l., No. 33, the OLD CUSTOMS HOUSE, the finest remaining C18 block in the city, brick-fronted, eight bays and three storeys, set on a high basement to accommodate the slope of the site, and with an exceptionally fine pedimented stone doorcase that would not be out of place in Molesworth Street, Dublin, or in the Bedford estate in London. In the hall there are still sections of wainscot panelling, and a Rococo string in the remodelled double-return staircase has the date 1741 in an acanthus wreath of carved wood. Long may this vestige of early Georgian Derry remain. Uphill on the r. the BANK OF IRELAND, 1869 by *Sandham Symes*, a high palazzo-style block with a console-bracketed cornice and segmental aedicules to the first floor.

RICHMOND STREET, on the l. opposite Castle Street, leads SE, through full-scale planners' demolition, across LINEN HALL STREET, where only old steps remain, to the EAST WALL. Here the Y.M.C.A. BUILDING, a large two-storey, stucco-fronted hall with gable pediment, is by *J. G. Ferguson*, 1866.* Note the heads of Luther, Calvin, Knox, and Cranmer high up in the entablature and out of harm's way. Set obliquely to it, further beyond the wall, is ST COLUMB'S HALL, a Temperance establishment built in 1888 to lavish Baroque designs of *Croom* and *Toye*. This veritable palace of abstinence has a grandiose cut-stone front that curiously ignores its steeply sloping site: two storeys slipping down to three, with a tripartite façade, rusticated below and divided on the upper floor by Corinthian pilasters. Each section is lit by a group of three round-headed windows. The centre is emphasized by a bowed portico that follows a concave–convex–concave profile, and by a statue group over an attic pediment with figures of Erin, Temperance, and Vulcan carved by *C. W. Harrison* of Dublin. The roof line is balustraded, with French pavilion roofs rising from either end. T-shaped plan. Much plainer hall behind the show front.

From St Columb's Hall turn r., either within the walls up East Wall, or outside up ORCHARD STREET, where small brick houses, all now mid C19, huddle against the slope of the city wall, with one bastion breaking through between them. At FERRYQUAY GATE the townscape is enhanced by an elegant Italianate stuccoed block, four storeys high, and very square, rising well above the wall. Across FERRYQUAY STREET, which leads back into the Diamond, the wall continues as ARTILLERY STREET, Past the heavily modelled cement façade of *E.J. Toye*'s CONVENT OF MERCY SCHOOL of 1911, to NEW GATE. Here steps lead up to CHURCH WALL, with more C19 houses huddling against the fortifications and one C17 corner bartizan.

Facing New Gate, the SYNOD HALL of 1879, a stuccoed two-storey block with a gable pediment, occupies the site of the theatre built about 1795. LONDON STREET runs r. from here, passing the CATHEDRAL PRIMARY SCHOOL of 1891 by *J. G. Ferguson*, red brick in a Flemish Gothic style with a corner circular stair-tower. And so into the open space at the E end of the cathedral churchyard. Turn r. into PUMP STREET, which retains on its SE side a fine sequence of eight late Georgian brick houses, many now part of the CONVENT OF

* Burnt and to be demolished 1978.

MERCY. The main house, a big, seven-bay, three-storey block, has a fine tripartite door with an elliptical fanlight and fluted Tuscan columns. Three pleasant houses also remain at the s end of the E side. At the bottom of Pump Street, FERRYQUAY STREET leads l. back into the Diamond. Low scale with poor modern buildings. The PHOENIX ASSURANCE on the l. is architecturally just what Derry does not want. The Diamond leads l. and back into Bishop Street past the DISTRICT PROBATE OFFICE, 1861, a two-storey brick block with checked window reveals, completely painted crimson. Then past the end of London Street, with some old houses with exposed sash boxes and stone eaves cornices which suggest an early date, to No. 24, THE NORTHERN COUNTIES CLUB, lavishly remodelled by *Alfred Forman* in 1902 and now a five-bay, three-storey block with a giant order of Composite pilasters across the upper floors of the entire front, expanding to half-columns on the end bays and supporting conical slate roofs. A. E. McCANDLESS & CO. opposite was originally the Imperial Hotel, built by a Mr Greer of Omagh about 1846. It is a large three-storey, six-bay stuccoed block with a channelled ground floor and an inappropriate modern door.

(b) Outside the Walls

A tour outside the walls might begin in SHIPQUAY PLACE below the NE face of the city wall. The Guildhall (*see* p. 389) rises opposite on its island site. Beyond on the l. is the biscuit-coloured block of the NORTHERN BANK, 1866 by *Thomas Turner* and one of his best commercial designs. Built of Scottish sandstone, this sophisticated palazzo-style block breathes an air of Glasgow rather than Derry. Three storeys high and, like the Guildhall, on the end of an island site, with a six-bay frontage and four-bay sides. Ground floor divided by wide piers with banded rustication – copied from Rochead? – with round-headed windows between. Ashlar for the floors above, with grouped Ionic pilasters at the chamfered corners, and big Roman aedicules with segmental pediments on the first-floor windows.

A loop can be made by crossing to the bank and taking GUILDHALL STREET on its r. to HARBOUR SQUARE. The COMMERCIAL PAPER COMPANY, behind the bank, is of 1892 by *E. J. Toye*. Tidy. Ground-floor arches in sandstone with carved keystones; brick above. Beyond are the Harbour Offices (*see* p. 390). Past the front of these, CUSTOMS HOUSE STREET leads back to Shipquay Place. Opposite are the POST OFFICE and CUSTOMS HOUSE, sturdy stone-faced blocks of 1876 with round-headed windows and big eaves. On the corner the NORTHERN COUNTIES HOTEL is of 1899, a symmetrical red-brick block with high end gables and an extravagant two-storey, five-bay arcade between the gable ends. From here the triangular WATERLOO PLACE opens out, with WATERLOO STREET leading s, uphill, to Castle Gate and Butchers' Gate. STRAND ROAD, a long, straight commercial street lined almost continuously by later C19 three-storey blocks, leads N. To the l. in SACKVILLE STREET are some late Georgian terraced brick houses. Take the next street to the l. off Strand Road, GREAT JAMES STREET, rising steeply with a succession of two-bay, three-storey houses stepping regularly uphill. Half-way up on the l. is the portico of Great James Street Presbyterian Church (see p. 387), with a big cubic ashlar-fronted three-storey house before it, the former manse beyond. At the top of the hill St Eugene's Cathedral (see p. 383) rises up grandly just beyond the crossroads with Francis Street.

Here another short loop may be made to the l. down Francis Street and then through the cathedral grounds by the main gate and out at the N side opposite the gates to Brook Park. FRANCIS STREET has some good brick and stucco houses of about 1840. For the cathedral precinct and the schools see p. 384. BROOKE PARK was purchased with a bequest of £15,000 left by James Brooke in 1865 for the establishment of a people's park in Derry. GWYN'S INSTITUTE, 1840 by *Thomas Jackson*, built in the park, was burnt out in 1973. (Jackson has indeed fared badly, as his Ulster Bank of 1858, a big classical affair in Waterloo Place, was also bombed and has since been demolished.) The Institute had a gauche C19 Palladian appearance, with three ashlar blocks, almost the same size and each with high gable pediments, linked by deeply recessed two-bay wings. The centre block was of three bays, the others were only two-bay, with their windows more widely apart. Rusticated ground floor. The shell remains at the time of writing. The gate lodge, a nice classical design, is also by *Jackson*.

INFIRMARY ROAD, crossing in front of the gates to the park, leads N past Christ Church (see p. 384) to, on the r., Clarendon Street. It passes (r.) the CRAIG MEMORIAL HALL of 1878, a small Gothic hall in green schist and sandstone, and (l.) the OLD INFIRMARY of 1810 by Soane's pupil *Robert Woodgate*, a long, seven-bay, three-storey block with forestanding porch, much reworked and encumbered by the additions made by *M. A. Robinson* in 1900. CRAWFORD SQUARE, with big stuccoed houses developed between the late 1850s and the 1870s to designs of *Robert Collins*, lies to the N off NORTH-LAND ROAD.

We return by CLARENDON STREET, opposite the Infirmary, 5 a fine succession of big, warm brown-brick houses stepping down the hill – fine, but never intended to be very grand, as the ubiquitous two-bay fronts with squashed windows on the ground floor make clear. Georgian in character, though mostly post-1845. Half way down QUEEN STREET crosses, closed to the r. by the vista of Great James Street Church with, nearer at hand, the vigorous red and yellow brick façade of the CITY 118 FACTORY, 1863 by *Young & Mackenzie*. A substantial seven-bay, three-storey frontage can be seen on Queen Street, but there is much more round the corner in PATRICK STREET, repeating the same rhythms with bold sculpted keystone faces on the main ground-floor arches. Following Queen Street in the opposite direction, on the r. are Nos. 13–16, four excellent Georgian-style terraced houses with good Ionic or Tuscan doorcases. Each is a three-bay, three-storey house, with a railed area, a semi-basement, and steps to the front door. Opposite is the wayward Reformed Presbyterian Church (*see* p. 387). The end of the street is closed by the wall of *Johnston*'s former asylum. At this turn r. past the handsome BAY VIEW TERRACE of *c.* 1870 and into STRAND ROAD again. The Technical College on the l. (*see* p. 391) closes the view out of the town. We return to the r., passing Strand Road Presbyterian Church and the neo-Georgian corner façade of the NATIONAL BANK, 1927 by *J. P. McGrath*.

(c) *Commercial and Factory Buildings*

The commercial and mercantile monuments of Derry are grouped mainly in the bow of land, between the E and N walls of the city and the river, from CRAIGAVON BRIDGE to Shipquay Place. The bridge, with two decks, the lower one originally for the railway companies, is by *Mott, Hay & Anderson* of London. It crosses the Foyle in five spans and was opened in July 1933. The earlier iron swing bridge here, of 1863, was designed by *John Hawkshaw*. The double level has had a bad effect on CAR-LISLE SQUARE, which now partly obscures the large brick block of the FACTORY, formerly Tillie and Henderson, on its SW side. This is by *J. G. Ferguson*, 1856, with French quoin pilasters and mansard roofs to big four-bay corner blocks that tie down its long façades. The FACTORY, formerly Robert Sinclair & Co., just out of the Square on the l., is of a more conventional character. 1863 by *A. McElwee* of Derry. Domestic, apart from its scale, with two brown-brick, four-storey frontages in ABERCORN ROAD and WAPPING LANE, and an elegant curved corner entrance, framed for the height of the building by quoin pilasters with a scrolled clock above the top storey. In the opposite direction, CARLISLE ROAD climbs in a dog-leg to Ferryquay Gate. Past the Perp Presbyterian Church, HAWKINS STREET leads l., up hill, to the HORACE STREET FACTORY (Welch Margetson & Co.), 1872 by *J. G. Ferguson*, much more powerful than the same architect's factory by the bridge, and probably the most confident and satisfying of all the industrial buildings of Victorian Derry. It is a massive block in Ruskinian Gothic, three storeys and eighteen bays long, with an arcaded basement that is well adapted to the changing levels of the site. The detail is rich but well controlled, with pink brick walls built out into corbelled cornices at each floor level and enlivened with sandstone voussoirs and green schist string courses flush with the face of the bricks. Perhaps to be truthful it is more G. E. Street's *Brick and Marble in the North of Italy* that lies behind Ferguson's style here. Or did he really copy the idiom of the former W. F. Bigger's Stores at Nos. 83–95 FOYLE STREET? This too is red-brick, Italianate Gothic, built in 1870 by *Young & Mackenzie* on a gently bowed site almost a third of the way along the route which was once the mercantile heart of the city. An excellent design.*

Foyle Street can be reached from Horace Street by turning l. into Carlisle Road, past the Gothic Methodist Church (*see* p. 388) and up to Ferryquay Gate. Here BRIDGE STREET (under redevelopment at the time of writing) doubles back downhill to the r., with Foyle Street on the level at the bottom. Lined with big, plain brick warehouses, the road was like a canyon built by commerce, but most on the riverside have now gone. Those on the l. are first the remains of Bigger's Building, then on the corner after SUGAR HOUSE LANE, No. 81, P. O'KANE & CO., a vigorous early Victorian five-bay, three-storey stucco block, crisply detailed, with arcaded shop windows, composite pilasters, and recessed window panels on the upper floors. Next Nos. 69–79, a thirteen-bay, three-storey FACTORY, the upper floors arranged as pairs of arcaded stucco window panels between thin strip pilasters. 1860? Nos. 3–17, the COM-

* Bombed in May 1976 and mostly demolished.

MERCIAL BUILDINGS of 1883, are by *J. G. Ferguson* again, a clever long façade of four shops with offices on two floors above and a central archway opening to a yard behind. Of squared rubble-faced masonry with ashiar window surrounds and richly sculptured imposts for the arches of all the windows. On the ground floor, narrow doors alternating with wide shop windows and separated by paired stone colonnettes. The carving of the springing stones here is delightful. On the keystones of the large arches heads representing the continents with which Derry men traded. (The attic courses, above the eaves cornice, have been renewed in artificial stone which can never match the rest.)

(d) Later Factory Buildings

The later factory buildings are scattered. The STAR FACTORY, in Foyle Road by the river at the S end of the city, is of 1899 by *Daniel Conroy*, a bold, stone-built facade of ten wide segment-headed windows built up to four storeys with a central clock turret. ROSEMOUNT FACTORY in Park Avenue is of 1904 by *M. A. Robinson*, a mammoth classical block, four storeys high, with pedestals, giant columns, and entablatures providing the vertical articulation. The WILKINSON FACTORY, Strand Road, 1921 by *R. E. Buchanan*, is in a C20 pared-down classicism but still giant in scale: three storeys and a blank attic, with fifteen bays of metal windows framed in vertical panels, all contained within forestanding terminal blocks. Now a supermarket. EBRINGTON FACTORY, Elvington Street, is a high, flat-roofed rectangular brick block, built in 1900 by *Daniel Conroy* across an older block.

BOOM HALL. 3.5 km NE. Near the shore of Lough Foyle, by the site of the boom placed across the river during the siege of 1689. A fine large classical villa built about 1770 by Robert Alexander (*c.* 1731–1790), a younger brother of the first Lord Caledon, it consists of a rather severe two-storey block with a basement on its entrance front, becoming three-storey where the ground falls away on the river side. It is built of coursed rubble with cut sandstone details. The five-bay entrance front was possibly intended to have had a giant-order portico, though this was never built. In the centre of the garden façade a big canted bay decorated on the first floor with a regular Roman aedicule. In the early C19 the house was the residence of several

Protestant Bishops of Derry. It is at the time of writing shamefully neglected by the local authority, whose road proposals and
new Derry bridge may not be deflected to save a fine house.

BROOK HALL. 4.5 km NE. An unusually fine late Georgian villa
described in 1802 as 'a modern edifice, lately finished on a very
elegant plan'. In the C18 the place belonged to the Wray family,
though this house was probably built for Sir George Fitzgerald
Hill, M.P. for Derry and Clerk of the Irish House of Commons,
after whose death, as Governor of Trinidad in 1839, it was
bought by Henry Barre Beresford, who owned it in 1846. By
1856 it had passed to the Gilliland family. There are two periods
to the building: the original house of Sir George Hill of *c.* 1790,
and a low single-storey entrance front added presumably by
Beresford. The plan of the first house is indeed elegant, with
a central oval entrance hall – laid with the longer side across
the axis – opening to a deep saloon with a segmental bow that
is answered inside by a curved wall with paired niches, either
side of a central door. To the S a big square drawing room again
with a segmental bow, and on the N a delightful, finely detailed
cantilevered oval staircase. The original house was just one
room deep, with the hall and saloon expressed as shallow bows
on each front. The new single-storey front across the entrance
is not so stylish, though it provides a Nash-like loggia of coupled
Ionic columns by way of a porch, and a new entrance hall –
on the same axis – top-lit with stylishly rounded corners. Contemporary with this addition is the pretty Regency-style
veranda that runs round the S and E sides of the house.

THORNHILL COLLEGE. 5.5 km NE. A large Baronial house by
Turner & Babington, built in 1882–5 for a Mr A. A. Watt 'in
a C16 style modified to suit modern requirements'. There is
more of Thomas Turner here than his local partner Hume Babington. The exteriors are dull, big and bland, with crow-
stepped gables, plain cross-mullioned windows, and very little
modelling. The irregular entrance front, with a door at one
corner and a gabled service block, lacks the *porte cochère* and
Irish tower intended to rise behind it. The front overlooking
the river and containing the principal rooms is symmetrical,
with square gabled bays at either end and a canted bay in the
centre. Inside, the *raison d'être* of the house is one immense
central hall, arcaded on two floors and lit by a huge staircase
window on the SW side. This hall is classically treated and
comes, of course, straight from Sir Charles Lanyon, with whom
Turner had trained. The house is now a convent of the Sisters

of Mercy with a big modern school in its grounds. It replaces an earlier house said to have been built before the siege.

BALLINAGARD. 6 km NE. The second home of the Hart family from Muff. Originally a standard, if substantial, five-bay, two-storey rubble-built house of the later C18. Improved by the addition of shallow segmental bays in brick across each side, and a big canted bay with a separate slate roof, not quite in the centre of the old front.

CULMORE POINT. 7 km NE. A triangular artillery fort was built here about 1610 to command the channel leading up to Derry. Pynnar described it as 'recently completed' in 1618, and the *Calendar of State Papers* reported that it had '12 guns mounted on the wall *en barbette*' in 1622. During the interregnum a large work was begun to take in an area of three or four acres round the fort, but it was never completed, and what was raised was demolished after 1662 on the advice of Major Legge, an English officer appointed to report on the state of the fortifications after the Restoration. The FORT today looks like an early C19 folly tower, about 20 ft square, with three floors of mullioned windows on its E face and battlements on the top. Its walls are probably still those of the C17 guard house within the triangular defence works.

HOLY TRINITY, CULMORE PARISH CHURCH (C of I). 1865–7 by *J. G. Ferguson*, a miniature cruciform church in rubble schist with sandstone dressings. Three-bay nave. Two-bay chancel. Big Dec W window and an offset N porch with octagonal belfry and stone spire above.

The ruined gabled WALL in the churchyard is part of the C17 garrison church demolished by James II in 1689.

CULMORE PRIMARY SCHOOLS. 1867 by *Thomas Turner*. A long, low design with paired gables at either end, those to the N of two storeys.

BALLYARNET PRESBYTERIAN CHURCH. 4.5 km N. 1848. A gabled hall with Gibbs surrounds to the windows and corner quoins.

GLENGALLIAGH HALL. 4.5 km NNW. 1847, built for a family called Brown. A surprising house, for its late C19 half-timbered gables give it a suburban look that almost obscures its Early Victorian Tudor elements; yet these survive intact inside, with a plaster-vaulted vestibule, pretty Gothic doors, and a long central hall lit by an oculus in the ceiling and a big Perp window at the far end with pretty coloured glass. Battlemented single-storey bay-windows at the side and back.

DOHERTY TOWER. 5.5 km NNW. One massive pier of rubble stone wall about 13 ft thick and over 25 ft high rises on the edge of an outcrop of schist. It is curved on the outer face and decorated with two bands of coursing where the stones are laid on their sides to present a broad boulder face running round the tower. This is all that remains of the castle and tower said to have been built in the C15 by Neactan O Donnell for his father-in-law O Doherty. It was captured in May 1600 by Sir Henry Docwra, who garrisoned it with 150 men. In 1608 it was in the possession of Sir Cahir O Doherty.

ELAGHMORE. 5.5 km NNW, opposite Doherty Tower. A big five-bay, two-storey house within a park. Late C18.

CREEVAGH HOUSE. 4.5 km WSW. Shrouded in woodlands. A large, plain late Georgian house built by the Babington family c. 1780. The usual five-bay, two-storey block enhanced by a freestone ashlar front with corner quoins and Gibbs surrounds to the windows. Inside is a delightful cantilevered oval stair, small in scale, lit by a half-landing window and roofed by a deeply coffered dome. The entire basement of the house is finely vaulted in brick.

WINDMILL FARM. 5 km WSW. A large L-shaped farmhouse, two-storey, with a five-bay front and four-bay wing. In the yard behind is a complete early C19 windmill tower still with its roof.

GOVERNMENT HOUSE. 3 km SW. A mid C19 Italianate house with canted bays, a square veranda, and horizontal rustication. Now a Christian Brothers monastery.

MILTON LODGE. 3.5 km SW. Mid to late C18, built on a hillside overlooking the Foyle. Three bays wide, with a central bow overlooking the river. Three-storey on this side, two on the other. Nice pedimented front door taken from Paine's *Practical Carpenter*. S of the house is a very large range of arcaded barns and farm buildings, unusually grand and in a stylish Italianate manner, with a two-storey arcaded pediment at one end. All in brick and looking about 1840.

MULLENNAN HOUSE. 6 km SW. A large, two-storey mid C19 house built as two square blocks with rendered walls and yellow brick chimneys. In mature Victorian grounds with many conifers. Built by the Harvey family.

BALLOUGRY PRIMARY SCHOOL. 4.5 km SW. A picturesque single-storey school of c. 1870 with projecting paired gabled ends in the manner of *Thomas Turner*.

EAST NEIGHBOURHOOD

WATERSIDE. This suburban district on the E bank of the Foyle developed in the C19 round the approach roads to Foyle Bridge. Recently it has been much cut about by new roadworks and housing clearances. The RAILWAY TERMINUS at the bottom of BOND'S HILL, built for the Northern Counties Railway in 1873 to designs of *John Lanyon*, is Italianate, of boulder-faced squared sandstone. The clock tower and part of the façade were demolished after bomb damage in 1974. Former UNION WORKHOUSE, N of GLENDERMOT ROAD, by *George Wilkinson*, the usual Elizabethan design in two ranges with three-storey, double-gabled ends to the main block. EBRINGTON BARRACKS, between the river and LIMAVADY ROAD, were laid out in 1839 with regular Georgian-style rendered blocks set round three sides of a parade ground, open on the W side to the river. The central E block is a three-storey, fifteen-bay terrace, flanked by long single-storey blocks with central pediments, and then a pair of five-bay, two-storey houses, all built in a line. Two-storey houses, of the same date but less regularly disposed, mark the sides of the parade ground, with later ranges of brick buildings of 1850 and 1917 behind. In ST COLUMB'S PARK are the ruins of ST BRECAN'S CHAPEL, reputedly C16, rectangular and rubble-built. The EVERGLADES HOTEL, VICTORIA ROAD, by the river SW of the town, is by *J. J. Tracey*, 1976, attractive and carefully detailed.

PREHEN. 2.5 km SE of Craigavon Bridge. A robust early Georgian classical house, reputedly dated 1745, and marked with the initials M.P. on an attic rafter. Whatever the date may be, the initials are hardly necessary to suggest an attribution of the house to the Derry architect *Michael Priestley*, whose personal style is stamped all over the design. The house is not large, but its proportions are ample, with a four-bay entrance front of two storeys and four-bay sides, the main rooms opening off an entrance hall 17 ft square and returning in a U-shape round a set of front and back stairs, built side by side, immediately behind the hall. This gives three regular elevations with a rear that is recessed in the centre. Attractively provincial four-bay, two-storey façade with a high hipped roof and regularly disposed chimneys set behind a solid eaves parapet such as Priestley used at the court house and at Port Hall, Lifford. The centre two bays are slightly advanced and marked, as are the outer corners, with sandstone quoins. A bold pedimented door with a Gibbs surround set between the middle windows of the ground floor creates a sense of tension in the classicism that recurs in the upper-floor windows, whose keystones impinge on the main cornice below the parapet. There is no frieze. A pediment rises out of the parapet over the central two bays, once again like Port Hall. The interior detail is of a robust early C18 kind. Black and white marble hall with a big timber stair behind with handsome handrail whorl. Fine brick-vaulted basement. Splendid loft, with perfect C18 timbers. High coved ceilings on the first floor. The house was built by Andrew Tomkins of Prehen and descended through his daughter Honoria to the Knoxes of Rathmullen and Moneymore, from whom Bishop Knox, who built so much in Derry in the early C19, was descended.

LOUGH DERG*

ST PATRICK'S PURGATORY

Lough Derg is a large piece of water in a declivity among shallow hills some 240 m (800 ft) above sea level in s Donegal. It has several small islands, two of which – Saint's Island and Station Island – have long been associated with the penitential exercises for which the place is famous.

A monastery was founded at Lough Derg by St Patrick or by St Dabeoc, whom some writers believe was the priest who presided over 'St Patrick's Purgatory' in the C6. Some time after 1132 the Augustinian rule was introduced and the community became a priory under the superiority of Armagh. The priory was plundered in 1196 and in 1207 but was restored and survived in some form until 1632, when Sir James Balfour and Sir William Stewart raided Lough Derg and demolished the buildings. For centuries this remote, desolate lough had attracted pilgrims from all over Europe, and though the conduct of the priory's affairs had not always been above scrutiny – Sixtus IV ordered an inquiry in 1479 and in 1497 Alexander VI ordered the original 'Purgatory' to be demolished – the fame of the place was sufficient for pilgrimages to continue despite obstruction in the C17 and specific mention in an act of Queen Anne prohibiting pilgrimages in general in 1704. The centre of pilgrimages today is the smaller Station Island, the farthest distant of any from the shore. Its buildings

*Not visited.

began to be reconstructed by Father O'Doherty, prior in the mid
c18, who in 1763 erected the church of St Mary there.

SAINT'S ISLAND. The cave which formed the retreat of 'St
Patrick's Purgatory' in the Middle Ages was on this island near
the shore. It was closed by Alexander VI in the late c15 and
the station moved in 1502 to Station Island. It was however the
Saint's Island community that was broken up in 1632 by the
Bishop of Clogher, James Spottiswood, who described the
'Purgatory' as 'a poor beggarly hole, made with some stones
lay'd together with men's hands without any great art and after
covered with earth'. He also broke up 'the Circles and Saints
Beds' and 'undermined the Chappell, which was well covered
with shingles'. Only the traces of stone walls with two rectangular enclosures remain.

STATION ISLAND. The present architectural development of
this small island, a mere 380 ft long, began in the mid c18 under
the prior, Father O'Doherty. It is now almost completely
covered with buildings of which the large centrally planned
CHURCH OF ST PATRICK by *William A. Scott* is the most
recent. Designed in 1921 and built in phases from 1924 by
T. J. Cullen after Scott's death, it is a massive neo-Romanesque
pilgrimage church, octagonal, with short cruciform arms, flanking circular towers to the entrance portal, and primitive Norman arcades outside. In 1912 *Scott* had also designed the grim
NEW HOSTEL block, a three-storey concrete frame, with
modern battlements, providing space for 220 cubicles. The
OLD PILGRIMS' HOSPICE, a three-storey stone-built block
erected by Father James McKenna in 1880–2, has been spoilt
by the removal of its gables and the addition of a clumsy mansard roof. Beside it are four substantial two-storey Georgian
houses in an irregular curve in front of ST MARY'S CHURCH,
a modest four-bay lancet hall with a gabled porch, statue niche,
and short chancel, built (with the square campanile beside it)
in 1870 at a cost of £500.

The penitential stations or Saints' Beds are between the two
churches, grouped round the one tree on the island, a sycamore.
The oldest structures at present remaining on Station Island,
they are now no more than circular rings of dry stone wall, 1
to 3 ft high, and, with the exception of St Molaise's Bed, which
is 16 ft in diameter, only 10 to 12 ft across. The STATUES in
front of the Old Hospice are the Virgin Mary, 1882 by *O'Neill*
of Dublin, and St Patrick and St Joseph, bought in Carrara
by the Bishop of Clogher and erected in 1891. – ST PATRICK'S

CROSS. The spiral shaft of a C12 cross taken from Saint's Island.*

C6   LOUGH ESKE   DO

CHRIST CHURCH (C of I). Isolated on a rural hillside, a two-bay harled hall with a short chancel and a square two-stage tower which now looks distinctly Scandinavian, having gained a crossed saddleback upper storey. The windows have timber Y-tracery. Three-light Dec E window.

113 LOUGH ESKE CASTLE. A picturesque Elizabethan-style mansion with an offset, four-storey tower, heavily machicolated, and supported by battlemented wings. All, except one wing, burnt out in 1939. The design is highly successful and must rank as the *chef d'œuvre* of its architect, *Fitzgibbon Louch* of Derry. Note the splendid corbelled heads below the battlements all round the house. The castle was built for Thomas Brooke between 1859 and 1861; a ballroom was added by Maj. Gen. H. G. White in 1914. It occupies the site of an earlier Brooke mansion of 1751 which was itself a rebuilding of the original Jacobean house. A date-stone of 1621 with the initials W.H. & I.M. is in the yard.

Traces of older castles, N of the house and on O'Donnell's Island in the lough, are minimal.

MACAMOOSH FORT *see* DRUMHALLAGH

J3   MACOSQUIN   LD

A scatter of houses about a C19 church marks the centre of the parish of Camus-juxta-Bann. Here *c.* 1218 the O'Cahan family founded a Cistercian abbey, and an earlier Christian community existed from the C6 at Camus by the River Bann. In the Jacobean Plantation the parish was granted to the Merchant Taylors, who had built a strong house, seven houses, and a church by 1619.

HIGH CROSS OF ST COMGAL. 4.5 km E, in the graveyard by Camus House. The pedestal and shaft of a cross standing about 8½ ft above the ground. Now much defaced, though clearly of the logical figure pattern popular in the northern crosses (cf. Arboe and Donaghmore), with four figure scenes on the E and

---

* The most complete accounts of the traditions and buildings on Lough Derg are given in Rev. D. Canon O'Connor, *St Patrick's Purgatory, Lough Derg* (Dublin, 1903 and Alice Curtayne, *Lough Derg* (Dublin, 1944).

w faces and interlace and bosses on the sides. Probably late C9 to early C10.

St Mary, Camus-juxta-Bann Parish Church (C of I). A hall and tower church of rubble, virtually rebuilt in 1826. Tower of three stages with octagonal finials and Perp detail. Polygonal chancel and sacristy by *Welland & Gillespie*, 1867. A carved stone with architectural detail in front of the tower is the only fragment of medieval work from the Cistercian abbey, though a small lancet walled up on the N side is known locally as the 'leper window'.

Macosquin Presbyterian Church. 3 km SE. T-plan Gothic of 1786, rebuilt in 1887.

Former Rectory. 1770. A tall three-storey house with a three-bay front and five-bay back. Modernized about 1800.

Camus House. 4.5 km E. A late Georgian, five-bay, two-storey house with a central fanlight.

Churches in the area. At Killeague, 3.5 km S, a gabled pebbledashed C of I hall; at Ringsend, 6.5 km SW, a Presbyterian five-bay hall of 1897 with box pews.

MAGHERA   LD *J5*

Maghera takes its origin and its name from the foundation of an early Christian monastery here by St Lurach about the C6. His church was given cathedral status in place of that at Ardstraw from about the mid C12 until 1254, when the see was transferred to Derry. However remote, it is the remains of this Christian community that give the place its most remarkable monument. The town is now, as always, a busy thoroughfare E of the Flenhane pass that leads over the Sperrins to Dungiven and to Derry. Its appearance is mainly C19, with one long street mostly of two-storey houses with minor roads leading off on both sides.

Maghera Old Church Ruins. In a graveyard at the E end of the town. The rubble-built shell of a nave and chancel with a stepped four-stage tower at the W end. In use continually until 1819: plaster still clings to the inside W gable. The E end is gone, but the walls stand entire, with segment-headed window openings. The chancel is 21 ft by 29 ft, the nave 21 ft by 38 ft; larger than usual. The centre window on the S wall has traces of its C17 sandstone side mullion. This must date either from 1622, when the church was repaired 'at the cost of the parishioners', or from after 1641, when it was burnt. The aumbry base with grooved decoration at the E end of the chancel is

earlier, and far earlier still the carved W entrance portal, now
masked – but also preserved – by the C17 square tower. In form
the doorway bears comparison with that at Banagher (also in
Co. Derry), with a massive flat lintel recessed within a wider
and higher outer stone frame. The jambs of both are noticeably
battered, i.e. tipped in towards the centre line. Like Banagher
too, the lintel inside the church is contained within a round-
headed arch – but the great difference between the two is the
rich sculptural decoration on the face of the Maghera lintel and
on what remains of the jambs of the door. The lintel, now much
defaced, carries a scene of the Crucifixion centrally placed over
the door (widened later by about a foot on the N side) with
groups of figures standing in a row on either side. Christ is
clothed; two angels appear above each arm of the cross, and
a soldier with a spear and sponge below. On the outer jambs
are interlace and spiral patterns that have been compared with
Bewcastle Cross in Cumbria of the C7 and with Clonfert in Co.
Galway of the later C12. Comparison of the portal frame with
Banagher might support a date about 1100, though the figures
of apostles beyond Christ's l. arm are comparable to those at
White Island, which have been dated c8. The condition of the
lintel and the dark corner in which it is make all pronounce-
ments vague.

The lower part of a SHELA-NA-GIG is built into the N side
of the tower about 20 ft from the ground.

ST LURACH, MAGHERA PARISH (C of I). Tower and hall type,
to a standard design by *John Bowden*, 1819. Pretty tapered tower
in three stages with big pinnacles. Dec timber windows to the
nave. Chancel in basalt rubble by *Welland & Gillespie*, 1864.

ST PATRICK. 2.5 km w. Built in 1825, rebuilt in 1912 by *J. P.
McGrath* of Derry. A stuccoed Romanesque hall with buttresses and wheel window in the gable. Impressive hammerbeam roof in pine inside. – MONUMENT. The Rev. John
McKenna P.P. † 1841. Neo-classical wall-tablet with a figure
of Faith standing beside a funerary urn. – STAINED GLASS.
Two late C19 windows with sixteen small scenes. Nice. In
memory of the Rev. P. Hassan.

PRESBYTERIAN CHURCH. Of 1800, and once a nice little
church. The regular congregation goes back to 1696, but apart
from its front the present building looks very recent. T-plan
with round-headed windows. Re-roofed, re-harled, and isolated in a sea of tarmac. Across the gable is a smaller three-bay
front in basalt with dressed quoins. An octagonal two-storey

belfry, in sandstone with an ogee cap, sits like a chessman over the central bay.

RECTORY. s of the old church. A gaunt cubic house built by the Rev. J. S. Knox in 1825 and on a grander scale than most Church of Ireland glebe houses. The style looks like *William Farrell*. Each front is of four bays by three storeys, with overhanging eaves and massed chimneys in the centre. A regular plan inside with fine quality plasterwork cornices.

ULSTER BANK. 1866 by *Thomas Jackson*. Two-storey, five-bay, very vaguely Venetian Gothic.

CHURCH RUINS, now no more than walls, are at CARROW-MENAGH, 2 km NW, 18 by 42 ft, and at MULLAGH, 1.5 km SW, a gable in a graveyard.

MAGHERABEG ABBEY *see* DONEGAL, p. 243

MAGHERAFELT   LD J5

Intended to be the lesser of the two settlements founded by the Salters' Company in 1609, Magherafelt proved to be better sited than its rival, Salterstown, and has developed despite the usual destructions in 1641 and 1689 into the major town of south County Derry, with a population (including the rural district) of over 34,500. As with most Ulster towns, the division between town and country is hard to determine, for although the very wide streets are often lined by big late C18 or early C19 terraced houses, there are many gaps and big open spaces with churches and trees in graveyards which, by their very isolation, militate against a sense of enclosed urban space. It is a pity that the parish church of 1664, which survived the Jacobite wars, was replaced by a new one in 1856. However a number of ambitious mid and late C19 buildings give the place some architectural distinction.

CHURCHES

ST SWITHIN, MAGHERAFELT PARISH CHURCH (C of I). 1856–8. A big church in black basalt with sandstone trim to its windows, buttresses and spire, all absolutely characteristic of *Joseph Welland*'s style. What is unusual is the building's height and scale: it must be one of Welland's largest and most ambitious designs. It is cruciform, with very wide N and S aisles expressed externally as separate gables, flanking a massive W tower, with stepped side buttresses, two-light Dec belfry stage, and broad broach-spire with one tier of lucarnes just above the broach. The windows are mostly three-light Dec with geo-metrical tracery, five-light to the transepts and six-light at the E end.

Inside, Welland's usual forms appear again, only richer. The entrance, by a side porch in one aisle, throws the grand sequence of two double-chamfered arcades – each of four arches – immediately into prominence. And they are grander than usual because the aisle ceilings have separate steeply pitched roofs with all the richness of exposed braced trusses, rafters, and side-braced purlins that Welland liked to use. In the nave, to compensate for the loss of a clerestory an unusual but not unsuccessful feature is the series of cusped trefoils arranged as continuous dormer lights, within the roof space, just above wall-plate level. Before the chancel the trusses double in the roof and then criss-cross diagonally over the transept crossing. As the roofs are elaborate, so too is the masonry, or more so than usual at this date. The wall plates are enriched with ballflower, the window reveals in the aisles have attached colonnettes, and the chancel has paired colonnettes supporting a double-chamfered arch with keel mouldings. A nice feature is the big two-centred arch at the opposite end of the chancel, opening into the full height of the tower, and extending the overall length of the building to almost 120 ft. The church cost £8,000, of which the Salters' Company paid half and the Ecclesiastical Commissioners a further £1,000. – MONUMENTS. To Radulpus Whistler † 1657 a double wall-tablet with Ionic moulding, salient entablature, and pilasters at the sides. Trans-ferred from the old church in 1858.

CHURCH OF THE ASSUMPTION. 1879–82 by *O'Neill & Byrne*. A conscious answer to St Swithin, with a similar though more slender steeple, 160 ft high, and an equally ambitious big nave, 112 ft long, though the style is now French rather than English Gothic. Many details are typical of their architects too: the plan, a long five-bay nave with lean-to aisles and an offset W steeple; the clerestory with paired cinquefoil lights, appearing on the side as just a narrow band between high roofs. O'Neill, as usual, is at his best in the spire, achieving a fine balance between decorated and plain surfaces, though as usual the but-tresses seem too thin.

The interior is impressive: the arcades supported on pink granite shafts with deeply undercut capitals carved by *Earley* of Dublin; the roof hipped and panelled in pine with braced trusses rising from corbel-stop heads; a gallery at the back in an extra half-bay; the sanctuary a polygonal apse with two-light Dec windows. – ALTAR. Seven-bay reredos in white marble with a central pinnacled canopy. – STAINED GLASS. Life of the Virgin by *Mayer & Co.*, 1898–1904.

MAGHERAFELT FIRST PRESBYTERIAN CHURCH. 1857. Apparently an early work of *Robert Young*, whose firm of Young & Mackenzie was to become the leading Presbyterian church architects in the later C19. Big, T-plan, in text-book E.E. style, with triple lancet windows in the 'transept' gables and a five-light lancet, with detached colonnettes in sandstone, on the main front. N of this gable is a four-stage tower spoilt by a meanly scaled sandstone belfry and broach-spire. It is cleaner and looks later. The rest of the church is in black basalt with sandstone trim of an orange-brown colour. Of all the denominations, the Presbyterians got the highest ground, but a dull design to go on it.

UNION ROAD PRESBYTERIAN CHURCH. 1867 by *Boyd & Batt*, a swaggering Lombardic design in stucco that might almost be a forerunner of John Corry's well known Elmwood Avenue church, Belfast. Gable front opening as a five-bay loggia on the ground floor. The elements are massive and brutal as only Batt knew how to make them: drum bases, stumpy columns, and vegetable capitals of the grossest sort. Above, a triple round-headed window flanked by single round-topped lancets. The sides by comparison are quite discrete, four bays of paired lancets.

METHODIST CHURCH. 1838. A three-bay rendered Gothic hall with stone quoins.

PUBLIC BUILDINGS

The bawn, castle, and houses built by the Salters' Company and described in 1622 have all gone. So too has the Market House built in the Diamond by the company in 1810, and the OLD COURT HOUSE of 1804, rendered and redesigned in the late C19, is now only a single-storey carcass. But the building that replaced it, in Union Road, is a more than worthy successor.

COURT HOUSE. 1874 by *Turner & Williamson*. A strong piece [100] of Victorian architecture, boldly massed and essentially free in style. The materials are coursed polygonal basalt and red brick with sandstone trim and slate roofs. The building might easily be a swagger seaside station. Round the court, a high gabled hall lit by porthole windows with crow-stepped gables and high chimneys, are grouped four square towers of various heights that end in high slated obelisk roofs. Further gabled and crow-stepped offices to one side. Between the towers on the front and E side a triple-arched loggia, vaguely Lombardic in character, with big undercut capitals. The building abounds in the paired round-headed windows that are typical of Turner's late style.

MID ULSTER HOSPITAL. Built round the former UNION WORKHOUSE of 1842 by *George Wilkinson*, the standard two-block design with double-gabled ends, now harled. Decent brown brick additions of 1952 and later.

TOUR

Apart from its churches, most of Magherafelt can be seen in a walk up Broad Street running uphill and due s to end in a big rose-bed roundabout at the crossroads of Queen Street, Market Street, and Rainey Street. At the bottom of BROAD STREET the OLD GAOL and BRIDEWELL of 1804, a small battlemented two-storey block with a big Gothick-arched entrance set within a court inside an archway of ashlar sandstone. Immediately w the OLD CHURCH RUINS, 1664, with parts of the s wall, both gables, and a tower – added in 1790 – still standing but all ivy-covered. The church was 20 ft wide, of rubble stone with brick openings. The RECTORY behind is a rectangular two-storey house on a high basement, originally of three bays, with a two-bay addition on the r. and a one-bay addition on the l. Overhanging eaves. Open pedimented doorcase on Tuscan pilasters. Church ruins and rectory make a nice green scene.

Broad Street itself preserves a good sense of scale. At the bottom on the r. the ULSTER BANK by *Blackwood & Jury*, ashlar-fronted classical of 1925, seven bays, with a stumpy Ionic colonnade to the ground floor. Next is a boldly gabled three-storey villa in basalt with a two-storey oriel at its s end. Something of an eruption in the street, it is followed by a terrace of three-storey houses and then the BELFAST BANK of 1922 by *Tulloch & Fitzsimmons*, as yet unspoilt, with lots of white timber, porches, corner bays, and red tile gables in the style of Nesfield. The other side of the street is just a series of pleasant terraced houses, three-storey and mostly stuccoed.

MAGILLIGAN

Magilligan is a famous triangle of flat land, the boundary of the

NE edge of Lough Foyle, with ten kilometres of beach and sand
dunes stretching in a slow curve from Magilligan Point to the
towering cliffs of Downhill. In the C18 the Earl Bishop of Derry
brought a road along the top of the 220 m cliffs that hem in Magilligan on the S and W. Then, in 1855, the railway came to run along
the bottom. Until then the area was decidedly cut off and has
retained, as a result, a wealth of vernacular cottages. It has no
proper centre, though the Belfast and Northern Counties Railway
halt may provide a reference point.

MAGILLIGAN HALT STATION. 1873–5 by *John Lanyon.* Red
   brick in an Italianate vernacular style with yellow and black
   brick, label moulds, and segment-headed windows.
BALLYMACLARY HOUSE. 0.5 km NE. A charming and surprisingly well finished gentleman's house on a miniature scale.
   Probably of about 1760; reputedly built as a summer residence
   for the Cather family, though ignored by C18 gazetteer and tour
   writers. L-shaped, with a S front built as a single-storey, five-
   bay wing with a wealth of fine sandstone detail: corner quoins;
   lugged architrave surrounds; and a wide projecting central bay
   which is the hall inside, with an entrance door flanked by narrow windows and framed by Ionic pilasters that break forward
   to half-columns on either side of the door. Inside, a dog-leg
   stair with heavy timber banisters leads to an attic floor lit
   through the gable ends.
MARTELLO TOWER. At Magilligan Point, 6 km NW. Built in
   1812 as part of the coastal defences during the Napoleonic
   Wars, a standard circular tower of thirty-four courses of Bally-
   harrigan sandstone with a machicolated protection at the wall
   head above the door. The walls, 13 ft thick, rise with a steep
   batter to support a domed circular chamber 30 ft in diameter
   inside. Most of the land here is owned by the War Department,
   and the tower is disfigured at the time of writing by a tarred
   addition at the top and half-demolished concrete huts at its
   base.
MAGILLIGAN PRESBYTERIAN CHURCH. 3 km W. 1863. A
   three-bay gabled hall of rubble basalt with Gibbs surrounds
   to the windows. The small buttressed bell-tower was added in
   1934.
TAMLAGHTARD CHURCH RUINS. 4 km SW. The remains of
   a long, thin, rectangular church, only 14 ft wide, with most of
   the wall standing to a height of 10 ft or more. Built of rubble
   slate and sandstone. Single-lancet E window with wide splayed
   reveals and a single-chamfered sandstone arched top. C13 at the

earliest, though the churchyard is said to contain the grave of St Aidan, Bishop of Lindisfarne, who retired to the monastery at Duncrum founded in 584 by St Colmcille. The grave is an incomplete MORTUARY HOUSE outside the E gable, similar to those at Bovevagh and Banagher. Burnt in 1642, the church was restored in 1660 and given by the Earl Bishop of Derry to Roman Catholics for use as a chapel when the new Tamlaghtard church was built.

ST AIDAN. 4 km SW. A long rendered hall of 1826, originally with paired doors on a five-bay side and, presumably, a side altar. Renovated in 1931 with a shallow chancel aisle with blind E.E.-type arcade behind. Huge gallery filling half the church.

ST CADAN, TAMLAGHTARD PARISH CHURCH (C of I). 3 km SW. A typical early hall-and-tower-type Georgian Gothic church. Three-bay nave. Square W tower with slender clasping buttresses, stepped battlements, and small battlemented blocks, filling out the tower at ground-floor level to the width of the nave. Built between 1778 and 1787, probably with the support of the Earl Bishop. Vestry and chancel by *Joseph Welland*, 1854. – MEMORIALS. Many plaques to the McCausland, Tyler, Gage, and Heygate families. The most notable are Conolly Gage † 1834, a plain white stele on a black background, and Conolly McCausland † 1794, a pedimented white marble plaque topped by an urn.

In the churchyard SE corner is the enormous black basalt plinth that marks the MAUSOLEUM 'of the families of Fruithill and Bellarena' on one side and of 'Marcus Gage of Streeve Hill and the Rev. Robert Gage of Tamlaght' on the other.

CROSS. At the higher NW corner of a long field 0.5 km NW of St Cadan's church. A tall stone, about 4½ ft high and 2 ft wide, with curved edges at the top and a raised cross of Lorraine on its face. Early C14?

CATHOLIC CHURCH. 1820–2, built for the Rev. Andrew Magonnel, who died from a fall from the scaffolding while the church was being built. The original design was possibly by *Robert Shepherd*. Four-bay hall with large Georgian-Gothic-shaped windows on the S side, in somewhat meagre Gibbs surrounds like those at Moate Church, Lisnaskea. Originally there were doors at either end below the gables and the altar was in the centre of the S wall. In 1922 *R. M. Butler* added the chancel

and bellcote gable and replaced the original windows with concrete tracery. This is extraordinarily good, three-light, with
wonderfully free tear-drop patterns at the top that give the
whole church a very distinctive appearance.

CHRIST CHURCH (C of I). 1841. Built as a chapel of ease for
Aghalurcher parish church. Originally a simple hall and chancel
with three lancets down each side and a three-light E window.
Roofed with a curious pivoted cast-iron truss, the web filled
with eleven diminishing circles. To this *Welland & Gillespie*
added a N transept and robing room in 1862.

METHODIST CHURCH. 1842. A three-bay harled Gothic hall
with Georgian-glazed sash-windows.

The village is one long street, extending from its early C19 bridge
of three segmental arches for about half a kilometre. Before the
bridge, N of the river, is an C18 house whose gable end termi-
nates the view up the main street better than anything modern
could do. The house has quoins and pronounced voussoirs to
its windows and doors with a carriage arch and stabling behind.
It is at the time of writing empty. The main street could be
attractive, with substantial C18 houses along its length, but
these have already begun to disappear under local authority
plans. In the middle of the street is the MARKET HOUSE of
c. 1830, three-bay, two-storey, with an arcaded ground floor
with iron gates. Almost opposite is the ORANGE HALL, originally an early C19 church with plain Y-tracery – possibly the
Presbyterian meeting house noted by Lewis in 1837. W of the
village is the former STATION, red brick, with segment-
headed windows with yellow and black brick trim.

DRUMGOON MANOR. 1.5 km SW. A large, square house built
by the Graham family about 1770. Three-bay, two-storey front
with diamond-cut quoins and square rusticated panels that
frame the main door. The house sits high on a basement, partly
brick-vaulted, and is approached by a long flight of steps. Inside, lugged door surrounds, a simple deep cornice in the hall,
and an C18 timber stair.

MALIN   DO F1

A tiny Plantation village set at the end of a creek of Trawbreaga
Bay. Rebuilt with twenty-eight good modern houses in the early
C19 and happily unspoilt. The Malin Hotel deserves a mention
for the tact with which it has been extended behind the old frontage, not along it. The jewel of the village is its C17 triangular

green, planted with limes and sycamores and, more recently, cherries.

CLONCHA PARISH CHURCH (C of I). An attractive tower and hall type church of 1827, placed centrally across the end of the green as seen from the bridge that enters the village. Harled, with stone trim and hood mouldings. Three-stage tower with battlements, thin strip buttresses, and square pinnacles. Timber Y-tracery with quarry glass.

MALIN PRESBYTERIAN CHURCH. 4 km WNW. An C18 gabled six-bay hall, now pebbledashed. Extended by 16 ft in 1868 and given its horseshoe gallery at the back. A single-storey, five-bay SCHOOL beside the church.

LAGG CHURCH. 5 km NW. Built in 1784, the first Roman Catholic church to be erected in Inishowen since penal times, on a simple T-plan with a three-bay nave. Harled and whitewashed.

MALIN HALL. A substantial house built by George Harvey, High Sheriff of Co. Donegal, in 1758. A square block with hipped roof and leaded central platform. Two storeys on a basement. Four-bay front, the entrance door, framed by a Tuscan aedicule in stone, just fitting between bays two and three. Three-bay sides with a Dutch-gabled wing to the E. Segment-headed windows in brick. Inside, the usual five-panel doors and lugged surrounds.

FRIAR'S CELL. 1.5 km WNW at Ballelaghan. A primitive single-cell structure built of two drystone walls against an overhanging rock to form a chamber roughly 8 ft by 5 ft. On the N side a small door, 1½ ft wide and 3 ft high. The outer part of the room is roofed with stone slabs sloping down from the rock, leaving a chimney hole in the centre.

_Fi_   MALIN HEAD   DO

The most northerly point of Ireland, marked by an early C19 SIGNAL TOWER, five-sided, with machicolated corners on the landward side, the same as the towers at Inishkeel and Glencolumbkille.

CLONCA OLD CHURCH. 5 km E of Malin Head on the N coast, below a steep cliff. An early monastic site with rectangular ruins of a late medieval church, 35½ ft by 15½ ft inside. The N, S and E walls remain, with splayed square-headed windows on the E and S. The site is associated with St Morialagh of Clonca, and secular abbots are recorded until the early C17.

THE WEE HOUSE OF MALIN. A rock-cut cell in the cliff opposite.

MALIN MORE AND MALIN BEG   DO *A6*

Small farming communities on the most westerly points of
Donegal, remote and seemingly protected from change. The
houses are still almost all thatched, with huge peat stacks beside
them. The fields are cultivated in strips running down to the rocks
in front of each house.

TEMPLECAVAN, in the fields SW of Malin Beg, is a ruined drystone church, 15 ft by 29 ft externally. The side walls are earth-
covered, but the gable stands to about 7 ft, with two small square
openings to a mural chamber and a niche on the inside.

MANORCUNNINGHAM   DO *E4*

A small village on the crown of a hill above Lough Swilly, by-
passed by the main road, with a church at its S end.

RAYMOCHY PARISH CHURCH (C of I). Built in 1792 at a cost
of £646. A three-bay lancet hall, harled, with a pretty W tower
(actually N) straight from Toytown, in three stages, with elongated battlements at the top and pinnacles of equilateral
triangles on tall plinths. The chancel, with a big Dec window,
and the vestry are of 1910.

RAYMOCHY OLD CHURCHYARD. 1 km S. Substantial remains
of Raymochy Old Church. The usual rectangular structure of
the C17. This dates from 1609 and preserves, among the nettles
and ivy, a perfect Planter's Gothic E window. Three lights of
double Y-tracery mullions in a round-headed arch. The mullions are irregular octagons in section and of sandstone. The
rest of the church coursed rubble slate.

BALLEEGHAM ABBEY. 3 km NNE. The ruins of a massively
simple church of the Third Order of Franciscans founded by
the O'Donnells late in the C15; suppressed and the lands
granted to James Fullerton in 1603. The setting and its present
state combine to make Balleegham memorable. It is directly
on the shore at the end of a short cul-de-sac, with nothing but
an empty cottage built against its N side. Its W door faces the
tides, with Killydonnell Abbey, another Franciscan house, a
little to the N on the opposite shore. Inside, the church is a
tunnel of green, for the most luxuriant ivy has taken charge

of its high walls, billowing over their tops in glossy dark clouds. Even without the ivy the abbey church must always have been striking, and strikingly dark. Its proportion is approximately four cubes, 80 ft by 20 ft wide and about 20 ft in height – a proportion that is found in other churches of this period at Magherabeg and Drumachose. The church is lit almost entirely at its E end by two pointed lights on the S wall and a fine E window of the C15, the best preserved in North West Ulster. Three lights with a transom and graceful uncusped flamboyant tracery. The wide splayed reveal is closed by a single-chamfered relieving arch inside. Credence cavities in the chancel end of the N and S walls, two doors, and what might be a holy water recess. What was the purpose of the flight of corbel steps below the E window? The church is built of granite boulders and slate with sandstone dressings.

ST COLUMBA. 2.5 km SE, at Drumoghill. Mid C19 Gothic. T-plan.

LESLIE HILL. 2.5 km S. A two-storey, three-bay late Georgian house of c.1830. Simple details.

MASSMOUNT see ROSNAKIL

MELLON HOUSE see MOUNTJOY FOREST

E3   MILLFORD   DO

A modest little place in a countryside described in 1846 as 'unspeakably less dreary than the many and extensive solitudes of other districts of Donegal'. That means that it is unspectacular, agriculturally improved, and pastoral in appearance.

ST PETER. 1961 by *Corr & McCormick*. A clean, uncompromisingly modern church with a hint of Basil Spence's Coventry Cathedral in its design. The plan is an elongated hexagon extended at either end to form a porch (w) and the sanctuary (E). The sacristy is another lower hexagon joined by a glazed brick link, and the bell-tower a separate hexagon only flattened and pierced. The walls are white and the windows wide rectangles subdivided by vertical pine shafts. Both the splayed walls and the slatted pine roof on tapering pilotis inside seem hints from Spence. And perhaps the whole conception of what a modern church should be comes from the same source. It is attractive, once you have noticed it, to find that a church dedicated to the fisherman Peter has its seats arranged in herringbone pattern about a central axis, and attractive too to find as easily read religious art as the reredos TAPESTRY of the Miraculous Draught of Fishes by *Colin Middleton*. The church indeed is full of contemporary art. – STAINED GLASS. SS. Columcille, Adamnan, and Comgall by *Patrick Pollen*; SS. Patrick, Brendan, and Eunan (Adamnan again by his other name!) by *Patrick Pye*; SS. Malachy, Brigid, and Attracta by *Phyllis Burke*; and St Garvan by *Imogen Stuart*, who also worked the ceramic STATIONS OF THE CROSS. – The crowing cock WEATHERVANE on the sacristy is by *Ian Stuart*.

ST COLUMBA, TULLYFERNE OLD PARISH CHURCH (C of I). 1858–60 by *Joseph Welland*. A nice, unspoilt, chunky Gothic Revival church with big angle buttresses. Five-bay lancet nave with bellcote, and short chancel. Three E lancets. Interior as originally designed. High roof with braced kingpost trusses and exposed rafters. Single-chamfered chancel arch.

LORETO COLLEGE. On a hill w of the town. 1964 by *Simon Leonard* of *W. H. Byrne & Son*. A large but compact group of new buildings. Three-storey teaching block on a concrete frame – a little monotonous but decently proportioned. Before it a cube-like four-storey block for teaching and accommodation, nicely handled, with thin paired windows on the upper floors. The CHAPEL is a seven-bay pointed portal-frame hall with zigzag roof and thin copper flèche.

OTHER BUILDINGS are two PRESBYTERIAN CHURCHES of 1837, one T-plan, the other a four-bay hall; and the former UNION WORKHOUSE, 1 km SW, a nine-bay, two-storey Elizabethan block of the mid C19 by *George Wilkinson*, derelict at the time of writing.

MONEA

A country parish containing the finest Plantation castle in Ulster.

CASTLE. Monea is picturesquely sited in the grounds of Castle- 37 town House, at the bottom of a steep hill on a small plateau above a lake. Built of hard local limestone with sandstone dressings, the outer walls are well preserved and give a good idea of what the castle must have looked like when functioning as an important house, though with such a Scottish-looking building, it is hard to imagine the thatch that originally covered its roofs.

The castle was built from 1618 by Malcolm Hamilton of Portaferry, who had been Chancellor of Down in 1612 and in

1623 was to become Archbishop of Cashel. In plan it is a rectangular tower house, 54 ft by 20 ft and three storeys high. It is
protected by the usual vaulted ground floor – here divided into
three main chambers – with a pair of dramatic circular towers
flanking the short w side, where the only entrance was. It is
these towers that give the castle its eminently Scottish appearance, for both are corbelled out at the attic-storey level to provide square caphouses with the crow-stepped gabled roofs that
are characteristic of so many C16 and C17 Scottish houses.
Arranged symmetrically as a pair and linked by a segmental
arch that spans the space between them above the second-floor
window, the towers ensure that the entrance front composes
into a building of unusual grandeur. The plan in its basic form
is reminiscent of the C16 Thirlstane Castle in Lauderdale, but
at Monea the grand round towers are confined to the w front
and replaced on the E by small angle bartizans corbelled out
from the wall head. Like all Plantation castles, the house was
fortified by a bawn, part of which remains, including the traces
of two circular flankers to the N. Details that may be noted are
the fine bolection moulding to the main door, the gun loop in
the s tower beside it that covers the entrance, and the machicolation above, provided by the arch linking the caphouses
already mentioned. Inside, the door gave access to a circular
stair in the N tower that led to the great hall on the first floor,
generously illuminated by big windows with recessed seats
along the s wall. The bedrooms were on the floor above. The
kitchen appears to have been at the E end on the ground floor,
where a water slop is placed in the s wall. There is a small spiral
stair in a turret in the N wall and a lavatory shoot coming down
from the bedroom floor at the E end.

Monea was taken by the insurgents in the 1641 rising. In
1688 it was the residence of Gustavus Hamilton, Governor of
Enniskillen, and it survived the Williamite wars intact. A fire
about the mid C18 led to its ultimate abandonment.

CASTLETOWN. The house in whose demesne Monea Castle now
stands. It is a square two-storey mid C19 block in stucco, with
three-bay front and side elevations. The front has a curving
bow porch with a tripartite round-headed window above. Console architraves to the ground floor.

ST MOLAISE, DEVENISH PARISH CHURCH (C of I). 1890 by
Sir Thomas Drew, erected in memory of John Dawson O'Brien
of Castletown D.L. An attractive multi-gabled sandstone
church built round the simple battlemented tower of its C18

predecessor. Notions of historical propriety have not affected Drew here. The design makes good use of lancet windows, a c13-type chancel arch with fillet moulds on the shaft, two mid-c14-type cluster columns in the chancel itself, and an authentic cusped two-light Dec window brought from Devenish Abbey and representing now the only surviving tracery of the 1449 restoration of *Matthew O'Dubigan*. The interior is delightful, all biscuit stone and pale wood tones, with timber wagon roofs to the nave and chancel. – FONT. A black stone bowl on an octagonal shaft, also from Devenish Abbey.

CATHOLIC CHURCH. 1908 by *William Scott*. A stone-built hall with lancet windows, a bellcote, and a rose window in the w gable. Simple but pleasing interior with a hammerbeam and cross-trussed roof.

TULLYKELTER CASTLE. 1 km s of Monea church. The ruins of a c17 strong house built by James Somerville, a planter from Cambusnethan in Ayrshire. Set on the crown of a hill, yet apparently a house as opposed to a bawn. The main range ran N–S, with projecting forebuildings at either end of the E front, and a central projecting block on the w front. The ruins are now entirely covered in ivy and partly adapted as farm buildings. No detail remains except for part of a moulded door surround.

HALL CRAIG. 2 km s of Monea church. A plain stone-built farmhouse of three storeys, a good deal altered since it was built in 1721. It retains however a fine open scrolled pediment above the main door, with characteristically attenuated proportions.

MONEYMORE   LD J6

Moneymore is in the centre of the area of Co. Derry granted to the Drapers' Company in 1609. At the time of Pynnar's Survey in 1619 it had an ancient castle protected with flankers and battlements, a bawn 100 ft square with a wall 15 ft high, a water mill, a malt house, six limestone houses, and six half-timbered houses as well as a conduit head, 14 miles away, that conducted water in pipes to the town. Pynnar described Moneymore as 'the best work that I have seen for building', and it clearly was one of the most sophisticated of the Jacobean Plantation towns. Like so many, it was sacked in 1641, not by Sir Phelim O'Neill, that ubiquitous agent of destruction, but by a follower called Cormick O'Hagan, who held the Drapers' castle for the native side for several years. Subsequently Moneymore was let to the Rowley family, whose lease expired in 1817. The castle, described as 'one of the most perfect in Ireland', had been pulled down about 1760 to make room for a public house, and the town when the Drapers took over once more was generally dilapidated. On the advice of their surveyor *Jesse Gibson* the company embarked on a general rebuilding of the town, spending some £30,000 between 1817 and 1822 on buildings that give the place its essential character today.

DESERTLYN PARISH CHURCH (C of I). 1829–32 by *William Joseph Booth*, surveyor to the Drapers' Company that paid the total cost of £6,000. Burnt out in January 1889 and restored by *William Fullerton* by October 1891. A large Norman Revival design, all in ashlar sandstone, with the usual panelling of window bays and corbelled eaves. Tower, five-bay nave and aisles, short chancel. Three-light round-headed E window. Big but dull. Inside, an open pitch-pine roof. – PULPIT. Caen stone.

MONEYMORE FIRST PRESBYTERIAN CHURCH. In 1818 the old church was reported to be 'not worth repairing', so this was built in 1821 in its stead. It is a typical large two-storey hall with a three-bay pedimented gable front. Round-headed windows. Inside, a nice panelled gallery supported on eight fluted Tuscan columns. Box pews. Restored in 1937.

MONEYMORE SECOND PRESBYTERIAN CHURCH. Pre-1837; paid for partly by the Drapers' Company. A four-bay classical gabled hall. Flanked by a pair of ashlar houses with timber pediments.

ST JOHN. 1956 by *J. O'Doherty*. A nine-bay harled hall with a gabled front and an offset brick tower with a curious glazed lantern top. Ugly porch. This church replaces a small building of 1771 and a larger church, once again contributed to by the Drapers' Company, of 1831.

CHURCH RUINS. 2 km NW. The remains of a small rectangular church in a graveyard. Parts of the S wall and a corner of the E gable stand to a height of about 8 ft. No details remain.

Thanks to the Drapers' Company the village has more buildings of quality than many twice its size. They are all in the MAIN STREET, grouped, almost like a stage set, round the T-junction at the S end. In the centre, closing the view, is the former Free School of 1820, now the ORANGE HALL, a simple symmetrical group similar to that put up by the Fishmongers at Ballykelly, with a three-bay, two-storey teacher's house with a hipped roof, flanked by a pair of tall, single-storey schoolrooms with pedimented ends. The school is presumably by *Jesse Gibson*, as is the OLD MARKET HOUSE of 1818 on the W side of the street.

Symmetrical, or as near symmetrical as possible, with a pedimented three-bay centre (surmounted by a mid Victorian timber bell-turret), linked by single-bay, two-storey sections – one with a pend – to two substantial four-bay houses with forestanding Tuscan columned porches, one rather spoilt now with petrol pumps and a shop. Opposite, the street changes scale and the Drapers change architect, to *W. J. Booth*, whose NEW MARKET HOUSE is of 1839, a solemn, austerely detailed three-storey block. The front, of ashlar sandstone, is eleven bays long, with a pair of substantial terraced houses flanking a central triumphal carriage arch with pedestrian passages either side, so that the whole is like some gigantic Palladian window at ground level. Above, the windows of the top storeys of the houses continue across the arch, with a large plain pediment over them. On the pediment are long projecting mutules such as Jones used at St Paul's Covent Garden which, in their rusticity, seem not inappropriate for a grain market.

THE MANOR HOUSE. A modest classical house of the later C19. Five-bay, three-storey front, the centre section balustraded, the outer bays with tripartite windows.

SPRINGHILL. 1 km SE. Set in its well-wooded demesne, Springhill is one of the prettiest houses in Ulster, not grand or elaborate in its design, but with very much the air of a French provincial manor house. To Sampson, writing in 1802, it brought to mind 'something of the ancient dignity of resident landlords', and the view of its main façade glimpsed down a long avenue still does much the same today.

Springhill is a Conyngham house, the home of a Scottish Plantation family from Ayrshire, whose oldest Irish member was a William Conyngham who settled in the townland of Ballindrum in 1609. The present house dates from after the rising of 1641, reputedly from 1658. It looks later rather than mid C17, though the basic T-plan of the old house, most apparent at the back, bears comparison with earlier houses, e.g. the Salters' Company castle on Lough Neagh nearby. In 1780 a pair of wide canted-bay pavilions was added to either end of the house by William Conyngham, and about 1820 the house was further extended by a new dining room on the SW. No architects' or masons' names are known.

Today the entrance is a seven-bay, two-storey front, with the 58 flanking bay-windowed rooms added by William Conyngham, all harled and whitewashed. The windows, particularly those flanking the main door in the centre, have the characteristic narrow proportions of the late C17 in Ireland – two panes wide instead of three, giving a sudden change of rhythm about the middle bays. The house is flanked by long single-storey ranges of offices of the C18, thought to occupy the site of an earlier bawn. They have pretty ogee gables, Gothick sash-windows, and finely cut urn finials. The later C18 extension of the front meant that the walls linking the offices to it had to be curved back in wide bows instead of following the more standard quadrant pattern. This increases the sense of enclosure before the house.

Behind the façade a comfortable jumble of roofs, slate-hung walls, and chimneys takes over from the order of the front, with a big round-headed window on the staircase the most prominent feature. A long beech avenue in a line with the entrance drive extends from the back of the house.

Inside, the HALL is panelled in a late C17 style with bold bolection mouldings. The rooms on either side have wainscoting that looks of about 1720. The STAIR is unusually fine, 5 ft wide, with nicely turned banisters alternately plain and with spiral flutes. The later C18 DRAWING ROOM has a black marble chimney-piece with Tuscan columns (1820s) and a bold modillion cornice. The GUN ROOM retains some of its early C18 oak panelling round the fireplace and on the ceiling cornice. Now a property of the National Trust.

MONGAVLIN CASTLE *see* ST JOHNSTOWN

C6   MOUNTCHARLES   DO

A pretty village of C18 and early C19 houses straggling along a ridge of hills. The place was developed by the family of the Marquess Conyngham, whose principal estates were in Co. Meath. Their house here and the churches are at the SE end of the village.

MOUNTCHARLES PARISH CHURCH (C of I). 1861. An attractive Ecclesiastical Commissioners' church built of coursed rubble with sandstone dressings. Three-bay hall with short chancel and s porch. Paired lancets to the nave; stumpy buttresses and bellcote. The interior very characteristic of *Welland & Gillespie*, with double-chamfered chancel arch, triple-lancet E window, and an exposed trussed roof alternating kingpost and cross trusses. Intact even to the Gothic oil lamp brackets on the side walls.

CHURCH OF THE SACRED HEART. A trim stone-built hall of
c. 1870 with a polygonal apse. Six bays. Lancets, with a rose
window in the w gable. – ALTAR. 1897.

THE HALL. A tall square house built before 1778 for Lord
Conyngham and looking rather as if a Dublin town house had
been transported to the countryside. There are two fronts,
harled, with stone quoins and trim and a high solid parapet that
completely hides the roofs, giving the building a rather bald
appearance. Three-storey on a basement. The entrance front
(N) is of three bays, the garden façade of five, with hardly any
windows at the sides. The architectural detail is unusual. The
front door is in a Venetian window pattern with rusticated
Tuscan pilasters, hidden now by a charming Gothick porch of
Regency wrought-iron work. The garden door is finer (and
later?) with a lugged architrave and pediment above. Inside,
the details look c. 1750: square window reveals, not splayed;
lugged six-panel doors; and a Tuscan-columned recess in the
dining room.

In the WALLED GARDEN, on axis with the N front,
is a large brick alcove with similar arches at the end of the terrace on either side.

SALT HILL HOUSE. 2.5 km SW, overlooking Donegal Bay.
Built as the agent's house for the Conyngham estate in the late
C18. Five-bay, two-storey front on a high basement, the middle
bay breaking forward with a shallow gable basement. The stair
is possibly a remodelling of about 1820. In the drawing room
a pane of glass is inscribed 'Miss Lee come and see J.P.B. 1852'.

WOOD LODGE. w of Salt Hill House. A tiny Regency parsonage:
three-bay cottage with central attic gable. Derelict at the time
of writing.

KILLYMARD OLD CHURCH. 1.5 km E. The ruins of a small rectangular church. w gable and N wall still standing, long and
grass-covered.

MOUNTFIELD   TY G6

CHAPEL OF EASE (C of I). 1826. A tiny rubble-built church of
two bays with a double Y-traceried E window and a delightful
two-stage tower, chamfered half-way up the second stage and
supporting a slender octagonal spire. Cost: £830, with a grant
from the Board of First Fruits.

CATHOLIC CHURCH. A six-bay harled hall with buttresses and
round-headed windows. Painted dark blood red.

MAINE CHURCH. 4 km SW. A three-bay hall, with offset porch and slated square spire.

HOLY TRINITY. 5 km S at Drumnakilly. 1843. A low rubble-built cruciform church in the Tudoresque idiom of *William Farrell*. The nave has apparently been extended to the W at a later date, but in the same style. W bellcote. Clear quarry-glass lancet windows.

MOUNTJOY CASTLE. 'Upon Lough Chichester, beside the old fort. Fair castle of stone and brick covered with slate and tile begun in the late Queen's time and finished by His Majesty, of earth well ditched and flanked with busworks.' Such is the account in the *Calendar of State Papers for Ireland* in 1611. The castle was completed by Francis Roe in 1602 and named after Lord Mountjoy. Lough Chichester is of course Lough Neagh. The old fort and the flanking earthworks appear in a survey drawing made by Robert Richardson for the Earl of Dartmouth in 1682, but all trace of both has vanished. Mountjoy was taken by Sir Phelim O'Neill's troops in 1641 and evacuated and burnt by them in 1642. Retaken by British forces in that year, it was burnt two years later, before Sir Phelim's troops again regained possession. Granted to Lord Dartmouth in 1683, it was garrisoned as a military station under James II and William III.

The plan of the castle is a typical Elizabethan fort – like those in Paul Ive's *The Practice of Fortification* (1589) or in Buonaiuto Lorini's *Fortificazione* (1609). A large hall, 30 ft by 20 ft inside, is flanked by four corner towers approximately 12 ft square inside, with the outer sides carried to a salient angle to expose attackers to a raking fire from the corners of each flanker. Though much battered, the walls are still substantial, rising to two storeys: the lower of boulder rubble with dressed quoins, the upper of Tudor brick. Both floors inside are brick-lined. The ground floor is copiously provided with single-splay gun loops. There is a draw-bar socket in the door at the SE. The centre 'hall' was once square but has been extended N and S with new brick walls, possibly in the late C17.

ST BRIDGET. 1834. A small five-bay rendered hall with pine-panelled ceiling and gallery inside.

MOUNTJOY FOREST   TY *F6*

A district in the country N of Omagh celebrated in the past for the great forest of over 200,000 trees planted from about 1780 by the patriot improver, Luke Gardiner, aided by John McEvoy, the author of the statistical survey of Co. Tyrone. Mr Gardiner, created Baron Mountjoy in 1789 and Viscount in 1795, was killed at New Ross in the '98 Rebellion, and his son, who became Earl of Blessington, lived mostly abroad and squandered his inheritance, taking £30,000 annually from his Irish estates. The forest is now only a remnant straddling the River Strule in Cappagh parish. Gortnagarn Bridge, 4.5 km N of Omagh, provides a convenient reference point.

DUNMULLAN OLD CHURCH. 3 km N. The ruins of an oblong church, 62 ft by 22½ ft, fairly well preserved, with a short later transept added on the S side. Late C16 or early C17, with more detail remaining than usual. E window with three round-headed lancets, the mullions of octagonal section, with a stepped label mould. W window with paired square-headed lights. The SW corner is of dressed stones cut like a continuous colonnette running from the ground to the eaves. Rubble-built semicircular arch to the S aisle. – MONUMENT. In the transept a primitive classical aedicule with trefoil-shafted columns on double lotus-like pedestals flanking an elaborate armorial achievement. The coat of arms, a sow with a litter of pigs. Probably late C17.

CAPPAGH PARISH CHURCH (C of I). 1 km SW. A pretty Georgian Gothic church sited opposite Old Mountjoy Forest, where the river takes broad sweeping curves through cornfields. Built in 1768 at the sole expense of the then Rector, Dr Gibson. Hall and tower type with a particularly elegant masonry spire, the plan following the earlier pattern for such churches with the tower contained between a flanking vestry and store, not freestanding. Polygonal apse and new windows by *Welland & Gillespie*, 1870. Chancel steps and embossed trussed roof of 1917. – MONUMENT. C17 tablet in the tower with rope mouldings and angels, removed from Dunmullan Old Church in 1968 – the bicentenary year.

KNOCKMOYLE CHURCH. 2 km NW. Mid C19. T-plan, with galleries and a nice panelled roof with exposed braced trusses that cross in the centre. Y-tracery. At one end of the T an early C19 three-stage stone tower with quoins. The broach-spire looks a later addition.

MOUNTJOY PRESBYTERIAN CHURCH. 3 km WNW. A crisp

little Victorian church. Six-bay lancet hall in rubble stone with
w bellcote, porch, and diagonal buttresses. Probably built after
1862, when the Rev. John Gilmour became minister.

OLD MOUNTJOY. An endearing jumble of a house, by Gortnagarn Bridge, formerly Mountjoy Cottage. The core is a modest
five-bay, two-storey range, one room thick and built of
broached stone. This can be identified clearly on the s side. It
was built by the first Lord Mountjoy, or by his father Charles
Gardiner of Rash House nearby, who died in 1765. On Lord
Mountjoy's death in 1798, his son, Charles John Gardiner,
began to carry out grandiose schemes on his estates. Rash
House was to be rebuilt, a little theatre was constructed in the
forest, and the cottage gained a miscellany of castellated additions which have all the character of amateur work. A long range
was added on the NE, and at the W end of the old house a great
room was built at a higher level, with a delightful Gothick
plasterwork cornice and a big mullioned window in a turreted
gable end. The drawing room in the centre of the old house
gained a nice Ionic marble fireplace and oak and laurel garlands
in plaster on the ceiling.

ERGANAGH RECTORY. 0.75 km N. Rebuilt in 1836, a solid stone
house, larger and more architectural than most, with the
recessed panel decoration and cubic massing characteristic of
William Farrell, who may well have been the architect. Three-
bay, two-storey, with a four-bay back and a segmental bow to
one side.

RASH HOUSE. 3.5 km N W of Omagh. Across the Strule from Old
Mountjoy. Nothing came of the Earl of Blessington's schemes
to rebuild Rash (the home of the Gardiners throughout the
C18) until 1850, when the present shooting lodge came into
being. The plan is a very pure C18 double-pile type, which may
mean that the house was cut down rather than rebuilt, or else
that the new lodge was influenced by the old plan. A hall in
the middle with rooms on either side (front and back) connecting to extra rooms, laid across either end of the block, and projecting (front and back) in wide canted bays. The appearance
now, with segmental central door and shallow slate roofs, is
typically early Victorian. The pair of carved lions by the door,
from Clonleigh by Lifford, have brothers or near relatives at
Greenhill by Brookeborough, at Clover Hill, Inver, and there
were apparently two more at Rosapenna near Carrigart.

ULSTER AMERICAN FOLK PARK. At Camphill, 0.5 km w. A
group of reconstructed and new 'historic' buildings centred

around the homestead from which various members of the Mellon family emigrated to America from 1808 until about 1830.
In 1968 the old house – a single-storey, thatched cottage with
heavy porch, sash windows each side, and an extension to the
r. and a shed to the l. – was restored by the Mellon family and
presented to the Scotch–Irish Trust, for whom it is administered by the National Trust. This has become the centre of
a folk park dealing with the principal waves of emigration to
America in the C18 and C19, and with the different culture that
Ulstermen encountered in their new homes. The buildings,
designed by *Robert McKinstry* and built through Enterprise
Ulster as a government-funded scheme, include an imaginative
RECEPTION CENTRE, described by one review as 'one of the
most elaborate interpretative buildings in the United
Kingdom'; a reconstructed T-plan MEETING HOUSE; a
WEAVER'S COTTAGE; SCHOOL; and – for the new world –
a Pennsylvania LOG FARM HOUSE and LOG BARN to suggest
the character of the Mellons' new home in America.

MOVILLE   DO *G2*

A seaside resort on the w shore of Lough Foyle formed in the
valley of a small river, the Bredagh. Bought by Samuel Montgomery, a Derry merchant, in 1768 and developed from 1780. The
centre of Moville has more of a sense of place than a lot of bigger
Ulster towns, with a square planted with trees, substantial houses,
and three principal streets. The heyday of the town corresponds
with the heyday of Derry, from the mid to the late C19, when
Moville became a popular watering place served from 1832 by
steamers that plied up and down Lough Foyle. A town noticed
in *Slater's Irish Directory* of 1856 as 'sheltered from the westerly
gales by the Squire's cars and Craignamaddy mountains' obviously had the right priorities for development. Numerous trim
villas along the shore prove that this was so. The atmosphere is
nice: the architecture undistinguished.

COOLEY CHURCHYARD, 1.5 km w, is the most interesting old
   site, remarkable for its cross and skull house. St Patrick, who
   ordained Oengus son of Ailill here, founded a monastery that
   soon became celebrated for its wealth and of which notices continue to the C12. The CROSS just outside the graveyard wall,
   10 ft high and set in a long stone base, is a plain monolithic
   slab, shaped like a High Cross, with the short arms and head
   joined by a nimbus with the usual segmental perforations.

More unusual is the irregularly placed hole in the upper arm of the shaft. The SKULL HOUSE, popularly associated with St Finnian, abbot of the monastery, is a large tomb-shrine, house-shaped, and similar to the more finished shrine at Banagher in Co. Derry. It is of rubble stone with a solid stone gabled roof standing 9 ft high. A small rectangular slit lights the NE gable, and at the other end is an opening at floor level with bones inside. The CHURCH RUINS in the NW corner of the graveyard are now no more than a gabled E wall with a splayed square-headed window, and the long S wall of another building. Before the Reformation one of these had served as a parish church. The other is presumably the ruins of the chapel built in 1622 that continued in use until its destruction in 1688.

ST COLUMB, MOVILLE PARISH (C of I). A moderate Gothic design of 1858 by *Welland & Gillespie*. Nave and chancel with offset S porch surmounted by an octagonal belfry and spire. This, unlike the rest, is of ashlar sandstone, most probably a later addition, as the original design shows a tower and spire *adjoining* the porch, marked 'cancelled' on the drawing. Standard interior with high braced kingpost trusses to the roof and exposed rafters. E window of three cusped lancets.

PRESBYTERIAN CHURCH. 1862 by *J. G. Ferguson* of Derry. A crib of St Columb, without of course the chancel, but with the offset turret and spire to give punch to the gable elevation.

CHURCH OF ST PIUS X. 1953 by *W. J. Doherty*. An ambitious rectangular block using high-quality materials – granite and slate outside, mahogany within – but too aggressive to settle happily in this seaside town. Moreover the design is not logical. The massive copper lantern, a twelve-sided polygon riding importantly above the entrance front, only lights a gallery at the back of the church. Inside, a series of good modern Stations of the Cross, a sycamore statue of St Pius, and an honest wooden figure of St Joseph, this last by *J. Haugh*, 1959.

PRIVATE HOUSES are NEW PARK of 1776, the original Montgomery house; CARNAGARVE HOUSE, 1 km NE, an early C19 stuccoed house, two-storey, with big canted bay-windows squashing a domed curvilinear cast-iron conservatory between them; GORTGOWAN, a rustic classical cottage on the shore, with a columned porch and a Diocletian window in a gable above; and ROCKVILLE, built for the Misses Montgomery by *J. G. Ferguson* in 1865 – a picturesque gabled cottage with battlemented bay-windows, label mouldings, and a conservatory.

OTHER BUILDINGS are the swaggering ST EUGENE'S
SOCIETY TEMPERANCE HALL, stucco Baroque of 1887; the
CUSTOMS AND COASTGUARD HOUSES, by *J. H. Owen*, two
seven- and eight-bay, two-storey blocks by the shore, clean and
simple mid-C19 Board of Works; and the FOYLE PILOTS
HOUSE, three-bay, three-storey stone with red brick trim.
RED CASTLE. *See* p. 476.

RED CASTLE. *See* p. 476.

MOY   TY *J8*

The plan of Moy is said to have been drawn up by the Earl of
Charlemont and modelled on Marengo in Lombardy. Though no
evidence supports either tradition, the town was certainly laid out
for the Earl, prompted, it seems, by the discovery of limestone
quarries at the Moy just across the Blackwater from Charlemont,
Co. Armagh. In 1755 the Earl's stepfather, Thomas Adderley,
wrote: 'should you think of giving encouragement to build a town
there it will be a treasure'. The work was begun about 1763 and
must indeed have been unusually attractive, though lack of proper
planning has recently done much to spoil the effect. Moy consists
of one long rectangular market place, planted with trees and
entered by a main street in the middle of the shorter sides, the
s leading to Charlemont, the N to Dungannon. The W side is lined
with C18 houses of two and three storeys; so are the ends, but
at the E the line of houses is broken by a broad green opening
to the parish church and glebe house. The other three churches
of Moy were built under the second Earl's direction that every
religious denomination should be represented in the town.

ST JAMES, MOY PARISH CHURCH (C of I). Rather a mixture.
Built originally in 1819 as a tower and hall type, with an elongated tower ending in pinnacles and Irish battlements and a
four-bay nave. In 1863 *W. J. Barre* proposed enlargements for
the church including a new belfry and broach-spire for the
tower, a s aisle, a s transept, and a short polygonal chancel. The
work was begun but left incomplete at Barre's death in 1867.
The spire was not built, and in 1868 *Sherry & Hughes* altered
the design, changing the apse and adding a N transept. Barre's
design looked fine; the half-completed result is messy. The
interior is best, similar to his work at St Anne Dungannon, with
a heavy timber trussed roof, deep double-chamfered arches to
the s aisle, and painted iron gasoliers.

CATHOLIC CHURCH. 1833. A big square hall of two storeys with
a pitched roof and a forestanding porch extended to form a

Lombardic tower with a three-arched belfry and a flat pyramid roof. Ashlar stone front with diamond-cut quoins. Relieving arches to doors and windows. Renovated in 1929 by *G. J. Robb*, who possibly added the top to the tower. – STAINED GLASS by *Mayer & Co.*, six saints in *quattrocento* niches. *Ashlin & Coleman* were also consulted here.

METHODIST CHURCH. 1860, also by *W. J. Barre*. A four-bay red-brick hall with round-headed lancets trimmed in yellow brick. Chunky bellcote, rose window, and porch at the gable front.

PRESBYTERIAN CHURCH. Mid C19. A small five-bay lancet hall and porch, harled, with stone dressings.

MARKET HOUSE. In the middle of the W side of the square. Built by Lord Charlemont in 1828 with a five-bay, two-storey front. Arcaded at the centre and ends, and surmounted by a pediment. Now a garage and largely spoilt.

ROXBOROUGH CASTLE. *Barre*'s masterpiece, a French château of 1865 contrived for Lord Charlemont out of a plain Georgian house of 1738, has been demolished. Only the gates and lodges remain and, in the grounds, an C18 FOLLY TOWER, a symmetrical FARMYARD COURT with a three-bay farmhouse, and a group of U-shaped STABLES, with stone pediments.

GRANGE. 2.5 km N. A rural community including two bigger houses and a Quaker meeting house. The MEETING HOUSE is a simple C18 four-bay hall in red sandstone rubble with brick trim and with a half-hipped roof. The ground is beech-lined and has handsome diamond-rusticated gatepiers. The community settled here in 1600. GRANGE PARK, built probably by H. H. Handcock about 1800, is a five-bay, two-storey house with attics, but three-bay on the ground floor, with big tripartite windows flanking the door. THE GRANGE is very similar save for its porch and overhanging eaves.

MOYOLA PARK *see* CASTLEDAWSON

A tiny border village between Co. Derry and Co. Donegal, with an unusual cottage with a thatched hipped roof in the main street.

MUFF PARISH CHURCH (C of I). Built in 1737 by the Harts of Kilderry: a three-bay harled hall with segment-headed windows. Refitted in 1835 with pretty three-light cross mullions in timber.

CHURCH OF THE SACRED HEART. 1961 by *M. A. Fitzpatrick.*
A nine-bay hall with angle-headed lancets. Dull, and built in
nasty materials.

PRESBYTERIAN CHURCH. 1 km w at Knowehead. 1865. A
simple hall church with a stucco temple front of four widely
spaced Tuscan pilasters. Round-headed windows between. Box
pews and a gallery inside.

KILDERRY HOUSE, on the shore by the village, was built by
the Hart family and is apparently of two periods. The older
part, all harled, is a two-storey block, three rooms wide across
each front, with in the middle of the entrance façade a semicircular bow incorporating a good pedimented doorcase surmounted by a Palladian pattern window that looks of about
1770. To this core wings have been added, projecting on both
fronts and with the angles on the entrance façade filled in with
canted sections. When was this done? The label mouldings over
the windows of the additions suggest the early C19, as does the
oversailing eaves cornice and the shallow conical roof given to
the central bow, like the round-tower roof at Nash's Cronkhill
or the similar roof proposed by *John Hargrave* in his unexecuted
scheme for Fort Stewart, Ramelton, nearby. This front was
originally flanked by brick outbuildings linked by low quadrants to the main house. On the N, opening off a drawing room,
is a pretty hexagonal summer-room that looks like Hargrave
again, but on the garden front it is the centre of the house,
rebuilt in brick with a canted-bay projection and low sash-windows, that looks the most recent alteration. An intriguing building, recently restored and converted into flats.

BIRDSTOWN HOUSE. 5.5 km w. A sad case of an early C19 enthusiasm for picturesqueness spoiling a perfectly competent
provincial classical house. Birdstown was a standard seven-bay,
three-storey gentleman's seat with Georgian glazed sash-windows nicely diminishing in height on the top floor. The centre
three bays projected slightly and were crowned by a pediment
with a semicircular window to light the attic. Closely similar
to Leslie Hill, Co. Antrim, of 1755, Birdstown presumably
dates from the same time, but its classicism has been stripped
and replaced by coy bargeboards and gables too thin for the
house's true origins not to peep through. The pediment has
gone, a gabled porch has been added, and on the E side is a
large, lopsided addition of only two storeys, though as high as
the rest of the house, a four-bay block with angled end bays
and a bargeboard gable over the centre two. The windows on

the ground floor of this addition are very tall and open almost
to ground level. Inside are eight-panel mahogany doors; those
of the original house are mid C18 in six panels. The original
family were Maxwells.

HOLY TRINITY, OLD TULLANISKIN PARISH CHURCH (C
of I). A picturesque group. Cruciform, with nave and W tower
of 1793. The tower is in two stages with ashlar strips at the
corners and Irish battlements as at Moy. Nave, now two-bay,
with stone Y-traceried windows. Transepts, three-sided apse,
and vestry all added by *Welland & Gillespie* in 1864. Dec E window. Inside, pine gallery of 1823 and exposed roof trusses. In
the churchyard a BULLAUN with two holes.

40 ROUGHAN CASTLE. 1 km NE. A redoubtable strong house built
by Sir Andrew Stewart in 1618 and belonging later to Sir
Phelim O'Neill, executed for his rebellion in 1653. For ideal
plans this ranks almost with Augher Castle: a central room, 20 ft
square, is flanked by exceptionally fat round towers at each
corner, 8 ft in diameter inside, converting to square rooms in
the upper floors. Moulded string courses, as at Castlecaulfield,
divide each floor, and a corbelled round-headed arch connects
the corner towers on the S face above the second-floor window.
The entrance was by a door in the NW tower with a spiral stair
immediately inside. The ground floors of the towers each have
several musket loops. The main hall was timber-floored. Fireplaces remain at two levels.

ROUGHAN HOUSE. An elegant two-storey, three-bay stucco
house with overhanging eaves and a shallow hipped roof.
Regency in appearance, but perhaps as late as 1840.

FURLOUGH LODGE. 1 km SE. Strikingly situated above the
Torrent River. A small five-bay, two-storey Georgian house
with a dressed sandstone front and a square central porch. The
front looks about 1820, but the house dates from before 1786.

ANNAGINNY LODGE. 1.5 km WSW. A mid Georgian house,
originally thatched. Burnt and rebuilt in the later C19 in a half-
timbered Tudor style by Colonel R. J. Howard. Almost symmetrical, with projecting gables at the ends of the front and
a three-bay recessed loggia between. The end gables, now tile-
hung, are presumably those of the old house but are hard to
recognize under their Tudor skin. The interior is dark, with
a curiously angular oak stair. Art Nouveau leaded lights, Jaco-

bean carved oak pilasters, and embossed leather paper heavily
gilt.

CANAL AQUEDUCT. Built by the Board of Public Works as part
of the Tyrone Canal from 1746 to 1752 at a cost of £20,000.
According to the Ordnance Survey Memoirs for Tyrone 'a civil
engineer named Ducart attempted to execute this'. *Davis
Ducart* certainly worked at Lissan House nearby and possibly
also at Florence Court and Limavady.

NEWTOWNBUTLER   FM F10

In many ways this small Fermanagh village is a typical Ulster
microcosm, with a representative building for most denominations, a court house, a hotel, a market house, and a station. None
is in any way special but none is mean, and the village can boast
some attractive Regency cottages as well and a Tudor-style school.

GALLOON PARISH CHURCH (C of I). 1821, rebuilt after a fire;
the original church dated from the C17. Large, cruciform, with
simple Gothic detail and cusped Y-tracery windows. At the W
end a massive square tower, harled, of four storeys, with a
strong batter to the upper two storeys and battlements at the
corners. A plaque on this reads 'North Clarke & Jo. Robinson
Ch.Ws. AD 1814', so the tower may pre-date the church itself.
Inside is a Georgian gallery supported on cluster-shafted
columns and a pretty plaster ceiling. Re-seated 1889.

CHURCH OF THE IMMACULATE CONCEPTION. A little S of
the village, in fields. 1886 by *George L. O'Connor*. A biggish
four-bay nave with one-bay chancel and side chapels. Rendered
Gothic with sandstone trim. At the W end (actually E) is an elaborate four-storey tower, buttressed, with geometrical tracery to
the belfry and a green copper spire – a little too narrow to be
successful.

METHODIST CHURCH. By the parish church. 'Erected 1834'.
A two-bay hall with a porch, Y-tracery, and a stone Gibbs surround to the door.

THE MARKET HOUSE on the W side of the main street near the
centre is the grandest public building, a big two-storey block
of about 1830, with an arcade of four segmental arches across
each floor filled in with windows and doors. Over the central
two bays an eaves pediment, the eaves supported by heavy,
block-like mutules typical of *W. D. Butler* of Dublin, to whom
the design is attributed. Recently restored as a church hall.
Butler certainly designed the COURT HOUSE of 1828–30, a

plain, T-shaped building a little down hill, with the court room in the leg of the T, the bridewell and houses in the crossbar. The only architectural feature here is the porch, severely Greek, with a segment-headed lunette, wreaths, and incised decoration *à la* Soane. The builder was *Jonathan Tilson*, an 'architect' from Belturbet, seven miles away in Co. Cavan. The LANES-BOROUGH ARMS HOTEL between the market house and the court house is good for the streetscape. It is an attractive early C19 hotel, five bays by three storeys, of rubble stone with brick trim. Free-standing Tuscan porch with an unusual fanlight above the door, made to contain a lantern.

In the C19 Newtownbutler benefited considerably from the improved communications in the area, first by the Ulster Canal linking Lough Erne and Lough Neagh, and then in 1859 by the Irish North West Railway linking Dundalk and Enniskillen. Both are now defunct. The engineer for the line was *Sir John MacNeill* and the architect of the stations *William G. Murray*. The STATION here cost £1,400 and was opened in 1860. A little E of the village, it is in E.E. manorial style, L-shaped, with a shouldered arcade of two bays as an entrance porch. Now a nicely maintained private house.

MAGHERAVEELY CHURCH. 5 km ENE. A three-bay lancet hall with tiny porch and bellcote.

MANOR HIGHGATE. 2.5 km ENE. An early C19 three-bay, two-storey house with a big central chimney and low eaves like Oak-field by Knockballymore.

DRUMBROUGHA'S CASTLE. 3 km WSW, by the lough shore. A long line of stone wall with traces of square returns: nothing more.

GALLOON ISLAND. *See* p. 302.

GALLOON ISLAND. *See* p. 302.

A long street of a village distinguished by the Catholic church on an open site in the middle of the N side and by the castle ruins further N.

CATHOLIC CHURCH. 1861 by *E. W. Godwin*, one of Ireland's favourite High Victorian Englishmen but here at his most modest. A long, low church of nine bays with a big roof cut into by the gables of two porches on the S side. Y and plate tracery. Bellcote. There was originally a segmental apse at the E end, but this was replaced in 1971 by a coy flat-roofed neo-Gothick E chapel by *Seamus Shesgreen & Associates*. The gallery inside is by *Daniel Conroy* of Derry, 1902. The old chapel which Godwin's church replaced was built in 1810.

ALL SAINTS (C of I). Consecrated in 1722 as a chapel of ease to the church at Taughboyne and opened in 1728. Now a straightforward early C19 hall and tower type church, the tower built in 1808 by William Forward of Castle Forward, later third Earl of Wicklow. Primitive Gothic with thin clasping buttresses and Y-traceried windows. Refitted by *Joseph Welland* in 1846. Polygonal apse added *c.* 1910. Big alien lychgate in memory of the Rev. A. G. Stuart of Bogay, 1920. – MONUMENTS. Three modest yet elegant classical tablets: to William Forward † 1770 by *Richard Kelly* of Dublin, an oval inscription above a cupid's head; to Eleanor Forward † 1807, a Tuscan aedicule surmounted by a coat of arms; and to the second Earl of Wicklow † 1815, a tablet surmounted by a coat of arms in relief.

PRESBYTERIAN CHURCH. A jaunty rubble and sandstone Gothic hall of 1881. Five bays, buttressed, with a bellcote and a big Dec central window.

THE CASTLE. Possibly the successor to Burt Castle. A large seven-bay, two-storey house on a semi-basement, by the main street but built at r. angles to it. Early C18. Plain harled, with the centre three bays slightly projecting, and some stone detail. The interior has big simple plaster cornices, wainscot panelling, and corner fireplaces like those at Buncrana Castle. Empty and neglected at the time of writing.

CASTLE FORWARD. E of the village. Once the seat of the Forward family, Earls of Wicklow. A nine-bay, two-storey house with a Tuscan columned porch. Now a ruin. Building accounts date the house to 1735–9, though the remains look later.

STONE ALTAR. McParland's *Statistical Survey of Donegal* of 1802 gives the following delightful account: 'In the deer-park, in the beech grove is a flag five feet in diameter, perfectly circular, and regularly indented with holes half an inch deep, and one inch diameter: it is raised on other stones eighteen inches high. Is this a druidical altar? Is it and its hieroglyphics emblematic of lunar worship? Or what then?'

RECTORY. 1825. A three-bay, two-storey house with a two-bay wing.

BOHULLION DISTILLERY. Extensive early C19 buildings with two brick chimneys. Derelict at the time of writing.

BURT CASTLE. 2.5 km N of Newtowncunningham. These ruins can be seen from miles around sitting up, black and a little menacing, on a knoll about 200 ft above Lough Swilly. The castle may be a foundation of the time of Henry VIII, as a medallion of about 1525 with the O'Doherty arms and a coin of 1547 were found near the site. Both the plan and the extensive provision of musketry loops in the present structure suggest that what is there now is of the late C16. The plan of Burt is an importation, not Irish, but typically Scottish. It is built on the 'three-stepped' or Z-plan of which there are over sixty examples in Scotland, mostly in the NE, but also in Orkney and Shetland. The closest equivalent to this Irish castle is Claypotts near Dundee in Angus, built between 1569 and 1588. Claypotts has the same plan: a strong rectangular block, vaulted on the ground floor and divided into two chambers, with strong round towers projecting from diagonally opposite corners to provide an effective and unobscured field of fire along all the walls. This sort of attention to defence and to artillery is commonplace among the castles of the Protestant planters of the next century, as indeed is the Scottish borrowing, but both are unusual in the work of native Irish proprietors.

The first documentary reference to Burt is in the grant of lands to Sir John O'Doherty in 1587. It is shown on a map of 1599 made during Elizabeth's campaigns in Ulster as 'the strong castel of Burt in possession of Huboy [O'Doherty]' and as surrounded on three sides by water with a strip of bog cutting off the fourth. Burt at its fullest extent is unusually well 34 recorded in a view taken in 1601 that shows the tower defended by four cannon and surrounded by a defensive square wall with casemates – similar to the surviving casemate at Doe Castle – covering two walls of the enclosure, just as the round towers cover the walls of the castle itself. These outworks have now completely disappeared, and the area of the enclosure is sub-divided by modern field walls. At Sir Cahir O'Doherty's rebellion in 1608 the castle was captured by the English, and was held as an important garrison point for several years. Still in use as a fortified house and bawn in 1690, it was abandoned early in the C18 and unroofed by 1833.

The ruins are substantial: walls $5\frac{1}{2}$ ft thick, built of large stone boulders bedded in shell mortar and originally harled. The main ground-floor chamber, $12\frac{1}{3}$ ft by $16\frac{1}{2}$ ft, was originally vaulted; the upper floors joisted. A turnpike stair in the SW tower is protected by four gun loops to each complete turn. At first-floor level the vaulted mural chamber, $11\frac{1}{2}$ ft by $5\frac{1}{2}$ ft, preserves a bolt socket in the jamb of the door. Traces of wattle shuttering are on the vaults here. Garderobe in the NE

tower. Fireplaces for the upper storeys on the E wall. The
towers originallly rose higher, with a gabled roof between
them: the wall-head today is almost level.

BURT CHURCH RUINS. By the shore NW from the castle the
walls of a rectangular church, approximately 60 ft by 20 ft. The
octagonal shafted mullions of the E window built into the wall
are clearly early C17. Small window opening at the W end of
the s wall; traces of an arch and lintel on the N wall. Slab to
the Rev. Andrew Ferguson † 1725; thirty-six years minister
of Burt.

BOGAY HOUSE. 4 km E of Newtowncunningham. Supposed to
be of the mid C18, though in appearance earlier. A simple design, but of more architectural quality than usual. Double-pile
plan with fronts of five bays, two storeys, and a semi-basement.
High hipped roof with three dormers in the middle of the s
front and regularly grouped chimneys. A provincial house still
in the tradition of Sir Roger Pratt, though almost a century
later. The detail minimal but effective: Tuscan aedicule porch;
console-pedimented central window on the s front, eaves string
course and cornice all in sandstone. Interior with six-panel
doors in lugged surrounds like Dunmore and Oakfield nearby.
Ground-floor windows of an elongated late C18 type. Stone
stair.

NEWTOWNSTEWART   TY F6

Originally Lislas, described by the *Traveller's New Guide* of 1815
as 'a neat small town pleasantly situated on the River Mourne',
with a network of roads 'leading to the different little villages
scattered in the remote parts of this mountainous district'. The
town is by an important junction of three rivers, a strategic position that is proved both by the siting of a great O'Neill castle just
behind it and by the role it played in Sir Phelim O'Neill's rebellion
when he took the place in 1641 and thereby cut off all government
communication with this part of Tyrone. The present town was
founded by William Stewart on land granted by Charles I. James
II, who lodged here in 1689, had the place burnt on his retreat,
and it was not rebuilt by the Stewarts until 1722. Later in the
C18 it became the property of the Gardiner family, under whom
it was considerably improved, with paved streets and a piped
water supply, though by the mid Victorian age its boom period
was over.

ST EUGENE, ARDSTRAW PARISH CHURCH (C of I). Nicely

set at the head of the street and approached by steps through old c18 gatepiers. Date-stone below the E window 1724. This church is a rebuilding by Dr John Hall of the first church, erected in 1622 and destroyed by King James's army. Hall and tower type, with irregular nave windows. The tower in three stages with a spire added in 1806. Altered inside in 1858, in 1867 by *Welland & Gillespie*, and in 1909, when the chancel was rebuilt. – BELL, now in the church porch. Given by Sir William Stewart in 1679 and 'enlarged' by Lord Mountjoy. – STAINED GLASS. E window, 'The Ascension', by *Heaton, Butler & Bayne*; P. S. Martin window, 'Christ's Charge to Peter', 1952 by *Clokey*. – MONUMENTS. The Rev. John Hall, builder of the church and glebe house, † 1735. A sophisticated grey and white marble aedicule with a Baroque coat of arms. – Katherine, daughter of Sir William Stewart Kt, † 1634. A plain slab.

ST EUGENE. 1 km NE. A plain rectangular church altered to a T-shape in 1823 by the Rev. Philip Porter P.P. Queen-post trussed roof with high galleries inside. The belfry and steeple, put up in 1834, are said to be the first in the Catholic diocese since penal times. The present timber belfry and spire is of 1904 by *E. J. Toye*.

FIRST NEWTOWNSTEWART PRESBYTERIAN CHURCH. The congregation dates from about 1650, though there was no church at Newtownstewart until 1804. The present church is of 1909 by *Robert Young*, a wide hall and tower with a short spire, Gothic, with two windows above a central pointed door in the gable. Dressed sandstone.

METHODIST CHURCH. 1818; a plain hall.

NEWTOWNSTEWART CASTLE. On Castle Brae, at the foot of the main street. A large Plantation house built by Sir Robert Newcomen, the father-in-law of Sir William Stewart. Three storeys, about to be roofed at the time of Pynnar's Survey in 1619. Very much a house rather than a castle, though only the S wall with three crow-stepped gables remains intact. Dismantled by order of James II in 1689 and not rebuilt. Details worth note are the brick-lined flues and octagonal star-shaped chimney like those at Rathmullen; the mullioned windows with square label heads; and the portion of a large window in the E wall with a classical cornice moulding and part of a date 16—. A half-round stair survives on the W wall.

OTHER BUILDINGS in the town are, next to the castle, the HOTEL, a substantial five-bay, two-storey Georgian block with quoins; the TOWN HALL, stuccoed, with a central gable, 'erected by B. Gillespie' in 1886; the CASTLE YARD ARCHWAY dated 1827; and, in the street S of the castle, a carriage ARCH of 1838 by D.B., with a primitive keystone face and rock-faced voussoirs. The disused G.N.R. STATION dates from 1891 and the OLD BRIDGE of six arches from 1727.

HARRY AVERY'S CASTLE. 1 km NE. Two massive D-shaped towers fronting a rectangular block form the entrance before the main dwelling house of this C14 castle, named after Henry Aimbreidh O'Neill who died in 1392. Built round a polygonal knoll flattened and converted into a bailey, the castle had a surrounding curtain wall facing the sides of the knoll and rising above it. Excavations have shown this to have been between 5 and 8 ft thick, though little now remains beyond the gatehouse towers and part of a square interval tower on the E side of the bailey. The gatehouse, the only means of entry to the enclosure, had a narrow spiral stair in the SW tower leading to the main hall, a rectangle immediately behind the two towers, on a level with the bailey behind it. The low vaulted chambers in each tower have traces of wattle shuttering on their ceilings. Segmental vaulted mural chambers at first-floor level, that on the E with a garderobe shaft. The castle represents an interesting stage of development between the full strength of Norman castles like Greencastle and Carrickfergus with functional defensive gateways and separate keeps, and the later tower houses of the C16 and Plantation periods. Destroyed in 1609 and systematically robbed of stone ever since.

CORICKMORE ABBEY. 5.5 km ENE. Built on a promontory above the meeting of the Owenkillew and Glenelly rivers, the monastery was founded for Franciscans of the Third Order about 1465 and continued until 1603, when it was granted to Sir Henry Piers. In 1837 there were 'some highly picturesque remains of this abbey affording an idea of the original extent and elegance of the buildings'. Today the ruins are very overgrown. The church was the characteristic long rectangle of C15 Franciscan houses ending in a two-light E window, the centre mullion of which still stands, with elaborate quasi-classical mouldings on the interior similar to those at Raphoe Cathedral. Some carved gable stones are in the graveyard.

WOODBROOKE HOUSE. 2.5 km W. Granted to the Buchanan family about 1624. Rebuilt about 1800. Two storeys on a high basement, with steps to the front door. Provincial Gibbs surround and wide tripartite windows each side. Five-bay on the

first floor. Built by a linen merchant; there is a bleaching green
behind the house.

CHURCHES in the area are: KILLYMORE CHURCH, 4 km E, a
four-bay rendered hall with quoins and pointed windows
CORICK PRESBYTERIAN CHURCH, 5.5 km NE, of 1800, a
similar four-bay hall; and DOUGLAS PRESBYTERIAN
CHURCH, 5 km NW, a four-bay harled hall and porch.

F7   OMAGH   TY

For the writers of gazetteers the most striking feature of Omagh
seems to have been the fire of 1743 that destroyed the entire place.
Other Ulster towns wear a uniformly nineteenth-century air without the cachet of having lost their earlier buildings in a universal
disaster, but Omagh has this as its excuse. It had a monastery
for Franciscans of the Third Order, founded in 1464 and existing
until after 1603, and a castle, the *Oigh Maigh* or seat of the chief,
which gave its name to the town. *The Annals of the Four Masters*
record its capture in 1471, and parts of it survived until the year
of the fire. The site is an obvious one for a town and a chief's
castle, set in a declivity in open and fertile country at the point
where the Carnowen and Drumragh rivers meet to form the
Strule. At the Plantation Captain Ormond Leigh built a fort with
a timber house and many dwellings, described in the *Calendar of
State Papers* for 1611 as 'a place of good import, upon all occasions
of service and fit to be maintained'. Much of this Plantation town
was built on the Franciscans' lands.

The present town ignores its rivers. One long street – Market
Street and then High Street – runs in a straight line and sharply
uphill to the court house and clustered spires of the two main
churches, both of the late C19. A modern loop road to the N,
Drumragh Avenue, cuts round the side of the town across the
river, where the technical college, schools, and county offices of
the C20 are to be found. Uninspired and generally rather clumsy
in design, they are better out of the town than in it.

CHURCHES

CHURCH OF THE SACRED HEART. 1893–9 by *William Hague*.
By far the most ambitious piece of architecture in Omagh, set
at the top of the town and dominating both the court house
and the Church of Ireland St Columba beside it. As so often,
the exterior is only a façade, with a long, plain, Puginesque
gabled nave and lean-to aisles behind. The chancel is expressed

by a step in the roof ridge, and the side chapels at the ends of the aisles have independently gabled roofs. What makes the church memorable is its fine entrance front: an elaborate essay in French Gothic with twin towers, defined by clasping buttresses above the first-floor level and identical until above the belfry stage, flanking a huge Dec window with a central wheel. Above the belfry rise two c14-type spires with lucarnes and many crockets at the angles. That to the s is shorter and more heavily detailed, giving rise to the usual stories of money running out, though it is clear that Hague designed two different spires.

The interior is memorable. The nave and aisles are articu- 122 lated by a seven-bay arcade supported on massive polished granite columns in a long rhythmic procession. Heavily undercut sandstone capitals with naturalistic floral decoration, lilies of the valley, fritillaries, etc. High clerestory with a busy hipped hammerbeam roof on corbel stops with the heads of Irish saints. Chancel with a high five-light geometrical E window (actually w) and a panelled wagon roof. Side chapels with double tierceron-vaults. – STAINED GLASS. E window. Naturalistic Last Supper, Adoration of the Sacred Heart, and Crucifixion in the rose.

ST COLUMBA, DRUMRAGH PARISH CHURCH (C of I). 1870 by *J. E. Rogers*. A large, striking church in a heavy Gothic style. Cruciform, though unconventionally planned inside, with deep transepts screened by a two-bay arcade – a plan type taken over by big Catholic churches in the 1880s – and vestigial aisles. w front with an elaborate geometrical traceried window. Offset tower and broach-spire to the N. The interior is a big wide space with exposed hipped roof trusses and heavily carved capitals to the columns. – STAINED GLASS. Many mid to late C19 pictorial windows. E window 1862 (and therefore saved from the earlier church) by *O'Connor* of London, showing four saints in niches with four of the seven acts of mercy. – w window to Samuel Galbraith of Clanabogan † 1864; eight parables. – N aisle, *Heaton, Butler & Bayne*, 1887, Christ healing the lame man – well drawn but rather brown.

OMAGH FIRST PRESBYTERIAN CHURCH, Dublin Road. Reputedly by *Vincent Craig*. Of reddish brown sandstone with a densely packed frontage of gable, squat porch, and chamfered octagonal bell tower masking a wide hall with double-gabled 'transepts' at either end.

TRINITY PRESBYTERIAN CHURCH, John Street. 1856. A

four-bay lancet hall of rubble stone with bellcote, transepts, and polygonal apse.

METHODIST CHURCH, James Street. 1857. A six-bay lancet hall with a gabled 'church' frontage divided into three parts by buttresses. Paired doors. Contractor (and architect?) Mr *Mullan*.

PUBLIC BUILDINGS

93 COURT HOUSE. Impressively set, and intended to impress, the court house looks down the hill from the head of the High Street. It is of 1814 by *John Hargrave*, with a long wing to the S added by *W. J. Barre* in 1863. Hargrave's model is that of a standard English Palladian country house of the later C18. Five-bay façade of two storeys with a temple-front portico added in 1820 at the top of a massive flight of twelve steps. The detailing is distinctly wayward. The portico, following no doubt the pilaster responds which preceded it, is Tuscan, but Tuscan of a very lanky variety, with shafts almost ten times the diameter of the column, whereas the Vitruvian rule for this order is never more than seven. The entablature by contrast is oddly reduced in scale and, where it extends across the façade of the main building to corner pilasters, omits the architrave completely, which necessitates a detached block above the corner capital. Other details are more orthodox: a rusticated ground floor with round-headed sash windows; ashlar above, with the first-floor window sills forming a continuous string course. In the S wing Barre continued Hargrave's main lines for five more bays but, through missing out the pilasters and portico, adroitly regularized his mannerisms. A smaller scale for these offices, plus a dip in the ground, leaves room for two storeys within the rusticated section of the façade, with the windows of both floors contained within high relieving arches to good Italianate effect. At the N corner of the court house in George's Street is a periwigged figure of Justice, apparently of the late C17 or early C18, set up above the first window bay in 1854. The interior is dull. Altered in 1906 by *W. H. Byrne & Sons*.

LORETTO CONVENT AND GRAMMAR SCHOOL, Brook Street. 1859. The original building is either by *J. Neville*, as reported in the *Dublin Builder*, or by *Hadfield & Goldie*, as stated in *The Builder* in 1860. L-shaped, of stone, with simple Victorian Gothic details. Three storeys on a high basement. Five bays with a two-bay addition joined by a round stair-turret. Hipped slated roof. Perhaps the addition, with a tall Gothic chapel behind, is by Hadfield & Goldie. It is strikingly effective inside: a five-bay hall with paired cusped lancets, a high boarded wagon roof with angel-head corbels to the trusses, and STAINED GLASS by *Mayer & Co*. The new school buildings are by *Vincent Murnaghan*.

OMAGH HOSPITAL. 2.5 km ESE. A large hospital complex built round the original lunatic asylum of 1847–53 by *William Farrell*. Farrell's asylum, one of the second series erected by the Irish Board of Works at a cost of £35,000, is a daunting three-storey range in an oppressive institutional Elizabethan style, sixty-two window bays long. Symmetrical, though broken by varied projections with grouped brick chimneystacks and massive square stair-towers with octagonal cupolas exactly like those on Wilkinson's workhouses. In 1863 extensive additions were made by *George Boyd*, and in 1895–9 a New County Infirmary was built by *C. A. Owen*, who also designed the Catholic and Protestant chapels of 1901 and 1903. The New Hospital of 1937 is by *V. H. Murnaghan*, the New Omagh Hospital of 1970 by *W. H. McAlister & Partners* of Derry.

TOUR

A tour of Omagh should begin with its principal churches and the court house, all grouped in a small triangle of streets, CHURCH STREET, JOHN STREET, and GEORGE'S STREET. It is here that the town has a satisfactory urban feeling, with big three-storey Georgian and early C19 houses curving in terraces round the streets. In Church Street, No. 13 is a handsome three-bay, three-storey stucco-fronted house with a pretty elliptical fanlight. Opposite, Nos. 4 and 6 are tiny old cottages, each two-bay and two-storey.

The HIGH STREET, leading E from the portico of the court house, at first in a wide funnel but narrowing to normal proportions, is the focus of the best commercial buildings in the town. Near the court house, on the l., the MUNSTER AND LEINSTER BANK of 1923 by *Morris & Kavanagh*, a late Portland stone classical façade, two-bay, three-storey, with an engaged Ionic order on the ground floor. Shortly below it the ULSTER BANK of 1909, a detached block typical of the Art Nouveau classicism of its architects, *Blackwood & Jury*, with bulging columns and balusters. It faces the finest High Victorian building in the town, the PROVINCIAL BANK OF IRELAND of 1864, built by a Mr McGaughey and almost certainly designed by *W. G. Murray*. Italian Gothic in sandstone. Four-bay, three-storey, with 97 a heavily detailed entrance and a big *cornicione* decorated with undercut ivy-leaf sculpture. The bank is flanked by big stuccoed Georgian houses at Nos. 11, 13, and 19, all apparently of about 1780, with stone quoins and eaves cornice and one with a Gibbs surround to its door. Further downhill on the l. is the BELFAST BANK, a five-bay, three-storey classical block in red brick and sandstone, designed as a post office by *J. L. Donnelly* in 1902.

Towards the end of the High Street, BRIDGE STREET leads l. to Mountjoy Road past the large new TECHNICAL COLLEGE by *Storie, Lynch & Partners* of 1968. Too massive and too boxy to be successful: a four-storey main block with low forestanding wing with zigzag roof. At the crossroads the lively Venetian Gothic ORANGE HALL of 1869 faces the TYRONE COUNTY HALL of 1962 by *Ostrick & Williams*, a friendly three-storey block in biscuit-coloured brick with concrete mullions, the corner entrance and stairs arranged in a glassy box. Turning r. at the crossroads, DRUMRAGH AVENUE, a new by-pass, leads back across the Strule to Market Street. It passes on the r. the 1914–18 WAR MEMORIAL, a granite pylon with a bronze plaque (signed *S.R.P.*) of an ascending angel with a wreath and two dead soldiers below. Further down the road on the l. is the re-sited INNISKILLINGS' SOUTH AFRICAN WAR MEMORIAL of 1904 by *Sydney March*, cast in copper by *Elkington & Co.*, a grand, heroic figure in a swirling mantle holding aloft the crown of victory with brooding figures crouched or sitting on minor plinths on either side. Across the river in MARKET STREET is the COUNTY CINEMA of *c.* 1930, North West Ulster's only attempt at the contemporary International Modern Movement in Mendelsohn's idiom and not without success. The BANK OF IRELAND here is of 1894 by *Millar & Symes*, brick and red sandstone, with big Dutch curled gables and cross mullioned windows. The street is characterized by long straight blocks of substantial late c19 terraces. Nos. 25–33 and Nos. 35–41 are both good blocks, the latter of four Victorian shops with cast-iron composite columns. The modern F. A. WELLWORTH's store sets a poor example for future developers. Market Street leads w back to the High Street.

In CASTLE STREET, w of the court house and churches and on the w bank of the river, is a little precinct entered through a pointed archway. This was the site of the old PRISON, built in 1796 and rebuilt by *John Hargrave* in 1823. Various late

Georgian terraced houses remain, together with the octagonal
three-storey sandstone block of Hargrave's GOVERNOR'S
HOUSE. It has a gallery on the first floor and short wings on
either side.

NEIGHBOURHOOD

The eastern suburbs of Omagh contain some interesting minor
country houses. The grandest is KNOCKNAMOE CASTLE,
2 km ENE, a flamboyant Jacobean house built in brown sandstone by the Stack family in 1875. The entrance porch – with
paired Tuscan columns and strapwork balcony above – the
curly gables, and the square turret with ogee copper cupola are
all details from the *Lanyon* office, or if not from Lanyon
directly, from his pupil and sometime assistant *Thomas Turner*.
Near Knocknamoe to the N is MULLAGHMORE HOUSE, a
charmingly unsophisticated double pile that is little more than
a cottage. Late Georgian (*c.* 1800). Two-storey, three-bay, with
pretty paired Gothic glazed windows and timber mullions.
LISNAMALLARD HOUSE nearby is smaller still, also late
Georgian and also two-storey and three-bay, with an odd
hipped roof and pretty fanlight. ST LUCIA BARRACKS of
c. 1835 are stone-walled, with two-storey stone ranges and later
three-storey gabled blocks of *c.* 1860: architecturally a dis-
orderly clutter.

There are two interesting houses on the E bank of the Drumragh.
First CREEVENAGH HOUSE, 1.5 km ESE, built by the Auchin-
leck family, presumably about 1810, long, low, and two-
storeyed, rendered, with stone quoins and wide overhanging
eaves. Three-bay, though given unusual scale by the use of tripartite windows throughout, with a polygonal single-storey
central porch. The interior is unusually handsome: a complete
neo-classical villa with a double return staircase symmetrically
planned on the axis of the hall, fine Grecian plasterwork, and
a heavily architectural character to the doors and fireplaces
of the main rooms. The hall floor is paved in Italian marble
– black, white, and terracotta-red – with scenes of the seven
ages of man. EDENFEL, 2 km ESE, a large multi-gabled and
aggressively picturesque villa with decorative bargeboards, hip
knob, and ornamental chimneys, was built in 1862 for a Captain
Buchanan to designs by *Boyd & Batt*.

There are three churches in the E vicinity. The ruins of DRUM-
RAGH CHURCH, 3 km S, in an old graveyard just after Drumragh Bridge, consist of the walls of a rectangular early C17 build-

ing reputedly burnt by Cromwellian troops. The side walls are
low, but both gables stand. Double-chamfered window reveals.
A little more remote, 4 km to the SE in open country, is a derelict
C of I church, with a four-stage tower and spire of 1854.
At CREEVENAGH CEMETERY, 1.5 km SE, a pretty chapel
of c. 1860, a gabled hall with Dec end windows and a gabled
porch in the middle of one side. Cusped lancets. DRUMRAGH
CATHOLIC CHURCH at Knocknamoe, 2 km ENE, is the old
chapel of Omagh. Partly thatched and partly slated at the time
of the Ordnance Survey Memoirs, it is now T-plan, with late
Georgian galleries in each arm. High trussed roof and short
sanctuary. STAINED GLASS. Crucifixion by *Mayer & Co.*, 1904.

LEARMOUNT FOREST. A large, ashlar-fronted Elizabethan
mansion built in 1830 by Henry de la Poer Beresford. Two-
storey front with five gables, the centre one broken with an ogee
profile with a porch below. On the E was the older house,
dressed up as a four-bay, three-storey castellated wing, with
the slender round corner turrets typical of the Morrisons – this
part recently demolished. The main house has opulent plasterwork and a big double return staircase on an axis with the front
door.

LEARMOUNT CHURCH (C of I). 1831. A tiny three-bay lancet
hall with diagonal buttresses, spiky bellcote, and porch. In the
graveyard is a monument to David Little, who lived to be 114.

ST MARY. At Altinure, 0.5 km NW. A good, solid, simple church
of about 1870. Just a nave and chancel with a plate-tracery
wheel window in the gable, Gothic bellcote, and lean-to s porch.
The roof with broad bands of two colours of slate. Recently
remodelled inside by *Liam McCormick & Partners*.

CARNABANE CHURCH. 3 km W. Mid C19, T-plan, with lancet
windows and three galleries inside.

STRAIDARRAN HOUSE. 3 km N. A delightful small country
house in a park-like setting with a tiny lake and a ruined church
in its grounds. The house, five windows wide, is single-storey
at the front, with half-hipped gables and a double perron rising
to a segment-headed fanlight door. On the W is a long, five-
bay castellated wing with a carriage arch in the centre flanked
by thin flat turrets. This is said to have been added by a family
called Hunter about 1830.

CHURCH RUINS. N from the house in a small enclosure. The

walls of a church of 18 by 24 ft. The w gable remains with one small window. C17?

PARKANAUR   TY *H8*

Now the Thomas Doran Training Centre for handicapped child- 83 ren. A large, rambling, Elizabethan-style house built princip- ally to designs of *Thomas Duff* of Newry. Parkanaur was origin- ally an O'Donnelly property. In the C17 it was granted to the Caulfields, and in the 1770s was bought by John Henry Bur- ges, who had made a fortune in the East India Company and who built a small two-storey gabled cottage as an occasional residence here in 1802–4. In 1820, when Burges settled on the estate, the cottage was enlarged, and in 1839 his son John Ynyr Burges, who had inherited considerable property in England the year before, re-cased the old work and then added a new w wing in 1843, all to Duff's design. Building had finished by 1848 except for the interior of the drawing room, completed in 1854, and the free-standing office block in a court behind the main house added about 1870. A plaque above the archway leading to the court is inscribed: 'This house and offices were built by John Ynyr and the Lady Caroline Burges without plac- ing any debt upon the property A.D. 1870.'

The growing importance of the house from retreat, to home, to seat is reflected in the graduated scale of the different parts. On the s front the 'cottage' is the first three bays on the E, with gabled entrance porch in the centre. It is followed by a project- ing larger gable and two more gabled bays – the first extension – and then by the new work by Duff turning w. This is a grand terraced front, detailed in much the same manner as Duff's Narrow Water Castle, Co. Down, with octagonal shafts at each projection of the façade, a big bay-window, and an upper oriel. The interior contains a great hall lit by three large Perp win- dows, with a Tudor-arched screen and minstrels' gallery at its s end. Much older work has been imported, notably the Jaco- bean chinmeypiece with male and female caryatids and the dining-room chimneypiece with Ionic columns and grotesque heads, dated 1651. A pretty mid C18 Baroque organ case is in the gallery.

PETTIGOE   FM and DO *D7*

A small border town, partly in Fermanagh and partly in Donegal and almost on the shore of Lower Lough Erne. Built largely of stone, it is set in fertile lush country, though the bleak Donegal moors that run up to Lough Derg are never far away. In the C18 and C19 the place benefited from the custom of pilgrims passing through it to St Patrick's Purgatory on Lough Derg. Its main interest today lies in the ruined castle just outside the town.

32 TERMON CASTLE. 1.5 km SW, in the grounds of Templecarne Glebe House. The interest of Termon Castle, built by the Mac-Grath family, the hereditary *coarbs* of Lough Derg Monastery, lies in its pronounced Irish character. Details of its design – the flat-headed, cross-mullioned windows on the W side, and the open ground floor unprotected by a vault – suggest that it is late in date and of the early C17 rather than Elizabethan. It has indeed marked similarities to Derryhevenny in Co. Galway built as late as 1643, and like that castle it ignores completely the pattern established by Jacobean planters nearby, the Brookes at Donegal or the Scottish families that built castles at Balfour, Monea, and Tully.

Termon was the birthplace of the apostate Franciscan friar Myler MacGrath, the Catholic Bishop of Down in 1565, who two years later reformed under Queen Elizabeth and became Protestant Bishop of Clogher and then Archbishop of Cashel, a see that he enjoyed for thirty-two years. As he died in 1603 Myler can hardly have built the present castle, but his Protestantism probably gave his son James MacGrath (to whom the estate was re-granted in 1610) sufficient status in the Plantation situation to build such an extensive and so strong a house. The plan, a tower and an extensive bawn, is common enough for the early C17, but it is the character of the architecture that is distinctly Irish: the batter at the base of the tower, the stepped Irish battlements, and the aggressively pointed machicolated corbels on the wall head. The castle is near the shore, with a bawn about 85 ft wide extending some 60 ft to the NW. It is defended on the landward side by two round flankers, with gun loops to provide raking fire along the walls and on to the field. The tower, 37 ft by 31 ft, with a round stair projecting at the NE corner, appears to have been connected to the bawn at its NW and SE angles, leaving only the two sides that faced the lough exposed to attack. These are protected by horizontal gun loops in the basement and by a machicolated wall head.

The entrance, a low Gothic door in the SE corner, is defended by two close-range gun holes (one on the N side at heart height, the other hidden in the joint of the masonry at the apex of the arch). There is also a murder hole in the passage just inside.

The walls at ground level are 6 ft thick, diminishing in width in the upper floors. The main apartments on the top two floors were lit by handsome mullioned and transomed windows in the s w front. Traces of the fireplaces in these rooms remain, as well as the curve of the secondary stair that joined the top floors in the N W corner. The main stair in the round tower began only at first-floor level. At its entrance a stone hinged socket may still be seen. The big square window reveals are all massively simple. Termon was clearly always a severe place, devoid of interior architectural decoration.

In the campaign of 1649–50 Cromwellian troops under Colonel Henry Ireton bombarded Termon, demolishing the courtyard side of the tower house, which has remained a ruin ever since.

TEMPLECARNE GLEBE HOUSE. 1.5 km S W. Built in 1813, with a pleasant two-bay two-storey front with tripartite windows and a shallow slate roof. Irregular four-bay wing with a yard behind.

TEMPLECARNE PARISH CHURCH (C of I). Neo-Norman of c. 1838, very like Farrell's church at Ballyshannon, with the same shallow panelled side walls with rows of 'peg' corbels at the top. A five-bay hall with porch and bellcote. Box pews inside. – GATEPIERS. Mid C18, with ball finials.

PETTIGOE CATHOLIC CHURCH. Early C19. A six-bay hall with Georgian Gothic sash windows down one side. E bellcote in dressed stone. Inside, a primitive classical altar aedicule with a big broken pediment.

THE WATERFOOT. 2 km S W. Across the river from Termon Castle and therefore in Fermanagh. A pleasant Georgian house built by the Barton family, L-shaped, with a long, low, two-storeyed front of five windows overlooking the lough; the stairs are in the short arm behind. White harled, with wide overhanging eaves that look about 1790. The rooms inside have pretty doorcases and ceilings. To this house, about 1831, Col. H. W. Barton added a block at the w end and a kitchen wing, both to designs of *J. B. Keane*. Keane's block is also two-storeyed, but higher, with large windows, though in the same simple style with big eaves. Projecting from the kitchen wing is a charming circular larder. Horseshoe-shaped WALLED GARDEN N of the house.

CARN CHURCH RUINS. 2.5 km N. A graveyard with some C18 memorial slabs crudely carved with coats of arms and flanked by primitive columns.

Churches at CASHELENNY, 8 km N W, are both simple early C19

halls. The CATHOLIC CHURCH is of four bays, with pointed
windows, a w bellcote in stone, and a balanced porch and vestry
at either end; the CHURCH OF IRELAND, of three bays, has
Georgian Gothic sash-windows.

F5   PLUMBRIDGE   TY

A village at the foot of the narrow and steep valley of the Glenelly
River that runs uphill from here for about 15 km to the lower
slopes of Sawel, which at 2,240 ft is the highest peak in the Sperrin
range. The bald mountain heights form a bleak background to
the narrow valley, which has itself the air of a half-forgotten world
full of derelict thatched cottages, gardens run to seed, and a few
simple churches.

CHURCH OF THE SACRED HEART. By the bridge, in a field
  filled with beech trees. 1896. A big cruciform church in dark
  red rock-faced sandstone. Tower and incomplete belfry. Four-
  bay nave, arcaded across the transepts. Hipped pine-panelled
  roof to the sanctuary. Windows triple lancets and paired Dec
  lights with a quatrefoil rose above at the E end.

UPPER BADONEY PARISH CHURCH (C of I). 5.5 km E. 1784.
  Hall and tower type with Dec stone windows and a short
  chancel added by *Joseph Welland* in 1859. Two-stage battlemented tower, harled, with a cornice.

ST PATRICK. At Cranagh, 10.5 km E. Later C19. A seven-bay
  rendered hall with an end porch, chancel, buttresses, and bellcote. E window with geometrical tracery. Trussed hammerbeam
  roof of unusual extravagance. Opposite, the old Catholic
  church, T-plan, of 1814.

EDEN CHURCH. 1.5 km E. A five-bay harled hall with pointed
  windows.

CAMPBELL HOUSE. w of Plumbridge. A handsome six-bay
  harled farmhouse with some tripartite windows on the ground
  floor. Plaque: 'Hugh Campbell Built this House in the year of
  our Lord 1786 Most Noble Duke Argyll VIVEA NOSTRA
  VOCO.'

ST MARY. At Aughabrack, 7 km N. Built in 1897 by the Rev.
  J. McClinchey and reconstructed by the Rev. P. Gormley in
  1941, the later architect *W. J. Doherty*. Cruciform Gothic with
  a short apsed sanctuary. Ceiling panelled in pine.

POMEROY   TY H7

A small upland village on the crown of a hill granted to Sir Arthur Chichester by James I but said to derive its name from the gift of some apples made by a local peasant woman to William III – *pommes au roi* – in 1690. The present layout is due to the improvements begun in 1770 by the Rev. James Lowry, who, with typical c18 rationalism, planned a tidy square with the main street entering in the s E and s w corners and a third street joining in the middle of the N side. But the church, now in its centre, was originally 6.5 km away at Crossdernott.

ATADESERT PARISH CHURCH (C of I). A curious mixture, but an essential accent in the middle of the town square. Built in 1841 to relieve pressure on the parish church that could 'not afford sufficient accommodation for the congregation during the summer months' – swollen no doubt by visiting Lowrys with a consequent increased attendance by the tenantry. The church of 1841 is a simple four-bay hall with a skinny gable end, decorated with dummy lancets. To this a s aisle was added with paired lancets and high gable end, and a handsome and reassuringly solid three-storey belfry tower and squat spire at the w end. The tower and probably the aisle date from 1877 – after the disestablishment of the Church of Ireland – and were erected by John and Armar Lowry 'as a tribute of attachment to their birthplace'. The interior has a triple lancet E window, a rear gallery in the nave, and a single-chamfered triple arcade to the aisle.

CATHOLIC CHURCH. 1912 by *W. H. Byrne & Son.* A moderate T-plan church on the model advanced by Toye at Gortin, Ardara, and elsewhere – that is, a long hall with two-bay arcaded transepts. Built of squared rubble sandstone with granite quoins. Faintly Norman, with a w bellcote and a big wheel window in the gable. Colonnettes with cushion capitals round the door. The usual airy interior with a panelled pine roof with alternating braced trusses.

PRESBYTERIAN CHURCH. 1802, 'restored' in 1926. Gabled six-bay lancet hall with pretty quarry glass.

POMEROY HOUSE. The square stone house built by James Lowry about 1780 has been demolished. Only some outhouses remain. The estate is now a forestry school.

LOURDES GROTTO. Between the square and the Catholic church, backing on to the foundations of the original T-plan Catholic chapel. The tenacity of old ways in Pomeroy is well illustrated by the fact that about 900 Catholics still regularly attended open-air masses outside the village as late as 1846.

ST JOHN. 3 km ENE, at Slatequarry. 1843. A simple five-bay Gothic hall with a Dec E window. Built by W.McC.

POMEROY PARISH CHURCH. 6.5 km ESE, at Crossdernott. A typical later C18 hall and tower type church. The site was granted in 1778: the church consecrated in 1782. Tower in three stages with thin diagonal buttresses and a blind arcaded Gothic parapet like Carrickmore. N transept added in 1862 by *Welland & Gillespie*, who also replaced the nave windows with the present cusped Y-traceried designs.

PORT HALL *see* LIFFORD

A popular place for a seaside holiday, with villas and small hotels, all late C19, dotted about the s shore of Gweebarra Bay. The best buildings here are both on islands: the ruined churches on Inish-keel, accessible at low tide from Tramore Strand, and the fort on Doon Lough.

INISHKEEL CHURCHES AND CROSSES. This island was the site of an early Christian monastery of which St Conall Coel was abbot in the mid C6. The remains of the churches appear to date from the C13 and later. The cross slabs may be C8. – ST MARY'S CHURCH. To the E, a small nave, 17 ft by 32 ft, with a later chancel of 13 ft by 19 ft. The s and N walls of the chancel are almost complete, with a widely splayed narrow window opening of the C13 on the s side. Note too the rounded shaft on the s corner of the chancel. Only the s side of the nave remains to any height, rebuilt at its w end with curiously chan-nelled stones re-used in the wall. Pointed s door with segment-vaulted reveal inside. – ST CONALL'S CHURCH. A long rect-angular church with substantial remains of the E and w gables and the s wall. Built of shore boulders with granite trim to the door and windows, of which there are three, all narrow lancets. The effect of this building that has sagged and settled is very much that of an C18 romantic folly. It is however C13. The church is 49 ft long and rather narrow at 16½ ft. Portions of the s wall were rebuilt when St Conall's memorial stone was laid inside in 1967. – The CROSS SLABS are E of St Mary's Church. (1). The stem of a cross standing 4 ft high. The E face is covered with four repeated patterns of an elaborate interlace knot.

Raised slab shaft in the w face. (2). A cross slab with an incised Latin cross on each face filled with very worn interlace. On the e face two figure panels under the arms of the cross (barely visible); on the w a carving of a horse and a wheel with swan-like birds above the cross arms. Françoise Henry suggests that these may refer to the legend of the children of Lir who had been turned into swans and were restored to human form by St Brendan. Further e two c18 gravestones, one of 1727, both with primitive skull and crossbones like Humpty Dumpty.

DOON FORT. 1 km s of Portnoo. An oval fort with massive dry stone walls occupying an entire island in the middle of Doon Lough (boats are available at the e end of the lough). This fort must be compared with the Grianan of Ailech between Derry and Burt, with Dun Aengus and others in the Aran Islands, and with Staigue Fort in Kerry. For the visitor to Donegal it is the perfect complement to the Grianan; for while that sits high on a commanding hill, Doon rises menacingly from the black water that surrounds it. Forts were built as places of communal refuge in the centuries preceding the Christian era and survived in remote districts into the later Middle Ages. Conor O'Boyle, Tanist of Boylagh, was slain here by one of the rival O'Boyle factions as late as 1530.

The walls, built with a characteristic batter, rise to about 15 ft and are about 8 ft wide at the top, with a low parapet running round the outer edge. As at the Grianan there is one entrance only, a passage 15 ft deep in the middle of the s side, wide at first but tapering to 5 ft 9 in. inside. It is not roofed. Mural passages run from the entrance gate e and w, the latter rising by internal steps to the wall top. The passage roofs are of a beehive drystone construction. Within the oval enclosure four flights of steps lead to the top of the wall: one e of the entrance, another on the n wall opposite, and two facing each other and running in opposite directions at the w end of the s side. Conservation work was carried out here in 1954 by Donegal County Council on behalf of Bord Fáilte.

ST CONALL AND ST MARK, INISHKEEL PARISH (C of I). 1825–8. Tower and hall type church of coursed rubble with thin clasping buttresses to the tower and Georgian Gothic sash-windows.

KILTOORIS LOUGH RUINS. 3.5 km SW. The CASTLE on O'Boyle's Island is now little more than a section of wall with a mural passage. The CHURCH, by the edge of the lough, s of the island, has a w gable and parts of the s and n walls of a rectangular nave of $13\frac{1}{2}$ ft by 28 ft. Flat-headed door and window with stone lintels. A round hole in the stone for a pivot at the r. side of the door. Late medieval.

PORTORA CASTLE *see* ENNISKILLEN, p. 287

E2   PORTSALON   DO

A late C19 holiday HOTEL developed by the Earl of Leitrim, with battlemented tower, bay-windows, and crow-stepped gables (on a podium of montbretia), stands above a small harbour whose pier was extended in 1888–91. The hotel enjoys an unrivalled view along Ballymastocker Bay to Knockalla Head, where a dramatic scenic road was completed in 1970.

ALL SAINTS (C of I). 1962–3 by *W. L. Roworth*. A four-bay hall with triangular-headed windows, rubble stone surrounds, and a rubble porch and chancel. Half-hearted and thoroughly nasty architecture, though this is not the opinion of the clergy, who call it 'an outstanding example of what can be achieved with very limited resources'.

89 KNOCKALLA FORT. 5 km SE of Portsalon pier. An artillery ground and tower like those at Greencastle and Rathmullen, but the situation here is terrifying, with the ditch on the S side of the tower running down to a precipice. Like Rathmullen the tower has two windows, gun ports at basement level firing into the ditch, and a single fortified gate. To protect the tower from the hill the profile on the W has a stepped parapet with embrasures at the top for rifle fire. Early C19, built to control, with Dunree Fort and battery opposite, the entry to Lough Swilly. Now a private holiday house.

J2   PORTSTEWART   LD

Portstewart owes its first development in the early C19 to two local landowners – John Cromie and Henry O'Hara. Cromie built the first house in 1792, and it was he who named the town after the Stewarts of Ballyleish. From a few fishermen's huts it had by the 1830s become what Lewis calls 'a delightful and well-frequented residence' with a long line of villas extending the length of the shore. 'Look at the little snug harbour of Portstewart,' wrote Thackeray in 1842; 'a hideous new castle standing on a rock protects it on one side, a snug row of gentlemen's cottages curves round the shore facing northwards, a bath-house, an hotel, more smart houses face the beach westwards defended by another mound of rocks. In the centre of the little town stands a new-built church; the whole place has an air of comfort and neatness which is seldom seen in Ireland.' But the price of provincial refinement also struck Thackeray: he noted the 'demure heads in crimped caps peeping over blinds at him' as 'he walked on the beach. The sea was not more constant roaring than scandal was whispering.' This genteel society would not allow the railway company a station in the town but kept the trains at a mile's distance at Cromore Halt so that the other C19 resort just along the coast in Co. Antrim – Portrush – developed at the expense of Portstewart, which has remained much the smaller of the two north coast holiday towns.

AGHERTON PARISH CHURCH (C of I), in the Diamond. 1839. Originally a five-bay hall of squared rubble basalt with sandstone quoins and lancet windows. In the middle of one long side, a square entrance tower of four stages with battlements and slender finials. The upper two stages have polygonal shafts at the corners. Chancel and sacristy of 1879 by *Thomas Drew*, with a Norman chancel arch supported on paired colonnettes and a wagon roof. – PULPIT. 1893. Stone octagon with colonnettes. – MONUMENT. Colonel John Eliot Cairnes † 1847. Marble slab with martial trophies by *Thomas & W. Fitzpatrick* of Belfast.

Local faction is recorded in the story told by Mr Girvan of how the new church was first built opposite the ruins of Old Agherton Church; the population refused to walk the mile to it, however, so the present building took its place. The church was erected on Mr Cromie's property, much to the chagrin of Mr O'Hara, who put up opposite a row of thatched cottages with ash pits in front, let free to tenants, 'provided that they burn tar during hours of Divine Service on Sunday'.

ST MARY, STAR OF THE SEA. On the Crescent facing the sea. Lombardic Romanesque by *W. J. Moore* of Belfast, 1916. Very bold in brown basalt with a wealth of yellow sandstone detailing that in this sea-blown situation is still as bright and clean as if it were newly built. Three-bay front with a gabled central bay projecting over a large wheel window set in a circular arch. Outer bays with an arcaded upper floor. Offset campanile on the N side of the nave with a finely carved belfry stage. Inside, a wide Romanesque hall with wall-stop beams, opening on the S through a two-bay arcade to the Lady Chapel.

ADAM CLARKE MEMORIAL METHODIST CHURCH, Heath-

mount. 1861 by *W. J. Barre*. On top of a hill. Once an aggressive seaside fortalice with a jagged tower with flying buttresses
straddling the nave like a very picturesque reworking of the
Irish Franciscan Friary theme. Sadly, part of the tower was
blown down in 1884, and in 1914 the whole was removed and
the tower tidied away into a decorous gable. Nave and single-
bay chancel, s porch and – now – N and s gables in the centre
of the nave. Basalt and sandstone with Dec tracery.

PRESBYTERIAN CHURCH. 1905 by *Vincent Craig*, replacing an
earlier hall of 1827. Emphatically up-to-date, with flamboyant
Art Nouveau Gothic windows, segmental arches, scalloped
battlements to the tower, and loose hood mouldings that flow
about the façade. A big hall, with low transepts at the E end,
polygonal apse, and a tall, offset W tower – a curiously orthodox
plan for a Nonconformist congregation. Rendered, with red
sandstone details and a red tiled roof. Note the big buttress that
interrupts the main W window and the joggled keystones of the
main arches. Flimsy arcaded aisles inside.

TOWN HALL. 1934 by *B. Cowser*. In plum-red brick with a
Roman tile roof, Lutyensesque, with a symmetrical two-storey
front to the sea. Five thin windows in the middle of the first
floor open on to a balcony.

DOMINICAN CONVENT OF ST MARY. Perched on the edge
of the cliffs at the W end of the town. The core of the convent
is the seaside toy castle built by Henry O'Hara in 1834. The
Ordnance Survey Memoirs thought it 'displayed little taste',
and indeed it was very old-fashioned for its date – a square
stucco castle of three storeys with square corner towers rising
a little higher than the body of the house. When O'Hara died
ten years later the house was enlarged. Two canted bays were
built out from, and entirely filled the space between, the corner
towers on the N and W sides and a new seven-bay battlemented
front was built across the s side. The only remaining glimpse
of the old castle is at the back of the convent complex, where
its E side remains largely unaltered with quaint pointed windows and circular lights to the attic storey. The rubble battlemented wall round the cliff path was built about this time,
reputedly for famine relief. The convent was bought in 1917
by the Dominican sisters, who added the battlemented E wing
in 1929 and the CHAPEL by *Padraig Gregory* in 1935. The
modern SCHOOL BLOCK continuing the line of these buildings
is by *Brian Gregory*, 1963–5.

TOUR

Though there is little in Portstewart of individual quality, the situation of the town, the sea air, and the general spruceness will recommend a walk to many. The parish church in the DIA-MOND, a square of mostly early C19 two-storey houses, is an obvious starting point. From here CHURCH STREET, parallel to the main frontage along the shore, leads NE past the two Nonconformist churches to the high ground at Heathmount. Here the road turns r. and then l., skirting an open space of common, and then descends to the shore road at the top of the town. Turn l. here to return along the entire length of THE PRO-MENADE, Portstewart's major attraction, made up for the most part of substantial three- and four-storey houses with brightly painted fronts, facing a small fishing HARBOUR at the N end. About the middle is a large three-storey double house with nice segmental bows and a central carriage arch, now called Toronto House and Foyle View. The WAR MEMORIAL STATUE of 1924 is by *Roslyn* of London.

At its s end The Promenade leads into THE CRESCENT, past the Catholic church and town hall to the cliff path that skirts the wall of O'Hara's castle and leads to LOW ROCK CASTLE, a dumpy two-storey villa with big drum towers at either end built about 1820. Nearby at THE BIRRINS is a rubble basalt ICE HOUSE built on the shore and covered with grass sods. Brick-vaulted within. From here a path goes up from the shore to suburban development that leads l. back to the Diamond.

NEIGHBOURHOOD

AGHERTON OLD CHURCH RUINS. 1.5 km S. Recorded in the papal taxation roll in 1305 and in the Down Survey of 1656. Dismantled in 1826. The walls remain of a rectangular church built of lime and basalt stones. The W gable is intact. Three segment-headed windows and a door at the S side.

CROMORE HOUSE. 1.5 km SE. Originally Ballyleish, a Stewart house which by 1778 had passed to the Cromie family. It is of two dates. The earlier centre is a four-bay, two-storey house of dressed sandstone on a semi-basement with diamond-cut quoins at the rear, and a low office wing on the E, seven-bay on a basement – in a countrified Palladian style. A volume of plans sold in the 1960s showed that there were once two office pavilions, or two were intended, to flank the main block.

In 1834 John Cromie enlarged Ballyleish, and it was probably he who changed its name. Between the main house and office wing he added a new block as high as the old house with another at the w end to balance the main elevation. The new ends are two-bay at the back of the house but have enormous square windows, slightly stepped forward, on the s front. Linked to these is a pair of large Doric porticoes, that on the E fronting the office wing and forming an entrance to the house, that on the w built as a free-standing conservatory to balance the façade. No architect is known for either portion of the house, but both were more than competent. The interior has a fine hall, paved in black and white marble, with a screen of Ionic columns and an exceptionally fine mid C18 CHIMNEYPIECE in coloured marble with female herms and Rococo frills and rosettes.

The GATE LODGE, with an arcaded gabled porch, is of a type often employed by *Charles Lanyon*, who might conceivably have superintended the additions to the house.

BALLYREAGH CASTLE. 3 km NE, on the coast. Though this C16 promontory fort is recorded in the *Preliminary Survey of Ancient Monuments of Northern Ireland* of 1940, in the late 1960s the local authority tidied up the coast-line and removed 55 ft of a wall about 4 ft thick that stood intact to a height of 13 ft for almost half its length and had splayed musket loops on the interior. The wall was built at the head of a ditch cut across a triangular promontory with sheer cliffs rising to about 15 m (50 ft) as its protection on the E and w. The local authority could not remove the promontory, but since its defensive wall has disappeared the place is hard to find. The fort belonged to the McHenrys, whose garrison fled in 1584 at the approach of Sir John Perrot.

BALLYWILLAN OLD CHURCH. 4 km E. The ruins of a big barn-like church standing virtually intact in a high windswept grave-yard. Until 1842, when it was abandoned, this was the only pre-Reformation church in Co. Derry still in use. It is built of rough-coursed basalt with limestone trim and preserves more features than usual in ruined churches in Ulster. The plan is long, 75 ft by 16 ft inside, and various dates are represented in the masonry. First, on the N wall, two narrow round-headed lancets with curious elongated hood mouldings, like those of St Molaise's church, Devenish, which cannot be later than the early C13. Inside on the E wall is a round-headed AUMBRY with clustered roll-mouldings of a similar date. The E window had two paired lancets probably of the C14, but only traces of their arches remain above the segment-headed opening of the present C17 E window. The w gable has one upper lancet. – MONUMENT. In the s w corner of the church a mid C18 slabstone with heraldic achievement.

MAGHERABOY HOUSE. 4 km E. A mid C19 stuccoed villa with rich Italianate detailing. Three-bay, two-storey, with an Ionic pedimented porch and single-storey canted bays on each side. Aedicule windows and console cornice above. Rich plasterwork cornices inside.

BALLYWILLAN PRESBYTERIAN CHURCH. 4 km E. 1899 by *W. J. Anderson* of Coleraine. T-shaped, with an ambitous Institutional Gothic tower of Perp character, offset beside the w gable. Black basalt with sandstone trim.

PREHEN *see* LONDONDERRY, p. 405

RAMELTON   DO *E3*

TULLYAUGHNISH OLD CHURCH. Built by Sir William Stewart and almost completed at the time of Pynnar's Survey of 1619. The usual long rectangular hall, 26 ft by 72 ft inside. The walls and gables all stand to their original height, with massive buttresses at the E end. The most interesting feature is the well preserved Perp E window of four lights with rather jumbled mullions above. The confusion and debased appearance are caused by a tracery dagger re-used from a late medieval church and clumsily incorporated upside down above the middle mullion. Outside on the gable over the window is a highly decorated C12 stone with an arch of bead moulding and two beasts, taken from the Romanesque church of St Columb on Aughnish Island.

TULLYAUGHNISH PARISH CHURCH (C of I). In hilly country a little s of the town. 1822–6 by '*Mr Nixon* of Strabane architect'. A six-bay buttressed lancet hall with a huge roof almost as high as the tower it adjoins. This was raised in the mid C19. Not attractive, though obviously an expensive job, with lots of ashlar work.

ST MARY. A large cruciform church in coursed stone rubble with provision for a centrally placed w tower, never completed. Wide nave of three bays with short transepts lit by three lancet gable windows and starred trefoils at the sides. E window geometrical Dec. Statue in a niche over the tower door. It looks about 1880.

FIRST RAMELTON PRESBYTERIAN CHURCH. 1906 by *Young*

& Mackenzie. A big hall with a lavish Perp front. Turreted stair
to the gallery N, gabled centre, and a big three-storey tower
with a broach-spire on the S. Built of coursed slate rubble with
red sandstone trim. The foundation stone was laid on 3 August
1906 by Lt. Col. John Campbell Fullerton, perhaps a descen-
dendant of Sir James Fullerton to whom so much of Donegal
had been granted by James I.

SCOTS CHURCH. A three-bay gabled Gothic hall of 1838 renovated in 1905, when the front gained stone buttresses, a respectable Gothic door, and stone windows with Dec tracery.

TOUR

Ramelton is one of the few towns in Donegal that is large enough
and sufficiently urban in character to justify a peregrination.
Its population is still under 1,000, but the concentration of the
buildings all on one side of the river and principally on one
side of the street gives it an apparent extent that invites perusal.
The town was founded in the C17 by Sir William Stewart, one
of the principal beneficiaries of the Jacobean Plantation, who
by 1620 had built forty-five houses. The River Leannan, flowing in a broad slow reach and navigable as far as Ramelton,
was the key to its prosperity, a prosperity that was marked by
corn mills, a brewery, bleach greens, linen works, and a salmon
fishery, all established by the early C19.

The main street, extending in a slow curve along the river frontage, is the place to start. It runs almost half a mile from Bridge
End on the W to the quays on the E. It is lined by trees and
has much of the air of an C18 mall, with a succession of big
three-storey Georgian houses at the W end facing the river. The
NORTHERN BANK, like a large classical villa in sandstone and
brick, is by *G. W. Ferguson*, 1903. About half-way along, the
main street divides at a small early C19 house, rubble with brick
trim. From here the river is lined by substantial warehouses
with a particularly fine group of four big buildings at the
extreme E end looking back towards the town. Mid C19. One
warehouse is dated 1864. Behind these is a good late Georgian
house of *c.* 1820, a three-bay, three-storey block with a hipped
roof, central chimneys, and pretty fanlight doorway. The
RAMELTON PUBLIC HALL facing it dates from 1878 and is
by *Young & Mackenzie*. It is a vigorous gabled hall in squared
green rubble stone with yellow brick trim. Paired entrance
doors below a big balcony; three round-headed lancets above.
From here the street runs uphill to the SW, where the spire of

the Presbyterian church on the Letterkenny Road can be seen.
Opposite are the old church ruins. The churches are already
out of the town in an open setting. All the roads downhill lead
back to the Main Street.

NEIGHBOURHOOD

KILLYDONNELL FRIARY. 3.5 km SW. Founded in 1471 by Cal-
vagh O'Donnell as a Franciscan Tertiary house; suppressed
about 1603, when the friars' lands were granted to Captain Basil
Brooke. The ruins comprise a church of 20½ ft by 80 ft with a
deep S transept 32 ft long with paired altar recesses on the E
side, now used for family burying grounds. Conventual buildings remain on the N and E sides enclosing a space where
cloisters may have been. The walls are generally obscured by
ivy and few architectural details can be seen. The S chancel window is a segment-headed recess with a relieving arch. E window
Dec, with remains of a quatrefoil in the centre. On the N wall
E end are traces of a moulded surround to a cavity, possibly once
sedilia. In the NE range the buildings are barrel-vaulted. The
friary is in the grounds of Fort Stewart and contains the mausoleum of the family made out of one of these vaulted rooms.

OLD FORT STEWART. 5 km E, by the shore below Ballygreen
Point. Of the fortified house and bawn erected by Sir William
Stewart about 1619 only a circular and a salient flanker of the
bawn remain. The walls are 4½ ft thick. The circular flanker is
among shrubs by the shore. The salient flanker, exceedingly
sharp like the bow of a ship, is stranded in the middle of a field
and covered in luxuriant ivy. The walls are entire, 24 ft long,
with a rebate 4 ft deep checked for musket fire. The bawn was
presumably demolished to provide stone for the present Fort
Stewart House.

FORT STEWART. 4 km ESE. A large, plain country house of the
mid C18. The main front is three-storey, of seven bays, with
two-bay, single-storey wings continuing in a direct line with
the front of the house. N wing heightened later. An enormous
yard with farm offices behind. In 1823 *John Hargrave* of Dublin
made designs for Sir James Stewart for a Picturesque Italianate
house with a round tower like Nash's Cronkhill to replace the
present building. Nothing came of this, but the present Ionic
porch and pretty entrance hall with segmental plaster vaulting
may well be his work. The plasterwork in the main ground-
floor rooms is also early C19.

FERRY HOUSE by the shore on this estate is a low, two-storey, seven-bay block – possibly originally thatched. Mid C18 panelled doors inside.

ARDRUMMAN HOUSE. 4 km SSE. Minimally Tudor, of about 1830. A gabled house with label mouldings and mullioned sash-windows. Two-storey: the front to the lough three symmetrical bays. Entrance front seven-bay, irregular.

CASTLEGROVE. 5.5 km S. The oldest part is supposed to date from 1695, when the Grove family moved from Castle Shannahan. It has been twice rebuilt since then. The present appearance is that of a large, trim 1820s house. Of two storeys, with a shallow slate roof behind the eaves cornice. Four irregularly spaced windows on the entrance side, and four larger, regular ones round the corner facing the lough. The Tuscan doorcase with flanking windows and forward-stepped centre offers the clue as to how the house developed. It is obviously mid C18 and equally obviously not in its original position. It opens to a hall and then, in the middle of the house, to a staircase set at r. angles to the entrance front. What appears to have happened, and this is borne out by the floor levels upstairs, is that a mid C18 house, two rooms deep and looking out to the lough, has had an extra suite of rooms built in front of it, blocking the original door on the E, which was then moved round to the front. The new rooms have Greek border plasterwork and rosettes. Adjoining the house on the W is a large Regency conservatory.

CLARAGH. 2.5 km WSW. A very odd late Victorian house: odd in its situation with the main door tucked against a hill thickly planted with trees; odd in its severe clean lines; and oddest in its curious red brick mouldings, doors, and chimneys set against squared rubble walls of red sandstone. There is a picturesque conservatory on the garden front shielding the service wing. The doors and stair rails inside look about 1880.

MOYAGH HOUSE. 4 km WNW. An L-shaped two-storey villa by *J. G. Ferguson*, 1878, burnt in 1912 and rebuilt in 1919 by *J. H. H. Swiney*, using the original walls. The present cast-iron Gothic veranda is composed of pieces of Strabane railway station.

A place of considerable interest: yet a visitor arriving in the triangular Diamond at Raphoe will be surprised to discover that he is in a cathedral town. The small scale of the place, the meagre church, despite its high tower, and the hills and hedgerows all round have little in common with most European episcopal capitals. Raphoe is very Irish: Irish in its lack of consequence and in the clear break that its buildings mark in the cultural and religious life of the place.

The origins of Raphoe are early Christian. St Colmcille founded a monastery here in the C6 and the cathedral is dedicated to Adamnan, or St Eunan, a native of Raphoe who was a monk here before he became Abbot of Iona in 679. However this may be, all that is left to record the early church is two pieces of a carved lintel and the dedication. Of medieval Raphoe fine sedilia and some stone details remain. Everything else is post-Reformation, Protestant and militantly so. The triangular plan of the Diamond dates from the C17 Plantation. The substantial houses that line its sides are of the Georgian ascendancy, while from a hill rising higher than the cathedral itself ruins of the fort-like bishop's palace dominate the town.

ST EUNAN'S CATHEDRAL (C of I). The Georgian clergy of the Established Church in Ireland took a rather simple view of church architecture. Buildings were best if they could be seen for miles around; so Raphoe Cathedral was given its enormous plain tower in 1737. Built of coursed rubble, it is the first thing one sees, four storeys high and checked in slightly at each floor. It has a round-headed belfry opening on each side at the third storey, a clock on the fourth, and battlements at the top. The nave that it shields from view is little wider than the tower, probably early C17, and has a low pitched roof that rises to barely half the height of the second storey of the tower. Projecting from the middle of the s side of the nave is a striking Baroque porch with volute-scrolled gable and depressed round-headed arch. It is possibly Jacobean, though more probably, to judge from the more elaborate door inside, later C17. The choir in a direct line E is as long as the nave and made to look bigger with a higher-pitched roof and bold E gable. All C13 in appearance, though the crisp masonry marks the chancel out as a restoration of 1892.

Such is the outside appearance of St Eunan's. Fragments of earlier work remain in or have been incorporated into the walls, but the basic structure today is post-medieval, built up and worked over by a succession of Protestant bishops. Of these the first was George Montgomery, chaplain to James I, by whom he was nominated Bishop of Raphoe, of Clogher, and of Derry, all in 1605. A re-used lintel in the s porch with part

of an inscription by Bishop Andrew Knox suggests that it was
he, Montgomery's successor, who rebuilt the nave (but not the
porch), re-using fragments of C15 sculptural detail, notably two
foliated label stops to the mullioned window on the S side.
Bishop John Lesley built the palace from 1636, demolishing
the remains of the round tower of the old monastery to do so.
In 1702, when John Pooley succeeded as Bishop, the complete
rebuilding of the cathedral that was to be continued by his successor, Bishop Nicholas Foster, began. Pooley donated the font
in 1706 and left a legacy to add N and S transepts to the church
– a programme that was carried out by Foster from 1716, before
he added the tower at his own expense. Thus the cathedral
became a plain cruciform structure, harled outside, and fitted
up with box pews, an Ionic bishop's throne with tester, a gallery, and plastered walls within.

This pleased well enough for a century or so; then criticism
began. In 1876 *The Architect* characterized the cathedral as 'the
most neglected church in the diocese though situated in the
richest part of Donegal'. In 1888 *Thomas Drew* contributed a
detailed article on the results of excavations in the graveyard
and explorations behind the plaster, and in 1892 a medievaliz-
ing re-restoration began under his direction. Originally he
proposed merely to screen the C18 transepts with a new arcade,
but in the executed scheme they were completely removed and
the choir extended back to abut directly on to the end of the
nave.

INTERIOR. Drew's interior is a fine one: certainly better
than the Georgian design it replaces, if the big, bare spaces of
Clogher Cathedral may be taken as a guide. The church is
approached through the CONSISTORY COURT – a chamber
redolent of characters from Trollope that doubles as a baptistery. Small box pews before the bench and Bishop Pooley's
FONT of 1706, a sixteen-sided alabaster bowl on a circular shaft,
on the N side. The court, with the vestry on the S, occupies the
first 14 ft of the C17 nave. Within the church proper, the nave
is roofed with exposed kingpost trusses. A double-chamfered
chancel arch, supported on half-round columns, opens to the
choir – the nave seating running through to the level of the old
transepts – and here the effect of Drew's higher roof is properly
felt, with robustly braced trusses that repeat the profile of the
arch stepping E to the triple lancet window. The 'restoration'
was inspired by the discovery of three SEDILIA arches and
a PISCINA recess at the E end of the S wall, with a small window

above. The mouldings, capitals with trefoil leaves, and nail-head bands are of C13 character and prompted Drew to introduce further features of this date, namely the E window, and most particularly the effective ranges of lancets with wide splays that meet at a sharp arris and return to the next lancet. Similar windows appear in the C13 cathedrals at Cashel and Ardfert and are presumably Drew's sources. Here there are four such lancets on the S wall, to the N two.

FURNISHINGS. SCULPTURE. In the vestibule the l. half of an early Christian carved lintel stone of the late C9 to early C10. 16 The style is close to that of the crosses at Armagh and Monasterboice, with stumpy rounded figures packed into a tight space and filling it completely. The subject is the Arrest in the Garden. Christ is held by two figures in the centre with Peter (the third figure from the l.) cutting off the ear of one of them, Malchus, the servant of the high priest. This panel was once thought to be the base of a cross: that it is a lintel is apparent by its continuation in a now much battered stone built into the outside N wall of the nave. In the top r. hand corner the outstretched arm of Christ on the cross, Christ's head, and an angel hovering above may be made out, indicating that the central scene of the lintel was a Crucifixion that links up with the small kneeling figure on the extreme r. of the panel in the vestibule. These fragments are presumably from the W portal of the main church of the early monastery. – Inside the S porch, fragments of late C15 sculpture, notably the stiff pictorial scene of a stag attacked by dogs worked into a label stop. – STAINED GLASS. In the S choir windows the Evangelists, 1906, signed *Olahta Theirinn.* – PULPIT. A late C19 white stone octagon with colonnettes. – BISHOP'S THRONE. Oak chair dated 1665. – MONUMENTS. Tablet to the wife of Dean Adair, 1618. – Alice Samwells Moore, wife of Bishop Hopkins, 1681, a Corinthian aedicule with an open segmental pediment and a coat of arms. – The Rev. William Bisset, 1834, a large Jacobean Revival mural tablet.

BISHOP'S PALACE. The typical Irish architectural has-been, 41 tenanted by pigeons and cows. The palace was built as a fortress by Bishop John Lesley in 1636 to overawe the local populace. It was taken by Cromwellian soldiers in 1650 and plundered by the troops of James II in 1688. It was restored under Bishop Pooley and again about the mid C18, when large windows were made in its walls. Shortly after 1835, when the Protestant diocese of Raphoe was united with Derry, the building was burnt down by a man who hoped to obtain a cheaper lease of the demesne if there were no residence on it.

The gutted shell today offers evidence of different dates of work that is not easy to make out, and becomes more complex as the walls rise higher. The plan, a typical Renaissance fortified palace – things like it are in Lorini's *Fortificationi* of 1609 – is a square, 46 ft inside, divided symmetrically by a spine wall (now incomplete) and fortified at each corner by a salient-angled bastion-like tower, 12½ ft square inside, with shot holes to cover the fronts of the house. The walls, of coursed rubble, are 4 ft thick and harled on the exterior. All this is Bishop Lesley's work, as are the small double-barred C17 windows with splayed reveals in the basement of each tower. The bishop's foundation stone is on the NE tower, inscribed: IO LESLAEVS EPS RAPOT IMVM POSVIT LAPIDEM 17 MAII 1636 SUPREMVM 19 AVG 1637 TRANSLAT SVAE 5°. Much C18 brickwork inside. The W tower is cross-vaulted in brick at basement level. On the main (E) front a handsome Gibbs surround with pediment over the door is identical to *Michael Priestley*'s door at Lifford Court House and suggests that he may have been responsible for the C18 rebuilding.

The palace is now of four storeys, counting the basement. Lesley's work perhaps rose no higher than a little below the top of the second main floor. Here the salients on the towers are dispensed with and the walls check back to a square form. The top floor, now battlemented with curious dummy bartizans, was remodelled by the last bishop, William Bisset, shortly after his elevation. The evidence of the window returns at this level on the E and W fronts suggests that the attic floor was lower in the C18 and lit by semicircular lights. The coats of arms on the E front might further explain the building's story.

OLD ROYAL SCHOOL, immediately N of the palace ruins. Founded by James I in 1608, rebuilt in 1737. A two-storey, five-bay block extended (in the late C18?) by an extra storey (note the extra height between the first- and second-floor windows) and by the addition of single-bay projecting wings that reproduce the English Palladian formula of a terminal Venetian window, surmounted here by a tripartite design rather too high up. Perhaps the original school had single-bay wings flanking the two-storey block. From the mid C18 the E wing served as the Diocesan Library.

ST EUNAN. On the Convoy Road. A delightful small church of 1874 by *Timothy Hevey* and a notable monument in the revived Hiberno-Romanesque style. Admirably economical. A gabled hall with a high roof rising without intermission into a semicircular apse, in form reminiscent of James Brooks's London churches of the 1860s which Hevey, as he spent years working as a draughtsman for *The Irish Builder*, will have known. And Hevey gave Raphoe back its round tower status by means of a belfry attached to the N side of the W gable, neatly adapted as a stair to the gallery inside, ending outside in the characteristic conical roof, here in slate. Spare and simple interior, with a braced-truss pine roof and gallery. The trusses round the apse are supported on detached column shafts with Celtic-pattern capitals on figure head corbels. – ALTAR FLOOR. Interlaced pattern in mosaic with a central pelican.

PRESBYTERIAN CHURCHES. There are two, almost identical. The earlier one in the Diamond now functions as a hall. It has a cement-rendered classical front of 1860, pedimented, with Ionic pilasters and a recessed centre with two Ionic columns. A four-bay church lies behind, with rounded windows and a hall below. The second church, in the Convoy Road, is of 1876, bigger and just the same except that it lacks the free-standing columns and has a curious bracketed order.

The W side of the DIAMOND contains the best houses: three of the mid C18 at the S end, and the CLERGY WIDOWS' HOUSE founded by Bishop Foster at the N end, a substantial three-bay, three-storey design with an ashlar stone front. In the centre of the Diamond the MARKET HOUSE, early C19, of unusual form, with a yard enclosed by pyramid pavilions. Sadly neglected at the time of writing.

OAKFIELD. 1.5 km NE. Built as the Deanery in 1739 at a cost 56 of £1,680 and happily still complete. Like Bogay House nearby (*see* Newtowncunningham), the elevations still have a C17 character, or at latest Queen Anne. A neat two-storey block, square, with five regular bays to the E, S and W and a screened yard to the N. Wide eaves on a stone cornice with a stone string course immediately below. Three dormers over the centre bays of the E and W fronts and a Tuscan aedicule to the main door. In other words the entrance front is not essentially different from Inigo Jones's design for Lord Maltravers at Lothbury in the City of London of 1638 – but Oakfield is over 100 years later! Such is the provincial time-lag. Inside, some nice C18 detail remains: a good scale-and-platt stair with turned timber balusters, lugged door surrounds, and a study with original wainscot panelling. The drawing room was altered in the early c19, when the windows were lowered and the doors gained fluted entablatures. Basement vaulted in brick.

Rathmullen is one of the prettiest villages in Donegal: pretty for its sandy beaches, painted houses, and the mature trees that skirt the surroundings; and a village worthy of the name for its concentration of churches, houses, a friary, castle, and fort all in a small area. Never a famous place, it has witnessed at least two historic Irish happenings: the capture in 1587 of Red Hugh O'Donnell, who was lured aboard a disguised merchant ship to sample wines and was carried a prisoner of Deputy Perrot to Dublin; and the flight of the Earls of Tyrone and Tyrconnell, who left their native country on 14 September 1607 in a Spanish ship that had been sent to Rathmullen.

St Mary's Friary. The Carmelite friary, dedicated to the Blessed Virgin Mary, was founded according to the records of the Irish Province of the Order in 1403. Most accounts however give the date of the foundation as 1516, the year in which the Four Masters record the fall of Rathmullen Castle to an O'Donnell attack; so it may be that the friary was restored in that year or refounded after the Mac Sweeny lords of Fanad returned to the place. The 'founder' of this period was Owen Roe Mac Sweeny. The friars remained at St Mary's till 1595, when their church was plundered by George Bingham, who sailed into Lough Swilly from Sligo and carried away vestments, chalices, and other objects. Bingham was later murdered by one of the crew. According to the Four Masters, the friars returned to restore the buildings, which are shown complete with a N range and orchard in a map made of the English campaign in Lough Swilly in 1599. At the Plantation the friary was granted to Sir James Fullerton, who assigned the buildings to Sir Ralph Bingley for use as a barracks. About 1617 the Protestant Bishop of Raphoe, Andrew Knox, obtained the manor from Turlogh Oge Mac Sweeny and converted the buildings into a fortified house, with the chancel retained as a private chapel. Later in the c17 this was used as the parish church. It was abandoned only in 1814.

36   The double function served by the friary in its later years is evident in the buildings that remain today. Of the church there is the chancel, chancel tower, and some remains of conventual buildings to the N. Bishop Knox's house occupies the

s transept and the nave, both considerably heightened and rebuilt.

The original friary plan was a standard one; a long church, almost 80 ft by 21 ft wide, with side altars in a s transept, and the living quarters to the N on a line with the side of the chancel. A cloister, now vanished, was in the NW corner. (The arrangement is essentially the same as that of the C15 Franciscan houses at Donegal and Killydonnell and many others.) Normally a friary church was divided into an area for the laity, the nave, and an area for the friars, the chancel. The division, which was at first made by a wooden screen, came to be marked by a tower crossing the nave, as here, with a double-arched vestibule between the two main spaces. As often happens in Irish friaries, the tower is much smaller in plan than the nave that it crosses, rising like a big square chimney through the ridge of the roof. With such a plan, the walls to support the tower must impinge on the space of the church, reducing the width of the crossing arches to modest – and one might add inexpensive – proportions. The result inside is visually very characteristic, for the arched crossing focuses the view from the nave on to the altar and E window and almost completely screens the sides of the chancel. Outside, a smaller square tower with spiral staircase was added (later?) on the s of the crossing tower, giving the friary a memorable profile with a thin but now unusually wide tower rising above the ruins.

Architectural details from the original buildings are limited. The E window was a complex three-light cusped design, mid C15, with a tracery pattern that is difficult to reconstruct convincingly. s chancel window two-light Dec, with a vesica-shaped head and an elaborate hood moulding with label stops carved with faces. Double-chamfered crossing arches, the inner supported on tapering stops with a crudely moulded impost cornice. Perhaps this is the work of 1516. The N door in the vestibule leads to the cloisters and friars' quarters of which the E wall and N gable remain. In the gable is a cross-mullioned window checked on the inside to take wooden shutters in the lower lights. Beside it, a stair in the thickness of the gable leads to a corner bartizan added by Bishop Knox. Note at the top of the window reveal the pierced stone to provide a pivot for the door to the stair. More alterations appear on the transept E wall, with two arched reveals walled up by the Bishop, who replaced them with small mullioned two-light windows with segmental arches inside. Between is a fireplace which looks rather old-fashioned for the early C17 but is presumably the Bishop's work as well.

The rest of the friary is now the fortified house. The transept S gable, with three flat-headed mullioned windows under label mouldings, is like that of an English manor, but round the corner the w side and the nave are emphatically Scottish: the building has become a typical L-shaped tower house with even a projecting square in the re-entrant angle that will have housed the main stair. The door is here, on the w wall, with a moulded sandstone frame, surmounted by the initials AN KN SE and the date 1618 (now almost illegible). Above the door by a chimney-breast is a small machicolation to protect it. The windows have typically Scottish half-round mouldings, and the corners of the nave are protected at roof level by two fine angle bartizans on moulded corbel courses. On the w gable, which is crow-stepped, two jagged brick chimneys shaped like eight-pointed stars. Inside, the interest of Bishop Knox's house is slight. None of the subdivisions remains, the windows are walled up, and most of the N wall has been demolished.

RATHMULLEN FORT. The C16 military map referred to above shows a castle similar to Inch on the point now marked by trees a little SW from the friary. A village cross stood between the two. Castle and cross have vanished, but the strategic significance of the site did not escape a wartime administration haunted by the memory of Wolfe Tone's arrival in Lough Swilly in the *Hoche* in '98 and by the fear of another French-backed Irish rising. The fort, designed about 1810 in conjunction with the battery on Inch Island, is the result. Devotees of military architecture will find it an evocative monument. A battered ashlar tower of five sides, surrounded by a ditch and a steep grass glacis, defends the fort on the landward side. Gun ports at basement level are trained along the ditch. The gate, fortified by three gun ports on either side, is in the S ditch. The tower, entered from the court at first-floor level and lit by one window N and S, has a single vaulted room with vaulted cellars below. On the roof are circular mountings for two guns with 360-degree cover. The walls of the enclosure have arcaded case-mates and emplacements for five guns along the shore side. In the present century the escarpment has proved a good spot to grow cabbages and leeks.

ST COLUMB, KILLYGARVAN PARISH (C of I). 1814. A small hall and tower type church. The tower is of ashlar blocks in three stages with diagonal buttresses but no pinnacles. Three-bay hall. Chancel and interior refitted by *Hume Babington* and *R. E. Buchanan* in 1887. Modest but unspoilt, with a pine-panelled ceiling and a panel-fronted gallery. – STAINED GLASS. In the N window a pretty, early Victorian design with Evangelists' symbols and bright, clear colours. In memory of Thomas Batt of Rathmullen House, † 1857.

ST JOSEPH. Gothic, of *c.* 1900. A rendered six-bay hall with stone trim and stone buttresses. Paired lancets flank a statue of St Joseph on the W gable. High kingpost trussed and braced roof with panelled ceiling inside. A decent, tidy design.

PRESBYTERIAN CHURCH. 1872. A chunky Gothic hall in squared rubble, five-bay, with bellcote and S porch beside the gabled end.

GLENCROSS CHURCH. 3 km NW, on a desolate moorland site. Built in 1792 by the Rev. D. J. McElwee, a large T-plan church with crossed Y-tracery lancets in timber and clasping buttresses with finials to the entrance gable. Otherwise utterly plain.

GLENALLA CHURCH (C of I). 5.5 km W. A charming exercise in Victorian high-mindedness (or high-handedness) built *c.* 1870 by Thomas Bernard Hart († 1880), 'that his tenants living among secluded mountains might worship therein to the Glory of God'. A pleasant, unobtrusive little church, Dec Gothic, with white tracery and trim to contrast with the local stone, bands of fish-tail slates on the high roof, and an arcaded bellcote with a solid stone spire poised precariously on the gable between nave and chancel. Double-chamfered chancel arch. Light and bright inside.

GLENALLA HOUSE, beside the church, is large, mid C19, of no special interest or style, but its COTTAGES and SCHOOL are picturesque with gables, bargeboards, and quarry glass.

Between Rathmullen and Kinnegar Strand to the N are two houses, RATHMULLEN HOUSE (originally The Lodge), stuccoed early C19, built by Lt. Col. Knox, with three canted bays with wide overhanging eaves on the main front, and FORT ROYAL, a classical Italianate house with entrance tower built by Charles Rae in 1807 and enlarged by him about 1837. Both are now hotels.

RAY

DO *C2*

RAYMUNTERDONEY OLD CHURCH. The ruins of a rectangular late C16 or C17 church sitting up in a walled graveyard by the river Ray. The four wide segment-headed windows on the S

wall do not look early, though the w door has a pointed head.
Remains of a C17 mural tablet inside on the w wall.

HIGH CROSS. Lying on the grass in front of the church ruins
a plain cross, 20 ft 9 in. high, with a pierced nimbus and two
raised squares on the ends of the cross bar. It is broken into
four pieces and has a hole through the shaft at the lower end.
The cross, carved from Muckish stone, is said to have been intended for Tory Island but was given rather reluctantly by St
Colmcille to one of his disciples, Fionán, who had recovered
his prayer book for him. Such a pretty story can hardly relate
to what is lying in the grass now. The scale and design are of
a mature High Cross pattern of the C10 and certainly not of
the mid C6 of St Colmcille. The holed stone disc at its foot and
another in the church are ancient mill stones. The fragment
of a BULLAUN and PILLAR STONE also in the graveyard are
presumed to date from an early Celtic foundation on the site.

ST PAUL, RAYMUNTERDONEY PARISH (C of I). 2.5 km E of
Falcarragh, by the road. A three-bay harled hall with w porch
built in 1803 for £500. Its Dec windows in stone and low N
aisle were added in 1864.

RAY GLEBE HOUSE. E from the church across the road. A big
rectangular rectory, three-bay, three-storey, with centrally
massed chimney. Rather like *William Farrell*'s work.

A district on the w shore of Lough Foyle between Moville and
Muff with church ruins, rural churches, and two substantial
houses in the vicinity.

ST FINIAN, UPPER MOVILLE PARISH CHURCH (C of I). 1850
by *Joseph Welland*, consecrated in 1853. A chunky cruciform
church, very typical of its architect, with a three-bay lancet
nave, short transepts, chancel, w porch, and lumpy bellcote.
All in sharp square coursed rubble with sandstone dressings.
The transepts lit by paired lancets with a sexfoil above; triple-
lancet E window. Interior with transept arches and crossed
trusses before the chancel.

In the churchyard are the ruins of the FORMER CHURCH
built in 1747 by Col. Edward Cary of Whitecastle and Edward
Cary of Castle Cary, a big three-bay hall with a round-headed
E window and the remains of a bellcote.

ST COLUMBA. 3 km SW. 1871. A striking, large hall running
along the side of a hill above the shore. Five bays of paired lan-

cets, a polygonal apse, and an emphatic W end with a massive
bellcote capped by a high stone roof and a wrought-iron grille.
All this is very much in the style of *Timothy Hevey*, as is the
bold but economical interior with high roof and alternating
braced and scissor trusses.

MOVILLE OLD PRESBYTERIAN CHURCH. 1.5 km NE. 1827.
A handsome four-bay harled hall with large round-headed windows. Now ruinous.

RED CASTLE, one of the most substantial older houses in Co.
Donegal, was described by Sir Walter Scott in 1814 as 'a large
good looking mansion with trees and a pretty vale sloping upwards from the sea'. It was a house of the Wray family, traditionally
C17 though possibly early C18. Nine-bay, two-storey block on
a basement, with high hipped roof, regular chimneys, and a
leaded platform between. Originally small gabled dormers were
set in the roof over alternate bays, but these have recently been
replaced – when the house became a hotel – by continuous strip
dormers that destroy much of the historic appearance of the
place. The windows too appear to have been altered in the early
C19. The house has gained a later porch, and the interiors have
been re-worked on several occasions. On the shore front, however, a terrace wall with a central gate and end piers topped
by ball finials of *c.* 1730 still survives.

WHITE CASTLE, 5 km SW, also noted by Scott, was built by the
Carys apparently in the late C18. It is now a charming whitewashed villa in a miniature park, of two storeys, with a canted
bay in the centre of the entrance front flanked by tripartite windows. Only one room deep except in the middle, where there
is a stair behind the octagonal entrance hall. The end elevations
appear as shallow segmental two-bay bows (with third-floor
windows tucked in like slits below the eaves). The style of the
house has much in common with Killygordon House and Edenmore near Ballybofey and may well be by the same provincial
yet not unsuccessful designer.

ROSNAKIL

DO E2

A rural district described in the mid C19 as a hamlet but now too
broken up to have any recognizable centre. Two churches lie by
the shore road running N from Carrowkeel.

CHURCH OF CHRIST THE REDEEMER, CLONDEVADOCK
PARISH CHURCH (C of I). C17, at least in origin – see the slab
to William Cuningham † 1693 on the S wall. Described in 1729

as in good repair, of stone and clay with thatch. Restored about 1830 and tidied up in 1868 by *Welland & Gillespie* but no more than that. Now a three-bay rendered hall, rather low, with round-headed windows and timber Y-tracery. Bellcote with typical churchwarden's chimney beside it. Note the C17 corbel-stop face built into the N gatepier.

MASSMOUNT CHURCH. One of the most moving buildings in Donegal. The name and isolated position of the church, on an exposed outcrop above an inlet of Mulroy Bay, both recall Penal days. Large, white, and prominently placed, the building is like a monument to a tenacious faith, and it must be one of the earlier Catholic churches in the county. Like Rosslea church, at the opposite end of the area covered in this volume, it is a long hall with the altar in the middle of one wall (s) and galleries round the other three sides. Georgian-glazed windows with 104 timber Y-tracery. The interior is wonderfully crisp and clean, unaltered since the middle of the last century and preserving an ambitious classical altar framed by big fluted columns with a heavy entablature above. Similar fluted columns support the galleries, whose undersides are panelled in pine. The architecture of Massmount is anything but sophisticated, and not perhaps for purists; yet there is a lot of quality in this design which few later C19 and few modern churches can equal. The date is not clear. It may very well be pre-1819, the year of the tombstone to the Rev. Francis Gallagher set against the s wall outside. A Catholic church is recorded at Rosnakil in 1785 built by the Rev. Joseph Friel P.P.

MOROSS CASTLE. Half-way between the two churches, 1.5 km w, on the coast. A rubble-built fragment on a rocky island connected to the shore by a causeway. One corner of a square tower about 20 ft high with a mural passage at the bottom.

LEAT BEG CHURCH (C of I). 5 km w. Mid C19. A tiny hall and porch, with square-headed windows. Gaelic cross on the w gable.

ROSNAKIL GLEBE HOUSE. 1 km E of Massmount. 1795. A big three-bay, two-storey front with console-bracketed entrance door. Regular offices behind.

A small village built round a T-junction; redeveloped in 1970 by *Storie, Lynch & Partners*. Near the w end is a nice two-storey terraced house of *c.* 1820 with a good Ionic doorcase. The OLD SCHOOL is of 1852, a stone-built hall.

ST TIERNEY. A large Georgian hall of *c.* 1800. Four bays with Y-tracery to which was added a tower at one end and a porch at the other in 1834. The interior has an altar in the middle of the longer E wall and a gallery round the other three sides supported on quatrefoil columns in cast iron. This is the early Catholic chapel plan like Massmount in Donegal and the Old Church at Garrison, and it makes for an interesting interior. Lewis in 1837 described the church in glowing terms: 'the interior is highly embellished; the windows are enriched with stained glass; and over the altar is a fine painting'. The altar itself is framed by an unusually ambitious essay in classical carpentry with paired fluted Tuscan pilasters and salient entablatures. This is probably the work of *W. H. Byrne & Son* who built the parish house and made Gothic and classical schemes for the altar in 1929. Long may it remain.

CLOUGHMORE, CHAPEL OF EASE (C of I). 2.5 km SE. On the border with Co. Monaghan. 1828. An extremely spiky hall and porch church with a pretty W end, set at the head of a T-junction. Harled walls with stone trim and buttresses and unusually pretty thin tracery windows.

AGHADRUMSEE CHURCH (C of I). 5.5 km W. A medium-sized hall and tower type church built in 1819–20. Three-bay hall with Y-tracery. The tower crenellated and pinnacled. Restored in 1875–8, when the chancel and vestry were added. The bell dates from 1899 and the church was restored again in 1920.

CATHOLIC CHURCH. At Killygorman, 5.5 km W. A large hall-type church of *c.* 1850, harled, with four bays of Y-tracery windows.

ROSSNOWLAGH

ST JOHN, ROSSNOWLAGH PARISH CHURCH (C of I). 1830. A rendered three-bay hall and porch with lancet windows and bellcote capped by composite stone fleur-de-lys. Chancel recess.

FRANCISCAN FRIARY. 1950 by *Downes, Meehan & Robson* of Dublin. A U-shaped, two-storey range of buildings, rendered, with granite surrounds to doors and windows and very shallow pitched roofs. The chapel on the N side has an offset campanile – a sort of modern equivalent of the Lombardic style of church. The interior is simple but not a great success.

ROTTEN ISLAND*   DO
                  2.5 km E of Killybegs Harbour

LIGHTHOUSE STATION. A harbour light designed and built by
George Halpin in 1837–8 was first exhibited on the night of 1
September 1838. The whole station is in its original form,
though converted to an automatic acetylene light in 1958 and
to automatic electric in 1963.

              ROUGHAN CASTLE *see* NEWMILLS

G6   ROUSKY   TY

A mountainous district of Tyrone, E of Gortin and cut by two
branches of the Owenkillew River. Here four modest rural
CHURCHES are set in the hilly countryside: ROUSKY, 6 km E
of Gortin, erected in 1800 and rebuilt in 1882 by the Rev. Peter
McGeown P.P., T-plan, with three galleries; GREENAN (C of
I), 3.5 km ENE of Rousky, a three-bay lancet hall of 1852 with
porch and bellcote; SHESKINSHULE, 6 km ESE of Rousky, mid
C19, a five-bay hall with Y-tracery in wood; and BROUGH-
DERE, 11 km E of Rousky, of 1876, a five-bay lancet hall with
quarry glass and stone trim.

B4   RUTLAND ISLAND*   DO

FORMER FISHING STATION. This island, divided from the
mainland at Burton Port by a narrow sound, was known until
the late C18 as Inishmacadurn. About 1780 herrings set here
in such enormous quantities that, as the means to cure and
transport them were inadequate, they were used as manure on
the fields for miles around. In 1783 a company was formed supported by the Marquess Conyngham and with a grant from
the Irish Parliament to develop the island as a fishing station.
In compliment to the then viceroy, the Duke of Rutland, the
place was then renamed Rutland Island.
   The company spent over £40,000 laying out a fishing station,
custom house, barracks, sail and net factory, and several streets
of houses, and for a number of years it was estimated to have
realized well over that sum annually in profits from the fish.
Then the herring moved away as mysteriously as they had
come, and to complete the disaster the sand dunes broke at the
                       * Not visited.

back of the island and, carried by great gales, half buried the town. In 1793 the fishery failed entirely and has never revived to anything beyond a modest scale.

The quay and a street of ruined houses running down to it may still be seen from Burton Port.

ST ERNANS *see* DONEGAL, p. 243

ST JOHN'S POINT   DO B7

A rocky neck of land jutting out into Donegal Bay, over 10 kilo- 4 metres long and rarely more than half a kilometre wide. Wonderfully quiet, with spectacular views along the coast to Muckros Head and Slieve League.

BALLYSAGGART FRIARY. At Fanegaragh on the SE coast halfway to St John's Point. This Tertiary Franciscan house was probably founded by the Mac Swiney Banagh about the end of the C15. It lasted no more than a century, as the community was driven out about 1602 on the defeat of O'Neill and O'Donnell at Kinsale. Today the place seems totally forgotten. It consists of a group of thatched cottages by a small beach and quay, with the gable and N wall of the friary church a little to the w. The church was rectangular, some 67 ft by 20 ft, and built of coursed red rubble stone. The gable stands almost entire, with an elegant two-light traceried E window, crisply carved. In the s wall traces of a window with sedilia below – note the carved capital – and a rectangular aumbry in the corner.

ST JOHN'S POINT LIGHTHOUSE. A harbour light built at the 92 request of local traders to mark the s side of the entrance to Killybegs Harbour. Representations were first made in February 1825, and the Ballast Board approved the works in 1829. The lighthouse and surrounding court of buildings were designed by *George Halpin* and cost £10,507 8s. 5d. The light, first exhibited on 4 November 1831, was converted to acetylene in 1931 and to automatic electric in 1962.

The buildings surrounded by a whitewashed enclosing wall form a powerful group at the end of the point. The tower of two storeys with a corbelled gallery round the light was originally slate-hung. Behind it is a neat rectangular court of single-storey houses and offices with a rudimentary classical eaves cornice. All in immaculate order, trim and shipshape.

'But a sorry collection of a few houses' is the description of the *Parliamentary Gazetteer* of 1846. The same holds good today; but if St Johnstown is little more than a location, various historical interests are focused conveniently here. The parish name, Taughboyne, is a corruption that means 'the house of Baithen', recalling St Baithen, the son of Brendan, a disciple and kinsman of St Colmcille and his successor at Iona in the late C6. The dedication of the Catholic church today is to that saint. Under James I, as part of the Plantation plan, St Johnstown was given borough status. It never grew, but the ground, owned first by Hamiltons, then Forwards, and finally Howards, brought £15,000 in compensation for the disenfranchisement of this particular rotten borough to the Earl of Wicklow in 1801, and that went to pay for one of Ireland's most spectacular Gothic Revival houses: Shelton Abbey in Wicklow. Here the Plantation has left its mark not so much in architecture as in the size of the Presbyterian community, with four congregations within a few miles. The foundations of these bodies are generally C17 but their buildings are more recent.

102 ST BAITHEN. 1857–60. The best building in the area, by *E. W. Godwin,* recently ruined inside by modernization. It is a small, severe church in rubble slate with sandstone trim. Nave and chancel with s porch and short transepts. Steeply pitched gables giving the high sheer roofs beloved by Godwin. Oddly pinched and personal tracery, the carving – especially the w window – by a Mr *Doherty* of Derry. Double bellcote over the E gable. Inside, a double-chamfered chancel arch supported on colonnettes. Broad trussed roof. Walls painted pale blue splatter-dash!

TAUGHBOYNE PARISH CHURCH (C of I). 3 km N in open fields. A long, low hall of four bays with harled walls and stone Y-tracery windows filled with quarry glass. Battered lower courses at the E end, with a three-light Victorian Dec window; bellcote on the w gable. All this looks very ordinary, but the church is in fact of 1627, and that was a rebuilding of the medieval structure. Evidence of this is the inscription and coat of arms by the N door, 'Thomas Bruce Rector Haec Ecclesia 1627', and the C15 label stop and two fragmentary beasts with knotted tails built into the wall by the door.

ST JOHNSTOWN PRESBYTERIAN CHURCH. Founded by the Rev. William Gray in 1724 and substantially rebuilt in the early C19 as a plain hall, with box pews and a gallery. The thin Gothic tower is of 1849.

MONGAVLIN CASTLE. To the S. The ruins of a rectangular castle of Scottish character built about 1619 by Sir John Stewart and recorded in Pynnar's Survey that year. The castle was occupied until the mid C19 and appears in the *Dublin Penny Journal* as a tall three-storey block with angle bartizans corbelled out at each corner. Only the S wall remains intact, with chimneys on the ground, first, and second floors. Parts of three bartizans also survive. The remains of a brick-lined oven are in the SW corner – remarkable for the unusually small size of the hand-kneaded bricks. On the second floor is a complete fireplace with dowel-type mouldings. Checks in the reveals of the ground-floor windows show that these were protected by an iron grille. In the early C19 Mongavlin was said to be haunted, and the noise of the wind in its roofs made a young servant hang himself.

DUNMORE HOUSE. 3 km NW, at Carrigans. A substantial if plain 60 country house of mid C18 date, set high on a hill with a view across the River Foyle. Nicely proportioned two-storey façade of five bays with a two-bay wing to the E, rendered, with stone eaves, quoins, and slant basement course. The windows are segment-arched. Completely detailed Venetian window in stone set above a central glazed Doric porch of the early C19. At the back attempts at regularity end. The staircase projects from the middle as a separate short wing. Inside, Dunmore preserves much good provincial C18 detail, including a big dentil cornice in the hall and pretty scalloped mouldings in the drawing room. The doors are generally of five panels with lugged 61 architraves, the most elaborate in the dining room. The STAIR is the best feature of the house: a timber scale-and-platt type 62 amply scaled, with three turned balusters to each step. The Doric cornice and splayed windows with fans in the cover of the reveal in the library in the E wing look early C19 like the porch. The basement is brick-vaulted throughout.

A date-stone set in the gatepier at the side of the house refers somewhat cryptically to the history of the place. 1620 is presumably the date of the first building here. The property passed after the death of D.H. (David Harvey) to W.M. (William McClintock), who had married Harvey's only daughter Elizabeth in 1685. William was succeeded by his son J.M. (John

McClintock), a captain in the Donegal Militia in 1745 and presumed builder of Dunmore. The dates 1678, 1709, and 1742 under the initials of the three men bear no obvious relationship to family history and may be building dates. If so, 1742 will be the date of the present house.

PROSPECT HILL. E from Dunmore. Once a McClintock dower house: a pretty three-bay, single-storey cottage with tripartite windows and a lovely view of the Foyle.

At Carrigans a number of single-storey cottages of Regency pattern-book character.

CHURCHES in the area: CRAIGDOOISH Chapel of Ease (C of I) at St Johnstown, a mid C19 hall and apse; KILLEAR Church (C of I) at Carrigans, a three-bay stone hall with a chancel of 1856 by *A. Hardy*, the Ecclesiastical Commissioners' local man.

PRESBYTERIAN CHURCHES are at CROSSROADS, 5.5 km NNE, a small hall of 1783, and at CHURCHTOWN, 3 km NNE. The latter, originally of 1644, is now a T-plan church with details that look about 1840. Charming late Victorian Gothic interior with galleries on cast-iron columns.

PRESBYTERIAN CHURCH. Built by the Rev. Thomas Dickson in 1794. T-plan.

ROCKDALE. 1 km W. A tall, square house, three-storey on a high basement, set impressively above the road. White-harled, with a shallow hipped roof. Garden front of four bays: the entrance with tripartite Tuscan doorway, Palladian window above, and segmental attic storey light. Handsome iron railings to the basement area. Proto-Victorian, though the stone yard behind is dated 1827 and the walled garden 1823. Built for James Corry Lowry, a younger son of the family at Pomeroy.

TULLYLAGAN MANOR. 1 km E. A late classical villa of 1828. Two storeys on a high basement with flat pilaster strips to the corners and big consoles to the eaves. Three-bay front with central forestanding porch surmounted by a tower. Nice neo-classical plasterwork cornices inside. Much disfigured by the removal of the earth in front of the house, turning it into a three-storeyed design with heavy steps to the front door. Hideous sun-room above the porch.

SESKINORE

SESKINORE HOUSE, the home of the McClintock family from about 1800, has been demolished, and its park is now a government forest with a caravan park in the outbuildings of the house. It was a two-storey stucco-fronted building with projecting central pediment and Tuscan *porte cochère* in the manner of Lanyon, all added in 1862 by Col. George Parry McClintock, who had got married two years before. Though the house has gone, the Colonel's church remains.

SESKINORE CHAPEL OF EASE (C of I). 1873 by *Robert A. Ferguson* of Londonderry. High Victorian Gothic in black stone with sandstone trim. Four-bay nave, short chancel, and a high gabled front with bellcote and wheel window above a gabled porch.

CATHOLIC CHURCH. Mid C19. A long rendered hall with short transept arms and stucco hood mouldings.

PRESBYTERIAN CHURCH. Three-bay harled Gothic hall.

SION MILLS

'In the county Tyrone, and within a distance of little more than three miles from Strabane, is to be found one of the most interesting establishments it has ever been our good fortune to visit in any country. We have inspected manufactories of much greater extent than the "Sion Mills", but have never witnessed with greater gratification the practical and efficient working of a fine moral system. The mills are situated on the river Mourne, which is one of the best water powers in Great Britain, the supply being not only large but constant. About eighty-horse power is now employed to drive eight thousand spindles; yet but a small portion of the water is necessary for the purpose. Instead of the hot furnace, long chimneys, and dense smoke, rendering still more unhealthy the necessarily close atmosphere of manufactories devoted exclusively to the spinning of flax and tow into linen yarn, there is a clean, handsome, well-ventilated building, where nearly seven hundred of a peasantry, which, before the establishment of this manufactory, were starving and idle are now constantly employed; and the air is as pure and as fresh as on the borders of the wildest prairie, or the boldest coast. The bare fact of such a population being taught industrious habits, and receiving *full* remuneration for their time and labour, is a blessing – but not the only one: agricultural labour is not neglected, because five out of the seven hundred are women and girls – creatures who, but for the spirit and enterprise of the Messrs. Herdman, (to whom, and the Mulhollands of Belfast, Tyrone is indebted for this establishment,) would be found cowering over the embers of their turf fires, or begging along the way-sides for morsels of food. But this system of social order and social industry is not, as we have said, the only advantage enjoyed at Sion Mills. Cottages, of simple construction, but sound and comfortable, have been built for the workmen and their families; a school is established, and to the Sunday-school the Messrs. Herdman themselves attend, taking the greatest interest in the educational progress of their workpeople, and distributing *motives* to improvement, lavishly and judiciously. Nor are they behind London in the idea, that "the people" may derive benefit from the introduction of more refined tastes into the business of everyday life. The traveller's ear is refreshed, if he pass along during the long evenings of winter, or the bright cheerful ones of summer, by the music of a full band; and instead of the saddened hearts and saddened features he has been led to suppose inseparable from the crowded factory, he hears a chorus of cheerful voices, or the echoes of dancing feet.'

Such is the account of Sion Mills in Mr and Mrs Samuel Hall's *Tour in Ireland* of 1843, and the ethos of improvement that emanates from their rich prose, describing this type of New Lanark in Ulster, is still present today. There by the river sits the big spinning factory: an early Victorian industrial giant in a verdant landscape of grass and chestnut trees with a trim improved village beside it. The assertion of one worker who spoke to Mrs Hall that 'from the day the first stone of the Sion Mills was laid he nor his never knew hunger' is amply supported by the public spirit of the architecture of the place, developed by the Herdman family from 1835. What strikes the visitor today however is a later village of the 1880s and 1890s built in the black and white idiom of Ernest Newton or Norman Shaw to designs of Emerson Tennent Herdman's brother-in-law, the London architect *W. F. Unsworth.*

CHURCH OF THE GOOD SHEPHERD (C of I). By *W. F. Unsworth*, dedicated in 1909. Unsworth chose a church in Pistoia as the model of his design, which is in an unusually elaborate Italianate Romanesque style with paired square campanili at the east end flanking a deep semicircular apse, and further bow-ended projections, like side chapels, at the altar end. Otherwise the design is a big five-bay gabled hall lit by five huge Diocletian windows, high up on each side, with a complex though modestly scaled entrance front whose centrepiece is another bowed projection (to accommodate a stair to the gallery inside) flanked by low lean-to entrance porches. The whole, worked in two contrasting types of stone, is decidedly odd in a Co. Tyrone setting.

Inside, where the setting is unimportant, the design is more convincing, with a big spare timber roof and an Italianate altar raised dramatically by seven steps above the congregation in a marble chancel. A paired lectern and pulpit, each faced in grey and green Connemara marble, provide the balustrade to the steps leading to the barrel-vaulted chancel, which ends in a semi-dome and is pierced at the springing of the vault by eleven circular clerestory lights, nicely calculated to emphasize the weight and thickness of the walls. In the vestibule is the tomb of Brigadier General A. St Quentin Ricardo, who played a leading part in completing the church.

ST TERESA. 1963 by *Patrick Haughey*. A severe, clean design, excellently detailed and well finished. The church is a long, low rectangle built as a steel frame of twelve bays with grey brick infill and a continuous clerestory strip just below the roof, opening only at the altar end to full glazed windows. The front is dominated by a long slate sculpture of the Last Supper by *Oisin Kelly*, really an incised drawing, based on the looped and swirling patterns of Romanesque design. Kelly also did the sculptured FONT inside. STAINED GLASS by *Patrick Pollen*.

SION PRESBYTERIAN CHURCH. 1865 by *J. G. Ferguson* of Derry, a characteristic design, with a florid Dec W window and an offset tower and spire rising above a side porch. Flint stone with sandstone dressings, the spire of yellow brick.

HERDMANS LTD FLAX SPINNING MILLS. The Sion Mills came into being as an industrial complex when James Herdman, his brothers John and George, and Andrew Mulholland of Belfast bought an unfinished flour mill from the Marquess of Abercorn and turned it into a flax spinning mill in 1835. This is the date inscribed on the segmental ashlar stone archway that is still the entrance to the main complex of the mills. Behind it and towering above all the other mill buildings is the main factory block, sixteen bays long and four storeys high, with re- iterated segment-headed windows the length of its ashlar front and, at the SW corner, an imposing Italianate six-storey stair tower. This block is by *W. H. Lynn* of *Lanyon, Lynn and Lanyon* and uses the idiom established by Lanyon in Belfast and Co. Antrim in the 1840s and 1850s. The foundation stone was laid in 1853. It is built with a running brick vault fireproof construction typical of the mid C19 and has since been extended by an an extra six bays, massively buttressed at its s end. Behind, on the river side, are lower sheds: the sixteen-bay TURBINE AND GENERATING HOUSE, and the STABLES and TOW PREPARING ROOM, a fifteen-bay, three-storey brick range that was part of the original spinning mill and is now the oldest building on the site. The mill chimney dates from 1877.

The growth of the industry is charted in the buildings. Beside the entrance arch is a delightful small-scale Victorian office building in brick with stone quoins and trim that looks about 1860. The PREPARING ROOMS date from 1884. Then, at r. angles to the archway and extending in a single-storey wing of twenty-seven bays, the extension of 1907. Further s are store buildings of 1908, and finally the NEW MILLS built in rustic brick in 1946 and 1951.

SION HOUSE. In 1884 the core of this house, a regular stuccoed Italianate mansion in the manner of Lanyon built in 1842 by James Herdman of Sion Mills, was re-faced, re-roofed, expanded and extended into one of the most exotic architectural flowers of the region, a huge and – in its context – very unlikely half-timbered Tudor mansion house. The architect, as always in Sion Mills, is *W. F. Unsworth*. He gave the house a red tile roof with high gables at either end and the soaring faceted brick chimneys that were high fashion in the 1880s. The hall and stairs are panelled in pine with Elizabethan-style balusters, and there is (or was, for it has been partly replaced in utilitarian brick) an elaborate Jacobean veranda and gallery along the garden front. The GATEHOUSE on the main road is a jolly two-storey half-timbered affair reminiscent of, and as pretty as, the C16 gatehouse at Stokesay. The STABLES are similarly picturesque, with a high roof, a tile-hung gable, and an elaborate ridge bellcote.

OTHER BUILDINGS. The wide grass verges and tree-lined road provide an attractive setting for more half-timbered work by *Unsworth*: the RECREATION HALL built for the benefit of Messrs Herdman & Co.'s employees in 1882; and (now used as church halls) the NEW INSTITUTE of 1895 and OLD ST SAVIOUR'S CHURCH, half-timbered like the rest and with a red-brick bellcote, opened for worship in May 1895 though never consecrated. The PUBLIC ELEMENTARY SCHOOLS of 1879 are double-gabled, with the grouped round-headed windows that Thomas Turner so often used. The former GREAT

Northern Railway Station is by *William H. Mills*,
1883. Trim polychrome brick.

SNOWHILL *see* LISBELLAW

SPRINGHILL *see* MONEYMORE

STEWART HALL   TY J7

The regular five-bay Georgian house built by Viscount Castlestewart and described in the *Post Chaise Companion* of 1786 as
'a most superb edifice with extensive and beautiful parks and
demesnes' has passed through various transmogrifications since
it was built about 1760. A long rectangular block 56 ft deep with
an 88 ft front, it should be two storeys on a basement, but has
been cut down to one storey with the proportions of a bungalow.
An L-shaped Georgian wing behind and to one side still stands
to the full height of the old house, the junction masked by a
grandiose late C19 Baronial tower of crude and heavy detail,
with mullioned windows, corner stair-turret, and angle bartizans at roof level. The original house was plain but finely detailed, harled all over, with a sandstone basement course,
quoins, and a fluted string course between the ground and first
floors that has now become the eaves. The main door is tripartite, with a salient entablature supported on Tuscan
columns. The upper-floor front was of six bays. Inside a square
hall, open through an arcade at the back to the staircase, which
had open ironwork banisters and a carved rail.★

STABLES, w of the house, in a curious court, arranged as
a quarter-circle. Those on the N are in a symmetrical block with
a three-bay arcaded centre under a rude pediment, surmounted
by a hexagonal bellcote with concave pyramid roof. Two-storey
wings each side of four bays, the ground floor with blind
segment-headed arches that continue round the court, except
in the centre of the curved side, where a small four-bay block
containing a Gothic estate chapel breaks forward.

The WALLED GARDEN is dated 1832. Before it is a FOLLY
WALL, castellated, of rubble stone with brick corbelling and
a plump round tower at either end.

STEWARTSTOWN   TY J7

A little town laid out by Sir Andrew Stewart, who had a grant

★ The house was completely demolished after bombing in 1973.

in the district from James I and built a castle and bawn here in 1608. The town is grouped round an oblong square lined by small-scale two-storey houses with some lime trees. At its s end is a substantial early Georgian house with a five-bay, two-storey façade. The town is at the time of writing run down and sprawling in an uncontrolled way.

ST PATRICK, DONAGHENRY PARISH CHURCH (C of I). Built in 1694, the 'lofty square tower and side aisles' added 'recently' in 1837. Reconstructed in 1875, burnt out in February 1877, and rebuilt extremely quickly (the church was reopened the same October) to designs of *William Fullerton* of Armagh. Of the older church only the tower remains, similar to if not identical with Holy Trinity, Newmills, and therefore of about 1795. (Dated initials inside of 1810 and 1813.) The new church is cruciform, harled, with stone trim. Three-bay nave. Dec windows. Interior with intersecting kingpost trusses over the crossing. Single-chamfered arch to the chancel.

ST MARY. An attractive T-plan church built in 1845 for the Rev. James Lennan P.P. Short projecting sanctuary lit by a big geometrical-traceried window beside which a tower and spire have been added. The style is unusually solid and good: three-storey tower with diagonal buttresses and elegant broach-spire. A recent remodelling has removed the tops of the corner buttresses of the church – a pity.

FIRST PRESBYTERIAN CHURCH. 1851 by *J. McNea* of Belfast. A five-bay lancet hall, harled, with cut-stone gable front. Octagonal shafts flank the door, which has a Y-traceried round-headed window above. Corner finials.

METHODIST CHURCH. 1843, rebuilt in 1878. T-plan, rendered, with diagonal buttresses.

MULLATAIN. A large L-shaped brick and rubble house with segmental bows round the sides of the main front. Two-storey with five-bay front; the door, originally in a segmental arch in the centre, has been moved to the side. There was a house here in 1786, but this looks more like 1810.

BARNHILL HOUSE. 0.5 km E. A miniature Palladian villa. Mid C18 (the seat of the Rev. Dr Lill in 1786), with some pretensions to architecture. Five-bay, two-storey front flanked by quadrant garden walls ending in miniature square pavilions with pyramid slate roofs. The centre bay of the house has diamond-cut rustication round the door, with keystone and pediment. Above are a Venetian window and a segmental attic light, squashed into a small eaves pediment. The interior had mid Georgian lugged door surrounds, six-panel doors, and a solid timber stair, three banisters to a tread. A pretty house that, left to fall down, was burnt out in 1973.

DONAGHENRY RECTORY. 1.5 km WNW. A high four-bay, three-storey harled house with a porch. One row of dummy windows, as at Termon rectory. Late C18.

DRUMCAIRNE HOUSE. 3 km E. Now in a government forest, but still a Charlemont house. Substantially early C19 but much altered. Three-bay, two-storey front with a splendid view SE to Lough Neagh and the Mountains of Mourne. Shallow hipped roof with overhanging eaves on thin paired consoles. Curious double sash-windows with French doors below and a big Tuscan porch. STABLES with a battlemented gabled wall behind.

ALBANY PRESBYTERIAN CHURCH. 6 km E at Kilcolpy. 1838. A large three-bay pebbledashed hall with round-headed windows and half-hipped gables.

BELLMOUNT. 4 km E. A largish three-bay, two-storey Georgian house of about 1830. The wide hall and six-panel doors inside suggest an earlier origin.

STRABANE   TY F5

Strabane has grown from a castle built by the Earl of Abercorn, the grantee under the Jacobean Plantation, to become the second town of Co. Tyrone, with a population of over 9,300. It is a border town, connected to Lifford in Donegal by a bridge across the united Finn and Mourne rivers that here become the Foyle. It is the largest town directly on the border and, like Derry, has paid heavily for its position in recent bombing campaigns.

The history of the place is one of gradual development to the late C19 and then of gradual decline until recent years. Some houses were built with the castle before 1609, when the commissioners for the Plantation made their survey of the six counties, and by the time of Pynnar's Survey, ten years later, the Earl had built a limestone school, a church was under erection, and there were eighty houses either of stone or of wood with 120 families. In 1641 Sir Phelim O'Neill, who destroyed so many of the Plantation settlements, actually took the Countess of Abercorn hostage. The castle was retaken by Colonel Hamilton after some years, but the town surrendered in 1688 to James II, who used it as a base for his attack on Derry. In the early C18, with the introduction of linen manufacturers, the place began to grow, and by 1777, when it appears in Taylor and Skinner's *Roads of Ireland*, it had developed into a sizeable town with the beginnings of a suburb on the s bank of the River Mourne. It remained the property of the Earls of Abercorn, who in 1755 had the Lifford Bridge rebuilt by a Mr Ramsay, and who in the following year employed the local architect, *Michael Priestley*, to provide an extensive plan for new streets with 300 houses. These improvements struck contemporaries as remarkable, but the scale of much of the development was modest. Though the main streets were built up, in the lanes the houses were to be only 12 ft high, their sole pretension to architecture that they were slated rather than thatched. In 1766 Priestley was working for the Earl, rebuilding Strabane Town Hall – a building which gave a good deal of trouble and for which *Sir William Chambers* provided a design for the steeple – and in 1802 *Robert Woodgate* was drawing up plans for a further extension, called the New Town, to be built round the basin where a new canal, four miles in length, connected Strabane to the navigable reaches of the Foyle. By 1824 its linen business ranked as the third most important in all Ireland, and in 1837 Lewis records 836 houses. The town was then 'strikingly prepossessing' with 'thriving orchards attached to the houses, and in the immediate neighbourhood, producing apples, pears and cherries in abundance'.

In the Victorian age the appearance of the town changed a good deal. The churches and Priestley and Chambers's Town Hall were all rebuilt; gas light was introduced in the 1850s; banks appeared, and in 1876 a flamboyant memorial clock tower by *Timothy Hevey* was added to Abercorn Square. Yet while these improvements took place, emigration reduced the population from some 7,000 before the famine to about 4,000 in 1889. At the time of writing Strabane is a town without much architectural focus, threatened by new roads, and run down.

<h3 style="text-align:center">CHURCHES</h3>

CHRIST CHURCH, CAMUS-JUXTA-MOURNE PARISH CHURCH (C of I). On the site of the C17 church. 1874 by *John Kennedy* of Londonderry in competition with eight other architects. Built of pale grey limestone with red sandstone trim. A satisfyingly solid church, cruciform, with a three-bay arcaded nave, aisle, and a massive belfry tower with half-round stair-turret and broach-spire. The details mainly E.E., with large geometric tracery in the chancel window. Inside there is a nice humane scale and sense of enclosure, with a high pointed barrel-vault to the nave. The Bishop of Derry gave the site, and the foundation stone was laid by the Countess of Abercorn, which patronage no doubt accounts for the substantial feeling the church still has. – STAINED GLASS. In the E window a highly pictorial Last Supper of 1879. – N transept window in memory of James Hugh McClay, the builder of the church. – MONUMENT. Inscribed tablet in the porch to 'Wil Hamilton Sometime Provost of Strabane 1640'.

CHURCH OF THE IMMACULATE CONCEPTION. 1895 by *William Hague*. A huge cruciform sandstone church with a tall W steeple flanked by two-bay gabled and pinnacled wings. French mid C13 window details; the effect rich but cluttered. The best element is undoubtedly the upper part of the steeple that rises above the W door: above a big window that lights the gallery, it chamfers into an octagonal belfry flanked by solid polygonal angle pinnacles that overlap the cornice of the spire. The type is of course early C13 and probably owes a good deal to Burges, who gave the motif some currency in Ireland after work began at St Finbar's Cathedral, Cork.

Inside, a four-bay arcade of pink granite columns with round sandstone capitals, a clerestory, and a hipped, panelled, very high roof with web trusses filled with timber tracery. Chancel arch on polygonal columns, with a panelled wagon roof. – PULPIT, ALTAR, and ALTAR RAIL. Lavish designs in white and coloured marble with gold mosaic. – STAINED GLASS. Pictorially lavish too.

STRABANE FIRST PRESBYTERIAN CHURCH. 1955 by *Thomas* 128 *Houston*. A large pink brick hall, nicely handled, in a modern Scandinavian idiom. Segment-topped windows and a clerestory of little slots, a large mullioned window in the gable end flanked by doors in recessed stone frames, and a massive rectangular brick tower offset on one side, square in plan, with a square columned bellcote on top. The interior is a little like a lecture theatre. – STAINED GLASS. E window by *Morris & Co.*: 'Christ and the Little Children'.

The congregation here was founded about 1659. The church replaces one of 1871 in E.E. Gothic by *J. G. Ferguson*.

ST MARY, MELLMOUNT. 1970 by *Patrick Haughey*. A larger and harsher version of the church at Dunnamanagh. Clerestory fascia in copper, nine bays wide, on each side. Rounded stone corner. However fine, surely not a design to build twice.

PUBLIC BUILDINGS

TOWN HALL. On the site of an earlier building, at the head of Market Street and Main Street. An essential element for Strabane, if only for its townscape value. Mid C19, an arcaded three-storey block set behind a wonderfully provincial municipal steeple, a degenerate though likeable heir of James Gibbs, square in plan and of five stages: the ground floor with channelled rustication and one elliptical open arch; above a Venetian window flanked by corner Tuscan pilasters; the third stage a smaller square with Corinthian pilasters and forestanding aedicules at the sides; the fourth a clock flanked by pilaster strips; and the summit an octagonal classical cupola with ogee lead dome. Set at the head of the street where the roads divide, the building gives an impression at least fleetingly similar to that of Gibbs's St Mary le Strand. Bombed in 1972.*

COURT HOUSE. Built in 1807 at a cost of £1,200 and repaired by *John Hargrave* in 1825. A tall three-bay, two-storey block on a high basement with the court house projecting at the rear.

GRAY'S PRINTING SHOP, 49 Main Street. A pretty, late Georgian shop-front, slightly curved, with four slender Tuscan pilasters and a central door. Gray's shop, restored by the Northern Ireland committee of the National Trust, is a remarkable survival from an age when Strabane was an important publishing centre. Fifty books were published in the town between 1779 and 1840, and there were two newspapers, the *Strabane Journal* of 1771 and the *Strabane News-letter* of 1780. The interest of this particular shop, with its upper-floor print-works in the yard behind, lies in its connection with John Dunlap, the printer of the American Declaration of Independence, who is traditionally thought to have begun his trade as a boy at Gray's Printery. In the print-works are a Columbian Press, an Albion Press, and three Platen Presses, all of the C19.

CONVENT OF THE SISTERS OF MERCY, Mount St Joseph. A plain six-bay, two-storey block with an asymmetrical classical porch, enlarged to the N by a long block with a two-bay front which converts the plan to an L-shape. At the junction a thin Gothic tower with paired belfry windows and a parapet round a stumpy spire. The angle bartizans are just like those Robert Adam might have given to a stable block. These are probably the additions made by *William Hart* in 1870. The CHAPEL is later, a large four-bay hall with paired round-headed lancets

* Now demolished.

with an earlier(?) and more elegant tower and broach-spire that look like *John O'Neill.*

Apart from the churches and Gray's shop, there is now little to lure the architecturally curious round the town. Those who respond to the bare bones of a built environment and can see as much in the mind's eye as is actually before them may enjoy the undulating lines of the Main Street, with its varied roof levels and gradually changing directions, or the narrow vernacular buildings in Market Street, or the big mid Georgian houses which were probably part of Priestley's plan lining the s side of Meetinghouse Street. These are all good things that could make Strabane architecturally worthwhile, but they are not the things that planners or the architects who work for modern commercial interests are inclined to respect. Most new buildings are bad, and the older ones are at the time of writing allowed to decay.

A short circular tour might start in the BOWLING GREEN, an open square at the SE end of the town with Christ Church on the NW side and a row of decent early C19 Georgian houses opposite. At the N by the side of the church is a block of three stucco houses, the middle one with nice cast-iron balconies, and beyond in NEW TOWN STREET, set sideways to the road, is VICTORIA HOUSE, a six-bay, three-storey block of the early C19 with a segment-headed central door divided by four Ionic columns. Newtown was an area whose development was superintended by *Robert Woodgate,* Soane's assistant, who had come to work at Baronscourt, so the house could perhaps be his design.

Now back to the Bowling Green and s along BARRACK STREET, past the Church of the Immaculate Conception (*see* p. 493). R. at the crossroads and r. again into MEETINGHOUSE STREET, running along the side of the Mourne, with some biggish terraced houses towards its w end. The Meeting House used to back on to the river, but has long since gone. No. 21 is where John Dunlap, the printer, was born. At the w end, by the TOWN HALL, keep l. down MAIN STREET, joined on the l. by BRIDGE STREET, which leads to the fine late C18 BRIDGE that crosses the Mourne on eight masonry arches. Opposite the end of the street Lord Abercorn built a market house on an arcaded ground floor in 1751, but that too has gone. Just beyond the junction on the r. is Gray's printer's shop (*see* p. 494), then the PROVINCIAL BANK, 1892 by *R. Watt,* four-

bay, three-storey, with a Tuscan order on the ground floor.
CASTLE STREET on the r. passes the NORTHERN BANK of
1922, at a corner site with CASTLE PLACE, an adroit piece
of mannered classicism in Portland stone and red brick by *H.
Seaver*. Then the BELFAST BANKING CO., 1881, a three-
storey, four-bay sandstone block with a pedimented oriel; and
the POST OFFICE, five-bay neo-Georgian with pediment,
temp. George V. Beyond in ABERCORN SQUARE, really a
crescent, the ULSTER BANK is by *Thomas Jackson*, 1861, a
charming piece of commercial classicism, cunningly sited in the
middle of the curve to gain support from its neighbours. Two-
storey with four high arches on the ground floor – the outer
two are doors – with emphasized quoins and voussoirs, and a
big keystone that runs into the string course above. Corinthian
cornice at the top and balustrade above. All in dressed sandstone to show that the bank had funds. The eight-bay red and
yellow brick terrace immediately beside it spoils Jackson's hopes
of a symmetrical setting but is good of its kind. Possibly by
J. P. McGrath and as late as 1904. The bare traffic island in the
centre of the crescent was once the site of *Timothy Hevey*'s
HUMPHREY MEMORIAL CLOCK TOWER AND FOUNTAIN,
a vigorous Gothic extravaganza of 1876 that deserved not to
be demolished. The 'square' continues s as an ordinary street to
CASTLE PLACE, passing on the r. a fine group of early Victorian shop-fronts, THE ARCADE, and then a Doric doorcase
that may be late c18 and PACKIE DOHERTY's nice Ionic front
with a proper classical entablature as the name board. The
HIBERNIAN BANK is a marble-faced vertical horror, just what
ought not to be here. Straight across, Market Street leads back
to Meetinghouse Street and then l. back to the Bowling Green.

NEIGHBOURHOOD

The suburbs across the Mourne are pretentious and ugly.
Beyond CARRICKLEE, 2 km SW, is a vaguely Elizabethan-style
house built by John Herdman of Sion Mills in 1891. GALLARY
HOUSE, 3.5 km SSW, is a plain harled house of about 1790 with
pilasters to the entrance door. The OLD HOSPITAL AND
WORKHOUSE in the w sector of the town preserve the standard
five-bay Tudor front of *George Wilkinson*'s designs. 1840.
THE WILSON HOUSE. 3 km E, at Dergalt. A typical Tyrone
crofter's cottage. The home of James Wilson, who emigrated
to America in 1807 and whose grandson was the American
President Woodrow Wilson. Restored by the Northern Ireland

Committee of the National Trust and preserving the characteristic Tyrone feature of a single upper room reached by a ladder and slated, whereas the rest of the cottage is thatched.

STRANORLAR

Stranorlar and Ballybofey are really the same town: the first N of the river Finn – a famous salmon river; the other, described by Lewis as a 'village', on the S bank. Ballybofey is no more than three or four streets but it has a good town scale, some substantial buildings of late C18 appearance, and a Market House. Stranorlar, though bigger, is untidy both architecturally and literally – too much cement, pebbledash and waste paper. The setting in a fertile valley below barren hills is fine; the town is negligible. It has moreover lost its big house, Drumboe Castle, the seat of the Hayes family, of which only the plantations and a picturesque Gothic gate dated 1876 remain. Another recent loss is the more vigorous commercial Gothic railway terminus for the Finn Valley Railway built in 1862 to designs of a Mr *Clayton* of Brixton – miniature like the railway itself but with a raffish clock tower and a centre spire that added at least an accent to this featureless place.

St Mary. The one architectural moment of the town, handsomely set immediately over the bridge from Ballybofey: an ambitious Gothic church of 1859 designed by *William Nicholson* of Manchester and built entirely in stone. The exterior is a little thin, though relieved by a flamboyant tower that was not completed till 1897. Seven-bay nave with aisles, trefoil-lit clerestory, and a two-bay chancel with flanking side chapels. The tower, incorporating an entrance porch, occupies the western bay of the S aisle. E.E. details, with odd paired lancets to the aisles decorated with corbel heads at the top of the lower mullion. E window of five lights with intersecting Y-tracery. The arcades inside on octagonal piers with stilted arches. Open trussed roof supported on colonnette shafts that rest on apostles'-head corbels. – Altar. A lavish Gothic design with a pinnacled tabernacle in Caen stone and yellow marble.

St John, Stranorlar Parish Church (C of I). An undistinguished tower and hall type church, originally of 1729–33, with additional N and S transepts and a short chancel almost doubling the size of the church – alterations of 1863 by *Frazer, Ferguson & Frazer* of Derry. The tower is of coursed rubble in three stages with primitive Gothic finials; the nave harled; the additions rubble again.

PRESBYTERIAN CHURCH. A rendered Gothic hall of 1906, presumably by *J. McIntyre*, whose Presbyterian church at Convoy
this follows closely: it has the same tripartite front – Dec window
in the centre, porch to the l., and a squat tower ending in a
triangular slate roof to the r. Four-bay hall behind.

FORMER MARKET HOUSE. At the E end of Ballybofey. 1862.
A tidy three-bay, two-storey stone-built block with yellow brick
cornice and window trim, flanked each side by market walls
and big round-headed stone arches.

EDENMORE HOUSE. 1.5 km E of Ballybofey, on the S bank of
the Finn. Almost all the 'seats' in the area are now derelict or
demolished. Edenmore is the exception. The house looks of
about 1810 or 1820. It is harled and whitewashed, of two
storeys, with a central canted bay. What gives it elegance are
the long flanking wings screening the yards behind and ending
in canted bay pavilions. The whole is long and low, with a pattern-book look, unusual in these parts.

ROCKFIELD. 1.5 km S. A pretty late Georgian house built by a
Mr Johnston. Five-bay, two-storey, on a basement, with a nice
fanlight flanked by Tuscan columns.

CHURCH OF THE ASCENSION (C of I). At Meenglas, 3 km SW
of Ballybofey. A tiny three-bay hall with round-headed windows built in 1961 to replace the 'very large and dilapidated
building' once attached to Meenglas Castle – now also gone.

ST PATRICK. 8 km N at Drumkeen. Mid C19. A large five-bay
lancet hall with provincial Gibbs surrounds and timber Y-
tracery sashes.

KNOCKFAIR. 2 km NNE. A nice two-storey thatched house with
a three-bay front, harled walls, and stone quoins. C18 five-panel
doors inside.

TYRCALLEN HOUSE. 3 km NNE. A five-bay, single-storey
shooting lodge built about 1800 by Sir Henry Stewart, who also
had an observatory here.

SWATRAGH   LD *J4*

A cluster of buildings on a curving road with four churches in
the vicinity.

KILLELA PARISH CHURCH (C of I). 1852 by *Joseph Welland*.
A nice design that Welland also used at Derryvullan, with nave,
long chancel, and S porch with an offset miniature spire beside
it. The details the usual E.E. with diagonal buttresses. Paid for
by the Mercers' Company.

St John Baptist. A large five-bay hall with Y-traceried windows and four-stage gabled tower. Reputedly of 1839. The windows have label mouldings, and there are octagonal shafts at the corners of the tower. Interior re-fitted by *E. J. Toye* in 1927, with a flamboyant Gothic altar in white marble.

St Eugene, Craigavole. 2.5 km N. 1855. A modest yet attractive early Victorian Catholic church. Five-bay lancet hall, Georgian-glazed and built of basalt. Tower with quatrefoil pierced parapet and round corbelled finials. Box pews and a small gallery on cast-iron columns inside.

Swatragh Presbyterian Church. A five-bay stuccoed gabled hall.

TAUGHBOYNE *see* ST JOHNSTOWN

TEMPO   FM *F8*

A secluded little village, consisting of one main street on the w side of Tempo Manor demesne. Some nice houses with columned porches.

Tempo Parish Church (C of I). Hall and tower type church of *c.* 1780. Georgian Gothic. Plain three-stage tower with quoins and finials. Four-bay hall and chancel. Originally a chapel of ease for Enniskillen parish in the old 'Pubble' district. The present arrangement inside is of 1866 by *Welland & Gillespie*, who added the chancel, porch, robing room, and a new pulpit. – stained glass. E window Pre-Raphaelitesque, 1893, in memory of Sir William Emerson Tennent.

Church of the Immaculate Conception. 1826. A four-bay Gothic hall built side on to the street. Tower of rock-faced stone blocks added in 1907. Sanctuary, baptistery, and sacristy of 1938. Ghastly pale yellow leaded lights – the nadir of church architecture.

Methodist Church. At the top of an alley with a box hedge round the ground before it, a two-bay hall of 1836, Georgian-Gothic glazed on one side.

Tempo Manor. By *Sir Charles Lanyon* in his most winsome Jacobethan Manorial style. Quite irregular, with seven curly gables (convex becoming ogee) dotted about the fronts. At the side of a projecting end wing on the entrance side a sizeable campanile, chamfered from a square to an octagon above the bell stage and ending in a candle-snuffer roof. The house is really an inflated cottage and looks it. One-storey, with attics lit by big round-headed windows in the gables. It would not be impossible to imagine its various components as parts of some mid Victorian rural railway station or charity school. That is its idiom.

Tempo in the C18 belonged to a branch of the Maguire family. In 1815 it was bought by a Belfast banker, William Tennent. When he died of cholera in Belfast in 1832, it passed to his only surviving daughter, who had married James Emerson, later Sir James Emerson Tennent. Sir James pulled down the old Maguire house and commissioned Lanyon to build a new one in 1862, adding the billiard-room wing and the campanile in 1867. Of the Maguire house all that remains is the STABLE COURT to the NE, a two-storey, four-bay block beside it reputedly the old kitchen. Inside, the house has a comfortable rather than an architectural character. There are however a big Elizabethan-style chimneypiece initialled J.E.T. 1863, and two exceedingly pretty Irish Rococo chimneypieces, with a flower basket and a medallion portrait on the transoms, saved from the Maguire house.

The grounds are a splendid example of mid-Victorian garden taste, now mature and very beautiful. The house sits on a terraced lawn with a square gravel path running round it and steps going down the banks. It overlooks a long lake fringed with rhododendrons and evergreens and fir trees. In the lake is the island 'Tempo Deiseal', which means right-hand-wise or sun-wise, that gives the manor its name and which according to C19 legend 'was used by Druidical sun worshippers'.

CREAGH METHODIST CHURCH. 3.5 km E. Three-bay harled hall with small porch and sacristy. Round-headed windows.

TERMON CASTLE *see* PETTIGOE

Js   TOBERMORE   LD

KILCRONAGHAN PARISH CHURCH (C of I). 1855–8 by *Joseph Welland*, a very typical work in excellent condition. Six-bay nave with separate chancel, short N aisle, and S porch. All of black basalt with sandstone trim. Triple lancet window at the E end. Roof with exposed rafters, braced purlins, and elaborate kingpost trusses. Two-bay arcade to the aisle and a double-chamfered arch to the chancel.

FORT WILLIAM. 1 km NE. A substantial late Georgian house of *c.* 1790. Two-storey, five-bay front, all harled and white-

washed. Dressed-stone Gibbs surround and cornice to the main
door.

OTHER CHURCHES: PRESBYTERIAN, 1897, a four-bay Gothic
hall; CARSON MEMORIAL BAPTIST, 1892, classical, with
gable pediment and single-bay wings at the side.

TORY ISLAND*   C1

A rocky island 12 km N of Horn Head whose sinister, lowering
silhouette can be seen from much of the north Donegal coast. It
was the stronghold of the Fomorians, a legendary race of gigantic
pirates whose leader was the one-eyed Balor. St Colmcille is supposed to have founded a monastery here in the c6. In 612, according to the *Annals of Ulster*, the monastery was destroyed in a
marine raid, but the church was rebuilt four years later and the
community survived until 1595.

MONASTERY RUINS. At West Town, the principal village on
the island, are the remains of two rectangular churches – one
10 ft by 9 ft with rounded corner stones – a round tower, and
two crosses. The ROUND TOWER is built of red granite
boulders with mortar made of sea shells. Its form is unusual,
reflecting the materials of which it is built in the width of its
base – $51\frac{1}{2}$ ft in circumference – and the incline of the walls.
It is 51 ft high, with a door $8\frac{1}{2}$ ft above the first offset of the base,
arched with narrow flat stones. Near the town is a CROSS
SHAFT, 6 ft high, broken, but with a figure carved on one side.
The TUA CROSS, by the landing pier at West Town, is $6\frac{1}{2}$ ft
high, T-shaped, made of a monolith of mica slate.

CATHOLIC CHURCH. 1857–61 by *E. W. Godwin*. A 'graceful little
Gothic church' that cost £392.

LIGHTHOUSE. A sea light on a low stretch of granite at the NW
point of the island, in a prominent position for vessels crossing
the Atlantic. Built from 1828 to 1832 at a cost of some £16,563
to designs of the Ballast Board's engineer, *George Halpin*. The
light was originally catoptric but was altered in 1862 to dioptric.
It was first exhibited on the night of 1 August 1832.

CHURCH RUINS also exist at INISHDOOEY, a small off-shore
island 7 km S of Tory.

TRILLICK   TY *F8*

CASTLE MERVYN. 1.5 km N. The ruins of a Plantation castle

* Not visited. Information on Godwin from Rory O'Donnell.

built *c.* 1630 by Lord Castlehaven. The s w gable still stands, with a big fireplace on the ground floor and a brick-lined oven. Rubble-built, with no architectural detail remaining. Much overgrown.

TRILLICK PARISH CHURCH (C of I). High Victorian Gothic, built in 1872 by the Archdale family in a new parish created in that year. Dec windows. Hall and chancel with offset porch. Belfry turret with a broach-spire. All in dark red sandstone.

KILSKEERY PARISH CHURCH (C of I). 3.5 km wsw. A big, rough church on a hill. Mid Georgian Gothic of 1790. Hall and tower type, with an elongated four-stage rubble tower with Irish battlements. Paid for by the Rev. Thomas Hastings. The original spire was taken down and re-erected in 1830. Five-bay nave. Improved in 1890 by *Thomas Elliott* of Enniskillen, who added a new ceiling, pews, floor, vestry, and E window.

KILSKEERY CATHOLIC CHURCH. 2.5 km w. Mid C19. A six-bay hall with sanctuary and three-storey battlemented tower.

ORATORY OF THE SACRED HEART. A modern hall of ten concrete portal frames, like a school gym; disappointing.

METHODIST CHURCH. 1833. A two-bay hall.

KILSKEERY GLEBE HOUSE. Opposite the parish church. A large, handsome Georgian rectory of 1775. Three-bay, two-storey front with high attic above. Four bays at the back. The interior with heavy plasterwork cornices and lugged door and window frames. Derelict at the time of writing.

CORKHILL HOUSE. At Kilskeery, by the river, in a secluded little valley. Three-bay, two-storey Georgian on a semi-basement. Steps to the front door. Tripartite windows either side.

A country parish three miles N of Enniskillen on the shores of Lower Lough Erne.

ST MICHAEL, TRORY PARISH (C of I). 1.5 km sse of Trory Bridge. A simple hall and tower type church rebuilt and consecrated in 1778. The tower is the most remarkable part of the church, with a particularly jagged silhouette provided by pinnacled Irish battlements, as at Ballinamallard, but with the added decoration of short lengths of string course set like quoins at the top corners of the tower. The interior was originally of just three bays, Georgian-Gothic glazed, with a short wing to the N containing the Archdale and Richardson family pews, neatly divided down the middle with a fireplace for each family.

Single-bay chancel of 1862 by *Welland & Gillespie*. The E window is a five-light cusped lancet. The chancel roof with hammerbeam trusses contrasts oddly with the coved and flat plaster ceiling of the rest. – STAINED GLASS. In the E window the Resurrection, by *Hughes* of London, 1880. Attractive patterns of roses and lilies in the outer windows. – In the side windows Supper at Emmaus and a charity group, both of 1892. – First nave window, a sombre Christ.

WHITEHILL CATHOLIC CHURCH. 2.5 km N of Trory Bridge. A rectangular mid C19 hall with three Gothic windows and a side porch.

METHODIST CHURCH. 0.5 km SE of Trory Bridge. Prettily set among trees, a small three-bay Gothic hall with a porch, harled, with quoins. Flat ceiling inside. Built according to local tradition by Mr Halliday of Trory Mill.

TRORY BRIDGE AND MILL. A single-arch stone bridge inscribed 'Built by Con. Connolly under the inspection of Edward Archdale Esq AD 1817'. Cost £1,100. By the bridge are the ruins of a watermill built by John Halliday. Early C19. Boats from Lough Erne used to ply up the river as far as the mill.

ST ANGELO. 1 km W of Trory Bridge. A three-bay, two-storey farmhouse in an idyllic position with long views across Lough Erne. In the last C19, when it belonged to the Lowrys of Pomeroy, it was given a more picturesque form, with half-timbering over the entire upper storey, three gables with finials, a red tile roof, and a gabled porch. Nicely detailed with dowels to join the timbering. Only the diamond-cut quoins of the original house remain to prove its C18 origin.

ROSSFAD. 1.5 km NW of Trory Bridge. A square, solid house that looks about 1780, built by the Richardson family. Three storeys on a high basement with a three-bay front and back and a deep four-bay side. The windows nicely proportioned, diminishing from floor to floor. Original hall and a fine wooden stair with turned balusters. Porch and E service wing of 1889. A curving stone screen wall is said to incorporate parts of a previous Maguire house.

TULLY CASTLE *see* CHURCH HILL

ULSTER AMERICAN FOLK PARK *see* MOUNTJOY FOREST

E5   URNEY   TY

CHRISTCHURCH, URNEY PARISH CHURCH (C of I). 1864–
   6 by *Welland & Gillespie*. A nice crisp design in coursed rubble
   stone. Cruciform, with a polygonal apse, double N transept, and
   a gabled first bay on the S of the nave to allow for possible expansion. Tower and broach-spire between nave and N transept.
   Wheel window in the W gable. Characteristic Commissioners'
   interior. – STAINED GLASS. S window of 1894, 'Suffer the little
   Children', by *A. L. Moore* of London. – MONUMENT. Taken
   from the old church. To William Maxwell † 1789. Draped urn
   in marble with bay-leaf garland.
OLD CHURCH RUIN. 1723, a rectangular hall, 24 by 60 ft, with
   round-headed windows on the S side and a small brick porch.
URNEY PRESBYTERIAN CHURCH. Congregation founded in
   1654. T-plan. Old Y-tracery windows now mostly replaced. The
   building is said to date from 1695 but looks no older than the
   mid C19.
URNEY PARK. Early C19. Built for Sir James Galbraith. A
   straightforward small classical block, two-storey, three-bay,
   with corner quoins, and a four-columned Tuscan porch in
   stone.

                   WALWORTH *see* BALLYKELLY

C7   WARDTOWN   DO
                       3 km WNW of Ballyshannon

A great gaunt house, roofless since early this century, yet still of
   unusual interest. Its ruins sit high above the Erne, staring over
   dunes and sand, and are visible from far across the estuary. The
   house was built by a General Folliott in 1740 to an exceptional
   plan, similar to the small conceits by Vanbrugh but on a larger
   scale. It is an absolutely symmetrical, three-storey castle with
   three half-round towers across the entrance front and one in
   the middle at the rear. Three rooms occupy the centre, each
   21 ft square, with windows to front and back. The entrance hall
   has apsed ends, expressed as towers in the middle of both fronts.
   The end towers are round rooms 13 ft in diameter with identical
   big square stair-wells behind them. The windows of the basement, barrel-vaulted throughout, have segmental pocket vaults.
   In the saucer domes of the tower rooms, also vaulted, some
   exceptionally delicate grotesque plasterwork. The plasterwork

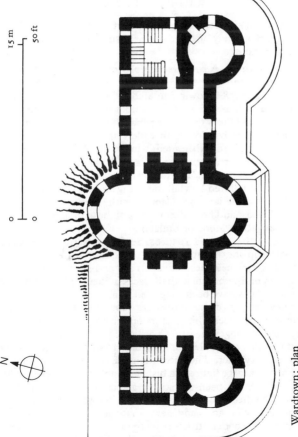

15 m
50 ft

N

Wardtown: plan
Alistair Rowan, redrawn by Stephen Gage

in the main ground-floor rooms was arranged in lugged panels. The whole house rose to a level of sophistication unusual in Ireland at this date. Its rigid symmetry (even to doubling the staircases) and its unusual architectural quality suggest a designer of some pretensions: but who? Pearce, the most likely choice, had died by 1733.

WHITE CASTLE *see* REDCASTLE

E8   WHITE ISLAND   FM

An island one kilometre long in Lower Lough Erne, N of Castle Archdale. Boats may be hired on the N shore of the lough immediately opposite.

CHURCH RUINS. A small rectangular cell, 20 ft by 39 ft inside, extensively repaired by General Archdale in the 1840s and restored in 1958 following an archaeological excavation of the site. The walls are 3 ft wide at the sides and 3 ft 3 in. at the gable ends. Little of the W or N walls remains. In the E wall is a narrow square-headed window with widely splayed reveals; in the S wall, a small round-headed window with a checked and chamfered external reveal and a large Irish Romanesque doorway, both re-erected. The doorway has two colonnettes to the jambs, and pointed bowtell mouldings to the voussoirs above. Probably of the late C12. Capitals with interlace and leaf patterns. Impost and hood decorated with bead mouldings. Inside a square FONT stone or bullaun.

14 SCULPTURED STONE FIGURES. Set for protection under a concrete slab inside the rebuilt N wall of the church are eight figures found at various times between 1840 and 1958 built into the masonry of the church, with the faces hidden, or buried nearby. Various dates have been suggested, ranging from the C7 to late medieval. Five of the figures are represented with the same dumpy round feet – like castors on a piece of furniture – that are used to suggest a sitting position in the C10 *Book of Deer*, and it seems probable that they date from around this period or a century later. The excavations of 1958 discovered one of the finest, a large figure of a bishop or abbot with a crozier and bell, which has been tentatively associated with Abbot Constans who died about 777 and who is known to have founded a monastery on an island here. Excavations have shown that there was a wooden structure on the site before the C12 church, and the figures are presumably related to this. Several have

sockets or mortices cut in the top of the heads, which suggests that they were used in an architectural context, possibly to frame a portal or sedilia, as one has interlace patterns down the r. side. An alternative theory – and it is an attractive one first put forward by Françoise Henry – is that the figures were used as caryatids to support the steps of the ambo (a raised preaching platform or chair), in which case they may possibly have been used in pairs.

The figures, with the exception of a ninth head found in the 1960s and not shown, are, from N to S: (1) a single head wearing a bonnet; (2) an unfinished figure, head and body; (3) a short figure with curly hair like a cap holding a shield and sword – a little like a hot-water bottle – and wearing a penannular brooch on the l. shoulder; (4) perhaps a pair for (3), with the same hair cap, holding two rams or, more probably, two griffins; (5) a tonsured monk touching his cheek with his l. hand and holding a staff in his r., with a pouch hanging from his girdle; (6) the bishop figure, wearing a hood and carrying a bell and crozier; (7) a badly mutilated figure seated in a habit with a book on his knees; (8) a grotesque figure with puffed-out cheeks that sits cross-legged with hands holding back her thighs to expose the genital area. This is a sheila-na-gig, that is a female fertility cult figure.

Various fanciful theories have been proposed for the identity of the figures. Father O'Driscoll suggested that they represented the seven deadly sins; another theory linked Nos. 3, 4, and 5 to an incident in the Tripartite Life of St Patrick where St Patrick (5) resuscitates Euna (4), the son of King Leaghaire (3), who had choked when eating mutton – hence the rams he holds – when Patrick was trying to convert the king to Christianity by fasting. A more simple interpretation, and it is one that is supported by early Christian iconographic tradition, is proposed by Helen Hickey. According to her, three, or possibly four, of the statues may be taken to represent different aspects of Christ. Thus (3) is to be read as an armed Christ, the King of Glory, returning in power at the Second Coming; (4) is Christ again, holding two griffins, whose fabulous forms, half eagle half lion, symbolize the dual nature of Christ as both divine and human; (5) is an unusual representation of King David, to be identified by the shepherd's staff in his right hand, the gesture he makes towards his mouth indicating his role as the author and singer of the Psalms; (6) the statue with the crozier and bell may be St Anthony of the Desert – a common early Christian type – or else Christ in his role as Abbot of the World (and if the latter is the case, then 5 and 6 together might represent the Old and the New Testaments, which would be particularly appropriate for a pulpit or reading platform); (7) is Christ holding a gospel book; and (8), the lewd female figure, is 'an illustration of Lust and a warning to the monks against the sins of the flesh'.

The church and figures are enclosed by a dry stone wall. In the SW corner is an incised CROSS SLAB inscribed with the name *concnain* across the top and *fod* at the bottom.

DAVY'S ISLAND.* S of White Island. Here is the wall of a church or cell that belonged to the Augustinian abbey of Lisgoole.

* Not visited.

GLOSSARY

Particular types of an architectural element are often defined under the name of the element itself, e.g. for 'dog-leg stair' see STAIR. Literal meanings, where specially relevant, are indicated by the abbreviation *lit*. Of the terms here defined, not all are necessarily used in this volume. The abbreviations E.E., DEC, and PERP, referring to stylistic subdivisions in English Gothic architecture, have little relevance to Irish medieval patterns. They are retained here principally because they provide a convenient shorthand with which to indicate the character of much C19 Gothic Revival architecture in Ireland which, particularly in the first half of the century, was often based on English models.

ABACUS (*lit*. tablet): flat slab forming the top of a capital, *see* Orders (fig. 16).

ABUTMENT: the meeting of an arch or vault with its solid lateral support, or the support itself.

ACANTHUS: formalized leaf ornament with thick veins and frilled edge, e.g. on a Corinthian capital.

ACHIEVEMENT OF ARMS: in heraldry, a complete display of armorial bearings.

ACROTERION (*lit*. peak): pointed ornament projecting above the apex or ends of a pediment.

AEDICULE (*lit*. little building): term used in classical architecture to describe the unit formed by a pair of columns or pilasters, an entablature, and usually a pediment, placed against a wall to frame an opening.

AGGREGATE: small stones added to a binding material, e.g. in harling or concrete.

AISLE (*lit*. wing): passage alongside the nave, choir or transept of a church, or the main body of some other building, separated from it by columns or piers.

AMBO: raised platform or pulpit in early Christian churches.

AMBULATORY (*lit*. walkway): aisle at the E end of a chancel, usually surrounding an apse and therefore semicircular or polygonal in plan.

ANNULET (*lit*. ring): shaft-ring (q.v.).

ANSE DE PANIER (*lit*. basket handle): basket arch (*see* Arch).

ANTAE: (1) flat pilasters placed at the ends of the short projecting walls of a portico or colonnade, which is then called *In Antis*. *See* Orders (fig. 16). The bases and capitals of antae differ from, and are more simple than, the columns of the order that they accompany. (2) the side walls of a building projecting at the gables, typical of many early Christian churches in Ireland.

ANTEFIXAE: ornaments projecting at regular intervals above a classical cornice. *See* Orders (fig. 16).

ANTHEMION (*lit*. honeysuckle):

A   P   A   P   A

Fig. 1. Anthemion and
Palmette Frieze

classical ornament like a honeysuckle flower (*see* fig. 1).

APSE: semicircular (i.e. apsidal)
extension of an apartment. A
term first used of the magistrate's end of a Roman basilica,
and thence especially of the
vaulted semicircular or polygonal end of a chancel or a
chapel.

ARABESQUE: type of painted or
carved surface decoration, often
with a vertical emphasis and
consisting of intertwined foliage

scrolls sometimes incorporating
ornamental objects or figures.

ARCADE: a series of arches supported by piers or columns.
Blind Arcade: the same applied
to the surface of a wall. *Wall
Arcade:* in medieval churches, a
blind arcade forming a dado
below windows.

ARCH: for the various forms *see* fig.
2. The term *Basket Arch* refers
to a basket handle and is sometimes applied to a three-centred
or depressed arch as well as the
type with a flat middle. *Transverse Arch:* across the main axis
of an interior space. A term used
especially for the arches between
the compartments of tunnel-
or groin-vaulting. *Diaphragm
Arch:* transverse arch with solid
spandrels spanning an otherwise
wooden-roofed interior. *Chancel*

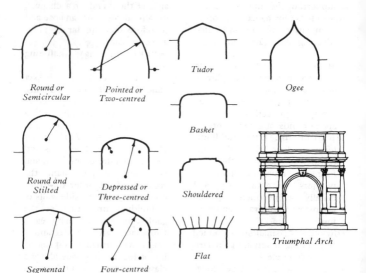

Round or   Pointed or   Tudor   Ogee
Semicircular   Two-centred

Round and   Depressed or   Basket
Stilted   Three-centred

                                         Shouldered

Segmental   Four-centred   Triumphal Arch
                                         Flat

Fig. 2. Arch

Arch: across the W end of a chancel. *Relieving Arch:* incorporated in a wall, to carry some of its weight, some way above an opening. *Strainer Arch:* inserted across an opening to resist any inward pressure of the side members. *Triumphal Arch:* Imperial Roman monument whose elevation supplied a motif for many later classical compositions.

ARCHITRAVE: (1) formalized lintel, the lowest member of the classical entablature (*see* Orders, fig. 16); (2) moulded frame of a door or window. Also *Lugged* (Irish) or *Shouldered Architrave*, whose top is prolonged into lugs (*lit.* ears).

ARCHIVOLT: under surface of an arch or the moulded band applied to this curve. Also called Soffit.

ARRIS (*lit.* stop): sharp edge at the meeting of two surfaces.

ASHLAR: masonry of large blocks wrought to even faces and square edges.

ASTYLAR: term used to describe an elevation that has no columns or other distinguishing stylistic features.

ATLANTES: male counterparts of caryatids, often in a more demonstrative attitude of support. In sculpture, a single figure of the god Atlas may be seen supporting a globe.

ATTACHED: description of a shaft or column that is partly merged into a wall or pier.

ATTIC: (1) small top storey often within a sloping roof; (2) in classical architecture, the top storey of a façade if it appears above the principal entablature of the façade.

AUMBRY: recess or cupboard to hold sacred vessels for the Mass.

BAILEY: open space or court of a stone-built castle; *see also* Motte-and-Bailey.

BALDACCHINO: free-standing canopy over an altar or tomb, usually supported on columns. Also called Ciborium.

BALLFLOWER: globular flower of three petals enclosing a small ball. A decoration used in the first quarter of the C14.

BALUSTER (*lit.* pomegranate): hence a pillar or pedestal of bellied form. *Balusters:* vertical supports of this or any other form, for a handrail or coping, the whole being called a *Balustrade. Blind Balustrade:* the same with a wall behind.

BARBICAN: outwork defending the entrance to a castle.

BARGEBOARDS: projecting inclined boards, often decoratively pierced and carved, fixed beneath the eaves of a gable to cover and protect the rafters. Common in C15 and C16 architecture and revived by Picturesque designers in the C19.

BARROW: burial mound.

BARTIZAN (*lit.* battlement): turret, square or round, corbelled out from a wall or tower of a castle, church, or house. Frequently at a corner, hence *Corner Bartizan.*

BASE: moulded foot of a column or other order. For its use in classical architecture *see* Orders (fig. 16). *Elided Bases:* bases of a compound pier whose lower parts are run together, ignoring the arrangement of the shafts above. Capitals may be treated in the same way.

BASEMENT: lowest, subordinate storey of a building, and hence the lowest part of an elevation, below the main floor.

BASILICA (*lit.* royal building): a Roman public hall; hence an aisled building with a clerestory.

BASTION: one of a series of projections from the main wall of a fortress or city, placed at intervals in such a manner as to enable the garrison to cover the intervening stretches of the wall. Post-medieval and developed for use with artillery (first at Rhodes), bastions are usually polygonal or semicircular in plan.

BATTER: inward inclination of a wall.

BATTLEMENT: fortified parapet, indented or crenellated so that archers could shoot through the indentations (crenels or embrasures) between the projecting solid portions (merlons). After the invention of gunpowder had made them obsolete, battlements continued in use as decoration until at least the C17. *Irish Battlements:* a system where the up-and-down rhythm of merlons and embrasures is interrupted at the corners, which are built up in a series of high steps, typical of late medieval architecture in Ireland.

BAWN (*lit.* ox fold): defensive walled enclosure attached to, or near, a tower house or Plantation castle.

BAYS: divisions of an elevation or interior space as defined by any regular vertical features (arches, columns, windows, etc.).

BAY-WINDOW: window of one or more storeys projecting from the face of a building at ground level, and either rectangular or polygonal in plan. A *Canted Bay-Window* has a straight front and angled sides. A *Bow Window* is curved. An *Oriel Window* projects on corbels or brackets from an upper floor and does not start from the ground.

BEAKHEAD: Norman ornamental motif consisting of a row of bird or beast heads with beaks biting usually into a roll moulding.

BELFRY (*lit.* tower): (1) bell-turret set on a roof or gable (*see also* Bellcote); (2) room or stage in a tower where bells are hung; (3) bell-tower in a general sense.

BELL-CAST: *see* Roof.

BELLCOTE: belfry as (1) above, with the character of a small house for the bell(s).

BILLET (*lit.* log or block) FRIEZE: Norman ornament consisting of small blocks placed at regular intervals (*see* fig. 3).

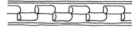

Fig. 3.   Billet Frieze

BLIND: *see* Arcade, Balustrade.

BLOCKING COURSE: plain course of stones, or equivalent, on top of a cornice and crowning the wall.

BOLECTION MOULDING: convex moulding covering the joint between two different planes and overlapping the higher as well as the lower one, especially on panelling and fireplace surrounds of the late C17 and early C18.

BOND: in brickwork, the pattern of long sides (stretchers) and short ends (headers) produced on the

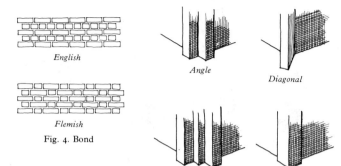

English

Flemish

Fig. 4. Bond

Angle

Diagonal

Set-back

Clasping

Fig. 5. Buttresses at a corner

face of a wall by laying bricks in a particular way (*see* fig. 4).

BOSS: knob or projection usually placed to cover the intersection of ribs in a vault.

BOW WINDOW: *see* Bay-window.

BOX PEW: pew enclosed by a high wooden back and ends, the latter having doors.

BRACE: *see* Roof (fig. 22).

BRACKET: small supporting piece of stone, etc., to carry a projecting horizontal member.

BUCRANIUM: ox skull, used decoratively in classical friezes.

BULLAUNS: boulders having an artificial basin-like hollow. Now frequently regarded with superstition, they are found at early monastic sites and killeens and were probably used for pounding and grinding grain.

BULLSEYE WINDOW: small circular window, e.g. in the tympanum of a pediment. Also called *Œil de Bœuf*.

BUTTRESS: vertical member projecting from a wall to stabilize it or to resist the lateral thrust of an arch, roof, or vault. For different types used at the corners of a building, especially a tower, *see* fig. 5. A *Flying Buttress* transmits the thrust to a heavy

abutment by means of an arch or half-arch.

CABLE MOULDING or ROPE MOULDING: originally a Norman moulding, imitating the twisted strands of a rope.

CAMBER: slight rise or upward curve in place of a horizontal line or plane.

CAMPANILE: free-standing bell-tower.

CANDLE-SNUFFER ROOF: conical roof of a turret.

CANES: *see* Quarries.

CANOPY: projection or hood over an altar, pulpit, niche, statue, etc.

CANTED: tilted, generally on a vertical axis to produce an obtuse angle on plan, e.g. of a canted bay-window.

CAPITAL: head or top part of a column; for classical types *see* Orders (fig. 16); for medieval types *see* fig. 6. *Elided Capitals:* capitals of a compound pier whose upper parts are run

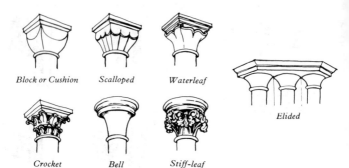

Block or Cushion   *Scalloped*   *Waterleaf*

Elided

Crocket   *Bell*   *Stiff-leaf*

Fig. 6. Capitals

together, ignoring the arrangement of the shafts below.

CARRIAGE ARCH: *see* Pend.

CARTOUCHE: tablet with ornate frame, usually of elliptical shape and bearing a coat of arms or inscription.

CARYATIDS (*lit.* daughters of the village of Caryae): female figures supporting an entablature, counterparts of Atlantes.

CASEMATE: in military architecture, a vaulted chamber, with embrasures for defence, built in the thickness of the walls of a castle or fortress or projecting from them.

CASEMENT: (1) window hinged at the side; (2) in Gothic architecture, a concave moulding framing a window.

CASTELLATED: battlemented (*q.v.*).

CAVETTO: concave moulding of quarter-round section.

CELLURACH: *see* Killeen.

CELURE or CEILURE: panelled and adorned part of a wagon roof above the rood or the altar.

CENTERING: wooden support for the building of an arch or vault,

removed after completion.

CHAMFER (*lit.* corner-break): surface formed by cutting off a square edge, usually at an angle of forty-five degrees.

CHANCEL (*lit.* enclosure): that part of the E end of a church in which the altar is placed, usually applied to the whole continuation of the nave E of the crossing.

CHANTRY CHAPEL: chapel attached to, or inside, a church, endowed for the celebration of masses for the soul of the founder or some other individual.

CHEVRON: zigzag Norman ornament.

CHOIR: (1) the part of a church where services are sung; in monastic churches this can occupy the crossing and/or the easternmost bays of the nave, but in cathedral churches it is usually in the E arm; (2) the E arm of a cruciform church (a usage of long standing though liturgically anomalous).

CIBORIUM: canopied shrine for the reserved sacrament. *See also* Baldacchino.

CINQUEFOIL: *see* Foil.

CLAPPER BRIDGE: bridge made of large slabs of stone, some built up to make rough piers and other longer ones laid on top to make the roadway.

CLASSIC: term for the moment of highest achievement of a style.

CLASSICAL: term for Greek and Roman architecture and any subsequent styles inspired by it.

CLERESTORY: upper storey of the nave walls of a church, pierced by windows.

COADE STONE: artificial (cast) stone made in the late C18 and the early C19 by Coade and Sealy in London.

COB: walling material made of mixed clay and straw. Also called *Mud Wall*.

COFFERING: sunken panels, square or polygonal, decorating a ceiling, vault, or arch.

COLLAR: *see* Roof (fig. 22).

COLONNADE: range of columns supporting an entablature.

COLONNETTE: small column or shaft in medieval architecture.

COLUMN: in classical architecture, an upright structural member of round section with a shaft, a capital, and usually a base. *See* Orders (fig. 16).

COLUMNA ROSTRATA: column decorated with carved prows of ships to celebrate a naval victory.

COMPOSITE: *see* Orders.

CONSOLE: ornamental bracket of compound curved outline (*see* fig. 7). Its height is usually greater than its projection, as in (*a*).

COPING (*lit.* capping): course of stones, or equivalent, on top of a wall.

CORBEL: block of stone projecting from a wall, supporting some feature on its horizontal top sur-

(*a*)　　　　　　(*b*)

Fig. 7. Console

face. *Corbel Course:* continuous projecting course of stones fulfilling the same function. *Corbel Table:* series of corbels to carry a parapet or a wall-plate; for the latter *see* Roof (fig. 22).

CORINTHIAN: *see* Orders (fig. 16).

CORNICE: (1) moulded ledge, decorative and/or practical, projecting along the top of a building or feature, especially as the highest member of the classical entablature (*see* Orders, fig. 16); (2) decorative moulding in the angle between a wall and ceiling.

CORPS-DE-LOGIS: French term for the main building(s) as distinct from the wings or pavilions.

COURSE: continuous layer of stones etc. in a wall.

COVE: concave soffit like a hollow moulding but on a larger scale. A *Coved Ceiling* has a pronounced cove joining the walls to a flat surface in the middle.

CREDENCE: in a church or chapel, a side table, often a niche or recessed cavity, for the sacramental elements before consecration.

CRENELLATION: *see* Battlement.

CREST, CRESTING: ornamental

finish along the top of a screen, etc.

CROCKETS (*lit.* hooks), CROCKETING: in Gothic architecture, leafy knobs on the edges of any sloping feature. *Crocket Capital: see* Capital (fig. 6).

CROSSING: in a church, central space opening into the nave, chancel, and transepts. *Crossing Tower:* central tower supported by the piers at its corners.

CROWSTEPS: squared stones set like steps to form a skew; *see* Gable (fig. 9).

CRUCK (*lit.* crooked): piece of naturally curved timber combining the structural roles of an upright post and a sloping rafter, e.g. in the building of a cottage, where each pair of crucks is joined at the ridge.

CRYPT: underground room usually below the E end of a church.

CUPOLA (*lit.* dome): small polygonal or circular domed turret crowning a roof.

CURTAIN WALL: (1) connecting wall between the towers of a castle; (2) in modern building, thin wall attached to the main structure, usually outside it.

CURVILINEAR: *see* Tracery (fig. 25).

CUSP: projecting point formed by the foils within the divisions of Gothic tracery, also used to decorate the soffits of the Gothic arches of tomb recesses, sedilia, etc.

CYCLOPEAN MASONRY: built with large irregular polygonal stones, but smooth and finely jointed.

DADO: lower part of a wall or its

decorative treatment; *see also* Pedestal (fig. 17).

DAGGER: *see* Tracery (fig. 25).

DAIS: raised platform at one end of a room.

DEC (DECORATED): historical division of English Gothic architecture covering the period from *c.* 1290 to *c.* 1350.

DEMI-COLUMNS: engaged columns, only half of whose circumference projects from the wall.

DIAPER (*lit.* figured cloth): repetitive surface decoration.

DIOCLETIAN WINDOW: *see* Thermae Window.

DISTYLE: having two columns.

DOGTOOTH: typical E.E. decoration applied to a moulding. It consists of a series of squares, their centres raised like pyramids and their edges indented (*see* fig. 8).

Fig. 8. Dogtooth

DONJON: *see* Keep.

DORIC: *see* Orders (fig. 16).

DORMER WINDOW: window standing up vertically from the slope of a roof and lighting a room within it. *Dormer Head:* gable above this window, often formed as a pediment.

DORTER: dormitory; sleeping quarters of a monastery.

DOUBLE PILE: *see* Pile.

DRESSINGS: features made of smoothly worked stones, e.g. quoins or string courses, projecting from the wall which may be of different material, colour, or texture. Also called *Trim.*

DRIPSTONE: moulded stone projecting from a wall to protect the lower parts from water; *see also* Hoodmould.

DRUM: (1) circular or polygonal vertical wall of a dome or cupola; (2) one of the stones forming the shaft of a column.

DRYSTONE: stone construction without mortar.

E.E. (EARLY ENGLISH): historical division of English Gothic architecture covering the period 1200–1250.

EAVES: overhanging edge of a roof; hence *Eaves Cornice* in this position.

ECHINUS (*lit.* sea-urchin): lower part of a Greek Doric capital; *see* Orders (fig. 16).

EDGE-ROLL: moulding of semicircular or more than semicircular section at the edge of an opening.

ELEVATION: (1) any side of a building; (2) in a drawing, the same or any part of it, accurately represented in two dimensions.

ELIDED: term used to describe (1) a compound architectural feature, e.g. an entablature, in which some parts have been omitted; (2) a number of similar parts which have been combined to form a single larger one (*see* Capital, fig. 6).

EMBATTLED: furnished with battlements.

EMBRASURE (*lit.* splay): small splayed opening in the wall or battlement of a fortified building.

ENCAUSTIC TILES: glazed and decorated earthenware tiles used for paving.

ENGAGED COLUMN: one that is partly merged into a wall or pier.

ENTABLATURE: in classical architecture, collective name for the three horizontal members (architrave, frieze, and cornice) above a column; *see* Orders (fig. 16).

ENTASIS: very slight convex deviation from a straight line; used on classical columns and sometimes on spires to prevent an optical illusion of concavity.

ENTRESOL: mezzanine storey within or above the ground storey.

ESCUTCHEON: shield for armorial bearings.

EXEDRA: apsidal end of an apartment; *see* Apse.

FERETORY: (1) place behind the high altar where the chief shrine of a church is kept; (2) wooden or metal container for relics.

FESTOON: ornament, usually in high or low relief, in the form of a garland of flowers and/or fruit, hung up at both ends; *see also* Swag.

FILLET: narrow flat band running down a shaft or along a roll moulding.

FINIAL: topmost feature, e.g. above a gable, spire, or cupola.

FLAMBOYANT: properly the latest phase of French Gothic architecture, where the window tracery takes on undulating lines, based on the use of flowing curves.

FLÈCHE (*lit.* arrow): slender spire on the centre of a roof.

FLEUR-DE-LYS: in heraldry, a formalized lily as in the royal arms of France.

FLEURON: decorative carved flower or leaf.

FLOWING: *see* Tracery (Curvilinear; fig. 25).

FLUTING: series of concave grooves, their common edges sharp (arris) or blunt (fillet).

FOIL (*lit.* leaf): lobe formed by the cusping of a circular or other shape in tracery. *Trefoil* (three), *Quatrefoil* (four), *Cinquefoil* (five), and *Multifoil* express the number of lobes in a shape; *see* Tracery (fig. 25).

FOLIATED: decorated, especially carved, with leaves.

FOSSE: ditch.

FRATER: refectory or dining hall of a monastery.

FREESTONE: stone that is cut, or can be cut, in all directions, usually fine-grained sandstone or limestone.

FRESCO: painting executed on wet plaster.

FRIEZE: horizontal band of ornament, especially the middle member of the classical entablature; *see* Orders (fig. 16). *Pulvinated Frieze* (*lit.* cushioned): frieze of convex profile.

FRONTAL: covering for the front of an altar.

GABLE: (1) peaked wall or other vertical surface, often triangular, at the end of a double-pitch roof; (2) the same, very often with a chimney at the apex, but also in a wider sense: end wall, of whatever shape. See fig. 9. *Gablet*: small gable. See also Roof.

GADROONING: ribbed ornament, e.g. on the lid or base of an urn, flowing into a lobed edge.

GALILEE: chapel or vestibule usually at the w end of a church enclosing the porch; *see also* Narthex.

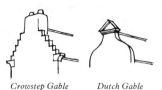

Crowstep Gable   *Dutch Gable*

Curvilinear or Shaped Gable at wall-head

Fig. 9. Gables

GALLERY: balcony or passage, but with certain special meanings, e.g. (1) upper storey above the aisle of a church, looking through arches to the nave; also called tribune and often erroneously triforium; (2) balcony or mezzanine, often with seats, overlooking the main interior space of a building; (3) external walkway projecting from a wall.

GARDEROBE (*lit.* wardrobe): medieval privy.

GARGOYLE: water spout projecting from the parapet of a wall or tower, often carved into human or animal shape.

GAZEBO (jocular Latin, 'I shall gaze'): lookout tower or raised summer house overlooking a garden.

GEOMETRIC: historical division of English Gothic architecture covering the period *c.* 1250–90. See also Tracery (fig. 25). For another meaning, *see* Stair.

GIBBS SURROUND: C18 treatment of door or window surround,

seen particularly in the work of James Gibbs (1682–1754) (*see* fig. 10).

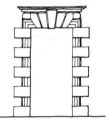

Fig. 10. Gibbs Surround

GLACIS: in military architecture, a bank, extending in a long slow slope from a fort, on which attackers are exposed to fire.

GLEBE HOUSE: a house built on and counting as part of the portion of land going with an established clergyman's benefice.

GNOMON: vane or indicator casting a shadow on to a sundial.

GROIN: sharp edge at the meeting of two cells of a cross-vault; *see* Vault (fig. 26a).

GROTESQUE (*lit.* grotto-esque): classical wall decoration of spindly, whimsical character adopted from Roman examples, particularly by Raphael, and further developed in the C18.

GUILLOCHE: running classical ornament formed by a series of circles with linked and interlaced borders (see fig. 11).

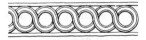

Fig. 11. Guilloche

GUN LOOP: opening for a firearm.
GUTTAE: *see* Orders (fig. 16).

HAGIOSCOPE: *see* Squint.

HALF-TIMBERING: timber framing with the spaces filled in by plaster, stones or brickwork.

HALL CHURCH: (1) a medieval or Gothic Revival church whose nave and aisles are of equal height or approximately so; (2) a church which is simply a rectangular gabled hall. Often in Ireland there is a simple tower at the w end, hence the term used in this series: *Tower and Hall Church.*

HAMMERBEAM: *see* Roof.

HARLING: *see* Rendering.

HEADER: *see* Bond.

HERM (*lit.* the god Hermes): male head or bust on a pedestal.

HERRINGBONE WORK: masonry or brickwork in zigzag courses.

HEXASTYLE: term used to describe a portico with six columns.

HOODMOULD: projecting moulding above an arch or lintel to throw off water. When the moulding is horizontal it is called a *Label*.

HUNGRY JOINTS: *see* Pointing.

HUSK GARLAND: festoon of nutshells diminishing towards the ends (*see* fig. 12).

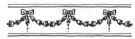

Fig. 12. Husk Garland

IMPOST (*lit.* imposition): horizontal moulding at the spring of an arch.

IN ANTIS: *see* Antae, Orders (fig. 16), and Portico.

INDENT: (1) shape chiselled out of a stone to match and receive a brass; (2) in restoration, a section of new stone inserted as a patch into older work.

INGLENOOK (*lit.* fire-corner): recess for a hearth with provision for seating.

INTERCOLUMNIATION: interval between columns.

IONIC: *see* Orders (fig. 16).

JAMB (*lit.* leg): one of the straight sides of an archway, door, or window.

KEEL MOULDING: *see* fig. 13.

KEEP: principal tower of a castle. Also called Donjon.

KEY PATTERN: *see* fig. 14.

KEYSTONE: middle and topmost stone in an arch or vault.

KILLEEN or CELLURACH (*lit.* a cell or church): a walled enclosure, used until recent times for the burial of unbaptized children. Often near old monastic sites.

KINGPOST: *see* Roof (fig. 22).

LABEL: *see* Hoodmould. *Label*

Fig. 13. Keel Moulding

Fig. 14. Key Pattern

Stop: ornamental boss at the end of a hoodmould.

LADY CHAPEL: chapel dedicated to the Virgin Mary.

LANCET WINDOW: slender pointed-arched window, often in groups of two, five, or seven.

LANTERN: a small circular or polygonal turret with windows all round crowning a roof (*see* Cupola) or a dome.

LAVATORIUM: in a monastery, a washing place adjacent to the refectory.

LEAN-TO: term commonly applied not only to a single-pitch roof but to the building it covers.

LESENE (*lit.* a mean thing): pilaster without base or capital. Also called pilaster strip.

LIERNE: *see* Vault (fig. 26b).

LIGHT: compartment of a window.

LINENFOLD: Tudor panelling ornamented with a conventional representation of a piece of linen laid in vertical folds. The piece is repeated in each panel.

LINTEL: horizontal beam or stone bridging an opening.

LOGGIA: sheltered space behind a colonnade.

LOUVRE: (1) opening, often with lantern over, in the roof of a building to let the smoke from a central hearth escape; (2) one of a series of overlapping boards placed in a window to allow ventilation but keep the rain out.

LOZENGE: diamond shape.

LUCARNE (*lit.* dormer): small window in a roof or spire, often capped by a gable or final.

LUGGED: *see* Architrave.

LUNETTE (*lit.* half or crescent moon): (1) semicircular window; (2) semicircular or crescent-shaped surface.

LYCHGATE (*lit.* corpse-gate): wooden gate structure with a roof and open sides placed at the entrance to a churchyard to provide space for the reception of a coffin.

LYNCHET: long terraced strip of soil accumulating on the downward side of prehistoric and medieval fields due to soil creep from continuous ploughing along the contours.

MACHICOLATION: in medieval military architecture, a series of openings at the top of a wall head, made by building the parapet on projecting brackets, with the spaces between left open to allow missiles or boiling liquids to be dropped on the heads of assailants.

MAJOLICA: ornamented glazed earthenware.

MANSARD: *see* Roof (fig. 21).

MARGINS: dressed stones at the edges of an opening.

MAUSOLEUM: monumental tomb, so named after that of Mausolus, king of Caria, at Halicarnassus.

MERLON: *see* Battlement.

METOPES: spaces between the triglyphs in a Doric frieze; *see* Orders (fig. 16).

MEZZANINE: (1) low storey between two higher ones; (2) low upper storey within the height of a high one, not extending over its whole area.

MISERERE: *see* Misericord.

MISERICORD (*lit.* mercy): shelf placed on the underside of a hinged choir stall seat which, when turned up, provided the occupant with support during long periods of standing. Also called Miserere.

MODILLIONS: small consoles at regular intervals along the underside of some types of classical cornice. Typically a Corinthian or Composite element.

MOTTE: steep earthen mound forming the main feature of C11 and C12 castles.

MOTTE-AND-BAILEY: post-Roman and Norman defence system consisting of an earthen mound (motte) topped with a wooden tower within a bailey, with enclosure ditch and palisade, and with the rare addition of an internal bank.

MOUCHETTE: motif in curvilinear tracery, a curved version of the dagger form, specially popular in the early C14; *see* Tracery (fig. 25).

MOULDING: ornament of continuous section; *see* the various types.

MUD WALL: *see* Cob.

MULLION: vertical member between the lights in a window opening.

MUNTIN: post forming part of a screen.

MURDER HOLE: small rectangular trap in the ceiling of an entrance passage in a castle or tower house.

NAILHEAD MOULDING: E.E. ornamental motif, consisting of small pyramids regularly repeated (*see* fig. 15).

NARTHEX: enclosed vestibule or

Fig. 15. Nailhead Moulding

covered porch at the main entrance to a church; *see also* Galilee.

NEWEL: central post in a circular or winding staircase; also the principal post when a flight of stairs meets a landing.

NICHE (*lit.* shell): vertical recess in a wall, sometimes for a statue, and often round-headed.

NIGHT STAIR: stair by which monks entered the transepts of their church from their dormitory to attend services at night.

NOOK-SHAFT: shaft set in an angle formed by other members.

NORMAN: *see* Romanesque.

NOSING: projection of the tread of a step. A *Bottle Nosing* is half-round in section.

OBELISK: lofty pillar of square section tapering at the top and ending pyramidally.

ŒIL DE BŒUF: *see* Bullseye Window.

OGEE: double curve, bending first one way and then the other. *Ogee* or *Ogival Arch: see* Arch (fig. 2).

ORDER: (1) upright structural member formally related to others, e.g. in classical architecture a column, pilaster, or anta; (2) one of a series of recessed arches and jambs forming a splayed opening. *Giant* or *Colossal Order:* classical order whose height is that of two or more storeys of a building.

ORDERS: in classical architecture, the differently formalized ver-

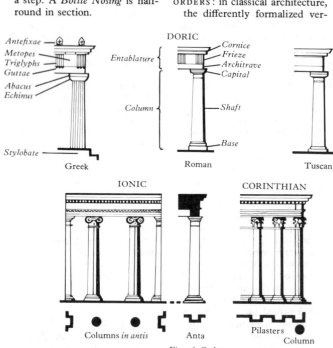

Fig. 16. Orders

sions of the basic post-and-lintel structure, each having its own rules of design and proportion. For examples of the main types *see* fig. 16. Others include the primitive Tuscan, which has a plain frieze and simple torus-moulded base, and the Composite, whose capital combines Ionic volutes with Corinthian foliage. *Superimposed Orders:* term for the use of Orders on successive levels, usually in the upward sequence of Doric, Ionic, Corinthian.

ORIEL: *see* Bay-window.

OVERHANG: projection of the upper storey(s) of a building.

OVERSAILING COURSES: series of stone or brick courses, each one projecting beyond the one below it; *see also* Corbel Course.

Pₐ ALLADIAN: architecture following the example and principles of Andrea Palladio, 1508–80.

PALMETTE: classical ornament like a symmetrical palm shoot; for illustration *see* Anthemion, fig. 1.

PANTILE: roof tile of curved S-shaped section.

PARAPET: wall for protection at any sudden drop, e.g. on a bridge or at the wall-head of a castle; in the latter case it protects the *Parapet Walk* or wall walk.

PARCLOSE: *see* Screen.

PARGETING (*lit.* plastering): usually of moulded plaster panels in half-timbering.

PATERA (*lit.* plate): round or oval ornament in shallow relief, especially in classical architecture.

PEBBLEDASHING: *see* Rendering.

PEDESTAL: in classical architecture, a stand sometimes used to support the base of an order (*see* fig. 17).

Fig. 17. Pedestal

PEDIMENT: in classical architecture, a formalized gable derived from that of a temple, also used over doors, windows, etc. For the generally accepted meanings of *Broken Pediment* and *Open Pediment see* fig. 18.

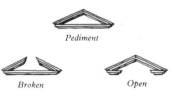

Pediment

Broken *Open*

Fig. 18. Pediments

PEND: covered archway passing through a terraced building to give vehicular access to gardens or yards behind. Also called a *Carriage Arch.*

PENDANT: hanging-down feature of a vault or ceiling, usually ending in a boss.

PENDENTIVE: spandrel between adjacent arches supporting a drum or dome, formed as part of a hemisphere (*see* fig. 19).

Fig. 19. Pendentive

PERISTYLE: in classical architecture, a range of columns all round a building, e.g. a temple, or an interior space, e.g. a courtyard.

PERP (PERPENDICULAR): historical division of English Gothic architecture covering the period from c. 1335–50 to c. 1530.

PERRON: see Stair.

PIANO NOBILE: principal floor, usually with a ground floor or basement underneath and a lesser storey overhead.

PIAZZA: open space surrounded by buildings; in the C17 and C18 sometimes employed to mean a long colonnade or loggia.

PIER: strong, solid support, frequently square in section. Compound Pier: of composite section, e.g. formed of a bundle of shafts.

PIETRA DURA: ornamental or scenic inlay by means of thin slabs of stone.

PILASTER: classical order of oblong section, its elevation similar to that of a column. Pilastrade: series of pilasters, equivalent to a colonnade. Pilaster Respond: pilaster set within a loggia or portico, or at the end of an arcade, to balance visually the column which it faces. Pilaster Strip: see Lesene.

PILE: a row of rooms. The important use of the term is in Double Pile, describing a house that is two rows thick, each row consisting of three or more rooms.

PILLAR PISCINA: free-standing piscina on a pillar.

PINNACLE: tapering finial, e.g. on a buttress or the corner of a tower, sometimes decorated with crockets.

PISCINA: basin for washing the communion or mass vessels, provided with a drain; generally set in or against the wall to the S of an altar.

PLINTH: projecting base beneath a wall or column, generally chamfered or moulded at the top.

POINTING: exposed mortar joints of masonry or brickwork. The finished form is of various types, e.g. Flush Pointing, Recessed Pointing. Bag-rubbed Pointing is flush at the edges and gently recessed in the middle of the joint. Hungry Joints are either without any pointing at all, or deeply recessed to show the outline of each stone. Ribbon Pointing is a nasty practice in the modern vernacular, the joints being formed with a trowel so that they stand out.

POPPYHEAD: carved ornament of leaves and flowers as a finial for the end of a bench or stall.

PORCH: covered projecting entrance to a building.

PORTAL FRAME: a basic form of pre-cast concrete construction where walls and roof are supported on a series of angled concrete beams which, meeting at the ridge of the roof, form 'portals'.

PORTCULLIS: gate constructed to

rise and fall in vertical grooves at the entry to a castle.

PORTE COCHÈRE (*lit.* gate for coaches): porch large enough to admit wheeled vehicles.

PORTICO: roofed space, open on one side at least, and enclosed by a row of columns which also support the roof (and frequently a pediment). A portico may be free-standing: more usually it forms part of a building, often in the form of a projecting temple front. When the front of the portico is on the same level as the front of the building it is described as a *portico in antis*.

POSTERN: small gateway at the back of a building.

PREDELLA: (1) step or platform on which an altar stands; hence (2) in an altarpiece the horizontal strip below the main representation, often used for a number of subsidiary representations in a row.

PRESBYTERY: the part of the church lying E of the choir. It is the part where the altar is placed.

PRINCIPAL: *see* Roof (fig. 22).

PRIORY: monastic house whose head is a prior or prioress, not an abbot or abbess.

PROSTYLE: with a row of columns in front.

PULPITUM: stone screen in a major church provided to shut off the choir from the nave and also as a backing for the return choir stalls.

PULVINATED: *see* Frieze.

PURLIN: *see* Roof (fig. 22).

PUTHOLE or PUTLOCK HOLE: putlocks are the short horizontal timbers on which during construction the boards of scaffolding rest. Putholes or putlock holes are the holes in the wall for putlocks, and often are not filled in after construction is complete.

PUTTO: small naked boy (plural: putti).

QUADRANGLE: inner courtyard in a large building.

QUARRIES (*lit.* squares): (1) in stained glass, square or diamond-shaped panes of glass supported by lead strips which are called *Canes*; (2) square floor-slabs or tiles.

QUATREFOIL: *see* Foil.

QUEENPOSTS: *see* Roof (fig. 22).

QUIRK: sharp groove to one side of a convex moulding, e.g. beside a roll moulding, which is then said to be quirked.

QUOINS: dressed stones at the angles of a building, usually alternately long and short.

RADIATING CHAPELS: chapels projecting radially from an ambulatory or an apse.

RAFTER: *see* Roof (fig. 22).

RAGGLE: groove cut in masonry, especially to receive the edge of glass or roof-covering.

RAKE: slope or pitch.

RAMPART: stone wall or wall of earth surrounding a castle, fortress, or fortified city. *Rampart Walk:* path along the inner face of a rampart.

RANDOM: *see* Rubble.

RATH: circular or near-circular enclosure consisting of one or more earthen (or occasionally stone) banks with ditches outside, classified as univallate, bivallate, or trivallate. Most date from early Christian times and housed single farms or served as cattle enclosures for the farms. Also called *Ring Forts*.

REBATE: rectangular section cut out of a masonry edge.

REEDING: series of convex mouldings; the reverse of fluting.

REFECTORY: dining hall (or frater) of a monastery or similar establishment.

RENDERING: the process of covering outside walls with a uniform surface or skin to protect the wall from the weather. *Stucco*, originally a fine lime plaster finished to a smooth surface, is the finest rendered external finish, characteristic of many late C18 and C19 classical buildings. It is usually painted. *Cement Rendering* is a cheaper and more recent substitute for stucco, usually with a grainy texture and often left unpainted. Shoddy but all too common in Ireland. In more simple buildings the wall surface may be roughly *Lime-plastered* (and then whitewashed), or covered with plaster mixed with a coarse aggregate such as gravel. This latter is known as *Roughcast* or, in Scotland and the North of Ireland, as *Harling*. A variant, fashionable in the early C20, is *Pebbledashing*: here the stones of

Fig. 20. Rinceau

the aggregate are kept separate from the plaster and are thrown at the wet plastered wall to create a decorative effect.

REREDOS: painted and/or sculptured screen behind and above an altar.

RESPOND: half-pier bonded into a wall and carrying one end of an arch. *See also* Pilaster Respond.

RETABLE: altarpiece; a picture or piece of carving standing behind and attached to an altar.

RETROCHOIR: in a major church, an aisle between the high altar and an E chapel, like a square ambulatory.

REVEAL: the inward plane of a jamb, between the edge of an external wall and the frame of a door or window that is set in it.

RIB-VAULT: *see* Vault.

RINCEAU (*lit.* little branch) or antique foliage: classical ornament, usually on a frieze, of leafy scrolls branching alternately to left and right (*see* fig. 20).

RING FORT: *see* Rath.

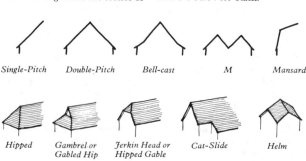

Single-Pitch   Double-Pitch   Bell-cast   M   Mansard

Hipped   Gambrel or Gabled Hip   Jerkin Head or Hipped Gable   Cat-Slide   Helm

Fig. 21. Roof Forms

RISER: vertical face of a step.

ROCK-FACED: term used to describe masonry which is cleft to produce a natural, rugged appearance.

ROCOCO (*lit.* rocky): the light-hearted last phase of the Baroque style, current in most Continental countries between *c.* 1720 and *c.* 1760, and showing itself in Ireland mainly in light classical elements and scrolled decoration, especially in plaster-work.

ROLL MOULDING: moulding of semicircular or more than semi-circular section.

ROMANESQUE: that style in architecture which was current in the CII and CI2 and preceded the Gothic style (in England often called Norman). (Some scholars extend the use of the term Romanesque back to the CIO or C.)

ROOD: cross or crucifix, usually over the entry into the chancel. The *Rood Screen* beneath it may have a *Rood Loft* along the top, reached by a *Rood Stair*.

ROOF: for external forms *see* fig. 21; for construction and components *see* fig. 22. *Wagon Roof*: lined with timber on the inside, giving the appearance of a curved or polygonal vault.

ROPE MOULDING: *see* Cable Moulding.

ROSE WINDOW: circular window with patterned tracery about the centre.

ROTUNDA: building circular in plan.

ROUGHCAST: *see* Rendering.

RUBBLE: masonry whose stones are wholly or partly in a rough state. *Coursed Rubble*: of coursed stones with rough faces. *Random*

Rubble: of uncoursed stones in a random pattern. *Snecked Rubble* has courses frequently broken by smaller square stones (snecks).

RUSTICATION: treatment of

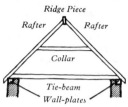

Common Roof Components

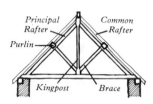

Roof with Kingpost Truss

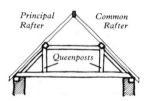

Roof with Queenpost Truss

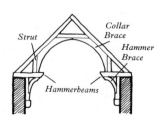

Hammerbeam Roof

Fig. 22. Roof Construction

joints and/or faces of masonry to give an effect of strength. In the most usual kind the joints are recessed by V-section chamfering or square-section channelling. *Banded Rustication* has only the horizontal joints emphasized in this way. The faces may be flat but there are many other forms, e.g. *Diamond-faced*, like a shallow pyramid, *Vermiculated*, with a stylized texture like worms or worm-holes, or *Glacial*, like icicles or stalactites. *Rusticated Columns* may have their joints and drums treated in any of these ways.

SACRAMENT HOUSE: safe cupboard for the reserved sacrament.

SACRISTY: room in a church for sacred vessels and vestments.

SANCTUARY: area around the main altar of a church (*see* Presbytery).

SARCOPHAGUS (*lit.* flesh-consuming): coffin of stone or other durable material.

SCAGLIOLA: composition imitating marble.

SCALE-AND-PLATT (*lit.* stair and landing): *see* Stair (fig. 24).

SCARCEMENT: extra thickness of the lower part of a wall, e.g. to carry a floor.

SCARP: artificial cutting away of the ground to form a steep slope.

SCISSOR TRUSS: roof truss framed at the bottom by crossed intersecting beams like open scissors. Frequently used in C19 churches in conjunction and alternating with kingpost trusses. Where the scissors occur with each rafter and are not formed into separate trusses the structure would be called a scissor-beam roof.

SCREEN: in a church, usually at the entry to the chancel; *see* Rood Screen and Pulpitum. *Parclose Screen:* separating a chapel from the rest of the church.

SCREENS or SCREENS PASSAGE: screened-off entrance passage between the hall and the kitchen in a medieval house, adjoining the kitchen, buttery, etc.

SEDILIA: seats for the priests (usually three) on the S side of the chancel of a church.

SET-OFF: *see* Weathering.

SHAFT: upright member of round section, especially the main part of a classical column. *Shaft-ring:* motif of the C12 and C13 consisting of a ring like a belt round a circular pier or a circular shaft attached to a pier.

SHEILA-NA-GIG: female fertility figure, usually with legs wide open.

SHOULDERED: *see* Arch (fig. 2), Architrave.

SILL: horizontal projection at the bottom of a window.

SLATE-HANGING: covering of overlapping slates on a wall, which is then said to be *slate-hung.*

SNECKED: *see* Rubble.

SOFFIT (*lit.* ceiling): underside of an arch, lintel, etc. *See also* Archivolt.

SOLAR (*lit.* sun-room): upper living room or withdrawing room of a medieval house, accessible from the high table end of the hall.

SOUNDING-BOARD: horizontal board or canopy over a pulpit; also called Tester.

SOUTERRAIN: underground

stone-lined passage and chamber.

SPANDRELS: surfaces left over between an arch and its containing rectangle, or between adjacent arches.

SPIRE: tall pyramidal or conical feature built on a tower or turret. *Broach Spire:* starting from a square base, then carried into an octagonal section by means of triangular faces. *Needle Spire:* thin spire rising from the centre of a tower roof, well inside the parapet. *Helm Spire: see* Roof (fig. 21).

SPIRELET: *see* Flèche.

SPLAY: chamfer, usually of a reveal.

SPRING: level at which an arch or vault rises from its supports. *Springers:* the first stones of an arch or vaulting-rib above the spring.

SQUINCH: arch thrown across an angle between two walls to support a superstructure, e.g. a dome (*see* fig. 23).

SQUINT: hole cut in a wall or through a pier to allow a view of the main altar of a church from places whence it could not other-

Fig. 23. Squinch

wise be seen. Also called Hagioscope.

STAIR: *see* fig. 24. The term *Perron* (*lit.* of stone) applies to the external stair leading to a doorway, usually of branched or double-curved plan as shown. *Spiral* or *Newel Stair:* ascending round a central supporting newel, usually in a circular shaft. *Flying Stair:* cantilevered from the wall of a stairwell, without newels. *Geometric Stair:* flying stair whose inner edge describes a curve. *Well Stair:* term applied to any stair contained in an open well, but generally to one that climbs up three sides of a well, with corner landings.

STALL: seat for clergy, choir, etc., distinctively treated in its own right or as one of a row.

STANCHION: upright structural

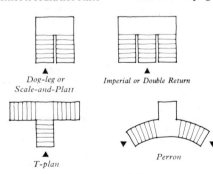

Dog-leg or Scale-and-Platt

Imperial or Double Return

T-plan

Perron

Fig. 24. Stair

member, of iron or steel or reinforced concrete.

STEEPLE : a tower together with a spire or other tall feature on top of it.

STOUP : vessel for the reception of holy water, usually placed near a door.

STRAINER : *see* Arch.

STRAPWORK : C16 and C17 decoration used also in the C19 Jacobean revival, resembling interlaced bands of cut leather.

STRETCHER : *see* Bond.

STRING COURSE : intermediate stone course or moulding projecting from the surface of a wall.

STUCCO (*lit.* plaster) : (1) smooth external rendering of a wall etc.; (2) archaic term for plasterwork.

STUDS : intermediate vertical members of a timber-framed wall or partition.

STYLOBATE : solid base structure on which a colonnade stands.

SWAG (*lit.* bundle) : like a festoon, but also a cloth bundle in relief, hung up at both ends.

TABERNACLE (*lit.* tent) : (1) canopied structure, especially on a small scale, to contain the reserved sacrament or a relic; (2) architectural frame, e.g. of a monument on a wall or freestanding, with flanking orders. Also called an Aedicule.

TAS-DE-CHARGE : stone(s) forming the springers of more than one vaulting-rib.

TERMINAL FIGURE or TERM : upper part of a human figure growing out of a pier, pilaster, etc. which tapers towards the bottom.

TERQUETRA : *see* Triquetra.

TERRACOTTA : moulded and fired

clay ornament or cladding, usually unglazed.

TESTER (*lit.* head) : bracketed canopy, especially over a pulpit, where it is also called a sounding-board.

TETRASTYLE : term used to describe a portico with four columns.

THERMAE WINDOW (*lit.* of a Roman bath) : segmental or semicircular window divided by two mullions. Also called a *Diocletian Window* from its use at the baths of Diocletian in Rome.

TIE-BEAM : *see* Roof (fig. 22).

TIERCERON : *see* Vault (fig. 26b).

TILE-HANGING : *see* Slate-hanging.

TIMBER FRAMING : method of construction where walls are built of timber framework with the spaces filled in by plaster or brickwork. Sometimes the timber is covered over with plaster or boarding laid horizontally.

TOMB-CHEST : chest-shaped stone coffin, the most usual medieval form of funerary monument.

TOURELLE : turret corbelled out from the wall.

TOWER AND HALL CHURCH : *see* Hall Church.

TOWER HOUSE (Scots and Irish) : compact fortified house with the main hall raised above the ground and at least one more storey above it. A C15 type continuing well into the C17 in its modified forms.

TRACERY : pattern of arches and geometrical figures supporting the glass in the upper part of a Gothic window, or applied decoratively to wall surfaces or vaults. *Plate Tracery* is the most

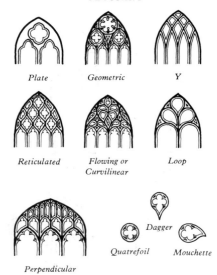

Plate Geometric Y

Reticulated Flowing or Curvilinear Loop

Perpendicular Quatrefoil Dagger Mouchette

Fig. 25. Tracery

primitive form of tracery, being formed of openings cut through stone slabs or plates. In *Bar Tracery* the openings are separated not by flat areas of stonework but by relatively slender divisions or bars which are constructed of voussoirs like arches. Later developments of bar tracery are classified according to the character of the decorative patterns used. For generalized illustrations of the main types *see* fig. 25.

TRANSEPTS (*lit.* cross-enclosures): transverse portions of a cross-shaped church.

TRANSOM: horizontal member between the lights in a window opening.

TREFOIL: *see* Foil.

TRIBUNE: *see* Gallery (1).

TRIFORIUM (*lit.* three openings): middle storey of a church treated as an arcaded wall passage or blind arcade, its height corresponding to that of the aisle roof.

TRIGLYPHS (*lit.* three-grooved tablets): stylized beam-ends in the Doric frieze, with metopes between; *see* Orders (fig. 16).

TRIM: *see* Dressings.

TRIQUETRA: a symbolic figure in the form of a three-cornered knot of interlaced arcs, common in Celtic art. Hence also *Terquetra*, a knot formed of four similar corners.

TRIUMPHAL ARCH: *see* Arch.

TROPHY: sculptured group of arms or armour as a memorial of victory.

TRUMEAU: stone mullion supporting the tympanum of a wide doorway and dividing the door opening into two.

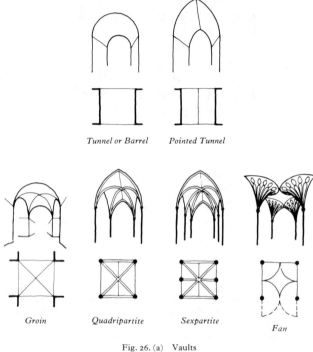

Tunnel or Barrel   *Pointed Tunnel*

Groin   *Quadripartite*   *Sexpartite*

Fan

Fig. 26. (a) Vaults

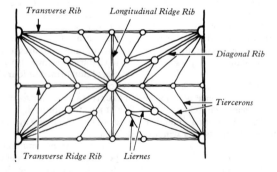

Transverse Rib   Longitudinal Ridge Rib

Diagonal Rib

Tiercerons

Transverse Ridge Rib   Liernes

Fig. 26. (b) Ribs of a Late Gothic Vault

TRUSS: *see* Roof.

TURRET: small tower, often attached to a building.

TUSCAN: *see* Orders (fig. 16).

TYMPANUM (*lit.* drum): as of a drum-skin, the surface between the lintel of a doorway or window and the arch above it.

UNDERCROFT: vaulted room, sometimes underground, below the main upper room.

VAULT: ceiling of stone formed like arches (sometimes imitated in timber or plaster); *see* fig. 26. *Tunnel-* or *Barrel-Vault:* the simplest kind of vault, in effect a continuous semicircular arch. *Pointed Tunnel-Vaults* occur in Irish late medieval castles but are otherwise rare. *Groin-Vaults* (usually called *Cross-Vaults* in classical architecture) have four curving triangular surfaces produced by the intersection of two tunnel-vaults at right angles. The curved lines at the intersections are called groins. In *Quadripartite Rib-Vaults* the four sections are divided by their arches or ribs springing from the corners of the bay. *Sexpartite Rib-Vaults* are most often used over paired bays. The main types of rib are shown in fig. 26b: *transverse ribs, wall ribs, diagonal ribs,* and *ridge ribs.* *Tiercerons* are extra, decorative ribs springing from the corners of a bay. *Liernes* are decorative ribs in the crown of a vault which are not linked to any of the springing points. In a *stellar vault* the liernes are arranged in a star formation as in fig. 26b. *Fan-vaults* are peculiar to English Perpendicular architecture and differ from rib-vaults in consisting not of ribs and infilling but of halved concave cones with decorative blind tracery carved on their surfaces.

VAULTING-SHAFT: shaft leading up to the springer of a vault.

VENETIAN WINDOW: *see* fig. 27.

Fig. 27. Venetian Window

VERANDA(H): shelter or gallery against a building, its roof supported by thin vertical members.

VERMICULATION: *see* Rustication.

VESICA (*lit.* bladder): usually of a window, with curved sides and pointed at top and bottom.

VESTIBULE: anteroom or entrance hall.

VILLA: originally (1) Roman country-house-cum-farmhouse, developed into (2) the similar C16 Venetian type with office wings, made grander by Palladio's varied application of a central portico. This became an important type in C18 Britain, often with the special meaning of (3) a country house which is not a principal residence. Gwilt (1842) defined the villa as 'a country house for the residence of opulent persons'. But devaluation had already begun, and the term implied, as now, (4) a more or less pretentious suburban house.

VITRIFIED: hardened or fused into a glass-like state.

VITRUVIAN SCROLL: running ornament of curly waves on a classical frieze. (*See* fig. 28.)

Fig. 28. Vitruvian Scroll

VOLUTES: spiral scrolls on the front and back of a Greek Ionic capital, also on the sides of a Roman one. *Angle Volute:* pair of volutes turned outwards to meet at the corner of a capital.

VOUSSOIRS: wedge-shaped stones forming an arch.

WAINSCOT: timber lining on an internal wall.

WALLED GARDEN: C17 type whose formal layout is still seen in the C18 and C19 combined vegetable and flower gardens sometimes sited at a considerable distance from a house.

WALL-PLATE: *see* Roof (fig. 22).

WATERHOLDING BASE: type of early Gothic base in which the upper and lower mouldings are separated by a hollow so deep as to be capable of retaining water.

WEATHERBOARDING: overlapping horizontal boards, covering a timber-framed wall.

WEATHERING: inclined, projecting surface to keep water away from wall and joints below.

WEEPERS: small figures placed in niches along the sides of some medieval tombs; also called mourners.

WHEEL WINDOW: circular window with tracery of radiating shafts like the spokes of a wheel; *see also* Rose Window.

INDEX OF PLATES

INDEX OF ARTISTS

INDEX OF PATRONS AND CLIENTS

Drapers' Company, 248, 423, 424, 425
Drummond, Sir John, 270, 271
Drummond, Rev. William, 331
Dunbar family, 185
Dunbar, Sir John, 36, 225
Dundas family, 35, 143
Eccles, Charles, 296
Eccles, Daniel, 296
Edwards, Edward, 381
Edwards, Hugo, 181
Ely, Marquess of, 275
Enniskillen, Countess of, 191
Enniskillen, 1st Earl of, 298
Enniskillen family, 189
Erne, 1st Earl of, 50, 223, 338, 349, 359
Erskine, Sir James, 113, 292
Faulkner, J., 328
Fishmongers' Company, 38, 58, 121, 122, 123, 294, 424
Flannagain, Gilbert Ua, 225
Folliott, General, 44, 504
Ford, Mr, 357
Forward family, 439, 482
Forward, William, 439
Foster, Nicholas, Bishop of Raphoe, 468, 471
Friel, Rev. Joseph, 478
Fullerton, Sir James, 335, 419, 472
Fullerton, Lt. Col. John Campbell, 464
Gage family, 140, 251
Gage, William, 140
Galbraith, Sir James, 504
Galbraith, Samuel, 189
Gallagher, Rev. Peter, 221
Gardiner, Charles, 430
Gardiner, Charles John, 430
Gardiner family, 430, 441
Gardiner, Luke, 429
Gaussen family, 124, 126
Gervais, Rev. Francis, 193
Gibson, Dr, 429
Gillespie, B., 443
Gilliland family, 402
Gilmour, Rev. John, 430
Gladstane family, 194

Gore family, 356
Gore, Sir Ralph, 144
Gormley, Rev. P., 454
Graham family, 417
Gray, Rev. William, 483
Greer family, 339, 397
Grocers' Company, 272
Grove family, 466
Haire, James, 235, 236
Haire, Rev. William, 195
Hall, Dr John, 442
Halliday, John, 503
Hamilton, Sir Claude, 271
Hamilton family, 35, 121, 135, 151, 159, 161, 214, 271, 333, 482; see also Abercorn
Hamilton, Gustavus, 422
Hamilton, Rev. H., 187
Hamilton, James, 151
Hamilton, John, 151, 243, 244
Hamilton, Malcolm, 351, 421
Hamilton, William, 311
Handcock, H. H., 434
Hanna, Rev. T., 112
Hansard, Sir Richard, 347, 348
Harrington, Thomas Knox, 261
Hart family, 220, 403, 434, 435
Hart, Captain George Vaughan, 220
Hart, Thomas Bernard, 475
Harvey, David, 483
Harvey family, 404
Harvey, George, 418
Hassard family, 137
Hassard, George, 139
Hastings, Rev. A., 335
Hastings, Rev. Thomas, 502
Hayes family, 497
Heath, Captain, 290
Herdman, James, 488
Herdman, John, 496
Hervey, Frederick, see Bristol
Heygate, Sir Frederick William, 140
Hezlett, Isaac, 111
Hill, Sir George Fitzgerald, 402
Hogsherd, Rev. Robert, 210
Holmes, Rev. Mr, 195

INDEX OF PLACES